Who Owns the Media?

Competition and Concentration in the Mass Media Industry
Third Edition

Benjamin M. Compaine
Douglas Gomery

LEA

2000

LAWRENCE ERLBAUM ASSOCIATES, PUBLISHERS

Mahwah, New Jersey   London

Lawrence Erlbaum Associates, Inc., Publishers
10 Industrial Avenue
Mahwah, NJ 07430

Cover design by Kathryn Houghtaling Lacey

Library of Congress Cataloging-in-Publication Data

Compaine, Benjamin M.
Who owns the media? : competition and concentration in the
mass media industry / Benjamin M. Compaine, Douglas Gomery.—3rd ed.
p.   cm. — (Communication)
Includes bibliographical references and index.
ISBN 0-8058-2935-0 (cloth : alk. paper) — ISBN 0-8058-2936-9 (pbk. : alk.
paper)
Mass media—Economic aspects—United States. 2. Mass media—Political
aspects—United States. 3. Mass media—Ownership—United States. I.
Gomery, Douglas. II. Title. III. Communication (Hillsdale, N.J.)
P96.E252 U68 2000
302.23'0973—dc21

99-089794
CIP

Books published by Lawrence Erlbaum Associates are printed on acid-free paper,
and their bindings are chosen for strength and durability.

Printed in the United States of America
10   9   8   7   6   5   4   3   2   1

Who Owns the Media?

Competition and Concentration in the Mass Media Industry
Third Edition

LEA's Communication Series
Jennings Bryant/Dolf Zillmann, General Editors

For a complete list of titles in LEA's Communication Series, please contact Lawrence Erlbaum Associates, Publishers

To Megan Rose Compaine: daughter, advisor, friend, and media player of the next generation

and

to Marilyn Moon, public servant and policy analyst extraordinaire.

Contents

Tables and Figures

Tables

Figures

FOREWORD

Considering Who Owns the Media

Seems nearly everybody talks about the media these days. Some bemoan what they see or hear and others celebrate the cornucopia of entertainment and news that daily becomes more widely available to more households. Some are concerned about the potential impact of violent or other antisocial behavior depicted on the theater or home screen and others argue the media do not in themselves "cause" anything to happen. Some see bias in media news reports and others revel in being able to see distant events in their own homes just as they are happening. Some argue the media have lowered national tastes and others see a host of uplifting publications and programs. To a degree, each of these conflicting observations is on the mark.

The volume you hold—really the third edition of a title first issued 21 years ago—analyzes who owns the media, an issue about which only a relative handful of people seem to complain. Yet the real answers to most of the everyday expressions of concern about or praise for media lie with the owners and managers of American print, film, and electronic media companies. These institutions provide the media content that takes up a substantial part of daily life for millions of Americans, as well as the advertising that helps the commercial world hum. Yet, with some obvious exceptions (e.g., Rupert Murdoch or perhaps the broadcast television networks), few of these owners are known outside media industry circles.

The same thing was true two decades ago when Benjamin Compaine first pulled Kenneth Noble, Thomas Guback, and me together to assess what was known about who owned the media in the late 1970s. In an intense few months we assembled what data were available and offered a survey of who owned what. We revised, reconsidered, and expanded these findings just 3 years later. Now, 20 years after that initial effort, Compaine and the University of Maryland's Douglas Gomery have undertaken a far more daunting task; trying to make ownership sense out of a very different media industry at the dawn of a new century—and the millennium.

Two Decades of Change

As an indicator of what Compaine and Gomery faced as they began their task back in 1997, consider just how much American media have changed in those two decades since the first edition. First and foremost the number and variety of media choices available to most American households are now far greater. When this book first appeared in 1979, the typical household received only a handful of television channels over the air—and only 20% of homes had access to cable systems that typically provided up to a dozen channels. Just three national networks dominated television prime time, attracting 90% of the audience. A typical home might also choose from among perhaps 10 or 15 radio stations, see movies at a few surviving downtown and newer suburban movie theaters, read one daily newspaper (or possibly two in the biggest markets), and visit an odd assortment of mostly small newsstands and bookstores. There was virtually no home video (although introduced in 1975, few homes could afford the equipment), only a handful of pay cable or cable networks (CNN was a year away; the Weather Channel and MTV two), no multiscreen cinema theaters, no CDs, and of course, no home computers (save in a few California garages), let alone World Wide Web services (an "unk-unk" back then, as defined in Chapter 7). We lived in what today seems like a benighted era.

Now young people react with amazement at the dearth of media choices we enjoyed back then (there were even fewer earlier). They cannot imagine a world without home video, video rental/sales stores, more than 100 satellite-delivered cable (or DBS) networks, multi-megascreen cinema complexes, CD players (and the "Walkman," which appeared just as the first edition of this volume was published), personal computers with ready Web access, huge book and music stores either in malls or on the Internet, or laptops and cellphones, for that matter. We had none of these two decades ago. A few of us could tune to one service that today's youth never knew—a limited over-the-air subscription television (STV) industry that has since disappeared.

Over the same period, the face of American business generally has also changed dramatically as manufacturing's primacy has given way in the information age. Whereas in 1979 we compared the media to what were then the nation's largest firms—industrial giants such as General Electric and Exxon—today Compaine and Gomery use Microsoft and other software firms that often did not exist two decades ago to draw comparative measures of size and scope.

The story of these two decades is not, of course, totally one of change, for some long-term trends have continued or even accelerated. The number of daily newspapers continues to decline making the one-newspaper town even more the national norm (the end of daily newspaper competition in San Francisco was announced as these words were being written). Television and radio station numbers grow steadily larger despite fears of further audience splintering. And magazines, which seem to rise and fall with the seasons and continually redefine what niche media are all about, also continued to grow in total numbers.

Defining the Elephant

The hugely more complex media ownership patterns and dwindling ownership regulation of today are described and assessed in the text and many tables and charts that follow. Where two decades ago we could write discrete chapters about well-defined separate industries (including newspapers, books, magazines, movies, broadcasting, and cable), those industry terms are today melding as both technology and economics drives a process of convergence. Indeed, one whole chapter (7) describes and assesses Internet Web services that were totally unforseen in the first two editions of this book.

Overall expansion of most media industries in recent years has come about in part because of a distinct change in the relation of media and government. Compaine and Gomery make clear just how much government's role has substantially declined since this book first appeared. Where the FCC once had stringent ownership controls concerning radio and television stations, most are gone and the rest have been liberalized. One entity can now operate several radio stations in a given market, which is a situation long banned by now-obsolete "duopoly" rules. (And again, literally as this foreword was being composed, the FCC announced plans to eliminate key duopoly restrictions for television stations in large markets as well.) No longer are movie studios enjoined from owning theaters. Television networks can own programs and program companies or vice versa, as Disney's acquisition of ABC in the mid-1990s made clear. And many former cross-media ownership rules have likewise disappeared thanks to the rise of a laissez-faire ideology in Congress and regulatory circles.

The Disney motion picture studio owns not only a radio-television network (ABC), but also cable channels and cruise ships. One news and public affairs cable network, MSNBC, is a cooperative venture between a traditional television network and computer software giant (Microsoft). By 1999, AT&T had become a giant in cable TV system ownership (see the beginning of Chapter 5), in large part to pave its re-entry into the local telephone business. It is increasingly difficult to tell where radio broadcasting begins and the music industry ends. Interlocking contracts and ownership agreements among media firms are both complicated and ever-changing.

And looming larger every day is the Internet, with its promise—or threat—of still further dramatic change. As detailed in Chapter 7, few are the media outlets or owners today without their requisite Web pages to which they often refer on the pages or screens of their more traditional media. Few are the television stations that have not lost viewers to those spending hours with their computers (broadcast television networks collectively attract fewer than half the nation's homes in what used to be TV's prime time). Few are the bookstores not concerned about sales increasingly lost to giant chain stores that did not exist two decades ago (Borders and Barnes & Noble) or to the Internet's Amazon or chain store web sites. And few are the other retail businesses not worried about how the Internet is changing buying and advertising patterns. Thus far at least, no one entity controls, let alone owns, the Internet. Microsoft has perhaps come the closest with its strong attempt to dominate access to the new medium by tightly bundling its Internet Explorer browser and Windows 98 operating software, and fighting a federal antitrust action as a result.

The authors' separate concluding chapters (9 and 10) are an especially appealing addition to this revised study. Compaine and Gomery see somewhat different elephants as they survey the media ownership landscape, and that helps to illustrate the many varied ways of considering this often controversial data. Compaine is a bit more optimistic and laissez-faire than is Gomery, and their positions parallel those of many other observers.

DOES OWNERSHIP REALLY MATTER?

In the end, of course, one must ask whether this concern about who owns the media really matters. To what extent, if any, do changing patterns of ownership have an effect on media content, economic functions, or audience impact? Surprisingly little research has been done on these topics—only marginally more than we could draw on two decades ago. Too much is assumed or anecdotal, merely suggesting results from ownership changes. Many are the unsubstantiated complaints concerning monopoly control's presumed negative impacts. Those very concerns underlay years of FCC regulations of electronic media ownership and periodic congressional forays into the topic. In fact, most research concludes with a "Scotch verdict" of not proven. In other words, having diversified or consolidated ownership appears to have little impact on the content provided. Indeed, more than a half century ago, economist Peter Steiner demonstrated in his Harvard dissertation that oligopolistic or even monopoly ownership of multiple radio stations in a given market might actually provide more diversified programming to listeners.

On the other hand, media ownership consolidation appears far more likely to have substantial and lasting economic impact—especially in local markets—and that is where policymakers are focused today. Soon after Congress deregulated radio ownership in 1996, for example, the Justice Department issued regulatory guidelines to limit owners of multiple stations from controlling more than half the advertising revenues in major markets. Likewise, while opening up broadcast station ownership on the one hand, the Federal Communications Commission has tightened rules concerning attribution of minority (but in fact controlling) ownership on the other.

Another factor on which relatively little research has thus far appeared is whether such economic dominance of a media business in one or more regions serves to prevent new entry by other potential competitors. Common sense—and data from newspapers and some other fields such as telephone or data communications—suggests that a monopoly incumbent provider of service has a variety of means either to prevent that entry or to make it prohibitively expensive. Whereas "interconnection" has not been the issue among media services as it has in telecommunications (but it is becoming so, as this is written, competitors are clamoring for access to AT&T's last-mile cable connections as vital to their access to end users), the lessons are useful. As both the 1934 Communications Act and the amendments contained in the 1996 Telecommunications Act also seek to broaden media ownership by attracting new players, the role of such regional monopolies will bear close watching in coming years.

The fact-filled chapters that follow are a commendable effort to detect patterns of and provide insight into a constantly changing panoply of media owners and institutions. In no other single place can you find such a combination of background and current status of what is, admittedly, a fast-changing target. In their work combining description, analysis, projections, and insight, Compaine and Gomery have served us all well.

—*Christopher H. Sterling*
George Washington University

Preface

The primary objective of this book is to update a series begun 20 years ago with the first edition of *Who Owns the Media?* (WOTM?) in 1979, and its 1982 update. Much has happened in 17 years, and we wish to bring that portrait current to 1999 by providing data points and trends over that time. Secondarily, this new edition offers an opportunity to evaluate the forces and trends identified in the earlier editions, and map new ones that have arisen since then.

SOME HISTORY BEHIND *WOTM?*

As is sometimes the case in our decision processes, *Who Owns the Media?* was largely the outcome of serendipity. In 1977, Ben Compaine was director of books and studies for a small publishing company, Knowledge Industry Publications, Inc. (KIPI). It was a period of some merger activity, particularly in book publishing and newspapers and the Federal Trade Commission (FTC) announced a symposium on the subject of media ownership and concentration. KIPI was approached by a midlevel executive of CBS, Inc. about creating a report for them on trends in media mergers. As a publisher, not a research company, KIPI management thought it would be conflict of interest to be engaging in proprietary research. However, Efrem Sigel, the editor-in-chief, did spot an opportunity. He suggested to Compaine and publisher Elliot Minsker that this might be a timely topic for a book.

The idea behind the book was to gather hard data on the trends in the media industry sectors: circulation, audience, advertising, prices, titles, subjects and, of course, ownership and its changes. They knew that most policy discussions about media ownership tend to start with anecdotal, individual complaints: stories about an author who did not get published because of some real or perceived corporate interference or an editor who claimed she made decisions based on what she thought the corporate office wanted or some news segment that was or was not aired due to some actual or imagined corporate self-interest. But what was really known? Was there a body of valid and reliable research that provided support for various hypotheses about the direction and effects of media ownership?

The editorial viewpoint of the book, it was agreed, was to start with a blank slate. Compaine assumed, based on exposure to the media's owns reports of mergers and acquisitions, that there was growing consolidation. But the book was not conceived to try to support or undermine any particular ideology or point of view. Time was short and the topic was hot. The FTC symposium was months away. Compaine, who had recently completed his PhD dissertation on the newspaper industry, had a head start in that area. The plan was to do an edited volume, drawing on the contributions of experts in each of the traditional media segments. Compaine called a former professor of his at Temple University, Chris Sterling, who had written extensively on broadcast and cable regulation. Sterling agreed to the tight time frame for the first draft (three months) and suggested Tom Guback, of the University of Illinois, as someone who knew the film industry well. Compaine turned to Ken Noble, a top publishing analyst at PaineWebber, for the book publishing section. Compaine took on the magazine chapter, as well as being general editor of the book and pulling together the conclusions.

Working with a condensed publishing schedule, Compaine and the KIPI staff managed to have bound hard copies off the press barely nine months from the project's inception. Typically, it takes a publisher at least that long to get bound books after they have the completed manuscript. And this was before authors provided their text in digital form. The first edition was greeted with generally positive reviews in the trade press as well as the *New York Times*. The second edition, only three years later, was primarily an update. The major change was the addition of Chapter 8, "Who Owns the Media Companies?" in response to one of the comments in a review.

THIS EDITION OF *WOTM?*

And that is where *WOTM?* was frozen until now. The initial goals of the publisher and editor were largely confirmed by the way the book was used. It was cited in subsequent articles, research and publications as often in support of someone's position of increasing concentration as in cases suggesting healthy continued competition. Over the years Compaine had been asked repeatedly to revise the 1982 edition. But the effort is considerable, and there were always other projects that seem to take precedence. But in 1995, at the Broadcast Education Association conference in Las Vegas, Chris Sterling suggested it was timely to re-do the book, and while Sterling passed on the opportunity to update his chapters, we are happy to have him provide the foreword to this edition. Neither Tom Guback nor Ken Noble, part of the original group, was available. Fortunately, Douglas Gomery, whose column "The Economics of Television" is a regular feature of the *American Journalism Review*, willingly took on the task.

The current edition is coauthored by Compaine and Gomery, a departure from the previous edition's contributions edited by Compaine. The authors' individual contributions are noted in the following chapters, but this preface and the afterword were joint efforts.

The basic structure of the previous volume was followed with several substantial additions. Most obvious is the added chapter by Compaine covering the online information business. This looks primarily at the use of the Internet and the World Wide Web as both a complement and competitor to the established media. Gomery added a second half to the radio chapter, covering the recorded music industry. Music publishing is often part of other media companies, makes up a large portion of the content of radio and plays a large role in theatrical films and, increasingly, the Internet.

We have made a few structural changes as well. In Chapter 5, Gomery considers television as a single industry, whether viewed via terrestrial broadcast, cable or satellite. Thus, competition, rather than the artifact of regulatory regime, is the organizing principle. Similarly, Gomery analyzed all the venues of the film industry together—theatrical film, pay TV, and home video. We are convinced these additions and changes better organize the understanding of these industry segments.

OBJECTIVES OF THE BOOK

In the end, the objective of the original editions holds for this one as well: "To bring together as much relevant data as feasible on the nature and degree of competition and ownership in the mass media business." The motivation then, as now, was to provide an empirical context for the continuing debate on the structure of the traditional media segments. By 1999, it had become readily apparent, however, how artificial traditional boundaries have become. The real action and issues rests on the borders between and beyond the conventional industries.

Another objective, inescapable given the title of this volume, was specifically to identify the owners of media properties. This included the corporate owners and, to the limited extent possible, many of the largest individual and institutional owners of the media corporations themselves. The book explores the extent of concentration in the media industries at the end of the 1990a, and compares then-current levels with those of previous periods.

Third, this volume preserves what many users said was a strength of the previous editions: the noticeably different voices of the authors. In those volumes, Chris Sterling wrote from his forte as a historian of the media, particularly regulation. Ken Noble was a financial analyst. Tom Guback wrote from what has been called in academic circles the "critical [of capitalism]" perspective. And Compaine took more of a managerial economist's perspective.

In this volume, readers will readily find a difference in both style and substance between the authors. Compaine maintains his data-mongering, stick-to-the-facts approach. Gomery follows the industrial organization framework for analysis as he has laid out in a companion book.[1] The input/output (I/O) model begins with analysis elements of market structure, the focus of this edition of WOTM?

This has led to a rather unique ending to this edition: two concluding chapters. Although the two authors probably agree more than they disagree on the interpretation of the data, it would have looked like the literary equivalent of a pretzel had we written a common conclusion with which we both felt comfortable. But such differences of analysis and interpretation define the very debates of media ownership. When, for example, Compaine sees that the merger of cable companies should be positive for greater competition in the merging arena of telephony and data transmission, Gomery looks at the same events and expresses concerns about AT&T's domination of the consolidation in the cable industry. Such interpretations are what policy debates are about. So our third objective is to highlight these differences and encourage readers to join in (not that anyone seems to need an invitation) at their seminars, board rooms or rule-making proceedings.

HOW TO USE THIS BOOK

How readers use this book depends on their motivation for holding it. There is no need to read it sequentially. Each of the first chapters is relatively self-contained. Some readers, however, might find greater context by reading the concluding chapters first: In understanding where each author comes out, there may be greater understanding of the analysis each lends to his chapters. On the other hand, other readers might find this "pollutes" them, or creates a predisposition to a certain slant. They may prefer—and we would not discourage—such readers to make their own analyses and then check out our conclusions later. In addition, this book serves as a data baseline in 1999.

But most of all, we hope it serves as an analytical primer for mass media industries, a mapping of these important communication and entertainment industries. A map helps travelers get from point A to point B. On the physical roads themselves, the landscape may change over the years: gas stations open and close, fast food restaurants spring up, housing developments are built or old buildings are torn down. But those changes do not affect the reality that the road still goes from point A to point B. So we hope that *WOTM?* continues to serve that function in understanding the forces behind acquisitions, divestitures, mergers, start-ups, regulatory changes and the like. Tracking those daily developments is the role of weekly newsletters and instant Web updates. Besides its static presentation of data series that end in 1996 or 1999, *Who Owns the Media?* should help readers understand *why* these things happen, as well as what *contexts* may be appropriate for analyzing their import.

NOTE ON A BIBLIOGRAPHY

We considered and discarded the value of adding a bibliography at this point. To have compiled a bibliography of all or most of the works cited would have required adding 20 or 30 pages to an already thick volume. We could have created some sort of selected bibliography, but that would have added a layer of criteria and debate. In the end we felt the endnotes serve as a rather exhaustive bibliography—one reason for using the endnote form rather than footnotes. We hope you understand this decision and find it reasonable.

NOTES

1. Alison Alexander, James Owers and Rod Carveth, *Media Economics: Theory and Practice*, 2nd ed. (Mahwah, NJ: Lawrence Erlbaum Associates, 1998).

ACKNOWLEDGMENTS

I'd like to thank Douglas Gomery for signing on for this venture and for seeing it through with resolve, professionalism, and patience. I also acknowledge the many students, faculty, media professionals and regulators who over the years have volunteered how useful previous editions of *Who Owns the Media?* were to some facet of their work. I suppose I should thank (or curse?) my friend and colleague Russ Neuman, at this date at the Annenberg School at the University of Pennsylvania, for frequently nudging me to re-do the book and reminding me how useful it was. Special mention, although he will be surprised, to Scott DeGarmo, an entrepreneur in a magazine editor's body, for generously sharing with me an expensive and very useful database of magazine publishing information. The folks at Lawrence Erlbaum, most especially editor Linda Bathgate and editorial director Lane Akers, were remarkably patient and supportive as this project met more than the standard amount of delay.

Finally, I make a special mention of my daughter, Megan. She wasn't born when the last edition of *WOTM?* was published and is still too young to understand this book. But Megan would come into my office at home after school or camp, ask what I was doing, and provide the relief that made me aware time and again that as wrapped up as we—I—could get in the arcane details of media ownership, there were other things that were more important, like learning the definition of "portcullis" in the third grade. Megan is also part of a generation that I see growing up with a different set of assumptions about the media than were held by my generation, which was in turn different from the view of my parents' cohort. "Cable" and "television" mean the same thing. Throwing a video tape in the VCR or exchanging e-mail or moving between a CD-ROM based encyclopedia and an online reference page is routine and transparent. She may look back at this edition of *WOTM?* in 10 years and ask why we had separate chapters on newspapers, magazines, and television. Why indeed?

—Benjamin M. Compaine

Douglas Gomery thanks Ben Compaine for inviting him to work on this important revision. Although I served as the primary author for Chapters 2, 4, 5, 6, and 9, Ben's comments surely made my work far better. I thank two University of Maryland students—Daniel Pickett and Meredith Traber—for their considerable research help. Students such as Daniel and Meredith remind one how worthwhile and fulfilling teaching can be.

T. P. Moon helped in many ways, too many to list.

I again thank Marilyn Moon for her wise counsel, for her help with economic and public policy analysis, and for her constant model of professionalism. For those reasons, and so much more, I dedicate this book to her.

—Douglas Gomery

1

The Newspaper Industry

Benjamin M. Compaine

The state of the newspaper industry at the end of the 1990s is not good, although individual publishers remain healthy and profitable. This apparent paradox is easily explained. On the one hand, since 1987, newspaper circulation has steadily declined. Circulation based on per household measure has been falling for decades. The number of newspapers has fallen. The amount of time those who look at newspapers spend with them is down. The percentage of total advertising revenue that goes to newspapers has shrunk. There are fewer cities than ever with fully competing newspapers each day.

On the other hand, those newspapers that have survived the thinning out of the 1970s and 1980s, in true Darwinian fashion, are more efficient, have positioned themselves better and, arguably, have provided a better product for their readers. More often than not they are part of multinewspaper groups. Gone are independents like the *Philadelphia Bulletin*, the *Washington Star* and the *Houston Post*. Although there are fewer advertising dollars for newspapers, they are split among fewer establishments. Although circulation is lower, declines are not uniform. In cities where a single publisher remains, circulation is higher, but it is less than the combined circulation of the two papers that used to be there.

For the most part, the newspaper groups of 1998 were the same as in 1980: Gannett, Knight-Ridder, Lee Enterprises, McClatchy among them. But there has been an ebb and flow. Thomson, which had owned more newspapers than any other group, was selling off many of its papers to concentrate on financial information and online distribution. Harte-Hanks has divested all its papers to focus on direct marketing. News Corp., which seemed poised to become a major player in newspapers, retained only the *New York Post*, having gone on to concentrate on broadcasting and film production.

Besides these trends, the other big development for newspapers has been the coming of the World Wide Web. Although in 1982 the Internet was not foreseen as the vehicle for the electronic newspaper, the development of something like it was being discussed:

> The technology that transformed the internal methods for producing the newspaper in the 1970s, i.e., computers and video display terminals, was threatening to reach out to the world of the consumer. Systems were being put in place to create what might be

1

called the electronic newspaper, videotext, or data base publishing. Whatever the term, implicit was the promise that the consumer would be able to get all or much of the content of the newspaper delivered via some electronic highway. Telephone lines were one route. The cable that brought in video was another. Over the air, via broadcasting, was yet a third pathway.[1]

It took another 15 years until this potential started to become a reality. By 1998, 492 daily newspapers had versions available on the Web.[2] After some early experiments with subscriptions, all but a few retreated to an advertiser support model. Few, if any, could be truly said to be profitable. And even those were generating only a fraction of the revenue of the mainstream print product. But the Web was showing the way for newspaper-like content that bypassed the economic bottlenecks of the costs of printing and distribution, opening the way for both new and nontraditional providers to offer content to consumers (see Chapter 7).

This chapter examines the players in the newspaper industry in the late 1990s and the research that addresses concerns of chains and ownership structure. Consistent with most of the other chapters, it looks in particular at the changes in the industry since the early 1980s.

GENERAL CHARACTERISTICS

With its origins in the United States dating back to the earliest colonial days, it should not be surprising that the newspaper industry is economically mature. Table 1.1 shows it has been declining in relative economic terms for nearly four decades, from accounting for 0.8% of gross domestic product (GDP) to under 0.5%. Advertising revenue (Table 1.2), although increasing in absolute terms, has been falling consistently since the 1930s. In 1998, expenditures on television advertising was 23.5% of the total, as compared with 21.8% for newspapers. It was not until the mid-1990s that television advertising (broadcast and cable) surpassed newspapers. Circulation has been falling for years, with daily circulation of 56.2 million in 1998, which is 11% below the peak of 63.1 million reached in 1973 (see Table 1.3). This decline is more substantial in light of the increase in the number of households—the primary purchasing unit for newspapers—by 44% in this period.

There were 1,489 daily newspapers of general circulation in 1998, a level that has been declining steadily since the 1980s. In addition, there were about 8,000 other newspapers, including about 295 foreign language and ethnic dailies, professional, business and special service dailies.[3] Whereas this chapter concentrates on the daily newspapers of general interest, the less than daily newspapers are a vigorous part of the industry structure. They are also the most robust segment. As seen in Table 1.4, weekly newspapers have achieved significant circulation growth, both in average size and in aggregate numbers.

The newspaper industry is one of the country's largest manufacturing employers. Newspaper employment reached its peak at 542,000 in 1989 and declined substantially over the next few years (Table 1.5). It had dropped nearly 12% by 1996, before a modest upturn in 1997. This is about twice the level of the decrease in the number of

TABLE 1.1

Newspaper Shipments and GDP, Selected Years, 1960–1995 (in current $)

	GDP (in billions)	Newspaper Shipments (in millions)	Newspapers as % of GDP
1960	$ 513	$ 4,100	0.80
1970	1,011	7,000	0.69
1982	3,242	21,276	0.66
1990	5,744	35,235	0.61
1995	7,265	35,576	0.49
1996	7,636	37,225	0.49

Source: U.S. Department of Commerce.

TABLE 1.2

Newspaper Advertising as Percent of Total Advertising, Selected Years, 1935–1997

	% of All Advertising	Newspaper Ad Revenue (in millions $)
1935	45.1	$ 762
1945	32.0	921
1955	33.6	3,088
1965	29.0	4,457
1975	29.9	8,442
1985	26.6	25,170
1995	22.5	36,092
1998	21.8	43,925

Sources: Newspaper Association of America, *Facts About Newspapers, 1999*, Table 9, Web site at www.naa.org/info/facts99/09.html, accessed July 23, 1999; Compaine, *The Newspaper Industry in the 1980s* (White Plains, NY: Knowledge Industry Publications, 1980), p. 59.

TABLE 1.3

Daily Newspaper Circulation in the United States, Selected Years, 1920–1998

	Daily		Sunday	
	Number	Circulation	Number	Circulation
1920	2,042	27,791	522	17,084
1930	1,942	39,589	521	26,413
1940	1,878	41,132	525	32,371
1950	1,772	53,829	549	46,582
1960	1,763	58,882	563	47,699
1970	1,748	62,108	586	49,217
1980	1,745	62,202	736	54,676
1990	1,611	62,324	863	62,635
1995	1,533	58,193	888	61,529
1998	1,489	56,182	897	60,061

Sources: 1920–1980: *Editor & Publisher International Year Book*, annual editions. 1990–1998: Newspaper Association of America, *Facts About Newspapers, 1999*. Tables 11 and 12, Web site at www.naa.org/info/facts99/, accessed July 23, 1999.

TABLE 1.4
Weekly Newspapers Circulation Growth, Selected Years, 1960–1998

	Total Weekly Newspapers	Average Circulation	Total Weekly Circulation
1960	8,174	2,566	20,974
1970	7,612	3,660	27,857
1980	7,954	5,324	42,348
1985	7,704	6,359	48,989
1990	7,550	7,309	55,181
1995	7,915	9,425	79,668
1998	8,193	9,067	74,284

Sources: Newspaper Association of America, *Facts About Newspapers, 1999*, Table 27, Web site at www.naa.org/info/facts99/, accessed July 23, 1999. 1995 and 1998 figures not comparable to previous years due to changes in how NAA collects its data.

TABLE 1.5
Newspaper Employment Compared to Total U.S. Civilian Employment,
Selected Years, 1970–1997 (Index: 1987 = 100)

	Newspaper Employment (in thousands)	Growth Index	Total U.S. Civilian Employment (in thousands)	Growth Index
1970	399	74	78,678	70
1980	503	94	99,303	88
1985	516	96	107,150	95
1990	539	101	117,914	105
1991	506	94	116,877	104
1992	509	95	117,598	105
1993	513	96	119,306	106
1994	504	94	123,060	109
1995	491	92	124,900	111
1996	478	89	126,708	113
1997	509	95	129,558	115

Sources: Calculations based on data from Newspaper Association of America, *Facts About Newspapers, 1997*; U.S. Bureau of Labor Statistics, Household Survey.

daily newspapers and a third greater than the decline in daily circulation. Overall, newspaper employment has decreased while civilian employment has increased.

Profitability

Interest in starting, buying and owning newspapers is a positive indicator of the financial health of the industry. The rapid rate with which newspapers have been bought at increasingly higher multiples of dollars per reader or earnings is a sign of a prosperous industry. Table 1.6 lists the revenues and profits for publicly held companies that derive a substantial portion of their revenue from newspaper operations. Net profit margins in 1997 ranged from about 15.1% for Gannett to 5.5% for Hollinger. In a year, any given firm may deviate substantially from industry norms or even its own norms. In 1997, Dow Jones showed a $802 million loss, which reflected the write down in the

TABLE 1.6
Revenue and Profit for Publicly Owned Newspaper-Owning Firms, 1997

Firm	1997 Revenue (in millions)	Profits (in millions)	Return on Revenue (%)
Gannett	4,730	713	15.1
Times Mirror	3,319	250	7.5
Knight-Ridder	2,877	413	14.4
New York Times	2,866	262	9.2
Hollinger, Inc.	2,180	120	5.5
Tribune Co.	2,720	394	14.5
Dow Jones	2,576	(802)*	—
Washington Post	1,956	282	14.4
A. H. Belo	1,248	83	6.7
E. W. Scripps	1,242	158	12.7
Central Newspapers	716	82	11.4
McClatchy Company	642	69	10.7
Lee Enterprises	439	64	14.6
Median			11.4

*Reflects write down of value of Telerate unit, sold in 1998.
Sources: Company reports.

value of its Telerate operation prior to its sale. The previous year, Dow Jones showed a $190 million profit, which was a 7.7% return on sales. Conversely, 1997 was a dramatic improvement for the New York Times Co., which showed only a 3.2% return in 1996. The median percentage return on sales for this group was 11.4%, making 1997 a very good year. The comparable figure for 1980 was 8.5%.

Table 1.7 compares this group of newspaper firms with the median net profit margins for selected groups from the *Fortune 1000* list for 1997. In the full list, the Publishing and Printing sector had the seventh highest median of 37 categories. The 13

TABLE 1.7
Median Return on Revenues, Selected Fortune 1000 Industries, 1997

Industry	Median
Wholesalers	1.1%
Food and Drug Stores	1.7
Food	3.3
Motor Vehicles and Parts	3.3
Chemicals	6.1
Securities	6.2
Telecommunications	7.3
Computers, Office Equipment	7.4
Publishing, Printing	8.2
Metal Products	9.0
Newspapers*	11.4
Pharmaceuticals	16.1
The 1000 Median	5.5

*From Table 1.6.
Source: *Fortune*, April 26, 1998.

newspaper firms in Table 1.6 would rate third on the *Fortune* list, with a median about twice as high as the *Fortune* median. This is roughly comparable to the long-term performance trend of the publicly owned newspaper companies.

Industry Structure

By conventional economic measures, the newspaper industry would seem quite competitive. Table 1.8 shows that in 1947 the four and eight firm concentration ratio for newspapers was 21% and 26%, respectively. The four largest newspaper publishing companies in 1992 accounted for 25% of industry shipments. The eight largest accounted for 37% of shipment value. These ratios are similar to the book and magazine publishing sectors of the publishing industry.This compares, just to choose several unrelated industries for context, with 63% and 77%, respectively, for the soap and other detergent industry (SIC 2841); 70% and 77%, respectively, for commercial printing, gravure; and 34% and 49%, respectively, for bread, cake and related product manufacturing. Compared to the median concentration ratios for all manufacturing industries, newspaper publishing, in 1992, was considerably less concentrated at all size levels.

A more sophisticated measure of the degree of concentration in a market is the Hersfindahl–Hirschmann Index (HHI). In this calculation, the index number increases as the number of firms declines and the inequality in the largest and smallest increases. HHIs of 1,800 or greater represent industries of great concentration. Index numbers at or below 1,000 are signs of no concentration.[4] In 1992, the newspaper industry had an HHI of 241, compared to 1,584 for soap and detergents, 396 for breads and cakes and 2,310 for commercial printing, gravure. The median HHI for all manufacturing industries in the United States was 509.

However, unlike most manufactured goods, the market for a national audience and national advertising is confined to a handful of newspapers: the *Wall Street Jour-*

TABLE 1.8
Share of Total Dollar Shipments by Largest Firms in Publishing Industries, Selected Years, 1947–1992

	Newspapers (SIC 2711)	Periodicals (SIC 2721)	Book Publishing (SIC 2731)	Median All Manufacturers
1947				
4 largest	21%	34%	18%	NA
8 largest	26	43	28	
50 largest	NA	NA	NA	
1967				
4 largest	16	24	20	NA
8 largest	25	37	32	
50 largest	56	72	77	
1992				
4 largest	25	20	23	37
8 largest	37	31	38	52
50 largest	70	62	77	87

NA: Not available.
Sources: U.S. Bureau of Census, Census of Manufacturers, *Concentration Ratios in Manufacturing*. This is undertaken every five years, with results available three years after the census date.

nal, *USA Today* and the *New York Times*, and to a lesser extent the *Christian Science Monitor*. Among them, they had about 4 million circulation in 1996, counting only the 414,000 of the *New York Times'* 1.1 million daily circulation that is outside its 31 county trading area.[5]

At the national newspaper level, the *Journal* accounted for 45% of circulation, *USA Today* for 42%, the *Times* for 10% and the *Monitor* for 2%. In 1980, only the *Journal* and *Monitor* were national newspapers, with the *Journal* accounting for 90% of national newspaper circulation. *USA Today* was started by Gannett in 1982 as the first true general, mass interest national newspaper. Notwithstanding the relatively unconcentrated nature of the newspaper industry at the national level, both the advertising and the circulation market for most newspapers is far more local.

COMPETITION AND GROUP OWNERSHIP

This section covers the state of competition newspapers face and what the roles of various group owners may be. A "group" is generally defined as the ownership of two or more daily newspapers in different cities by a single firm or individual. Newspaper competition traditionally refers to separate ownership of two or more general interest daily newspapers in the same city. It will be seen, however, that "competition" may also be given a broader definition.

Background

In the heyday of multinewspaper cities and many independent owners, newspapers were thin—even big city papers were often only eight pages in 1900. Type was still hand-set until the Linotype came into widespread use at about the same time.[6] Many daily newspapers were designed to appeal to a select group, and there was a newspaper that expressed the political views of seemingly every faction that sprang up. Newspapers did not really compete for the same audiences. Using modern terminology, newspaper engaged in monopolistic competition.[7] James Bennett wrote in his first issue of the *New York Herald* in 1835:

> There are in this city at least 150,000 persons who glance over one or more newspapers every day and only 42,000 daily sheets are issued to supply them. We have plenty of room, therefore, without jostling neighbors, rivals, or friends, to pick up at least 20,000 or 30,000 for the *Herald*, and leave something for those who come after us.[8]

Today, a newspaper in a multinewspaper territory can grow primarily by taking a subscriber from another newspaper.

In the 1880s, the cost of newer, faster presses and Linotypes, and the demands of the new advertisers for circulation, brought about economies of scale that demanded a newspaper be sold at a low price to a mass audience. The cost of entry increased as well. Increased specialization required by the technology of 1900 reduced the extent to which newspapers could depend on job printing during off hours as a means of subsidizing competing newspapers.[9]

Improved transportation made it possible for a single paper to distribute to a larger territory, and the telephone and telegraph also aided the same papers in covering the further away suburbs. Advertisers could also depend on customers patronizing their stores from a broader area and could therefore make use of the broadened circulation. Other trends at the beginning of the 20th century included:[10]

1) A decline in the political partnership that had demanded that each group have a newspaper representing its view resulted in a need for fewer newspapers.
2) Advertisers found it cheaper to buy space in one general circulation newspaper than in several with overlapping circulation.
3) The Associated Press' rules for new memberships, providing exclusive territorial franchises, made acquisition of a newspaper with membership the easiest way for a nonmember in the same market to join.

Radio, then television, made inroads into newspaper functions. Perhaps the most significant lesson from this is that, despite increasing competition from newer media, newspapers have remained an important mass medium.

That interest in the printed format of the newspaper remains firm is illustrated by the makeup of those companies who purchased a newspaper in 1997: Of the 66 transactions involving dailies, in 55 cases the buyer owned at least two other daily newspapers. And, in other cases, the purchaser already published weekly or "shopper" newspapers.[11] These purchases continued the trend toward group ownership of newspapers and away from the independent, locally owned paper. In 1923, for example, there were 31 newspaper groups that owned a total of 153 newspapers—or about 7% of all dailies. By 1954, the number of chains had tripled to 95. The number of groups reached 167 in 1978, but started consolidating by the 1980s. By 1996, 126 groups published an aggregate of 1,151 newspapers, accounting for 76% of the total number of dailies and 82% of daily circulation.

As newspaper groups have grown, competition among newspapers within cities has diminished. Table 1.9 follows the steady decline in the number of cities with competing papers. In 1923, 502 cities had two or more directly competing newspapers. By 1996, only 19 cities, or 1.3% of all cities and towns with daily newspapers, had head-to-head newspaper competition. On the other hand, more cities had their own daily paper in 1996 than in 1923 or in 1963. This indicates that the publishers followed the population and the retailers from the cities to the suburbs. In effect, newspapers became decentralized.

Table 1.10 identifies the cities with competitive newspapers. In addition to the 19 cities that had newspapers under separate ownership in 1997, another 16 cities had newspapers that operated under the agency shop provision of the Newspaper Preservation Act (see p. 49). In these cities, a single firm handles all business and production for the two papers. Separate firms own and manage the papers themselves, presumably guaranteeing editorial independence.

Thus, there are actually two related trends in the area of newspaper ownership: the apparently increased concentration of ownership, and the decrease in intracity newspaper competition.

TABLE 1.9

Number of Cities with Daily Newspapers and Competing Daily Newspapers, Selected Years, 1923–1996

	Number of Cities with Daily Paper	Cities with Two or More Dailies*	% of Total Cities with Two or More Dailies
1923	1297	502	38.7%
1933	1426	243	17.0
1943	1416	137	9.7
1953	1453	91	6.3
1963	1476	51	3.5
1973	1519	37	2.4
1981	1534	30	2.0
1996	1488	19	1.3

*Includes only fully competing newspapers under separate ownership. Does not include papers publishing under joint operating agreements.

Sources: 1923–1973: James Rosse, Bruce Owen and James Dertouzos, "Trends in the Daily Newspaper Industry, 1923–1973," *Studies in Industry Economics*, No. 57, Dept. of Economics, Stanford University, p. 30. 1981 and 1996: compiled from *Editor & Publisher International Year Book*, 1981 and 1997.

TABLE 1.10

Cities with Competing English-Language Newspapers, 1997

Competitive Newspaper Cities	Agency Shop Cities
Mountain Home, AR	Birmingham, AL
Los Angeles, CA	Tucson, AZ
Pleasanton, CA	San Francisco, CA
San Diego, CA	Honolulu, HI
Aspen, CO	Evansville, IN**
Denver, CO	Fort Wayne, IN
Montrose, CO	Detroit, MI
Washington, DC	Las Vegas, NV
Chicago, IL	Albuquerque, NM
Boston, MA	Cincinnati, OH
Columbia, MO	York, PA
Berlin, NH	Chattanooga, TN
Trenton, NJ	Nashville, TN*
New York, NY	Salt Lake City, UT
Pittsburgh, PA	Seattle, WA
Wilkes-Barre, PA	Charleston, WV
Kingsport, TN	
Manassas, VA	
Green Bay, WI	

*JOA dissolved and Nashville Banner ceased operations in 1998.
**JOA dissolved in 1998.

Source: *Editor & Publisher International Year Book, 1997*; Newspaper Association of America, *Facts About Newspapers, 1999*, Table 26, Web site at www.naa.org/info/facts99, accessed July 23, 1999.

Concentration of Ownership

Concentration of ownership in the U.S. newspaper business has not changed much during the 20th century as measured by the percent of circulation accounted for by the largest and smallest circulation newspapers. As seen in Table 1.11, the largest 25% of newspapers actually accounted for a lower percentage of daily circulation in 1996 than it did in 1923. A similar breakdown of the largest 10% and 1% of firms shows a parallel decline.

Figure 1.1, which graphs the largest 25%, 10% and 1% of newspaper circulation share, shows that the largest newspapers, regardless of ownership or independence, have accounted for a remarkably constant percentage of total circulation over the decades. As the number of newspapers has declined, the number of papers in each percentage group has, of course, shrunk. But these trends also make clear that over-all newspaper circulation has declined faster than has the number of daily papers. Fewer papers and publishers are contending for a shrinking audience.

An International Comparison

Comparing concentration in the United States to other countries has limited validity due to the different industry structures. France, for example, has a mixture of 18 general interest national, 8 specialized (e.g., sports) and 36 regional dailies. The United Kingdom combines a choice of 11 national dailies with 89 regional dailies. Germany, on the other hand, is more like the U.S. model, with 396 local newspapers and 6 national papers. Canada is closest to the U.S. model, with 105 primarily local dailies.[12]

Recognizing the limits in this inexact comparison, there is still some value in comparing ownership in some selected developed countries. Compared to the 60% of circulation accounted for by the top 10% of U.S. newspapers, the comparable figure in France is 32%, in the United Kingdom it is 73% and in Canada it is 46%. By the measure of the percentage of aggregate circulation accounted for by the largest

TABLE 1.11
Percentage of Total Daily Circulation Accounted for by Largest
and Smallest Newspapers, Selected Years, 1923–1996

	Smallest 25%	Largest 25%	Largest 10%	Largest 1%
1923	2.2%	82.5%	64.9%	22.6%
1933	2.2	84.2	67.4	23.4
1943	2.2	84.3	66.6	22.4
1953	2.3	83.6	66.6	21.1
1963	2.4	83.0	65.7	22.1
1973	2.8	80.4	66.3	20.6
1978	3.0	78.9	61.3	19.8
1996	2.8	78.1	59.8	20.5

Sources: 1923–1973: Rosse, et al., "Trends in the Daily Newspaper Industry 1923–1973," p. 28; 1978: compiled from *Editor & Publisher International Year Book, 1979*; 1996: compiled from *Editor & Publisher International Year Book*, 1997 CD-ROM database.

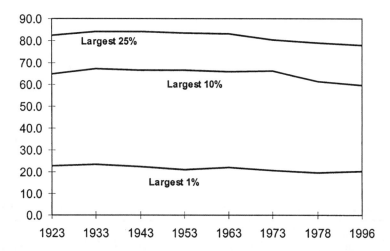

FIG. 1.1. Percentage of Circulation Accounted for by Largest Newspapers. Source: Table 1.11.

firm in each country, the United States is far less concentrated. Whereas the largest chain in circulation, Gannett, accounts for about 10% of U.S. daily circulation, Germany's Axel Springer Verlag accounts for 23% of that country's circulation. In the United Kingdom, News International papers control 36% of circulation and the second largest chain, Mirror Group, controls another 22%.[13] Canada's Southam, Inc. accounted for 29% of the daily circulation in 1996.[14]

Chain Ownership

The desire to own groups of newspapers—for whatever reasons—has long been compelling. E.W. Scripps started his chain in the 1880s. By 1900, there were eight major chains, including Scripps-McCrae, Booth, Hearst, Pulitzer and the Ochs papers. In 1908, according to Frank Munsey, "There is no business that cries so loud for organization and combination as that of newspaper publishing. The waste under existing conditions is frightful and the results miserably less than they could be made."[15]

Table 1.12 clearly shows that after decades of a steady increase in the number of group owners and the number of dailies they control, the increase in the number of groups may be ending. As various groups merge, the number of groups is likely to decrease and the average size of groups is likely to increase. Still, a typical group is small, with the median owning four newspapers. The median total circulation of a newspaper group is just shy of 73,000 copies daily.

It took until 1997 for the Gannett chain to achieve the potential impact in total circulation as was achieved by Hearst at its circulation peak in 1946. In that year, its newspapers had a combined circulation of 5.3 million, or 10.4% of total daily circulation, all in traditional local newspapers. In 1997, the largest chain in circulation, Gannett Co., had a circulation of 6.0 million, accounting for 10.5% of all daily circulation. This includes about 1.7 million from USA Today, the national daily it started in 1982. The group of chains in Table 1.13 were chosen to show the two dominant chains for 1946 (Hearst and Scripps) and the three largest in 1998 (Gan-

TABLE 1.12
Number of Daily Newspaper Groups and Dailies they Publish, Selected Years, 1910–1996

	No. of Groups	No. of Dailies in Groups*	Average Size of Group (number of papers)	% of Total Dailies Group-Owned	% of Daily Circulation of Group-Owned Dailies
1910	13	62	4.7	2.4	N.A.
1930	55	311	5.6	18.9	43.4%
1940	60	319	5.3	17.0	N.A.
1953	95	485	5.1	27.0	45.3
1960	109	552	5.1	31.3	46.1
1970	157	879	5.6	50.3	63.0
1980	154	1139	7.4	65.3	72.9
1996	129	1146	8.9**	76.2	81.5

N.A.: Not available.

*Before 1954, the number of dailies may be overstated because morning and evening editions of some papers were counted as separate papers.

**Median group owns four newspapers.

Sources: 1910–1970: "Number of Dailies in Groups Increased by 11% in 3 Years," *Editor & Publisher*, February 23, 1974, p. 9., except % of dailies *Historical Statistics of the United States: Colonial Times to 1970* group owned for 1910, U.S. Census Department, Series R244-257, p. 810. 1980: calculated from *Editor & Publisher International Year Book*, 1981, pp. I-357–I-363. 1996: calculated from *Editor & Publisher International Year Book*, 1997 CD-ROM database. In some cases, the database yields different results from those *E&P* publishes in the printed directory.

TABLE 1.13
Newspaper Circulation by Selected Group Owners, Selected Years, 1946–1998

Group	1998	1980	1966	1946
Gannett Co. Inc.	10.7%	5.7%	1.9%	1.2%
Knight-Ridder Inc.	6.9	5.6	4.0	3.4
Newhouse Newspapers	4.9	5.1	5.0	1.0
Hearst	2.3	2.1	4.4	10.4
E. W. Scripps	2.4	2.4	4.8	4.4

Sources: *Editor & Publisher International Year Book*, 1947, 1967; American Association of Newspapers, *Facts About Newspapers, 1981*, and *Facts About Newspapers, 1999*.

nett, Knight-Ridder and Newhouse). These five chains, among the few that existed over that span, accounted for 20.4% of daily circulation in 1946 and 27.2% of a relatively smaller industry 50 years later. If *USA Today* were eliminated from Gannett's and total U.S. circulation, this group would account of 24.2% of total circulation.

Much of the activity of these groups over the years has involved swapping properties. As some chains have grown, others have shrunk or disappeared. The Hearst chain has either bought or established more than 40 dailies—merging some, selling others, suspending several. In 1940 there were 17 Hearst papers, leading all chains in combined circulation.[16] By 1998, there were only 12 Hearst newspapers, ninth in total circulation. At one time, Frank Munsey had six newspapers in New York, Washington, Baltimore and Philadelphia. They were all merged, sold or suspended.[17]

The term "group," as popularly defined, is somewhat misleading. The tabulation in Table 1.14 shows that more than half of the so-called chains consist of 4 or fewer newspapers, and usually small ones at that. At the other extreme, there are 27 firms that own 10 or more newspapers. Among them, they own 750 newspapers (as compared to 629 in 1980). The median number of papers owned by the total of 129 groups is 4, compared to an average of nearly 9, indicating a skewed proportion at the high end.

Rank by Circulation

The 15 largest groups, ranked by circulation in Table 1.15, accounted for just over 50% of all daily circulation in 1998. Even without *USA Today*, Gannett Co. has a considerable edge over Knight-Ridder for the distinction as the group with the largest circulation. Knight-Ridder had less circulation in 1980 than in 1998 even though it had 6 more newspapers in 1998. Gannett's circulation per newspaper was about the same as in 1980, but it owned 5 more local newspapers. Newhouse remains the largest of the privately owned companies. Dow Jones includes the 1.8 million circulation national *Wall Street Journal*, as well as the 19 papers of the 600,000 circulation Ottaway group.

In 1998, the 10 largest groups owned 273 newspapers, somewhat of an increase from the 238 papers owned by the 10 largest groups in 1980 and mostly due to the inclusion of MediaNews Group, which owns an unusual combination of several big city newspapers and some very small town dailies. Measured against a smaller population of dailies

TABLE 1.14
Distribution by Number of Newspapers in Groups, 1996

No. of Newspapers in Group	No. of Groups	% of Group Newspapers	% of Newspapers Group Owned
2	35	27.1	6.1
3	20	15.5	5.2
4	13	10.1	4.5
5	8	6.2	3.5
6	10	7.8	5.2
7	9	7.0	5.5
8	3	2.3	2.1
9	3	2.3	2.4
10	1	0.8	0.9
11–15	7	5.4	7.3
16–20	10	7.8	15.5
21–25	1	0.8	1.9
26–30	4	3.1	9.6
31 +	5	3.9	30.2
Totals	129	100.0	99.9

Average group size: 8.9 papers
Median group size: 4 papers

Source: Calculated from *Editor & Publisher International Year Book*, 1997 CD-ROM database. In some cases, the database yields different results from those *E&P* publishes in the printed directory.

TABLE 1.15
Largest Newspaper Publishing Firms, by Circulation, 1980 and 1998

1998 Rank	Firm	Daily Circulation		No. Daily Newspapers	
		1998	1980	1998	1980
1	Gannett Co.	5,994	3,563	74	81
2	Knight-Ridder	3,872	3,493	33	39
3	Newhouse Newspapers	2,781	3,167	23	28
4	Times Mirror Co.	2,370	2,316	9	4
5	Dow Jones & Co.	2,311	2,339	20	21
6	New York Times Co.	2,253	1,108	20	9
7	MediaNews Group	1,828	*	51	*
8	E. W. Scripps*	1,330	1,515	20	15
9	Hearst Newspapers	1,319	1,321	12	13
10	McClatchy Newspapers	1,311	358	11	5
11	Tribune Co.	1,264	1,195	4	8
12	Cox Enterprises	1,121	2,854	16	19
13	Thomson Newspapers	1,031	**	50	67
14	Freedom Communications	960	**	28	31
15	A. H. Belo	896	333	7	7
	Total	28,410		378	
	% of total daily circulation	50.6%			
	% of all daily newspapers			25.4%	

*Group did not exist in 1980.
**Group not among the 15 largest in 1980.
Sources: 1998: Newspaper Association of America, *Facts About Newspapers, 1999*. 1980: Compaine, et al., *Who Owns the Media*, 2nd ed., Tables 2.16 and 2.17.

in 1998, the largest groups held 18% of the total number of dailies in 1998 as compared to 14% in 1980. In 1998, the 10 largest groups accounted for 23.1 million daily circulation, an increase of 1.1% from the 22.9 million circulation of the 10 largest groups in 1980. However, with total circulation lower in 1998 (see Table 1.3), as a proportion of total circulation it rose modestly to 41%, up from 37% for the 10 largest in 1980.

Rank by Number of Daily Papers

The firms with the greatest number of daily newspapers under common ownership are listed in Table 1.16. In sum, they account for 14% of the total number of chains and own 42% of the total number of daily newspapers.

Although Gannett is the largest group based on circulation, a new group of players dominates the list of largest publishers based on the number of newspapers owned. Hollinger, Inc. a Canadian firm that, with the exception of the 500,000 circulation *Chicago Sun-Times*, consisted mostly of small town newspapers of under 10,000 circulation. (Hollinger is also the parent company of Southam, Inc., Canada's largest newspaper publisher.)

Tables 1.15 and 1.16 are based on 1996 data. Subsequently, there were some shifts, as firms changed their business strategies. In 1997, Knight-Ridder bought four of the

TABLE 1.16
Largest Newspaper Groups, by Number of Daily Newspapers in Group, 1996

Rank	Firm	Number of Daily Newspapers
1	Hollinger International*	105
2	Gannett Co. Inc.	88
3	Thomson Newspapers Inc.**	73
4	Donrey Media	48
5	Knight-Ridder Inc.	32
6	Morris Communications	29
7	Ogden Newspapers	28
8	Freedom Communications	27
9	MediaNews Group	26
10	Newhouse Newspapers	22
11	The New York Times Co.	20
11	Dow Jones & Co. Inc.	20
13	Park Communications	19
13	Lee Enterprises	19
15	Journal Register Co.	17
15	E. W. Scripps Co.	17
15	Howard Publications	17
15	Cox Enterprises Inc.	17
	Total	624
	% of total newspapers	41.5%

*Hollinger sold many of its smallest papers in 1997 and 1998, with only 55 remaining as part of the group in mid-1998.

**Thomson retained 58 daily newspapers in the United States in 1997.

Source: Calculated from *Editor & Publisher International Year Book*, 1997 CD-ROM database and corporate reports.

Capital Cities/ABC newspapers that Walt Disney owned after it acquired that company, including the *Kansas City Star* and the *Fort Worth Star-Telegram*.[18] Disney decided it did not want to be in newspaper publishing. But Knight-Ridder also sold four newspapers, including the 100,000 circulation paper in Long Beach, California, and a Gary, Indiana, daily. Harte-Hanks, which owned 29 dailies in 1980, sold off its papers to several other groups and moved out of the newspaper business. Hollinger did not even exist in the U.S. market until 1986. Thomson, another Canadian-based firm, sold many of its newspapers (some to Hollinger) to concentrate in electronic and financial media.

The largest firms by both circulation and number of papers are slightly larger and account for a greater proportion of circulation and newspapers than a similar compilation in 1980. In that year, the 10 largest groups by circulation accounted for 37% of daily circulation versus 43% in 1996. The 14 largest groups of newspapers accounted for 26% of the newspapers in 1980, as compared to 37% in 1996.[19]

Is the Newspaper Industry Unduly Concentrated?

From the perspective of a local retailer or real estate broker, whether the local paper is one of dozens owned by a group or the only daily newspaper property of a local family, the issue is almost universally the same: If the local daily newspaper is the most efficient medium for them to reach their market, then they have no choice. Similarly, for the local resident, who feels it useful to read about the local sports teams, the issues in town government, the developments on the school board or the sale items at the supermarket that week, there have been few alternatives to buying the daily newspaper, regardless of the form of ownership.

However, there is the more philosophical, but quite emotional, debate concerning whether a society that has lived with the myth of a diverse and independent press is in danger of being ill-served by having fewer owners than ever being able to put their editorial voice—directly or indirectly—in front of a substantial proportion of the population.

The data indicate, with no room for ambiguity, that the daily newspaper industry is generally more concentrated in the sense that fewer owners have control over more newspapers and circulation. But that leaves open three questions:

1) What standard of concentration is appropriate, from either a legalistic view or a media critic view?

2) Is there any evidence to date that current trends in ownership and management have ill-served the public beyond anecdotal stories or unsubstantiated "fears"?

3) Is this discussion moot as the result of the proliferation of other media, from weekly newspaper and shoppers and other direct mail, to dozens of cable stations and networks, and ultimately to the low cost, unmediated opportunity for both commerce and commentary the Internet has opened up?

Responses to the legal part of the first question will be left to the Federal Trade Commission and the Justice Department, which have their own economic criteria. And media critics must decide for themselves about what satisfies their own criteria.

The second question is addressed later. And the third question is taken up both in Chapter 7, as well as in the concluding comments to this volume.

Effects of Concentration

There is a difference of opinion between those who would agree with Munsey that concentration of ownership may improve newspapers, and those who believe that chain ownership results in fewer editorial "voices," hence more homogeneous newspapers and a general reduction in quality. This second viewpoint was expressed at least as far back as 1930: "It cannot be maintained that the chain development is a healthy one from the point of view of the general public. Any tendency which makes toward restriction, standardization, or concentrating of editorial power in one hand is to be watched with concern."[20]

This conflict was highlighted in an exchange of opinions in the *Columbia Journalism Review*, involving Gannett's purchase of the *Honolulu Star-Bulletin*. An evaluation of the changes made at that paper after Gannett came in noted that two positions, including the Washington correspondent, were eliminated; 12 columns, including the surfing column and a "Nautical Notes" feature and two comic strips were cut; the Copley News Service was canceled; a final edition was canceled, moving up the final deadline 75 minutes; 30 printers lost their regular positions and were put on a "daily basis"; three engravers were laid off; and overtime was eliminated. Gannett brought in a new publisher who told reporters that the cuts were needed for economic reasons and that the Honolulu paper was fourth from the bottom in year-to-year revenue improvement in the Gannett chain.[21]

In a response to that criticism, the managing editor of the *Huntington* (WV) *Advertiser* (which became a Gannett paper as part of the deal with Honolulu) wrote that the same type of things happened when the *Star-Bulletin*, then an independent paper, had itself bought the *Advertiser*. But he claimed that when Gannett took over, virtually every member of the news staff got a raise, lingering union problems were settled with three years back pay and the dingy newsroom was renovated; reporters were given a voice in policymaking and choosing their own editor; there was greater editorial freedom for columnists and reporters; and ad salespeople were given commissions as well as salary. The Huntington papers were encouraged to do investigative reporting, even to the extent of damaging previously "untouchable" community leaders. The editor wrote that the paper was opening up communication channels with the community and providing more leadership.[22]

Concerns for Newspapers as Part of Groups

The potential harm of group ownership lies in the concentration of financial, political and social power in relatively few people. This has been the central argument of media critic Ben H. Bagdikian. He has expressed fears that the media in general and newspapers in particular are increasingly controlled by "a new kind of central authority over information—the national and multinational corporation."[23] He sees a handful of men and women controlling what the rest of us read, see and hear—or don't get to read, see and hear. Central to his thesis is that newspapers are big business and therefore the owners of these properties will have the same presumably conservative economic interests of big business in general, coloring the coverage of politics, business and social affairs in a way that favors the dominant views of big business.

Bagdikian is not alone in raising such alarms. From the critical academic sociologist Herbert Schiller to the well-regarded CBS news producer Fred Friendly, warnings have come about the dangers, whether real or potential, of the alliance of capitalism and the media. Although there are always some anecdotal stories to support such conspiracy theories, other anecdotal evidence (as well as more elaborate and controlled research) suggests a far more complex and ambiguous outcome.[24]

Research on Media Structure and Ownership Effects

How realistic are these concerns? Research on media ownership and structure has become more sophisticated and widespread since the 1970s. Today, studies look at three related issues:

- How chain-owned newspapers and individually owned newspapers differ, if at all, in editorial content, advertising pricing, interactions with the community and workforce-related matters.

- How, if at all, newspapers that face direct or indirect local competition differ from those that do not have local daily competition.
- How the corporate structure of a newspaper may affect the editorial content and/or business policies of newspapers. This area is of the most recent vintage and addresses, most specifically, the concerns of those who worry about the effects of capitalism on journalism.

Chains Versus Independent Papers

One of the insights that seems to have grown out of the research in the 1980s and 1990s is that differences along several dimensions of newspaper content and policies seem more related to the size of the newspaper and its corporate parent than to whether it is part of a chain. This was perhaps suggested by an unpublished study that found that chains spread out over several regions were consistently less homogeneous in their endorsement of presidential candidates, indicating that the small, personally managed regional chains tend toward *tighter* editorial control than the more visible national groups.[25]

In his own review of 17 studies on the subject, David Demers found few differences in editorial page content between chain and nonchain newspapers. The "critical model" holds that chain newspapers publish fewer editorials about local issues, fewer editorials critical of mainstream groups and ideas and exercise greater control over what editorial editors write, all because, according to the "critical model," they are more afraid to offend advertisers, sources or readers.[26] Demers' review found that only 3 of the 17 studies supported this critical hypothesis. Seven showed no relation or mixed results. And 7 studies "suggest that chain organizations are more vigorous or create conditions conducive to greater diversity."[27]

In his own study, he used a formulation of what he called "corporate structure" and "entrepreneurial" newspapers. Among the characteristics that determine a corporate structure are a clear-cut division of labor, a hierarchy of authority, a formalistic personality and a complex ownership structure. By contrast, an entrepreneurial newspaper is structurally simple and tends to be managed and owned by the same individual or family. This formulation recognizes that a small nonchain newspaper has more in common with the typical "chain" of three or four small regionally based papers than it does with the *New York Daily News*, which in 1998 was the only newspaper in its corporate family.

Demers found that the more a newspaper exhibits the corporate form, the greater the number of editorials and letters to the editor, the greater the number of local staff written articles and the greater the editorials and letters are likely to be critical of mainstream groups or sources.

David Coulson and Anne Hansen used the sale of the highly regarded *Louisville Courier-Journal* to Gannett Co.[28] in 1986 as a more localized test for change by a large corporate chain on an independent newspaper. The *Courier-Journal* had been owned by one family since 1918 and it was their only newspaper. The researchers empirically evaluated 20 issues of the paper from two years before Gannett's acquisition and an equal number two years after it took over the paper. They found that the newshole—the amount of space devoted to nonadvertising content—increased substantially. Stories were slightly shorter, but there were many more. The amount of hard news stories increased, whereas the number of features increased even more. The number of staff written stories increased substantially, but not as much as the number of wire service stories. Only 2% of copy was from Gannett News Service. The number of local news stories increased by 30%, as did the number of column inches devoted to local stories.

Certainly there are stories of corporate owners exerting their editorial preferences. William Randolph Hearst Jr. demanded that his papers support the Johnson–Humphrey ticket in 1964 (although he let each paper make its own decision in 1968 and they split 8-5 in favor of Nixon–Agnew). In 1972, James M. Cox required his nine newspapers, including the *Atlanta Journal and Constitution*, to endorse the Nixon ticket. What the two examples have in common, significantly, is that they are cases where the corporations were closely held. That is, they did not have public stockholders for which the management had a fiduciary responsibility.

This is consistent with research showing that publishers and owners of family- or independently owned newspapers exert greater control over the editorial process than at group-owned newspapers. Or, conversely, that editors at chain newspapers tend to have greater latitude in determining editorial policy. Drawing from surveys of hundreds of editors of newspapers, the findings of Wilhoit and Drew were that the owner or publisher at 46% of family- or independently owned newspapers exerted great (30%) or moderate (16%) influence on the priority of topics on the editorial page. At group-owned newspapers, the owners or publishers exerted similar degrees of influence—from 13% (publicly owned) to 16% (privately owned).[29]

Ultimately, whether or not group ownership improves or degrades a newspaper depends on the criteria established for making such judgments, the state of the newspaper when the new owner arrives and, more importantly, which chain is doing the buying. Indeed, a key study set out to measure the quality of group-owned and independent papers, both privately and publicly held.[30] The study identified eight categories of newspaper quality: commitment to locally produced copy, amount of nonadvertising copy, ratio of nonadvertising to advertising space, number of interpretive and in-depth stories, amount of graphics, number of wire services, story length, and reporter workload.

The sample encompassed 31 independent and 49 group newspapers of a variety of sizes. Recognizing that larger newspapers have greater resources than smaller papers, the researchers rated the papers on both an absolute basis and then included a circulation-related factor. After statistical analysis, the study found that ownership by a group, privately or publicly owned, had "no systematic effect on news quality"; that taking the sample of independent newspapers as its own group, they would rank in the middle or just below the middle of the groups studied; that even within groups newspapers were not homogeneous in news quality; and that although size of the newspaper could have a substantial effect on quality, some smaller groups produced "better newspapers than would be expected, while some of the groups with larger circulation papers . . . [produced] newspapers that do not have as much quality as would be expected." These findings are consistent with the mixed results of other studies comparing group and stand-alone newspaper ownership. Whether a newspaper has higher or lower quality depends on both the policy of the owners and the financial resources available to the individual publisher.

Thus, single newspaper ownership is no guarantee of integrity or quality, nor is ownership by a group necessarily a negative for readers or advertisers. Walter Annenberg, when he owned the *Inquirer*, and William Loeb, the late publisher of the *Manchester Union Leader*, are cited as examples of controversial owners of single papers. It is generally agreed, for example, that the Knight-Ridder organization dramatically improved the editorial quality of the *Philadelphia Inquirer* and *Daily News* after purchasing them from independent owner Walter Annenberg. Gannett, as just seen, has a more mixed reputation.

John C. Quinn, former senior vice president for news for Gannett, on a speech at an International Press Institute conference, explained:

> Newspaper concentration may multiply the anxiety over evil; it also increases the capacity for good. And a publisher's instinct for good or evil is not determined by the number of newspapers he owns. A group can attract top professional talent, offering training under a variety of editors, advancement through a variety of opportunities. . . . It can invest in research and development and nuts and bolts experience necessary to translate the theories of new technology into the practical production of better newspapers.
>
> Concentrated ownership can provide great resources; only independent, local judgment can use the resources to produce a responsible and responsive local newspaper. That measure cannot be inflated by competition nor can it be diluted by monopoly.[31]

Can the Corporate Structure Have a Positive Influence?

The overall consistency of studies that show that large group, corporate and public ownership have had a neutral to positive effect on the editorial side of newspapers, while at the same time focusing greater attention on profitability, is apparently counterintuitive, at least to those who assume the worst about big business.

Why might corporate newspapers in many cases be an improvement over entrepreneurial ones?

- Less concern about profitability. People who have been in business for themselves or have managed a small business know that financial concerns are never far from mind. Getting a loan from the local bank for a capital expenditure can be difficult and expensive. On the other hand, although publishers of corporate newspapers may have pressure to meet profit goals set by the corporation, the local managers do not have to be concerned about meeting the weekly payroll. Capital improvements may be bankrolled via the parent at far more favorable terms than less credit-worthy small businesses.
- Fewer ties to the community. The prototypical myth holds that the local, small town publisher has ties to the community, whereas the hired guns from the corporate chain come and go with no such attachment. However, in journalism, where local reporters, editors and publishers are today expected to be watch dogs, this outsider role may actually work in the public's favor. Reporters and editors who are on a career path are more likely than the home grown variety to hold professional norms and values and to place more emphasis on reporting honestly than parochially.
- Greater distance from political pressure. For similar reasons, as with fewer community ties, corporate editors know they have a job elsewhere if they offend the local political powers. It is less likely that their girlhood friend is now the town manager or head of the local chamber of commerce.

- Greater resources. With corporate marketing departments behind them, the local managers are often able to sell more advertising, at a higher rate than a stand-alone or small chain operation. Although some of this extra income may go to improved profit margins, there is substantial evidence that some is also returned to the local newspaper to improve editorial content—and hopefully bolster circulation (or at least slow its slide).

Not all these factors are at work in all corporate newspapers all the time. But they help explain the preponderance of evidence that the larger chains and corporate papers tend to be equal to or superior to noncorporate newspapers.

Boundaries Between "Church and State"

In the decades after World War II, there seemed to grow in larger, corporate newspapers a belief that there was a high wall that kept apart "the lofty church of the newsroom and the sordid counting room" of the enterprise.[32] In smaller, family run newspapers, of course, such a figurative barrier was unlikely, as the same person, or family, often served as both editor and publisher. The prevailing standard at the corporate newspapers was that the reporters and editors needed to cover what had to be covered and write what had to be written, without concern about how readers or advertisers reacted.

But facing declining circulation and advertising share, publishers at corporate newspapers have suggested that the wall must at least be permeable. James Batten, who rose from reporter to chairman of Knight-Ridder, admitted that "we were, after all, 'the press,' beholden to no one." But, he continued, "the days when we could do newspapering our way, and tell the world to go to hell if it didn't like the results, are gone forever."[33]

At Times Mirror's *Los Angeles Times*, this issue gripped the newsroom in 1998 when the publisher assigned a business executive to work with each section of the paper: Sports, Business, Metro, Life & Style, etc. It was part of a plan to find ways to attract new readers. The *Times*, which had a peak of 1.4 million circulation in 1991, had watched it drop to 1.1 million in 1997.[34] The concern of some journalists was that if advertising executives hinted that an article might offend a big advertiser, then it might pressure journalists to pull punches in articles. Some fear that even without direct hints, the fact that reporters and editors even think about the financial implications of what they are doing can taint their work.

However, even those who have been critical of journalistic practices have recognized that failing to understand the need to attract readers and advertisers leaves the "church" with fewer resources to do any job. James Fallows, a former editor of *U.S. News and World Report* tried to put such efforts in perspective. "What they [the *Times*] are doing has the potential to cause problems. But every publication is in business and they need to do well as a business. How this works depends on the execution."[35]

Why the Chains Keep Buying

The pace of merger activity ebbs and flows with general economic trends. In relative terms, the early part of the 20th century saw the greatest period of consolidation in the industry, as seen in Figure 1.2. Between 1910 and 1930, the number of dailies in groups

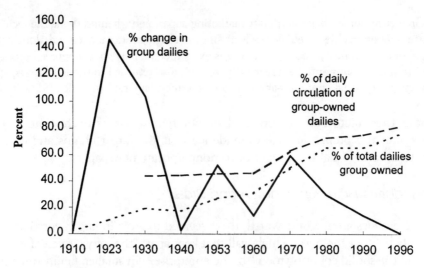

FIG. 1.2. Changes in Percentage and Number of Grouped-Owned Dailies and in Group Circulation, Selected Years, 1910–1996. Source: Table 1.12.

increased from 62 to 311—more than 400%. After World War II, there was another spurt of chain growth. However, the percentage of newspapers that were part of groups remained in the mid-40% range from 1930 to 1960. Starting with a consolidation from 1960 to 1970 that saw the number of dailies in groups increase from 31% to 50%, the 1970s through the 1990s saw the proportion of circulation accounted for by newspapers as part of groups grow to 82%. At the same time, the number of actual newspapers that were part of groups remained virtually unchanged between 1980 and 1996. And the number of groups, at 157 in 1970, had fallen to 129 by 1996.

The trends seen in Figure 1.2 indicate a shift in acquisition and consolidation patterns. By the 1980s, the weaker papers had long been bought or closed. By the 1990s, the pattern was for small chains to combine with one another or to sell to larger groups. So newspapers that had been part of a chain continued to be in a chain, only the ownership changed.

Why had newspapers continued to be a desirable investment in some quarters?

Profit

Newspapers *can* be a profitable investment. The median operating profit on the newspaper publishing sector for the publicly held media groups in Table 1.6 was about twice that of all publicly owned businesses. These, of course, are the survivors of a shrinking industry.

Scarce Commodity

Newspaper properties are attractive because they are a scarce commodity. With a finite market of good, potentially profitable properties, competition to buy them is strong. Quite a few companies in the newspaper business have actually sold other media interests so as to invest more heavily in newspapers. This includes Pulitzer, which sold its broadcast division and bought the Scripps League newspapers in 1996, and Times Mirror Co., which has shed its cable and broadcasting properties while expanding its reach in newspaper. The alternative of starting a newspaper of any size is not attractive. There just are not that many areas that can support a paper that do not already have one. In the 1960s, Cowles Communications spent three years trying to establish the *Suffolk Sun* in competition with *Newsday* on Long Island and eventually gave up. *Newsday*, a Times Mirror newspaper, in turn spent years trying to extend *Newsday* in the New York City market, ultimately abandoning the effort in 1995 at a cost of $250 million just to close down the effort.[36]

Professional Management

As profitable as newspapers can be, under the professional management of chains they can be even more so. The objective of a family-owned business is often different from one that is publicly owned or professionally managed. Minimizing taxes and maximizing cash, rather than earnings per share or return on investment, may be the objective of private owners. Earnings can also be increased by bringing in professional managers and using the sophisticated business and financial services many of the chains make available. The Gannett group has used a marketing team that was sent to any local paper in the chain to provide in-house consulting to find ways to boost circulation and advertising. One analyst explained why this makes a difference:

> I think the motivation of the earlier newspaper groups was essentially to be important people in the cities in which their operations were located. This orientation made them somewhat reluctant to be aggressive in pricing, advertising and circulation rates. The new managers have no such relationships.[37]

The ideal form of synergy of group management can be illustrated in the unique nature of Gannett's Suburban Newspapers group. A plant in Harrison, New York, prints nine of the dailies in the group, including three zoned editions of one of the papers. The papers, primarily afternoon editions, range in circulation from 3,300 to 45,000. The papers have some separate editorial staff, but share a common building and production equipment and can afford technology that would be prohibitive to any one of the papers alone. Moreover, certain common features and advertising inserts are combined with local news and advertising, enabling each paper to be something more than it might be otherwise. It has what might be termed a "critical mass" needed for certain newspaper economies.

Cash

Newspaper chains tend to generate large amounts of cash, not only from profits but from depreciation and amortization of goodwill. They also carry low debt in relation to invested capital as compared to other businesses. Lee Enterprises, which had a net profit of $54 million in 1997, generated an additional $30 million in cash through depreciation and amortization. In addition, tax laws allow firms to accumulate undistributed profits to buy other communications properties, and as such are exempt from tax provisions on excess accumulated profits. This encourages further acquisition.

There exists little convincing evidence that being part of a group provides any advantage in gaining advertising. Most newspaper advertising is derived from local sources and the small amount of national advertising comes mostly through advertising agencies. Similarly, few chains provide economies in purchasing supplies, and even labor negotiations tend to take place at the local level.

The Case of MediaNews Group

There is a human tendency, it seems, to look for simple answers, to seek black-and-white distinctions, to hold absolutes of good and bad. It rarely is that clear. And so it is with the ownership and management of newspapers. William Dean Singleton and his MediaNews Group may be a good case study.

Singleton got his experience working for others. When appointed publisher of the *Trenton (NJ) Times*, one of his first decisions was to fire one fourth of the staff. In 1983 he started his own company. From its earliest acquisition, a 24,000 circulation paper in Woodbury, New Jersey, the company and its part-owner, Singleton, picked up the reputation as being ruthless in its management because they cut back on newsroom and most other expenses, including trimming staff. At first it bought mostly small papers, but eventually it bought the *Houston Post*—which it proceeded to sell to its competitor, the *Chronicle*, which promptly closed it down. In 1998, he acquired the *Long Beach Press-Telegram* from Knight-Ridder. Singleton soon cut 100 of 500 staff jobs and cut the salaries of those who remained.[38]

Singleton could have been the poster-boy for greedy chain owner. But, on the other hand, Singleton had a story to tell. Papers are often sold because there is something wrong—like too many staffers or people in the wrong position. "Starting years ago, we could only afford to buy troubled papers, so we did lots of changes . . . ," one of his former editors explained, citing Singleton's willingness to buy the dying Oakland *Tribune*. "That paper was within minutes of extinction, and we saved it." Says Singleton, "Nobody enjoys trimming a paper's cost, but when it's losing money, you have to strengthen it."

Singleton can also point to the *Denver Post*, purchased from Times Mirror in 1987 as another fire sale. But by making the hard decisions that Times Mirror would not, the *Post* turned around, both as a financial and editorial entity. In 1998, its circulation exceeded that of the *Rocky Mountain News*.

There may also be an upside with this breed of owners for the journalists who crave their independence. Most newspaper entrepreneurs who choose newspapers instead of pharmaceuticals or fast food franchising do so for their business interests. Many are in it for the financial gains they expect, not because of an ideology. The former editor of the *Denver Post* said that one of Singleton's beliefs was not to interfere with editorial operations.[39] The quickest path to losing circulation today might be for an owner of a single paper or a group to alienate a segment of its readers by deviating editorially from journalistic standards on the news pages or by being extreme in its editorial pages.

Table 1.17 lists some acquisitions as well as sales and, where available, the price paid.

TABLE 1.17

A Sampling of Mergers and Acquisitions in the Daily Newspaper Industry

Purchaser	Property Purchased	Seller	Year	Price (where known)
Knight-Ridder	Kansas City Star, Ft. Worth Star-Telegram, Wilkes-Barre (PA) Times Leader, Belleville (IL) News-Democrat	Walt Disney Co.	1997	$1.65 billion
Knight-Ridder	Lesher Communications	Lesher Communications	1995	$360 million
Knight-Ridder	The Monterey County Herald and San LuisObispo Telegram-Tribune	E. W. Scripps	1997	Swap for Boulder Camera
E. W. Scripps	The Boulder (CO) Daily Camera	Knight-Ridder	1997	Swap for Monteray and San LuisObispo papers
E. W. Scripps	6 dailies	Harte-Hanks	1997	$625 million
Gannett Co.	10 dailies	Multimedia Inc.	1995	$2.3 billion*
McClatchy Newspapers	Raleigh News & Observer	News & Observer Publishing Co.	1995	$1.4 billion
South Coast Newspapers	The Times Advocate in Escondido The Californian in Temecula	Times Advocate Co.	1995	
Walt Disney Co.	Newspapers including Kansas City Star, Ft. Worth Star-Telegram	ABC/Capital Cities	1997	$18.9 billion
MediaNews Group	Long Beach Press-Telegram	Knight-Ridder	1997	$50.7 million for all four papers
Community Newspaper Holdings	Milledgeville Union-Recorder, Boca Raton News, Newberry Observer	Knight-Ridder	1997	
Hollinger	Johnstown Tribune-Democrat	MediaNews Group	1996	six small dailies, several weekly newspapers, and $31.4 million
Hollinger	Times-West Virginian and The Meadville Tribune	Thomson	1998	
Media General	28 daily newspapers, 10 TV stations	Park Communications	1996	$710 million
McClatchy Newspapers	Minneapolis Star & Tribune, other businesses	Cowles Media Co.	1997	$1.4 billion*
Dow Jones	Portsmouth (N.H.) Herald	Thomson Corporation	1997	swap for Sun City (AZ) News-Sun
Various	32 daily newspapers in US, 14 in Canada	Thomson Corporation	1996–97	$900 million

*includes other media holdings, some of which acquirers subsequently sold.
Sources: Company press releases, 10-Ks, trade publications.

STRATEGIES FOR GROWTH IN CHAINS

Over the years, newspaper firms have followed diverse strategies for growth. They all recognize to varying degrees, however, that growth can come about only through new ventures or acquisition. This is due to the mature nature of the newspaper industry. Internal profit growth from circulation and advertising gains is slow. The savings from the electronic production technology of the 1970s were a welcome, but one-shot phenomenon. Other than a common recognition of the need for some sort of outside growth, chains have evolved several overlapping approaches: acquisitions of additional newspapers or diversification into allied media (i.e., broadcasting and cable, magazines and book publishing, and most recently, electronic information services).

Broadcasting

Of the 21 newspaper firms listed in Table 1.18, 12 had broadcast interests in 1996. Newspapers were involved in the earliest days of radio and television. They were among the pioneer users of wireless telegraphy as a news-gathering tool. The *New York Times* received the initial message from a transatlantic service in 1907.[40] They were also among the first to try out commercial broadcasting. As is often the case, some publishers entered into the business as a new opportunity, and others wanted to hedge their bets should radio become a real threat to newspaper circulation or advertising. Another motivation was the prestige it could bring them in their communities by taking the lead in these new enterprises.[41]

Over time, some publishers increased their broadcast interests, while others cut back or eliminated broadcasting. Among the latter are Times Mirror and Knight-Ridder. On the other hand, the Washington Post Co., Hearst and E. W. Scripps are among those that have increased their investments in broadcasting. Still, what makes these all *newspaper* publishers with diversification in broadcasting is that each of these firms got its start in newspapers and still derive more revenue (although not necessarily profit) from its newspaper operations.

Magazines and Book Publishing

Five of these newspaper publishers have enough revenue from magazine publishing to be considered a separate line of business. Four are book publishers. Some publishers have a long history of participation in other publishing formats. Hearst has been involved in magazine publishing almost as long as with newspapers (see Chapter 2) and probably has greater revenue from magazines than from newspapers.[42] With its purchase of the Conde Nast group in 1957 and subsequent acquisitions like *The New Yorker* (1985) and *Wired* (1998), the Newhouse interests have built a substantial magazine group. Times Mirror and the New York Times Co. have waxed and waned in involvement in magazines as well as books. In 1980, Newhouse purchased book publisher Random House from RCA (for $60 million), then sold it as a much more prosperous enterprise to Bertelsmann in 1998 (for more than $1.2 billion). Times Mirror Co. had a long association with book publishing with its Matthew

TABLE 1.18
Diversification of Newspaper Publishers, by Revenue Source, 1996

	% from Newspapers	% from Broadcasting	% from Cable	% from Books	% from Magazines	% from Business Information Services	% from Other Sources
A. H. Belo	56	44					
Central Newspapers	100						
Dow Jones	58					42	
Gannett	81	12					7
Hollinger	100						
Independent Newspapers	100						
Knight-Ridder	82					18	
Lee Enterprises	73	27					
McClatchy Newspapers	100						
Media General	63		37				
MediaNews Group	100						
New York Times	90	3			7		
Pulitzer Publishing	57	43					
E. W. Scripps	49	23	21				7
Thomson	26					74	
Times Mirror	60			32	9		
Tribune Co.	58	37		5			
Washington Post	46	19	12		22		
Hearst	25	15		10	35		15
Newhouse	30	10	25		35		
Cox Enterprises	35	15	27				23

Source: *Communications Industry Report*, 15th ed. (New York: Veronis, Suhler & Associates, October 1997).

Bender & Co., C. V. Mosby and other imprints, all of which were sold in 1997 and 1998. Thomson became a major book publisher with its 1996 acquisition of legal publisher West Publishing, although it was primarily interested in its electronic publishing sector.

Cable

Five of these newspaper companies had investments in cable operators and, in several cases, in programming services (see Chapter 4). For a time, newspaper-based companies "discovered" cable systems for investment. Unlike broadcasting, few major newspaper companies had the vision or plan to be among the pioneers in cable. A few, however, such as Cox, did invest early. By 1981, Cox had more than 1 million subscribers in its systems. Times Mirror and Newhouse were also major investors. Tribune Co. and the New York Times Co. had small interests.

By the late 1990s, however, many newspaper companies had sold their cable interests, most prominently E. W. Scripps, which sold its systems to Comcast in 1996 for $1.6 billion.[43] Newhouse bailed out of broadcasting but increased its stake in cable systems and programming.

Newsprint and Paper Products

With newsprint accounting for roughly 15% of the total expenses of large circulation newspapers, a few publishers have tried their hand at vertical integration by investing in newsprint manufacturing or, in the case of Times Mirror, in wood and paper products broadly. Most have either totally abandoned or cut back on this strategy as being an unprofitable allocation of resources. Times Mirror sold off its entire paper products subsidiary. Dow Jones has sold its newsprint investment, but the New York Times Co., Cox, Media General and Knight-Ridder are among those who maintain equity investments in newsprint plants. It is not a meaningful income stream for any of these companies. These investments have served mostly as a hedge against occasional bubbles of increased newsprint costs as well as less occasional shortages.

Electronic Information Services

The Business Information Services category in Table 1.18 refers primarily to electronic information services tailored for business rather than consumer users. Only three publishers had meaningful revenue in 1996. One of those, Knight-Ridder, acquired Dialog Information Services from Lockheed in 1988 for $353 million and sold it in 1997 for $420 million—all in all making this a poor investment.

Although most newspaper publishers were involved in electronic publishing in the late 1990s via Web sites on the Internet (see Chapter 7), some had looked at elec-

TABLE 1.19
Diversification of Newspaper Publishers, 1980 and 1996

	1996	1980
Same or more in newspapers		
McClatchy Newspapers	100%	100%
Independent Newspapers	100	100
Central Newspapers	100	100
New York Times	89	70
Gannett	79	77
Media General	64	44
Times Mirror	61	47
Less in newspapers		
Lee Enterprises	72	73
Washington Post	45	47
Knight-Ridder	86	90
Tribune Co.	56	67
Cox Enterprises*	35	61
E. W. Scripps	60	83
Dow Jones	60	93
Newhouse*	30	75
Hearst*	25	60
Thomson	22	100

*Estimates.
Sources: 1996: Table 2.18; 1980: *Who Owns the Media?*, 2nd ed., p. 53.

tronic delivery of information as a business opportunity long before the Internet
became a mass medium. With its business markets, Dow Jones had been delivering
breaking financial news via wireline services for years. Its information services business accounted for 37% of its 1997 revenue. It was also a leader in charging consumers for its World Wide Web based information services.

Thomson has engaged in a strategic plan to sell off many of its small newspapers
(often selling to another Canada-based company, Hollinger International), while
keeping the *Toronto Globe and Mail*, one of Canada's premier newspapers. In 1996
and 1997 alone, it sold 46 daily newspapers. By 1997, only 22% of Thomson's revenues were from newspapers. In 1991, it bought Macmillan's Professional and Business Reference Publishing followed by JPT Publishing, including the Institute for
Scientific Information, which it claims is the world's largest commercial scientific
research database. In 1994, Thomson acquired the reference database service, Information Access Company, from Ziff Communications. Thomson used its proceeds
from selling its newspapers to purchase West Publishing in 1996, a leading publishing of law books, increasingly accessed online.

Both Times Mirror and Knight-Ridder made what, in retrospect, were premature
investments in consumer online information services in the early 1980s. Neither service found a market, floundering on expensive hardware, slow access and proprietary
systems. Despite, or perhaps because of, this experience, Knight-Ridder was one of the
earliest to embrace the emerging consumer electronic information market of the
1990s, with its Mercury Center service from its San Jose newspaper. The *Los Angeles
Times*, Times Mirror's flagship newspaper, relaunched a consumer service on Prodigy as
a proprietary service, but by 1996 had moved it to the World Wide Web.

See Chapter 7 for further descriptions of newspaper company involved in electronic information services.

. . . And Newspapers

Yet through it all, some publishers continue to stay focused on the newspaper business: McClatchy and Central are among some of the older public companies.
Hollinger, a relatively new company that established itself in Canada, bought its first
newspaper in the United States in 1986. It bailed out the ailing *Chicago Sun-Times*
and a group of suburban Chicago dailies in 1994. It continued buying very small
town papers, but in 1998 purchased the Gary, Indiana, *Post-Tribune* (circulation
65,000) from Knight-Ridder, while selling some of its smallest papers.

And new investors have enough faith in the profitability of newspaper to join the
industry. Leonard Green & Partners is an investment company. Some of it major
investors are the state pension funds of California, Michigan and Pennsylvania. In
1997, it paid $310 million to buy 56 dailies, 34 paid weeklies and 77 free papers with
a combined circulation of 900,000—all spread through 11 states, with major clusters
in southern Illinois, Missouri, western New York, Pennsylvania and California—
from Hollinger Inc. and organized them as Liberty Group Publishing.[44]

Why did Liberty Group Publishing invest in newspapers? The community newspapers the firm has purchased from Hollinger are big moneymakers, with an average

profit margin of more than 30% on revenues. One of the partners in Leonard Green summed it up:

> Despite the sad talk about declining newspaper circulation and the growth of interactive media, [partner Peter] Nolan thinks papers are a tremendous investment, particularly in smaller markets where local papers face less competition from radio, television or the Internet. What's more, he said, his conversations with advertisers have convinced him that revenues will continue to grow.
>
> Said Nolan, "We're contrarian investors. While everyone's running to radio, running to TV, running to electronics and the Internet, we think that creates an opportunity with newspapers. It's a very mature industry but it's far from dying. We're very bullish on newspapers."
>
> "There's no fat in the machine that needs to be cut out," Nolan commented. "They're running pretty darn well. We have absolutely no plans to reduce staff. In fact, we'll be hiring."[45]

Another chain that started in the newspaper business with a clear sense of newspaper trends, MediaNews Group, was profiled previously. It started acquiring daily newspapers in 1983. In 1998, it published 35 dailies and more than 100 weeklies and shoppers in 11 states, including the *Denver Post*. In 1997, it acquired the *Long Beach (CA) Press-Telegram* from Knight-Ridder and the *Los Angeles Daily News*.

Table 1.18 is useful to see the range (or perhaps the lack to range) of firms whose primary business is publishing daily newspapers. But it is static—a snapshot. As the previous descriptions show, many publishers have had a variety of strategies. This reflects a typical business pattern: Some managers and owners like to have a "portfolio" of investments. Others believe in focusing on one or two things they know best. Some owners may see opportunities with a limited time horizon. Others invest out of fear of what they might miss. A change in ownership or management may bring changed priorities. Sometimes management will embrace a strategy that has worked in the past. Other managers come in and want to make their own mark.

Most of all, the environment in which publishers—and all business—operates is dynamic. When cities were growing, literacy climbing, standards of living rising, newspapers benefitted. Advertisers wanted to reach consumers with disposable income. Industrial workers may have felt more need to know about the world around them than the generation that lived on the farm. Buses and trolleys let people live further from their work, and also gave them some idle moments to read a newspaper going to or from. In such an environment, newspapers could grow and thrive.

Radio, television, the movement to the suburbs, replacement of sitting on the bus with driving in the car, direct mail and shopper papers are among the many changes facing the publisher of dailies. Their markets stopped growing. They could remain profitable only by outlasting their direct competition, offering some combination of content, pricing, delivery service and "branding" to hold on to their readers and thereby their advertisers. Strategies that involved concentrating ever more on newspapers had to be weighed against alternatives, such as putting scarce resources (personnel as well as capital) in other ventures. In previous decades, those alternatives included other print media or broadcasting, then cable. In the first decade of the

21st century, investing in newspapers can have limited appeal, and only then under conditions that overcome the powerful trends against the prospects of traditional newspapers.

Why Independent Papers Keep Selling

For every purchase, there must be someone willing to sell. Privately held independent newspapers are being pressured to sell for several reasons. "Greed, taxes and internecine struggles among dozens of stockholding heirs have helped speed the dissolution of family-owned papers."[46] But economic trends that have already been identified have also persuaded families to sell: declining circulation, rising newsprint prices, the movement of businesses and readers from downtowns to suburbs, competition from new technology and global media chains and buyers willing to pay more for a newspaper than it may be worth.

Weak Management

Rising costs and competition—including the investment in online sites, wages, newsprint and presses—require strict controls and profit planning, which small independents cannot always get or do not have the resolve to implement. Groups can attract bright young people and give them publisher titles. Groups can have specialists who can set up control systems for each paper, without any one of them having to be burdened by full development costs. Likewise, the chains can have production specialists to help in evaluating technology. With little or no history in a community, new owners can often make the hard choices that need to be made to allow a newspaper to thrive—or just survive.

Family Squabbles

A newspaper company represents "stored value." Although the founding family and a succeeding generation or two may have had a commitment to journalism, over time the great grandchildren, cousins and others sometimes grow apart. " 'Few family businesses endure to the fourth generation in America,' says Howard Muson, publisher of *Family Business Magazine*."[47] Some family members see their assets tied up in a newspaper that may be returning little to them in dividends, but has grown to be worth tens or hundreds of millions of dollars. Some family members want access to this wealth and have enough stock to make themselves heard. " 'What holds a family business together is shared values and commitments,' according to Frank Blethen, publisher of the *Seattle Times* and member of the family that control a majority of the stock. 'You can create corporate structures, classes of stock, trusts and arrangements, a framework to perpetuate family ownership. But in the end, there has to be family harmony.' "[48]

But as families expand, differences of opinion are likely to increase. At the *Oakland (CA) Tribune*, family problems led that paper to sell to Combined Communications in 1977.[49] Both the father and grandfather of the publisher were former U.S. Senators. With the paper to use as a power base, business was secondary. Some family members involved in management in 1976 complained that the paper was being run "more for civic pride than profit."[50] "The idea of a family-owned newspaper in the future is not probable," concluded the publisher of the family-owned *Louisville (KY) Courier-Journal* in 1977.[51] He was indeed prophetic, as his family sold the paper to Gannett in 1986.

In 1996, the *Brockton Enterprise* in Massachusetts, owned and managed by the Fuller family for 115 years, was sold to a newly formed media company, Newspaper Media Co. The immediate issue for the afternoon paper was sharply decreasing profits in 1995, due to skyrocketing newsprint costs and declining ad revenues. But this was only the catalyst for long simmering family differences. Fuller family members had been at odds over whether to sell the struggling family legacy. The paper's publisher, Myron F. Fuller, said he considered buying out the interests of the remaining family shareholders, but could not afford it and therefore agreed to the sale.[52]

The McClatchy Company, although publicly owned, is still largely controlled by the founding family. In 1997 it acquired Cowles Media, another longtime family-controlled company whose flagship paper was the *Minneapolis Star Tribune*. "Family pressures lead to Cowles's decision to put itself on the [sales] block."[53] At the time, Cowles shares were valued at half the rate of other media companies and some family members wanted to use their share of the assets for their own purposes. A similar family dispute lead to the sale of the *Des Moines Register & Tribune* to Gannett in 1985.[54]

Some of the larger publishers have managed to take advantage of the markets for public capital by setting up two classes of stock, with voting power remaining with the founding family, but all stockholders sharing dividends and appreciation, if any. Six of the 10 largest newspaper companies in the United States are so structured, among them Dow Jones, The New York Times Co., Tribune Co., Times Mirror Co., as well as The Washington Post Co. and The McClatchy Company.

These arrangements make it difficult for an unwanted acquirer to buy the company. But they have a downside. First, they tend to depress the stock value relative to similar companies with more conventional ownership. Investors tend to reduce the value of stock that does not include full voting rights. It also means that a small group of family member stockholders—or even an individual—has enough voting power to force a break-up of all or some of the company's assets.

This is what happened to Dow Jones in 1997. The descendants of the founding Bancroft family control 70% of the voting stock. Several family members were becoming dissatisfied with the direction of the company. In particular, the company had planned to invest $650 million in its Dow Jones Markets division, a part of the company that faced entrenched competition and had not been doing well. As a result, whereas the value of an investment in Gannett, Knight-Ridder or The New York Times Co. has increased more than 40% in 1997, Dow Jones stock went up less than half that rate. Under pressure from several family members, Dow Jones management sold the underperforming division instead of investing more in it.[55]

Financial Weakness

Smaller companies do not have as many financial resources to cope with the results of several years of losses during a recession, or to compete with shoppers, radio stations, cable or television operators all seeking the same local advertisers. Sometimes they are not able to recover from a poor investment. Larger chains, in newspapers as in any other field, are likely to have greater latitude to make up for a downturn in one segment of their business or a bad investment. Often it is the stockholders who face lower earnings and stock prices (as Dow Jones' experience with its Telerate investment) instead of immediately turning to the layoffs that might face a small firm with shallow financial pockets.

Two so-called independent publishers—one large, one small—illustrate these factors. The context in which Frank Blethen, the Chief Executive of the company that publishes the *Seattle Times* was discussing family squabbles was that of pressure from Knight-Ridder to buy the company. Knight-Ridder owns 49%, but appoints only 4 of 12 members of the Board of Directors. Blethen admitted that Knight-Ridder's involvement with the company had its benefits, but resented its attempts to pressure the family to sell out the other 51%.[56]

But how did Knight-Ridder get 49% ownership in the first place? During the Depression, Ridder Brothers, Inc., already a chain owner, provided the money to stave off impending bankruptcy of the second generation of the Times' family owners. That interest became part of Knight-Ridder when the Knight and Ridder chains merged.

A similar scenario faced the family that owned the *Berkshire Eagle* in western Massachusetts for more than a century. The *Eagle*, a 32,000 circulation paper, had a solid reputation for quality journalism, having won several prestigious prizes, including the Pulitzer for Editorial Writing in 1973.[57] But it embarked on an ambitious real estate project in the late 1980s to renovate an old factory to use for the newspaper's offices as well as rental space for others. A minor recession drove down real estate values in the New England economy and the owning family was deep in debt. Its major asset was the newspaper company, which it sold (including three other small dailies) to MediaNews Group.

Taxes

Estate Taxes. Taxes, inheritance taxes as well as tax rates of sales of property, may be the most important variable in determining why and when newpapers get sold. Indeed, a statistical study by Dertouzos and Thorpe[58] that looked at various motivations for selling newspapers found that in the early 1980s by far the most compelling explanation for newspaper chains was the tax laws. Although the Economic Recovery Act of 1981 and subsequent revisions to the tax code since then reduced some of the most glaring negative motivations, tax regulations continue to play a role in sales and mergers.

Estate tax laws were initiated in 1916 more as a social measure to redistribute wealth than as a revenue raiser. In 1997, that tax rate for estates greater than $600,000 was 37% and went as high as 55% on estates greater than $3 million.[59] A valuable newspaper property that is privately held is a taxable asset in the estate when the principal(s) die. The estate must pay the tax on the value of the property. If the estate is not well endowed with cash or other marketable securities to sell, then the heirs may be forced to sell the newspaper to pay the taxes on it. In the absence of rigorous estate planning, at the death of the principal owner, the newspaper or newspapers are valued by the Internal Revenue Service at their market value. Thus, a small newspaper or small family-owned group that generates perhaps $500,000 annually on annual sales of $10 million may be valued at $15 million, leaving the heirs with a tax bill of perhaps $7 million. Few families have the means to pay such a sum without selling off the assets that caused them. Even with estate planning, the estate tax can be formidable. Says one newspaper executive, "Some families have had to lay off employees, substantially cut capital investment or sell their newspapers. . . . Borrowing that much could cripple a family's ability to invest in and grow the business."[60]

To cope with estate taxes, most families engage in rigorous, complicated and expensive planning, providing for ownership successor strategies that lower tax obligations. But even that has its costs on the operation of the newspapers. Notes William Morris, head of the family-owned Morris Communications, "Instead of the business using the money to expand and grow, it must use part of the income for defensive measures [to minimize tax]."[61]

The 1976 Tax Reform Act, which changed the method of determining the valuation of an asset in an estate, was specifically identified as a primary motivator in the sale that year of the family-owned *New York Post* to another family-owned but obscure newspaper company, Australia's News Corp.[62]

Favorable Tax Treatment of Stock Swaps.   Another aspect of the tax structure encourages selling to publicly owned groups rather than to individuals or other family-controlled companies. Private companies generally make their purchases with cash—they have little else to offer the selling company. The sellers, therefore, must pay a capital gains tax (20% in 1998, but as high as 36% previously) on the difference between their investment in their newspaper(s), which is often almost negligible if in the family for many years, and the purchase price. Publicly owned companies, on the other hand, have another option—stock in their company that has a known market value. If the exchange is for stock in the purchasing firm, then the swap is tax free, until the seller decides to sell the purchasing firm's stock. With stock, the sellers can parcel it out to family members and even employees and let them each decide if they want to sell some or all of it whenever they see fit and pay capital gains tax only on the amount of stock sold. In strong economic times, publicly owned companies have another advantage over private ones. As their stock price increases, they need to offer fewer shares for any given purchase price. For example, if acquiring company Alpha has stock trading at $10 per share and they want to buy publisher Beta for $20 million, they would give the owners of Beta 2 million shares. But if strong profits and a strong economy help drive Alpha's stock to $15 per share, they need to offer only 1.33 million shares to make up a $20 million purchase.

High Offering Prices

Depending on the perspective, it could be called prudence or greed when huge sums are offered for newspapers that yield modest incomes and profits to their owners. There are a finite number of daily newspapers and little expectation that new ones can be started in most communities. Thus, the demand by those who like the newspaper business seems to be greater than the supply of papers and small chains for sale. Hence independent and small chain publishers are simply being over-whelmed with offers and money. "Ultimately, economics will control," noted Robert Singleton, former Knight-Ridder chief financial officer and past member of the *Seattle Times*' Board of Directors. "Dangle enough money, somebody'll get greedy, and the Blethen family will cave."[63]

For one or, more likely, some combination of these reasons, individual newspapers and small groups that have sold themselves to larger entities in the 1990s were the *Raleigh News & Observer* and the *Minneapolis Star Tribune* (both to McClatchy), the *Quincy Patriot Ledger* (to a new company, Newspaper Media) and the *Asbury Park Press* (to Gannett). Of course, there is another, quite strategic reason: Some owners and investors may believe that the long-term outlook for newspapers is not attrac-tive. They see the declining circulation and advertising share, competition from older and newer media formats and may decide that they should bail out now.

John Morton, a longtime analyst and observer of the newspaper industry, as well as a broker, summed up the activity in sales: "What all this signifies is that newspa-pers is a business, and in time the imperatives of business overcome all other con-siderations, regardless of whether the family business is a big chain or a small paper in the boondocks."[64]

DECLINING COMPETITION
AND THE "MONOPOLY" NEWSPAPER?

Of more concern to some observers than the growth of chains per se is the perceived decline of newspaper competition within individual markets. Whereas 502 cities had two or more competing newspapers in 1923, including 100 cities with three or more papers, by 1998 that figure had decreased to 34 cities, including those with joint operating agreements. And only two cities, New York and Chicago, have three competing ownerships of English-language general interest daily newspapers.

However, the few U.S. cities with competing newspaper firms accounted for 20.8% of all daily circulation, down slightly from 22.8% in 1980. This was still a sig-nificant decline from 1923, when 88.8% of newspapers were sold in cities with mul-tiple competing newspapers.

It should not be surprising that larger cities are more likely to be able to support competing newspaper firms. Even at the peak of newspaper competition, many smaller towns had a single newspaper. Yet only 8 of the 19 cities with fully compet-ing papers have over 100,000 circulation, and 13 of 15 cities with joint operating agreement newspapers were larger than 100,000.

However, whether or not newspapers are local "monopolies" may involve a more complex response than might first appear. Corollary questions concern what consti-tutes a monopoly and whether newspapers that face no direct daily newspaper com-petition provide an inferior editorial product compared to those with direct compe-tition. Has the changing structure of the newspaper industry at the local level lessened the diversity of points of view available to readers? Have the results of

declining direct competition resulted in a monopoly price structure for the advertisers and subscribers?

Economic Structure of Newspapers

The production of a traditional newspaper is a manufacturing process. It utilizes
machines: terminals, typesetters, plate makers; raw materials: newsprint paper and ink;
passing though a fabrication process: a printing press that smears ink on the paper,
folds and trims the paper before being passed on to other machines that stack, bundle,
tie or wrap the newspapers and direct them to a loading dock. From there, they must
be distributed just as lettuce or tennis shoes. Trucks may take the newspaper to wholesalers, who further distribute papers to retailers for sale to customers or to cars and
trucks that take the newspapers to coin-operated boxes or individual homes.

  Thus, an understanding of why most towns have only a single newspaper derives
from an analysis of the economics of manufacturing, in particular economies of scale.
Most critical is the notion of "first copy cost." All manufacturing operations can
generally assign the costs of production to either "fixed costs" (those needed for any
level of production) and "variable costs" (those that change as levels of production
change). Fixed costs plus variable costs equals the total cost of producing a product.
In newspaper publishing, the fixed or first copy costs include virtually all editorial
and advertising sales salaries and part of the circulation staff: all the costs associated
with taking the words, photographs, advertising copy created by reporters and editors and ads sold and typesetting them, creating a printing plate and mounting it on
the printing press. Thus, before the presses roll each day, the publisher has incurred
substantial costs.

  For a typical daily, the first copy cost is from 40% to 45% of total costs.[65] Clearly,
the greater the number of newspapers that can then be printed (and sold), the lower
the average cost per copy. Second, the cost of publishing additional pages declines
as the number of pages increases at any constant level of circulation. This is true, in
part, because the cost of running the press does not increase proportionally to the
number of pages printed at the same time. Finally, the expense of distributing one
newspaper in a given locale to a group of subscribers is less than several firms each
covering that territory for the same number of total subscribers.

  Variable costs are all those that change with levels of production. For newspapers,
these include, most significantly, newsprint and ink, which together account for
15% to 20% of total expenses. Wear and tear on the press and electricity to run them
are other variable costs. Some costs are hard to allocate. A fleet of delivery trucks is
a fixed cost until it is time to replace the truck. If circulation is down and the trucks
have not been delivering a full load, then more papers may be put on another truck
and the older one not replaced, moving it from a fixed to a variable cost.

  The rate at which variable costs increase depends on the "marginal" cost of production. In orange juice manufacturing, an additional quart has significant marginal cost: the cost of oranges, packaging and the cost of shipping that quart are a substantial portion of the total price of the quart of juice. For a newspaper, the marginal
cost is not much: primarily newsprint and ink. Reporters do not get paid more for

extending the press run another copy. Nor do editors or classified ad takers. Assuming there is room on the truck, the transportation cost is almost invisible.

Figure 1.3a shows how the fixed and variable costs combine for total cost for a typical manufactured good, such as an automobile or orange juice. Figure 1.3b illustrates how the fixed cost (or first copy cost) of a newspaper compares to the variable costs. It is meant to show that for most manufactured goods, the variable costs are a substantial part of the total cost—labor and material associated with additional units. In contrast, for newspapers, a high proportion of total costs is the first copy (this holds true for magazines and books, even more so for television and online).

What all this means in practice is that a newspaper with 50,000 circulation is far less expensive to publish than two newspapers each with 25,000 circulation. Even more important in understanding the demise of local competition is that if one newspaper can get a significant lead over its rival in circulation, then it has a huge economic advantage. If a 15,000 circulation newspaper is trying to compete with a rival that sells 60,000 daily, then it faces a similar cost structure—for reporters, wire services, presses, trucks to get out to all parts of the city. But it gets less revenue from their advertisers, who obviously expect to pay less to reach 15,000 rather than

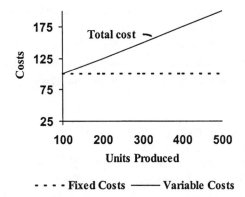

FIG. 1.3a.   Illustrative Manufactured Product Costs.

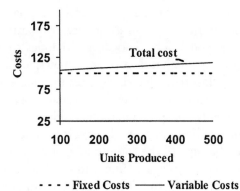

FIG. 1.3b.   Illustrative Newspaper Production Costs.

60,000 households. This, then, is what is meant by economies of scale. It also represents a major economic barrier to entry for anyone considering starting up a new
paper in competition to an entrenched one.

As the second paper falls behind, it must cut staff, offer fewer features and get
thinner; and it eventually sells out to the rival or folds it doors and slips quietly into
the night. This is a major part of the story of the demise of intracity newspaper competition.

The Market for Newspapers

In the world of economics, the "market" for a product or service may refer to two
parameters. One is the market for the *product*: The market for tomatoes are all those
who buy tomatoes and tomato-based product—like sauces. The market for 35 mm
film are all those amateur and professional photographers who take photographs
with 35 mm cameras.

A second use of "market" is a *geographical reference*: The Cleveland market is an
area that includes the suburbs of that city. A geographical market can be global—
IBM can provide its services in much of the world—or quite local, such as a plumber
whose business is in the Cleveland suburb of Shaker Heights.

Newspapers (and most magazines) are unlike most other products because their
product market is less well defined. Is the market for the newspaper the reader who
buys the papers or the advertiser who, in effect, is buying access to the readers? The
bulk of the newspaper's revenue comes from advertisers. But unless it produces a
product that readers find useful, they stop buying the newspaper, reducing the value
to advertisers.

Competition and Advertising Rates

Competition for the advertiser market could include competition among newspapers for local and national advertisers, competition between metropolitan newspapers and nearby smaller dailies and weeklies and competition between newspapers
and other media.

One researcher found that "consumers [advertisers and readers] receive no benefits from the assumed economies of scale" and "consumers pay higher prices under
monopoly with no compensating increase in quality or quantity of product."[66] But
other research is more equivocal. John Langdon concludes that "concentration of
daily newspaper circulation in the hands of a single newspaper does appear to raise
the general [national] and classified advertising rates to some extent." But he added
that his study lacked statistical results for retail advertising levels, the area in which
the consequences of monopoly power in a market could be expected to be the greatest. He further stated that milline rates for advertisers may actually decrease following a merger in a market, because of the "dominance of circulation over concentration";[67] that is, any increase in agate line rates is more than offset by the
proportionately greater increase in circulation of the combined daily. This comes
from the previously discussed economies of scale: The cost associated with publishing one newspaper with a given circulation is lower than those of two newspapers

each with a portion of that circulation. The advertiser also avoids having to pay for duplicate readership of the competing papers.

For the most part, there has been scant attention paid to intermedia competition. There are some cross-elasticities between newspapers as an advertising vehicle and other media: direct mail, shopper papers, Yellow Pages, radio, local and national television and increasingly online-based options. Metropolitan newspapers may also have some competition from city magazines. However, publishers believe they do have greater latitude in setting advertising rates if they run the only newspaper in town. An increase in ad rates of from 15% to 30% has reportedly followed after the demise of a competing newspaper or formation of a joint operating agreement.[68] Even this, however, is subject to interpretation: Does this reflect the higher circulation of the surviving newspaper?

Although other media may not be perfect substitutes for newspaper advertising, newspaper publishers believe they face competition from other media and some research supports them.[69] A study that interviewed 131 advertising decision-makers in six small newspaper communities generally supported the contention that newspapers compete with other media, particularly among more knowledgeable advertisers (e.g., national and regional chains that used inserts). Less knowledgeable advertiser decision-makers who used run-of-press advertising (presumably smaller, local establishments) were less likely to consider non-newspaper alternatives if advertising rates increased.[70] Although case law has not recognized other media as viable competition for newspapers, they would seem to be for certain classes of advertisers.

One study tried to evaluate whether other media were substitutes for national newspaper advertising.[71] The finding was that the coefficients of cross-elasticity of demand for newspapers and eight other media (subsets of network television, network radio billboards and magazines) was in all cases less than zero. This indicated that national advertisers would not divert budgets from other media to newspapers in proportionate response to lower ad rates at newspapers or higher ad rates in the other media. This study, however, only examined the national geographic market and would need to be extended to the local retail market for greater relevance. Long-term trends, however, have suggested that advertisers have indeed replaced newspapers with other media. This can be seen in two comparisons:

- In 1935, newspapers accounted for 45% of all advertising expenditures;[72] radio had 7%. Ten years later, as radio matured, it had 15% of expenditures, whereas newspapers fell to 32%. In that same period, magazines jumped from 8% to 13% of advertising. Thus, these two media accounted for an additional 13% of advertising—newspaper share fell 13%. Between 1950 and 1960, the first decade of television, newspaper advertising share fell nearly 8 points and television garnered 10%.

- In 1950, national advertising in newspapers accounted for 16% of all national advertising. That had fallen to under 9% by 1970 and to half that (4.5%) in 1997.[73]

It is reasonable to assume that some advertisers felt that radio and television were substitutes—or indeed superior to—newspapers. Advertising that used to be in newspapers (when they and magazines were the two major national media) has clearly been diverted to other media, presumably radio and television.

This substitutability can be seen cleanly in the diversion of advertising dollars from broadcasting to newspapers (and magazines) by cigarette manufacturers after advertising of their product was banned from broadcasting in 1971. In 1970, only 3.9% of cigarette advertising expenditures were devoted to newspapers. Broadcasting accounted for 61% of advertising expenditures. By 1975, with no expenditures on broadcasting, newspapers received 21% of cigarette advertising dollars, or an increase from $14 million in 1970 to $104 million in 1975.[74] What is a substitute may depend on the alternatives.

Why Advertisers May Prefer a Single Paper

Advertisers have an interest in the number of newspapers in their communities. Publishers derive from 20% to 30% of revenue from circulation, which for a fat city daily may not even cover the cost of the newsprint and ink used to print the paper. The bulk of newspaper revenue comes from advertisers, whose interest is in reaching an audience they believe consists of many potential customers. Publishers know they can justify a higher charge to advertisers as their circulation increases. But because of the economies of scale just discussed, a single newspaper in a given location can typically offer an advertiser a lower rate than competing papers reaching the same total market.

This declining long-run average cost curve, however, is balanced by other factors that produce a practical limit on the extent to which a newspaper can expand:

- A large metropolitan daily faces rising transportation costs and other distribution expenses, which may actually increase as circulation extends over a wider geographical area. This can be overcome somewhat, but at a high fixed cost, through suburban printing locations.
- The more limiting factor, preventing unlimited national expansion, is the highly localized demand of newspaper content. As the newspaper spreads out, it must become less complete in covering the local news of various communities and in serving the need of local advertisers who do not want to pay for readers in areas far from where they do business. It is this need to specialize in providing services for a geographically segmented audience and advertiser that ultimately offsets the economy of scale effects and determines the geographical extent of local newspaper circulation.

Indeed, it was a conscious decision of many publishers in the 1990s to cut back on circulation in remote areas of little interest to local advertisers that were therefore unprofitable.[75]

Although a widespread phenomenon, it was probably seen most dramatically in Iowa, where the *Des Moines Register* had long billed itself as "The Newspaper Iowa Depends Upon." Circulation of the paper peaked in the early 1960s at about 350,000 daily and more than 500,000 on Sunday. But small cities like Waterloo, Cedar Rapids and the cluster known as the Quad Cities on the Mississippi were growing while rural Iowa withered. These towns had their own dailies that grew with them. Daily circulation ebbed in the outer reaches of Iowa. Faced with declining circulation and the cost of running both the *Register* and the evening *Tribune*, the Cowles family closed the *Tribune*. Since 1985, when Gannett bought the paper, circulation outside the metropolitan area (called the "Golden Circle"), has dropped by almost 70,000 daily, some due to cancellations and the rest due to the shrunken circulation area. The daily circulation of the *Register* in 1997 was about 165,000 and Sunday circulation was about 279,000.[76]

The paradox is that in the process of cutting back, mostly good things have happened to the *Register's* newsroom, as well as to other Iowa dailies, readers and advertisers. Although circulation is down, eliminating the costs of money-losing circulation has contributed to bringing profits up. As a result, Gannett invested $51 million in new presses and a manufacturing plant reportedly offering unprecedented printing speed, zoning capability and graphics quality to the *Register*.[77]

Moreover, the other papers in the state have flourished. When Bill Monroe, executive director of the Iowa Newspaper Association, joined the association in 1980, only two or three newspapers in the state were morning dailies. "Publishers adjusted to the Register's delivery to survive and wound up getting better," Monroe says. "We have 92 percent penetration of newspapers in the state of Iowa," he added. "Show me another state that has that kind of penetration. Show me a place where Des Moines pulled out and it left a void. You can't. These other papers have gotten stronger and stronger."[78]

Defying national trends, the circulation of the *Cedar Rapids Gazette* in the east climbed steadily to almost 70,000 a day and the *Omaha World Herald*, which had all but replaced the *Register* in west and northwest Iowa, sold about 25,000 newspapers a day in the state.

In the process, the newshole of the *Register* increased 10% and the newsroom grew from 190 under the Cowles family to 205 under Gannett. According to the publisher, the newsroom's budget grew faster than inflation, local coverage expanded and major enterprise stories continued.

Charles C. Edwards, Gardner Cowles' great-grandson and the last family member to serve as publisher of the *Register*, taught journalism briefly after retiring. "I felt like a dinosaur bringing these issues of journalism and profit into the classroom. All these kids were here for was to get a job." Concluded one observer, "And if there are going to be jobs for them, there have to be profitable newspapers. The key is finding the formula for making money and producing excellent journalism at the same time."[79]

Rosse's Umbrella Model

One element of newspaper publishing in the 21st century is highlighted in the *Des Moines Register* case, and elsewhere. Although not many cities have head-to-head direct newspaper competition, newspaper publishers feel there is plenty of competition.

The "umbrella hypothesis"[80] model is as robust today as when introduced in 1975. The model recognizes that whereas few cities have more than one daily newspaper, these newspapers nevertheless compete with other newspapers. That is, most regions of the country have a metropolitan newspaper whose circulation extends well beyond the central city, perhaps for hundreds of miles. The circulation falls off as the distance increases, but within this circulation area are "satellite cities," each with its own daily circulation that goes beyond its borders. Dailies in these level two cities may have circulation in smaller communities, which may in turn have their own local dailies. Even within the smaller community, there may be weekly newspapers, "shoppers" and other specialized media.

Figure 1.4 illustrates how each level throws an "umbrella" over the lower levels. Level one papers draw advertising from national and regional advertisers, as well as local in-city stores. They are also the most subject to competition from broadcast media and cable, as they compete for the major national and international news as well as the advertising revenue. Newspapers at the second and third levels compete with each other only in the fringes of their natural markets, but they must compete with the papers above and below them.

The second and third level newspapers exist because of the needs of local readers and advertisers, which cannot be adequately fulfilled by the metropolitan daily. Even zoned editions of the big city papers cannot provide the complete coverage of local government, school boards and sports teams, or the Main Street shopkeepers in the surrounding towns.

The reality of intercity competition is apparent in many large cities. Within a 30-minute (nonrush hour) drive of Boston's City Hall are daily newspapers in Quincy, Brockton, Lowell, Lawrence, Framingham, Lynn, Haverhill, Gloucester, Salem, Wakefield and Woburn. Even the second tier cities bump into each other: Lowell and Lawrence are separated by 16 miles of highway; both are evening papers with circulation exceeding 50,000.

The *Camden Courier Post*, with 90,000 circulation, is about one mile across the Delaware River from center city Philadelphia and its two Knight-Ridder newspapers.

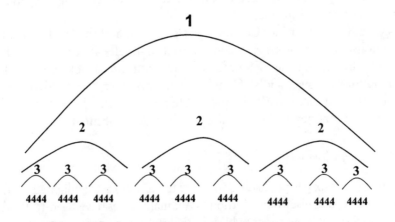

Key:
Level 1—Newspaper in large metropolitan center
Level 2—Newspapers in satellite cities
Level 3—Local dailies
Level 4—Weeklies and other specialized media

FIG. 1.4.   "Umbrella Model" of Newspaper Competition. Source: James N. Rosse, "The Evolution of One Newspaper Cities," discussion paper for the FTC Symposium on Media Concentration, pp. 50–52.

"Monopoly" newspapers in New Jersey cities across the Hudson from New York include those in Newark, Bergen County, Jersey City and Passaic County. Daily newspapers in Santa Monica, Glendale, Pasadena, Torrance, Long Beach and Costa Mesa are among many in the shadow of the *Los Angeles Times.*

In each case, the second tier newspapers have to contend with a metropolitan paper that casts a shadow over its domain. They are often fighting for the same national and regional advertisers: inserts from Home Depot and K-Mart, run-of-press advertising from local department stores that blanket the area. They contend for readers who, because of cost or time, have tended to get only one paper, the "local local" or the metro local. The metropolitan newspaper, on the other hand, finds that it may be stymied in its attempt to grow outward from the central city as its market becomes more geographically dispersed. Typical was the situation of the *Miami Herald*, a Knight-Ridder newspaper. Suffering with declining circulation and advertising, its options for geographic growth are limited. "The newspaper has in recent years faced energetic competition from the Fort Lauderdale Sun-Sentinel, based in Broward County,"[81] immediately north of the *Herald's* base in Dade county.

Competition and Content: Effects on the Editorial Product

Most attention in research and among media critics is paid to the role of competition in determining the quality of the newspaper as a consumer product. The general theme is that competition should pump up the adrenalin of the newsroom as well as demand that publishers devote greater resources to the quality and content of the "product" than if they had the market to themselves. However, once departing from anecdotal stories, the research confirms that good and improving newspapers are a function of many variables well beyond the existence of direct newspaper competition. Just as compelling as the case for competition to result in a better newspaper is the reverse: Newspapers competing for dwindling share of advertising dollars and for a declining base of competition have few resources to devote to improved salaries, added bureaus and wire services, more reporters or new presses. A "monopoly" newspaper, with advertisers and readers to itself, can use the economies not only to improve profitability, but to improve the paper to try to hold on to those readers and advertisers.

In fact, most studies have found that readers perceive little difference between competing and noncompeting newspapers. And researchers have found little to substantiate the view that lack of local competition itself produces inferior journalism.

Dating back to studies in 1954, researchers have found few significant differences in content between competitive and noncompetitive newspapers. Any differences seem to be random, such as one study that reported a significant difference in reporting news of accidents and disasters, in which case competing papers carried more such news.[82] Another study found that nine types of news coverage were perceived by readers to be better after mergers than before. Overall, reader attitudes in Atlanta, Louisville, Minneapolis and Des Moines were slightly more favorable after mergers eliminated head-on competition.[83]

Further research has found that competing dailies do not guarantee the "marketplace" of ideas, which is the oft-cited rationale behind the need for competing newspapers. In examining pairs of competing papers in small cities, an investigator found only one pair that showed any tendency to compete by "issue," and there the competition was along partisan lines.[84]

Several studies have tried to determine what effect the demise of a competitive situation had on the content of the surviving newspaper in a community. Four studies in the United States and two in Canada were somewhat contradictory, some showing a decline on quality, others showing no significant changes.[85] One studied content and reader perception during a period of head-on evening competition in Bloomington, Indiana, and contrasted this with a time when one of the papers was about to fold (moderate competition), as well as a period five months after one of the competing dailies closed down. According to the hypothesis, under conditions of intense competition, a daily would devote more of its nonadvertising space to local content and sensational and human interest news and features than under conditions of noncompetition. Another hypothesis predicts that readers would perceive no difference in the quality of the two competing papers or notice any difference in the amount of local news in the remaining noncompetitive papers.[86]

In fact, the findings substantiated neither of the hypotheses. Local news content did not decline when competition ended, nor did the proportion of "immediate reward" items (e.g., sports, crime, accidents, etc.). And consistent with some previous studies, the results confirmed that readers found no perceived difference in the surviving newspaper. Readers of the papers were aware, however, of quantity differences in the two papers. On the other hand, one of the earliest studies of a specific newspaper market during competition, during a transition with minimal competition, and a period after one competing newspaper closed down reported that the percentage of space for local news, features, pictures and opinion was greater in the competitive period.[87] One of the Canadian studies found some similar differences, but several concluded that competition had no "socially significant effect" on the content of the newspapers.[88]

Yet another study looked at multiple relations on the fairness and balance of newspapers, analyzing the effects of group ownership, competition and reporter workload.[89] Although the results were clear, the implications were less so. The study found that newspapers with direct competition were less fair in their coverage than papers without competition. The authors speculated that there is "less pressure to be fair and balanced because alternate voices are available."

Another study, looking only at differences in pairs of competing newspapers, found that "leading" newspapers in each pair did have some common characteristics.[90] In comparing 46 newspapers in 23 markets, eliminating operations with joint operating agreements and pairs where one paper had circulation more than twice the circulation of its rival, the researchers found:

- The amount of content in each of 20 editorial categories was almost the same.
- Leading newspapers have more advertising space.
- Leaders used more news services.
- The leader was more likely to be the newer newspaper.
- In format, the trailing paper had larger pictures and fewer stories on page one.

Overall, these authors found "few content and relatively few consistent format differences." This is consistent with studies that have detected no relation between competition and an index of quality[91] and another that found few effects of competition on diversity of content.[92]

In general, this lack of difference among competing and within noncompeting newspapers may have several explanations. It could indicate that the constraints of having to sell to a mass market dictate certain formulas that editors have honed over the years, Moreover, as editors often work their way up, moving from paper to paper, they share common training ground that they all generally follow when they run a newspaper. There may also be an element of media responsibility that editors feel, particularly when they know they are the only newspaper in town. Publishers also may be particularly sensitive to accusations of abusing "monopoly" power. They may have learned as well that they must meet certain minimum standards to hold on to subscribers and the advertisers who want a decent circulation and rate. In all likelihood it is a combination of several or all of these or other factors. Perhaps it takes more than two newspapers competing directly to provide the niche for a paper that can be more specialized, controversial or otherwise significantly different. Finally, there may be artifacts from the manner in which researchers have measured the effects of competition, looking at such surrogates as newshole or wire service subscriptions, which may or may not be valid measures themselves.

In trying to bring some closure to the issue of competition and content, a researcher studied a sample of monopoly, competitive and Joint Operating Agreement newspapers (see p. 49). His results showed that competition did have a measurable effect on content, but added that "it is difficult to determine if the overall effect of competition is to improve the product."[93] Newspapers facing intense competition may need to differentiate themselves and to prove they are a substitute for the competitor. So one may spend more money on wire services and reporters to fill their newshole, but they may get this added allocation by reducing another area, such as the size of the newshole itself. This may explain the mixed research results of competition: Whether or not it improves the product may depend on the way the qualities of "better" are determined. Considering just one variable, for example, are more stories by local reporters in a smaller newshole "better" than using more wire service copy but having a larger newshole?

Just as there may be some degree of substitutability of other media for newspapers from an advertiser's perspective, so may other media be partial substitutes for newspapers as sources of news and other information. Television is the dominant source for news for most people at 69%, as compared to 37% for newspapers.[94] Research has suggested that this may not be the best state of affairs for the republic. A study that looked specifically at the role of newspapers and television in informing the public on political issues yielded carefully qualified "circumstantial evidence that competition and diversity are important social indicators of resources for political education."[95] The authors suggest that television is not as effective as newspapers in conveying a political candidate's policy positions and that therefore the decline in the number of newspapers, especially competing newspapers in the same city, is cause for some concern.

Competition and Online Access

In mid-1998 there were 492 general circulation daily newspapers available online via the Internet.[96] This represented about one third of all daily newspapers. One year earlier there were only 197. In addition, there were 29 sites provided by broadcast networks and 216 television stations were listed with Web sites.[97]

The utility, the business model, the economics, and the consumer response to online media was still in its infancy in 2000. It undoubtedly will have an impact on consumer use and advertiser expenditures. The impact of online access may well make moot any concerns about concentration of ownership of the media in denying users access to a variety of opinions, news sources, entertainment, culture and commerce. For not only does online access give a consumer in a one-newspaper town the tool to seek out news from elsewhere, it allows smaller entities, such as weekly newspapers, an avenue for daily involvement with readers. It blurs the line between text, audio and video, as "newspaper" sites add video clips and audio playback, such as a news conference, to their articles. At the same time, television networks and stations can and are providing longer text articles that expand the information that accompanies voiceovers on the 30-second or 2-minute presentations they make on the air.

It is not obvious who the winners and losers will be online. Time Warner's CNN site competes with Gannett's *USA Today* site. News Corporation's *Times of London* can compete with the *New York Times*. Advertisers may not only have their own sites for promotion, but, like the Ragu site (sauces), add enough entertainment or information content to become destination sites on their own. Chapter 7 explores the online phenomenon in greater detail.

Cross-Media Ownership

Same Market

The outcome of noncompetitive newspapers in a particular market may be mitigated by the existence of competing media (i.e., television, radio and magazines). What is potentially more insidious for readers and advertisers would be the situation where more than one major medium in a locality is under the same ownership. This is reflected in concern about cross-media ownership. In 1940, 23% of the broadcast outlets (radio at the time) were owned by newspapers in the same market. In 1974, the Federal Communications Commission restricted new combinations of newspapers with broadcast stations in the same community. By 1995, only 19 of 734 television stations in the 100 largest markets were under common ownership with the newspaper in that market.[98]

As in other areas, the effects of broadcast–newspaper cross-ownership has not produced definitive outcomes in their value or harm to their community. One of the most frequently cited studies reported on Zanesville, Ohio, where the city's only newspaper, radio station and television station were under the same ownership.[99] In comparison with those who lived in similar cities with greater media diversity, Zanesville residents used the news media less and were less well informed than residents in comparison cities, got less news than residents in two comparison cities with competitive media, used less nonlocal media than those they were compared with and reported high public acceptance of the media.

Other studies yield conflicting findings on the effects of newspaper–broadcast affiliations. One found that media with concentrated ownership covered the news in greater depth because it had more resources. But another concluded that television stations owned by newspapers carried less locally originated programming. Although one researcher found that newspaper-owned television stations departed more frequently from the norms of objectivity, he saw no other differences in the news sources and practices of television stations owned by newspapers. A researcher calculated that newspaper–television cross-ownership increased story overlap between the co-owned media by 17% compared to similar independently owned media. This additional homogenizing effect was judged to be potentially harmful to the public. The same study cited a Federal Communications Commission staff report that newspaper-owned television stations provided more local news, nonentertainment and entertainment programming than other television stations.[100]

With the number of television–newspaper cross-ownership cities low and decreasing, combined with the large number of options available via cable and direct broadcast satellite, this piece of media concentration has become a minor issue compared to the situation prior to the FCC's 1974 ban.

Newspaper and Broadcast Common Ownership

Although newspaper–broadcast co-ownership in the same market has almost disappeared, several of the largest newspaper publishing companies are also among the large broadcast station licensees, but fewer than in previous years. Table 1.20

TABLE 1.20
Television Holdings of Largest Newspaper Publishers, 1998

Rank	Firm	No. of TV Stations	% of TV Households
1	Gannett Co.	20	16.2
2	Knight-Ridder	NA	NA
3	Newhouse Newspapers	NA	NA
4	Dow Jones & Co.	NA	NA
5	Times Mirror Co.	NA	NA
6	New York Times Co.	NA	NA
7	MediaNews Group	NA	NA
8	McClatchy Company	NA	NA
9	E. W. Scripps	9	9.8
10	Hearst Newspapers	12	9.5
11	Thomson Newspapers	NA	NA
12	Tribune Co.	18	35.5
13	Cox Enterprises	8	9.4
14	Hollinger International	NA	NA
15	Freedom Communications	NA	NA

NA: Not applicable.
Sources: Federal Communications Commission, "Review of the Commissions Broadcast Ownership Rules," Notice of Inquiry, MM Docket No. 98-35, March 12, 1998, Appendix A.

includes the largest newspaper companies from Table 1.18, showing the reach of their television holdings, if any. In addition to the largest newspaper groups in this table, other, smaller publishers with broadcast holdings include A. H. Belo, Media General, Lee Enterprises and the Washington Post Co. The trend in the 1980s and 1990s has been for newspaper companies to shed their broadcast holdings to concentrate in publishing or other areas. Among them are Times Mirror, Knight-Ridder, Pulitzer, Harte-Hanks and Newhouse. On the other hand, News Corp., the largest broadcast group, sold off its newspaper holdings, as did Capital Cities/ABC after being acquired by the Walt Disney Company in 1998. A smaller group of newspaper owning companies have added to their broadcast holdings: Gannett, Tribune Co., Hearst and Cox.

Overall, the percentage of television stations in the 100 largest markets owned by companies with newspaper interests as well declined from 28.0% in 1973 to 24.7% in 1989 and further to 22.5% in 1995.[101]

ANTITRUST AND LEGISLATIVE ACTIVITIES

As part of the only industry specifically mentioned for protection in the Constitution, newspapers have been largely, although not completely, immune from judicial and legislative tampering. The key case that did affirm the government's ultimate right to insure freedom of expression was the *Associated Press* (AP) case.[102] The AP, a cooperative financed by member newspapers to provide news accounts to all, had a policy of restricting competition by making it extremely expensive to buy a new membership in a city where there were already newspaper members. The government sued the AP on antitrust grounds. The AP held out the First Amendment as its defense, as well as the theory that newspapers were not covered by the Sherman Act because they were not engaged in interstate commerce. The Supreme Court disagreed. More important than the substantive ruling against the AP's restrictive practice, the Supreme Court's ruling clearly placed newspapers within the jurisdiction of antitrust legislation. It is surely in the government's power to preserve the free dissemination provided for in the First Amendment: "Freedom to publish is guaranteed by the Constitution, but freedom to combine to keep others from publishing is not. Freedom of the press from governmental interference under the First Amendment does not sanction repression of that freedom by private interests."[103]

Over the years, newspaper companies have faced antitrust issues such as competition among newspapers in a geographical area, pricing of adverting, pricing of subscriptions and fixing of retail prices of the paper. Some of the practices that were called into question are almost moot, as there are so few cases where newspapers are competing head to head.

An example of an antitrust case involving newspapers that eventually had to be resolved in a 1951 Supreme Court decision was *Lorain Journal Company v. United States*. The *Lorain Journal* was the only daily newspaper in this Ohio town. When a radio station in Lorain went on the air, the *Journal* refused to accept advertising from customers who also advertised on the local radio station. The Court ruled against the newspaper in an antitrust case. The Court held that the newspaper's right to chose advertisers is tempered by its responsibility to not engage in behavior designed to drive out potential competition.[104]

The area of antitrust that is most prevalent involves combinations of newspapers in geographical proximity to one another. The Justice Department has virtually ignored newspaper combinations at the national level. As was pointed out previously in this chapter, when measured in the national market, no chain comes close to challenging the thresholds that determine economic oligopoly and monopoly.

Newspaper Preservation Act

With the rights of the government firmly established in the *Associated Press* case, in the 1960s the Justice Department brought an action against the two newspapers in Tucson, Arizona, which had formed a joint operating company to handle advertising, business and production matters, leaving editorial staffs and policy in the hands of the separate owners of the two papers. Forty-two other newspapers in 21 cities had similar joint operating agreements. Using *Tucson* as a test case, the government charged the two papers with price fixing, profit pooling and market allocation. In 1969, the Supreme Court upheld a summary judgment supporting the government's charge.[105] This ruling brought action on a bill that had been introduced in Congress in 1967 to protect such arrangements. The Newspaper Preservation Act was passed in 1970, in effect providing an exemption to the 44 newspapers in the existing 22 joint agreements.* The Act did, however, limit the right of future agreements, which must be approved by the Justice Department on a case-by-case basis. There are also sanctions for abuse of the legalized combination by the joint newspapers to prevent further competition in the market, but these have never been applied.

The concept of joint operating agreements has had its supporters and critics, with segments of the newspaper industry itself of divided opinion. The proponents of the legislation argued that two separate editorial voices were a better alternative than the single voice that would exist if an otherwise marginal paper were forced out of business or taken over entirely by the stronger paper. The opposing view has been voiced not only by many small, independent dailies, but by the *New York Times* and the Newspaper Guild as well. It was their contention that daily and weekly papers in the prosperous suburbs, in effect, were substituting for the failing metropolitan newspapers. The joint operating agreements could therefore lessen competition within the city and at the same time promote an unfair advantage over existing or potential rivals.

Critics of the Newspaper Preservation Act have cited, in particular, the loose interpretation of the Act by the Justice Department in those cases where it has approved new joint agreements since 1970, such as the 1979 decision affecting the Scripps-Howard's *Post* and Gannett's *Enquirer* in Cincinnati and the 1989 decision supporting the combination in Detroit of Knight-Ridder's *Free Press* and Gannett's *Evening News*. First, they note the ability of chain-owned papers to do "creative accounting" to make contributions to corporate overhead or to purchase services

---

*At one point, the bill was called the Failing Newspaper Act. Obviously, someone wanted to put a better face on a sad situation.

from corporate headquarters at rates that help make the paper look less profitable. A money-losing newspaper could have some benefit for a chain in the form of tax writeoffs to balance profits from other properties.[106]

Second, whereas the law supposedly mandates that joint agreements should be approved only as a last resort, when no other buyer for the paper can be found, this has left room for ambiguity. Does the owner of the "failing" paper have to accept any offer presented? For example, in hearings on the Cincinnati agreement, it was reported that Larry Flint, publisher of *Hustler* magazine, made a serious offer for the *Post*. Nonetheless, E. W. Scripps Co., owner of the *Post* and petitioner for the joint agreement, rejected the offer.[107]

This position, however, was upheld by the U.S. Court of Appeals in a 1983 ruling affirming approval of a joint agreement in Seattle between the *Post-Intelligencer*, the "failing" newspaper owned by Hearst, and the *Times*, in which Knight-Ridder had a minority ownership. The Court agreed with the U.S. Attorney General who had to approve the joint operating agreement. He argued that there was no evidence presented indicating that any new owner could have succeeded where Hearst had failed. The Court's opinion added that the *Post-Intelligencer's* "trend toward failure is irreversible under any management."[108]

The fine line that the Justice Department must walk in determining the applicability of the Newspaper Preservation Act for new applicants is the partial loss of competition in approving the agreement against the possibility that if the agreement is not approved, then one of the newspapers will cease to exist completely. It is half a loaf or no bread. Newspaper unions and employees, as well as advertisers, need also consider the options.

There is a danger that if the weaker paper is discouraged by Justice Department policy to delay too long in seeking a joint agreement, then it will be so close to failure that the stronger paper would have no incentive to enter into an agreement. The stronger paper need only hold on for a short time and it could have the market to itself when the weaker paper folds. This is what happened in Philadelphia and Cleveland in 1982, when the *Bulletin* and the *Press*, respectively, closed down. In both cases, the papers had years of small but manageable losses, which suddenly turned into huge losses. By the time they made overtures to the stronger papers, there was little leverage to get them to enter into a joint agreement.

These were exactly the issues facing the Justice Department in one of the most contentious of all petitions for a joint agreement between the Detroit papers in 1986. This followed years of spirited competition between Knight-Ridder's *Free Press* and the *Evening News*, purchased by Gannett in 1985. The *Free Press* was the second place paper for years, accounting for about 35% of the advertising linage of the two papers in 1986.[109] In 1979, Knight-Ridder executives determined to spend whatever it took to overtake the *News*. The paper slashed advertising rates and held down subscription prices. The *News* matched the *Free Press* and both papers lost money in the battle. To hold on to circulation, the *News* continued selling for 15 cents weekdays, less than any other Gannett paper and lower than the more prevalent 25 cents. The *Free Press* reported annual losses of between $11 million and $14 million between 1981 and 1986.

In a hearing before an administrative law judge for the Justice Department, the unions at both newspapers opposed the joint agreement, fearing the loss of 1,500 jobs. They and others argued that Knight-Ridder and Gannett set out to lose enough money so they could qualify for the joint agreement. The judge agreed and refused to grant permission for the JOA. However, the ruling was reversed by the Attorney General, who concluded there was no way the *Free Press* "could extricate itself" from probable collapse.[110]

What can be said for the Newspaper Preservation Act is that it has indeed kept alive some semblance of metropolitan newspaper competition in those cases where it has been applied. But in only one case has a weaker paper eventually gotten healthy enough to reclaims its independence from a JOA. This was the *Anchorage (AK) Daily News*. It was first saved in a JOA with the competing *Times* in 1974. But charges by the *Daily News* that the *Times* mismanaged the joint arrangement lead to a break-up in 1978, leaving the owning Fanning family back where it started, with a money-losing newspaper and few resources to subsidize it. Its circulation under the JOA had dropped from 12,000 to 8,000. It was rescued by the McClatchy group in 1979, which invested heavily in new presses, facility and staff. Circulation rebounded within three years to 39,000, but the paper ran at a loss until 1992, when its formerly stronger rival closed.[111]

In another case, the two dailies in Chattanooga, Tennessee, published under a joint operating agreement from 1942 until 1966. At this point, the JOA expired. But neither company was profitable on its own. A second marriage in 1970 returned them to financial health.[112] In effect, joint operating agreements preserve the status quo. To that extent, it may be viewed as making the best of the reality of diminished prospects for multiple daily newspapers in the crowded media mix.

Geographical Limitations

Neither Congress nor the appropriate executive bodies have found a need, or the authority, to pursue wide-ranging structural changes in the newspaper industry. Following a period of apparent media consolidation in the 1970s, the Federal Trade Commission (FTC) held a two-day public symposium in 1978 on whether there was harmful concentration of ownership within all mass media. In 1980, the FTC staff concluded there is "relatively little the Commission can do" about the increasing number of one newspaper towns because economies of scale are the primary reason they exist.[113] The FTC further stated that it is difficult to challenge newspaper chains on antitrust grounds because their papers usually operate in separate geographical markets.

Newspaper groups do have to show some sensitivity to antitrust laws in the nature of where they do business. The Justice Department has shown little activity concerning number of newspapers owned or even total circulation. But under some circumstances they have been prevented from making acquisitions. For the most part, the chains have been careful not to buy papers that have overlapping distribution and thereby lay themselves open to charges of controlling all papers under the "umbrella."

The most notable case in this arena was in 1970, when Times Mirror was forced to sell the *San Bernardino Sun* and *Telegram* because of an antitrust ruling based on the predominance of the *Los Angeles Times* in southern California and the lessening of competition that would result if the nearby San Bernardino papers were run by the same owner. The point that geographical proximity, not overall size of the chain, is the key to control, is underlined in that it was the larger Gannett chain that took the San Bernardino papers off of Time Mirror's hands.

Similarly, Gannett's suburban newspapers in Westchester County provide the basic local papers for a large contiguous area in suburban New York City. However, they all compete under the dominating influence of the large metropolitan papers that are widely available in their territory.

Newspapers may be testing the limits of geographic concentration in pursuing the strategy of clustering, such as Gannett's Westchester group. In 1997 and 1998, Gannett assembled another cluster in New Jersey, where it joined its longtime newspaper in the southern and western part of the state, the *Camden Courier-Post* with the newspaper in Vineland, New Jersey, and four newspapers, including the *Asbury Park Press* in the northern and eastern part of the state. These later four papers are within a 90 mile line of each other. But they are also all under the umbrella of the *Newark Star-Ledger* and, to a lesser degree, the New York newspapers. The Camden and Vineland newspapers are in the shadow of Knight-Ridder's Philadelphia metropolitan papers.

Similar clusters are taking shape elsewhere, without reaction from the either the Federal Trade Commission or the Justice Department. In northern California, MediaNews Group purchased the Oakland newspaper, adding it to papers in Hayward, Pleasanton, Fremont and San Mateo. These are not only under the umbrella of nearby San Francisco's two dailies, but a dozen second and third tier dailies contiguous with their trading areas.

NEW PLAYERS AND NEW COMPETITION

In 1980, the newspaper industry was suddenly shaken by the possibility that they might face a new and powerful competitor: American Telephone & Telegraph (AT&T). Back then, AT&T was almost synonymous with the telephone industry. AT&T made some noises about making their Yellow Pages directories available online, via telephone line to television sets. To the newspaper executives, this sounded like a threat to their most profitable sector, classified advertising.

Although the scare of that scenario never materialized, and AT&T itself was broken up—first by the 1982 antitrust settlement and further in 1996 by market forces—newspaper companies confronted even greater competition 20 years later. The rapidly declining prices of computing, personal computers and other forms of "smart" boxes were rapidly expanding the base of Internet users.

More ominous, perhaps, is that the barriers to entry to the newspaper business, which have traditionally been the substantial up-front capital costs for presses, distribution trucks and staff, have been sharply lowered. In the world of electronic distribution, a modest personal computer and a firm providing a Web site hosting service for a price that is less than what many people pay for cable service is all that is necessary to create a Web site that offers some piece of the newspaper package. With only a relatively small additional investment, firms can—and have—created sites that offer what newspapers have offered: rental apartment, used car and real estate listings; local events calendars; sports; movie reviews and local theater times; and so on.

Incumbent publishers, to be sure, tend to have a built-in advantage at first. They have the "brand equity"—the local presence and, they hope, the credibility—to ward off online competitors. But the mere threat that electronic services of all stripes (from individual entrepreneurs to deep pocket competitors from outside industries) will be creating a level of potential competition that will require publishers to respond. The alternative may be to face the perils of those who withered and perished in the past. See Chapter 7 for more on the ownership of online information services.

SUMMARY AND DISCUSSION

The concluding paragraph of the newspaper chapter of the 1982 edition of *Who Owns the Media?* is just as applicable in 1999:

> Thus, we should not be surprised to see even fewer multi-newspaper towns. And, while the familiar newspaper may continue to be around, . . . its competitive position must be analyzed in the context of the other media, both those which are already in existence and those which will likely become more prevalent in this decade.[114]

The issue of concentration of newspaper ownership and the proliferation of one-newspaper firm cities continues to raise great passions among interested parties. It is not hard to find examples on an individual case basis for some corporate policies that would seem to be counter to good journalism or even good long-term business sense. On the other hand, stepping back from specific examples yields a more objective evaluation based on the full spectrum of evidence.

First, it should be clear that even with the mergers and acquisitions in the industry, in 1998 no newspaper or chain dominated the nation's news dissemination. Even the largest group accounted for circulation similar to the largest group in 1946. Although there is indeed greater concentration measured by size of groups or proportion of circulation accounted for by groups, by any standard of economics, law or even logic, the ownership of newspapers was still widely dispersed in 1998. The control over total circulation by the largest chains has not changed in any substantive way that affects the behavior or economics of newspapers.

Second, although economists may have been able to justify the benefits of being part of a chain-owned newspaper, a wealth of research has further shown the generally benign effects of bigness in the real world. The overwhelming weight of the research has shown that, with snapshots taken over several decades, corporately owned newspapers and "monopoly" newspapers are, overall, either indistinguishable from family-owned papers or, by some accounts, superior.

There is little empirical evidence that either chain-owned newspapers or newspapers in single-firm cities as a group provide poorer service to readers or advertisers than independent or competing newspapers. In the short run, some newspapers (corporate or independent) can take advantage of their local monopoly status. But examples also exist that demonstrate how a chain owner improves a newly acquired paper. None of the research or subsequent events would change a conclusion of the 1982 Rand study that found an "absence of evidence that group newspapers, on the average, operate in a manner which is measurably different from independents."[115]

The long-term trend toward one-newspaper firm cities is largely driven by economics. Circulation continues to slide among the best as well as the poorer papers, in cities with competition and in those with only a single newspaper. There is more competition than ever for the attention and money of the consumer audience. A newspaper has never gone out of business for lack of editorial material. It needs readers so it can get advertisers. All owners know this. Advertisers, who want to reach that audience, also have more choices than ever. Moreover, postmortems of closed papers disclose a consistent pattern: In large measure, advertisers, from whom newspapers derive the bulk of their revenue, are reluctant to support competing newspapers when a single firm can provide the audience coverage they need more economically and hence at lower total advertising rates. The sizable first copy cost and the expense of distribution over a given territory tend to favor consolidation of newspapers.

Given the decline of newspaper as a printed product, consolidation may not only be natural but healthy. Family companies in a mature, highly competitive arena are less likely to have the resources or the management depth to keep going. They may be more likely to have to make compromises in editorial standards to remain viable. Or, shunning that ethical choice, they may close up shop. On the other hand, profitable corporations have a greater capability—although not always the resolve—to outlast cyclical downturns, spread the costs of investments over multiple newspapers, stare down challenges from a disgruntled advertiser or an unhappy city counselor.

Certainly the chain owner has the potential to dictate editorial policy. Some do in the endorsement of political candidates (although the question of how much real impact such editorials have is still unresolved) or in ordering certain articles to be printed. Other owners, however, use the same power to demand higher editorial standards. In the end, newspapers are a local product and must fulfill the needs of a community. Most chain owners appear to recognize this and give individual editors and publishers maximum latitude. Furthermore, under the umbrella model, even many one-newspaper communities appear to face intercity competition, as well as that from weekly and "shopper" newspaper rivals; there is also competition from broadcast and cable television, radio and, increasingly, online information.

Finally, in the last analysis, there are really no alternatives to the current structure of the industry. It would be difficult if not constitutionally impossible to create some antitrust standard for newspapers based on some perceived editorial or public service rather than the economic considerations that are currently in place for all businesses. Could there be some limit that says that no company can account for more than 25% of total national circulation, or have more than 10% of all newspapers? This is not likely.

The Future

Possibly the greatest challenge facing the owners of newspapers in the opening decade of the 21st century will be making the transition from paper-based to electronically based businesses. The discrete boundary between a daily newspaper, weekly newspaper, a Web site from a broadcaster, a software company or a new information provider is far less distinguishable when they may all be accessed via the same video screen.

The newspaper industry, like its broadcasting and other print brethren, will find it increasingly difficult to separate its own turf from those of others who used to play in separate arenas. Not only do Cable News Network and ABC News compete online with the *New York Times* for audience and advertisers, but local upstarts may be competing with the daily in every city and town. Banks, food stores, the schools, the Little League are among many who may reach audiences directly instead of being filtered by the daily newspapers. These new sources do not have the tradition of journalist standards that newspapers maintain, but it remains to be seen how important that is to audiences.

There may be good reasons why local newspapers will maintain an advantage over these alternatives: maybe one-stop "shopping" (but smart technology may erode that), maybe the brand identity, the infrastructure, the good will that most newspapers have in their communities. But the one key factor that publishers must face is that the online world provides their customers (i.e., readers and advertisers) with more options than ever. Radio and television undercut the world of newspapers. These have contributed to the need for consolidation in the newspaper industry. The online world will only add greater competition. Existing newspapers will need to adjust to thrive, or even survive.

NOTES

1. Benjamin M. Compaine, et al., *Who Owns the Media?*, 2nd ed. (White Plains, NY: Knowledge Industry Publications, Inc., 1982), p. 27.
2. Compiled from the directory of online newspapers, by state, from the *American Journalism Review*'s Web site, ajr.newslink.org/statnews.html. on Aug. 9, 1998.
3. *Editor & Publisher International Year Book*, 1997, CD ROM database for weekly, foreign and specialty newspapers.
4. Alan B. Albarran, *Media Economics* (Ames, IA: Iowa State University Press, 1996), p. 50.
5. *Editor & Publisher International Year Book*, 1997 and 1980. National circulation data for the *New York Times* is from its 1997 10-K report, March 2, 1998, accessed via Edgar Online on Web site at www.edgar-line.com.
6. Alfred McClung Lee, *The Daily Newspaper in America* (New York: Macmillan, 1947), pp. 120–122.
7. See Albarran, p. 33. This is a structure where there are many sellers offering similar products, but not perfect substitutes. For example, despite the large number of book titles, a textbook on organic chemistry is not a substitute for a romance novel. Similarly, a cable channel that is all sports is not a viable substitute for a viewer who prefers comedy shows.
8. John Tebbel, *The Compact History of the American Newspaper* (New York: Hawthorne Books, Inc., 1963), p. 97.
9. Bruce Owen, Economics and Freedom of Expression (Cambridge, MA: Ballinger Publishing Co., 1975), p. 48.

10. Frank Luther Mott, *American Journalism*, 3rd ed. (New York: Macmillan, 1962), p. 635.
11. Compiled from data provided by Bolitho-Cribb & Associates on Web site at www.imt.net/~jcribb/publish.html. BoLitho-Cribb is a newspaper broker and the data is drawn from press releases announcing sales and acquisitions of newspapers. It may not be comprehensive.
12. "World Press Trends," 1997 ed. (Paris, France: World Association of Newspapers).
13. Ibid.
14. *Editor & Publisher International Year Book*, 1997, CD-ROM database.
15. Tebbel, p. 242.
16. Willard G. Bleyer, *Main Currents in the History of American Journalism* (Boston: Houghton-Mifflin, 1927), p. 413.
17. Tebbel, pp. 219–220.
18. Knight-Ridder, Inc., *Annual Report, 1997*.
19. 1980: Compaine, et al., pp. 42–43. 1996: Tables 2.16 and 2.17.
20. Oswald Garrison Villard, "The Chain Daily," *The Nation* 130 (1930), pp. 595–597, as cited by Gerald L. Grotta, "Changes in the Ownership of Daily Newspapers and Selected Performance Statistics, 1950–1968: An Investigation of Some of the Economic Implications of Concentration of Ownership" (unpublished doctor's dissertation, Southern Illinois University, 1970), p. 5.
21. Denby Fawcett, "What Happens When a Chain Owner Arrives," *Columbia Journalism Review*, November/December 1972, pp. 29–30.
22. Letter to the Editor from C. Donald Hatfield, *Columbia Journalism Review*, January/February 1973, pp. 65–66.
23. Ben H. Bagdikian, *The Media Monopoly* (Boston: Beacon Press, 1983), p. xv. The phrase remains the same in the Preface to the 5th edition, 1997.
24. Indeed, I have always found something of a paradox in Bagdikian's alarms about how big business mass media will want to suppress stories harmful to its political or financial interests, while at the same time his book, highly critical of the media masters, has gone through five editions. And—more to the point—is favorably reviewed in the mainstream press and is repeatedly cited by journalists working for the papers and broadcasters presumably controlled by the men and women of which he is so critical.
25. Danial Wackman, et al., "Chain Newspaper Autonomy as Reflected in Presidential Campaign Endorsements," *Journalism Quarterly* 52.417 (Autumn 1975). In this study, a group was defined as "three or more dailies in different cities under the same principal ownership or control," p. 413.
26. David Demers, "Corporate Newspaper Structure, Editorial Page Vigor and Social Change," *Journalism & Mass Communication Quarterly* 73.4 (Winter 1996), pp. 857–877.
27. Ibid, p. 858.
28. David C. Coulson and Anne Hansen, "The Louisville Courier-Journal's News Content After Purchase by Gannett," 72.1 (Spring 1995), pp. 205–215.
29. G. Cleveland Wilhoit and Dan G. Drew, "Editorial Writers on American Daily Newspapers," *Journalism Monographs* 129 (October 1991), p. 31.
30. Stephen Lacy and Frederick Fico, "Newspaper Quality & Ownership: Rating the Groups," *Newspaper Research Journal*, Spring 1990, pp. 42–56.
31. Robert L. Bishop, "The Rush to Chain Ownership," *Columbia Journalism Review*, November/December 1972, pp. 14–15.
32. Iver Peterson, "Publishers Spread the Word: Realities of News Business Changing," *New York Times*, June 9, 1997, on Web site at www.nytimes.com/yr/mo/day/news/financial/newspapers-updating-media.html.
33. Ibid.
34. James Sterngold, "A Growing Clash of Visions at Los Angeles Times," *New York Times*, October 13, 1997, p. D-1.
35. Ibid.
36. Times Mirror Co., *10-Q Report, Securities and Exchange Commission*, November 14, 1995.
37. Robert E. Dallos, "Bidding Sends Prices Higher in Newspaper Acquisitions Binge," *Los Angeles Times*, January 9, 1977, p. VI-5.
38. Lori Robertson, "From Woodbury, New Jersey, to Prime Times," *American Journalism Review*,

March 1998, on Web site at www.newslink.org/ajrlorimar98.html/. The following account is drawn from this article.

39. Ibid.

40. Alfred McClung Lee, "The Daily Newspaper in America" (New York: Macmillan, 1947), p. 557.

41. Christopher Sterling and John Kittross, *Stay Tuned* (Belmont, CA: Wadsworth Publishing Co., 1978), p. 105.

42. As privately held companies, Hearst, Cox and the Newhouse interests do not report revenues for any of these businesses. Some insight into their revenue have been gleaned from public-owned entities in which these companies hold controlling interest (e.g., Cox Communications—cable; Hearst-Argyle Broadcasting—TV and radio).

43. E. W. Scripps Company, *1997 10-K Report*, March 27, 1998.

44. Robert Neuwirth, "Instant Newspaper Chain," *Editor & Publisher Interactive*, December 6, 1997, on Web site at www.mediainfo.com/ephome/news/newshtm/recent/120697.

45. Ibid.

46. Susan Paterno, "Independent's Day," *American Journalism Review*, October 1996, on Web site at www.newslink.org/ajrseattle.html.

47. Ibid.

48. Ibid.

49. Gannett acquired Combined Communications in 1979, then sold the *Oakland Tribune* to its editor and his wife, Robert and Nancy Maynard, in 1983. On the verge of extinction (its circulation fell to half its 1979 level), the *Tribune* was rescued by MediaNews Group in 1992.

50. "A Bitter Family Squabble Put Oakland's *Tribune* on the Block," *Business Week*, February 21, 1977, p. 60.

51. "The Big Money Hunts for Independent Newspapers," *Business Week*, February 21, 1977, p. 59.

52. "Brockton, MA, Paper Sold to Newly Formed Media Group," *Media Daily* 4.143 (July 25, 1996).

53. Steven Lapin and Richard Gibson, "McClatchy to Buy Cowles media in Deal Valued at $1.4 Billion," *Wall Street Journal*, November 17, 1997. Interactive Edition.

54. Ibid.

55. John Sullivan, "Outsider's Insider: Next Generation Dow Jones' Heir Bill Cox III Speaks Again, After Leaving Payroll," *Editor & Publisher*, September 27, 1997, p. 16ff. Having subsequently sold its Dow Jones Markets business between September 1997 and July 1998, Dow Jones stock increased 19%—among its peers only Gannett had a better performance.

56. Paterno.

57. George Garneau, "Singleton Buys Eagle Publishing," *Editor & Publisher*, August 19, 1995, p. 21.

58. James N. Dertouzos and Kenneth E. Thorpe, *Newspaper Groups: Economies of Scale, Tax Laws and Merger Incentives* (Santa Monica, CA: Rand Corp., 1982), pp. 4–8.

59. David B. Martens, "Death and Taxes," *Presstime*, March 1997, on Web site at www.naa.org-presstime/9703/p397est.html.

60. Ibid.

61. Ibid.

62. "Dolly's Last Surprise," *Newsweek*, November 29, 1976, p. 84.

63. Paterno.

64. John Morton, "Chains Swallowing Other Chains," *American Journalism Review*, n.d., on Web site at www.newslink.org/ajrmortja97.html.

65. Robert G. Picard, "The Economics of the Daily Newspaper Industry," in Alison Alexander, James Owers and Rod Carveth, *Media Economics*, 2nd ed. (Mahwah, NJ: Lawrence Erlbaum Associates, 1998), p. 121.

66. Grotta, pp. 77–79.

67. John Langdon, "An Intra Industry Approach to Measuring the Effects of Competition: The Newspaper Industry" (unpublished doctor's dissertation, Cornell University, 1969), p. 159.

68. Robert G. Picard and Jeffrey H. Brody, *The Newspaper Publishing Industry* (Boston: Allyn and Bacon, 1997), p. 43.

69. John Dimmick and Eric Rothenbuhler, "The Theory of the Niche: Quantifying Competition Among Media Industries," *Journal of Communications* 34.1 (Winter 1984), pp. 103–119; James

Rosse, "The Decline of Newspaper Competition," *Journal of Communication* 30.2 (Spring 1980), pp. 65–71.

70. Ken Smith, "Intermedia Competition for Advertising in Small Daily Markets," *Journal of Media Economics* 8.4 (1995), pp. 29–45.

71. John C. Busterna, "The Cross Elasticity of Demand for National Newspaper Advertising," *Journalism Quarterly* 64.2–3 (Summer–Autumn 1984), pp. 346–351.

72. From Table 2.x.

73. 1950 and 1970: calculated from *Historical Statistics of the United States, Colonial Times to 1970*, T 444–471, p. 856. 1997: *Facts About Newspapers, 1998*, Newspaper Association of America, Table 9.

74. U.S. Federal Trade Commission, "FTC Report to Congress for 1994 Concerning Cigarette Sales, Advertising, and Promotion, Pursuant to the Federal Cigarette Labeling and Advertising Act," on Web site at www.ftc.gov/os/9610/94cigrp.htm.

75. John Morton, "Saving Money, But at a Price," *American Journalism Review*, n.d., on Web site at www.newslink.org/ajrmortj_f97.html.

76. Mark Lisheron, "The Retrenching Register," *American Journalism Review*, November 1997, on Web site at www.newslink.org/ajrdmr.html.

77. Ibid.

78. Ibid.

79. Ibid.

80. James N. Rosse, "Economic Limits of Press Responsibility," No. 56 (Palo Alto, CA: Department of Economics, Stanford University, 1975).

81. Felicity Barringer, "Publisher of Miami Herald Resigns," the *New York Times* on the Web, August 5, 1998, at www.mediainfo.com/ephome/news/newshtm/stop/stop.htm.

82. Raymond B. Nixon and Robert L. Jones, "The Content of Competitive Vs. Non-Competitive Newspapers," *Journalism Quarterly* 32 (Summer 1956), pp. 299–314.

83. Raymond B. Nixon, "Changes in Reader Attitudes Toward Daily Newspapers," *Journalism Quarterly* 31 (Fall 1954), pp. 421–433.

84. Gerald Borstell, "Ownership, Competition and Comment in 20 Small Dailies," *Journalism Quarterly* 33 (Spring 1956), pp. 220–222.

85. Galen Rarick and Barrie Hartman, "The Effects of Competition on One Daily Newspaper's Content," *Journalism Quarterly* 43 (Fall 1966), pp. 459–463. John C. Schweitzer and Elaine Goldman, "Does Newspaper Competition Make a Difference to Readers?" *Journalism Quarterly* 52 (Winter 1975), pp. 706–710. David Stakun, "Content Analysis of the Bloomington *Herald-Telephone* During and After Publication of the Competing *Courier-Tribune*" (Unpublished master's thesis, Indiana University, 1980). Katherine Trim, Gary Pizante and James Yaraskavitch, "The Effects of Monopoly on the News: A Before and After Study of Two Canadian Newspaper Towns," *Canadian Journal of Communications* 9 (1983), pp. 33–56. Maxwell McCombs, "Content Analysis of the Montreal and Winnipeg Newspapers," Syracuse University, 1984 (photocopied). From literature review in Stephen Lacy, "The Effects of Intercity Competition on Daily Newspaper Content," *Journalism Quarterly* 64.2–3 (Summer–Autumn 1987), pp. 282–284.

86. Schweitzer and Goldman.

87. Rarick and Hartman.

88. McCombs.

89. Stephen Lacy, Frederick Fico and Todd Simon, "Relationships Among Economic, Newsroom, and Content Variables: A Path Model." *Journalism Quarterly* 2.2 (1989), pp. 51–66.

90. David H. Weaver and L. E. Mullins, "Content and Format Characteristics of Competing Daily Newspapers," *Journalism Quarterly* 52 (Summer 1975), pp. 257–264.

91. Lee Becker, Randy Beam and John Russial, "Correlates of Daily Newspaper Performance in New England," *Journalism Quarterly* 55 (Spring 1978), pp. 100–108.

92. Robert Entman, "Newspaper Competition and First Amendment Ideas: Does Monopoly Matter?" *Journal of Communication* 35.3 (Summer 1985), pp. 147–165.

93. Stephen Lacy, "The Effects of Intercity Competition on Daily Newspaper Content," *Journalism Quarterly* 64.2–3 (Summer–Autumn 1984), pp. 281–290.

94. "Primary Media Sources of News," Roper-Starch Worldwide, on Web site at www.nab.org/Research/.

95. Peter Clark and Eric Fredin, "Newspapers, Television and Political Reasoning," *Public Opinion Quarterly* 42, p. 157.

96. Eric K. Meyer, "An Unexpectedly Wider Web for the World's Newspapers," *AJR Newslink*, on Web site at www.newslink.org/emcol10.html.

97. Ibid., on Web site at www.newslink.org/tel.html and www.newslink.org/nett.html. These were counted on August 9, 1998.

98. Herbert Howard, "TV Station Group ownership and Cross-media Ownership, A 1995 Update," *Journalism Quarterly* 72.2 (Summer 1995), pp. 390–401.

99. Guido H. Stempel III, "Effects on Performance of a Cross-Media Monopoly," *Journalism Monographs* No. 29 (June 1973), pp. 10–28.

100. George Litwin and W. H. Wroth, "The Effects of Common Ownership of Media Content and Influence" (Washington, DC: National Association of Broadcasters, July 1969); H. J. Levin, *The Policy on Joint Ownership of Newspapers and Television Stations* (New York: Center for Policy Research, 1971); J. A. Anderson, "The Alliance of Broadcast Stations and Newspapers: The Problem of Information Control," *Journal of Broadcasting* 16; all cited by W. Phillips Davison and Frederick T. C. Yu, *Mass Communications Research: Major Issues and Future Directions* (New York: Praeger Publishers, 1978), p. 48; William T. Gormley, *The Effects of Newspaper–Television Cross Ownership on New Homogeneity* (Chapel Hill, NC: Institute for Research in Social Science, University of North Carolina, 1976), pp. 211–215.

101. Herbert Howard, "Group Ownership of Newspapers and TV Stations," *Journalism Quarterly* 51.4 (Winter 1974), pp. 715–718; Herbert Howard, "TV Station Group Ownership and Cross-Media Ownership, A 1995 Update," *Journalism Quarterly* 72.2 (Summer 1995), pp. 390–401.

102. *Associated Press v. United States*, 326 U.S. 1 (1945).

103. Ibid., at 20.

104. *Lorain Journal Company v. United States* 342 U.S. 143 (1951).

105. *Citizen Publishing Co. V. United States* 394 U.S. 131 (1969).

106. Celeste Huenergard, "Scripps Hoping for Quick Decision in Cincinnati Case," *Editor & Publisher*, February 6, 1979, p. 19; Michael Parks, "A Merger Plan Under Fire," *Advertising Age*, June 19, 1981, pp. S12–13.

107. Celeste Huenergard, "Cincinnati Post called 'Unsaleable' at Hearing," *Editor & Publisher*, September 23, 1978, p. 12.

108. Jonathan Friendly, "Court Ruling Appears to Ease Newspaper Business Mergers," *New York Times*, May 14, 1983, p. 9.

109. Joseph B. White, "Knight-Ridder's No-Lose Plan Backfires," *Wall Street Journal*, January 4, 1988, p. 6.

110. Andy Pasztor and Joseph B. White, "Meese Clears Detroit Pact on Newspapers," *Wall Street Journal*, August 9, 1988.

111. "Anchorage Daily News," on Web site at www.adn.com/49/fannings.html ff.

112. "JOA—A 50-Year Record of Newspaper Life-Saving," *Editor & Publisher*, March 13, 1982, pp. 14–15.

113. "Why the FTC Is Stepping Away from Media Probes," *Advertising Age*, January 28, 1980, p. 14.

114. Compaine, p. 81.

115. Dertouzos and Thorpe, p. 6.

2

The Book Publishing Industry

Douglas Gomery

The printed book remains one of the most important forms of mass media in 1999. The advent of motion pictures, radio, television and, in recent times, cable television and home video were expected to kill the book industry. Printed text was seen, by this crude version of the substitution effect, to be gradually and virtually eliminated. But book publishing is as it has ever been. Although often thought of as a small-time backwater media business, versus the high-flying television or movie industry, book publishing has survived continuing consolidations and mergers and continues to provide opportunities for newcomers. Book publishing is as active and important—indeed more important—than ever. Forget any notion that book publishing is languishing. A staggering 1.3 million book titles were in print at the start of 1997; of these, 140,000 were published in 1996. The figure approached and exceeded one and half million by 1999. Consider that in 1947, the first edition of *Books in Print* listed 85,000 titles representing 357 publishers. The 1996 edition listed 49,000 book publishers. This is evidence that there is not one single book market, but many small ones (e.g., trade, children's, textbooks, and others analyzed below).[1]

Consider how brisk U.S. sales were in 1998 with a total of $23.03 billion, which is a 6.4% increase over 1997, according to the Association of American Publishers. Overall trade sales ($6.15 billion) were up 6.5%, with adult and juvenile paper bound books showing double-digit growth (10.2% and 13.8%, respectively). The education market showed continued vigor: elementary and secondary (el-hi) sales ($3.3 billion) rose 10.3%; higher education sales were up 8.2% to $2.9 billion. The following other sectors showed healthy growth: professional, $4.4 billion (up 6.3%); mass market paperbacks, 1.5 billion (up 5.6%); university presses, $391.8 million (up 6.5%); standardized tests, $204.6 million (up 6.9%); and subscription reference, $767.4 million (up 4.2%). The only sector showing a significant downturn was mail order sales (down 9.7% to $470.5 million), continuing the slide begun in 1997.[2]

Book selling and buying seems robust, particularly if the focus is on change and growth during the 1990s. On average, 128 new books were issued every day, including holidays. Super stores helped this a great deal, and so has the Internet. Los Angeles emerged as the book buying capital of the nation. And although Generation "X" did purchase less than its share, these individuals typically settled down at age 30, at which time their book buying sharply increased. But, the statistics show all-over growth, despite the demands and lures of home video and cable television. And, the Internet and World Wide Web are not likely to dampen book sales either.[3]

The growing number of mergers and acquisitions redefined the industry. In March 1998, for example, Germany's private Bertelsmann AG became the largest publisher in the world when it took over Advance Publication's (also private) Random House—then the largest trade publisher in the United States—and moved to the point of selling an estimated 40% of all the trade books sold worldwide (under its Dell, Doubleday and other labels). The Bertelsmann AG deal, worth an estimated $1.5 billion, rocketed Bertelsmann AG into first place in sales of trade books in the United States, with longtime leader Simon & Schuster dropping to second place. Then, in October 1998, the expanded Bertelsmann AG bought half share in the Web bookseller barnesandnoble.com and sought to dominate the Internet market and to overtake pioneer Amazon.com. Finally, in November 1998, Barnes & Noble announced it would take over Ingram, the largest distributor in the United States. At the time, nobody knew that Barnes & Noble would not consummate the deal; but, at the start of 1999, the U.S. book publishing industry was dominated by a German company in partnership with a New York City-based bookseller.[4]

Part of this was simply the book publishing industry participating in a national trend of corporate consolidation. So many mergers had not taken place since the early part of the 20th century. In 1997, for example, over $1 trillion mergers took place in the total economy. And this total was 50% higher than that of 1996, which was itself a record year. The book industry was part of this trend (as analyzed later), touching all phases—publishing, distribution, the rise of the superstore, selling over the Internet. Whereas book publishing was dominated by 10 companies, music had 5 controlling corporations and film had 6. But, in the 1990s, there continued to be no insurmountable barriers to entry into book publishing, with room for new niche entrants. There was developing controversy, as critics lamented the increasing concentration and others defended the mergers and acquisitions of an industry making the transition into the age of the Internet.[5]

Mark Crispin Miller argued that seven companies dominated book publishing in 1998: Bertelsmann AG, Pearson PLC, Viacom, News Corporation, Time Warner, Hearst and Holtzbrinck. He lamented that only two independents, W. W. Norton and Houghton Mifflin, remained. Miller believed that writers would have less places to get books published, best selling would become even more predominant a motivation and these powerful companies would limit the nation's freedom of expression. Investment banker and biographer Porter Bibb disagreed, pointing to mismanagement—uncontrolled manufacturing costs, ill-conceived seven figure advances to authors and the increasing rate of returns from bookstores—as the forces pushing consolidation. Other industries were modernizing and going global, so why not book publishing? Why not praise Bertelsmann AG and Barnes & Noble for seeking to sell over the Internet, and offer the average customer more choices to buy and read? Miller and Bibb were in agreement that book publishing was changing, but Miller saw these changes as a negative force and Bibb viewed this as a transition that would prove good for author and reader alike.[6]

One point is evident in both points of view. In particular, this merger trend would continue, in part fueled by favorable demographics, as the Baby Boomers age and use their growing finances and leisure time to buy and read. Older Americans have always been the heaviest readers, and this was the fastest growing group within the U.S. population in the 1990s. Furthermore, with record enrollments in elementary and high schools, and anticipated increases in college and university enrollment in the next century, the future looks bright for textbook sales. And, in 1999, amidst the hype for the first new *Star Wars* film in a generation, the book version became a hot title and shot to the top of the "best seller" lists even as the movie was being released. Despite talk of a TV-obsessed nation, book selling and reading were moving to record levels.[7]

KNOWING IS HARD

Yet measuring this growth precisely in terms of statistics is hard. Many publishers are small in size, and others are private corporations (like Bertelsmann AG), who are not required to release sales data. With mergers, publishing divisions buried within corporate structures do not report separate book publishing information. Government data is long out of date and so, as seen in Tables 2.1 and Table 2.2, we only are learning "officially" of the changes in the 1990s. And the government's restrictive definition of a book publisher severely undercounts the number of publishers. R. R. Bowker named near 20,000 entries, but the Bureau of the Census lists just over 2,000. The difference is in what is counted. The Census requires that a publisher meet a minimum level of business activity with at least one paid employee during the year, plus an employee identification number, plus book publishing as its primary

TABLE 2.1
The Official U.S. Government Count:
Number of Book Publishing Companies

	Book Publishing Companies
1997	*
1977	1,652
1982	2,007
1987	2,182
1992	2,503

*1997 data not issued as of September 15, 1999, but will be available on Web site at www.census.com, 1997 Economic Census, Manufacturing-Industry series, NAICS Subsector 323117, "Book Printing."

Source: U.S. Department of Commerce, Bureau of the Census, *1992 Census of Manufacturers: Newspapers, Periodicals, Books, and Miscellaneous Publishing* (Washington, DC: USGPO, 1994), Table 27A-1.

TABLE 2.2
The Official U.S. Government Count: Number of Employees,
Establishments and Value of Shipments (in millions)

	Number of Establishments	Number of Employees	Value of Shipments
1963	993	46,800	$ 1,534.6
1967	1,022	52,000	$ 2,134.8
1972	1,205	57,100	$ 2,856.8
1977	1,745	59,500	$ 4,793.9
1982	2,130	67,100	$ 7,740.0
1987	2,298	70,100	$12,619.5
1989	2,298	73,900	$14,074.0
1992	2,652	83,800	$17,126.4
1997	*	*	*

*1997 data not issued as of September 15, 1999, but will be available on Web site at www.census.com, 1997 Economic Census, Manufacturing-Industry series, NAICS Subsector 323117, "Book Printing."

Sources: U.S. Department of Commerce, Bureau of the Census, *1992 Census of Manufacturers: Newspapers, Periodicals, Books, and Miscellaneous Publishing* (Washington, DC: USGPO, 1994), Table 27A-1; *1987 Census of Manufacturers: Newspapers, Periodicals, Books, and Miscellaneous Publishing* (Washington, DC: USGPO, 1988), Table 27A-6; *1977 Census of Manufacturers: Newspapers, Periodicals, Books, and Miscellaneous Publishing* (Washington, DC: USGPO, 1978), Table 27A-5.

business. The net result is a vast number (in excess of 16,000) of "book publishers" that do not meet these minimal standards. Best sources of statistics in 1999 came from the Web site, www.bookwire.com, which includes *Publishers Weekly* information and the files of the official Book Industry Study Group.[8]

The industry-funded authority is the Book Industry Study Group, which in 1999 projected book sales to increase more than 5% per annum. Niche markets were now worth billions of dollars. Book club sales were expected to vault past $1 billion; college textbooks were projected to exceed $2.6 billion. Sales of children's, mass market paperbacks and professional books continued to grow as well. But remember, these are numbers funded by the industry, which seeks to put as good a face on its prospects as it can, and they remain gross categories, rarely defined by publisher and thus making analysis of ownership and its relative and changing rankings difficult.[9]

Thus, it must be acknowledged up front that any analysis of the book publishing industry is limited by the lack of up-to-date, truly comparable statistics. Definitions of what constitutes a publisher vary widely; partial reporting plagues every number cited here. No one really knows how many books are published each year. It is estimated that more than 50,000 titles are published annually, but some analysts go as high as 70,000 titles. Honestly no one knows. With many small publishers starting and ceasing operations each year, there is no central authority that can establish the figure precisely. The best single ongoing source that surveys the data at hand is complied by the scholarly publication, *Publishing Research Quarterly*, prepared by William S. Lofquist. Lofquist surveys the sales figures for the industry by the basic categories, including domestic activity, book prices and international activity. His valiant work ought to be consulted by anyone who seriously wishes to keep up with the statistics on book publishing—at least those that are available.[10]

A SHORT HISTORY

The book industry is the oldest of the mass media, predating the founding of the United States. Then, as now, there are three components to the book industry. First, publishers have a contract with authors to write a manuscript. The publisher then turns this manuscript into a finished book and then either directly distributes or subcontracts distribution of the books to booksellers. Retailers have long sold books from bookstores, but later branched out to general department stores and college and university bookstores. Publishers also sell directly to the public via direct mail, through telephone orders and, by the late 1990s, the Internet. Since the beginning, as an economic good for trade, the book has never—save in rare experiments—been advertising supported, but a direct sale. This book may be entertainment with a mystery, a guide on how to repair the kitchen or an historical treatise on the settling of the American West. The first bookstores were in Eastern cities—indeed publishers have long concentrated in major cities—but as the nation was settled, they were gradually set up in every state.[11]

From the beginning, three types of books were pioneered: mass selling trade books, school textbooks and scholarly tomes. Mass sellers have always drawn the most attention. In the 19th century, these were aimed at the literate public, and included fiction and nonfiction titles. As education became more important to American life, textbooks (aimed at college, high school and elementary school students) become a specialty of book publishing. The passage of the Morrill Act in 1865 brought research universities and the beginning of scholarly publishing. Although mass selling trade books were aimed at all readers, only scholars purchased university press books, and these never sought to make a profit. For textbooks, the "buyer" was a school district, or the instructor of a college course who assigned the texts. The textbook industry may have begun as an educational (read: nonprofit) business, but over time it became a valuable profit making part of the book publishing industry. If there is a date marking the start of U.S. book publishing, it was probably when printers began printing and selling works such as Benjamin Franklin's *Poor Richard's Almanack*.[12]

Through the 19th century, books were expensive and sales were measured in the thousands at best. Only the affluent citizens, with extra time and money, possessed them. Thomas Jefferson, for example, owned one of the biggest collections in the United States. He later donated this collection to begin the Library of Congress in Washington, DC, which is now the largest library in the world. He had but 6,500 volumes, which is less than the inventory of a small bookstore today. But the 19th century saw big changes in the U.S. book industry. More Americans learned to read. Faster printing techniques were developed. And better means of transportation allowed distribution to all parts of the growing nation. The industry was moving from elite audiences to mass marketing. The bestseller was created. At this time, companies like Charles Scribner's Sons were founded, and New York City became the center for trade publishers.

Harriet Beecher Stowe's *Uncle Tom's Cabin*, through its popularity in the 1850s, became the first mass market bestseller in the history of U.S. publishing. She published *Uncle Tom's Cabin* in hardcover, which appeared a couple of weeks before the last installment was serialized in the magazine *National Era.* By January 1853, more than 200,000 copies had been sold as readers sought to find the ending. Stowe received more than $10,000 in royalties for the first three months of sales, and the book industry—authors writing, publishers printing and distributing and booksellers retailing—had begun.[13]

Nineteenth-century books meant expensive hardcovers. Books remained relatively expensive as late as the Great Depression of the 1930s. In 1914, however, an important change took place: Books gained a special class for mailing. This law promoted distribution by rail—later truck—across the United States. This, in turn, led to book clubs, which sent titles to members of a club, and the bestseller (usually fiction and a biography). Thus, during the early 1900s, book purchase and reading was a middle-class phenomenon. The Book-of-the-Month Club was created in 1926, and the Literary Guild was founded the following year. Academic programs began postulating the "great books." The *New York Herald-Tribune* introduced a separate book review section, and after 1930 book discussions went on the radio.[14]

Still, until the 1940s, the book industry remained a collection of small companies, often family owned. The paperback revolution would change all that. From 1952 to 1970, industry sales increased more than 10% a year. During the 1970s, it grew by more than 15% a year. By 1989, the book business was a big business figured at sales of $14 billion a year when counting all three categories of books. The paperback, and the rise of mass education, also meant a real surge for the sale of textbooks to colleges, universities and elementary and secondary schools.[15]

The key to the growth of the book industry was paperback's lower prices. The handful of publishers in operation during the early 1900s grew to about 500 by the close of World War II. By 1992, the number of publishers had risen above 30,000. Led by inexpensive copies of Dr. Benjamin Spock's *Pocket Book of Baby and Child Care* and mysteries galore—sold in not just book stores, but in bus stations, grocery stores and later Kmarts) bestseller lists were created; the first and most important appeared in the *New York Times* in August 1942. As late as 1949, hardcover trade books and paperbacks sold in equal proportions, about 175 million copies each. By the mid-1950s, paperback sales swamped hardcover sales and hardcovers have never again come close. At the same time, universities expanded because of the GI Bill, and the textbook industry started measuring sales in thousands of copies. Even the handful of university presses began to generate a list of all research state universities plus two dozen private universities.[16]

Such sales—measured in the billions of dollars—saw book publishing become a big business. In the 1960s, a wave of mergers swept the book industry. Many smaller houses were absorbed into conglomerates, which began an era of restructuring that continues today. Random House was purchased by RCA (then owner of NBC) after Random House had absorbed both the Alfred A. Knopf and Pantheon imprints. Holt, Rinehart and Winston, itself the product of two mergers, became part of CBS. But these acquisitions did not last; the 1970s ended the growth spurt that began in 1945.[17]

A second wave of mergers commenced again in the boom of the 1980s. Simon & Schuster acquired textbook giant Prentice-Hall, and RCA and CBS sold out to others. Still, over time, the book industry remained one of the more open and least concentrated of the mass media. With the innovation of the personal computer, it seemed everyone wanted to become a publisher. Niche publishing became key: specialized books were aimed at children, mystery readers, romance lovers and novel freaks, for example. By the 1990s, the trade book and textbook publishing industry had fully become part of the conglomeratization of the mass media. Noted publishers are now part of massive organizations, such as Time Warner (Little, Brown), Bertelsmann AG (Bantam Doubleday Dell) or News Corporation (HarperCollins). The largest book publisher based in the United States in the 1990s was Simon & Schuster, owned by conglomerate Viacom (more noted for its Paramount Hollywood studio). Viacom also owned leading textbook publisher Prentice-Hall.[18]

Major book publishers became buried in conglomerates more famous for other mass media products. Until 1998, the Newhouse newspaper chain owned Random House. Magazine publisher Reader's Digest was a major player in book publishing with its book division. McGraw-Hill was noted for its business information and magazine *Business Week*, but was ranked as a top book publisher. And, until 1999, the Hearst Corporation, owner of William Morrow and Avon imprints, was better known for its magazines and newspapers. More of these mega-publishers created not only bestsellers, but also a line of religious books, textbooks, reference books and some scholarly books. This era of conglomerates contrasted with the state of the industry before World War II when book publishers were small enterprises—nationally based, personally owned, mostly partnerships.

Single titles became blockbusters. In 1991, for instance, 5 hardcover novels published in the United States sold over one million copies; more than 50 sold over 100,000 copies. The top 10 bestsellers together in 1983 sold fewer copies than the top bestseller of 1993, *The Bridges of Madison County. Bridges of Madison County* remained on *Publishers Weekly*, the key trade publication, bestseller list until October 1995, for a total of 161 weeks. Indeed, in 1993, a total of 9 books sold more than one million copies each. The number of fiction and nonfiction that sold more than 100,000 copies in 1993 also set a record at 157 titles. All were aimed at a particular audience, and in rare cases—making for legends within the business—became bestsellers. For example, Tom Clancy wrote *The Hunt for Red October* on an IBM electric typewriter in his spare time and published it with the tiny technical house, The Naval Institute Press of Annapolis, Maryland. In 1984, *The Hunt for Red October* hit only a few bookstores, but sold surprisingly well. Putnam Berkley issued it as a paperback, and within a decade Clancy's income jumped to $15 million per year. He became the inspiration for frustrated novelists who were convinced they could do better than what was out there.

The latest trends in bookselling in the 1990s included the failure of discount stores (such as Crown) and the rise of superstores (with in excess of 100,000 books, such as Borders Books & Music) into all major U.S. communities. Even with the rise of Internet selling, these superstores have become the sites for national tours to promote the next bestseller (as seen in Table 2.3).

Technology added venues. By the 1990s, customers began to expect books in audio editions, pitched at the growing number of home cassette players and car stereos, and large print versions, aimed at the visually handicapped. Indeed, by the 1990s, professional narrators (e.g., Frank Muller) pushed sales past $2 billion per annum, double that of 1994. The pay is modest, typically $100 to $150 per finished

TABLE 2.3
Writing and Selling: Examples of Promotional Campaigns, 1997

Author Title	Publisher Date Published Print Run	Promotion
Kitty Kelley The Royals	Time Warner's Warner Books September 23, 1997 1,000,000	5-city book tour; interviews on "Larry King," all network morning shows; ads in Entertainment Weekly, Vanity Fair, the New York Times
Paula Barbieri The Other Woman	Time Warner's Little, Brown September 10, 1997 750,000	11-city book tour; interviews on 700 Club and Oprah; ads in U.S. Today, the Los Angeles Times, the Chicago Tribune, Time, People
Whoopi Goldberg Whoopi	Hearst's Morrow/Rob Weisbach October 1, 1997 450,000	10-city book tour; interviews on 20/20, The Tonight Show and Rosie O'Donnell; promotion on cross-country train ride
Kelly Flinn Proud to Be	Advance's Random House October 1, 1997 300,000	15-city book tour; interview on 20/20; ads in U.S. Today, People, Army Times, Stars and Stripes, network radio
Stephen E. Ambrose Citizen Soldiers	Viacom's Simon & Schuster November 1, 1997 250,000	10-city book tour; interviews on Today and Charlie Rose; Veterans of Foreign Wars magazine
Anita Hill Speaking Truth to Power	Bertelsmann's Doubleday September 19, 1997 150,000	10-city book tour; interviews on Dateline NBC and Today; ads in the New York Times and the Los Angeles Times
J. Anthony Lukas Big Trouble	Viacom's Simon & Schuster October 14, 1997 65,000	Memorial 8-city book tour by the late Mr. Lukas' friends, including David Halberstam, Nicholas Lemann and Patricia Nelson Limerick

Source: New York Times, October 12, 1997, p. B13.

recorded hour, and most readers do it as a part-time job. But to the big companies the additional revenue boosted their bottom lines.[19]

"Desk top publishing" sought to break the trade book Boston to New York to Washington, DC editorial axis. By 1997, there were presses located in every state in the union, with sizable distribution arms working to get their products in the hands of desiring customers. Table 2.4 shows that more books have been published, fully half of the titles ever published in the United States issued since 1970. In the 1990s, it settled in at about 100 new titles issued per day, and a set of major publishers struggled and still managed to capture the bulk of this market. An oligopoly topped the book industry, but below them were more than 50,000 small presses, all offering books aimed at a certain niche of readers.[20]

As seen in Table 2.4, the future seems bright for the book industry as it has survived many challenges, technical changes and ownership acquisitions and mergers. Indeed, all of the other mass media (print, film, and electronic) have come about since the book started the mass production and distribution of ideas and pleasure centuries ago. And

TABLE 2.4
Total Book Sales

	Net Dollar Sales (in millions)	Percent Change from Previous Year	Net Unit Sales (in millions)	Percent Change from Previous Year
1989	14,110.8	+11.18	2,142.0	+6.92
1990	14,855.2	+5.28	2,144.3	+0.11
1991	15,568.7	+4.80	2,181.0	+1.71
1992	16,329.1	+4.48	2,192.3	+0.52
1993	17,394.4	+6.52	2,221.9	+1.35
1994	18,178.1	+4.51	2,274.4	+2.36
1995	19,485.0	+7.19	2,337.6	+2.78
1996*	19,944.2	+2.61	2,346.7	+0.39
1997*	20,965.2	+4.86	2,395.7	+2.09
1998*	22,117.1	+5.49	2,453.3	+2.40
1999*	23,380.9	+5.71	2,504.1	+2.07

*Indicates a Book Industry Study Group projection.
**Newly created Web site at www.bisg.com will update actual figures.
Source: Book Industry Study Group, Book Industry Trends 1995 (New York: Book Industry Study Group, 1995), pp. 2-4–2-9.

yet bookselling and publishing have never been healthier. The next section turns to a description of how the modern book publishing industry operates.

BASIC INDUSTRY OPERATION

The book industry is hardly complicated. It begins with publishers contracting with authors to write a manuscript. The publisher then turns this manuscript into a finished book. This feat is accomplished by editors, production workers and printers. This chain of operation is a well-known aspect of publishing. Less well known is the act of distribution, or getting the book from the printer to the outlet from which the customer buys it. The publisher (or a subcontracted party) then distributes these books to booksellers, originally by wagon, then by rail, now by air and truck.

But whereas publication gains the publicity (with bestseller lists and authors as celebrities), it is nonglamorous distribution that creates (like distribution in the other mass media) a true source of profits and power. In the family-owned, privately held Ingram Industries, Inc., which also includes 1,500 barges for hire, is a division that has evolved from a 1964 acquisition of a Tennessee textbook depository. In the mid- and late 1990s, Ingram Books had revenues measured in the billions, at least 10 times the size of the next largest distributor. Ingram Industries, Inc., which is currently worth $3 billion, ranks among the top 10 private companies in the United States. During the late 1990s, the Ingram Book Group handled about two thirds of the books that wended their ways through to bookstores, and in cooperation with the Publishers Marketing Association launched a program designed to include publishers with fewer than 10 titles on its database in the future. Ingram handled trade books, spoken audio, textbooks and specialty magazines from a dozen distribution centers located from Tennessee to California, from Virginia to Colorado, from Indiana to Oregon. Amazon.com certainly was more famous, but it was Ingram that distributed for the company.[21]

But Ingram, although the largest, is not the lone distributor of books. In an aggressive move in an unsettled time for wholesalers, the second-place distribution company, Baker & Taylor Books, planned in 1999 to nearly double warehouse space and added music and videos to its stock mix. The company expanded two of its four warehouses and moved the other two; this added a total of 650,000 square feet, which amounts to a 90% increase. The number of titles stocked at the warehouses increased by about 50,000, and the depth of stock also grew. The company also began drop-shipping from all warehouses to better serve Internet clients. Baker & Taylor Inc., the parent company, saw sales grow as publishers looked for an alternative to Ingram. Like other smaller wholesalers, the company benefitted from booksellers' negative reaction to the announcement that Barnes & Noble planned to buy Ingram.[22]

But it simply was not possible for small publishers and sellers to construct their own distribution network. The "Big Ten" did not need to depend on Ingram and Baker & Taylor. Nor did vast chains or Amazon.com. It was the small operators in the publishing industry that suffered because of a lack of control of distribution. And they would continue to be so, becoming a major power in book publishing meant the corporation had control over distribution.[23]

But, in the end, the book industry is all about buyers seeking a certain title. The thousands of titles sold have been categorized in any number of ways. *Publishers Weekly* names categories from "Agriculture" to "Travel." Others look for broader genre, here in alphabetical order as the 1990s end: from art to biography, business to fiction, history to literature, medicine to philosophy, psychology to religion, science to sociology. The relative proportions can be seen in the official government title output laid out in Table 2.5. This is a guide to the modern super bookstore with its shelves of history titles, but smaller shelves of books on music and poetry. Yet, despite the solid Census-driven numbers in Table 2.5, care must be taken in a fluid market where categories cannot easily be drawn. One can see this in the fudge factor of "general works," which could include overlapping subjects.[24]

By the mid-1990s, the available statistics describing the book industry were impressive indeed. Estimates as high as 60,000 new books each year have been set forth. (Consider that before World War II, less than 10,000 titles per annum were published.) Whatever the generalities, the numbers are indeed impressive. Consider just the adult trade book and children's sales denoted in Table 2.6. This means millions of sales, both for and to adults, and to adults for children. This indicates a healthy industry, with more books being bought for leisure-time reading.

But to the industry, the content is less important than the type of book and its associated selling practices. A sociology of a going-to-the-mall trade book may cover similar content to a textbook about the same subject matter, but the book publishing industry considers one a trade book and the other a textbook. Over the years, a certain set of internal categories has been developed. These categories are described to lay the groundwork for the analysis of the ownership of their producers and sellers.

Trade books dominate in the book public's mind because they are aimed at all readers, that is, they are of general interest, both in hardcover and paperback, covering fiction and nonfiction. These are the books ranked on the bestseller lists, which dominate shelf space in the bookstores. They are also sold by direct mail and

TABLE 2.5
The Official U.S. Government Count: U.S. Book New Title Output: 1992 and 1994

Category	1992	% of Total	1994	% of Total
Agriculture	558	1.15	401	0.99
Art	1,392	2.82	1,131	2.79
Biography	2,007	4.07	1,758	4.33
Business	1,367	2.77	1,294	3.19
Education	1,184	2.40	1,041	2.57
Fiction	5,690	11.55	4,765	11.74
General Works	2,153	4.37	1,666	4.11
History	2,322	4.71	1,899	4.68
Home Economics	826	1.68	768	1.89
Juveniles	5,144	10.44	4,271	10.52
Language	617	1.25	544	1.34
Law	1,063	2.16	836	2.06
Literature	2,227	4.52	1,854	4.57
Medicine	3,234	6.56	2,515	6.20
Music	346	0.72	271	0.67
Philosophy, Psychology	1,806	3.67	1,445	3.56
Poetry & Drama	899	1.82	776	1.91
Religion	2,540	5.15	2,148	5.29
Science	2,729	5.54	2,234	5.50
Sociology & Economics	7,432	15.08	6,232	15.36
Sports & Recreation	1,113	2.26	882	2.17
Technology	2,152	4.37	1,523	3.75
Travel	468	0.95	340	0.84
Total:	46,193	—	40,584	—

Sources: *Publishers Weekly*, March 7, 1994, p. S28; *The Bowker Annual: Library and Trade Almanac*, 40th ed. (New Providence, NJ: R. R. Bowker, 1995), p. 512.

TABLE 2.6
Trade Book Unit Sales, 1990–1997 (in millions)

	Adult Hardcover	Juvenile Hardcover	Total Hardcover	Adult Paperback	Juvenile Paperback	Total Paperback	Total Adult	Total Juvenile	Total Trade
1990	206.1	188.4	394.5	197.0	113.0	310.0	403.1	301.4	704.5
1991	213.0	203.3	416.3	199.1	122.2	321.3	412.1	325.5	737.6
1992	227.1	197.5	424.6	214.5	121.3	335.8	441.6	318.8	760.4
1993	237.2	187.4	424.6	223.2	115.1	338.3	460.4	302.5	762.9
1994	250.0	186.0	436.0	236.5	135.0	371.5	486.5	321.0	807.5
1995*	260.0	182.0	442.0	246.0	132.0	378.0	506.0	314.0	820.0
1996*	267.0	176.0	443.0	255.0	130.0	385.0	522.0	306.0	828.0
1997*	277.0	174.0	451.0	265.0	133.0	398.0	542.0	307.0	849.0

*estimated
Source: *Veronis, Suhler & Associates Communications Industry Forecast*, 9th ed., July 1995, p. 246.

through book clubs. Only rarely do scholarly, scientific and professional books—aimed at small targeted audiences—crossover into this category. Here the first edition is frequently printed in hardcover, which is then followed by a paperback edition. Often, this "reprint" is done by a different company after bidding for paper rights. In past years, the major publishers did it all and demanded authors and their agents sign away all rights in advance. In the 1990s, trade books held the largest share of the market, about one third of all book sales as measured by dollars sold and by units (i.e., books) sold. Hardcover bestsellers almost always cluster among celebrity books by television and movie stars, noted politicians and military officers and others who vault into the public's eye because of some famous (or infamous) act. The numbers are greater than $5 billion a year in sales, the largest category of sales in the typical categories discussed here, and about the same as the monies spent on going to the movies in theaters.[25]

Book clubs form a subunit of the trade category, and serve as specific means to sell trade books. These clubs sell steadily, but modestly, compared to other categories. Although this accounts for just about $1 billion sales per year, these clubs are not as important a share as they once were, because more customers shop by mail or the Internet or purchase their books at superstores. In 1982, book clubs had more than 10% of the share of adult trade books; by the mid-1990s, this had fallen in half and the clubs (particularly Time Warner's Book of the Month Club) had become valuable for their lists, which were used for target mass mailing and direct mail solicitation.[26]

Audio books should be considered an extension of the trade book segment. Americans spent well in excess of $1 billion for these recorded versions of bestsellers, and unlike book clubs—comparable in share of the market—audio is growing. In the mid-1980s, audio was but a quarter of a million dollars. This category started in the 1970s as the Walkman and other cheap, simple to operate and portable (as inside the automobile) tape players became widespread and replaced the cumbersome disc record player. This was an established niche by the 1990s, served by superstores, other retailing, mail order and World Wide Web means of purchase.[27]

Mass market paperbacks are aimed at a different audience than trade books, whether in hardback, paper, audio or sold through book clubs. Mass market paperbacks are not sold by bookstores, but can be found in grocery stores and drug stores, all nonbookstore outlets aimed at the once-and-done reader. They are small in size and printed on low quality paper, as compared with the average trade book, which is larger in size and printed on higher quality paper (hence meant to be saved and re-used). The 1990s witnessed a relative decline of mass market paperbacks, as Borders Books & Music and Barnes & Noble sold quality paperbacks to more customers. Still, the mass market star biography or lurid mystery remain popular and ubiquitous. In the mid-1990s, these accounted for about one twelfth of the sales of books by dollars, and far more by units because of their relatively low price versus other types of books. The basic strategy is to find a title that will sell in high volume so that the low price means sizable total dollars taken in—in toto, nearly $2 billion per annum. Examples might include any Tom Clancy, John Irving, Mary Higgins Clark or Sidney Sheldon fictional entry found in a grocery store, a Wal-Mart, an airport or some other retail situation where the traffic passing each day is high.[28]

Textbooks form the first and most important category of specialized books because they sell the most. They are aimed exclusively for sales at a captured audience, students, and are not chosen usually by buyers themselves, but by the teacher, professor or school district. Experts in a speciality write texts informed by consultants striking to fashion a bestseller. Texts are updated on a regular basis to capture new knowledge and trends as well as to force new sales. Although maintaining perhaps the lowest profile of all published categories, the elementary and high school textbook market is a big business, accounting for one eighth of all dollar sales for books in the United States in the mid-1990s, or one tenth of all books sold each year. The college and university textbook market is smaller, but still a sizable niche. Here, half are in paperback and half in hardcover, which amounts to billions of dollars per annum (as seen in Table 2.7).[29]

Certainly textbook sales can mean real money. For example, consider the case of an economics textbook by N. Gregory Mankiw issued in 1997. The author was paid $1.4 million by Harcourt Brace & Company for *Principles of Economics*, which became the nation's new sales leader in colleges and universities across the United States—indeed, around the world. The stakes are high: Each year some 900,000 college students across the United States take "Introduction to Economics" for the first time, and 600,000 buy a new book for the course. Publishers, in turn, collect some $30 million in revenue, which was split 35 ways in 1997. Harcourt was betting it could capture the lion's share of that revenue, and paid Mankiw an advance against royalties of $1 million plus an outright grant of $400,000 after a three-way bidding war in 1992. Mankiw gets $10.00 for each copy sold at the wholesale price of $49.00. Harcourt will not break even until it sells 60,000 copies, with 180,000 sales per year being the goal, or nearly one third of the market. Thus, in 1997, Harcourt set its sites on 3,500 university and college professors across the United States to sell them on the book, get them to adopt it and then have the students buy it. Mankiw and Harcourt wanted to knock-off industry leader McGraw-Hill's text by Campbell R. McConnell and Stanley L. Brue, as well as their classic by Paul Samuelson, which by 1997 had sold some 3.5 million copies since its original introduction nearly 50 years ago.[30]

TABLE 2.7
Unit Sales of Educational Books, 1990–1997 (in millions)

	Elementary/ High School	College	Total Educational
1990	209.3	136.9	346.2
1991	206.0	133.2	339.2
1992	208.3	136.6	344.9
1993	224.9	135.5	360.1
1994	210.8	136.1	346.9
1995	237.0	142.1	379.1
1996	245.5	149.0	394.5
1997*	265.0	150.7	415.7

*estimate

Source: *Veronis, Suhler & Associates Communications Industry Forecast*, 11th ed., July 1997, pp. 327, 343.

In 1999, textbooks and their ancillary product sales remained strong, often with annual double-digit gains in sales. As education became more of a public policy concern, the sales of textbooks rose. Pearson PLC's spending of billions of dollars attested in real ownership terms the importance of this unit. One 1998 estimate had Pearson PLC with a quarter of all textbooks sold in the United States—followed by McGraw-Hill, Harcourt General, Houghton Mifflin and Thomson, all with sales of $500 million more in 1997; the smaller companies will probably be absorbed after 2000. The economies of scale are vast in this sector, as Pearson PLC noted that it would save $130 million over two years by combining the Simon & Schuster units with its own vast textbook sales brands.[31]

Religious books form an invisible category like textbooks, are aimed at a particular audience like mass market paperbacks and sell in numbers measured in millions of copies. Many people lament the moral decline of the United States in the 1990s, but religious publishing is doing better than ever. Dollar sales approach book clubs and exceed mail order. Hardcover titles account for two thirds of sales based on two important niches. The first are key works (such as the Bible for Christians) and other key testaments for all variety of faiths. There are also other inspirational works from biographies and autobiographies to histories and celebrations. This category continued to grow well in the 1990s, passing $1 billion in annual sales; consider that, in the mid-1990s, there were some 50,000 religious titles in print.[32]

Children's books is another growing and lucrative niche, well known to anyone with young children. Macmillan established this as a separate category with the first juvenile department in 1920 called "Books for Girls and Boys." In 1942, the Little Golden Books imprint was launched. These 25-cent full-color picture books, compared to the average priced adult trade book at $1.50, was an obvious bargain. But the vast growth came after World War II with the Baby Boom. In 1945, in anticipation, representatives of 30 publishing houses with interest in children's books formed the Children's Book Council. In 1965, the Great Society of President Lyndon Baines Johnson recognized the trend and began the Elementary and Secondary Education Act, which provided funds to school libraries for nontextbook purchases. As the Baby Boomers, born between 1946 and 1964, had children, these young people and their parents demanded more children's books, and this market segment has continued to grow. By November 1997, the *New York Times* had published its 50th annual special edition of the Sunday "Book Review" section devoted to children's books.[33]

Indeed, it is fascinating to break apart the sales of books for children (juvenile) and adults (as seen in Table 2.8). Whereas children's books are surely major sellers, they do not come close to adult trade sales. The major children's publishers include Simon & Schuster, Little, Brown, HarperChildrens, Farrar Straus Giroux, and Viking Children's Books. Scholastic is another major player, but is not part of some larger conglomerate. Companies as diverse as Oxford University Press, Pleasant Company Publications and Talewinds issue selected titles. The aforementioned majors, plus Golden Books and Scholastic, make up the main sellers of children's hardcovers and paperbacks, which accounted for more than $2 billion per annum in the mid-1990s.

TABLE 2.8
Consumer Spending on Trade Books, Adult and Children (in millions)

	Adult Hardcover	Juvenile Hardcover	Total Hardcover	Adult Paperback	Juvenile Paperback	Total Paperback	Total Adult	Total Juvenile	Total Trade
1990	$2,921.1	$1,234.4	$4,155.5	$1,855.7	$ 486.6	$2,342.3	$4,776.8	$1,721.0	$6,497.8
1991	3,172.0	1,393.5	4,565.5	1,975.0	571.5	2,546.5	5,147.0	1,965.0	7,112.0
1992	3,595.0	1,381.3	4,976.3	2,207.8	612.9	2,820.7	5,802.8	1,994.2	7,797.0
1993	4,127.4	1,246.0	5,373.4	2,337.5	691.7	3,029.2	6,464.9	1,937.7	8,402.6
1994	4,528.6	1,336.8	5,865.4	2,668.2	737.5	3,405.7	7,196.8	2,074.3	9,271.1
1995	4,387.9	1,370.3	5,758.2	2,783.0	956.3	3,739.3	7,170.9	2,326.6	9,497.5
1996	4,195.0	1,490.0	5,685.0	2,833.0	1,112.0	3,945.0	7,028.0	2,602.0	9,630.0
1997*	4,369.8	1,476.0	5,845.8	2,945.5	1,090.4	4,035.9	7,315.3	2,566.4	9,881.7

*estimate
Source: Veronis, Suhler & Associates Communications Industry Forecast, 11th ed., July 1997, pp. 272–273.

Professional books are those aimed at specialists, including business people, lawyers, medical professionals and other science and technical workers. They usually appear only printed in hardcover editions, and often are meant to be kept for years as reference tools. They are very expensive per copy sold, and so although they sell fewer units than trade books, the revenues generated are impressive (as seen in Table 2.9). Ironically, top sellers in the 1990s have been computer books. More are being offered in paperback versions, with nearly two thirds now issued as such. But dollar sales, because of high prices sold to select niche markets, are still dominated by hardcover editions. Business books do well when the economy does not and specialists are looking for answers. Law books and medical books grow at top rates, as knowledge and specialty increase. Technical and scientific books from U.S.-based publishers are also important, in large part because of the vast university research community, and also because English continues to be the dominant language used for analysis and discussion in science and technology. In the mid-1990s, sales in this category mounted to nearly $4.0 billion per annum, with a great deal of diversity within (see Table 2.10). Law books, in themselves, are a huge market, as are medical books.[35]

TABLE 2.9
Unit Sales of Professional Books (in millions)

	Sales
1990	$148.6
1991	147.0
1992	152.9
1993	155.9
1994	161.7
1995	165.4
1996	163.6
1997*	164.2

*estimate
Source: *Veronis, Suhler & Associates Communications Industry Forecast*, 11th ed., July 1997, pp. 327, 343.

TABLE 2.10
Publishers' Sales of Professional Books, 1990–1997 (in millions)

	Business	*Law*	*Medical*	*Technical, Scientific, Other*	*Total*
1990	$527.9	$ 947.5	$526.3	$ 764.2	$2,765.9
1991	488.8	1,011.9	580.5	779.5	2,860.7
1992	490.3	1,128.1	622.7	865.6	3,106.7
1993	510.9	1,177.7	707.4	924.5	3,320.5
1994	560.0	1,299.0	754.1	993.1	3,606.1
1995	617.6	1,400.4	809.3	1,042.0	3,869.3
1996	666.1	1,495.0	860.3	973.2	3,994.6
1997*	720.0	1,547.6	902.3	1,006.4	4,176.3

*estimate
Source: *Veronis, Suhler & Associates Communications Industry Forecast*, 11th ed., July 1997, p. 329.

University press scholarly books should be seen in the same light as professional publishing, although they can and do publish trade-like titles and take aim at categories far broader than the business, law, scientific, technical and medical titles that are the core of professional publishing. There are university press books aimed at advancing knowledge for specialists, and their publishers usually do not seek to make a profit publishing scholarly books. These are typically serious nonfiction titles across a wide variety of disciplines and encompassing all forms of knowledge as it is reflected in the leading U.S. universities. More university presses have begun to issue fiction, including novels, short stories and poetry. Although small in number (somewhat more than 100 belong to the Association of American University Presses), their influence is great among teachers and scholars. Sales to university libraries remain important here as libraries and institutions purchased about 1 in 20 books. In 1995, sales came to more than $300 million, a small amount when compared to other categories.[36]

Selling and Pricing Decisions

There are no sales figures that conform totally and faithfully to these categories, but the information contained in Table 2.11 is quite helpful. Trade sells the most, followed by professional books. Education is the invisible seller, one where the choice and price are hardly at the selection of the buyer, but the instructor or school. In toto, there is a great deal of money in the sales of many kinds of books.

Whatever the category of sales, demand is strong and so the average price of a book is rising. In 1994, the average retail price of a new hardcover book was $42.97. Mass market paperbacks are cheaper and, in 1994, were reported at $5.74 retail. Trade paperbacks fall in the middle at $20.05 retail in 1994. The figures vary, with books on medicine costing $76.22 and mass market paperback fiction selling at $4.80 retail.[37]

Table 2.12 summarizes relative prices over time for trade books—both for children and for adults. Paperbacks remain cheaper but the price of adult paperbacks in the late 1990s is approaching the adult hardcover price of the early 1990s. The convergence is less obvious for children's books, but the trends are clearly the same. Demand is there and consumers are willing to pay more, despite the relatively inex-

TABLE 2.11
Estimated Book Sales, by Selected Category, 1994–1998 (in millions)

Segment	1994	1995	1996	1997	1998
Trade	5,541	5,655	5,626	5,826	6,150
Professional	3,606	3,869	3,995	4,227	4,400
Mail order	557	565	580	575	471
Mass market paper	1,392	1,347	1,533	1,608	1,500
University press	326	340	349	372	392
Elementary/high school	2,156	2,466	2,608	2,775	3,300
Higher education	2,177	2,325	2,486	2,659	2,900
Standardized tests	157	167	179	190	205

Sources: *Publishers Weekly*, March 18, 1996, p. 13; *Publishers Weekly*, July 7, 1997, p. 12; see Web site at www.netadvantage.standardpoor.com, "Publishing," 1999, p. 8.

TABLE 2.12
Average Trade Book Prices

	Adult Hardcover	Juvenile Hardcover	Total Hardcover	Adult Paperback	Juvenile Paperback	Total Paperback	Total Adult	Total Juvenile	Total Trade
1990	$14.17	$6.55	$10.53	$ 9.42	$4.31	$ 7.56	$11.85	$5.71	$ 9.22
1991	14.91	6.92	11.02	9.90	4.61	7.87	12.49	6.04	9.64
1992	15.70	7.21	11.83	10.38	4.82	8.30	13.14	6.26	10.26
1993	16.92	7.49	13.10	10.68	5.21	8.62	13.97	6.48	11.03
1994	17.68	7.34	13.38	11.33	5.00	8.89	14.64	6.29	11.29
1995	18.31	7.74	13.82	12.28	5.36	9.23	15.38	6.55	11.56
1996	18.81	7.97	13.87	13.00	5.56	9.44	15.94	6.72	11.63
1997*	19.25	8.20	14.36	13.70	5.80	10.01	16.55	6.97	12.20

*estimate

Source: *Veronis, Suhler & Associates Communications Industry Forecast*, 11th ed., July 1997, p. 270.

pensive nature of the other mass media—particularly "free" television and radio broadcasting.

Who purchases books in the United States in the 1990s? Each year, more than a billion books are sold, not counting used shops. Older persons purchase more trade books. Of 10 subject areas traditionally surveyed, popular fiction dominates sales with cooking a distant second. Thereafter, the subject categories rarely tally a great share of the market, illustrating the diversity of the types and genres of books sold. Well-off Americans purchase more books. The higher the education level attained, the more likely individuals are to buy a book. The top-selling season, not surprisingly, is the Christmas gift buying season stretching from Thanksgiving Day on. As the Baby Boomers age and gain more wealth, they purchase more books. And, as they raise families later and with a smaller number of children per family, they spend more on literature per child. Yet, in the end, the one surprising fact in book retailing, versus other forms, is that book publishers spend little on direct advertising, generally less than 1% of revenues. Another point is that price is not as important a measure as it is in other commodities.[38]

What does this mean to the industry as the 1990s end? Mark Crispin Miller is right that book publishing is dominated by a handful of huge corporations, but there are more than his seven when considering other than trade book publishers. Other categories of book publishing, analyzed later, need to be included. Moreover, in 1997, there were more than 20,000 U.S. book publishers issuing just a book or two per annum. Compared to other industries, book publishing is not highly concentrated. The one exception is educational publishing, which is concentrated into six or so companies. Bringing out a textbook requires lots of up-front capital and so there are real barriers to entry. Because these three- to five-year up-front costs are substantial, there are really no mom-and-pop textbook companies. This segment, highly profitable, is dominated by McGraw-Hill, Viacom, Inc., Harcourt General, News Corporation and Pearson PLC.[39]

Book publishing owners range from large media conglomerates (e.g., Time Warner, News Corporation and Viacom) to small, family-owned operations that issue a

handful of titles per year. In terms of sales, according to *Forbes* and its top 500 listing, Wal-Mart Stores, a big seller of books, ranked 4th; the Walt Disney Company,
a small publisher within a huge media enterprise, ranked 39th; Viacom, the largest
publisher with its Simon & Schuster division, ranked 103rd; and Time Warner,
owner of a major publishing house, ranked 128th. Others, even major publishers like
Reader's Digest and Harcourt General, were much further down the list. But this listing was based on data from public companies, based in the United States, and traded on a stock exchange.[40]

Whatever the statistical reporting problems and details of oligopolistic concentration, book publishing in 1997 followed cycles of boom and bust in sales. Consider that in 1996, according to the Association of American Publishers, total book
sales increased 4%, down from an increase of 6% the year before, when approximately 1.5 billion books were sold and totaling well in excess of $20 billion. Much-
heralded titles from major publishers lost money. These included Johnnie Cochran's,
O.J. Simpson's attorney, *Journey to Justice*; Ballantine paid a reported $3.5 million in
an advance, but sold only half its initial press run of 500,000 copies. And Cochran's
fellow attorney, Robert Shapiro, also received more than $1.0 million in an advance;
Warner Books issued *The Search for Justice*, which sold only half its initial printing.[41]

More book publishers were attempting synergy, linking the hawking of a book
with a movie or television program. Major publishing houses have to count on Hollywood "ancillary" funds to make a book profitable. Celebrity authors from Hollywood "pre-sell" millions of copies. Books have been a story source for the movies
since Hollywood began (e.g., *Uncle Tom's Cabin* and *Quo Vadis?*). Giant Hollywood
companies today (e.g., Viacom with its Paramount Pictures and Simon & Schuster
publisher divisions) seek to achieve synergy from books being made into movies. It
is expected that a successful book will be made into either a feature motion picture
or a television miniseries. Indeed, some examples of best-selling books turned into
blockbuster movies include *Raintree Country* (1940s), *Anatomy of a Murder* (1950s),
Jaws (1970s) and *Forrest Gump* (1990s).

In the 1990s, a million dollar payment for using a successful novel to make a hit
movie is hardly unusual. In 1996, *The Eleventh Plague*, a novel coauthored by John
Baldwin and John Marr, was optioned by Twentieth Century-Fox for $2 million!
John Grisham's work commands even more. And today television is an equal force.
Consider that by May 1997 TV talk show hostess Oprah Winfrey had promoted six
novels on her television show that went on to the bestseller lists. To the book publishing industry, having a novel picked by Oprah in 1997 was akin to winning the
lottery.[42]

Book publishing has accepted the Hollywood formula, and uses the star system in
the form of "celebrity" authors. Like Hollywood, book publishing in the 1990s had
its superstars—John Grisham, Tom Clancy, Danielle Steel, and Patricia Cornwell.
Like Hollywood, book publishing devotes the majority of its promotional resources
to "event books" by these superstars, and relies on their predictable huge sales.
Authors like Stephen King struck deals worth millions. For example, in November
1997, King signed a three-book deal with Simon & Schuster, the largest book publisher in the world. King's next novel, tentatively titled *Bag of Bones*, commanded an

unconventional deal in which he received nearly 50% of the profits. For this share of the profits, King took a mere $2 million advance, which is low for him. *The Dead Zone* put King on the bestseller lists in 1979 and 20 King books had appeared on the bestseller lists through late 1997 when he signed this new deal. After 18 years, King had become dissatisfied with Viking and decided to conduct an unusually public search for a new publisher. Viking, a division of the British publishing and media giant Pearson PLC, had agreed to pay rival star Tom Clancy more money. Clancy was earning $20 million a book while King was getting "merely" $16 million. King approached Simon & Schuster and gambled that he could sell more. Thus his deal, formulated like that of many Hollywood actors and directors, would mean even more money for him.[43]

King and company benefitted from the expansion of book retailing. The number of bookstores in the United States in 1996, by one compilation, included a vast number of religious stores (4,012), college bookstores (3,430), and discounters (led by Wal-Mart). There were 500 booksellers located in museums and art galleries, and more than 400 children's bookstores as well. In 1972, the top four bookstore chains accounted for just over 10% of all book sales. By 1990, Walden books (owned by Kmart) had more than 1,000 stores and alone accounted for that same percentage of sales. By 1995, Borders Books & Music had superstores from Alaska to Wisconsin to Hawaii to Washington, DC (with seven in this metropolitan region alone). By one authoritative estimate, in January 1997, there were more than 29,000 U.S. booksellers, with nearly 1,000 new ones added in 1996. About half the booksellers in the United States in 1997 were independents, the other half chains. And the future looked bright as Internet bookstores, led by Amazon.com., promised to open a vast new set of sellers.[44]

And this industry is global. The companies that sell the most books in the United States in 1999 are based in Germany (Bertelsmann AG) and the United Kingdom (Pearson PLC). This is a world market because citizens of Norway, Germany, Belgium, Switzerland, and Austria, for example, spend more on books per person than Americans, but the size and wealth factor in the United States make it the world's leading book-buying market—and the subject of this chapter. Publishers may be headquartered in any country, but their success is judged and their ownership is explained in terms of their sales in the United States.[45]

BOOK PUBLISHING'S BIG 10 OLIGOPOLY

There are major firms, but generally the book industry is not as concentrated as other mass media industries. Still there is a "Big 10." But, entry (and exit) as a small publisher or independent bookseller remains possible and frequent. Only in the distribution stage of book publishing are there pronounced economies of sale of operation. For example, Ingram entices larger publishers to economize through mass ordering and thus keep costs low and barriers to entry high as it handles vast numbers of titles. Ingram also benefits from vast ware units. Yet, joint efforts by smaller publishers, usually in the form of consortia that pool distribution activities, mean that a small publisher is not necessarily out of the business. Capital requirements are relatively low, and few specialized talents (including editors) are required. Although products are sharply differentiated—to the point where each title is unique in some sense—brand identification does not carryover from one title to another. That is, the customer looks to the author and to the content, not to the publishing house.[46]

Major houses dominate certain sectors of the industry they believe will generate the most profits. Consider trade books. Domination can best and most easily be appreciated after a glance at the *New York Times* bestseller list, where the same publishers appear year after year. In 1996, for example, the leaders in bestsellers, as complied by *Publishers Weekly*, saw Advance's Random House (by 1998 owned by Bertelsmann AG) in first place, followed by Bertelsmann's various imprints, Viacom's Simon & Schuster, News Corporation's HarperCollins and Time Warner's various imprints. These five had most of the books, most of the weeks on the hardcover lists and market shares from 20% to 13%. The same five dominated mass paperback bestseller lists as well. Indeed, *Publishers Weekly* found in the fiction category that approximately 90% of the top fiction titles were by writers who had previously enjoyed bestseller status. For nonfiction, the top sellers included titles by and about famous people in the news, followed by how-to-do titles. From 1992 to 1996, Advance's Random House had the highest share of hardcover and paperback bestseller titles, except in 1995 when Bertelsmann's Bantam Doubleday Dell imprints led the way. (It is no wonder—as analyzed later—that Bertelsmann AG in 1998 purchased Random House.) A single placement for a small publishing house (e.g., Regnery, Tor and Running Press) kept it in business, promising revenues to cover any forthcoming down turns in sales. Yet, with more than 50,000 small publishers, the odds were long that any single one would turn out a bestseller.[47]

Bestsellers are important because they provide a larger portion of revenues and profits for the 10 majors. Yet although publishing textbooks, professional books, and children's titles creates less fame, they regularly create significant profits. But, with all their attendant publicity, it is easy to think that bestsellers are the lone source of income for publishers. Indeed, as shown in Table 2.13, trade books typically trail children's books and textbooks as money makers. Also, medical professional books, business and law professional books and the operations of book clubs are geneally more profitable. The difference is that a bestseller can make up for a great deal of underachieving trade books, which end up being sold at a discount.

Thus, whereas it is easy to enter the industry and produce a small number of titles each year, becoming a Big 10 house dominating one or more of the categories is difficult. The 10 majors create one barrier to entry as more capital is required for advances. Successful trade book authors sign with major trade houses to get the widest possible distribution, and the largest possible royalty return. Authors prefer cash up front and smaller houses do not have that available. The public may not care about the long-standing reputation of a publishing house, but authors know that a history of widely selling books and of successful authors minimizes their risk. It would seem that goodwill, that most elusive of corporate values, accumulates slowly over time in book publishing, and relatively new firms, which are undercapitalized and have short histories, are at a comparative disadvantage.[48]

TABLE 2.13
Rare Look at Publishers' Estimated Pre-Tax Margins by Category of Book Titles (% of Net Sales)

Segment	1994	1995
Trade	14.3%	8.5%
Adult Hardbound	11.9	3.7
Adult Paperbound	15.2	12.2
Juvenile	19.0	5.8
Religious	8.9	17.0
Professional	14.6	13.9
Medical	19.2	19.7
Scientific & Technical	11.7	9.3
Business & Law	18.6	18.0
Book Clubs	20.8	19.2
Mass Market	9.8	13.4
Elementary & High School	17.2	16.3
College	10.3	12.2

NOTE: Margins are pre-tax and do not include certain corporate charges such as corporate staff compensation, legal and accounting fees and interest costs.
Source: *Publishers Weekly*, February 5, 1996, p. 13.

In the trade side, the industry is dominated by a handful of firms in a classic, albeit fluid, oligopoly. Why? Strategic marketing power on one side and global economies on the other provide at least two core reasons. First, when marketing through the modern media, a corporation needs to be able to react quickly as it finds profitable niches, develop products to satisfy these niches and then defend its new market from others who seek to copy and take away market share and profits. Second, the market has grown to be global. Information in English flows around the world in the same way as video images from CNN and movies from Hollywood and music from Big Five music companies. Whereas the focus of this discussion is book publishing in the United States, it must be recognized that this is a global industry, and it will become more so in the 21st century.

Both marketing power and globalization have made book publishers appealing targets for mergers and acquisitions. The giant book publishers—led by Bertelsmann AG and Pearson PLC—cover nearly all markets for books, and have chosen to concentrate on book publishing as their top priority. These firms have developed thousands of new titles each year, which could be built on for strategic thrusts and to invade new markets around the world. Moreover, as the value of the U.S. dollar fell, foreign publishing giants—principally in Europe—looked to U.S. book publishers as values to purchase. Unlike federal law that prevents foreign ownership and control of U.S. radio and television licensed broadcasting stations, the Constitution's First Amendment permitted a foreign company to purchase outright any book company willing to sell.

The 10 oligopolists—that is, 10 majors—spread risks. Media conglomerates in the 1990s (and earlier) took over book publishers in order to soak up the synergies associated with books as the basis of movies and television programs. This has been a trend in the late 20th century. Indeed, as early as the 1960s, there were 183 mergers and acquisitions in U.S. book publishing as the book industry rode the wave of general conglomeratization in the United States. The 1970s were marked by recession, so the number of mergers and acquisitions peaked in 1970—along with the crest of the general economy. But there were a number of significant acquisitions in the 1970s, such as Germany's Bertelsmann AG purchase of Bantam Books, which mark the beginning of the globalization of book publishing. During the 1980s, after a recession, the U.S. economy picked up and so did the number of mergers and acquisitions in book publishing. Indeed, between 1984 and 1988, there were more than 150 mergers in the book industry, almost as many as took place during the 1960s. So, in the 1980s, Bertelsmann AG further expanded by taking over Dell and Doubleday, Rupert Murdoch's News Corporation's acquired Harper & Row and later Collins, and the United Kingdom's Pearson PLC acquired New American Library and other companies. Between 1960 and 1989, noted scholar Albert N. Greco, there were 573 mergers and acquisitions in book publishing affecting the United States.[49]

Mergers and acquisitions have not been as frenetic in the 1990s, but takeovers and corporate absorptions continue to redefine the basic structure of the book industry. The early and mid-1990s, for example, saw Viacom's purchase of Paramount Communications and with it Simon & Schuster; then, in 1998, it sold its educational and references divisions to Pearson PLC. Thus, the rankings of the top 10 majors in the book oligopoly will continue to be fluid and changing. In Table 2.14 the industry-sponsored Book Industry Study Group set a top 11, and Standard & Poor's determined a different 11—depending on the category of sales (as seen in Table 2.15). Hearst was sold to News Corporation in 1999, so the 11 was reduced to 10. The discussion begins with the 1998-generated Standard & Poor's "new" 10

TABLE 2.14
Eleven Largest Book Publishing Firms in the United States, 1993 (in millions)

Parent Company (Publishing Entity)	1993 Book Revenue	% of Total Book Revenues of Top 20 Firms	% of Total U.S. Book Revenue
Viacom (Simon & Schuster)	$1,700	11.65%	9.77%
Reader's Digest	1,334	9.14	7.67
Newhouse (Random House)	1,150	7.88	6.61
Time Warner Book Group	1,079	7.39	6.20
Bertelsmann (Bantam Doubleday Dell)	1,010	6.92	5.81
News Corporation (HarperCollins)	1,003	6.87	5.77
Harcourt General	945	6.47	5.43
Thomson Publishing	904	6.19	5.20
Times Mirror	843	5.78	4.85
Pearson (Penguin-Addison Wesley)	674	4.62	3.87
McGraw-Hill	667	4.57	3.83

Sources: *BP Report*, December 19, 1994, p. 7; Book Industry Study Group, *Book Industry Trends 1995* (New York: Book Industry Study Group, Inc., 1995), pp. 2–4.

TABLE 2.15
Largest Book Publishers for U.S. Market, 1998

Company	Top Trade Publisher	Top Children's Publisher	Top Educational Publisher
Viacom			
(Simon & Schuster)	yes	yes	yes
Reader's Digest	yes	no	no
Hearst	yes	yes	no
Time Warner Book Group	yes	no	no
Bertelsmann			
(Bantam Doubleday Dell)	yes	yes	no
News Corporation			
(HarperCollins)	yes	no	yes
Harcourt General	no	no	yes
Thomson Publishing	no	no	yes
Houghton Mifflin	yes	yes	yes
Pearson			
(Penguin-Addison Wesley)	yes	yes	yes
McGraw-Hill	no	no	yes

Source: *Standard & Poor's Industry Surveys*, "Publishing," April 23, 1998, p. 10.

identified as the majors, always recognizing that the dynamics of these majors most likely will continue to change.[50]

The Top Two

Two of the 10 majors stand as the giants of the modern book publishing industry, selling thousands of titles each year in the United States. Yet, ironically, both are foreign based: Bertelsmann AG in Germany, by most measures the largest book publisher in the world, and Pearson PLC in Britain. Bertelsmann AG publishes in all sectors, save educational textbooks. It is far and away the leader in trade publishing. Pearson PLC publishes in all sectors, and is a giant in educational publishing. I take them up now.

Bertelsmann AG is a less well-known conglomerate than Time Warner or Disney because it is a private company and is based in Germany. Yet, even before its acquisition spree in the late 1990s, its Bantam Doubleday Dell books division generated revenues in excess of $1 billion per year in the United States (even more in the rest of the world). Noted imprints include Bantam Books, Doubleday, Anchor, Image Books, Dell, Delacorte, Dial Press, Delta and Laurel, as well as the Literary Guild book club. But insiders knew, and trade publications such as *Variety*, ranked Bertelsmann AG in the same league with Time Warner and Disney, even though obtaining precise data on Bertelsmann AG sales was not easy. Experts could only guess that as the 1990s ended, book publishing was equal—over even greater than Bertelsmann AG's other sizable divisions—music (see Chapter 5) and television in Europe, where for the latter Bertelsmann held a 50% stake in CLT-UFA, Europe's largest operator of independent television stations. Smaller, but profitable divisions, also included book clubs, literary and scientific publishing, daily newspapers, consumer magazines such as *Family Circle*, trade journals, radio stations, online services and printing plants.[51]

Bertelsmann AG was the leader in mergers and acquisitions as the 1990s ended. Indeed, no bigger deal transformed the industry than in March 1998 when Bertelsmann AG and Advance Publications, Inc. announced that Bertelsmann AG had agreed to purchase New York City-based Random House, Inc., the leading trade publisher in the United States. Bertelsmann AG had long been committed to expanding its presence in the English-language consumer trade book publishing business, and this mega-deal shot it to number one in trade book sales. The imprint name remained "Random House," but the plan was to fold it into Bertelsmann AG's book publishing division, Bantam Doubleday Dell. At that point, Bantam Doubleday Dell had offices not only in the United States, but also in Canada, the United Kingdom, Australia, New Zealand and South Africa.

The two executives behind the deal, Mark Woessner, Chairman and Chief Executive Officer of Bertelsmann AG, and Peter Olson, Chairman and Chief Executive Officer of Bertelsmann Book Group North America, proclaimed the importance of this acquisition, but because Bertelsmann AG was a private concern its value can only be estimated. The best guesses came in between $1 and $2 billion. This made Bertelsmann AG the top publisher of books in 1997—ahead of Pearson PLC, Viacom, Time Warner or News Corporation. One estimate in 1998 gave Bertelsmann AG and its Bantam Doubleday Dell Publishing Group, including Random House, a full sixth of the trade publishing business in the United States.

Bertelsmann AG, the third largest media conglomerate in the world behind Disney and Time Warner in 1999, sold more than $6 billion worth of books per annum. Indeed, in 1997, Random House, also owned by a private corporation called Advance Publications, Inc., sold more than an estimated $1 billion alone. For Bertelsmann AG, books constituted the core of its expanding media conglomerate.[52]

The head of book publishing was Peter Olson, who joined Bertelsmann AG in 1988. Through the 1990s, he had been responsible for the ever-expanding Bantam Doubleday Dell Publishing Group, Doubleday Direct, North America's largest direct marketing consumer book club business, as well as other operations in the United States. The Bantam Doubleday Dell group published not only trade fiction and non-fiction, but audio books for adults and young readers alike. As the 1990s ended, the company consisted of six editorially distinct, operationally interdependent publishing units in the United States: the adult divisions of Bantam Books, Doubleday, Dell-Delacorte and Broadway Books; Bantam Doubleday Dell Books for Young Readers; and Bantam Doubleday Dell Audio. Random House added the Random House Trade Publishing Group, the Random House Information Publishing Group, the Knopf Publishing Group, the Crown Publishing Group, the Ballantine Publishing Group, Random House Children's Publishing, Random House Audio, Random House Value Publishing, Fodors Travel Publications, Random House New Media and divisions in Canada, the United Kingdom, Australia, New Zealand and South

Africa. All these combined, the "new" Bertelsmann AG would see its books sales in the United States represent 35% of the Bertelsmann book sales volume worldwide.[53]

By July 1998, all the formalities had been completed, and the integration of the two companies began. Olson and his top executives moved to consolidate several long-established publishing units, and as might be expected, departures centered on top Random House division heads and editors—despite earlier assurances by Olson that the union would not erode the independence of Random House units. By May 1999, Random House had begun merging eight of its publishing units into four groups or divisions, including a combination of Bantam Books, the mass market paperback publisher with roots dating back to 1945, and Dell Publishing, the half-century-old publisher of popular authors like Danielle Steel and Thomas Harris. This reorganization saw Bantam and Dell in one group and Doubleday and Broadway Books in another unit, with Random House folded in, which created two mass market paperback powerhouses able to take full advantages of economies of scale in marketing and accounting.

Indeed, longtime staff from both sides decided working for such a large company was not what they liked about the book publishing industry. Some reorganization seemed just the normal process of consolidation in late 20th-century style. For example, in April 1999, the long expected restructuring of the Random House sales force took effect, and under the realignment, Random House trimmed several hundred employees in the United States. A major changes that took place was the breakup of a separate Ballantine sales force, as it was folded into a sales unit composed of Bantam, Broadway, Dell, and Doubleday.[54]

Other cases were more contentious and potentially more serious. Under the reorganization, Carole Baron, Dell's longtime publisher and editor, quit. Morton Janklow, the literary agent for bestselling author Danielle Steel, told the *New York Times* that Steel was upset because Baron had edited her books for two decades. Although this might have been a bargaining tactic, it may also reflect many authors' need for stability. Bertelsmann AG executives stated for the record that they had tried to find Baron a new position within the new company, but Baron said she was leaving simply because "my job doesn't exist." Book publishing editors were used to working in their own divisions, and found the cost-cutting consolidation of the "new" Bertelsmann AG restricting to their freedom to bid on and acquire manuscripts, sometimes in competition with other editors that were part of the same corporation. That system had provided authors with more opportunity to find markets for their work and, often, higher advances. Olson and company saved millions of dollars with consolidation, but in the process transformed the publishing industry, and set up an experiment that everyone was watching to see if and how it played out. And under the consolidation, trade publishing was not the only type of book that would be effected. For example, Bertelsmann AG also combined two longtime religious imprints, Water Brook Press and the Doubleday religious unit, as well as two trade scholarly publishers, Anchor Books (founded in 1953) and Vintage Books.[55]

Even specific projects were dropped in the reorganization. For example, the "new" Random House canceled its contract with Kim Masters, a contributing editor for *Time* and *Vanity Fair* magazines, to publish her book about Michael Eisner, the chairman of the Walt Disney Co., and his ascension to Hollywood power. Bert Fields, Masters' attorney, was representing former Disney executive Jeffrey Katzenberg in his dispute with Eisner, and contended that Random House's Broadway Books canceled the book (to be called *Keys to the Kingdom*) because Bertelsmann AG did want to offend Eisner, who as CEO of Disney might be helpful later. In particular, Disney's ABC television network offered a prime vehicle for book marketing. The "old" Random House had published Eisner's official memoirs, *Work in Progress*, and with its success Masters had contracted to write her exposé for the Broadway Books division of the "old" Bertelsmann AG. The struggle began as the consolidation was ongoing, and early in 1999 grew so serious that the "new" Bertelsmann AG requested that Masters repay a portion of her reported $700,000 advance. Bertelsmann AG knew how to market, and controversy needed to be controlled, not restrict access to vital tools such as ABC's *Good Morning America* and *20/20*. For the 1998 Christmas season that meant, for example, books by television newspersons who could gain high and free visibility for their works. NBC's Tom Brokaw hawked *The Greatest Generation* for Random House to the heights of the bestseller lists. Random House also published *The Century* by ABC's Peter Jennings as ABC and the ABC partially owned History Channel played complementary documentaries. With these pre-sold network TV titles, Brokaw's book moved to number one on the bestseller lists and Jennings' book moved to the third spot.[56]

Bertelsmann AG's purchase of Random House generated the most publicity, but it hardly represented its lone acquisition. In June 1998, Bertelsmann AG acquired Reed-Elsevier's half share in BCA, giving Bertelsmann sole and full ownership of the consumer book publisher. Through this purchase, Bertelsmann AG was once more demonstrating its long-term commitment to the future of the English-language consumer book business and particularly to direct marketing book club operations. BCA was formed in 1966 and became the United Kingdom's largest book club operation with both general and special interest clubs—including over two million customers. This deal offered economies of scale to Bertelsmann's Literary Guild and moved it to the top of the book club business around the world. In 1999, book clubs were still contributing sales from more than 5 million members.[57]

Directly targeting the United States, in October 1998 Bertelsmann AG and bookseller Barnes & Noble, Inc. announced a joint venture in online bookselling to be called barnesandnoble.com (later simply www.bn.com). Under the agreement, Bertelsmann AG paid $200 million for a 50% stake in the barnesandnoble.com—with each party also promising to contribute $100 million more to the capital of the joint venture. This was vertical integration pure and simple. Bertelsmann AG published the books, and Barnes & Noble took them and sold them online. Launched in May 1997, barnesandnoble.com had become the sixth largest e-commerce Web site in the United States by mid-1998, according to Media Metrix. Bertelsmann AG would continue to move forward separately in Europe with its BooksOnline venture, but in close cooperation with the ever-expanding barnesandnoble.com Web site in the United States. Through barnesandnoble.com and BooksOnline, Bertelsmann AG accumulated the vertical power to make more titles available and more easily accessible for millions of readers in the United States and Europe. Whereas the official announcement stressed how barnesandnoble.com carried the works of more than 25,000 publishers, the two partners recognized the alliance would seek to help Bertelsmann AG titles. This deal was the capstone to a series of strategic multimedia Bertelsmann AG partnerships, including an alliance in Europe with America Online.[58]

In November 1998, Bertelsmann AG acquired 82% of the German scientific publishing group Springer GmbH for an estimated $600 million. That deal acquired one of the most important scientific publishing houses in the world. With an international program spanning the gamut of scientific, technical and medical publishing, Springer boasted of scientific authors who had earned more than 120 Nobel Prizes. The group published close to 500 specialized journals, and pioneered the electronic dissemination of scientific information through its online service, LINK, used by academics, researchers and industry professionals throughout the world. Springer published over 2,000 books annually, and Bertelsmann AG combined its then-substantial scientific, technical and medical publishing divisions with the Springer units to effect cost savings. Almost one quarter of Springer's annual revenues comes from sales in the United States, with two thirds of its publications in English. STM became the new division.[59]

All these mergers and acquisitions were built on a book publishing history begun when Bertelsmann AG acquired Bantam Books in 1977. During the 1980s and 1990s, Bantam experienced an impressive period of growth as it published original fiction, issued best-selling "instant books," developed reference and educational works and published blockbusters titles such as *Iacocca*, which remained on the bestseller list for two years. In 1986, Bertelsmann AG acquired Doubleday Dell and formally created Bantam Doubleday Dell Publishing Group, Inc. and in the process fashioned such imprints as Bantam Audio Books, Bantam Classics, Bantam Skylark, Loveswept, New Age Books, Anchor, Currency, Dolphin, Image, Made Simple Books, Nan A. Talese Books, The Outdoor Bible Series, Perfect Crime, Delacorte, Dell, Delta, Island, Laurel and Double D Westerns. By 1995, the head of Bantam Doubleday Dell was bragging to *Publisher's Weekly* that his division was far exceeding "parent Bertelsmann's objective of achieving 15 percent return on assets."[60]

The offices of Bertelsmann AG in Gutersloh, Germany, a town of less than 100,000 persons, lie far from Madison Avenue. There is much speculation about the precise finances of this German conglomerate. In 1997, for example, *Forbes* reported that Reinhard Mohn and family controlled nearly 90% of the company, and thus were worth about $2.5 billion. And the family had announced its intentions to expand. In 1997, rumor had Bertelsmann buying HarperCollins, but Murdoch— after talking—decided not to sell. Bertelsmann publicly stated that it coveted HarperCollins for its children's list. The 1998 acquision of Random Hosue solved that problem.[61]

The Random House acquisition shocked the book publishing world because the Newhouse family, long owners of Advance Publications, Inc. and its Random House division, seemed to be doing well. But, as a private company, that conclusion was based on guesses. Yet imprints (i.e., Random House, The Modern Library, Times Books, Alfred A. Knopf, Pantheon, Schocken, Villard, Vintage, Fodor's, Crown and

Fawcett books) seemed to generate bestsellers in a range of appropriate categoreis. Samuel I. Newhouse, Jr., Chairman of Advance Publications, held a vast media fortune, focused on newspapers, magazines and cable television (including newspapers like the *New Orleans Times-Picayune* and the *Cleveland Plain Dealer*, and magazines like *Vogue, Architectural Digest, GQ* and *Bride's*). But because Samuel I. Newhouse, Jr. and his brother Donald Newhouse, owned 100% of Advance stock, they were free to sell out when a great offer came along. Bertelsmann AG made that offer. The Newhouses cashed in a decades-old $60 million investment in Random House and became even wealthier. Bertelsmann AG did this deal, and the others, because they figured it would bring the company more prominence and profit in the U.S. market. In 2000, Bertelsmann AG set out to boost its book sales from third place. By the end of 1998, for books alone, Bertelsmann AG had annual revenues of about $4 to $5 billion; again, because this is a private company, these are only estimates. Simply put, in 1998 Bertelsmann AG had become the biggest book publisher with a serious rival.[62]

Pearson PLC, a vast British-based media and software company, owned book publisher the Penguin Group and controlled imprints (i.e., Viking, Penguin, Dutton, Signet, Plume, Meridian, G. P. Putnam's Sons, New American Library, Grosset, Boulevard, Berkeley Books, Jove, Ace, Dutton, etc.), as well as newspapers, magazines, various multiventures, and television production, satellite television and film production in Europe. One estimate of book sales in the United States in 1996 placed Pearson PLC at $1.2 billion and $1.7 billion outside the United States. And this did not include the millions of dollars in revenues from the purchase of Putnam Berkley, which Pearson PLC bought in late November 1996 from MCA for $336 million; the $580 million spent for HarperCollins' educational line centered on Scott Foresman; or the 1998 acquisition of Simon & Schuster's education and professional and reference lines for $4.6 billion. By 1999, fully 50% of Pearson operating profit came from book publishing aimed at the U.S. market. If Bertelsmann led with noneducational book publishing in all their various incarnations, Pearson PLC led with educational publishing such as Prentice-Hall and Allyn & Bacon, and then trade publishing.[63]

Through the end of the 1990s, Pearson PLC represented a diverse company. It published the *Financial Times*, ran an interactive data company and Madame Tussard's Wax museum, owned half of computer software publisher called Mindscape and also owned half of investment banker called Lazard Brothers & Co. Before its acquisition spree starting in late 1996, Pearson PLC had three divisions: 1) Information publishing included the Spanish publishing group Recoletos and Pearson Professional Publishing; 2) educational publishing included Addison Wesley, and Longman; and 3) trade publishing centered on Penguin.[64]

Indeed, Pearson PLC's acquisition of Viacom's Simon & Schuster's educational and reference publishing unit for $4.6 billion redefined book publishing in the United States, for sheer size and for the movement of two longtime U.S.-based book publishers into the hands of European firms. In November 1998, the Pearson PLC purchase passed U.S. government approval, and in a single stroke—as Bertelsmann AG had done six months earlier—Pearson PLC's Addison Wesley Longman educational division leaped to the top of the textbook publishing market in the United States. Pearson, in 1996, had added the HarperCollins Educational line, and so after winning a bidding war against News Corporation, in 1999 the company expected to realize $275 million from the sale of assets related to its $4.6 billion purchase and then launch the most powerful and largest textbook publisher in history.

As seen in Table 2.16, this deal was considerable. Viacom's educational, professional and reference publishing businesses, which are part of Viacom's Simon & Schuster unit, then comprised one of the world's largest educational and computer book publishers. Simon & Schuster also encompassed major operations in reference and business and professional publishing. These operations had combined annual sales of approximately $2 billion. The businesses included operations in 43 countries and leading elementary, high school and higher education imprints such as Allyn & Bacon, Prentice-Hall, Silver Burdett Ginn, Globe Fearon and Modern Curriculum; pioneer technology-based learning companies such as Computer Curriculum Corporation, Educational Management Group and Invest Learning; major names in ref-

TABLE 2.16

Pearson PLC's Purchase of Viacom's Educational, Professional and Reference Publishing, 1998

Publishing Segment	Units Viacom Sold/Pearson Purchased
Education Technology	Computer Curriculum Corporation; Educational Management Group; Invest Learning; Modern Curriculum; Simon & Schuster Learning Technology Group; Red Rocket; Simon & Schuster Learning Products Group
Higher Education	Allyn & Bacon; Longwood; Brady; Gorsuch Scarisbrick; IRI Skylight; Merrill Education; Prentice-Hall; Prentice-Hall Engineering Science and Math; Prentice-Hall International; Prentice-Hall Business; Prentice-Hall Education, Career & Technology; Prentice-Hall Humanities and Social Studies; Prentice-Hall Regents; Alemany Press; Family Album U.S.; Prentice-Hall Professional Technical Reference; Simon & Schuster Custom Publishing
K–12	Prentice-Hall School; Silver Burdett Ginn; Cambridge; Globe Fearon
Business and Professional Publishing	Appleton & Lange; Bureau of Business Practice; Jossey-Bass/Pfeiffer; Master Data Center; New York Institute of Finance; Prentice-Hall Direct; Center for Applied Research in Education; Parker
Macmillan Publishing U.S.	Macmillan Publishing U.S.; Macmillan Computer Publishing U.S.; Alpha; Ilayden; Macmillan Technical Publishing U.S.; Que; Que E&T; New Riders; SAMS; Sams.net; Waite Group Press; Ziff-Davis Press; Lycos Press; Borland Press; Cisco Press
Macmillan Digital Publishing U.S.	Brady Games; Macmillan Online U.S.; MCP Software; SSI Macmillan Distribution
Macmillan Reference U.S.	ARCO Test Preparation; Audel; Baedekers Travel Guides; Betty Crocker Cookbooks; Burpee; Cassells; Check Chart; Frommers; GK Hall; Harrap Billingual Dictionaries; Howell Book House; JK Lasser; Macmillan Library Reference U.S.; Macmillan General Reference U.S.; Macmillan Travel U.S.; Schirmer; Scribner; Twayne; Thorndike; Unofficial Guides; Websters; New World; Weight Watchers Books
International Imprints and Divisions	S&S Canada; S&S Asia; S&S Australia; Simon & Schuster Europe; Simon & Schuster Latin America; Prentice-Hall of India

Source: Viacom corporate Web site at www.viacom.com.

erence and business and professional publishing, including Macmillan, Que, Bureau of Business Practice, Jossey-Bass, Prentice-Hall Direct, New York Institute of Finance and Appleton & Lange; and international publishing operations, including Simon & Schuster Asia, Simon & Schuster Latin America, Simon & Schuster Australia and Simon & Schuster Europe.

Unlike the more conservative Bertelsmann AG, Pearson PLC took on considerable debt, tripling what it owed. In March 1999, Pearson's education group reported a sales increase of 25% to $1.16 billion in 1998, including about $200 million in revenues from the Simon & Schuster properties that Pearson formally took control of in November 1998. Excluding sales from Simon & Schuster, revenues in the group rose 3% to $966 million. Total operating profit in the year 1998 increased 65% to $164 million, a figure that included profits of $36.5 million from the former Simon & Schuster divisions. The combination of Pearson's education and Penguin's consumer publishing businesses had total sales of slightly more than $2 billion in 1998 and posted an operating profit of $244 million.[65]

In 1998, the Simon & Schuster educational units reached more than four million students in 12,000 schools each day with electronic instruction, including on-demand interactive television and computer curricula. The division consisted of a Computer Curriculum Corporation, the market leader in delivering software to K–12 schools; the Educational Management Group, which delivered live, interactive, instructional television programming into 4,600 schools; the Modern Curriculum; the Learning Technology Group; and the Invest Learning Corporation. Simon & Schuster represented the world's largest higher education publisher, with market-leading books offered in every academic discipline. The Higher Education division was widely regarded as the leader in connecting print and new media, and had approximately 200 World Wide Web companion textbook sites by the end of 1998.

In 1998, Macmillan Publishing U.S., the reference division of Simon & Schuster, represented the largest computer and reference book publisher in the world. Annually, Macmillan published more than 2,000 new titles, with more than 30 million copies sold in 1996. It had international distribution channels in 117 countries. There were three operating units: 1) Macmillan Computer Publishing U.S., the world's largest computer book publisher; 2) Macmillan Reference U.S., which published library reference materials and "book franchises," including Frommer's Travel Guides, the Arco Test Prep series, the J. K. Lasser's Tax Guides and The Idiot's Guide Series; and 3) Macmillan Digital Publishing U.S., which in 1998 was second only to Microsoft in programming language software sales. In addition, Prentice-Hall Direct published health, self-improvement, business and education titles, and Appleton & Lange published textbooks and multimedia products for students and professionals in the medical and health care industry.

But this is not to say that there were no complications from Pearson PLC's purchase of part of Simon & Schuster. In May 1999, John Wiley & Sons acquired all but one of the approximately 55 college textbooks that the U.S. Justice Department ordered Pearson to sell before it would approve the purchase of Simon & Schuster's education division. According to the Wiley announcement, the company acquired unnamed college texts and instructional packages in biology/anatomy and physiology, engineering, math, economics/finance and teacher education. Wiley paid about $58 million for the materials, which together with an elementary school program generated revenues of some $35 million.[66]

In March 1999, Michael Lynton, CEO of Penguin, noted that although there had been costs associated with "repositioning the business," the company's book publishing "underlying" operating profits continued to rise. He declined to break out specific sales figures, making analysis somewhat difficult to precisely define, but all of Penguin's American divisions grew. The 1998 sales in the children's group rose to more than $150 million. The company announced Penguin's U.S. operation had an operating margin of more than 12%.[67]

Yet, even with the emphasis on educational publishing, remember that for trade book sales, according to one October 1997 ranking, Pearson PLC stood fourth, fueled by the Putnam Berkley deal. This, the most significant book industry merger of 1996, melded Penguin's strong backlist of steadily selling books with Putnam's bestsellers. The combined company represented about one of every eight books sold in the United States, with star authors such as Tom Clancy, Amy Tan and Patricia Cornwell. Pearson represented a true rival in the trade field to Bertelsmann AG's new powerhouse and to Viacom's Simon & Schuster. Indeed, in terms of an author's advance, Pearson PLC had made its biggest commitment to Tom Clancy, who received $50 million for two novels. Side deals promised Clancy in excess of $100 million for paperback rights, TV mini-series development (with NBC) and even books for young adults (a new Clancy venture).[68]

Three Ranking Media Conglomerates

The acquisitions and mergers begun in the late 1960s often saw expanding media conglomerates looking to enter the book publishing industry. This represented a pure synergy play. That is, a powerful and diversified company in television or film figured that book publishing represented a regular and continuing production of stories that could be turned into a TV series or feature films. Thus, by 1999, three major media conglomerates were seeking to factor book publishing into their collection of media properties, and to then leverage book publishing to expand profits in other media businesses they might own.

By some calculations, **Time Warner** represented the biggest media conglomerate in the world. This symbolized a vast multinational media company centered on television and film (as seen in Chapters 4 and 6) that also did books. According to one estimate, just $1 in $20 was generated by its book publishing division. In 1995, the estimate from books was $325 million out of a 1995 company total revenue of $8.1 billion. Mail order portions of Time Warner publishing include Time-Life Books, Book-of-the-Month Club, Sunset Books and Oxmoor House. This media conglomerate also includes movies, cable and satellite TV, cable TV franchises, television programming and feature film making from a major Hollywood studio, music, CNN radio, a vast array of magazines, theme parks and sports teams. And, indeed, in its Web site under publishing in the annual reports, the discussion is more about the famous magazines—*Time, Sports Illustrated* and the like—than about book publishing. Yet, even Time Warner officially admits that its Book of the Month Club (Bertelsmann AG's major rival to its Literary Guild) and direct marketing Time-Life books account for significant revenues, place dozens of books on the bestseller lists, and were enjoying solid (if unspectacular in the electronic age) growth from imprints such as Little, Brown, Warner Books, Time Life Books, Sunset Books, Leisure Arts and the Oxmoor House.[69]

The vast media conglomerate Time Warner was created in 1989 as Warner Communications, a major Hollywood studio and music company, and a leading publisher, Time, Inc., merged. The leading force behind the merger was Warner Communi-

---

PROFILE: Time Warner Inc.

Basic Data:
Headquarters: New York, NY
Web site: www.timewarner.com
CEO in 1999: Gerald M. Levin
1998 Sales (in millions): $14,582
1998 Net Profits (in millions): $168
1998 Assets (in millions): $31,640
Rank in 1998 Forbes 500—Sales: 102

Major Holdings:
Broadcast Television: The WB Network.
Cable MSO's: Time Warner Cable with clustered MSOs in New York City, Tampa Bay, Milwaukee, St. Louis, Houston and Raleigh & Duhram, NC.
Cable Networks: Turner Broadcasting (includes CNN, TNT & TBS), HBO, Cinemax, CNNSI (combining cable network and *Sports Illustrated* magazine), Turner Classic Movies, the Cartoon Network.
Film & Television: Warner Bros. Studio, WB Television (producing such shows as *ER* and *Friends*), Lorimar Television (syndicating such shows as *Dallas*), Quincy Jones Entertainment (producer of *Fresh Prince of Bel Air*), Warner Home Video, HBO Pictures, New Line Cinema movie studio, Fine Line Features movie distribution.
Magazines: *Fortune, People, Sports Illustrated, Time, Weight Watchers, Asiaweek, Money, Entertainment Weekly, Mad Magazine, Life.*
Music: Atlantic Recording Group, Warner Bros Records, Ivy Hill Corp. Elektra Entertainment, plus other labels.
Publishing: Warner Books, Little, Brown book publishers, Time-Life books, Book-of-the-Month-Club, History Book Club.
Other Interests: DC Comics, Six Flags Entertainment and Theme Parks, Atlanta Hawks (Professional basketball), Atlanta Braves (Major League baseball).

Significant Events:
1989: Time and Warner merge.
1996: The FTC reaches a settlement with Time Warner allowing its $6.2 billion merger with Turner Broadcasting.
1997: CEO Gerald M. Levin orders company-wide budget cuts of 3% to 5% to boost lagging stock price.
1997: Time Warner posts $30 million profit, with revenues reporting to climb 25% to nearly $6 billion, led by its cable TV MSOs and networks.
August 1997: Time Warner cable begins to sell and trade to custer MSOs to help lower $17 billion debt.
2000: AOL takes over.

cations CEO Steven J. Ross, who advertised his creation as the synergy to end all synergies. But Ross died in December 1992, and his empire fell to his former aide and protégé, Gerald M. Levin. Both Warner and Time had long distinguished histories, neither in book publishing per se. Warner began as a movie studio in 1924; Time began about the same time with Henry Luce's innovation of the weekly news magazine. Warner and Time Life book publishing came along as ancillary operations to the movie (and then TV business) and to magazine publishing. But book publishing did make money, and synergized with the other divisions of the company. The book division, although not a major part of the company's earnings, contributed steadily, and was regularly noted in the fine print of all annual reports issued by a company far more famous for CNN and HBO than book publishing.[70]

Viacom, Inc., although not as big a media conglomerate as Time Warner overall, was a player in book publishing until its sale in 1998 to Pearson. Viacom, as part of a strategic program to focus on its core entertainment TV and film assets (see Chapters 6 and 7, respectively), sold its educational, professional and reference publishing operations to Pearson PLC, and retained its consumer operations, which annually published more than 2,100 titles under 34 trade, mass market, children's and new media imprints. Viacom retained the investment banking firm of Morgan Stanley to identify qualified buyers, evaluated their proposals and in the end helped select Pearson PLC. Proceeds from the sale repaid corporate debt. In making the announcement, Sumner M. Redstone, Chairman and Chief Executive Officer of Viacom, said, "We have made a strategic decision that the future of Viacom lies in maximizing the value and potential of our core entertainment assets. The sale of our education, professional and reference publishing businesses will further refine that focus on software driven entertainment, unlock the substantial value of these undervalued publishing assets for our shareholders and dramatically improve our capital structure." Redstone rationalized the decision as fulfilling a desire to revert back to simple synergy—retain only the book publishing operations that might help its Paramount studio and Viacom's television operations make more profit. He retained those parts of book publishing that meshed with the remaining entertainment businesses and those able to deliver stories, and thus to integrate with other entertainment divisions and produce profits (as in the form of new book imprints for youth-oriented MTV and Nickelodeon brands, as well as books tied to Paramount Pictures' film releases).*

What remained was not inconsequential. Viacom's Simon & Schuster Consumer Book Group imprints, with thousands of fiction and nonfiction bestsellers behind them, still owned imprints with backlists that included the works of Dale Carnegie, Will and Ariel Durant, F. Scott Fitzgerald, Joseph Heller, Ernest Hemingway, Norman Mailer, Larry McMurtry, E. Annie Proulx, Bertrand Russell, Richard Rhodes, William Shirer, Edith Wharton and Thomas Wolfe. In 1997, the Simon & Schuster Consumer Book Group published 56 New York Times Bestsellers, including 11 number one bestsellers. Simon & Schuster's Consumer Book Group's Trade imprints

---

*As we go to press, in late 1999 Viacom proposed to acquire CBS. The deal, when and if finalized, would formally combine the two companies sometime during the spring of 1999. See Douglas Gomery, "The Company That Would Be King," *American Journalism Review*, December, 1999, page 66.

included Simon & Schuster, Scribner, Scribner Paperback Fiction, Lisa Drew Books, The Free Press, Fireside, Touchstone, Simon & Schuster Editions and Kaplan Books. Pocket Books was still an historic name and a sizable force defining the mass market division of the Simon & Schuster's Consumer Book Group with imprints that included Archway Paperbacks, Minstrel Books, MTV Books and Washington Square Press. Simon & Schuster's Consumer Book Group's Children's Publishing was a field leader, with the following imprints: Aladdin Paperbacks, Anne Schwartz Books, Atheneum Books for Young Readers, Little Simon, Margaret K. McElderry Books, Simon & Schuster Books for Young Readers, Simon Spotlight, Libros Colibri, Nickelodeon Books and Rabbit Ears Book & Audio. Simon & Schuster New Media combined the resources of audio and interactive. Indeed, Simon & Schuster's Consumer Book Group's Audio division ranked as the world's largest audio publisher in the 1990s. Finally, Simon & Schuster's Consumer Book Group's Web site—www.simonsays.com—offered live author events, reader reviews, reading groups, bulletin boards and access to information on 11,000 consumer group titles.[71]

Still more of the public purchased products from other Viacom divisions, which included Blockbuster Video, the MTV cable TV networks, Paramount Pictures, Paramount Television, Paramount Parks, Showtime pay TV Networks, television stations and movie theater screens in 12 countries. Viacom also owned the Spelling Entertainment Group, as well as a half-interest in Comedy Central and the UPN television network. National Amusements, Inc., a closely held corporation that operates approximately 1,100 screens in the United States, the United Kingdom and South America, is the parent company of Viacom, and Sumner Redstone controlled its stock and managed the company. He determined to sell off Simon & Schuster's educational, professional and reference book divisions. In 1997, he deemed that Viacom could be more profitable as a TV and movie company that also did consumer book publishing. Redstone had created the modern Viacom as part of his National Amusements in 1994 with his $10 billion accession of Paramount Communications.[72]

In March 1999, the "new" Simon & Schuster announced that revenues had remained flat while operating income fell. Simon & Schuster president Jack Romanos attributed this to disruptions caused by the divestiture of the consumer group's sister companies, as well as costs associated with creating a new corporate staff. He was simply in the process of reinventing the Simon & Schuster Consumer Book Group. He explained that Simon & Schuster's trade and children's divisions had good years, whereas the mass market paperback unit had a difficult 1998. Because of the volume of business Simon & Schuster does in mass market, and that the category often produces higher profit margins than the trade and children's operations, the new century would bring the challenge of how to revitalize mass market paperback sales. Although he believed the segment had a bright future, he correctly noted the company will need to adopt some different approaches to be successful, and he would do this by exploiting ties to Viacom's film and TV operations. Romanos estimated that approximately $40 million of revenue came from Simon & Schuster's relation with its parent company, citing such examples as the success of *Star Trek* and numerous movie tie-ins. The decline in earnings notwithstanding, Simon & Schuster still posted a respectable operating margin of 9.4% in 1998, as compared to a margin of 10.9% in 1997.[73]

PROFILE: Viacom, Inc.

Basic Data:
Headquarters: New York, NY
Web site: www.viacom.com
CEO in 1997: Sumner M. Redstone
1998 Revenues (in millions): $12,096
1998 Net Profits (in millions): $–48
1998 Assets (in millions): $23,613
Rank in 1998 Forbes 500—Sales: 130

Market Holdings:
Broadcast Television: Partner in UPN television network, owner and operator of broadcast television stations in Philadelphia, Boston, Washington, DC, Dallas, Detroit, Atlanta, Houston, Seattle, Tampa, Miami, New Orleans and Indianapolis, among others.
Cable Television: Owner of cable networks, including MTV, M2, VH-1, Nickelodeon, Nike at Nite, Showtime, The Movie Channel, The Paramount Channel (UK), Comedy Central.
Film & Television: Paramount Pictures Corporation (major Hollywood studio), National Amusements movie theater chain (with screens in 11 countries), Famous Players theater chain in Canada, Blockbuster Entertainment Group (home video), Blockbuster Pictures Holding Corporation (investments in films), Spelling Entertainment Group (television producer), Republic Entertainment (film and TV producer and distributor), Paramount Home Video, Worldvision Enterprises (television syndicator), Viacom International, United International Pictures.
Music: Blockbuster Music (retailer of music), Famous Music.
Publishing: Simon & Schuster, Prentice-Hall, Macmillan Publishing U.S., Schimer Books, Charles Scribner's Sons, Thorndike Press, Twayne Publishers, Pocket Books, Allyn & Bacon, Ginn books, MTV Books.
Other Interests: Viacom retail stores; Virgin Interactive Entertainment; Paramount Parks: Kings Island outside Cincinnati, OH; Kings Dominion, near Richmond, VA; Carowinds near Charlotte, NC; and Raging Waters, near San Jose, CA.

Significant Events:
1970: Viacom created as FCC rules that CBS can no longer syndication operations.
1987: Sumner Redstone's National Amusements, Inc. of Dedham, MA, buys controlling interest of Viacom, Inc. for $3.4 billion.
1996: Launches new cable network—TV Land.
1996: Sumner M. Redstone fires Paramount Pictures boss Frank Biondi and takes over.
1996: Creates M2: Music Television, a new "freeform" music television cable channel.
1997: Sells U.S. Cable networks to Seagram Ltd. for $1.7 billion.

Romanos certainly had a rich history from which to draw, probably the most fabled in the U.S. book publishing business. As mentioned previously, the innovations of its Pocket Books unit during the middle of the 20th century, literally defined the book publishing industry. During the mid-1990s, Simon & Schuster set a goal of obtaining half its book revenues from electronic publishing by the year 2000, and thus led the way to the additional sales from different forms, in this case CD-ROM, videodiscs and the World Wide Web. It also pioneered new ways to financially relate to star authors: In November 1997, Stephen King signed with Simon & Schuster for a small advance but a higher than standard share of the royalties. King bet he could continue to attract millions of buyers, and so rather than take a large advance up front, he partnered with Simon & ~ ~uster. They—author and publisher—bet that such a partnership would ~   o write more attractive books, and then let both parties reap th~ ˙   ˙s. The results are still not in, but the outcome will hel~   'ishing industry into 2000.[74]

  The ˙   'ized the biggest and most global of media
~   1 owned by Rupert Murdoch. With its
    ˙ll as newspapers, magazines, broadcast

ɔration Limited

M:
Bro.   ., Fox television stations,
  Inc   .ork, KTTV-Los Angeles, KRIV-
  Hou   .ashington, DC, among others), Her-
  itage   .n stations and program production).
Cable Te.   ws cable channel, Kids International, Internation-
  al Famì,   gional sports cable channels.
Film & Tele   ventury Fox-studio, Fox Video Company, Fox Broadcasting
  Company,   ventury-Fox Home Entertainment, BSkyN, the Sky Channel satellite
  service in ι ɔpe, STAR TV in Asia, JSkyB in Japan satellite television, Canal FOX in
  Europe, Sky Entertainment Services in Latin America, VOX and DF1 television in Germany.
Music: small music company.
Publishing: magazines, including joint deal with *TV Guide*, and *Good Food*; newspapers, including *The Boston Herald*, *The New York Post*, *The Sun* (London, England), *The News of the World* (London, England), *The Times* (London, England); HarperCollins book publishing.
Other Interests: CineBooks, Inc. (Computer systems), Los Angeles Dodgers (Major Leaguer baseball), 100 daily and weekly newspapers in Australia, Ansett Transport industries.

Significant Events:
1985: Rupert Murdoch buys Twentieth Century Fox-studio; establishes in the United States.
1986: Begins Fox television network.
1989: Starts Sky television and becomes a major force in TV in Europe.
1993: Acquires 64% of START TV in Asia.
1994: Spends $1.6 for rights to broadcast National Football League games.
1997: Acquires the 80% of New World Communications group not already owned for about $2.5 billion in securties, and with the new 10 television stations News Corporation becomes largest owner of TV stations in the United States.
1997: Agrees to buy Los Angeles Dodgers baseball team for $350 million.
1997: Agrees to buy International Family Channel cable network for $1.9 million.
1997: Rupert Murdoch's son James named president of News American Digital publishing, a new unit that will consolidate all of News Corporation's electronic pushing operations.
1998: Spins off Fox Group as IPO to raise cash for investment.

television, cable television and film as see in the Profile: The News Corporation Limited the book division, like with the "new" Viacom is a consumer trade division, driven by the synergy that it proffers to the dominating portions of News Corporation. One estimate placed book publishing at about 7% of News Corporation's total revenues, which approached $20 billion as the 20th century ended. During the final six months of 1996, operating profits fell by 66% to a mere $18 million, which was hardly what Rupert Murdoch expected. And so late in October 1997, Murdoch named Jane Friedman as new president and CEO of HarperCollins Publishers. She learned her trade with Advance Publishing's Random House, where she rose to executive vice president of Knopf Publishing Group, publisher of Vintage Books and president of Random House Audio Publishing.[75]

Murdoch, because the previous executive had done so well, did not change management. In an unusual move, in June 1997, HarperCollins began to drastically downsize its list of books, canceling at least 100 new titles and finished manuscripts in an unusual cost-cutting move. It was rare to cancel books when authors missed their contractual deadlines; this was usually tolerated. In the mid-1990s, HarperCollins had made some dazzling bets on celebrity and brand-name author books, paying a reported $4 million advance for the autobiography of comic Jay Leno. It seemed Murdoch could not make up his mind about the value of the synergy of book publishing with his television and motion picture properties. Indeed, in the mid-1990s, Murdoch was selling in an unusual move, proffering his educational divisions to Pearson PLC.[76]

HarperCollins did better thereafter, enjoying a strong fiscal 1999. As of February 1999, HarrperCollins posted rising sales and operating profits. For the first half of fiscal 1999, operating income increased by 54% to $40 million on a 11.5% gain in revenues to $426 million. Friedman argued that the strong performance was led by "stellar results" in the adult trade and children's groups. During the first six months of the fiscal year, HarperCollins had 21 bestsellers, and sales at Christmas were "very good." She also noted that the company experienced a significant increase in sales through online retailers. This pleased her new boss, Lachlan Murdoch, son of Rupert. The new role put the younger Murdoch in charge of News Corporation's book operations, as well as the *New York Post* newspaper. Seen as the heir apparent at News Corporation, Lachlan Murdoch tutored directly under his father, and all assumed he would take his father's place sometime after 2000.[77]

The Murdochs agreed to minor acquisitions. In March 1999, HarperCollins purchased Ecco Press of Hopewell, New Jersey, a small publisher of both fiction and nonfiction. Two of Ecco's current releases, *Feeding the Ghosts* by Fred D'Aguiar and *Hare Brain Tortoise Mind: How Intelligence Increases When You Think Less* by British psychologist Guy Claxton, had just sold out of their 5,500 first copy printings—big numbers for Ecco. The two very different titles found their readers in very different ways. *Feeding the Ghosts*, a poetic novel reminiscent of the Amistad incident but featuring a female-led slave-ship uprising, seemed to capture an audience online, in superstores and selling to libraries. Indeed, each month Ecco circulated a very selective catalogue of 100 titles to more than 7,000 public libraries (and to even more military base libraries around the world), which made a huge difference. By joining front, he partnered with Simon & Schuster. They—author and publisher—bet that such a partnership would cause King to write more attractive books, and then let both parties reap the benefits of the sales. The results are still not in, but the outcome will help define the U.S. book publishing industry into 2000.[74]

The News Corporation Limited symbolized the biggest and most global of media empires, and was associated, controlled and owned by Rupert Murdoch. With its HarperCollins division and its imprints, as well as newspapers, magazines, broadcast

---

PROFILE: The News Corporation Limited

Basic Data:
Headquarters: Sydney, Australia
Web site: N/A
CEO in 1997: Rupert Murdoch
1997 Revenues (in millions): $11,264
1997 Net Income (in millions): $564
1997 Assets (in millions): $30,832
Rank in 1998 Forbes International 500: 217

Market Holdings:
Broadcast Television: Fox Broadcasting Company (television network), Fox television stations, Inc. (owned and operated TV stations including WNYW-New York, KTTV-Los Angeles, KRIV-Houston, WFLD-Chicago, KDAF-Dallas and WTTG-Washington, DC, among others), Heritage Media, New World Entertainment (television stations and program production).
Cable Television: FX cable network, Fox news cable channel, Kids International, International Family Channel network, 15 regional sports cable channels.
Film & Television: Twentieth Century Fox-studio, Fox Video Company, Fox Broadcasting Company, Twentieth Century-Fox Home Entertainment, BSkyN, the Sky Channel satellite service in Europe, STAR TV in Asia, JSkyB in Japan satellite television, Canal FOX in Europe, Sky Entertainment Services in Latin America, VOX and DF1 television in Germany.
Music: small music company.
Publishing: magazines, including joint deal with *TV Guide*, and *Good Food*; newspapers, including *The Boston Herald*, *The New York Post*, *The Sun* (London, England), *The News of the World* (London, England), *The Times* (London, England); HarperCollins book publishing.
Other Interests: CineBooks, Inc. (Computer systems), Los Angeles Dodgers (Major Leaguer baseball), 100 daily and weekly newspapers in Australia, Ansett Transport industries.

Significant Events:
1985: Rupert Murdoch buys Twentieth Century Fox-studio; establishes in the United States.
1986: Begins Fox television network.
1989: Starts Sky television and becomes a major force in TV in Europe.
1993: Acquires 64% of START TV in Asia.
1994: Spends $1.6 for rights to broadcast National Football League games.
1997: Acquires the 80% of New World Communications group not already owned for about $2.5 billion in securities, and with the new 10 television stations News Corporation becomes largest owner of TV stations in the United States.
1997: Agrees to buy Los Angeles Dodgers baseball team for $350 million.
1997: Agrees to buy International Family Channel cable network for $1.9 million.
1997: Rupert Murdoch's son James named president of News American Digital publishing, a new unit that will consolidate all of News Corporation's electronic pushing operations.
1998: Spins off Fox Group as IPO to raise cash for investment.

television, cable television and film as see in the Profile: The News Corporation Limited the book division, like with the "new" Viacom is a consumer trade division, driven by the synergy that it proffers to the dominating portions of News Corporation. One estimate placed book publishing at about 7% of News Corporation's total revenues, which approached $20 billion as the 20th century ended. During the final six months of 1996, operating profits fell by 66% to a mere $18 million, which was hardly what Rupert Murdoch expected. And so late in October 1997, Murdoch named Jane Friedman as new president and CEO of HarperCollins Publishers. She learned her trade with Advance Publishing's Random House, where she rose to executive vice president of Knopf Publishing Group, publisher of Vintage Books and president of Random House Audio Publishing.[75]

Murdoch, because the previous executive had done so well, did not change management. In an unusual move, in June 1997, HarperCollins began to drastically downsize its list of books, canceling at least 100 new titles and finished manuscripts in an unusual cost-cutting move. It was rare to cancel books when authors missed their contractual deadlines; this was usually tolerated. In the mid-1990s, HarperCollins had made some dazzling bets on celebrity and brand-name author books, paying a reported $4 million advance for the autobiography of comic Jay Leno. It seemed Murdoch could not make up his mind about the value of the synergy of book publishing with his television and motion picture properties. Indeed, in the mid-1990s, Murdoch was selling in an unusual move, proffering his educational divisions to Pearson PLC.[76]

HarperCollins did better thereafter, enjoying a strong fiscal 1999. As of February 1999, HarrperCollins posted rising sales and operating profits. For the first half of fiscal 1999, operating income increased by 54% to $40 million on a 11.5% gain in revenues to $426 million. Friedman argued that the strong performance was led by "stellar results" in the adult trade and children's groups. During the first six months of the fiscal year, HarperCollins had 21 bestsellers, and sales at Christmas were "very good." She also noted that the company experienced a significant increase in sales through online retailers. This pleased her new boss, Lachlan Murdoch, son of Rupert. The new role put the younger Murdoch in charge of News Corporation's book operations, as well as the *New York Post* newspaper. Seen as the heir apparent at News Corporation, Lachlan Murdoch tutored directly under his father, and all assumed he would take his father's place sometime after 2000.[77]

The Murdochs agreed to minor acquisitions. In March 1999, HarperCollins purchased Ecco Press of Hopewell, New Jersey, a small publisher of both fiction and nonfiction. Two of Ecco's current releases, *Feeding the Ghosts* by Fred D'Aguiar and *Hare Brain Tortoise Mind: How Intelligence Increases When You Think Less* by British psychologist Guy Claxton, had just sold out of their 5,500 first copy printings—big numbers for Ecco. The two very different titles found their readers in very different ways. *Feeding the Ghosts*, a poetic novel reminiscent of the Amistad incident but featuring a female-led slave-ship uprising, seemed to capture an audience online, in superstores and selling to libraries. Indeed, each month Ecco circulated a very selective catalogue of 100 titles to more than 7,000 public libraries (and to even more military base libraries around the world), which made a huge difference. By joining

HarperCollins, Ecco would enter the 21st century with a huge marketing apparatus behind it, and would be expected to throw off profits far in excess of the average independent publisher.[78]

Still not everything had gone well at HarperCollins in the 1990s. In 1997, for example, News Corporation took an unusual charge of $270 million for Harper-Collins as it publicly disclosed it was restructuring its book division. This charge—said to be the largest in book publishing history up to that point—included costs associated with author's advances paid, but no manuscripts published. It also eliminated more than 400 of the 3,000 international employees of the company. Harper-Collins increasingly turned to cross-promotion, leading the book publishing industry into new methods by which to capture the public's attention. In February 1999, for example, it participated, along with industry leaders Bertelsmann AG and Pearson PLC, in a cross-promotion with Coca Cola to give away five by four inch 32-page excerpts of six novels in 45 million packages of Diet Coke. This campaign grew out of a focus group research sponsored by Diet Coke that saw a correlation between Diet Coke buyers and book buyers. The book excerpts included "works" by Elmore Leonard and Barbara Taylor Bradford and were promoted in grocery store displays. This seemed an efficient way to reach Baby Boomers who did not have time to go to a Borders or to shop online.[79]

In 1999, News Corporation purchased Hearst's book operations for $180 million. Hearst ended its book publishing business, but as a privately owned corporation it disclosed little information about its operations. The Hearst Books division in 1995 accounted for revenues estimated at $160 million of the company's total of $2 to $3 billion. For 1998, *Publishers Weekly* estimated that sales in the Hearst Book Group had grown past $200 million. In an annual letter to employees, issued in January 1999, Hearst president and CEO Frank Bennack, Jr., said that the 1998 financial performance of its trade book group (including imprints such as Avon Books, William Morrow & Co., Arbor House and Hearst Books) improved over 1997. Elaborating on Bennack's comments, Hearst Book Group president William Wright told *Publishers Weekly* that sales at Morrow and Avon both grew at double-digit rates during 1998. Although Bennack reported that Morrow had "notable sales growth" in 1998, he stated Avon's revenues increased at a faster rate than its sister publisher.

The strong performance of the two companies pushed total group revenues to record levels. Indeed, according to Wright, every imprint at the company showed growth in 1998. During the year, the Hearst Book Group had 6 titles reach the best-seller list, and 12 hit the mass paperback charts. The Hearst Book Group also had a healthy increase in backlist sales, "which gave a major boost to the bottom line," Wright observed. Among 1998's best performers at Morrow were the two trade titles *The Day Diana Died* and *We Are Our Mothers' Daughters*, both of which hit the top spot on the *New York Times* bestseller list. Morrow's cookbook division had a good year in 1998, led by Emeril Lagasse's *TV Dinners*. The Hearst Books imprint, which publishes books carrying Hearst magazine brands, doubled its output and saw sales and earnings double as well. Helping boost sales at Avon was *The New Diet Revolution*, which by early 1999 ranked as the longest running bestseller in Avon history. Other strong performers in 1998 included *What Looks Like Crazy on an Ordinary Day* (an Oprah's Book Club pick), *Serpent's Tooth*, *Dream a Little Dream* and *Petals on the River*. Avon added three new imprints in 1998 (i.e., Bard, Twilight, Spike) and planned to launch two more in 1999 (i.e., WholeCare, which will be devoted to health, and Tempest, an Avon Books for Young Readers fiction imprint). A history imprint, Post Road Press, was planned for spring 2000. Wright noted that the creation of new imprints was aimed at lessening Avon's dependency on the romance field. In toto, the Hearst Book Group planned to publish a total of approximately 1,000 titles in 1999, a minor increase over 1998.[80]

Four Units of Pure Media Conglomerates

Finally, four important book publishers function as part of pure conglomerates, or specialty media companies, and should not be associated with pure media conglomerates like Time Warner or Viacom. These may see book publishing as an extension of what the company already does, or just another unit in a diverse conglomerate. In the end, there is no pure synergy here—as there theoretically is for the four pure media conglomerates analyzed earlier—but simply that at one time book publishing seemed like an extension of, or was simply added to, corporate operations. These four companies analyzed both book publishing as a stand-alone division, which is profitable enough in the long run to generate profits equal to or better than what other investments the company might make. This seems to be creating an "other" category, but these four are undoubtedly some of the most important book publishers in the U.S. market.

The Reader's Digest Association is more famous as a magazine company that also has a direct mail book division. This is not a book publisher in the traditional sense, because these books cannot be bought at a traditional bookstore, a superstore or through Amazon.com or some other Web bookseller. They can only be obtained through direct mail from Reader's Digest, which started bookselling to exploit the multimillion dollar list it constructed through its long-running popular magazine. If the magazine can condense periodical articles, why not a book division that condenses published books? According to its own public pronouncements, the Reader's Digest Association is a global leader in publishing and direct marketing of products that inform, enrich, entertain and inspire people of all ages and cultures around the world. It publishes magazines, books and home entertainment products in the family, home, health, finance and faith categories. Revenues were $2.6 billion for the fiscal year ending in June 1998; headquarters was in Pleasantville, New York; book sales created less than one third of the revenues generated, which is hardly a small figure with Reader's Digest Condensed Books selling millions of copies per year (about half in the United States and half abroad).[81]

Still the magazine was not doing well in the late 1990s. The Reader's Digest Association had to begin to deal with its aging audience. Profits were sluggish in August 1997 when James P. Schadt resigned. Schadt sought to focus on younger readers and to create joint ventures, but nothing he did seemed to bring higher profits. Readership at the magazine remained stagnant. Here was yet another case of an executive very successful outside publishing (at Cadbury Schweppes PLC, at Pepisco and at Sara Lee, all successful consumer-oriented companies), who came on board in 1991

and was not able to turn the company in a new direction. He even began to experiment by selling at selected Borders or Barnes & Noble superstores. As the magazine
circulation stagnated, book (and music and home video) sales—combined on company ledgers—began to fall. All future executives would need to deal with the
demands of a Baby Boom, but as the 1990s ended cost-cutting seemed the only
means that would regularly contribute to the bottom line.[82]

In April 1999, the Reader's Digest Association announced a quarterly operating
profit of $34.3 million—up 58% from $21.7 million in the same 1998 period. Still,
revenues for the quarter were down 7% compared with the third quarter of 1998. The
profits came from abroad with major markets in Europe, especially Germany and the
United Kingdom, remaining strong. Thomas O. Ryder, Reader's Digest's new Chairman and Chief Executive Officer, argued that the company was ahead of schedule in
the cost reduction and re-engineering initiatives announced in September 1998.
Adjusted operating profit for the first nine months of fiscal 1999 was $149.8 million,
up 58% on a comparable basis. The improvement reflected lower promotion and
product costs. Revenues of $1,947.8 million for the first nine months of fiscal 1999
decreased 3% as compared with the first nine months of fiscal 1998; this reflected
primarily lower unit sales within books and home entertainment products in the
United States and the United Kingdom, and the significant scaling back of mailing
activity in Russia. In April 1999, the Reader's Digest Association seemed to be counting on its Books and Home Entertainment Products division to continue to plow
money into company profit ledgers by lowering promotion and product costs.[83]

Ryder, just as his predecessor, sought new joint ventures. For example, in May
1999, IDG Books Worldwide, Inc., and Reader's Digest Association announced
plans to market two popular IDG Books Worldwide titles through the Reader's
Digest Association's direct mail lists in the United States. Under the licensing agreement, Reader's Digest would reprint and distribute IDG Books' titles (e.g., *Teach
Yourself Computers*) first in English and then hopefully, as with magazines and other
books before them, in other languages in up to 40 countries worldwide. Market tests
showed a demand for these books because Reader's Digest, like IDG Books, was
known for simplifying information for consumers and then selling to a database of
over 100 million names. In 1999, IDG Books Worldwide was headquartered in Foster City, California, best known for its "For Dummies" and Cliffs Notes. At that
time, it had more than 1,000 book titles in print in English, plus translations in 36
languages around the world.[84]

The McGraw-Hill Companies, a longtime magazine publisher, also took steps to
increase its presence in book publishing in the 1990s. Although far more famous for
Business Week, this U.S.-based multibillion dollar company publishes some trade
books, but has concentrated extensively in the education and professional areas. In
1998, McGraw-Hill reported that sales by its educational and professional publishing division rose 3% to $1.62 billion, with operating profit for the year increasing
7.6% to $202.1 million. The gain was due to higher sales in the group's elementary
and higher education units, offsetting lower sales in the professional publishing
operations. Sales in the elementary unit rose 7.6% to $831.5 million, led by strong
results at Glencoe, SRA and CTB units. Solid gains in both the sale of frontlist and

backlist titles boosted higher education revenues 7% to $359.4 million. Revenues in the professional publishing unit fell 4.8% to $429.5 million, due to continued weakness in its Continuing Education Centers and softness in the Asia-Pacific markets.[85]

Whereas it owned and operated four television stations, published a wide range of magazines (e.g., *Business Week, Aviation Week, Architectural Record*) and controlled Standard and Poor's information services, McGraw-Hill had become a top five textbook publisher, primarily in the "invisible" elementary and secondary school market where school boards choose the texts. In addition, the company sought to develop professional book publishing, another category known only to specialists in medicine and business. Yet, in the late 1990s, the thrust was educational publishing. In 1996, McGraw-Hill added the former Times Mirror educational units. In 1999, McGraw-Hill agreed to acquire Appleton & Lange, Inc. for $46 million; Appleton & Lange publishes basic medical science books and clinical reference products.[86]

Harcourt General, Inc. through the 1990s was a conglomerate with publishing and the fabled Nieman Marcus department store chain as its other—at least until 1999. Because trade bestsellers made up but 3% of total book sales, like McGraw-Hill, Harcourt General's thrust was to the educational and professional markets. Yet, with imprints of Harcourt Brace Javonovich and Holt, Rinehart and Winston, the Dryden and Academic Presses and Harvest Books, this should not mean that this company represented some sleepy minor conglomerate company based in Chestnut Hill, Massachusetts. With revenues in excess of $3 billion per year, and book sales measured in the billions of dollars, books were one third of corporate revenues.[87]

Indeed, the late 1990s saw Harcourt General reinventing itself. In March 1999, Harcourt General announced that its wholly owned publishing and educational services subsidiary, known as Harcourt Brace & Company since 1993, was officially changed to Harcourt, Inc. This was part of a comprehensive re-branding campaign designed to strengthen a position to become one of the world's premier "lifelong learning companies." Brian J. Knez, Chief Executive Officer of Harcourt, Inc., argued that by uniting its education, training, assessment and professional information businesses under a common identity, this re-branded the company, and allowed it to leverage brand recognition across the broad spectrum of learning markets. Harcourt, Inc., like publisher Thomson analyzed later, wanted to be a full service anytime, anywhere, multimedia, knowledge-based solution company for people of all ages. A critical component of this re-branding process would be to open a dynamic, customer-focused Internet site that will offer seamless access to the wide range of Harcourt products and services. This new Harcourt site was launched at www.harcourt.com in March 1999. The Harcourt, Inc. re-branding campaign featured a new logo, and in addition to traditional classroom instruction, also focused on education and training for businesses and at home. Through Harcourt, Inc., a leading, global multimedia learning company, Harcourt General could provide educational, training and assessment products and services to classroom, corporate, professional and consumer markets.[88]

Also during spring 1999, Harcourt General, bending to Wall Street's preference for "pure-play" companies, announced plans to spin off most of its stake in Neiman Marcus Group and end Harcourt's control of the high-end retailer. Under its plan, Harcourt would distribute its stake to its own shareholders, leaving itself with 10%

of Neiman Marcus. In Spring 1999, the value of the spun-off shares was set at about $655 million. Harcourt General's CEO and dominant stockholder, Richard A. Smith, argued that as Harcourt entered into 2000 it was best to concentrate on books and media. At the time, Smith and his family owned about 28% of Harcourt, and controlled the company with 10 times the votes of other stockholders.[89]

This spinning off of Neiman Marcus took Harcourt back to its roots. Harcourt had been a longtime publisher, and in 1991 the Smith family, owner of General Cinema (see Chapter 6) purchased the book publisher—then known as Harcourt Brace Javonovich—for $1.5 billion. Two years later, General Cinema was renamed Harcourt General, and Smith and his family sold their movie theaters and concentrated on educational and professional book publishing. In 1997, Harcourt acquired the National Education Corporation, a provider of professional training services, and the Steck Vaughn Publishing Corporation, a publisher of elementary, secondary and college textbooks.[90]

Harcourt General was also an active player in the market for professional books. In August 1997, for example, it emerged as the winner in the contest to acquire Churchill Livingstone, the medical publishing unit of Pearson PLC. Harcourt General paid approximately $92.5 million in cash for Churchill, which had annual revenues of about $50 million, and added Churchill to a medical publishing portfolio that already included W. B. Saunders and Harcourt Brace de Espana S.A., a Spanish-language publisher of medical books. The acquisition of Churchill, which was then generating nearly two thirds of its revenues from outside the United States, was thought to strengthen Harcourt General's presence in the international market with books, journals and the newly developing market for CD-ROM titles.[91]

Although the Harcourt trade division accounted for only about 2% of the $1.8 billion in total sales recorded by the publishing and education company in fiscal 1998, division president Dan Farley argued that this unit had carved out its own special niche. Indeed, 1998 was the third year in a row the Harcourt trade division had made a profit; during 1996–1998, profits had more than doubled, and revenues topped $50 million. In addition, 1998 marked the third time in the 1990s that Harcourt was the American publisher of the Nobel Prize for Literature winner—Jose Saramago, Octavio Paz and Wislawa Symborska. Harcourt was able to turn the eminence of Saramago's Nobel into sales, shipping about 60,000 copies of his most recent novel, *Blindness*, and 25,000 copies each of Saramago's backlist just before the close of its fiscal year in October 1998. Harcourt focused on publishing serious fiction and nonfiction as a midsize house with a reputation for quality that its bigger rivals did not cultivate. Harcourt's adult division published about 45 hardcovers and 55 trade paperbacks annually during the 1990s, small figures compared to its major rivals. Approximately half of the output of Harvest, the division's trade paperback imprint, were original titles of history, politics and poetry. Its children's operation accounted for about 60% of the company's total revenues, with a main focus on quality picture books. The children's division, which at one point published more than 200 titles annually, by 1999 was releasing roughly 175 books per year.[92]

Overall, as of the late 1990s, Harcourt's book division was not doing well as it reorganized educational and professional lines, and absorbed new units such as the National Education Corporation. For example, in 1998, amortization of intangible assets associated with the National Education Corporation acquisition reduced operating earnings. Still, revenues from the company's Harcourt Brace publishing subsidiary stood at more than $1 billion per annum. The focus was directly aimed for long-run profit maximization. Here was a educational and professional publishing giant that was poised to concentrate on book publishing and lifelong learning, with the goal of growing past its larger rivals and (like Pearson PLC) join the top ranks of book publishers.[93]

Thomson Corporation, like the other three specialists, was far better known as a Canadian newspaper publisher than as major book publisher. According to the official Thomson line, during the 1990s, Thomson was increasingly an "information" company and grew more specialized as such. From 1995 to 1999, its information revenues grew by $2.4 billion, which is an achievement almost equivalent to creating a Fortune 500 company. (Total corporate revenues in 1998 rose 7% to $6.3 billion.) In 1998, its revenues from continuing businesses were $6.1 billion, making Thomson one of the largest corporations of its kind in the world. In March 1999, Thomson posted higher net income for 1998 due to profit gains at four of its five divisions. Net profits neared $2 billion per annum. It spun off its travel division and its health care information group and newspaper group continued to do well. Under the quiet direction of Chairman Kenneth R. Thomson, who controlled three quarters of the stock, the days of seeking to develop a chain of travel agencies, or operating the Hudson's Bay Company department stores, were gone. In 1997, *Forbes* ranked the Thomson Corporation as the 9th largest in Canada and the 309th largest in the world. In a rival 1997 survey, *Business Week*, done with different methodology, ranked the Thomson Corporation as the 4th largest in Canada and the 252nd largest in the world. The company's accounting methods make separating book publishing out difficult, but one estimate of book sales alone for 1996 placed Thomson at $1.5 billion in U.S. book sales, and at $2.5 billion elsewhere.[94]

Whereas the legal address of Thomson had long been Toronto, Canada, its headquarters and most of its North American staff for book publishing was located and based in Stamford, Connecticut. In the early 1990s, its travel business represented the top generator of revenues, but by 1999 Thomson was out of travel altogether. Its newspaper division, led by the notable *Toronto Globe and Mail*, moved to top revenue generator. Book publishing was one smaller part of the Thomson empire, with imprints such as educational's Wadsworth and Boyd & Fraser, Brooks-Cole, Chapman & Hall, Delmar and Van Nostrand Reinhold. Thomson also began to move into professional and legal publishing. In 1996 it acquired legal publishing giant West Publishing Company for $3.43 billion, then the largest book publishing merger in history. The venerable West Publishing Company, based in St. Paul, Minnesota, sold more than $1 billion of law books per year, and dominated legal online information. West represented a professional publishing jewel, generating millions of dollars in profits per annum, yet nearly invisible outside the legal profession. In short, during the 1990s, Thomson has been trying to reinvent itself as a publishing giant.[95]

In May 1999, leveraging its success in the traditional academic market, International Thomson Publishing renamed itself Thomson Learning and took direct aim (as rival Harcourt General was doing) at the academic and adult learning markets.

Its two divisions, Lifelong Learning Group and the Academic Group, formed the new Thomson Learning and reflected a new corporate vision and strategic direction. Thomson Learning entered the 21st century seeking to expand beyond traditional academic markets, targeting school-to-work professional certification programs; test preparation; corporate sourcing, selection, and learning; and continuing adult education. Thomson Learning will seek to bridge the learning gap between the classroom and the workplace. Thomson intends to take what it learned in its long history of working with students, instructors and academic institutions and apply it to meet the needs of adult learners and their employers. Thomson Learning's individual businesses will retain their brand identities, but the name change will bring all the businesses under a single vision, with an anchor brand that moves customers seamlessly from one Thomson Learning service to another.

Thomson Learning will bring together four already successful companies with complementary lines of products and services and a 1999 revenue base of nearly $250 million. These included:

1) AlignMark—Electronic sourcing and selection and learning and performance management products and services, including Accu-Vision and WisdomLink, to help corporations optimize their investment in human capital.
2) Course Technology—Computer and information technology courseware and courses for academic, corporate and lifelong learning.
3) Delmar—Vocational-technical and health care courseware and courses for academic, corporate and lifelong learning, including the recently acquired Singular Publishing.
4) Peterson's—Products and services that connect educational providers and educational consumers, including the recently launched CollegeQuest, GradAdvantage and TestPrep.

Thomson did not abandon the educational textbook market in which it had long been a leader. Thomson Learning's academic publishers will provide schools, colleges and universities with traditional text materials, multimedia and a growing list of new online services. With a 1999 combined revenue base of approximately $600 million, these companies included Brooks/Cole (a leading publisher of course materials and courseware for mathematics, science, engineering and statistics), Heinle & Heinle (a top brand in foreign language publishing and English as a second language), South-Western Educational Publishing (with products and services in a variety of subjects led by business and computer education), South-Western College Publishing (led by top selling textbooks in accounting and taxation, finance, economics, business law, management and marketing), Wadsworth (a college division for the humanities, social sciences, teacher education and nutrition), Thomson Learning Custom Publishing, Thomson Learning's International Group and the Nelson companies in Canada, Australia, the United Kingdom, Asia, Europe, South Africa and Latin America.[96]

Thomson also began to look to the future. In January 1999, Varsitybooks.com, an online college bookseller, announced a joint marketing agreement with International Thomson Publishers. Under the agreement, sales representatives from Thomson would pitch the virtues of Varsitybooks to professors, while sales through Varsity would help bolster the reps' bottom line. No money would exchange hands. The

Association of College Bookstores saw this as an invasion of their territory, and expressed concern about this development, as well as other Web incursions that promised to diminish their business monopolies on college and university campuses. In Fall 1998, Varsitybooks.com began with a modest five-school list, and then expanded its operations to include lists at 57 colleges; it increased its available titles from 250,000 to 500,000. An arrangement with the second largest distributor, Baker & Taylor, allowed for overnight shipping to many parts of the country, a feature Varsity then boasted as unique for a college cyber-retailer.[97]

The Rare Pure Book Company

Houghton Mifflin is not part of diverse holdings like the aforementioned majors. This is the smallest of the majors, and as a pure book company represented a throwback to the past. It concentrated on trade and educational publishing. Indeed, in educational publishing there was enough room for Houghton Mifflin not only to play, but to thrive. Established in 1832, Houghton also publishes children's books and trade titles, but with the $455 million acquisition of D. C. Heath & Company in 1995, it bet its future on textbook sales, principally in Kindergarten through 12th grade, but also in colleges and universities. In 1998, Houghton sold $861 million worth of books and related products. In 1999, Houghton Mifflin had a school K–6th grade division, a secondary school division in McDougal Littell and a college division, as well as a supplementary materials (i.e., Great Source) unit. The company publishes assessments (Riverside) and provides test administration technology and services for the academic, clinical, professional and corporate markets.[98]

Houghton Mifflin, in 1998, saw its K–12 publishing group boost net sales to a record $862 million. Excluding extraordinary and infrequent items, income after tax was $40.8 million, despite considerable expense of trying to bid for Simon & Schuster's educational units that Pearson PLC won. According to *Educational Marketer*, Houghton Mifflin ranked number one in K–12 textbook adoptions in 1998. Late in that year, Houghton Mifflin acquired DiscoveryWorks, a best-selling K–6 science program, from Silver Burdett Ginn Inc. Science was the only major discipline in which the school division had no product offerings, and it has been one of Houghton Mifflin's strategic goals to enter this market. DiscoveryWorks will allow Houghton Mifflin to participate in many state adoption opportunities in 2000 and beyond, including those in California, Florida, and Texas. McDougal Littell, Houghton Mifflin's secondary school division, was the clear leader in its market in 1998, according to *Educational Marketer*. Its literature and language arts programs gained share in California, Maryland, New York and other states. Its mathematics product line took commanding shares in Alabama, Oklahoma, Texas and in many open territory districts. The division's new programs in U.S. and world history also outsold the competition. In 1999, McDougal Littell added a new Spanish program, and a new edition of its literature series, *The Language of Literature*.

The college division is a market leader in the disciplines of mathematics, history, chemistry and modern languages. Nearly all its major textbooks have technology components, such as CD-ROMs and Web sites. For example, *Calculus* by Larson/Hostetler/Edwards was also offered in an Internet version, and *The American Pageant* by Bailey/Kennedy/Cohen came with *@history*, a CD with original source material tied to the text. This technology has created new packaging opportunities and improved backlist sales. The division also launched major initiatives in two rapidly growing areas of the college market in 1998, distance learning and online publishing. A license agreement was signed with Live Text Inc. to package and sell course management software suitable for distance learning courses. Online projects were signed in mathematics and education, and work began on development of a content database that will increase the number of products available online.

Houghton Mifflin's trade and reference division continues to develop popular, award-winning adult and children's publications. For example, *Snowflake Bentley*, written by Jacqueline Briggs Martin and illustrated by Mary Azarian, won the 1999 Caldecott Medal for excellence in illustration—one of the highest honors in children's literature. And, *American Pastoral*, by Philip Roth, received the Pulitzer Prize for Fiction in 1998. Houghton Mifflin trade was expanding. In April 1999, Wendy J. Strothman, executive vice president of the trade and reference division, announced that Beacon Press had entered into an agreement to have Houghton's trade and reference division handle sales and fulfillment starting in August 1999. Beacon had long been distributed to the trade by Random House. Beacon, which published about 100 books a year, would be Houghton's first trade client and there seemed to be room for more expansion into the next century.[99]

Houghton Mifflin Interactive has shifted its focus to concentrate on instructional software, aligning it more closely with the company's overall mission. The educational technology market, currently estimated at $700 million, is frequently funded separately from printed materials. Houghton Mifflin recently acquired the Little Planet Literacy Series from Applied Learning Technologies. Little Planet represented one of the leading technology-based pre-Kindergarten to grade three literacy series on the market.

Still Houghton Mifflin was in trouble in the 1990s. In April 1999, while Houghton Mifflin reported first quarter net sales of $84.3 million, an 18% increase over the 1998 figure, this generated a first quarter loss of $37.0 million. Although Houghton Mifflin was positioned to compete effectively in its markets, it did not have the deep pockets or the economies of scale to effectively compete with the majors above it. It depended on K–12 publishing, with that segment's first quarter net sales up 32% to $52.0 million. The school division, McDougal Littell, Great Source Education Group and the Riverside Publishing Company also reported double-digit net sales gains on far smaller bases. But college publishing net sales were down slightly, and trade sales were even. Houghton Mifflin would have to acquire more units, or think about selling out to one of the majors analyzed earlier.[100]

ASPIRANTS

With just 10 major book publishing companies, this industry was not as concentrated as the movie or music industries. Thus, barriers to entry seemed low enough that new firms were willing to take a chance. We take them up later, first by considering giant European-based publsihers that seek to sell more books in the United States.

For these four European media companies book publishing is a major unit of the corporation.[101]

Verlagsgruppe Georg von Holtzbrinck G.m.b.H. (hereafter simply Holtzbrinck) of Germany owned not only the Farrar, Straus & Giroux imprint (including Hill & Wang, Noonday Press and North Point), but also St. Martin's Press, W. H. Freeman and Henry Holt & Co. Because Holtzbrinck is a private company like Bertelsmann, their sales data is either a guess or old. In the late 1990s, book revenues from trade and educational sales were estimated to be one third of the company's total of $2 billion revenues. Holtzbrinck took most of its revenues from television and newspaper operations in Germany, and from magazines sold around the world (most notably *Scientific American*). Holtzbrinck was no small book publishing operation, but was still struggling to become a major publisher.[102]

Henry Holt, according to new publisher John Sterling in early 1999, has "not been profitable for a while," and thus he eliminated a number of jobs, cut its lists, and folded Owl Books back into the hardcover group. Holt was expected to reduce its list to 200 titles in 1999, and as Sterling noted, "A smaller list inevitably means a smaller staff." Cutbacks were also spurned by Owl's return to the hardcover group. Before Sterling came aboard in the fall 1998, he thought Owl could be more successful as a separate imprint. However, "in a marketplace where hard and soft imprints are commonly working together, and where sales and marketing are already integrated, it didn't seem to make sense any longer." He explained that books will continue to appear under the Owl imprint, but after 1999 there will be no more reprints of outside titles. This was notably bad news as Holtzbrinck tried to compete.[103]

In contrast, St. Martin's Press, as one of the largest trade book houses in the business, contained a dynamic college division, as well as a small division for reference works. St. Martin's represented a varied collection of imprints ranging from its self-described label, St. Martin's, to Picador, from Thomas Dune Books to Griffin, from the "Let's Go" travel series to Bedford Books. St. Martin's also distributed books for Rizzoli, Rodale, World Almanac, Consumer Reports and several other smaller imprints. All these familiar "American" brands were controlled by Holtzbrinck, with its headquarters in Stuttgart, Germany.[104]

Holtzbrinck executives knew they needed to extract more economies of scale, and thus lower costs, if the company ever expected to move into the ranks of the majors. It might seem a strange place to look, but the most visible portion of Holtzbrinck in the United States was in the middle of rural Virginia. During the fall 1997, Holtzbrinck opened a new $30 million high tech warehouse as its bet on an increasing book distribution presence in the United States. "I simply believe in America," explained Dieter von Holtzbrinck, the chairman of the company and the son of the founder. This 425,000 square foot warehouse looked to maximize efficiency of distribution; inside a visitor would see a gleaming industrial jungle of chutes and rollers and dangling laser wands, which would be used to "harvest" books and send them off quickly to paying customers. Holtzbrinck needed just 300 employees to ship what it hoped would be more than 60 million books annually. Computers and bar codes did the sorting, low wage workers simply packed what was sent down the line to them. The filled and sealed boxes were then collected by robotic "fork lifts," which travel along a narrow magnetic strip etched on a polished concrete floor, and sent on their way. Virginia was selected because of low labor costs and subsidies from state and local units of government. This seemed to be a trend as Ingram continued to dominate distribution, and the U.S. government seemed unhappy with a bookseller like Barnes & Noble vertically integrating upward (discussed later). The logical extension, therefore, would be for publishers to vertically integrate downward, as Holtzbrinck was doing.[105]

Reed-Elsevier, a joint venture of Reed International PLC of London, England, and Elsevier of Amsterdam, Netherlands, was best noted for its portfolio of 1,200 academic and technical journals, but was also a major book publisher. Reed-Elsevier is characterized as a member of the "Big Three" of legal publishing, which also includes Wolters Kluwer and Thomson of Canada. In 1993, Elsevier NV and Reed International PLC had amalgamated their operational activities by transferring their subsidiaries and other investments to two holding companies: Reed-Elsevier PLC (London) and Elsevier Reed Finance NV (Amsterdam). Reed-Elsevier specialized in the publishing and printing of scientific, professional and business information. This billion dollar company is most aptly represented as the publisher of *Publishers Weekly*. Reed-Elsevier's online service NEXIS-LEXIS ranked as the world's largest provider of online information, and Reed-Elsevier also published business and travel directories such as *The Official Airline Guide*.

In 1997, Reed-Elsevier tried to merge with its Dutch competitor Wolters Kluwer (see later), but backed away and instead purchased the Chilton Company (publisher of 39 trade magazines) from the Walt Disney Company for $447 million. This created a powerhouse global publisher of journals. Indeed, Reed-Elsevier figured the future lay in professional reference publishing, so in 1997 it agreed to sell its adult trade book division to Random House and to exit trade publishing altogether. One estimate of Reed-Elsevier's book business was totaled at about $600 million sales in the United States, and $1.4 billion elsewhere—about one fourth of the annual revenues of a corporation with more than $8 billion in total revenues.[106]

Reed Elsevier was purchasing and selling operations as it restructured. In April 1998, it paid $1.65 billion for Matthew Bender & Company (a legal publishing unit) from Times Mirror, who was exiting the book business, as well as its half share of Shepard's citation service. (Reed-Elsevier already owned the other half of Shepard's.) Bender, in the late 1990s, was a $250 million annual business. In June 1998, an agreement was reached whereby Bertelsmann AG acquired Reed-Elsevier's half share in the BCA trade publisher. For its part, Reed-Elsevier was simply continuing its strategy of withdrawing from consumer publishing in favor of professional and information markets. BCA was formed in 1966 and Reed had made it the United Kingdom's largest book club operation, with both general and special interest clubs.[107]

Yet whereas Reed-Elsevier was a company restructuring itself, it was posting declines in pre-tax profits. Reed-Elsevier's transition to the electronic age was so painful, that in 1998 the company reorganized top management. The boards, which had remained separate for Britain's Reed and for the Netherlands's Elsevier since the 1993 merger, were combined in 1998. Increasing competition from the Internet caused the newly merged company to make the costly transfer from paper publishing of specialized information to online publishing; as the conversion took place, no one was surprised by falling profits. Reed-Elsevier had a very broad range of businesses, and the goal was to continue to build content in science, legal, medical, business and tax publishing, not stepping outside these core interests.[108]

Wolters Kluwer NV of the Netherlands, in 1999, was an internationally operating publishing group with subsidiaries throughout Europe and the United States. Geographically, Wolters generated 55% of its sales in Europe, 32% in the United States, 2% in Asia Pacific and 11% in other countries. The company focused on business publishing, legal and tax publishing, educational publishing and medical publishing. Indeed, Wolters Kluwer offered its information products not only as books, but as periodicals and trade journals, newsletters, loose leaf publications, data banks, electronic libraries, diskette publications, CD-ROM products and increasingly online. The company was a leading legal publisher in Europe, with legal and tax publishing accounting for 44% of total 1998 revenues. Business publishing followed at 21%, medical and scientific publishing with 18%, educational publishing and professional training with 15% and other activities with 2%.

Wolters was also expanding in the 1990s. It bought New York's Plenum Publishing in 1998 for $258 million to bolster its scientific publishing. In the same year, it almost merged with Reed-Elsevier, but Wolters called off the deal after European Union regulators expressed concern. Wolters continued to expand with its February 1998 purchase of medical publisher Waverly, Inc. for $375 million in cash. Wolters' transition to the new electronic world went easier than it did for Reed-Elsevier. In March 1999, a year after backing out of a multibillion dollar merger with Reed-Elsevier, Wolters Kluwer NV achieved a measure of vindication when the Dutch science publisher reported an 18% gain in 1998. This contrasted brightly with a 3.4% decrease 1998 pre-tax profit reported by Reed-Elsevier. In all, Wolters leveraged growth through 30 acquisitions in 1998 focusing on the U.S. medical market and international scientific publications.[109]

Paris-based **Havas** in 1999 published books and specialized professional journals, and mounted trade exhibitions. It was France's leading school and reference book publisher, with the Larousse, Bordas, Nathan and Masson groups, and also a major trade book publisher with such imprints as Laffont, Julliard, Plon, Belfond and Presses de la Cité. This added to annual revenues near $9 billion in the 1990s. Havas was a 50–50 partner with Bertelsmann AG in France's leading book club; foreign assets included the Larousse group in the United Kingdom and the Anaya school, professional and trade groups in Spain. This meant little impact in the United States, but surely the basis and potential was there. Havas aspired to be a global publisher in all languages in the manner of Bertelsmann AG. Indeed its trade, reference, textbook and multimedia operations were headed by Agnès Touraine, trained at the Business School of Columbia University in New York City. With 51.7 billion francs in annual sales (some $9 billion at the 1998 conversion rate), Havas had the backing of a deep-pocketed owner—the 167-billion-franc ($29 billion in 1998) Vivendi (water supply, energy, waste disposal, transport and telecommunications)—which made it a logical candidate to leap to a major publisher in the United States.[110]

In the late 1990s, a small number of U.S.-based media giants sought to leverage their power into the creation of a major book publisher. For example, the Walt Disney Company, which is often listed as a small media enterprise (depending how one measures), formed the largest media company in the world along with Time Warner. In 1995, Disney spent $19 billion to acquire Capital Cities/ABC and began the imprint Hyperion, as well as others associated with its film division (Miramax) and its the cable television sports programmer (ESPN). Yet, this huge media company, with total revenues measured in the billions of dollars had trade book sales measured in the millions of dollars. Book publishing was a growing part of the Disney empire, and Disney management, led by Michael Eisner, sought the same synergies achieved by Viacom and News Corporation.

PROFILE: The Walt Disney Company

Basic Data:
Headquarters: Burbank, CA
Web site: www.disney.com
CEO in 1997: Michael D. Eisner
1998 Sales (in millions): $23,226
1998 Net Profits (in millions): $1,717
1998 Assets (in millions): $43,537
Rank in 1998 Forbes 500—Sales: 46

Market Holdings:
Broadcast Television: ABC Television Network, ABC owned and operated stations (e.g., WABC-New York City, KABC-Los Angeles, WLS-Chicago).
Cable Television: Ownership of networks: ESPN Networks, part owner of Arts & Entertainment & the History Channel, part owner of Lifetime, Toon Disney, as well as TV networks in Europe and Japan.
Film & Television: Hollywood Pictures, Touchstone Pictures, Walt Disney Pictures, Miramax studio, Walt Disney Television, Buena Vista Pictures Distribution, Buena Vista Home Video.
Music: Walt Disney Music Company, Hollywood Records.
Radio: ABC Radio networks, ABC owned and operated stations (e.g., WRQX-FM-Washington, DC, WABC-AM-New York City, WMAL-AM-Washington, DC).
Publishing: Disney Publishing Group.
Theme Parks: Disneyland (California), Walt Disney World (Florida), EuroDisney (Paris, France), Tokyo Disneyland; Disney-MGM Studio park.
Other Interests: The Mighty Ducks (National Hockey League), Anaheim Angels (Major league baseball), Disney retail stores, Broadway plays such as "The Lion King;", Disney Cruise Line, Disney Vacation Clubs.

Significant Events:
1995: The Disney Channel becomes available in the United Kingdom.
1996: Acquires 25% interest of the California Angels baseball team and takes on the role of managing general partner.
1996: Buys Capital Cities/ABC television network and stations and cable TV interests.
1996: Disney World celebrates its 25th anniversary.
1997: Michael Eisner's contract with Disney is extended to 2006.
1997: Fifteen million Southern Baptists threaten to boycott the Walt Disney Company, however boycott is virtually impossible because Disney ownership is so broad.
1997: CEO Michael Eisner exercises 7.3 million of his stock options worth more than a half billion dollars.
1998: Micael Eisner pushing memoir, *Work in Progress* (Random House).
1998: Disney acqiures 43% stake in Web portal Infoseek.

Disney certainly had the resources to become a major in book publishing. So, in 1996, Douglas Kennedy's *Big Picture* (from Disney's Hyperion imprint) received $750,000 worth of promotion and publicity, figures usually associated with the major publishing houses. By 1997, Disney's adult backlist consisted of more than 500 titles, with some 140 books published per annum. In the same year, Oprah Winfrey's *Make the Connection* sold more than two million copies. Here was a new company (started in 1991) that could move up to major status if it continued to put resources into book publishing and could effect true synergies from its other media products.[111]

Yet Disney struggled to make a go of it in book publishing. In April 1999, the Walt Disney Company admitted it had been going in the wrong direction, and announced a reorganization of its book publishing business. The Hyperion adult book group became part of ABC-TV, and a new entity, Disney Publishing Worldwide, was created to manage the other imprints. Bo Boyd, Chairman of Disney consumer products, and Anne Osberg, President of Disney consumer products, figured if Hyperion worked more closely with ABC, then the elusive synergies would be captured. Hyperion had already developed a number of imprints based on ABC units, such as Daytime Press and ESPN Books. By being directly connected to ABC, the theory was that ABC would feed resources that could provide material for best-selling books—as ABC had seen Peter Jennings do with *The Century* in 1998. The 21st century would see if such an experiment would actually work.[112]

But a few true, independent book publishers struggled. None had the monies of Disney, or even that of a Houghton Mifflin, but all sought to counterpunch and fit into an industry dominated by the 11 majors and a score of media conglomerates based in Europe and the United States. The major book oligopoly was loose enough to permit medium- to small-sized book publishers to enter and to exist as niche players on the margin (measured in millions rather than billions of dollars in sales).

John Wiley & Sons Corporation offered proof that success was possible. Wiley proved professional publishing was not solely the province of the majors. For example, in 1997, Wiley purchased not only VCH Publishing, a leading German-based international scientific, technical and professional publisher, but also the Preservation Press. Wiley was not lying down to the power of a Bertelsmann AG and still sought to grow. The purchase of VCH Publishing boosted Wiley's standing in the sales of medical, technical and scientific books while also driving up international revenues, which represented nearly half of Wiley's total sales (more than a half a billion dollars per annum as the 1990s closed). But scientific, medical and technical books represented only about half the company's revenues; Wiley engaged in educational publishing as well, and even nonfiction trade publishing. In 1999, Wiley had three divisions: scientific and technical, educational and professional and trade. The company's origins go back to the beginnings of U.S. publishing when in the 19th century Charles Wiley named the company after his sons. The company published 1,500 new titles each year, and was growing. Its New York headquarters offered the corporate center, but distribution centers in Colorado, Maryland, New Jersey and Illinois gave the company true power. With Wiley InterScience as its expanding online service, Wiley offered a model of an independent book publisher surviving in an industry where a corporation had to become a media conglomerate.[113]

The mid- and late 1990s were expansionary periods for Wiley: a parade of acquisitions and joint partnerships, factoring in the publishing program of Oliver Wight, Van Nostrand Reinhold's OS/2 operating system titles and Houghton Mifflin's college engineering list, as well as the mergers noted earlier. Wiley announced a strategic alliance with America Online to deliver online *The Ernst & Young Tax Guide*. The mid-1990s saw Wiley partner with the *Adweek* Magazines Group, Forbes and Byron Preiss Visual Publications, Inc. In 1996, Wiley purchased Clinical Psychology Publishing Company, a publisher of books and journals in the fields of clinical and educational psychology; the publishing operations of Technical Insights, a provider of print and electronic newsletters in various areas of science and technology; and two food science and technology newsletters from Lyda Associates. In 1997, Wiley formed book publishing alliances with the Internet publisher, Mecklermedia, and the company embarked on this electronic publishing initiative to augment its strengths in scientific, technical, medical and professional publishing. It continued to publish its journals in print as well. Wiley acquired Peter Brinckerhoff's Mission-Based Management series in 1998, which comprised three best-selling titles for nonprofit organizations from the Colorado-based publisher, Alpine Guild. In 1999, WILEY-VCH announced an agreement to acquire the book program of the German Materials Science Society, and in collaboration with the 3,000-member society, WILEY-VCH began developing titles under a joint imprint. It launched a scientific technical membership journal in mid-1999, titled *Advanced Engineering Materials*.[114]

In May 1999, John Wiley & Sons, Inc. announced its biggest deal, signing an agreement to purchase the San Francisco-based publisher, Jossey-Bass, from Pearson PLC. The acquisition, which was subject to a governmental review, cost $82 million in cash. Like Wiley, Jossey-Bass had a strong reputation as a publisher of highly regarded professional books and journals. The acquisitions of Jossey-Bass and other higher education titles from Pearson PLC (also announced in May 1999) strengthened Wiley's market positions in core business areas. (In 1999 John Wiley & Sons acquired all but one of the approximately 55 college textbooks that the Justice Department ordered Pearson to sell before it would approve the purchase of Simon & Schuster's education division.) Jossey-Bass, founded in 1967, published books and journals for professionals and executives, primarily in the areas of business, psychology and education and health management. Jossey-Bass also added important publishing relations with the Peter F. Drucker Foundation, the Center for Creative Leadership and Booz Allen Hamilton.[115]

Wiley primed for the future. The company launched Wiley InterScience in 1997 to provide full-text Internet access to 50 of the journals, as well as searchable content listings, abstracts and Web sites. This service fully implemented by 1998, at which point full-text presentation was available for virtually all of Wiley's 400 scientific, technical, medical and professional journals. Wiley placed a strategic focus on subject areas in which it has a competitive position, including the physical and life sciences, mathematics and engineering, and accounting, with an increasing presence in business, economics, finance, computing, modern languages and psychology. This added to Wiley's strength in the professional market, offering a full range of products for accountants, architects, engineers, contractors, lawyers, psychologists and other professionals. Because a substantial portion of Wiley's business comes from international markets in addition to offices in the United States, Wiley had operations in England, Germany, Canada, Asia and Australia to serve the needs of the local markets and explore opportunities for expanding the publishing programs.[116]

Yet Wiley was nowhere close to the size of a major publisher. In 1999, John Wiley & Sons, Inc. announced that net income for the third quarter of fiscal 1999 (ending January 31, 1999) advanced 50% to $13.4 million, as compared with $8.9 million in the previous year. Net income for the first nine months of fiscal 1999 increased 47% to $33.2 million, as compared with $22.7 million in the previous year. Revenues for the quarter increased 11% to $138.0 million from $124.4 million in the previous year. For the first nine months of fiscal 1999, revenues of $383.7 million were up 9% over the previous year's $352.3 million. Still, as long as it stuck to its niche, Wiley would continue to grow and demonstrate that an independent could survive and thrive.[117]

W. W. Norton, another independent publisher, was smaller, but could be defined as purer because it was privately owned by its employees. Norton must be considered a success for simply surviving. Norton avowedly declares itself a general trade publisher of both fiction and nonfiction, as well as a publisher of educational and professional books. In the 1990s, Norton averaged some 300 new titles per annum, from imprints that included its corporate name as well as Backcountry Publishing, Countryman Publishing and Foul Play Press. And Norton kept and maintained a strong backlist, with nearly 4,000 titles in print. Norton specialized and declared no aspirations to publish children's books, religious books or genre fiction, but prided itself on history, poetry and fiction that would stand the test of time.[118]

Scholastic Corporation did aim at children, but hardly with the size of Disney. Although most famous for its children's books (such as the popular *Goosebumps* series) in the 1990s, Scholastic re-launched into the grade school curriculum market, a $2 billion field. It spent $100 million developing reading, math and science programs for children over six years, and developed a successful line of reading texts, teacher's manuals and supplementary teaching materials. Scholastic did admit that breaking in to the mathematics market was harder than it imagined and in 1997 abandoned that effort. Richard Robinson, Chief Executive Officer and son of the man who founded the publisher in 1920, expected that by 2000, Scholastic would become a force in the K–6th grade market, building up for decades of selling books to the same children for their leisure time use. However, it was struggling to reach that goal.

In 1920, M. R. "Robbie" Robinson founded Scholastic Publishing Company in his hometown of Pittsburgh. The Western Pennsylvania Scholastic, covering high school sports, debuted in October 1920. Two years later, *The Scholastic*, a national magazine with literature and social commentary for high school English and history classes, was launched. In 1926, Scholastic published *Saplings*, its first book, which was a collection of the best student writing from the winners of the Scholastic Writing Awards. By 1957, 50 paperback titles had been published. By 1999, Scholastic was one of the largest publishers and distributors of English-language children's books in the world. In 1948, Scholastic entered the school book club business with

Teen Age Book Club (TAB; co-sponsored by Pocket Books), offering up classics for 25 cents each. By 1999, Scholastic was operating the largest school book club business in the United States, with 11 clubs serving preschool through junior high school students. To service these and other operations, by 1999 Scholastic's National Distribution Center provided warehousing, packing and order fulfillment (Jefferson City, Neosho and Moberly, MO; and Des Plaines, IL).

Books have only in the last two decades become an important part of the company, not simply a sideline. In 1986, the *Magic School Bus* book series, written by Joanna Cole and illustrated by Bruce Degen, debuted with the publication of its first hardcover called *The Magic School Bus at the Waterworks*. By 1999, Scholastic's *The Magic School Bus* had 10 original, hardcover titles in print, with more than 2.4 million hardcover copies sold, and more than 43 million paper editions sold. In 1986, the *The Baby-sitters Club* book series by Ann Martin debuted, which by 1999 had 335 books published, over 172 million books in print plus a television series, home videos, a Web site and a fan club. In 1989, Scholastic established its Professional Publishing division to focus on the needs of K–8 educators and the professional development market. By 1999, the division was publishing more than 110 new titles each year, including books geared to early childhood educators and at-risk learners.

These numbers were surely impressive, but in 1992 came the *Goosebumps* series of books written by R. L. Stine. By the mid-1990s, *Goosebumps* had become the number one best-selling children's book series of all time, with over 167 titles and 215 million books in print. By 1997 the *Goosebumps* video line, distributed by Fox Home Video, won the "Best Children's Video of the Year" Award from the Video Software Dealers Association. In 1996, Scholastic built on this success and acquired Lectorum, the largest distributor of Spanish-language books to schools and libraries in the United States, and Red House Ltd., a leading United Kingdom distributor of children's books to the school and home markets. (With this acquisition, Scholastic becomes the largest children's book publisher and distributor in the United Kingdom.) Also in 1996, Scholastic acquired Trumpet Book Clubs, serving preschool through grade six, from Bantam Doubleday Dell of Bertelsmann AG.[119]

But by the late 1990s, its *Goosebumps* children's series was slowing down, and the company struggled to find a follow-up. Revenues began to fall, down from the peak of $135 million in fiscal year 1996. Scholastic's other trouble spot came from softer sales in school book clubs. Like many nervous book publishers, Scholastic saw the future as electronic and international in scope, but this would require more than simply establishing a Web site. With the majors expanding their children's offerings, Scholastic began to experience deep-pocketed international competition. A key question involves what Scholastic can do to compete into the next century.[120]

Golden Books Family Entertainment offered a case study of how a respected children's niche publisher could get into trouble. Called Western Publishing Company until May 1996, former Simon & Schuster Chief Operating Officer Richard E. Snyder (and a group of investors) took it over for $65 million, and renamed the company after its most famous product. Snyder took direct aim at children's books, and challenged not only the majors but rival Scholastic as well. With about $300 million in sales per year, by the mid-1990s Golden Books Family Entertainment was no small company, but it was tiny compared to the multibillion dollar giants like Simon & Schuster and Bertelsmann AG. Snyder sought out partners to help, and signed up Hallmark Cards, George Lucas (for a series of *Star Wars* books) and Jim Hensen Productions (for Muppets books). He purchased Broadway Video company for $91 million in 1996 to gain access to characters from Lassie to the Lone Ranger. Still, Golden Books was reporting losses; it began to restructure and cut costs, all with decreasing revenues.[121]

In its 1999 10-K filing with the Securities and Exchange Commission, Golden reported a 1998 net loss of $128.6 million, as compared to a 1997 loss of $49.7 million. Revenues fell to $193.6 million from $242.5 million in 1997. Revenues in Golden's consumer division, comprising mainly its book publishing operations, fell 12% to $150.7 million. The decline was attributed to lower electronic and education category sales, higher returns and a temporary reduction in buying by major retailers like Kmart. The decline in revenues and higher operating losses resulted in a further downsizing, reducing employees to 950 at the end of 1998 from its 1,200 in 1997. Auditors Ernst & Young noted that Golden had operating losses, working capital deficiencies and negative cash flow, and was in default for all of its debt agreements. The company was set to go into bankruptcy.[122]

But, in April 1999, Golden Books struggled to save itself by generating funds through the sale of its adult division to St. Martin's for $11 million. St. Martin's Press, a unit of Verlagsgruppe Georg von Holtzbrinck, formally acquired Golden Books Family Entertainment Inc.'s adult publishing group—which included Golden Field Guides; Whitman Coin Guides; *The Seven Habits of Highly Effective Families*, written by Stephen R. Covey; Maria Shriver's *What's Heaven?*; and *Parents* magazine's *Parents Answer Book*. St. Martin's Press had already distributed all Golden Books' adult titles. The struggling Golden Books Family Entertainment then turned to concentrate on publishing children's books. But, its first stop was to file a plan of reorganization with the U.S. Bankruptcy Court in Manhattan. Unless some miracle turnaround can be effected, it seems that the company will be acquired by one of the majors, or possibly Disney.[123]

INDEPENDENT PUBLISHERS

Many aspire to publish important and meaningful books, make a profit and stay in business for the long run. These small publishers do not want so much to challenge or become a global major, or even a division of a media conglomerate. They seek to operate independently. Ironically, the easiest way to establish a new book publisher is to be spun off by a major publisher. *Niche* was the by-word for the small publisher. All small, independent publishers cannot be listed because this sector of the industry is too mercurial. The best information in 1999 is contained in *The Rest Of Us: The First Study of America's 53,000 Independent, Smaller Book Publishers*. For this study, the Book Industry Study Group sent a one-page questionnaire to the 53,479 publishing firms in the R. R. Booker *Books in Print* database in 1997. No responses from the large trade houses were included in the survey. Respondents ranged from brand new companies that have not yet released their first titles, to companies that have been in business more than half a century. Similarly, respondents ranged the sales spectrum from under $100,000 to $10 million or more in annual revenues.

The survey found that modern technology had provided small publishers with the opportunity to hold costs down with modest initial print runs. The most popular round numbers for first printings include 2,500, 3,000, and 5,000. Figures for back-list as a percentage of total titles published indicated that smaller and independent publishers tend to keep their books in print. On the average, publishers in the survey that have been in business for from 6 to 15 years were still selling more than three quarters of all the titles they have ever published. Publishers who had been in business for from 16 to 30 years reported that more than half the titles they had released were still in print and actively selling. Independent publishers in the survey were evenly divided between those who figured they had been negatively affected by superstores and those who reasoned the effect had been positive. Echoing this split, and incidentally underlining the complexity of the book business, several respondents checked both "positively" and "negatively." There was no way to survey all these small publishers, but surely opportunities remained for other publishers.

Indeed, the majors did not dominate in more narrow categories, and literally left the market open to independents—for the profit making and nonprofit publishing houses, often in surprising numbers. The best example is gardening, with some 100 presses claiming interest in this subject. These presses ranged from associations with gardening interest (e.g., American Association of Nurseyman and American Hibiscus Society) to major presses (e.g., Reader's Digest and Pearson PLC's Penguin imprint). Gardening in the 1990s represented a typical niche of passion. And so every Spring, Web sellers, superstores and independent booksellers set up places devoted to the subject of gardening, tailoring them to a specific region and to certain interests, with the hottest best-selling titles the most localized. The future for publishing and selling books on gardening looked bright with the aging of the Baby Boomers.[124]

Thus, with the rise of the personal computer and desk top publishing, "suddenly" small niche publishers seemed to spring up all across the United States. The history of independent publishing offers a fascinating examination of seeking a voice while still making money, all in an industry dominated by major houses. Literally thousands of minor companies and independent aspirants took hold, all as outgrowths of the turbulent 1960s, as independent-minded people sought to work outside the system and give voice to writers of fiction and nonfiction alike. Hundreds of little but thriving book publishers emerged. Look back to May 1968, when what became the Committee of Small Magazine Editors and Publishers, met at the University of California-Berkeley and by the end of that year had more than 100 members. These were small presses publishing small magazines, and then issuing books, one or two per year, from all corners of the United States.[125]

By the 1990s, there was no doubt that a small company could produce a high quality book. The problems lay in getting it distributed and sold. In 1965, the first annual *International Directory of Little Magazines and Small Presses* listed some 250 publishers. By the late 1990s, there were some 50,000 presses. Many published a single book per year; fewer, but hundreds literally, published dozens of titles per annum. *The Writer's Market Guide* listed these titles from book publishers that started with A&B Publishers Group of Brooklyn, New York (which published some dozen titles per year) and ended its alphabetic list with Zebra Books (which published more than 100 titles per annum of romance fiction for women) and Zoland Books (which published a dozen titles per annum on biography and art). *The Publishers Directory* used more than 1,000 reference pages to list book publishers, representing more than 1,500 pages of listings from A to Z—from A/A Minnesota, based in Minneapolis, Minnesota, which published works on the architecture of the state as well as the bimonthly magazine, *Architecture Minnesota*; to ZyLab Corporation, of Buffalo Grove, Illinois, which published works on data processing software.[126]

   Publishers Weekly sought to identify a score that exemplified the fastest growing and most promising of the 1990s. General Publishing Group of Santa Monica, California, in 1993, for example, had sales under $1 million; by the end of the century, sales topped $10 million. Growth was led by two show business-related titles: *Frank Sinatra: An America Legend* and *General Hospital*, both of which sold more than 120,000 copies. New World Library of San Rafael, California—based on the success of Deepak Chopra's *The Seven Spiritual Laws of Success*, both in paper and audio versions; *No Greater Love* by Mother Teresa; and New World's first work of fiction, *Papa's Angels: A Christmas Story* by Collin Wilcox Paxton—was also selling more than $10 million per year. Then, there was a travel book company, based in Manteo, North Carolina, called the Insider's Guide, Inc. Founded in 1982, this company published regional guidebooks written by local authors and updated annually. With two year growth of 208%, the company in 1997 expanded to an Internet site. It had sales of $1.8 million in 1995 based on 28 new titles that year. Exley Giftbooks, based in New York City, grew over two years at the rate of 170% for a parent company based in the United Kingdom. First opened in 1992, Exley Giftbooks deals in gift books not only through nonstores but also stationary stores and other retail gift selling chains to generate sales of about $3 million per annum. At about the same size and with about the same growth rate was Hoovers, Inc., formerly known as Reference Press and based in Austin, Texas, which provided business information. Wisdom Publications of Boston, Massachusetts, founded in 1989, sold well in excess of $1 million worth of books from 16 new titles in the mid-1990s. Wisdom concentrated on translations of teachings and commentaries on Buddhist masters, and original works by the world's leading Buddhist scholars. Taylor Publishing Company of Dallas, Texas, traced its growth to the success of its Positively for Kids series that was launched in the Spring 1995. The autobiographical children's book *Things Change* by Troy Aikman, the Dallas Cowboys' quarterback, was joined by *Count Me In* by Cal Ripken, Jr., the record-setting infielder for the Baltimore Orioles baseball team. Taylor also published in the growing niches of gardening and health.

   There were many others cited by *Publishers Week*—from cookbook companies to those specialized in fly fishing, bar tending, religion and New Age books. There seems nothing common save that each represents a niche too small for a major house but just right for a company generating sales between $1 and $10 million per annum. Niche-minded entrepreneurs needed to take a big risk, and expect returns far below what profit maximizing majors would require. This testifies to the health and competitiveness of a mass media industry all too often characterized by its major players, not by its diversity and ease of entry.[127]

Nonprofit Book Publishing

All of the aforementioned examples, and more, consist of profit-seeking operations with owners and share holders interested in growth and dividends. Yet the category of independent publishers is also highly populated by nonprofits, or book publishers seeking to achieve some other goal rather than making maximum profits pure and simple. Whereas the publicity and complaints surround the commercial presses that are famous and profit driven, there has always existed a strong nonprofit sector in book publishing. Nonprofit publishers are often affiliated with some large nonprofit institution, be it a museum, a religious organization, an educational institutions, or a hobby organization. In many ways, university presses comprise the most active, visible and representative component of this nonprofit sector.

A typical example is the University of Chicago Press. Since its creation in 1891, the University of Chicago Press, part of the important private university based in its namesake city, originally published only the work of its faculty. In 1905, this policy was reversed and it began to publish work by other authors. A university board must pass on all publications and, in the 1990s, the press issued about 250 works per year as well as scholarly journals. In 1993, the backlist, the heart of any university press, included more than 4,000 titles. The press does not have an endowment, but gains needed support as part of the overall University of Chicago budget. Some of its titles are bestsellers in the university press sense of the word; for example, the *Chicago Manual of Style*, first issued in 1906, sells about 20,000 copies per year. By the end the 1990s, the University of Chicago Press was publishing books in many categories.

The Oxford University Press was founded in the United Kingdom in 1478, making it the oldest publishing establishment in the English-speaking world. In the 1850s, the press sent sales representatives to the United States to sell Bibles, which remain one of the bestsellers. In 1895, the Oxford University Press opened a branch office in New York City, but it was not until the dark days of the Great Depression that the press initiated nonreligious book publishing, and not until 1950 was that separate branch actually incorporated in the United States. Since 1950, the New York City branch has been financially self-sufficient, with all its stock held by its British parent. Its catalog is an amalgamation of both American and British titles, making the Oxford University Press one of the leading importers of books into the United States. As a university press, Oxford has the primary goal of publishing books of the highest scholarly standards, but it also seeks out more widely salable trade hardcover and paperbacks to balance the losses from the more specialized and limited selling scholarly works. Its editorial functions—divided into seven divisions: bibles, economics and business, humanities, the social sciences, medicine and the sciences, music and journals—create about 1,500 new titles per annum and add to a backlist of more than 12,000 titles.[128]

Chicago and Oxford describe the leading, but also typical, university presses. Table 2.17 and Table 2.18 provide lists of the numerous others divided by those

TABLE 2.17
Public University Presses

Nearly every state university of major rank, with aspirations as a research center has such a press.

Indiana University Press, Bloomington, IN
Iowa State University Press, Ames, IA
Louisiana State University Press, Baton Rouge, LA
Oregon State University Press, Corvallis, OR
Pennsylvania State University Press, University Park, PA
Rutgers University Press, New Brunswick, NJ
Temple University Press, Philadelphia, PA
University of Alabama Press, Tuscaloosa, AL
University of Arizona Press, Tucson, AZ
University of Georgia Press, Athens, GA
University of Illinois Press, Urbana, IL
University of Massachusetts Press, Amherst, MA
University of Michigan Press, Ann Arbor, MI
University of Minnesota Press, Minneapolis, MN
University of Missouri Press, Columbia, MO
University of Nebraska Press, Lincoln, NE
University of New Mexico Press, Albuquerque, NM
University of North Carolina Press, Chapel Hill, NC
University of Oklahoma Press, Norman, OK
University of South Carolina Press, Columbia, SC
University of Texas Press, Austin, TX
University of Washington Press, Seattle, WA
University of Wisconsin Press, Madison, WI
University Press of Florida, Gainesville, FL
University Press of Kansas, Lawrence, KS
University Press of Mississippi, Jackson, MI
University Press of New England, Hanover, NH
University Press of Virginia, Charlottesville, VA

sponsored by tax payers through state-sponsored land grant universities in the United States, and those, like Chicago, sponsored by private universities. These lists are hardly comprehensive and do not include smaller university presses that publish a few books a year (e.g., Baylor University Press). But Tables 2.17 and 2.18 do give a sense of the scope and variety of presses not aimed at making profits but at extending the knowledge and research created at leading U.S. research universities.

Not all university presses are well funded. Consider the case of New York University Press. Squeezed by a declining library market and fiscally prudent administrators, New York University Press, like many other academic publishers, searched for ways to publish serious books while not requiring subsidies from its sponsoring institution. By the late 1990s, its lifeblood library sales were contracting. At the same time, universities reduced subsidies to inkind services such as telephones, e-mail accounts and technical support. In 1999 NYU Press had annual sales of about $6 million, a full-time staff of 18, plus 15 student interns. The press published some 150 books a year in 12 areas that ranged from traditional categories like history to more fashionable academic disciplines like cultural studies. The press also handled distribution for a "selective" group of publishers, including the Monthly Review Press, Berg Publishers, Rivers Oram/Poandor

TABLE 2.18
Private University Presses

Like state universities important private universities publish academic tomes (and more and more popular books, so-called middle list titles) as well.

Columbia University Press, New York, NY
Cornell University Press, Ithaca, NY
Duke University Press, Durham, NC
Harvard Business School Publishing, Cambridge, MA
Harvard University Press, Cambridge, MA
Johns Hopkins University Press, Baltimore, MD
MIT Press, Cambridge, MA
New York University Press, New York, NY
Princeton University Press, Princeton, NJ
Stanford University Press, Stanford, CA
Syracuse University Press, Syracuse, NY
University of Notre Dame Press, South Bend, IN
University of Pennsylvania Press, Philadelphia, PA
Yale University Press, New Haven, CT

NOTE: There are also the private Washington, DC-based think tanks. These are nonprofit and organized like universities as educational aspirants.

Brookings Institution Press
The Urban Institute Press
The American Enterprise Institute co-publishs with the MIT Press.
The Smithsonian Institution Press

and Lawrence & Wishart. It experienced only an occasional hit, such as it did in the late 1990s with *Kosovo: A Short History* by Noel Malcolm, which sold 15,000 copies during the period of the conflict in the Balkans. Because of unexpected timeliness, paperback rights sold to major HarperCollins for six figures. How could NYU Press best "compete" with large, well-funded presses (like those at Chicago, Oxford, Cambridge and Princeton) that were in the process of becoming "digital elites" actively involved in the new media, without the necessary resources?[129]

Yet university-related presses hardly represented the only nonprofit book publishers. Also note that most religious publishers sought to provide a service for certain religious communities, and were most often nonprofit. In 1999, scores of small houses such as the American Bible Society existed, but the leading religious publisher in the United States was Thomas-Nelson, Inc. of Nashville, Tennessee (one of the world's largest sellers of Christian Bibles). The American Bible Society was far more typical. Based in New York City, with a distribution center across the Hudson river in Wayne, New Jersey, the American Bible Society also published the Christian Bible in many forms (e.g., braille, on compact discs and on audio cassettes). The Bible, and related Christian texts, amounted to nearly 100 titles published each year, and nearly 8,000 titles in print in 1999.

Yet religious publishing in the United States has long been dominated by the profit-seeking Thomas-Nelson, Inc., with yearly sales of about $150 million and profits of about $10 million per annum. Thomas-Nelson published not only Christian Bibles, but also serious works about life, living, meaning and values. In 1997,

Thomas-Nelson started a children's division, and sold $10 million in the first year. In the future, Thomas-Nelson planned a series of books aimed at the African American market, more self-help titles and books on marriage and family from a Christian point of view.[130]

Religious publishing represents a mixture of profit and nonprofit companies. Consider the niche of children's publishing and the Children's Book Press with its overt agenda. Children's Book Press sought not to make profits per se, but to expand book publishing for small children from what its owners considered white bread "Dick and Jane" titles to books that included children named Aekyung, Nanabosho and Rashawn. Based in San Francisco, far away from Manhattan's publishing center and Scholastic and Golden Books, Children's Book Press was begun by Hariett Rohmer in her home in 1975. Two decades later, her enterprise tallied nearly $2 million in annual sales—with bestsellers (here judged to be more than 100,000 copies) such as *In My Family* by Carmen Lomas Garza, a bilingual picture book depicting the author's childhood growing up as a Mexican-American in Anglo-Texas.[131]

Indeed, those dissatisfied with what the majors published constitute the core of entrants to independent publishing. Although nonprofit educators and religious organizations make up the bulk of these entrants, the range of those dissatisfied has been and will continue to be vast and energetic. Thus, both profit-seeking and nonprofit-oriented entrants are expected. The majors will surely continue to dominate, but unlike the movie and music industry, they will rarely dissuade an entrant. This wide-ranging, diverse sector of the book publishing industry, never summing to vast dollar amounts of sales, accounts for thousands of small players.

BOOKSELLERS

The retail end of book publishing was changing in fascinating ways during the 1990s. As the decade began, most pundits would have predicted that the sales in bookstores (seen in Table 2.19) would surely have stagnated. But, as indicated in Table 2.1, sales took off. And, with the Internet making virtual book shopping possible, book sales continued to rise. Book buying was a "hot" activity in the 1990s, led by the building and opening of superstores like Borders and Barnes & Noble across the United States. Only after that "revolution" was accomplished, did sales through the Web, led by Amazon.com, begin its impact. And with no vertical integration, the book-selling sector is analyzed separately next.[132]

Borders, Barnes & Noble, and Books-A-Million stocked thousands of titles; independent bookstores remained much smaller. A generation ago, there were five times as many independent bookstores as chain stores, and the chains offered only slightly more titles per store than independent rivals. By the mid-1990s, Borders, Barnes & Noble, Crown and Books-A-Million were selling half of all books sold. The growth of the chains in the 1990s was nothing short of remarkable. As seen in Tables 2.20 and Table 2.21, there were less than 100 of these vast 100,000-title retailers as the 1990s began; by the mid-1990s, the total in operation neared 800 and was climbing rapidly. Their sales exceeded $3 billion and were expanding as well.[133]

TABLE 2.19
U.S. Bookstore Sales, 1990–1996 (in millions)

	Total
1990	$ 7,343
1991	7,731
1992	8,329
1993	9,042
1994	9,961
1995	10,264
1996	11,547

Source: *Publishers Weekly*, July 1997, special issue, p. 100.

TABLE 2.20
Growth of Superstores, 1991–1998 (in millions)

	Stores
1992	210
1994	469
1996	788
1998	1,056

Sources: *Publishers Weekly*, July 1997, special issue, p. 100; "Borders Group Profits Up 14% to $92 Million," *Publishers Weekly*, July 15, 1999, p. 10; "Sales Rose 8% at Top Chains in Fiscal '99, to $6.1 Billion," *Publishers Weekly*, May 3, 1999, p. 10.

TABLE 2.21
Growth of Four Largest Bookstore Chains, 1991–1999 (in millions)

Chain	1999 Revenues (Stores)	1991 Revenues (Stores)
Barnes & Noble	$3,006	$1,619
	1049	1343
Borders Group	$2,595	$1,139
	1420	1268
Crown Books	$ 225	$ 232
	79	257
Books-A-Million	$ 348	$ 73
	179	101

Sources: *Publishers Weekly*, July 1997, special issue, p. 100; "Borders Focuses on Stores to Drive Results in Fiscal '00," *Publishers Weekly*, April 19, 1999, p. 16; "Sales Rose 8% at Top Chains in Fiscal '99, to $6.1 Billion," *Publishers Weekly*, May 3, 1999, p. 10.

Barnes and Noble, Borders and Books-A-Million emerged as key retailers in their communities. They constantly sponsored promotions to lure in new customers (i.e., music recitals, art exhibits, teach-ins about the stock market, poetry readings, book discussion groups and signings by celebrity and relatively unknown authors). Publishers worked with radio and television to promote books sold by the superstores. Radio did best from stations affiliated with National Public Radio and television offered venues from the sweeping power of 60 *Minutes* and the *Today* show to C-SPAN's *Booknotes*, A&E's tie-ins with its *Biography* series, and the suggested readings issued by talk show hostess Oprah Winfrey. Indeed, when Oprah Winfrey's personal cook appeared on the talk show to promote her book, *In the Kitchen with Rosie*, this up-to-then modest seller shot to the top of the bestseller lists. Customers by the thousands descended on their local Barnes and Noble, Borders or Books-A-Million branch. This "Big Three" are discussed next.[134]

Barnes & Noble, Inc. emerged during the 1970s as a scrappy New York City–based chain—in business since the turn into the 20th century—and had but a single store as late as 1971. From that modest base, Barnes & Noble expanded, buying up mall chains such as B. Dalton and Doubleday and superstore pretender Bookstop of Austin, Texas. It even took over the fabled Harvard Co-op. In the mid-1990s, Barnes & Noble was opening about 50 superstores per annum, closing B. Dalton stores at a similar rate. By mid-1997, Barnes & Noble had 439 superstores, aiming for 500 before the turn of the century. For the fiscal year ending January 31, 1997, it reported net income of more than $50 million on sales of $2.5 billion. By 1999, superstore sales accounted for 82% of total revenues. In April 1998, Barnes & Noble officially became a Fortune 500 company—ranking 496th in revenues in the 1998 listing. In February 1999, Barnes & Noble, Inc. reported that retail sales for the fiscal year ending January 30, 1999, had reached $3.0 billion, an increase of 8.0% over fiscal 1998. Barnes & Noble superstore sales rose 12.0% to $2.5 billion, and contributed 84% of total retail sales in 1998.[135]

Leonard Riggio built the modern Barnes & Noble. When Riggio was a night student at New York University (NYU), he found the classes in business policy and management so dull that he dropped out in 1965. He pushed technological advances, reducing bookselling to bits and bytes and two-day delivery. At age 58 in 1999, with salt-and-pepper hair and Brooklyn still in his voice, Riggio was largely co-responsible (with the Borders brothers) for the book industry's metamorphosis during the 1990s—that is, the advent of the superstore. The *New York Times* properly noted that in the 1990s the book superstore came to dominate the literary landscape with airy temples of titles, comfortable chairs and the fragrance of espresso.

But all of Barnes & Noble's transformation began in the 1960s when, as a 24-year-old dropout, Riggio invested $5,000 of borrowed money in a bookstore called Student Book Exchange near the NYU campus. Six years later, in 1971, he bought Barnes & Noble, then a floundering bookstore in Manhattan's Flatiron district. Later Riggio expanded into popular books, buying the B. Dalton mall store chain in 1986. By 1999, his more than 520 superstores, plus 500 B. Dalton mall stores are so much a part of the landscape, and seen as so threatening by independent booksellers, that the conflict provided the storyline for the 1998 movie *You've Got Mail.*

In 1998, Riggio began to navigate his New York-based company through another metamorphosis—online bookselling. Barnesandnoble.com, Amazon.com and the Internet seemed to be the wave of bookselling's future. With the book industry's future in flux, Riggio is hedging his bets, anticipating that customers will feel equally comfortable lingering in Barnes & Noble superstores to scan the latest hardcovers, or shopping for exotic titles online or downloading a bestseller from a home computer into a 22-ounce electronic reader. He is building on others' early work, in this case Amazon's, much as he did before when he followed Borders Group with a cafe or expanded on Bookstop's development of the superstores.

Riggio is trying to lead his company on both sides of the divide, steadily building new superstores into a chain expected in 1999 to eventually number 1,000 (although the expansion has slowed to about 50 in 1999 from about 90 in 1998), while investing heavily in the Internet. Riggio was far behind as 1999 started, with Barnes & Noble online having but one ninth of rival Amazon's sales. Will Riggio's electronic offspring only speed the process, cannibalizing sales from his bricks-and-mortar outlets—a scenario that could place some of his superstores in the same jeopardy as the independent bookstores forced to close when they could no longer compete? Indeed, by offering discounts of up to 40% on hardcover books and 20% on paperbacks, barnesandnoble.com is already undercutting the superstores, although shipping and handling fees narrow the price difference.[136]

Yet, in the short run, Barnes & Noble's mid-1990s balance sheets recorded losses, based on its rapid expansion and opening new superstores. Closing B. Dalton stores did not help either. During late 1996 and early 1997, Barnes & Noble spent more than $172 million to make the final step in the transformation from a mall-based bookseller to a chain of superstores. Could it do the same thing as Barnes & Noble moved online?[137]

Moreover, expansion did not come without controversy. For example, in November 1997, Barnes & Noble was indicted on obscenity charges for selling three books that feature photographs of nude children by photographers Jock Sturges and David Hamilton. Although these works received some critical praise, a Tennessee county grand jury claimed they violated state obscenity laws by making them too accessible to minors. The grand jury noted under Tennessee law that published materials placed in racks above the reach of children or with wrapping that covered all questionable images was exempt from the law; their indictment noted that parents had complained and accused Barnes & Noble of making *The Last Day of Summer* and *Radiant Identities* by Sturges and *The Age of Innocence* by Hamilton too easily available. More seriously was the October 1997 deal linking Barnes & Noble to the New York Times Company and its fabled bestseller lists. Independent bookstores complained and stopped cooperating with the *New York Times* in reporting their sales. A war for the list ensued as 1997 came to a close.[138]

But, in October 1998, Riggio placed his bets as Barnes & Noble and Bertelsmann AG announced a joint venture for online bookselling in the United States—barnesandnoble.com. Under the agreement, Bertelsmann supplied $200 million for a 50% stake in the barnesandnoble.com joint venture. Each party will also contribute $100 million to the capital of the joint venture. Bertelsmann AG also contributed unspecified resources from its previously announced BooksOnline service. Combining Bertelsmann AG's resources with the strength of Barnes & Noble should accelerate its growth and development, but it still had a long way to catch Amazon.com. Through barnesandnoble.com and BooksOnline in Europe, owned by Bertelsmann AG, it accumulated vertical power to make more titles available and more easily accessible for millions of readers around the world. This would be an important business experiment to watch into 2000. But, as of 1999, all online booksellers were losing money.[139]

Borders Books & Music Group was the other pioneer in superstore bookselling. And it sold as many books as Barnes & Noble. Borders, based in Ann Arbor, Michigan, started to expand in the early 1990s. It consisted of a single campus bookstore in the heart of the University of Michigan, Ann Arbor, campus. Kmart bought in and then in 1995 sold it to the public. In September 1996, Borders opened a 38,000 square bibliophile and audiophile mall in Manhattan, in the very heart of Barnes & Noble's home territory. The average Borders store contained more than 100,000 titles plus more than 50,000 music selections. And then there were its coffee bars and couches. Borders pioneered book buying as fun.[140]

Borders policy required clerks to take written examinations to prove their worthiness. The company began in Ann Arbor, where in 1971 Tom and Louis Borders opened their used bookstore near the Michigan campus. They courted the countercultural and hired only staff who knew and loved books. But what really gave the company its edge was its computer inventory system that tracked each book electronically from order to sale. According to company lore, Louis Borders, former MIT mathematics whiz kid, modified a computer program he had developed to predict horse race winners to track book inventory and make sure the titles people wanted were always on the shelves. In 1992, the brothers cashed in and sold out to massive retailer and Waldenbooks owner Kmart. Kmart's corporate culture and Borders laid back intellectual operation clashed; three years later, Borders went public.[141]

But with growth has come controversy, not in terms of obscenity or corporate collusion (as is the case with Barnes & Noble), but unionization demands by employees who were no longer simply college students looking for some part-time work. After a year of negotiations, in October 1996, the Chicago Borders Books & Music store on Clarke Street in Chicago became the first store in the chain to have a union-negotiated contract after a vote of 28 for and 17 against. Borders' employees became members of the United Food and Commercial Workers Union local 881, and their two-year contract set in place in October 1997 called for a union shop, representing approximately 45 workers, and annual union dues of $204. Salaries would start at $6.50 a hour, with a 25-cent raise after six months, and another 25-cent raise after a year on the job. The standard work week was set at 37 hours, and the contract provided for a formal grievance procedure and a medical plan. In 1997, Borders workers organized in Bryn Mawr, Pennsylvania, and this became one of the rare instances of new unionization in the 1990s.[142]

During Spring 1999, Borders announced that its superstore sales increased 22.2% over the same quarter in 1998 to $409.4 million. On a comparable store basis, sales increased 4.0%, representing a significant turnaround from the prior quarter. During the quarter, 12 stores opened, bringing the total to 262 versus 206 in 1998. Its Web site, Borders.com (which began operation in mid-1998), increased sales 23.1% sequentially from the fourth quarter, totaling $3.2 million in the first quarter. Positive results from cross-promotions with the stores contributed to this increase. Waldenbooks sales declined 2.7% over the same quarter in 1998 to $186.5 million. On a comparable store basis, Walden sales declined 2.3%.

Consolidated sales were $618.7 million, an increase of 13.5% over the same quarter in 1998. Still, the Borders Group may not have been as flashy as Barnes & Noble or Amazon.com, but in 1998 it was a leading global retailer of books, music, video and other information and entertainment items with stores in the United States, United Kingdom, Australia and Singapore. Indeed, with cafe operations in nearly all of its stores, Borders represented one of the largest specialty coffee retailers in the United States.[143]

In late April 1999, the uncertain future many saw for Borders hit its executive suite with the resignation of CEO Philip Pfeffer after just six months. Borders took a one-time charge of about $3 million to pay for Peffer's "Golden Parachute." Pfeffer, at age 54, was a publishing veteran who was previously at Random House. Pfeffer also previously served as CEO of book and media wholesaler Ingram Distribution Group. When he joined Borders in November 1998, he promised to bring it up to speed with the aggressive expansion of industry leader Barnes & Noble and Internet powerhouse Amazon.com. Although he inherited the nation's most profitable bookseller, with profit twice the size of Barnes & Noble, he was still criticized for being slower to climb on the Web bandwagon. Instead, under Pfeffer, Borders focused on repainting superstores rather than the dramatic moves industry observers expected. So even as Pfeffer exited, Borders.com was tallying up one hundredth of the sales of Amazon.[144]

Borders seemed to have its peak as the Internet was drawing away customers. Whereas in 1999 it remained what the *Wall Street Journal* called "America's most profitable book seller," Amazon.com was still not making any money at all, and its profits for 1998 measured twice that of Barnes & Noble. After being spun off by Kmart in the mid-1990s, its annual 20% increases in profits seemed like a glory-filled past but not a glory-filled future. Borders let Amazon get a three-year head start into Internet selling, and the superstore fad seemed to have run its course. The trend was not upward—even with annual sales in 1998 in excess of $3 billion. The problem was that it hit its peak; Amazon.com was convincing customers to buy books online. And, Amazon's stock was worth $6.3 billion and Borders was worth about half that amount. The future seemed to be on the Web—at least that is what Wall Street figured in 1999.[145]

Books-A-Million, Inc., based in Birmingham, Alabama, and controlled by the Anderson family, trailed with but 148 stores in 17 states in 1997. In 1998, it was selling less than 2% of all books, one sixth of the total of Borders and of Barnes & Noble. But the regionally focused Books-A-Million was moving in the superstore direction, and by 1999 its superstores were producing the bulk of company revenues, far more than its smaller Bookland mall shops. Books-A-Million bet, like Borders and Barnes & Noble, that 20,000 or more square foot sales space could and should be made fun. "We have a saying at Books-A-Million that there's no whispering allowed," said Clyde Anderson, the company's president and CEO in 1997. "We want people to feel free to enjoy themselves. We're not just selling books, we're selling fun and entertainment. Our stores exhibit a real sense of theater and our associates are really at the heart of that feeling." Yet revenues at Books-A-Million, even with its increase of 7.1% in the fiscal year ending January 30, 1999 were but $347.9

million, or about one ninth of Borders' or Barnes & Noble's revenues. Books-A-Million was expanding slowly—to 175 superstores as 1998 ended. The company seemed to be at a turning point as it entered 1999.[146]

A book buying revolution was taking place. In toto, as 1998 ended, more than half of all book sales in the United States came through these chain superstores. The average paperback purchase of a mystery (fiction outsold nonfiction, with mystery and suspense the favorite national category) in the far West or Northeast was a women in a Barnes & Noble or Borders. Book shopping in the 1990s had become a "hip thing to do on Friday or Saturday night." People found the proper section, slipped into a cozy chair and waited for new people to meet with common interests. Once a meeting took place, then it was easy to slip over to the cappuccino bar and talk. Moms, Dads, grandparents and rebels all felt comfortable in a Borders, along with scheduled speakers, storytellers, musicians and the rest of the reading public. These bookstore chains culled the elements of the past—the library, the coffee shop and the church meeting room— and became the social place to see and be seen in the 1990s.[147]

In turn, this billion dollar segment of book retailing grew more influential. Book publishers regularly consulted representatives from Barnes & Noble and Borders for guidance about jacket covers, titles and expected customer demand. They recognized a common interest as bilateral oligopolists. There were a dominant set of major publishers and a dominant set of booksellers, and both could cooperate. This new era of book publishing and selling was a far cry from the intellectual seat-of-the-pants editorial decisions of the past. Before, publisher's representatives leisurely toured independent stores; by 1998, computers linked the majors and the superstores. No wonder that when editors at Random House could not settle on a dust jacket for Mario Puzo's *The Last Don*, they called their counterparts at Barnes & Noble for suggestions. But it is not only the major houses. More small publishers will make the trip to the Ann Arbor, Michigan, headquarters of Borders to see if they can convince the corporate buyer to stock one of their titles.[148]

Crown Books proved not all could make the superstore strategy work. Crown came to superstores late because it began in 1977 as a discounter. Based on an idea founder Robert Haft hatched for a college term paper, and operating out of Landover, Maryland, in 1996 Crown crested selling about $300 million in books and earned $4 million. With some 168 stores across the United States, by 1999 Crown was asking for relief from its creditors, principally mall owners and book publishers. Discounting has not worked in the face of the Borders' amenities and the access and ease of the Internet. Yet, for Crown, the analysis is far simpler; in city after city, Borders and Barnes & Noble pushed into Crown's market share and, through the mid-1990s, sales growth stalled and profits were elusive. The Crown Books widely advertised slogan, "You'll Never Pay Full Price Again," seemed less important than the competition's far greater selection and ambiance. With the growth era of the 1980s long behind Crown, the company attempted to restructure and close smaller 3,000 square foot stores, open Super Crown stores and close the outlets that made the company money a decade earlier. In 1997, Super Crown Warehouse stores with 15,000 square feet of retail space, still only half the size of a typical Borders or Barnes & Noble, were opened. Crown never caught up. In 1998 it filed for bankruptcy relief.

Its share of national sales fell below 2%. Executives placed the company up for sale and there was a real possibility that it would simply close up shop before a buyer could be found. The great experiment of discounting books, which looked promising in the 1980s, had proven an utter failure in the 1990s.[149]

Independent Booksellers

The superstores of the 1990s signaled an end of an era of independent bookstores. The late 1990s brought regular closings—at the rate of one per week. In 1992, independent bookstores had one quarter of the share of all adult trade books sold; by 1996 it was falling to one sixth; by the end of the 1990s, it was lower. For example, in 1997, so few independent bookstores remained in the Houston, Texas, area that their local trade group was disbanded. Like independent book publishers, independent booksellers became niche players, increasingly specializing in such areas as travel books or mystery books—some niche where they could carry even more stock than the Borders or Barnes & Noble. Long considered a leisurely literary-like profession, bookselling in the 1990s became a competitive enterprise. Newspaper headlines constantly told of independent bookstores being pushed out of business by the opening of a superstore down the block. By 1996, chains accounted for more than 271 million books sold as compared to 196 million sold by independents.[150]

The closing of long cherished independent bookshops became a national story in 1997 as New York City and Washington, DC stores closed, and the *New York Times* and the *Washington Post* began to report their stories. For example, in May 1997, Books & Company on Madison Avenue at 74th Street shuddered at the reason given in the *Times* as "pure economics"—costs of leasing space were rising and sales were falling. Across Manhattan Island on the Upper West Side three independent bookstores closed because they could not compete with a nearby four-year-old Barnes & Noble superstore. In Washington, DC, for more than four decades, Sidney Kramer Books had provided a place where the hard to locate public policy tract or obscure foreign policy book could easily be secured. In 1996, a Borders superstore opened one block away. Sidney Kramer Books had long survived a nearby B. Dalton, but the vast size, section and ambiance of Borders meant a $1 million loss in sales in a single year after its opening.[151]

This headline was repeated across the United States in the late 1990s. Yet there was life after the superstore. Christian bookstores, for example, added more diverse products—and even espresso bars—and prospered as niche players. One Olathe, Kansas, Christian bookstore patron summed up the new type of religious outlet: "It's sort of like a Christian Borders." These Christian super bookstores sold books, as well as music, videos, clothing, board games and limited edition art prints. Christian bookstores had existed for decades, usually as small mom-and-pop enterprises geared to providing the latest Bible commentary. But, as evangelical Protestants grew in numbers and wealth, and small store owners felt the wrath of a new local superstore, some expanded and prospered. In 1996, the Christian Booksellers Association numbered 4,000 stores, and its surveys indicated the typical store was getting bigger. The survey also indicated the typical store is more than likely to stay open in the evenings, have a well-lighted parking lot and to boast of its clean restrooms with baby changing tables and free diapers.[152]

Niche selling seemed to be growing in all forms. Consider those specializing in books for and about African Americans. In 1999 in nearly every large U.S. city, such a store existed: Afrocentric Books of Chicago; Black Images Book Bazaar of Dallas, Texas; Black Books Plus of New York City; Esowan Books of Los Angeles; Hue-Man Experience of Denver; and the Apple Book Center of Detroit. The Phenix Information Center of San Bernardino, California, was able to attract 10,000 people to a minor league baseball stadium for the appearance of Coretta Scott King in promotion of her newest book. Faron and Joann Roberts opened the Phenix for a mere $5,000 in a community of 174,000 people, only 17% of whom were African American, and faced off against two nearby superstores. Still, the Phenix was able to sell more than a quarter of a million dollars of books a year.[153]

Indeed there are survival stories in many cities. Powell's City of Books, located on the fringe of downtown Portland, Oregon, filled a large city block and offered more than 500,000 new and used books. It was a space that seemed more appropriate for a going-out-of-business sale for a furniture store (complete with cement floors and crude wooden shelves). In the early 1970s, there was but a single room of books for sale; in the late 1990s, there were seven rooms of books on 10-foot-high shelves and patrons use a map to navigate. Powell's sought to provide a community for booklovers and writers—as did Denver, Colorado's Tattered Cover bookstore—and offered a model of how to compete and localize a vast bookstore.

Nonbookstore Bookstores

A trend that few have noticed outside the book industry is the rising share of book purchases in nonbookstore bookstores like Wal-Mart or Kmart. Consider the case of the Best Buy discount chain (a major retailer of music, home videos, computer hardware and durable appliances), which in 1997 began selling books in 280 stores in 32 states. With annual sales of $8 billion, Best Buy knew how "to move product." Tests in stores in California, Minnesota and Florida found very favorable results, based on a synergy of sales of other entertainment and information items. Best Buy stores, which range from 30,000 to 58,000 square feet in space, carried 2,000 titles. These included bestsellers, romance novels and children's books, which are discounted from 45% for bestsellers down to 25% for children's books.[154]

Three successful models inspired Best Buy. First, price clubs emerged as a powerful force in book sales in the 1990s. These clubs, led by Wal-Mart's Sam's Club, generally charged a membership fee (usually about $25) so "members" could buy in bulk. In the case of books, the club purchased a sizable order of a few book titles—at a steep discount directly from the publisher—and then sold them to "members" at pennies above wholesale cost. Some independent bookstore owners complained they could purchase books in quantity from these clubs at a lower price than directly from the publisher. Price clubs rarely ventured from pre-sold celebrity volumes or those on the bestseller lists, but executives at Borders and Barnes & Noble did notice their impact on sales.[155]

The second model came from Target stores, a 35-year-old middle-class discounter division of the Minneapolis-based Dayton Hudson Corporation department store chain, which sold nearly $20 billion of merchandise from hundreds of U.S. stores. Target focused on the suburbs of large and middle-sized cities. The typical 125,000-square-foot Target store placed books near the electronics section. Two main book buyers and their staff made all selections for all stores, concentrating on adult trade titles, mass market paperbacks, children's books, romance novels, westerns, cookbooks, career guides and a smattering of regional guides. Target identified its typical customer as a female college graduate seeking an occasional book. In toto, in 1999, Target's "occasional" buyer mounted up millions of dollars of book sales, and made Target one of the most important and fastest growing booksellers in the United States.[156]

A third model is a version of small town America where the local bookstore was the local Wal-Mart. Wal-Mart offered nothing fancy, just the basic bestsellers. The Internet's Amazon executives admitted learning something about operating a massive inventory with computers to keep costs low from techniques developed at Wal-Mart. Wal-Mart's formula worked because, unlike Crown, it discounted a limited number of titles.[157]

But, in selected spots, the limited selection at the local Wal-Mart left an opening for a small town niche player. Hastings Books, Music & Video is one such small town chain. With little fanfare, Hastings Books, Music & Video opened 114 stores in 15 of the western states. In towns with only 10,000 or 20,000 people, Hastings Books, Music & Video became the community gathering place. Hastings combined the lure of book buying with the ability to rent the latest video or buy the newest compact disc. Founded in 1968 in Amarillo, Texas, Hastings added video to its music and books during the 1980s. And, as the company grew, it remained in the hands of the founding Marmaduke family, and the company headquarters remained in an old Sears catalogue center. Like its model, Wal-Mart, the tradition had been keeping costs of sales to a minimum. The Marmadukes hope to become as wealthy as Wal-Mart's Walton family, who started their business after World War II.

ONLINE SELLING

Yet the superstores, the Targets and the Wal-Marts were not the most notable change in bookselling in the 1990s. It was online technology that was fundamentally revitalizing bookselling. Although Amazon.com did not exist until 1995, by 1999 it was one of the most notable new brand names. Even while publishers were setting up their own Web pages (as seen in Table 2.22), Amazon was selling and listing millions of titles. Shopping on the Web site was something new that replaced toll free telephone numbers.[158]

Amazon.com became the leading Internet bookseller by offering a selection of millions of books, while actually stocking only a few thousand in a Seattle warehouse. The key to Amazon's success was "sell all, carry few"—with distributor Ingram Book Group initially handling most of the distribution. Amazon.com worked with a dozen wholesalers, but in 1999 still obtained nearly two thirds of its books through Ingram. Ingram was able to ship virtually all its orders the day they were received, meaning Amazon could promise most titles within 48 hours after the Web customer placed an order. Ingram's processing did not come cheap, requiring an

TABLE 2.22
Representative Publisher Web Sites, 1999

Acropolis Books, Inc	www.acropolisbooks.com
Addison Wesley Longman, Inc	www.aw.com
Bantam Doubleday Dell Publishing Group	www.bdd.com
Cambridge University Press	www.cup.org
Columbia University Press	www.cc.columbia.edu/cu/wp
Elsevier Science Inc	www.elsevier.com
Gallaudet University Press	www.gallaudet.edu/~gupress/
J. Paul Getty Trust Publications	www.artsednet.getty.edu
Harcourt Brace & Co.	www.harcourtbrace.com
HarperCollins Publishers	www.harpercollins.com
Harvard Business School Press	www.hbsp.harvard.edu
Harvard University Press	www.hup.harvard.edu
Henry Holt & Co.	marketplace.com/obs/english/books/holt/index.htm
Houghton Mifflin Co.	www.hmco.com
International Thomson Publishing	www.thomson.com
Iowa State University Press	www.isupress.edu
The McGraw-Hill Companies	www.books.mcgraw-hill.com
The MIT Press	mitpress.mit.edu
New York University Press	www.nyupress.nyu.edu
Ohio State University Press	www.sbs.ohio-state.edu/osu-press
Oxford University Press	www.oup-U.S..org
Penguin Putnam, Inc	www.penguin.com
Princeton University Press	pup.princeton.edu
Random House, Inc.	www.randomhouse.com
St. Martin's Press	www.stmartins.com
Teachers College Press	www.tc.columbia.edu
The University of Hawaii Press	www.eng.hawaii.edu/Manoa/Bldg/UHP.html
William K. Bradford Publishing Co.	www.wkbradford.com
Yale University Press	www.yale.edu/yup

Source: Association of American Publishers Web site at www.publihsers.org.

old fashioned warehouse chain to add a couple of percentage points above what the book costs directly from the publisher. In 1999, Amazon began to rapidly build its own alternative distribution system.[159]

Speed and dependability have meant that Amazon received mountains of good publicity, and generated sales that grew hundreds of percent per annum. However, as the year 2000 approached, Amazon had still not made a profit. In part, these "losses," based on hundreds of millions worth of sales, came about because founder and CEO Jeffrey Bezos was spending millions to build up Amazon's new distribution system. Amazon enlarged its own warehouse in Seattle, and added a new one in New Castle, Delaware, resulting in a sixfold increase in warehouse capacity.[160] To build its own distribution system, Amazon has borrowed heavily from, and hired talent away from, discounter Wal-Mart. Amazon.com's sales grew from $16 milion in 1996 to $148 milion in 1997 to $610 million in 1998, an amount it equaled in the first six months of 1999, albiet with added revenue from selling music and running auctions.[161]

But to stay hot, Amazon.com fashioned many ways to boost sales and postpone profit making. It sold bestsellers, first at 20% to 40% off, and then by mid-1999, at 50% off. Starting new sales lines required up-front investment. The losses edged into the hundreds of millions of dollars per annum, even as revenues increased past $1 billion a year. Still, independent book publishers and sellers across the United States had no choice but to establish their own Web sites and seek to offer something different than Amazon. What that would be was not clear, however. Certainly Amazon deserves credit for pushing interest in book buying on the Internet as Borders did for superstore bookselling earlier.[162]

The battle for online shoppers shifted into high gear in May 1999 when Amazon.com slashed bookseller prices by 50% in its Internet bookstore, a move that was quickly matched by its two principle competitors—barnesandnoble.com and Borders.com. By mid-1999, Amazon (which had expanded into the online auction market and had taken stakes in online retailing everything from pet supplies to groceries and pharmaceuticals) looked to be the Internet winner because of its discounting. Amazon.com's scale economies, product diversity and use of bestsellers as "loss leaders" provided an enormous advantage. Yet, in 1999, price cutting in the online book market would not have a major impact on profit margins for Amazon, because *New York Times* bestsellers represented less than 5% of Amazon's total book revenue. In the end, the trend would seem to be that Internet book retailers should benefit from the increased traffic drawn to their sites by the pricing competition. Amazon was also receiving fees for directing traffic to several online retailers in which it had invested, including Drugstore.com, Pets.com and HomeGrocer.com. The idea was that customers came for the discounted books and then bought other products.[163]

By building its own distribution centers Amazon was expected to lessen its dependence on Ingram. Ingram reported capacity in excess of 2 million square feet, slightly more than the 1.5 million Amazon will have when the expansion is complete. One of Amazon's new warehouses was formerly owned by Golden Books, which sold it in January 1999 for $2.2 million to a local real estate developer as part of its bankruptcy (analyzed previously).[164]

Amazon forced both Barnes & Noble and Borders to jump in and establish their own Web sites. In May 1997, Barnes & Noble, Inc. sued Amazon.com claiming that Amazon was falsely stating it was "the World's Largest Bookstore." Barnes & Noble asserted that it was the largest because it owned and operated 439 superstores and 569 mall stores in the United States, its own online sales site in conjunction with America Online, its barnes & noble.com Web site and stocked more books than Amazon.com. Still when Amazon.com went public in March 1997, growth had been spectacular: In 1996, Amazon had sales of $15.7 million, up from just $511,000 in 1995. Here was a speculative stock for risk takers only; even with the glow of its initial public offering, Amazon executives warned that no profits would be forthcoming in the foreseeable future. Even with the power of the superstores in the mid-1990s, Amazon could step in and take away millions of dollars in sales, and even generate new sales of books. As to the future, this sector of the industry will stabilize, but it would be difficult to predict the structure of the industry.[165]

OWNERSHIP AND THE FUTURE

Amazon.com surely underscored that even in the age of television, Americans still valued books. Books sales of all categories grew in the 1990s, thousands of new titles were issued and sales records were set. Giant foreign media conglomerates and their U.S. rivals were betting that book publishing was not only a growing business, but also provided important synergies with other media divisions. Moreover, niche book publishers arose faster than surveys could count them. As a healthy industry, book publishing may look toward a promising future.[166]

There have been cases of book publishing powerhouses that have bet otherwise. Consider the case of the Times Mirror Corporation, which is best known for its flagship newspaper the *Los Angeles Times*. In 1993, Times Mirror's book publishing division ranked as the ninth largest in the United States in terms of sales. But Times Mirror executives reasoned that bookselling would not expand, and so it sold off its book divisions and moved to concentrate on its newspapers (i.e., the *Los Angeles Times*, the *Baltimore Sun*, *Newsday* and the *Allentown (Pennsylvania) Morning Call*). Times Mirror CEO Mark H. Willes, who came aboard in the mid-1990s to "save" the company, swapped its college publishing businesses with McGraw-Hill's Shepard citation publication and then sold that. He then consolidated Times Mirror publishing, which in 1996 made up 29% of company revenues but 18% of earnings, and sold off pieces. In 1998 he tendered Times Mirror's legal publishing division to Reed-Elsevier for $1.65 billion in cash, and was out of book publishing.[167]

Surely the near term future would revolve around what would be the ultimate impact of the World Wide Web. In the fall 1998, Warner Books' catalogue looked a little different from previous catalogues. Alongside the blurbs, the jacket photos and the author bios sat small yet noticeable type, not dissimilar to the movement it represented: "Web Marketing," read the copy, hinting at author chats and cyber-placements. Greg Voynow, the new director of online marketing at Time Warner Electronic Publishing, understood its importance. "I think it reflected the mind set that is beginning to infiltrate this company," he says. "The Internet is an efficient way to get the word out about books." As 1999 began, online marketing had arrived at most medium-sized and large trade publishers, who had, until recently, lagged behind small independent publishers and self-published authors. When small publishers discovered the Web, large houses cautiously waited to gauge the Internet's value, shrugging it off initially as a "geek-inspired hysteria." For example, it was not until mid-1998 that Pearson PLC's Putnam half of Penguin-Putnam installed company-wide e-mail, nearly two years after self-published author Jim Donovan marketed and sold 75,000 copies of his *Handbook to a Happier Life* strictly through the Internet.

Still, in 1999, more questions remained than there were answers and formulae of what best to do online. What should be posted on a Web site? How do you bring people to a site, and how do you keep them there? What is the ultimate goal of bringing them there anyway: branding, sales, customer service or some strange form of 21st-century credibility that defies quantification? How do you integrate online and offline marketing departments—or is segregation ultimately the best policy? But if it has dawned on book publishing houses that they need to fashion ways to bring customers to their sites, they are also learning that, as Gertrude Stein might have said, "first you need a there, there." Major and independent publishers experimented with formats. Rough Guides, a Pearson PLC imprint, posted the contents of its entire list (numbering 100 titles) on the Web. Viacom's Simon & Schuster created a site for Stephen King's *Bag of Bones*, and sent the first chapter to fans by e-mail weeks before the book went on sale.

Despite exponential gains in personnel, online departments at the major publishers remained comparatively small. Viacom's Simon & Schuster employed but 40 people, Pearson PLC's Penguin-Putnam division only 6. In 1999, the online departments' future place in the hierarchy remained unknown. The dominant school of thought argued for extensions of sales, publicity and marketing departments. It was Larry Weissman, the associate director of online marketing at Random House, who formed the Publishers Web Association. Some marginal publishers like Scholastic gambled that fundamental change was necessary and created so-called extensive destination sites. At Scholastic, the company sought to make its site "a destination to enjoy great characters," in the words of Website coordinator Bill Wright, and to educate every reader to know the Scholastic name. But these were just two experiments, and the purpose of Internet marketing remained unresolved.

Looking toward 2000, the focus seemed to have switched from a new marketing tool to positive revenue generator. That revenue could come through many sources. Publishers such as Rough Guides have, through advertising, already generated extra cash. Yet one place that probably will not bring in any money will be direct sales. Viacom's Simon & Schuster remained one of the few large publishers to bet on direct sales in 1998, but minimized its site in 1999. In the end, book publishers will continue to grapple with questions of generating more profit using the Internet.[168]

Bookselling and publishing were thriving, but did all the mergers, acquisitions and expansions discussed here help or hurt the book buying public? Critics claimed they led to more central control, less dissemination of knowledge, and thus threatened the free movement of speech, a basic tenet of democracy. The end result, insisted these critics, was the creation of massive media conglomerates, able to dominate single markets with monopoly-like power, which in turn led to the loss of editorial independence and the rise of profit maximizing managers who were unconcerned with the contributions to democracy.[169]

Studies, including this one, indicate that through the 1980s and 1990s about half the books sold in the United States were published by a dozen companies. This is only an approximation. Yet, it means that half the books sold were published by other book publishers. And there is change among book publishing's majors. In 1980, the list included Grolier and the Encyclopedia Britannica. The former has grown little and fallen from the ranks of the majors and the latter is fighting for existence in a world of electronic encyclopedias. And Thomson, which did not make the list in 1980, was near the top in the 1990s.[170]

In terms of the exploitation of concentrated ownership, book publishing and sales have generated less problems than other mass media. But some do exist. In September 1996, after 17 years, the U.S. Federal Trade Commission (FTC) dropped its investigation of the largest U.S. book publishers. In making its decision to drop the proceedings, the FTC did not reach a decision on whether the publishers under investigation had in fact violated federal antitrust law, but rather decided that so much had changed in the industry since the late 1970s that further action on the matter was a waste of public resources. The decision brought to a close a proceeding that had focused on Random House, but involved all the major houses discussed earlier. Independent booksellers had complained that these publishers had violated the Robinson–Patman Act by favoring large bookstore chains with discounts not available to them. Discounts remain common, but unless the FTC or some other government agency re-opens the investigation, a court will probably never be allowed to judge whether or not this practice is illegal.

Indeed, in the 1990s, book publishing must be judged as a loose and open oligopoly. This is not to say that giant publishers such as Viacom's Simon & Schuster, and Time Warner's Warner Books, with their 7% or 8% shares of the market, might not have too much power, but to argue that they can dominate and restrict the flow of information seems exaggerated. In recent years there has been movement away from New York, Chicago and Boston to cities and towns in the South and West, with more publishing houses producing more titles through many new voices.[171]

An immediate problem concerned the vertical integration as exemplified by the failed merger of distributor Ingram with Barnes & Noble. This potential acquisition caused independent bookstores to complain to Congress, which then pressured the Federal Trade Commission to investigate, with the two parties finally calling off the alliance. Had the deal gone through, with Bertelsmann AG's participation in Barnes & Noble's Web site, the potential of a Bertelsmann, Barnes & Noble and Ingram combination could have fundamentally changed book publishing, selling and buying in the United States. Independence of companies was superior to vertical integration and cost-cutting through any means. Further testing of mergers, both vertical and horizontal, is certain after 2000.[172]

Independent booksellers used the Ingram plus Barnes & Noble merger as a test case. They organized one of the most elaborate opposition campaigns in the recent history of the book industry, with many petitions, e-mails and telephone appeals to the Federal Trade Commission and members of Congress. All sides had heard reports from inside the FTC that the Commission might delay or block the deal because it might give Barnes & Noble an unfair competitive position. Independent booksellers cheered when the merger was called off, rightly fearing they would not get the same treatment from Ingram as the Barnes & Noble superstore if the deal had gone through. This type of struggle will not go away. Small companies will continue to complain to Congress and the FTC about such deals. And they may succeed, as the independent booksellers did with regard to the Barnes & Noble and Ingram deal.[173]

NOTES

1. Jonathan Karp, "Decline? What Decline?," *Media Studies Journal* 6.3 (Summer 1992), pp. 45–53, established a nice portrait of this question and can also be found in the book that resulted from this journal issue: Everett E. Dennis, Craig L. LaMay and Edward C. Pease (eds.), *Publishing Books* (New Brunswick, NJ: Transaction Publishers, 1997), pp. 33–40.

2. Association of American Publishers (AAP) Book Sales, "Total $23.03 Billion in 1998." The sales figures were prepared by the Statistical Service Center, based on year-to-date data from the AAP December Monthly Sales Report, along with other information gathered during the year. See also Book Industry Study Group's *Book Industry Trends 1998* by the Statistical Service Center, which utilizing the 1992 Census of Manufacturers as its basis, reviews and forecasts book sales in dollars and units for 1992–2002. See also as well Standard & Poor's Industry Surveys, "Publishing," April 23, 1998, pp. 2–5.

3. Albert N. Greco, "The Market for Consumer Books in the U.S.: 1985–1995," *Publishing Research Quarterly* 13.1 (Spring 1997), pp. 3–40, surely the most extensive study of one decade done.

4. Standard & Poor's Industry Surveys, "Publishing," p. 1.

5. Christopher Farrell and Richard A. Melcher, "The Lofty Price of Getting Hitched," *Business Week*, December 8, 1997, pp. 36–37; Alan B. Albarran and John Dimmick, "Concentration and Economics of Multiformity in the Communication Industries," *Journal of Media Economics* 9.4 (1996), pp. 41–50.

6. Mark Crispin Miller, "And Then There Were Seven," *New York Times*, March 26, 1998, p. A31; Porter Bibb, "In Publishing, Bigger Is Better," *New York Times*, March 31, 1998, p. A27.

7. Gene Weingarten, "Instance 'Menace,'" *Washington Post*, May 21, 1999, pp. C1, C5.

8. See *Literary Market Place—1997*, the Directory of the American Book Publishing Industry (New Providence, NJ: R. R. Bowker, 1996).

9. Jim Milliot, "BISG Predicts a 5% Gain in Book Sales for 1997," *Publishers Weekly*, July 7, 1997, p. 12.

10. See, e.g., William S. Lofquist, "U.S. Publishing Industry: Statistical Series," *Publishing Research Quarterly* 13.2 (Summer 1997), pp. 83–88. The *New York Times* does as good a job as any newspaper of covering book publishing trends, as seen in Doreen Carvajal, "You Can't Read Books Fast Enough," *New York Times*, August 24, 1997, Section IV, pp. 1, 3.

11. I have drawn on the following sources: Benjamin M. Compaine, *The Book Industry in Transition* (White Plains, NY: Knowledge Industry Publications, 1978); Lewis A. Coser, Charles Kadushin and Walter W. Powell, *Books: The Culture and Commerce of Publishing* (New York: Basic Boos, 1982); John P. Dessauer, *Book Publishing: A Basic Introduction* (New York: Continuum, 1989); Datus C. Smith, Jr., *A Guide to Book Publishing*, rev. ed. (Seattle: University of Washington Press, 1989); Wendy S. Van de Sande (ed.), *Publishers Directory—1994*, 14th ed. (Detroit: Gale Research, Inc., 1994).

12. The following—when not noted—is based on the work of John Tebbel, which is best accessed in John Tebbel, *Between Covers: The Rise and Transformation of Book Publishing in America* (New York: Oxford University Press, 1987); and John Tebbel, *A History of Book Publishing in the United States*, 4 vols. (New York: Bowker, 1972, 1975, 1978, 1981).

13. Moira Davison Reynolds, *Uncle Tom's Cabin and Mid-Nineteenth Century United States: Pen and Conscience* (Jefferson, NC: McFarland & Company, 1985); Thomas F. Gossett, *Uncle Tom's Cabin and American Culture* (Dallas: Southern Methodist University Press, 1985).

14. Joan Shelley Rubin's *The Making of Middle Brow Culture* (Chapel Hill, NC: University of North Carolina Press, 1992) carefully chronicles these and other key developments in the making of a book middle-class culture in the United States during the first half of the 20th century.

15. See Betty Ballantine, "The Paperback Conquest of America," in Gordon Graham and Richard Abel (eds.), *The Book in the United States Today* (New Brunswick, NJ: Transaction Publishers, 1997), pp. 101–112.

16. Tom Huntington. "How Paperbacks Finally Changed Publishing," *Audacity* 5.2 (Winter 1997), pp. 34–42. See also John Bear, *The #1 New York Times Best Seller* (Berkeley, CA: Ten Speed Press, 1992), which chronicles top sellers through 1991. This ought to be read in conjunction with Daisy Maryles, "Making the Charts," *Publishers Weekly*, July 1997, special issue, pp. 32, 34, 36; and "People Who Shaped the Book Business," *Publishers Weekly*, July 1997, special issue, pp. 18–24, 26, 31.

17. Dan Lacy, "From Family Enterprise to Global Conglomerate," *Media Studies Journal* 6.3 (Summer 1992), pp. 1–13; David A. Garvin, "Mergers and Competition in Book Publishing," *The Antitrust Bulletin* 25.2 (Summer 1980), pp. 327–361; Compaine, *The Book Industry in Transition*.

18. John F. Baker, "Reinventing the Book Business," *Publishers Weekly*, March 14, 1994, p. 36.

19. Rodney Ho, "King of Audio Book Narrators Makes 'Readers' Swoon, " *Wall Street Journal*, April 10, 1998, pp. B1, B8; Trudi M. Rosenblum, "Audio at the Crossroads," *Publishers Weekly*, June 10, 1996, pp. 53–56.

20. "How We Got to Here, 1973–1997," *Publishers Weekly*, July 1997, special issue, pp. 14–16.

21. Anthony Bianco, "Inside a $15 Billion Dynasty," *Business Week*, September 29, 1997, pp. 64–65, 68, 72, 76; Bridget Kinsella, "Ingram, PMA Launch Program to Aid Small Publishers," *Publishers Weekly*, August 4, 1997, p. 24. On private companies, their power and lack of data, see Steve Kichen and Tina Russo McCarthy, "Wall Street? No, Thanks," *Forbes*, December 1, 1997, pp. 180–262. A firsthand report by an Ingram executive can be found in Steven J. Mason, "Wholesalers Burgeon on Speed and Service," in Graham and Abel, pp. 77–83.

22. Patrick M. Reilly, "Barnes & Noble Like to Build Centers of Distribution if Ingram Deal Fails," *Wall Street Journal*, June 2, 1999, p. B8; Patrick M. Reilly, "Barnes & Noble Close Book on Attempt to Buy Ingram, Amid FTC Objections," *Wall Street Journal*, June 3, 1999, p. B18.

23. John Mutter, "Baker & Taylor Books to Expand Warehouse Space by 90 percent, Add Music, Video," *Publishers Weekly*, May 24, 1999, from Web site at www.bookwire.com.

24. Gary Ink, "Output Bounced Back in '94," *Publishers Weekly*, April 29, 1996, pp. 32–34.

25. Standard & Poor's Industry Surveys, "Publishing," February 6, 1997, p. 4.

26. Al Silverman, "Book Clubs in America," in Graham and Abel, pp. 113–127.

27. Trudi M. Rosenblum, "Dressing Up Audio," *Publishers Weekly*, March 10, 1997, pp. 56–59, nicely summarizes the unappreciated importance of this billion-dollar sector of "book" publishing.

28. Robert Dahlin, "Men (and Women) Who Made a Revolution," *Publishers Weekly*, July 1997, special issue, pp. 51–52, 54, 56, 58, 60, neatly encapsulate the history of the development of this genre of publishing.

29. Cameron S. Moseley, "US School Publishing: From Webster and McGuffey to the Internet," in Graham and Abel, pp. 23–36.

30. Michael M. Phillips, "Economics Textbook Is Getting a Blockbuster Send-Off," *Wall Street Journal*, September 22, 1997, pp. B1, B8.

31. Doreen Carajal, "Sales of Textbooks Continuing to Defy Gloomy Predictions," *New York Times*, May 26, 1998, pp. A1, D4.

32. Nick Harrison, "Sacred Texts: It's Still the Good Book," *Publishers Weekly*, October 13, 1997, pp. 32–34, 36–37, 40; Werner Mark Linz, "A Religious Country Reflected in Its Publishing Industry," in Graham and Abel, pp. 1–10.

33. Charles E. Gates, "Children's Books: 500 Million a Year; Where Do We Go From Here?," in Graham and Abel, pp. 11–21.

34. Eden Ross Lipson, "Once Upon a Time, and for Years After," *New York Times*, November 17, 1997, pp. B1, B3, consistently and tellingly underscores the billions of dollars at stake in children's books. See also "Book Review," *New York Times*, November 16, 1997, pp. 25–54; Leonard S. Marcus, "Mother Goose to Multiculturalism," *Publishers Weekly*, July 1997, special issue, pp. 62–64, 66, 68, 70.

35. The *Veronis, Suhler & Associates Communications Industry Forecast*, 11th ed., July 1997, pp. 324–335.

36. Naomi B. Pascal, "Between Academe and the Marketplace: University Presses Face the 21st Century," in Graham and Abel, pp. 201–212.

37. Albert N. Greco, *The Book Publishing Industry* (Boston: Allyn & Bacon, 1997), pp. 132–133, 135.

38. Ibid., pp. 215–242.

39. Standard & Poor's Industry Surveys, "Publishing," February 6, 1997, pp. 8–9.

40. See "The Forbes 500s—Sales," *Forbes*, April 21, 1997, pp. 180–200, for information on publicly held companies; and Steve Kichen, Tina Russo McCarthy and Peter Newcomb, "The Private 500," *Forbes*, December 2, 1996, pp. 150–200, for those private companies.

41. Chris Petrikin, "Book Biz: Read It and Weep," *Variety*, May 12–18, 1997, pp. 77–78.

42. The history of Hollywood's long dependence on bestsellers as material for motion pictures is nicely summarized in Paul Nathan, "Ah, But You Should Have Read the Book," *Publishers Weekly*, July 1997, special issue, pp. 102–104, 106, 108.

43. Doreen Carvajal, "Who Can Afford Him? Stephen King Goes in Search of a Publisher," *New York Times*, October 27, 1997, pp. D1, D8; Doreen Carvajal, "Middling (and Unloved) in Publishing Land," *New York Times*, August 18, 1997, pp. D1, D6.

44. Dave Bogart (ed.), *The Bowker Annual*, 42nd ed. (New Providence, NJ: R. R. Bowker, 1997), p. 522; Karen Hallard (ed.), *American Book Trade Directory—1997–98*, 43rd ed. (New Providence, NJ: R. R. Bowker, 1997) offers the nearly 2,000-page listing of all the booksellers in the United States.

45. "Bookworms," *Washington Post*, April 18, 1998, p. A14.

46. For the history of any company, see *Hoover's Guide to Media Companies* (Austin, TX: Hoover's Business Press, 1996). For a contemporary capsule of the company see Hoover's Web site at www.hoovers.com. Know that for detail on public companies—without charge—one needs to consult the Web site of the U.S. Security and Exchange Commission, known as EDGAR, at www.sec.gov. Seek out the most recent annual report and most recent 10-K report.

47. Jim Milliot, "Book Sales Topped $20 Billion in 1996 But Growth Rate Slows," *Publishers Weekly*, March 3, 1997, p. 11; Daisy Maryles, "How the Winners Made It to the Top," *Publisher Weekly*, January 6, 1997, pp. 46–49.

48. There are a number of bestseller lists. This list is based on information gathered by the *Wall Street Journal*, which reflects nationwide sales of hardcover books during the week ending the previous Saturday and then published the following Tuesday. The *Wall Street Journal* used data from 2,500 B. Dalton, Barnes & Noble, Inc., Bookland, Books-A-Million, Books & Co., Bookstar, Bookstop, Borders Books & Music, Brentano's, Coles, Coopersmith, Crown, Doubleday, Scribners, Super Crown and Waldensbooks stores. The *Wall Street Journal* in typical fashion breaks the list into two parts, fiction and nonfiction (general), and casual inspection notes that most of the titles are from an imprint of one of the majors discussed later—at least those that issue trade books. In contrast, *Publishers Weekly* maintains and mounts specialized lists, including hardcover bestsellers, paperback bestsellers and children's bestsellers. The two former are dominated by the majors, whereas children's publishing is specialized enough that smaller companies, such as Scholastic or Greenwillow, can make it onto the lists. Amazon.com, as of 1999, ranks all the books it tenders.

49. Greco, *The Book Publishing Industry*, pp. 45–78.

50. See *Literary Market Place—1997*, pp. xi–xiv.

51. Herbert R. Lottman, "Bertelsmann Sales Rise 5% in Fiscal '96; Books Now No. 2," *Publishers Weekly*, September 30, 1996, p. 15; Doreen Carvajal, "Americans Buy Books, Foreigners Buy Publishers," *New York Times*, August 10, 1997, p. E4; "The Global 50," *Variety*, August 25–31, 1997, p. 34. See also Web site at www.bertelsmann.de.

52. I. Jeanne Dugan, "Boldly Going Where Others Are Bailing Out," *Business Week*, April 6, 1998, p. 46.

53. "Bertelsmann Acquires Random House, Inc. from Advance Publications," *Publisher's Weekly*, March 23, 1998; "Bertelsmann Purchase of Random House Completed," *Publisher's Weekly*, July 1, 1998, both from the Web site at www.bookwire.com. See also Web site at www.bertelsmann.de.

54. Jim Milliot, "Random House Restructures Sales Force into Three Groups," *Publishers Weekly*, March 29, 1999, found at Web site at www.bookwire.com.

55. Doreen Carvajal, "Bertelsmann Is Reorganizing Random House," *New York Times*, May 28, 1999, p. D1. See also Web site at www.bertelsmann.de.

56. Alex Kuczynski, "Random House Cancels Book on Eisner," *New York Times*, May 28, 1999, p. D2; Doreen Carvajal, "Cross Media Deals Mean Bonanzas for Publishers," *New York Times*, January 25, 1999, pp. C1, C4.

57. "Bertelsmann to Acquire Reed Elsevier Share of BCA," *Publisher's Weekly*, June 19, 1998, from Web site at www.bookwire.com. See also Web site at www.bertelsmann.de.

58. "Bertelsmann to Buy 50 Percent Stake in barnesandnoble.com," *Publisher's Weekly*, October 7, 1998, from Web site at www.bookwire.com. See also Web site at www.bertelsmann.de.

59. Doreen Carvajal, "Bertelsmann Signs Deal for Springer Verlag," *New York Times*, November 21, 1998, p. B2. See also Web site at www.bertelsmann.de.

60. Jim Milliot, "Strong Year Pushes Total BDD Revenues Close to $700 Million," *Publisher's Weekly*, August 28, 1995, p. 26.

61. "Subtext Perspective: Buy, Buy, Bertelsmann!," October 3, 1997, from Web site at www.book-wire.com.

62. On private companies, their power and lack of data, see Steven Kichen and Tina Russo McCarthy, "Wall Street? No, Thanks," *Forbes*, December 1, 1997, pp. 180–262; See also Thane Peterson and Richard Siklos, "Cautious Company, Risk Taking CEO," *Business Week*, November 9, 1998, pp. 146–147.

63. Jim Milliot, "Acquisitions Boost Pearson Books Sales to $1.5 Billion," *Publishers Weekly*, April 28, 1997, p. 11; Carvajal, "Americans Buy Books," p. E4; Hardy Green, "Superstores, Megabooks— and Humongous Headaches," *Business Week*, April 14, 1997, pp. 92–94.

64. Kimberley A. Strassel, "Pearson Post Drop in Profit, to Expand FT in U.S. Market, *Wall Street Journal*, March 18, 1997, p. B14; Heidi Dawley, Pearson May Be Poised for a Breakup," *Business Week*, September 2, 1996, pp. 54–55; Jim Milliot, "Value of Publishing Mergers Tripled in '96," *Publishers Weekly*, April 14, 1997, p. 12.

65. Jim Milliot, "Pearson Edn. Results Boosted by S&S Purchase," *Publishers Weekly*, March 15, 1999, from Web site at www.bookwire.com.

66. "Wiley Buys Pearson College Titles, *Publishers Weekly*, May 24, 1999, from Web site at www.book-wire.com.

67. "Penguin Putnam Posts Modest Gains in Transition Year," *Publishers Weekly*, March 15, 1999, found on Web site at www.bookwire.com.

68. Judy Quinn, "Clancy's Deals Top $100 Million," *Publishers Weekly*, August 25, 1997, p. 12; Jim Milliot, "Pearson Acquires Putnam Berkley for $336 Million," *Publishers Weekly*, October 3, 1996, p. 19.

69. Annual reports for Time Warner can be found on the official corporate Web site at www.time-warner.com.

70. Mark Robichaux, "Time Warner Posts $30 Million Profit, Bouncing Back from Year Earlier Loss," *Wall Street Journal*, July 17, 1997, p. B10. For historical background as to the merger of Time and Warner, see Chapter 6 of this book, and Connie Bruck, *Master of the Game: Steve Ross and the Creation of Time Warner* (New York: Simon & Schuster, 1994), for a biography of Steven J. Ross and his creation of Time Warner.

71. See Web site at www.viacom.com.

72. Jim Milliot, "S&S Revenues Top $2.3 Billion," *Publishers Weekly*, March 10, 1997, p. 12, and Web site at www.viacom.com.

73. Jim Milliot, "Sales at 'New' Simon and Schuster Rise 1%, Earnings Fall," *Publishers Weekly*, March 8, 1999, from Web site at www.bookwire.com.

74. John W. Verity, "A Model Paperless Library," *Business Week*, December 23, 1996, pp. 80, 82; G. Bruce Knecht, "Horror Story Author Stephen King, Simon & Schuster Set Novel Profit Deal," *Wall Street Journal*, November 7, 1997, p. B8; G. Bruce Knecht, "Macmillan's Order to Use Wholesalers Angers Booksellers," *Wall Street Journal*, September 4, 1997, p. B3.

75. Green, "Superstores, Megabooks," pp. 92–94.

76. Doreen Carvajal, "HarperCollins Cancels Books in Unusual Step for Industry," *New York Times*, June 27, 1997, pp. A1, C3.

77. Jim Milliot, "HarperCollins Posts Another Strong Quarter," *Publishers Weekly*, February 15, 1999, from Web site at www.bookwire.com. See also Web site at www.newscorp.com.

78. Calvin Reid, "Small Press Success: Some Ecco Jewels," *Publishers Weekly*, March 22, 1999, from Web site at www.bookwire.com.

79. Nikhil Deogun, "Book Samples to Be Served with Diet Coke," *Wall Street Journal*, October 23, 1998, p. B7; Carvajal, "Cross Media Deals," pp. C1, C4; G. Bruce Knecht, "News Corp. Takes a Charge on Book Unit," *Wall Street Journal*, August 5, 1997, pp. A3, A4; G. Bruce Knecht, "HarperCollins Reverses Get Tough Plan to Recover Advances for Canceled Books," *Wall Street Journal*, August 22, 1997, p. B13.

80. Patrick M. Reilly, "News Corp.'s HarperCollins to Acquire Avon, William Morrow from Hearst," *Wall Street Journal*, June 18, 1999, p. B2; Jim Milliot, "Hearst Book Group Posts Record Year in 1998," *Publishers Weekly*, January 25, 1999, from Web site at www.bookwire.com. See also Jim

Milliot, "Morrow Has Poor '96, Avon Does Better," *Publishers Weekly*, January 20, 1997, p. 266; Patrick M. Reilly, "Hearst Picks Sikes to Head Its Unit for New Media," *Wall Street Journal*, March 16, 1997, p. B7.

81. See Web site at www.readersdigest.com—plus as background *Hoover's 500: Profiles of America's Largest Business Enterprises* (Austin, TX: Hoovers Business Press, 1996), p. 411; and John Heidenry, *Theirs Was the Kingdom: Lila and DeWitt Wallace and the Story of the Reader's Digest* (New York: W. W. Norton, 1993).

82. Wendy Bounds, "Reader's Digest Net Rises 71%, Buoyed by Cost Cutting," *Wall Street Journal*, April 29, 1998, p. B14; G. Bruce Knecht, "George Grune Is Back at Reader's Digest, Replacing Schadt as Chief Executive," *Wall Street Journal*, August 12, 1997, p. B7; Geraldine Fabrikant, "Reader's Digest Chief Resigns as Expansion Ideas Falter," *New York Times*, August 12, 1997, pp. D1, D7; "RD Has Poor 3rd Qtr., Unveils $400M Marketing Plan," *Publishers Weekly*, April 14, 1997, p. 14; "Book Sales Slip at Reader's Digest," *Publishers Weekly*, October 18, 1996, p. 10.

83. Wendy Bounds, "Reader's Digest Net Rises 71%, Buoyed By Cost Cutting," *Wall Street Journal*, April 29, 1999, from Web site at www.wsj.com.

84. See Web site at www.idgbooks.com.

85. "Results Up at MHC Publishing Group," *Publishers Weekly*, February 1, 1999, from Web site at www.bookwire.com.

86. Jim Milliot, "McGraw-Hill Cos. Publishing Unit Takes Shape," *Publishers Weekly*, April 14, 1997, p. 34; John W. Verity, "A Model Paperless Library," *Business Week*, December 23, 1996, pp. 80, 82; *Hoover's 500*, p. 319; "The McGraw-Hill Companies, Inc." found in "The Fortune 500" on the *Fortune* magazine Web site at www.pathfinder.com/fortune.

87. Jim Milliot, "Harcourt Sales, Profits Up in '96," *Publishers Weekly*, March 10, 1997, p. 14.

88. See Web site at www.harcourt.com.

89. See Web site at www.harcourt.com.

90. Jim Milliot, "School Sales Lead Harcourt Growth," *Publishers Weekly*, February 12, 1996, p. 14.

91. Jean Richardson, "Harcourt to Acquire Churchill Livingstone," *Publishers Weekly*, August 25, 1997, p. 18.

92. Jim Milliot, "Harcourt Trade Division Enjoying Strong Run," *Publishers Weekly*, April 12, 1999, found at Web site at www.bookwire.com.

93. See Web site at www.streetlink.com\h\.

94. "Foreign Rankings—Canada," *Forbes*, July 28, 1997, p. 28; "The Business Week Global 1000," *Business Week*, July 7, 1997, p. 58.

95. Louise Gagne (ed.), *Publishers Directory—1998*, 18th ed. (Detroit: Gale Research, 1997), p. 1274; Carvajal, "Americans Buy Books," p. E4; Jim Milliot, "Value of Publishing Mergers Tripled in '96," *Publishers Weekly*, April 14, 1997, p. 12; Iver Peterson, "Thomson to Buy Legal Publisher in a $3.43 Billion Cash Accord," *New York Times*, February 27, 1996, pp. D1, D11; *Hoover's Global 250* (Austin, TX: Hoovers Business Press, 1997), pp. 514–515.

96. See Web site at www.thomcorp.com.

97. Steve M. Zeitchik, "Varsitybooks.com Partners with ITP," *Publishers Weekly*, January 25, 1999, from Web site at www.bookwire.com.

98. Jim Milliot, "Houghton Mifflin Sales Up 36%, Though Trade Sales Off," *Publishers Weekly*, February 3, 1997, p. 14; Barbara Carton, "Houghton Mifflin Is Seeking Ways to Make the Grade," *Wall Street Journal*, June 24, 1996, p. B4; Kirsten C. Holm, *Writer's Market—1998* (Cincinnati, OH: Writer's Digest Books, 1997), pp. 175–176. See Web site at www.hmco.com.

99. Judith Rosen, "Houghton Mifflin to Distribute Beacon Press," *Publishers Weekly*, April 5, 1999, from Web site at www.bookwire.com.

100. See Web site at www.hmco.com.

101. I include only those sizable book publishers based in Europe who seek to challenge Bertelsmann AG and Pearson PLC. My list is hardly meant to be comprehensive and would include, for example, the Lagardere Groupe—a French company with a book division called Grolier, which is better known for its magazines in 15 languages (including *Woman's Day* and *Car and Driver* in the United States)—if we intended to be complete. This Paris-based media powerhouse sold in 1996

reference and professional titles in the United States to the tune of $400 million, and an additional $1.2 billion outside the United States. It also sells children's books and its best known product to the general public is the *Encyclopedia Americana*.

102. Doreen Carvajal, "Americans Buy Books," p. E4; "Publisher in Germany Agrees to Buy Farrar," *Wall Street Journal*, November 1, 1994, p. B8.

103. John F. Baker, "Holt Cutting Titles, Jobs in Bid to Restore Profitability," *Publishers Weekly*, February 1, 1999, from Web site at www.bookwire.com.

104. "Genger, Richards to Move to Holt," *Publishers Weekly*, September 29, 1997, p. 17.

105. Bob Summer, "Holtzbrinck Opens State of the Art Va. Distribution Center," *Publishers Weekly*, September 15, 1997, p. 11; Doreen Carvajal, "Holtzbrinck's New Word on U.S. Publishing," *New York Times*, September 11, 1997, pp. D1, D4.

106. Felicity Barringer, "Times Mirror Sells Legal Unity to British Dutch Publisher," *New York Times*, April 28, 1998, p. D6; "Reed Elsevier and Wolters Kluwer Plan to Merge," *Publishers Weekly*, October 20, 1997, p. 10; "Reed Elsevier and Wolters Kluwer Merging," *New York Times*, October 14, 1997, p. D6; *Hoover's Global 250*, pp. 418–419; Carvajal, "Americans Buy Books," p. E4.

107. Robert Frank, "Reed Elsevier to Revamp Management Amid Painful Shift to Electronic Media," *Wall Street Journal*, August 7, 1998, p. B7; Lisa Bannon and Kimberley A. Strassel, "Reed Elsevier to Buy Two Units of Times Mirror," *Wall Street Journal*, April 28, 1998, p. A3. See also "Bertelsmann to Acquire Reed Elsevier Share of BCA," *Publisher's Weekly*, June 19, 1998, from Web site at www.bookwire.com.

108. See Web site at www.reed-elsevier.com.

109. Bill McIntosh, "WRAP: Wolters Kluwer Pft Shines; Reed Elsevier disappoints," *Wall Street Journal*, March 1999, found on Web site at www.wsj.com.

110. Herbert R. Lottman, "Touraine to Lead Havas Book Divisions in France," *Publishers Weekly*, February 8, 1999, from Web site at www.bookwire.com.

111. Jim Milliot, "Disney Publishing Had Strong '96, Looks for More Growth," *Publishers Weekly*, January 20, 1997, p. 263; Chris Petrikin, "Book Biz: Read It and Weep" *Variety*, May 12–18, 1997, p. 77.

112. "Walt Disney Company Restructures Publishing Group," *Publishers Weekly*, April 12, 1999, from Web site at www.bookwire.com.

113. "Wiley Buys Pearson College Titles," *Publishers Weekly*, May 24, 1999, from Web site at www.bookwire.com. See also Jim Milliot, "Wiley Looks to Acquisitions, Technology for Growth," *Publishers Weekly*, September 1, 1997, p. 14.

114. See Web site at www.wiley.com.

115. See Web site at www.wiley.com.

116. "Wiley Sales Jump 19% to $432M.," *Publishers Weekly*, June 30, 1997, p. 12.

117. See Web site at www.wiley.com.

118. Kirsten C. Holm, *Writer's Market—1998* (Cincinnati, OH: Writer's Digest Books, 1997), p. 229; Gagne, *Publishers Directory—1998*, p. 939.

119. See Web site at www.scholastic.com.

120. Jim Milliot, "Big Drop at Retail Hurts Scholastic in Fiscal '97," *Publishers Weekly*, September 8, 1997, p. 11; Jim Milliot, "Scholastic Looking for Rebound from Stock Plunge," *Publishers Weekly*, March 3, 1997, p. 12; "Scholastic Begins Reorganization of Book Group," *Publishers Weekly*, March 10, 1997, p. 11; Timothy L. O'Brien, "Scholastic Corporation Learns It's Best to Be Prepared for Class," *Wall Street Journal*, July 8, 1997, p. B4; Jim Milliot, "Lawsuit Filed Against Scholastic Over Stock Collapse," *Publishers Weekly*, April 14, 1997, p. 13.

121. "Golden Books Family Entertainment; Loss Narrows Amid Decline in Costs From Restructuring," *Wall Street Journal*, November 12, 1997, p. B14; David D. Kirkpatrick, "Golden Books Narrows Its Loss in Fiscal Period," *Wall Street Journal*, December 13, 1996, p. B6; Jim Milliot, "Golden Restructuring Will Cut 200 More Jobs," *Publishers Weekly*, December 10, 1996, p. 10; Lisa Gubernick, "The Best Revenge," *Forbes*, October 21, 1996, pp. 104, 106.

122. Jim Milliot, "Golden Lost $128 Million in '98, Seeks Approval for Reorganization Plan," *Publishers Weekly*, April 19, 1999, found on Web site at www.bookwire.com.

123. Patrick M. Reilly, "Will Golden Books' Next Chapter Be Its Sale?," *Wall Street Journal*, August 6, 1998, pp. B1, B4.

124. Lucinda Dyer, "Gardening Boys: Green Grow the Sales," *Publishers Weekly*, February 10, 1997, pp. 52–54, 56–60; Gagne, *Publishers Directory—1998*, p. 1280; *Literary Market Place—1997*, p. 10.

125. Jim Milliot, "Prospering in the Land of Giants," *Publishers Weekly*, November 18, 1996, pp. 32–34, 36.

126. Van de Sande, *The Publishers Directory*, and Joseph Barbato, "The Rise and Rise of the Small Press," *Publishers Weekly*, July 1997, special issue, pp. 39–40, 42, 44, 46, 48.

127. No better example of "lightening striking" can be found than in the experience of Northland Publishing, a small press based in Flagstaff, Arizona. For about a decade, Northland struggled to distinguish itself. In October 1996, in a six-minute segment on National Public Radio, children's book commentator Daniel Pinkwater waxed enthusiastically about *Monster Slayer*, adapted from a Navajo folktale by Vee Browne and illustrated by Baje Whitethorne, and the hardcover picture book, *Mystery of Navajo Moon*, by Timothy Green. Northland's David Jenny had taken "a shot in the dark" by sending a package of books to Pinkwater, who aired his praise on September 28, 1996. Northland's office telephone began ringing off the hook the following week as retailers asked to set up accounts, wholesalers beefed up their stock and educational institutions requested catalogs. People began going into Borders asking for those books specifically, and in a week sales went into five figures. Suddenly a struggling company was about to become one of the inspirational success stories of *Publishers Weekly*. See Milliot, "Prospering in the Land of the Giants," pp. 32–34, 36.

128. Holm, *Writer's Market—1998*, pp. 116–117; *Literary Market Place—1997*, p. 10.

129. Calvin Reid, "NYU Press: Publishing, Selling Serious Books in New Ways," *Publishers Weekly*, May 17, 1999, found on Web site at www.bookwire.com.

130. *Literary Market Place—1997*, p. 10; Holm, *Writer's Market—1998*, p. 104; Gagne, *Publishers Directory—1998*, p. 1273; Jim Milliot, "Nelson Sales Dip, But Profits Rise," *Publishers Weekly*, August 4, 1997, p. 24; Doreen Carvajal, "The Bible, a Perennial, Runs into Sales Resistance," *New York Times*, October 28, 1996, pp. D1, D10.

131. Julie Lew, "Small Presses Thrive in the Diversity Niche," *New York Times*, October 14, 1996, p. D7.

132. See Stephen Horvath, "The Rise of the Chain Superstore," in Graham and Abel, pp. 63–76.

133. John F. Baker, "Publishers Concerned by Superstore-Indie Struggle," *Publisher's Weekly*, September 18, 1995, pp. 10–11, 19.

134. Horvath, pp. 63–74.

135. Information for 1999 came from Web site at /www.shareholder.com/bks. See also G. Bruce Knecht, "Book Superstores Bring Hollywood-Like Risks to Publishing Business," *Wall Street Journal*, May 29, 1997, pp. A1, A6; Green, "Superstores, Megabooks," pp. 92–94; Patrick M. Reilly, "Holiday-Time Sales at Book Superstores Read Like a Thriller for Borders," *Wall Street Journal*, January 9, 1996, p. B9; Patrick M. Reilly, "Where Borders and Barnes & Noble Compete, It's a War," *Wall Street Journal*, September 3, 1996, pp. A1, A8; Sunita Wadekar Bhargave, "Espresso, Sandwiches, and a Sea of Books," *Business Week*, July 26, 1993, p. 56.

136. Doreen Carvajal, "Barnes & Noble Tries to Read a Hazy Future," *New York Times*, April 18, 1999, Section II, pp. 1, 6.

137. Jim Milliot, "Chain Sales Up 15% in First Half of Fiscal '98 to $2.4 Billion," *Publishers Weekly*, September 1, 1997, p. 9; Jim Milliot, "Barnes & Noble Says Business Overhaul Nearly Finished," *Publishers Weekly*, May 19, 1997, p. 11.

138. I. Jeanne Dugan, "Battle of the Best Seller Lists," *Business Week*, December 15, 1997, p. 38.

139. "Barnes & Noble Files for Web Unit IPO," *Wall Street Journal*, March 19, 1999, p. B8; "Bertelsmann to Buy 50 Percent Stake in barnesandnoble.com," *Publisher's Weekly*, October 7, 1998, from Web site at www. bookwire.com. See also Patrick M. Reilly, "Barnes & Noble Reports a Loss of $4.6 Million," *Wall Street Journal*, November 28, 1998, p. A6. See also Barnes & Noble's Web site at /www.shareholder.com/bks.

140. Green, "Superstores, Megabooks," pp. 92–94; Reilly, "Holiday-Time Sales," p. B9; Kirk Johnson, "A New Superstore of Books Enters the New York Fray," *New York Times*, September 4, 1996, p. B3; Milliot, "Barnes & Noble Says Business Overhaul Nearly Finished," p. 11.

141. Reilly, "Where Borders and Barnes & Noble Compete, It's a War," pp. A1, A8.

142. Calvin Reid, "Chicago Borders Ratifies Union Contract," *Publishers Weekly*, October 20, 1997, p. 10.

143. See Web site at www.bordersstores.com.

144. Thomas Jaffee, "Borders Overboard?," *Forbes*, September 21, 1998, pp. 104–106.

145. Patrick M. Reilly, "In the Age of the Web, a Book Chain Flounders," *Wall Street Journal*, February 22, 1999, p. B1; Patrick M. Reilly, "Borders Group Names Pfeffer CEO; Results Swing to Loss of $800,000," *Wall Street Journal*, November 13, 1998, p. B6; Jaffe, "Borders Overboard," pp. 104–106.

146. Jim Milliot and Calvin Reid, "Sales Rise, Earnings Fall at Books-A-Million," *Publishers Weekly*, March 29, 1999, from Web site at www.bookwire.com. Quotations from corporate statement issued on the Business Wire, October 8, 1997, announcing the opening of a new store in Meridian, Mississippi. A nearly identical statement for the opening of a superstore in Port Richey, Florida, can be found on the Business Wire of September 30, 1997. See also Jim Milliot, "Chains Earned Profits of $233 Million in Fiscal 1997," *Publishers Weekly*, May 26, 1997, p. 12; Jim Milliot, "Superstore Sales Rise 36 Percent, to More Than $3 Billion," *Publishers Weekly*, May 19, 1997, p. 10; William M. Stern, "Southern Fried Reading," *Forbes*, June 20, 1994, p. 91.

147. G. Bruce Knecht, "Book Superstores Bring Hollywood-Like Risks to Publishing Business," *Wall Street Journal*, May 29, 1997, pp. A1, A6; John Mutter, "More Than Half Now Buy Their Books in Chains—'PW' Survey," *Publishers Weekly*, May 12, 1997, p. 13; Roxanne Roberts, "High-Browse Fun," *Washington Post*, April 3, 1997, pp. C1, C8.

148. Jim Milliot, "Chain Sales Up 15% in First Half of Fiscal '98 to $2.4 Billion," *Publishers Weekly*, September 1, 1997, p. 9; Doreen Carvajal, "Book Chains' New Role: Soothsayers for Publishers," *New York Times*, August 12, 1997, pp. A1, D5.

149. Stephanie Stoughton and David Streitfeld, "Crown Wants Its Creditors as Owners," *Washington Post*, March 25, 1999, pp. E1, E3; Margaret Webb Pressler and Steven Ginsberg, "In Hopes That Experience Speaks Volumes," *Washington Post*, "Washington Business," July 20, 1998, pp. 12–14; Margaret Webb Pressler and Steven Ginsberg, "Crown Books Files for Reorganization," *Washington Post*, July 15, 1998, pp. C1, C12; Maryann Haggerty, "Ex-Rival Named President of Crown Books," *Washington Post*, December 31, 1997, p. D10; Margaret Webb Pressler, "How Crown Books Slipped Down the Best Seller List," *Washington Post*, September 22, 1997, pp. A1, A8; Jim Milliot, "Poor Quarter Prompts Changes at Crown Books," *Publishers Weekly*, September 22, 1997, p. 10; Jim Milliot, "Dart Said to Be Considering Sale of Stake in Crown," *Publishers Weekly*, September 15, 1997, p. 14; "Crown Books," "Washington Business," *Washington Post*, April 28, 1997, pp. 30–31; Zina Moukheiber, "The Price Is Right," *Forbes*, December 16, 1996, pp. 52–53.

150. Barbara Carton, "Bookstore Survival Stunts Have Scant Literary Merit," *Wall Street Journal*, June 3, 1997, pp. B1, B8; Green, "Superstores, Megabooks," pp. 92–94.

151. Dinitia Smith, "Epilogue for Another Bookstore," *New York Times*, January 18, 1997, pp. 15, 24; David Streitfeld, "Sidney Kramer Books Turns the Lights Out," *Washington Post*, May 1, 1997, pp. C1, C2.

152. The Christian bookstore growth trends are neatly summarized in Gustav Niebuhr, "Christian Bookstores Take Worldly Lesson," *New York Times*, July 25, 1996, p. A16. For the history of this type of bookstore read Nick Harrison, "All in the Family-CBA Style," *Publishers Weekly*, July 1997, special issue, pp. 76–78, 80. The CBA is the Christian Booksellers Association founded in 1950.

153. Andrea Adelson, "Black-Owned Bookstores Defend Niche," *New York Times*, October 6, 1997, p. D11.

154. Elizabeth Bernstein, "Best Buy Breaks into Book Market," *Publishers Weekly*, September 1, 1997, p. 9.

155. See "Retailer Categories in the United States and Canada," *American Book Trade Directory*, 41st ed., 1995–1996 (New Providence, NJ: R. R. Bowker, 1996).

156. Elizabeth Bernstein, "Target Hits Bulls Eye of Mid-List Book Sales," *Publishers Weekly*, July 7, 1997, pp. 22, 24.

157. "Wal-Mart Agrees to Settle Lawsuit Against Amazon," *New York Times*, April 6, 1999, p. C6; Emily Nelson, "Logistics Whiz Rises at Wal-Mart," *Wall Street Journal*, March 11, 1999, pp. B1, B8.

158. Dave Bogart (ed.), *The Bowker Annual*, 42nd ed. (New Providence, NJ: R. R. Bowker, 1997), pp. 539–572.

159. Rita Koselka, "A Real Amazon," *Forbes*, April 5, 1999, pp. 50–52.

160. Anthony Bianco, "Virtual Bookstores Start to Get Real," *Business Week*, October 27, 1997, pp. 146, 148.

161. Hoovers Online at http://www.hoovers.com, accessed July 22, 1999; Chris Stetkiewicz, "FOCUS-Amazon.com shares slide as losses mount," Reuters News Service Online, accessed July 22, 1999, at www.etrade.com/.

162. George Anders, "Amazon Plans to Offer 50% Discounts on Hardcover, Paperback Best Sellers," *Wall Street Journal*, May 17, 1999, p. B11.

163. Joelle Tessler, "Amazon Seen Emerging as Big Winner in Online Price Wars," from Dow Jones News Services, May 18, 1999, on Web site at www.wsj.com.

164. Steven M. Zeitchik, "Amazon.com to Open Its Fourth Distribution Center in Kansas," *Publishers Weekly*, April 19, 1999, from Web site at www.bookwire.com.

165. Peter DeJonge, "Riding the Wild, Perilous Waters of Amazon.com," *New York Times* magazine, March 14, 1999, pp. 36–41, 54, 68, 79–80; Jim Milliot, "Barnes & Noble Says Business Overhaul Nearly Finished," *Publishers Weekly*, May 19, 1997, p. 11; Patrick M. Reilly, "Barnes & Noble, Inc. Sues Rival Amazon.com," *Wall Street Journal*, May 13, 1997, p. B3; G. Bruce Knecht, "On-Line Book Retailer Amazon Sees Profit in Later Chapters, Files IPO," *Wall Street Journal*, March 25, 1997, p. B7.

166. Greco, "The Market for Consumer Books in the U.S.," pp. 3–40, offers an exemplary example of the fine work of Greco.

167. Felicity Barringer, "Times Mirror Sells Legal Unity to British Dutch Publisher," *New York Times*, April 28, 1998, p. D6; Frederic M. Biddle, "Times Mirror Co. to Review 3 Units; Disposal Is Possible," *Wall Street Journal*, November 25, 1997, p. B8; Jim Milliot, "Times Mirror Combines Bender and Mosby; Matthew Bender and Co., Mosby-Year Book Inc.," *Publisher's Weekly*, April 28, 1997, p. 14; Jim Milliot, "Times Mirror Reorganization Completed, Willes Says," *Publishers Weekly*, December 16, 1996, p. 11; Ronald Grover, "O.K., He Cut Costs. Now Can He Sell Newspapers?," *Business Week*, July 28, 1997, pp. 54–55; Jim Milliot, "Value of Publishing Mergers Tripled in '96," *Publishers Weekly*, April 14, 1997, p. 12.

168. Steven M. Zeitchik, "Outlook '99: No Place Like a Home Page," *Publishers Weekly*, January 4, 1999, from Web site at www.bookwire.com.

169. Patrick M. Reilly, "Luring Today's Teen Back to Books," *Wall Street Journal*, March 24, 1999, pp. B1, B4; Doreen Carvajal, "As Booksellers Suffer, Readers Depart," *New York Times*, May 3, 1999, p. C13.

170. Martin P. Levin, The Positive Role of Large Corporations in US Book Publishing," in Graham and Abel, pp. 225–244.

171. Albert N. Greco, "University Presses and the Trade Book Market: Managing in Turbulent Times," *Book Research Quarterly* 3 (Winter 1987–1988), pp. 30–35.

172. Patrick M. Reilly, "Barnes & Noble Draws Fire Over Plan to Buy Ingram Book for $600 Million," *Wall Street Journal*, November 9, 1998, p. B10.

173. Stephen Labaton, "Staff of F.T.C. Is Said to Oppose Barnes & Noble Bid to Wholesaler," *New York Times*, June 1, 1999, pp. A1, C9.

3

The Magazine Industry

Benjamin M. Compaine

The periodical business has remained relatively robust by constantly reinventing itself. It is highly responsive to fads and trends while at the same time supportive of titles that have published continuously for decades. Spurred in the 19th century by higher levels of literacy, as well as the twin steam-driven technologies of gravure for printing and railroads for distribution, magazines reached further into the population. Rising standards of living helped the advertising-driven business model take hold, keeping prices for readers well below the cost of production.

For much of their life, magazines served as *the* mass medium in American society. Now that other media, principally television, serve that purpose, magazine publishers exist largely by focusing on very specialized niches (e.g., cattle ranchers to brides-to-be). Publishers have become expert at co-opting trends that could have been far more deadly to the industry. Whereas television eroded the market for mass consumption good advertising, it provided the direct impetus for two of the most successful magazines of all times: *TV Guide* and *People*. Personal computers generated the market for dozens of highly popular and profitable periodicals. And the rise of the Internet has provided both an outlet for the content of publishers as well as the grist for still more magazines about it.

The mass circulation, general interest magazine is not quite dead. But very few remain. By far the largest portion of the magazine industry consists of special interest or limited audience publications, which may be consumer or business/trade oriented. Time Warner and Hearst are recognizable names in magazine publishing, but less well-known companies are among the top rank of publishers, including Bertelsmann, Ziff-Davis and Primedia.

Ownership trends in the periodical publishing business arouse far fewer emotions than developments in newspapers or television. Perhaps that is because periodical publishing is a relatively easy entry business. Although there are large corporate media companies at the top, small, independent publishers keep bubbling up from the bottom. Moreover, even small companies with modest circulation publications are often able to influence popular culture or a political debate with far greater notice than seemingly higher viability media.

The terms *magazine* and *periodical* are used interchangeably in this section. A magazine is defined as a publication that appears, or at least is intended to appear, on a regular basis with a minimum frequency of four times annually under a common title. Publications issued less frequently than quarterly are not counted in determining the size of publishing groups.

EVOLUTION OF MAGAZINES

Magazines evolved because of two unique characteristics that differentiated them from newspapers. First, as they did not have to carry up-to-the-minute news, they could rely on more leisurely delivery systems than newspapers, especially to rural areas. More importantly, in an age before television and radio, they were able to offer an advertiser national coverage. As Americans spent increasing amounts of money on raising their material standard of living, magazines benefitted from the expanding market for the goods and services advertisers offered.

Throughout the 20th century, magazines responded to the dynamics of several factors:

- more people with more money for discretionary spending;
- the spread of popular education;
- the increase in the amount of leisure time; and
- the need for specialized information for both hobbies and business.

Magazines have always faced competition in taking advantage of these changes. In the early years of the century, newspapers were the primary competition and, to a lesser extent, books. Soon movies became an important form of entertainment. Radio swept the nation in the 1920s, unmatched in speed of penetration until television came along in the 1950s. And inexpensive paperback books, getting under way just before World War II, became a major form of mass media. In the 1970s and 1980s, newsletters of all sorts combined the specialization of many periodicals with the immediacy of newspapers.

Under this barrage of competition, magazines nonetheless continued to expand, for in many ways each new medium helped the older ones. As book publishers have discovered that a successful movie helps boost book sales, so too have magazine publishers taken advantage of television. The popularity of televised spectator sports has stimulated sales of sports magazines. In 1998, *ESPN The Magazine* tried to ride on the coattails of the popular ESPN all-sports television network. News magazines find that newsstand sales jump in tandem with the same events that spike Cable News Network's (CNN) viewership.

Magazines Become More Specialized

Perhaps the most significant reason for the robust periodical industry has been its ability to adapt to a changing role in society. It is no longer needed as a national advertising tool for mass-oriented products. Television can supply far-flung regions with the same advertisement. Nor is it needed purely for entertainment, as television and the movies satisfy those needs. Magazines have changed, out of necessity as much as through foresight, into a medium for serving discrete interests within the mass population. Whereas most magazines used to be published for a mass readership, today even most of the so-called mass consumer magazines have narrowed their audiences down to definable proportions. Witness the development of magazines aimed not just at sports enthusiasts, but with a further specialization (e.g., *Condé Nast Women's Sports and Fitness*).

This specialization covers not just consumer magazines but the diverse information needs of business and the professions through a steadily increasing number of trade and association magazines, both paid and controlled (sent free to an eligible population) circulation. As with consumer magazines, business magazines serve the need of advertisers who wish to reach a well-defined audience for their product or service.

Number of Magazines Increasing

One indication of this specialization is a growing number of magazines, despite the leveling of total magazine circulation. In 1950, there were almost 6,600 periodicals of quarterly or greater frequency. In 1998, the number was over 11,800, although with deaths and births of many publications, the actual number of different titles is no doubt much greater.[1] The number of magazines peaked in the late 1980s and early 1990s. Most of the newer magazines have been small circulation, specialized publications serving alumni groups, industry associations, clubs, professional societies and the numerous consumer and trade interests that have emerged. But growth in total circulation has been less, because it takes many 25,000 and 150,000 circulation magazines to replace the mass circulation versions of *Life, Saturday Evening Post, Look* and *Colliers*. (Although the first two have reappeared, they are both structured to survive on less circulation than the six or eight million of their predecessors.)

Publishers have always been quick to sense new interests within the public and then establish new publications to cater to them. When the movies made Hollywood the center of attention for those curious about the private lives of the stars, *Photoplay* appeared and grew into a fat fan magazine. In 1934, with model railroad hobbyists numbering in the hundreds, an entrepreneur put out *Model Railroader*, a magazine whose circulation in 1998 was near 215,000. In 1951, when the aqualung made underwater adventure available to skilled swimmers, an enthusiast launched *Skin Diver*, selling 200,000 copies a month in 1998. Personal computing created yet another niche for publishers: *PC Magazine* (1.2 million), *PC World* (1.1 million) and *PC/Computing* (1.0 million) being among the consumer magazines. *PC Week, InfoWorld* and *PC World* are among the largest trade magazines. The Internet spawned its own publications, such as *InternetWeek*.

Whole categories have been created to meet new interests, and imitators have joined the successful innovators. There are magazines for gamblers, private pilots, brides-to-be, horse breeders, home decorators and fixer-uppers, antique collectors, followers of politics, sports, news, hair styles and psychology. Business periodicals exist for food engineers, automotive mechanics, consumer electronics, retailers, computer programmers and even for magazine publishers.

The Fragmenting Society

Whereas shared national radio and then television, which until the late 1980s programmed only a handful of networks, functioned to create a homogenizing of content and culture, magazines evolved as a medium for highly diverse interests. U.S. newspapers tended to serve specific geographic interests; television covered primarily common entertainment interests (less so as cable networks have evolved); publishers of magazines have been forced more than the other media to diversify for a variety of reasons:[2]

- *Job specialization.* A more complex society creates a need for specialized subgroups of managers, engineers, researchers and financiers. To meet the needs of these subgroups, many of which do not understand the language of the other, there are special publications tailored to their needs—the business and professional press.
- *The assertion of new freedoms and tastes.* American society has become more permissive, resulting in magazines that have responded to different groups asserting their potential of becoming new markets. This included magazines, such as *Ms.* or *Women's Sports*, that were different from the traditional women's magazines (i.e., *McCalls* or *Redbook*), or the sex magazines such as *Playboy* or *Hustler*. Youth was served by *Rolling Stone*, later by *Spin* and *Vibe*; Blacks by *Ebony* and *Jet*; and gays and lesbians with *Out Magazine*.
- *Spread of education.* In the second half of the 20th century, higher education became mass education in the United States. The proportion of adults that completed high school doubled between 1960 and the 1990s, and the proportion completing college tripled. The result has been the creation of a vast well-educated, literate audience (by historical standards) with a multiplicity of personal and intellectual interests.
- *A consumer haven.* With a market as vast and wealthy as that of the United States, almost any well-presented idea can create a highly lucrative, if limited, submarket for itself.
- *Increased opportunities to pursue interests.* More than just leisure time, Americans have the discretionary income to embrace a wide variety of pursuits, from bowling to camping, furniture building to wine making. People with similar interests join together, identifying with one another. Advertisers have adapted to new consumer trends by seeking out publications that will reach like groups of consumers. Among other things, they have learned that an individual will not react to a wine ad found in *TV Guide* the same as one that appears in *Gourmet*.

ROLE OF MAGAZINES

Throughout their history—and because of it—magazines have made substantial contributions to society and popular culture. First, by their very diversity, they have provided the populace with an inexpensive and open marketplace for an exchange of ideas, opinions and information, as well as a forum for debate. Among the over 10,000 periodicals in existence, there are magazines devoted to subjects from Ukrainian culture to the problems of retirement. This diversity has come at something of a price to the publisher: the high level of failure among the seemingly secure and established publications as well as the new ones. It has been calculated that of the 40 magazines with a circulation of over one million in 1951, fully 30% were no longer publishing by 1974.

Second, magazines play a role in the public enlightenment. Magazines have often taken the initiative in delving into national issues and problems, going back at least to the muckraking days of Ida Tarbell and Lincoln Steffens at *McClure's*. They have dealt with such concerns as the problems of equality, poverty in the midst of affluence, the decay of the cities, the administration of justice, the war in Vietnam, the corruption of politicians. In many cases, these issues were first brought up by the small, limited audience magazines and were then picked up for mass attention by the big magazines, sometimes years later. Consumer education has been a major topic for the *Journal of Home Economics* since the 1930s; the *New Republic* headlined "Consumers United!" back in November 1933. The tradition continues with niche magazines like *Mother Jones* initiating investigative articles often picked up by the major media.

Third, the magazine has long been the communicator and sometimes initiator of popular culture. The comic book heroes are an obvious example. But magazines also help create fads, in language as well as form. Often a scholarly journal will use certain words, such as "rubric." These words are picked up by the small circulation, high brow periodicals like the *New York Review of Books*, then make their way to an *Esquire*, and finally are adopted for ultimate diffusion by *Time* or *Newsweek*.

Fourth, magazines have provided a wide range of diversion—from sexual escapism to informative pieces on the space program.

Finally, they are instructors that help with daily living: They tell how to prepare food better, how to cope with the rigors of living in New York, how to order wine, how to build a platform bed, how to download files or tweak computer performance or where to go for a quiet vacation. *Better Homes & Gardens* once estimated that 2.2 million readers clip something for future reference from an average issue. *Hot Rod* has been found to be very popular in school libraries and is ordered in bulk by teachers who have determined that it holds great appeal for slow readers.

DEVELOPMENT OF THE INDUSTRY

The American magazine dates back to February 1741, when Andrew Bradford brought out *American Magazine, or a Monthly View of the Political State of the British Colonies*. His first issue beat Benjamin Franklin's *General Magazine* by three days.[3]

For the next 150 years, magazines existed on a small scale and with limited life: Bradford's effort died in three months, and Franklin's lasted only twice as long. Most magazines were for a small set of the educated and had limited circulations, with 2,000 to 3,000 being good-sized. The modern magazine can find its origins in two events of the late 19th century. In 1879, Congress acted to provide low cost mailing privileges for periodicals. This helped fuel the boom in publishing, already being fed by the growth in secondary education, as the number of magazines leaped from 700 in 1865 to 3,300 in 1885. Still, a large circulation was 100,000. Then, in October 1893, Frank A. Munsey announced a reduction in the subscription price of *Munsey's Magazine* from $3 to $1 per year and the single-copy price from 25 cents to 10 cents. Munsey was putting into practice what was then just an emerging concept, that by selling his magazine for less than its cost of production, he could achieve a large cir-

culation. His profits would come from the large volume of advertising a hefty circulation would attract. For the first time, publishers such as Cyrus Curtis, Edward Bok,
S. S. McClure and others began to provide magazines for the masses, filling the gap
between the "class" books such as *Harper's* and *Scribner's* and inexpensive pulp readers like the *People's Literary Companion*.

Munsey's idea worked. Circulation of his first 10-cent issue was 40,000. By April
1895, it was up to 500,000. This level was now economically feasible only because
the technologies of printing, paper and distribution had made print runs of that
magnitude logistically feasible. In the early 1900s, the characteristics of the modern
magazine had begun to emerge. Magazines had become low in price, typically costing 10 cents, sometimes 5 cents. Through this low price, mass production and mass
distribution, they had achieved undreamed of circulations. By 1900, the *Ladies'
Home Journal* was near one million.

The role of advertising became paramount. Publishers needed it to make their low
circulation prices work, and advertisers became attracted to magazines as a means of
reaching a national market. In attempting to serve wider audiences, magazine content was reaching out to appeal to new and diverse interests.

By the early 1900s, the magazine industry was dominated by giant publishers. In
1918, Curtis Publishing Co.'s three big magazines—the *Saturday Evening Post*,
Ladies' Home Journal and *Country Gentleman*—accounted for 43% of all national
advertising dollars spent in consumer and farm publications. In 1920, the five leading magazines in advertising revenues grossed $41.9 million, or 56% of the total. By
1997, however, such dominance had waned considerably. Time Warner, the largest
publisher in advertising revenue, accounted for 15.9% of the gross ad revenue of the
300 largest magazines, as compared to 16.3% of the total in 1980. The five largest
advertising revenue magazines (i.e., *People*, *Sports Illustrated*, *Time*, *TV Guide* and
Newsweek) together brought in 16 % of advertising revenue accounted for by 216
consumer magazines measured by the Publishers Information Bureau, as compared to
28% for the top five in 1980 and down from about 31% in 1973.[4]

If any single characteristic dominates the history of the magazine, it is its constant
state of flux. Since 1900, thousands of publications have come and gone. At the start
of 1995, 46 magazines on the market were at least a century old, and 832 were less
than a year old.[5] In 1930, 25 consumer and farm magazines had circulations in excess
of one million. Thirty years later, 15 were out of business. Yet others keep trying.
Many of the leading magazines in 1998 did not exist 10 or 20 years earlier, including *PC Magazine*, *Entertainment Weekly*, *Martha Stewart Living* and *Wired*.

THE COMPETITIVE NATURE OF MAGAZINE BUSINESS

Magazine publishing has been a vigorous, highly competitive business primarily
because of its economic structure. It has traditionally been an easy field to enter.
There are few structural barriers to entry: no need for large amounts of capital or regulatory walls. With a month or two credit from a printer, one or two people can put
out a first issue with almost no capital. Multimillion dollar full-blown national distri-

bution explosions from Time Warner or Condé Nast notwithstanding, magazine publishing is still possible for low rollers. Hugh Hefner reportedly assembled the first issue of *Playboy*, appropriately enough, from his bedroom, and *Rolling Stone* began in a loft.

Desktop publishing has helped create a new category of periodicals called "zines." These are low circulation publications with highly focused editorial. A zine "print run" may be several hundred photocopies of a single issue, although zine audiences range from as few as 25 readers to as many as 100,000. Examples of the narrow focus of the zine market are "girlzines" for teenage girls, with titles such as *Cupsize* and *Chickfactor*. One estimate calculated as many at 10,000 zines published in the United States in the mid-1990s.[6]

Besides its dynamic nature, a second pervasive feature of the industry is the central role of the entrepreneur: the individual with a concept. Time and again, the history of periodical publishing proves the role of the idea to be paramount. Money and initial execution are secondary. Hadden and Luce initiated the news summary magazine concept and got an edge that *Newsweek* is still trying to overcome. DeWitt Wallace did not do a mammoth marketing study before launching *Reader's Digest*; he just "felt" that it could sell and used his intuition to guide him. Publishing histories are dominated by the names of men (only more recently women), rarely organizations. It was Edward Bok who made the *Ladies' Home Journal* the largest circulation magazine in the world for a time and Cyrus Curtis who made the *Saturday Evening Post* into the most successful weekly of its time. Curtis could somehow sense a market for a new publication: Business associates and advertising people had advised him against starting the *Journal* and later the *Post*.

Theodore Peterson, author of *Magazines in the Twentieth Century*, divides publishers into two rough groups: the missionaries and the merchants. Their behavior is often similar, but their motivation differs. Those in the former group are publishers devoted to their cause, some "secular gospel." *Reader's Digest*'s Wallace preached optimism; Luce believed in the efficacy of photographs as vehicles for information and education; Harold Ross of the *New Yorker* strived for perfection; and Bernar Macfadden of *True Story* and *True Romances* used his publications to either directly promote his cause of bringing "health and joy through exercise, diet and the simple life" or to amass profits to further such ends through his foundation. John Johnston saw a niche to bring the successful formula of mainstream magazines to Black audiences, starting with *Negro Digest* in 1942, and three years later with *Ebony*.

The merchants are not particularly champions of some cause. They regard magazine publishing strictly as a profit-seeking business enterprise. Nonetheless, in pursuit of this, they often put out superior publications, such as S. S. McClure's *McClure's Magazine*. Condé Nast saw a niche for fashion publications catering to luxury-loving readers who would be attracted by slick, elegant publications, and the result was *Vogue, Glamour* and *Mademoiselle*. Wilford Fawcett and George T. Delacorte Jr. found profits in magazines edited for a lower level of sophistication. Fawcett's *Captain Billy's Whiz Bang* was followed by his copy of the confession magazines, then *Mechanix Illustrated*, which worked on the formula made successful by *Popular Mechanics*. Men copied *Esquire, Spot* followed *Life* and even *Superman* was imitated in the form of *Captain Marvel*.

Modern magazine founders likely have a mix of merchant and missionary. *Wired*, the first popular magazine to cover the new media in an innovative magazine format, was created by an entrepreneurial couple, Louis Rossetto and Jane Metcalf. Martha Stewart was the moving force behind *Martha Stewart Living*, initially bankrolled by Time Warner but later sold to her as part of an independent entity. Many of the computer magazines were started by people, such as Wayne Green, who were enamored with those new devices.

Magazine history is littered with a sense of déjà vu. Time Inc.'s *People* was preceded by Newsweek's *People Today*, introduced in 1950 as a 10-cent magazine "to portray . . . in words and pictures people in all their facets—at work, asleep, or very much alive." In 1900, there was *Shooting and Fishing* and *American Golf*; today there are *Field & Stream*, *Golf & Travel* and *Golf Digest*, among others. Periodically, publishers complain about the hardships being imposed by increases in second-class postage rates. Rate hearings in 1949 and 1962 produced the same complaints, but the resulting increases came and there was little change in the string of new magazines started, and no publication can trace its demise to the postal burden alone.

The industry is highly fragmented, so much so that no one company or group of companies dominates it. The largest general circulation magazine in 1997, *Reader's Digest*, accounted for 4.1% of per issue major consumer magazines sales, virtually the same as the 4.2% *TV Guide* accounted for in 1980, when it was the largest magazine (excluding association periodicals).[7] The great diversity of magazine editorial matter, combined with the considerable segmentation of interests within the population, ensures the existence of a large number of differentiated publications.

The great diversity of publishers and publications has its counterpart in a paucity of detailed information about the industry. Publishers are extremely close-mouthed about the economics of their operations; only a small minority report to the Publishers Information Bureau, which is an industry clearinghouse for advertising and circulation data. Most small publishing houses and many of the largest are privately owned and therefore need not release any of the details of their operation. Even many publicly owned firms lump operating figures of various enterprises together, making an analysis of magazine finances difficult.

SIZE OF THE INDUSTRY

The periodical publishing industry is a relatively small segment of the total industrial production, at .31% of 1996 Gross Domestic Product (GDP), but it accounts for 29% of shipments of the print mass media industry. After several decades of little growth, it experienced a strong rebirth through the 1980s: The value of shipments in 1990 was an estimated $20.7 billion, up 132% since 1980. During the same period, the overall economy, as measured by current dollar GDP, grew 52%. But, as seen in Table 3.1, the 1990s saw a slow down of that growth, with a 1990 to 1995 increase of only 15%, as compared to 26% for GDP. Industry employment in 1995 reached 123,000, less than one third the number of employees in the newspaper industry, although periodicals had shipments equal to almost two thirds that of newspapers. (The apparent efficiency stems in large

TABLE 3.1
Value of Periodical Shipments Compared to Gross Domestic Product, Selected Years, 1960–1995

	GDP (in billions)	Industry Value of Shipments (in millions)	Shipments as % of GDP
1960	$ 513	$ 2,133	0.42%
1970	1,011	3,195	0.32
1980	3,784	8,937	0.24
1990	5,744	20,746	0.36
1995	7,254	23,905	0.31

Sources: U.S. Bureau of the Census, *U.S. Industrial Outlook* and *Statistical Abstract of the United States*, annual editions.

measure from the fact that most newspapers do their printing in house, and most periodical publishers use third-party printers).

Circulation

As shown in Table 3.2, in 1997 the per issue circulation of the major consumer magazines was estimated at 366 million copies per issue, down slightly from the 369 million reached in 1990. Single copy sales accounted for 18% of the total, a proportion that has been falling almost continuously for decades. In 1980, single copy sales accounted for 34% of total consumer magazine circulation.

But of more interest is the calculation, also seen in Table 3.2, that circulation per adult has remained robust, unlike newspapers. It is actually above the level of the 1960s and 1970s. Average circulation per issue, at 621,000, is lower than in past decades, reflecting the larger number of magazines needed to sustain aggregate circulation growth.

TABLE 3.2
Circulation of All A.B.C. General and Farm Magazines in the United States, Selected Years, 1950–1997

	Number of Magazines	Single Copy (000)	Subscription (000)	Total Circulation (000)	Circulation Per 100 Adults	Average Circulation Per Magazine (000)	Single Copy %
1950	249	63,610	83,069	146,679	140.2	589	43.4%
1960	269	61,044	126,870	187,914	162.8	699	32.5
1970	303	69,761	175,545	245,306	182.9	810	28.4
1980	406	93,937	181,100	275,037	171.7	677	34.2
1985	474	80,540	240,866	321,406	182.8	678	25.1
1990	563	74,927	294,101	369,029	198.0	655	20.3
1995	583	65,462	297,655	363,117	187.6	623	18.0
1996	605	66,440	300,335	366,775	187.3	606	18.1
1997	590	66,350	29,9952	366,302	187.0	621	18.1

Sources: Circulation—Audit Bureau of Circulation records for January–June of each year. From Magazine Publishers of America, New York, NY. Population—U.S. Bureau of Census projected estimates of the resident population 18 years and older.

As television eroded individual magazines as a primary vehicle for mass market advertising, the demographics of readership or common lifestyle of the audience became more important than sheer numbers. Publishers referred to this as "quality" circulation. At about the same time, the new Postal Service replaced the old Post Office, with a mandate for various classes of postal service to cover its costs: Congress was determined to phase out the old second-class rate subsidy. Second-class rates alone went up 487% between 1971 and 1980. The result was that publishers claimed they would have to pass substantially greater costs to subscribers while putting greater emphasis on single copy sales. Some publications have traditionally built their distribution around emphasis on newsstand sales: *Playboy* long concentrated in this area, while some women's magazines—like *Woman's Day* (part of the Hachette Filipacchi), Bertelsmann's *Family Circle* and News Corporation's *TV Guide*—depended on single copy sales, relying on the supermarket checkout stand for viability. When Time Warner started *People*, it sold subscriptions only through offers in the magazine itself and then only at a price relatively close to the single copy price through newsstands and supermarkets.

But, in every one of these cases, the subscription model eventually won out, as second-class postage increases eased and concerns about paper costs became more critical: Newsstand sales involve returns and therefore waste, unlike subscriptions. In 1997, *TV Guide* was 2 to 1 subscriptions, *Family Circle* sold well over half its copies by subscription as did *People Weekly* (compared to 8% in 1980) and *Playboy* was about 4 to1 subscription to single copy.

Magazine Prices

Magazine prices advanced substantially faster than consumer prices in general during the 1970s. However, between 1980 and 1996, magazine subscription prices edged up less than prices in general. In 1980, the average subscription cost for consumer magazines was $19.87, whereas in 1996 it was up only 20% to $23.83. During that period, the Consumer Price Index rose 90%. Single copy prices increased about 50% in that period, still well under overall inflation.[8]

Number of Magazines

The number of periodicals in Table 3.3 includes consumer, business, farm, trade and academic publications, published at least quarterly. (Other compilations that use a less rigorous standard for periodicals, such as including annual publications, identified as many as 18,000 publications in 1998.) Between 1960 and 1980, the total increased by 13%. From 1980 to 1997, the increase was a far more robust 28%. Most of that increase was in quarterly and bimonthly periodicals. Monthly publication remained the most common interval, with slightly over one third of the periodicals appearing at that rate. Bimonthly publication also showed a strong preference, with much of the growth coming in the 1980–1990 period. The most dramatic shift was in the steep decline in the number of weekly periodicals, perhaps reflecting a lifestyle that made it burdensome for readers to make use of weekly magazines as well as the ability of television to satisfy the immediacy that weekly publications had filled in the past.

TABLE 3.3
Number of Periodicals by Frequency, Selected Years, 1950–1997

Frequency	1950	1960	1970	1980	1990	1995	1997	% change 1950–1997	% of total 1950	% of total 1997
Weekly	1,443	1,580	1,856	1,716	553	513	429	−70.0	21.9	4.5
Semimonthly	416	527	589	645	435	216	289	−30.5	6.3	3.1
Monthly	3,694	4,113	4,314	3,985	4,239	4,545	3,407	−7.8	56.0	36.0
Bimonthly	436	743	957	1,114	2,087	2,359	2,102	382.1	6.6	22.2
Quarterly	604	895	1,108	1,444	2,758	3,199	3,239	436.3	9.2	34.2
Total	6,593	7,858	8,824	8,904	10,072	10,832	11,408	43.6	100.0	100.0

Excludes less than quarterly and other frequencies.
Sources: *U.S. Statistical Abstract, 1997*, Table 906. Data from Gale Research Inc., Detroit, MI. *Directory of Publications and Broadcast Media*, annual editions.

Advertising

Magazine advertising revenue as a proportion of all advertising expenditures was stable in the 1990s, after enduring major inroads in its share of total advertising dollars following the growth of television. Magazines accounted for about 13% all advertising expenditures in 1945. That fell to as low as 5.2% in 1975, where it has remained, with small variations.

Table 3.4 shows that in 1997 about $9.8 billion was spent by advertisers in magazines, more than three times the level of 1980. Consumer prices in this period did not quite double. This is in contrast to newspapers, which showed weaker growth and continuing slide in the share of advertising expenditures.

Table 3.5, a tabulation of advertising revenue and pages in those general magazines that reported to the Publishers Information Bureau arm of the trade association, the Magazine Publishers of America, shows that magazine revenue gains were considerably greater than the actual pages of advertising. Between 1980 and 1997,

TABLE 3.4
Advertising Expenditures in Magazines, Selected Years, 1935–1997

	Magazines (in millions)	All Advertising (in millions)	Magazines % of Total
1935	$ 130	$ 1,720	7.6%
1950	478	5,700	8.4
1960	909	11,860	7.7
1970	1,292	19,550	6.6
1980	3,149	53,570	5.9
1985	5,155	94,900	5.4
1990	6,803	129,590	5.3
1995	8,580	162,930	5.3
1997	9,821	187,520	5.2

Source: "Estimated Annual Advertising Spending Details (1935–1997)," McCann-Erickson, New York. Accessed on Web site at www.mccann.com/res/asr.shtml.

TABLE 3.5
General Magazine Advertising Revenue and Pages Compared with GNP, Selected Years, 1945–1997

	Number of Magazines	Advertising Revenue	Advertising Pages	Average Revenue/Page	GDP* (in billions)
1945	97.0	286.7	NA	NA	213.4
1950	85	396.7	67,392	5,886	286.2
1960	79	380.0	74,861	11,087	506.0
1970	89	1,168.7	76,924	15,193	982.4
1980	102	2,846.1	114,705	24,812	2,626.1
1985	142	4,919.9	152,566	32,248	4,054.0
1990	167	6,753.3	171,689	39,335	5,568.0
1991	164	6,538.2	156,650	41,738	5,737.0
1992	173	7,141.9	163,514	43,678	6,046.0
1993	179	7,625.5	167,973	45,397	6,378.0
1994	185	8,504.6	180,589	47,094	6,947.0
1995	201	10,114.9	208,378	48,541	7,265.4
1996	208	11,179.2	213,781	52,293	7,636.0
1997	216.0	12,755.0	231,370	55,216	8,079.7

*Prior to 1960 measured in GNP.
Sources: Advertising—Publishers Information Bureau. GDP—U.S. Bureau of Economic Analysis.

revenue for these measured magazines was up 348%, but the number of advertising pages barely doubled. This is the result of a rapid escalation in average cost per thousand-page rate magazines. In 1980, an average black-and-white page cost $7.10 per thousand and a four-color page was $9.70 per thousand. In 1997, those rates were in excess of $22 and $29 per thousand, respectively.[9]

INDUSTRY STRUCTURE

There were 4,699 periodical publishing establishments in 1992, nearly two thirds more than the 2,860 periodical publishers in 1977, according to the 1992 and 1977 Census of Manufacturers. Just under 1,000 of these had 20 or more employees. However, thousands of periodicals are published by associations, universities or other entities that are not counted because publishing is not their principal line of business. The periodicals they publish can be roughly divided into two categories: consumer/farm and business. By far the largest revenue segment is general consumer magazines, accounting for 66% of combined magazine revenue. Farm publications make up only 3% of the market, with business, trade, organization and professional magazines accounting for the remainder.

Revenue Structure

Traditionally, magazines derived the bulk of their revenue from advertising. Depending on the size and type of periodical, the ratio between advertising and circulation revenue can vary greatly. Political magazines such as *The New Republic* or *The Weekly Standard* may look for circulation for 80% or more of their revenue. On the other hand, many "controlled circulation" business magazines depend on advertising for from 90% to 100% of their revenue.

For general consumer magazines, however, in the late 1960s advertising sales provided 60% of publishers' revenue. In the 1970s and 1980s, the general business strategy was to look for readers to pay a greater share of the cost of the publication, so that by the early 1990s circulation and advertising revenue, industrywide, were about equal. However, Figure 3.1 shows that publishers are again placing more of their fortunes in the hands of advertisers. Although circulation prices have risen at about the general rate of inflation, advertising rates have risen faster. This may reflect greater competition for consumer's discretionary media spending, which must incorporate video rentals and purchases, cable TV fees and Internet service provider fees, none of which existed among the mass audience until the 1980s and 1990s.

Production and Distribution Structure

The magazine business is a relatively easy one to enter as measured by capital needs because it is an almost pure "content" business. In terms of the information business map in Chapter 9, magazine publishing itself involves largely the services of the upper righthand corner of the map. Few magazines, for example, need to do their own typesetting (although the decreasing cost of photo typesetting technology has made this economically attractive to increasingly smaller publishers). Meredith Corp. is the only major publisher that prints its own publications. Almost all, from Time Warner on down, contract their printing to commercial printers. Many even contract out the subscription fulfillment process: the back shop operation involved in processing subscriptions and renewals. Finally, magazine publishers rely on third parties for delivery of their final product. Most publishers depend on the U.S. Postal Service to provide delivery, that being the only delivery service, including cable,

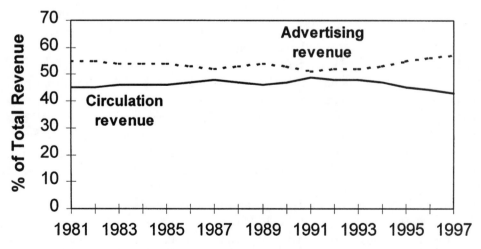

FIG. 3.1. Advertising and circulation revenue, 1981–1997. Source: *The Veronis, Suhler & Associates Communications Industry Forecast* (11th ed.), 1997, p. 300. Data from McCann-Erickson, VS&A Associates, Wilkofsky Gruen Associates, Magazine Publishers of America.

telephone and broadcasting, that has penetration to 100% of all households and institutions in the country.

Single copy sales are the greatest bottleneck in the consumer magazine structure. There are thousands of publishers. There are tens of thousands of retail outlets, from supermarkets to street corner kiosks. The Postal Service is a public utility that must deliver any publication that pays the posted tariffs. But the handful of private firms that distribute magazines to those retailers has contracted from 180 in 1995 to only 60 in 1998 (and the consolidation was continuing).[10] This has had a noticeable effect in the relation between distributors and publishers, as well as publishers and retailers.

For all the changes in the publishing business, the process of newsstand distribution has been singularly unique in its traditional nature. For decades, in most cities, there was a single wholesale distributor of magazines. Most were relatively small mom-and-pop businesses. Their role was to take bundles of magazines from publishers, make the rounds each week of the local retailers, remove the unsold copies of magazines (for which retailers got full credit) and stock the shelves and racks with current issues. The economics were simple: Wholesalers paid publishers 60% of the cover price for each sold copy. Retailers paid wholesalers 80% of the cover price. The wholesaler thus grossed 20% of the cover price of sold copies, although they had to handle more copies than were sold, having to distribute and take back unsold copies.

Although wholesalers were usually local monopolies and would seem to have leverage over any publisher that needed their service, in reality most were small enough that they did not have much clout with larger publishers. Their willingness to distribute an independent start-up magazine was often critical to young publications that could not afford the cost of direct mail campaigns for subscriptions. But usually these monopolies did take on new magazines, in some measure out of a sense of responsibility ("If I didn't no one else would" is how one wholesaler put it[11]), in another in the hope that the new magazine would grow to a profitable volume. With the fixed cost of the routes, adding a few more titles affected their costs little. Even so, not every niche publication can find its way into the retail channel.

It is somewhat of a paradox that this essential but sleepy business was not shaken up by publishers nor by the wholesalers' initiative for growth. Rather, several large national retailers were frustrated over the archaic magazine distribution system they faced. The change started when Safeway, a large West Coast supermarket chain, told wholesalers in part of its region that it would no longer deal with firms that only serviced a single city. Instead, they went out to look for competitive bids for wholesalers who would service an entire region. Other large retailers took the same approach. Wholesalers responded in two ways: one was with rapid mergers to create firms that could service larger regions. The second was with more attractive terms for retailers, the result of the competitive bidding against other newly regionalized wholesalers.

There were two benefits for regional and national retailers. First, they need to deal with fewer wholesalers, resulting in fewer accounts to pay and vendors to monitor. Kroger, a 1,300 store supermarket chain, has dropped from 95 to 5 wholesalers; Walgreen Drug Stores has reduced from 100 to 6 wholesalers. Wal-Mart claimed it was a "nightmare" paying the invoices of 305 wholesalers: Instead of the 20% margins they traditionally had, they are now able to negotiate from 25% to 30% discounts from cover prices.

Publishers, on the other hand, are split on the outcome of this new consolidation. Publishers of smaller magazine and would-be publishers have expressed the most concern. With retailers squeezing wholesaler margins, the wholesalers have tried to get steeper discounts from the publishers. It has also been feared that, with slimmer margins, wholesalers will focus on getting shelf space for more copies of the best-selling magazines, at the expense of slower moving publications. Initial evidence of this concern was only anecdotal. *The New Republic* reported that in the last half of 1997 its newsstand sales fell about 28%, to 4,907 weekly copies, from the similar period in 1995. In that same time period, subscriptions stayed even. The magazine's circulation director attributed the decline to the shrinking number of magazine stands on which it gets distributed.[12] Other small publishers see a silver lining, such as the improved distribution models that wholesalers have proposed that help determine the best outlets for different types of magazines, such as the health/fitness magazines of Weider Publications.[13]

Some large publishers expect to benefit. The chief executive of Time Inc. agreed that there were "too many magazines going through the system."[14] In one experiment, a supermarket chain cut the number of titles it displayed in several stores from 1,100 to 500. The outcome was an increase in magazine sales. This was attributed to greater attention to which titles would be displayed and the capability to give those titles better position on the rack.[15]

Some publishers view these distributors as being like common carriers: They must distribute to whoever needs them. Others believe they need to be more selective: "You don't need 40 titles on how to play golf," was how one summed it up.[16] What seems most likely is that smaller circulation magazines will need to pay more fees—perhaps a few cents for each copy returned—to get distribution.

Another paradox in the consolidation of wholesalers has been *greater* competition. Instead of what were essentially local monopolies, there are now multiple regional wholesalers who are bidding fiercely for the business of the retailers. The largest was Anderson News Co., a Tennessee-based firm with about 25% of the market. The second largest is Aramark Magazine & Book Services, Inc. A third major distributor, serving the Mid-West, is Chas. Levy Co.[17]

MAGAZINE PUBLISHER OWNERSHIP

Besides the considerable number and diversity of magazines, the periodical publishing industry shows relatively less concentration of ownership than large industries overall and a general decline in concentration between 1947 and 1992 (see Figure 3.2). Compared to newspaper and book publishing in Table 1.9, periodical publishing is marginally less concentrated. The steady dispersion of ownership and control in periodical publishing contradicts the myth of greater concentration. This gap between perception and reality is due largely to the high visibility of mergers but the difficulty of media coverage of the evolutionary growth of new players creating fresh magazine titles for changing markets. The list of group publishers in Table 3.10

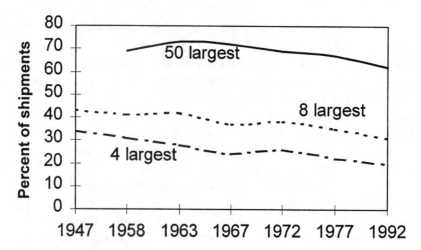

FIG. 3.2. Concentration ratios for periodical publishing, 1947–1992. Sources: U.S. Bureau of the Census, Census of Manufacturers, 1977, Table 7; 1992 Census of Manufacturers, Report MC92-S-2, "Concentration Ratios in Manufacturing," on Web site at www.census.gov/mcd/mancen/download/mc92cr.sum.

includes many names of sizable publishers who are far from the limelight. Even the largest mergers and acquisitions in 1997, in Table 3.18, includes few names that would be recognizable even to most media people.

The number of periodical publishing companies had also increased substantially by the 1992 Census of Manufacturers, with 4,390, compared with 2,860 identified periodical publishing firms in 1977, and an increase of 54% since the previous census. There were 2,430 publishing companies in 1967.[18]

Many of the largest circulation magazines are not necessarily found on the newsstand. In many cases, they are published by associations and are essentially a primary benefit that attracts membership. *National Geographic* (1997 circulation, 9 million, National Geographic Society), *Modern Maturity* (1997 circulation, 20 million, American Association of Retired People) and *Guideposts* (1997 circulation, 4 million, Guideposts) are among these magazines. Some of the largest and best-known magazines are also published by organizations that publish few, if any, additional periodicals: *Newsweek* (3.2 million, Washington Post Co.), *Reader's Digest* (15 million, Reader's Digest Association) and *Bloomberg Personal* (5.5 million, Bloomberg L.P.).

There were by one count about 315 multiple title publishers of consumer, farm and business periodicals identified by Standard Rate & Data Service (SR&DS) in mid-1981. (SR&DS itself did not provide the tally.) There is some double counting in that some groups, such as Ziff-Davis and Harcourt Brace Jovanovich, were included in both business and consumer/farm sectors. SR&DS lists only those publishers that accept advertising for their magazines. The listing is also incomplete, because Triangle (*TV Guide* and *Seventeen*) was not included and other publishers may have been omitted as well. Furthermore, many publications, such as academic journals, are not listed in any SR&DS publications, yet many of these journals do accept advertising and are published by groups.[19]

Using a measure and database not directly comparable, there were 210 multiple title groups in 1997. This compilation was restricted to magazines that 1) had their circulation confirmed by a recognized auditing service such as the Audit Bureau of Circulation, 2) accept advertising and 3) have single copies available for sale.[20]

For all these reasons, it is difficult to precisely measure the quantity of magazines that are published as part of multititle firms. It can be calculated that identifiable business and consumer/farm magazine groups published 1,464 audited titles of quarterly or greater annual frequency in 1997, a slight increase over the 1,429 titles in 1978. The proportion of publications from multititle publishers in 1997 was in the same 13% to 14% range of all periodical titles published as 1981.[21]

Group-Owned Versus Non-Group-Owned Magazines

As might be reasonably expected, there are some overall differences between magazines published as part of a group and those that are independent. Table 3.6 summarizes selected characteristics of the two types of ownership. The median circulation of non-group-owned consumer periodicals is about two thirds that of group-owned titles. This is to be expected: As an independent magazine becomes larger, more visible and presumably gains greater revenue and profit potential, it often becomes a more promising prospect either for purchase by a group publisher or for gaining the financial wherewithal to start or purchase additional publications itself, either way eventually becoming part of a group.

The subscription price of both types of magazines is quite similar, reflecting in part the common competition they face for the consumer's magazine budget and price expectations. They also must factor in the same postal rates and similar production costs. Single copy sales tend to be insignificant for most small magazines and therefore were not calculated here.

The basic cost per thousand (cpm) advertising rates are about the same for the group-owned and chain magazines in this sample. Large circulation mass audience magazines, regardless of ownership type, tend to have lower cpms than special interest magazines targeted to active participants in the subject matter of the magazines.

Largest Magazines

Table 3.7 lists the 50 largest magazines in 1997 by circulation per issue. Total circulation for the top 50 edged up almost 2% compared to 1980. The largest, *Modern Maturity*, is sent to all members of the American Association of Retired Persons. *TV*

TABLE 3.6
Selected Characteristics of Group-Owned and Independently Published Magazines

	Group-Owned	*Independent/Small Group*
Basic 1-year subscription	$ 23	$ 22
4-color ad cpm	$ 37.40	$ 36.05
Median circulation	1,009,000	707,000

Sources: Purposive sample of 26 group-owned consumer magazines and 17 independent or very small group-owned consumer magazines. Data on each magazine from *Oxbridge Directories of Print Media and Catalogs on CD-ROM*, third quarter, 1998. The universe of magazines was the *Advertising Age* compilation of the 300 largest magazines (by revenue), June 15, 1998.

TABLE 3.7

50 Largest Circulation Consumer Magazines and Their Owners, 1997

1997 Rank	1980 Rank	Magazine	Paid Circulation	Parent Company
1	7	Modern Maturity	20,390,755	American Association of Retired Persons
2	2	Reader's Digest	15,038,708	Reader's Digest Assoc.
3	1	TV Guide	13,103,187	News Corp.*
4	4	Better Homes & Gardens	7,605,187	Meredith Corp.
5	3	National Geographic	7,463,344	National Geographic Society
6	6	Family Circle	5,107,477	Bertelsmann
7	10	Good Housekeeping	4,739,592	Hearst Corp.
8	—	Consumer Reports	4,693,453	Consumers Union of U.S.
9	9	Ladies' Home Journal	4,590,155	Meredith Corp.
10	—	Cable Guide	4,544,778	TVSM
11	—	Taste of Home	4,504,700	Reiman Publications
12	5	Woman's Day	4,461,023	Hachette Filipacchi
13	8	McCall's	4,216,145	Bertelsmann
14	13	Time	4,155,806	Time Warner
15	—	Guideposts	3,730,400	Guideposts
16	20	People	3,608,111	Time Warner
17	21	Prevention	3,310,278	Rodale Press
18	22	Sports Illustrated	3,223,810	Time Warner
19	17	Newsweek	3,177,407	Washington Post Co.
20	12	Playboy	3,169,697	Playboy Enterprises
21	14	Redbook	2,889,466	Hearst Corp.
22	19	American Legion	2,734,318	American Legion
23	18	Cosmopolitan	2,701,916	Hearst Corp.
24	36	Seventeen	2,567,613	Primedia
25	30	Southern Living	2,474,463	Time Warner
26	—	Martha Stewart Living	2,339,799	Martha Stewart Living Omnimedia
27	11	National Enquirer	2,324,678	American Media
28	—	Highlights for Children	2,284,500	Highlights for Children
29	23	U.S. News & World Report	2,224,003	Mortimer Zuckerman
30	—	YM	2,221,937	Bertelsmann
31	25	Glamour	2,115,642	Advance Publications
32	27	Smithsonian	2,065,432	Smithsonian Institution
33	—	Country Woman	1,955,772	Reiman Publications
34	16	Star Magazine	1,948,247	American Media
35	—	Money	1,935,402	Time Warner
36	—	Teen	1,842,186	Petersen Publishing Co.
37	46	Ebony	1,819,431	Johnson Publishing Co.
38	24	Field & Stream	1,751,772	Times Mirror Co.
39	37	Parents	1,745,292	Bertelsmann
40	—	Country Living	1,697,742	Hearst Corp.
41	—	Country	1,599,155	Reiman Publications
42	44	Life	1,568,565	Time Warner
43	26	Popular Science	1,558,655	Times Mirror Co.
44	—	Golf Digest	1,529,671	New York Times Co.
45	—	Men's Health	1,511,345	Rodale Press
46	—	Woman's World	1,505,637	Bauer Publishing Co.
47	—	Birds & Blooms	1,476,434	Reiman Publications
48	42	Sunset	1,471,825	Time Warner

(Continued)

TABLE 3.7 (Continued)

1997 Rank	1980 Rank	Magazine	Paid Circulation	Parent Company
49	32	Popular Mechanics	1,425,692	Hearst Corp.
50	—	First For Women	1,408,419	Bauer Publishing Co.
		50 magazines, 1997	183,529,022	
		50 magazines, 1980	180,219,972	

1980 rank: — means title did not exist or was not in top 50.
Underlined are publishers with three or fewer magazines.
* Sold in 1998 to United Video Satellite Group.
Source: "Top 300 Magazines," Advertising Age, June 15, 1998. Omitted are magazines that are distributed as supplements of Sunday newspapers, such as Parade, USA Weekend and the New York Times Magazine.

Guide, which sold nearly 18 million copies per issue in 1980, fell behind longtime leader Reader's Digest, whose own domestic circulation fell from 18 million in 1980 to 15 million in 1997. The top 10 magazines accounted for 24% of the total aggregate per issue circulation of the magazines counted in Table 3.2, up slightly from the 22% for the 10 largest in 1980.

Of the top 10, 8 have long been among the leaders. Consumer Reports and Cable Guide are not only new to the top 10, but to the top 50 as well. They displaced McCalls and Woman's Day.

Most of the 50 largest magazines are part of groups. Some, like National Geographic, Playboy and U.S. News & World Report, are part of publishers with just one or two other titles. Most are parts of larger magazine publishing companies, such as Time Warner or Hearst, that have many publications.

Many of the largest magazines are published by associations and not-for-profit organizations, in which the magazine is a major "deliverable" for members. Among these are National Geographic, Smithsonian, Modern Maturity and American Legion. The compilation of largest magazines also contains the names of many publishers who were either not around or much smaller in 1980: Bauer Publishing, Reiman Publishing, American Media, Primedia, Martha Stewart Omnimedia, Mortimer Zuckerman. On the other hand, some large media companies that had substantial publishing interests in 1980 were largely or substantially out of the business in 1998: CBS, Inc., ABC (which had shut down or divested most of their consumer periodicals before being acquired by Disney) and Triangle Publications.

Leading Publishers

There are, to be sure, options in determining which are the largest magazine publishers. Three of these are: by the number of magazines published by groups, by total circulation of the groups magazines and by total magazine revenue.

By Number of Magazines

In 1998 there were thousands of organizations publishing one or more consumer, farm, trade, professional or scholarly periodicals. The American Automobile Association published 20 titles. Advisor Publications (Data Base Advisor et al.) had 12 titles. Hundreds of colleges and universities published magazines for their alumni. Professional and trade associations published magazines for their constituencies: for example, the 8,600 circulation monthly *Journal of Coatings Technology* from the Federation of Societies for Coatings Technology or *Stone in America*, a monthly from the American Monument Association. There is even the *Federal Law Enforcement Bulletin*, a 46,000 monthly from the Federal Bureau of Investigation (FBI).

Table 3.8 identifies the largest publishers by number of periodicals. The compilation of groups by number of titles introduces a number of players not found in either the largest revenue of circulation lists in Tables 3.9 and 3.10. Indeed, many are far from household names.

Primedia, once known as K-III, is composed of both trade periodicals and well-known consumer magazines. It purchased *Modern Bride*, once owned by Ziff-Davis; *Seventeen*, owned by Triangle Publications for many years and then News Corp.; and *New York* and groups of trade magazines (e.g, Intertec Publishing Co., with titles that include *Hay & Forage Grower* and *Modern Bulk Transporter*). United News & Media is largely unknown in the United States, but in 1998 was a $2.8 billion British media company. Its U.S. magazine holdings derive from the Miller-Freeman group of trade publications, ranging from *Computer Telephony* magazine to *Kitchen & Bath Business*. Reed-Elsevier, largely through its Cahner's subsidiary, publishes 74 trade magazines, but their aggregate 1997 circulation of 4.3 million does not put it among the largest publishers by that criterion. Kappa Publishing Group is part of Magazine Editorial Service, an obscure suburban Philadelphia operation. Most of its publications are bimonthly games and crossword puzzle periodicals, with titles like *All Number Finds*

TABLE 3.8
Largest Magazine Groups by Number of Periodicals, 1997

Rank	Publisher	# of Titles	Primary Types
1.	Primedia*	125	Consumer/Trade
2.	United News & Media	97	Trade
3.	Reed Elsevier	76	Trade
4.	Kappa Publishing Group	72	Consumer
5.	Petersen Publishing	54	Consumer
6.	Advanstar Communications	50	Trade
7.	Sterling/Macfadden	41	Consumer
8.	Harris Publications	39	Trade/Consumer
9.	Game & Fish Publications	38	Consumer
10.	National Mediarep	36	Consumer
11.	Penton Media	36	Trade
12.	Time Warner	28	Consumer
13.	Meredith	28	Consumer
14.	Thomson	28	Trade
15.	PennWell	26	Trade
16.	Fish and Game Finder Magazines	24	Consumer

*Does not include 38 titles purchased from Cowles Media in 1998.

Sources: *Oxbridge Directories of Print Media and Catalogs on CD-ROM*, third quarter, 1998; Corporate Web sites. Includes publications of quarterly or greater frequency.

and *Featured Crosswords*. But they also publish a few magazines with more traditional content, such as *American Astrology* and *World Boxing*.

What is very clear from this data—and the many additional groups with 10 or 20
titles—is the overwhelming variety and diversity among the magazines published by
these groups. Game & Fish Publications concentrates in highly regional versions of
game and fishing magazines, localized by state. They may be easily confused with
Fish and Games Finder Magazines, with a portfolio of state-specific titles ending in
"Fish Finder," such as *Louisiana Fish Finder*. Only by browsing through one of the
directories that list all the periodicals that can be called magazines can one appreciate the breadth of the periodical publishing business. Indeed, many of the descriptions used to describe the vastness of the World Wide Web today may be applied to
magazine publishing: overwhelming, targeted, easy entry, obscure sites and so on.

Few of the 12,000 periodicals that are in the Oxbridge Communications' *Directories of Print Media and Catalogs* in 1998 could be considered general circulation by
any stretch. Most are sent to targeted groups: members of trade associations, specific industries, consumer groups, professional societies. Two thirds of them seek out
advertising and many of those are totally supported by advertising. Only 13% of all
magazines, 1,522, have any newsstand circulation. (Of course, few newsstand operators could display even that number of titles, but many may be culled out by region
or local interests.) A larger proportion, 22%, are "controlled circulation" magazines.
In most cases, this means they are sent for free to subscribers who qualify, by reason
of membership or interest. Only 22% have their circulation audited by a recognized
organization such as the Audit Bureau of Circulation (ABC) or BPA International.
General advertisers want to be assured that circulation is as reported and will give
high credibility to magazines that provide audited data. The other 78% report their
circulation with no guarantees that they are accurate.

All in all, the 16 firms with the greatest number of magazine titles had, in 1997,
769 magazines, or about 6.5% of all periodicals published in the United States four
times annually or greater.

By Magazine Circulation

Having a large stable of periodicals does not necessarily translate into large aggregate circulation. With a single magazine, the American Association of Retired Persons claims greater circulation than all groups—except three. News Corp. was
among the leading groups primarily by virtue of *TV Guide*, which it subsequently
sold but in which it maintained an indirect minority interest. This compilation does
not include the circulation of *Parade*, the Sunday supplement distributed in about 38
million newspapers by the Newhouse group.

The predominance of the Time Warner publications is perhaps greater by another measure of circulation: total number of magazines sold in a year. Based on the calculation in Table 3.10, Meredith's circulation is 1% greater than Time Warner's, the
second largest publisher by this measure and 10% larger than Primedia's. Although
almost all the magazines of the other publishers are monthly or less frequency, Time
Warner has its four mass circulation weeklies (*Time*, *Sports Illustrated*, *People Week-*

TABLE 3.9
Largest Magazine Publishers in the United States, by Circulation, 1997

Publisher	Total Circulation per Issue* (000)	Number of Domestic Consumer Magazines
1. Meredith	31,734	28
2. Time Warner	31,344	28
3. Primedia**	28,970	61
4. American Association of Retired Persons	20,391	1
5. Bertelsmann	22,233	14
6. Hearst	20,470	21
7. Hachette-Filipacci	18,195	31
8. Reader's Digest Association	16,953	5
9. News Corp.***	15,450	3
10. Advance Publications (Newhouse)	14,338	17
11. Reiman Publications	11,750	7
12. National Geographic Society	10,937	3
13. Petersen Publishing	10,652	36
14. Disney	10,265	10
15. Rodale Press	9,139	13
16. Scholastic	8,689	19
17. Times Mirror	6,426	9

*Sum of one issue of each magazine, quarterly or greater frequency. Includes only consumers. Circulation as reported by publisher.
**Includes publications of Cowles Media, acquired in 1998.
***13 million of this is from *TV Guide*, which News Corp. sold in 1998 to United Video Satellite Group in exchange for a large minority equity interest in United Video.
Sources: *Oxbridge Directories of Print Media and Catalogs on CD-ROM*, third quarter, 1998; company Web sites.

ly, *Entertainment Weekly*), as well as the biweekly *Fortune*. If circulation is weighted by frequency, Time Warner's magazines sold over 1 billion copies in 1997. Meredith, on the other hand, has a stable of monthlies, bimonthlies and quarterly publications, as does Primedia. Thus, Meredith's cumulative annual circulation in 1997 was 269 million copies, about one fourth that of Time Warner. By this measure, News Corp., before the sale of the 13 million biweekly circulation *TV Guide* and with 2.2 million weekly sales of the supermarket tabloid *Star*, would have been rated the second largest published, with almost half the annual circulation of the Time Warner group.

Most of the groups in Table 3.10 can attribute all or most of their circulation to consumer magazines. Only Primedia has a substantial trade presence as well.

By Revenue

As might be expected, Time Warner is by far the largest magazine publisher in the United States based on revenue. Table 3.11 identifies the largest publishers by revenue derived from periodical publication. The number of domestic magazines in the table excludes the many editions that publishers such as Reader's Digest and Hearst publish or license globally. It also does not count separately overseas editions of domestic magazines, such as *Time Europe*. Hearst Corp., publisher of *Good House-*

TABLE 3.10
Largest Magazine Publishers in the United States, by Revenue, 1997

Publisher	Revenue from Magazines (in millions)	Number of Domestic Magazines
1. Time Warner	$ 3,071	28
2. Hearst	1,460	21
3. Advance Publications (Newhouse)	1,283	17
4. Reed-Elsevier	1,269	76
5. Thomson Corp.	937	28
6. Primedia	859	125
7. Reader's Digest Association	811	5
8. International Data Grp	787	13
9. Ziff-Davis Publishing	748	15
10. News Corp.	673	3
11. United News & Media	605	87
12. Hachette-Filipacchi	605	23
13. Meredith Corp.	568	28
14. McGraw-Hill	484	24
15. Bertelsmann	474	14

Sources: *Advertising Age*, 8/17/98, Leading 100 Media Companies, p. S10; *Oxbridge Directories of Print Media and Catalogs on CD-ROM*, third quarter, 1998; Hoover's Profiles Online; 10-K reports.

keeping and *Cosmopolitan*, among others, was a distant second. Revenue for Advance Publications, part of the Newhouse interests, are enhanced by advertising revenue from *Parade*, the Sunday newspaper magazine it publishes. However, neither *Parade* nor other weekend newspaper magazines are included in the total of magazines. *Parade* is purchased by newspapers and not directly by end users. *USA Weekend*, also a Sunday Gannett-published supplement, is likewise not included. McGraw-Hill is the only predominantly business periodical publisher in the group, although many of Primedia's publications (but not circulation) are trade and business periodicals.

Relative Consumer Magazine Group Size

Between 1980 and 1997 there was less change in the makeup of the size of periodical publishing groups than may be first indicated by Table 3.11. In that table, the percentage of all magazine publishing groups (defined as publishing two or more magazines) with aggregate circulation of 300,000 or fewer copies per issue increased from 38% to 58%. However, that may be due to the different sources used to calculate the two periods. The 1980 period counted groups that subscribed to SR&DS, and the 1997 data was derived from a larger universe of all periodicals. As the smaller groups would be least likely to participate with SR&DS, they are very likely to be underrepresented at the low end. Among middle level of groups—300,000 to 3 million circulation—the percentages are close. At the high end, the data suggests that the proportion of groups with many magazines or a few large circulation periodicals has actually declined. In 1997, only 13 groups out of 364 had aggregate circulation of 10 million or more copies per issue, or about 4% of that universe. In 1980, eight groups were of similar size. But with the same caveat about the source of

TABLE 3.11
Circulation Size of Consumer Magazine Groups, 1980 and 1997

Circulation Size	Number		Percent		Cumulative Percent	
	1997	1980	1997	1980	1997	1980
Under 300,000	203	33	56	38	56	38
300,000 to 999,999	81	20	22	23	78	61
1 to 3 million	53	14	15	16	93	77
3 to 10 million	14	11	4	13	97	90
Over 10 million	13	8	4	9	101	99
Totals*	364	86	100	99	101	99

*Does not equal 100% due to rounding.
Sources: 1997: Compiled from *Oxbridge Directories of Print Media and Catalogs on CD-ROM*, third quarter, 1998. 1980: Calculated from circulation reported in *Standard Rate & Data Service, Consumer-and Farm Magazines*, May 27, 1981.

the data, it may be reasonable to assume that the proportion of a broader consumer magazine universe would have been similar to 1997.

TRENDS IN NEW PUBLICATIONS

As noted previously, periodical publishing is a relatively easy entry enterprise. With printing, fulfillment and delivery all handled by outside parties, magazines may be started with investments of under $100,000. For larger publishers with deeper pockets, testing a new magazine as a one-shot publication is a modest investment.

The other side of the low cost, low risk equation is the historically low survival rate of new titles, regardless of the stature of the publisher. In 1973, about 127 new consumer magazines were announced or made their first appearance. Some of them were major, well-financed operations, such as *New Times* or *Viva*. Others were obscure and of uncertain origins, like *New Awareness* and *Alaska Geographic*. By 1981, not one of these was still a going concern.

Premature Obituaries

The doubters have written off the magazine's future six times during the 20th century.

1) After World War I, when the automobile became established as a legitimate business and pleasure vehicles for the masses, observers felt that people would no longer have time to read magazines.

2) In the mid-1920s, the radio was the source of dire predictions—who needs to read when you can just listen to the box?

3) Still later in that decade, the addition of "talkies" to the movie world added more cause for doom.

4) Then came television after World War II, the medium that did knock some magazines for a loop and, more than any other single factor, has changed the nature of other media.

5) In the late 1960s and early 1970s, the demise of such icons as the *Saturday Evening Post*, *Life* and *Look* convinced many that magazines had finally had it.

6) In the 1980s, the advent of video cassettes and the potential of video disks and video-text (a failed premonition of the World Wide Web) had some futurists again writing off the printed magazine as a viable medium.

But magazines have proven robust. Magazines have evolved and fulfill a different role than in the early decades of the 20th century. And perhaps having survived, the diviners of the future of media have not seemed to promote the World Wide Web as a new source for doubt about the immediate future of magazines. Indeed, it has spawned a variant dubbed "e-zines," magazines that are produced not in print but via the Web.

Turnover, New Titles and Interests

Because various sources use differing criteria for defining a magazine, it is difficult to pull together data on the number of new periodicals and their survival over an extended period. Figure 3.3 shows the year founded of some consumer magazines published at least quarterly that were still being published in 1998.

Many periodicals do not last long, often but not always because they are under-capitalized. A study of what happened to new magazines found that out of 102 magazines that were started in 1981, only 17% were still in existence in 1987.[22] Statistically, only 20% of magazines survived fours years after their start up. Perhaps more critically, the study found no difference between the survival rate of magazines started by the 100 leading media companies and all others. Moreover, far more magazines were started by smaller or nonmedia entities than by media companies. Of the 65 consumer magazines started between 1981 and 1983 that this study tracked, 12 were from the large media companies, and 53 were from all others. Among the magazines that large publishers launched and folded in this period were *TV-Cable Week* and

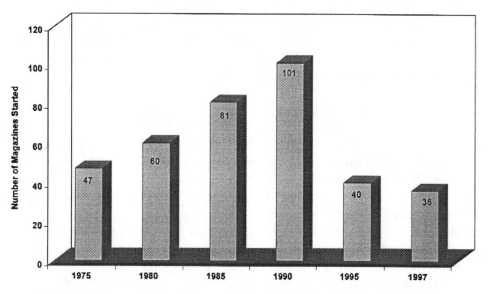

FIG. 3.3.   Year started for consumer magazines still published in 1998 ($n = 365$). Source: *Oxbridge Directories of Print Media and Catalogs on CD-ROM*, third quarter, 1998.

Picture Week, from Time Inc.; *Panorama*, from *TV Guide* publisher Triangle Publications; and *Playboy Guides to Fashion and Electronics* from Playboy Enterprises.

Clearly, magazine publishing is high risk, but it brings a constant stream of hopefuls into the marketplace each year. Entrepreneurial publishers are quick to respond to new interests, industries and trends. The increased penetration of cable television and other home video devices, such as the video cassette recorder, created a market of readers for such magazines as *Video Review* and *Videography*. More successful has been the proliferation of magazines serving the expanding personal computer market. Some, such as IDG's *Computerworld* and Reed-Elsevier's *Datamation*, date back to 1968 and 1957, respectively. But others, such as *Family Computing* (1994), have been started or repositioned to reflect the broadening base of personal computer users.

This profusion of new titles, added to the constantly changing titles over the years, has been the reason that magazines as an industry have been able to survive. As leisure time for most Americans has increased, publishers have discovered a great assortment of hobbies, cults and pursuits. Interests have become more diversified and publishers have always been quick to establish new magazines catering to them. Titles such as *Shooting and Fishing, American Golf Bird-Lore* and *Snap-Shots* may sound contemporary but were in fact the special interest publications of 1900. One can scarcely name a specialized subject that does not have its own publication. Moreover, as mentioned previously, as a title in a new category becomes successful, it is copied by others.

Even television has given a boost to some magazines. Although TV is blamed for the demise of the entertainment value of magazines, as another medium of information, television often whets the appetite of its viewers for more information. Thus, newsstand sales of news magazines, among others, jump during such major events as Watergate in 1973, the Gulf War in 1991 and the sex scandals that swirled around President Clinton in 1998. The success of *TV Guide* and then cable guides are, of course, linked closely to the penetration of television, and a publication such as *Sports Illustrated* can look to television's expanding coverage of sports as a factor in its success. Table 3.12 identifies some of the magazines introduced just in 1997. They cover a typically broad range of special interests and were started by a myriad of publishers, both established and new, groups and independent.

ROLE OF THE ENTREPRENEUR

Quite possibly, more than in any other industry, the success or failure, the mediocrity or acclaim, of a general interest magazine can be traced to a specific individual: a Hugh Hefner, De Witt Wallace, Henry Luce, Cyrus Curtis, a Bok, Gingrich, McClure or Ross. Magazines—that is, the best magazines—have long been closely associated with a personality. And although it does not have to happen, all too frequently when that individual passes from the scene, the magazine begins to fade also. It may survive, but as a different publication, reflecting the personality of another.

It is this observation that has led Clay Felker, former editor of *Esquire* and *New York Magazine*, to postulate the life cycle hypothesis of magazine longevity. "There

TABLE 3.12
Selected Magazines Introduced in 1997

Title	Publisher	Audience/Editorial Concept
@Austin	Capital Times Co.	A magazine about the people of Austin and what they're up to, the places worth seeing and the best things to see and do.
Alive	US Flies Alive	A magazine dedicated to the people shuttling between two worlds, the Arab world and the West.
Blue	Blue Media Ventures LLC	No existing American publication sufficiently celebrates the diversity of the planet and spirit of adventure one learns in discussing its details.
Capital Style	Roll Call, Inc.	The art of political living in our busy nation's capital.
Christian Motorsports Illustrated	CPO Publishing	CMI is a reader written forum for proclaiming the good news of Jesus Christ and his love.
Coastal Living	**Southern Progress (Time Warner)**	If you love the sand, the wind, the surf and the sun, then this is the magazine for you.
Condé Nast Sports for Women	**Condé Nast (Newhouse)**	A book devoted to women who love to play.
Gold Collector's Series: Eye of the Tiger	H&S Media	The only quarterly magazine dedicated to golf's greatest golfer, plus exclusive stories and more Tiger photos than anywhere else.
Icon Thoughtstyle Magazine	Icon Thoughtstyle Magazine	For those people who haven't wound up in the middle.
Jane	**Fairchild Publications (Disney)**	A magazine for the new woman.
Jump	**Weider Publications**	For girls who dare to be real.
Kid's Wall Street News	Kid's Wall Street News	A financial publication dedicated to all kids.
Ladies' Home Journal More	**Meredith Publications**	Not young, but good; fashion we can actually wear, and real problems.
Luxe	ASM Communications	Luxe features luxury marketing like no other magazine.
MAMM	POZ Publishing, LLC	Courage, respect, survival: These are the topics discussed in this magazine.
Maxim	Dennis Maxum, Inc.	The best thing to happen to men since women.
Milton	Berle-Moll Enterprises, Inc.	We smoke, we drink and we gamble.
Mode	Lewit and LeWinter, Inc., and Pantheon	A magazine that should conform to anyone's limited definition of beauty.
Mr. Food's Easy Cooking	Hearst	New meal ideas from America's favorite TV chef.
Muse	**The Cricket Magazine Group**	This magazine will show you that there are lots of things out there for children to be interested in.
North & South	North & South, Inc	A book to give the truth about "fresh" history.
Notorious	Notorious Partners, L.P.	A wide range of entertainment for all women and men.
Oxymoron	Oxymoron Media Inc.	Poetry, essays and special writings by selected authors.
Siren	Siren	If you're tired of reading only about orgasms, lipstick and sex, buy Siren
WE Magazine	WE, Inc.	This is a lifestyle magazine that specializes in people with disabilities.
Wine X Magazine	Wine X Magazine	For the young—Gen X—wine lovers.

Major magazine group publishers in **bold**.

Source: "30 Most Notable New Magazines for 1997," *Mr. Magazine*, on Web site at www.mrmagazine.com/nl/archive.cfm.

appears to be an almost inexorable life cycle of American magazines that follows the pattern of humans," wrote Felker, in the spring 1969 issue of *The Antioch Review*. That pattern is "a clamorous youth eager to be noticed; vigorous, productive middle-age marked by an easy-to-define editorial line; and a long, slow decline, in which efforts at revival are sporadic and tragically doomed."

This hypothesis strikes a logical note because magazines are so intensely personal. A successful editorial policy is more than just the assembling of data by a committee or an analysis of a market. "A key fact about magazines," noted Felker, is that unlike any other mass medium, "one man [sic] can influence every idea, every layout, every word that appears in print." Yet, a basic problem that faces the successful magazine is that both the publishers and their formulas become obsolete. And a corollary of this hypothesis is that the bigger the periodical is, the more reluctant it is to change.

Although some longtime publishers have been able to successfully launch new publications from corporate headquarters, some of the most original still come from individual entrepreneurs. In the tradition of entrepreneurs with a vision, Louis Rossetto and Jane Metcalfe started *Wired* in 1993 with a rather unique concept of capturing the newly blossoming digital culture in an analog format. The magazine received substantial media attention for its unique format and style. But, also in a frequently repeated tradition, in 1998 the founders sold it to Advance Publications, one if its early investors.

Steven Brill is a lawyer with a passion for the media. He was the founder of cable's *Court TV* as well as *American Lawyer* magazine. Both eventually became part of Time Warner. But in 1998 Brill started another magazine, *Brill's Content*, because of a professed concern for the state of journalism and a hope that the magazine ultimately would serve to improve the quality of journalism.[23] The first issue sold 325,000 copies.

The "visionary individual" hypothesis seems to have some validity just on its face. But it does not completely explain the success of many corporate start-ups and the remakes of older publications.

Corporate Start-ups

One of the significant trends in recent years has been the increased willingness of chains to undertake start-ups. Traditionally, the large firms have acquired existing publications: the survivors from the many start-ups undertaken by individuals and small publishers. The attitude of many large publishers was summed up by John Purcell, former executive vice president of CBS' now-defunct magazine group. Asked why CBS did not engage in more start-ups, he noted that some had been considered but added: "Bear in mind that the equivalent of starting a new magazine the size of *Road & Track*, with all its success, is just about the same as adding another issue of *Woman's Day*, which has a lot less risk."[24] CBS sold all its magazines in the 1980s.

Nonetheless, the high prices being paid for successful publications by acquisition-minded firms have made start-ups relatively more attractive, although some publishers are more likely to initiate new publications than others. Meredith, publisher of *Better Homes and Gardens*, for example, has created a stable of spins-offs over the years, including *Better Homes and Gardens American Woodcrafts Gallery*, *Better Homes and Gardens American Patchwork & Quilting* and *Better Homes and Gardens Kitchen & Bath Ideas*. Typically, these brand extensions were started as one-shot or annual publications. If successful, they were brought back as quarterlies and, as the market warranted, evolved into bimonthly or monthly publications.

Condé Nast, as part of Newhouse's Advance Publications, was not particularly known as a publisher of new titles. But it did introduce *Self* in 1978. In 1997 it started *Condé Nast Sports for Women*, then in 1998 acquired a more established competitor, *Women's Sports + Fitness*, and merged the two magazines to make *Condé Nast Women's Sports and Fitness*. Time Warner and Hearst are also among the leading companies that have been willing to start up new titles. Hearst's *Good Housekeeping* spawned *Country Living*, which in turn gave birth to *Country Living Gardner*. And so it goes, from the general to the special interest topics.

Time Inc., the publishing unit of Time Warner, has had a history of boldness in launching new magazines, often without the safety net of brand extensions. They have also been known to stick with an unprofitable publication for several years, in contrast to other well-financed publishers who allow a year or two in which to become profitable. Henry Luce kept *Sports Illustrated* alive for seven years before it made money. However, even Time was more willing to pull the plug on some of its more recent start-ups that did not catch on, such as *TV-Cable Week* and *Picture Week*. But it has also bankrolled successful start-ups, including *Entertainment Weekly* and *Martha Stewart's Living* (the latter spun off to a company owned by founding inspiration, Martha Stewart.*)

Large publishers are often the only ones who can provide direct competition with established major magazines. For years, for example, Time's *Sports Illustrated* was the lone major general interest magazine for followers of professional sports. In 1997, however, Disney, having acquired the ESPN all-sports cable network as well as a large magazine publishing division as part of its acquisition of Capital Cities/ABC, decided to create a competitor using the ESPN brand name. It was reported that Disney had budgeted $50 million to carry *ESPN Magazine* to profitability.[25]

TWO STRATEGIES: START-UPS AND ACQUISITIONS

As in any make or buy decision, there are cost tradeoffs in acquiring or starting a periodical. The first question is, "Do we want a title in this marketplace?" If yes, then the field of available publications can be scouted. The cost of available magazines must be compared to the cost of starting fresh. An important factor in the equation is the management that comes with a new publication. In developing a publication internally, a company must include the cost of the management time used in developing the new publication, an expense that would be far greater in most cases than in acquiring an existing magazine.

---

*In 1999 Martha Stewart Living Omnimedia became a publicly-traded company.

er as venture capitalist was adopted as a viable
strategy between corporate start-ups and shoestring entrepreneurial ventures by
some publishers. *Wired* had funding from Newhouse and the Tribune Co. *Martha*

TABLE 3.13
Outcome of 70 Consumer Magazine Start-Ups from 1969–1980

Title	Year Started	Original Publisher	Status in 1998
Ambiance	1978	entrepreneurial	out of business
Americana	1969	American Heritage	out of business
American Photographer	1978	entrepreneurial	out of business
Apartment Life	1969	Meredith	out of business
Astronomy	1978	entrepreneurial	published by Kalmbach
Backpacker	1973	entrepreneurial	published by Rodale
Black Enterprise	1970	entrepreneurial	still published
Blair & Ketchum's Country Journal	1974	entrepreneurial	out of business
Book Digest	1974	entrepreneurial	out of business
Byte	1970	entrepreneurial	published by McGraw-Hill
Calendar	1976	entrepreneurial	out of business
Dirt Bike Magazine	1972	Hi-Torque	Hi-Torque
Discover	1980	Time Inc.	Disney
Epicure	1972	CBS	out of business
Equus	1977	entrepreneurial	still published
Essence	1970	entrepreneurial	still published
Families	1980	Readers Digest	out of business
Firehouse	1976	entrepreneurial	Cygnus Publishing Co.
Food & Wine	1977	entrepreneurial	American Express Publishing
Gallery Magazine	1971	entrepreneurial	still published
Gambler's World	1972	entrepreneurial	out of business
Games	1977	entrepreneurial	Kappa Publishing*
Genesis	1972	entrepreneurial	still published
Geo	1979	Bertelsmann	out of business
Good Food	1973	Triangle	out of business
High Times	1979	entrepreneurial	still published
Horse, Of Course	1971	entrepreneurial	out of business
Human Nature	1978	Harcourt Brace Jovanovich	out of business
Hustler	1974	entrepreneurial	still in business
Inside Sports	1980	Newsweek	out of business
Intellectual Digest	1970	entrepreneurial	out of business
Kosher Home	1978	entrepreneurial	out of business
L'Officiel/U.S.A.	1970	entrepreneurial	out of business
Look	1972	Hachette-Filipacchi	out of business
Mariah	1976	entrepreneurial	out of business
Money	1973	Time Inc.	Time Warner
Moneysworth	1970	entrepreneurial	still published
Mother Earth News	1970	entrepreneurial	still published
Motorboat	1973	United Marine Publ	out of business
Ms.	1972	entrepreneurial	still published
New Dawn	1976	entrepreneurial	out of business
New Harvest	1979	entrepreneurial	out of business
Nuetsro	1977	entrepreneurial	out of business
Omni	1978	Penthouse	still published
On the Sound	1972	entrepreneurial	out of business
Oui	1972	Playboy	Laurant Publishing
Outside	1977	Rolling Stone	Mariah Media
Panorama	1980	Triangle Publications	out of business
People Weekly	1974	Time Inc.	Time Warner
Penthouse	1969	General Media	General Media
Petersen's Photographic Magazine	1972	Petersen Publishing	Petersen Publishing

(Continued)

177

Table 3.13 *(Continued)*

Title	Year Started	Original Publisher	Status in 1998
Pizzazz	1977	Cadence	out of business
Plants Alive	1972	entrepreneurial	out of business
Playgirl	1973	entrepreneurial	Crescent Publishing Co.
Quest	1977	entrepreneurial	out of business**
The Runner	1979	MCA	out of business
Sail	1970	entrepreneurial	out of business
Self	1979	Conde Nast/Newhouse	Conde Nast/Newhouse
Smithsonian	1970	Smithsonian Institution	Smithsonian Institution
Soap Opera Digest	1975	entrepreneurial	Primedia
Travel & Leisure	1970	American Express	American Express Publishing
Us	1977	New York Times Co.	Wenner Media
Vital	1977	entrepreneurial	out of business
Viva	1973	General Media	out of business
Your Place	1978	McCall's	out of business
WomanSports	1973	entrepreneurial	out of business
Working Mother	1979	McCall's	MacDonald Communications

*This *Games* may not be a direct descendant of the magazine started in 1977.

**There are several periodicals with the Quest name, but none appear to be related to this one.

"Original Publisher" indicates whether it was from an individual/small publisher ("entrepreneurial") or an established publisher. Status: "Out of business" means that the title is not listed in the *Oxbridge Directories of Print Media* (see source).

Sources: Titles, start year and publisher type: Compaine, et al., *Who Owns the Media?*, Table 4.16. Status in 1997: *Oxbridge Directories of Print Media and Catalogs on CD-ROM*, third quarter, 1998.

Stewart's Living was bankrolled by Time Inc. *George*, the progeny of the late editor in chief John Kennedy and executive publisher Michael Berman, was underwritten in 1995 by Hachette-Filipacchi for as much as $20 million.

Table 3.14 tracks the outcome of 70 consumer magazines started by both established publishers and entrepreneurs. Although many of the survivors from the entrepreneurs have become part of larger publishers, quite a few have remained independent. On the other hand, consistent with the 20% success rate for new magazines, a high proportion of large group ventures have long since disappeared. The periodicals in Table 3.13 were an opportunistic sample—drawn from available data rather than as a statistically valid sample. But in this group, the results of success for the small, entrepreneurial start-ups and those from larger chains and established players is about the same. Of the former group, 19 of 41 magazines, or 46%, were still published in 1997, in many cases by the founding company. Of the latter group, 12 of 24, or 50%, survived to 1997. In this sample, at least, there was little long-term difference in survivability between entrepreneurial start-ups and chain magazine publisher startups.

GROUP PUBLISHING

There is a good reason why most magazines are published by multimagazine groups: a single periodical, especially one of limited audience circulation, must carry too great a burden of overhead to make economic sense. The economies of scale are not great in magazine publishing, but the natural limits to the size of the consumer and business special interest magazines make acquisitions and start-ups a necessity if a company wishes to keep growing and spread its fixed costs. Once a periodical reaches a saturation point, ad revenue growth becomes limited to cost per thousand increases or total pages sold.

New York magazine is a simple example. From a start-up circulation of 50,000 in 1968, circulation grew rapidly to 391,000 in 1978. The rate of circulation growth was 35% from 1969 to 1970, 26% the next year, down to 10% in 1972 and slowed to 6% in 1973. Between 1973 and 1978, circulation grew an average of 2.7% annually. So after some heady growth, *New York* logically turned outside for further growth, first by its acquisition of the *Village Voice* and then started *New West* (which has since folded). *New York* eventually sold itself to Triangle Publications, which was acquired by News Corp., which sold off its magazines. *New York* became part of Primedia in 1991.

The numbers are tougher for most trade magazine. Very typical is *Teleconnect*, a very successful trade magazine. It is written for "people who buy, sell, install, use, manage, or maintain office communications systems of all kinds." This is a rather finite audience and its 1997 circulation of about 20,000 substantially exhausted the universe of potential subscribers. Advertisers for the magazine are similarly finite. At a cost per thousand of more than $100, neither Toyota nor Crest would find it an efficient buy. Rather, advertisers include Northern Telecom, Dialogic and a host of relatively small hardware and software providers to the large users of telecommunications.

A magazine such as *Teleconnect* may have potential revenue of $1 million to $3 million, depending on whether it actually sells subscriptions or, like most trade publications, gives them away. Once at that level, there are no horizons for an entrepreneur (e.g., Harry Newton and Gerry Friesen, who started *Teleconnect*) other than to start or acquire other magazines (which they did).

There are several economies that can result from having numerous publications under the same corporate banner:

- A publisher of well-established magazines has greater leverage in getting distribution of a new publication and may be able to negotiate a more favorable deal with a national distributor.
- Bulk acquisition of paper may be slightly less expensive and easier.
- Printing contracts can be negotiated en masse.
- Subscription fulfillment contracts for a small circulation periodical can be combined with other magazines for a more economical rate.
- In-house circulation staffs can be centralized.
- A good publishing group can also provide corporate research and management expertise, adding to this economic leverage.
- Finally, the most recent advantage for group publishing is the improved capacity for "data mining." This is, using sophisticated computer programs that can cull from subscribers lists of likely prospects for other goods or services that may be marketed by the publisher or offered to third parties.

On the other hand, most magazine operations must be run as separate entities. Many of their costs vary little from independent to group status. For example:

- Editorial staffs for each magazine are generally strictly segregated, often because of the disparate subject matter of the books: Conde Nast's *New Yorker* has little in common editorially with *Mademoiselle*.
- Advertising staffs are separate, although regional offices can be combined in a single facility and many groups of small magazines sell insertions on a package basis. Group publishers have experimented with shared ad sales staffs and have generally discarded them for sales by representatives designated for a particular magazine.
- Postage on subscription mailings is strictly per unit, and mailing cost for the magazines is figured separately for each title.

There are, then, modest economies of scale: some modest cost savings in printing, paper and production, some helpful leverage in distribution and, up to a point, the ability to spread some corporate overhead. Indeed, the largest group publishers often divide their publications into somewhat autonomous subsidiary groups, often with little interaction with the owning corporate structure other than in providing annual business plans with financial goals established by headquarters.

The quest for a chain then lies in the fact that magazine publishing is an industry with good margins, but on a small scale.

Acquisitions

While starting a new magazine has a certain excitement, buying an existing one is quicker, easier and not necessarily more expensive. The key is buying at the right price. Profitable periodicals either are not for sale or are available only at a high price, whereas unprofitable publications are usually in bad straits for a reason. Table 3.14 summarizes the largest magazine transactions in 1997. Note that most of these deals were for trade magazines, a natural result of there being more of such periodicals than consumer magazines.

"What you're buying is good will," noted an analyst at one of the most highly regarded special interest publication groups. Once a title saturates its market, opportunity for growth of circulation and ad revenue become tied to higher rates rather than more purchasers and ad pages. A publisher thus tends to seek another magazine.

Another observation is that all sellers are not the proverbial mom-and-pop operations and not all buyers are large media conglomerates. Disney, for example, inherited a large portfolio of magazines in its 1996 acquisition of Capital Cities/ABC. Analyzing the way these fit in with its strategic view, it decided to temporarily hold on to some (e.g., the Fairchild Publications) but to divest many others (along with several large daily newspapers).

The New York Times Co., News Corp., Ziff-Davis and CBS are among the large media companies who have been divesting themselves of magazines. Meanwhile new entities, specializing in magazine publishing only, such as Miller Publishing and Cygnus Publishing (both started by former magazine executives in 1996 with venture capital backing), Primedia (started in 1989 as K-III Communications) and

TABLE 3.14
10 Largest Magazine Sales of 1997

Publications	Seller	Buyer	Value
Chilton Business Group (39 trade magazines)	Disney	Reed Elsevier	$447 million
Casino Executive, International Gaming & Wagering Business plus trade shows and info services	T/SF Communications Corp	Veronis, Suhler & Associates Communication Partners Limited Fund II	$145 million
Institutional Investor	Disney	Euromoney Publications	$142 million
Computer Telephony, Teleconnect, Call Center, Imaging	Telecom Library	United News and Media (Miller Freeman)	$130 million
PTN (trade magazines)	Cygnus Publishing	Stanley Sills and Golder, Thoma, Cresses, Rauner	$97 million
American Lawyer and Corporate Counsel	Time Warner	U.S. Equity Partners, L.P.	$63 million
Farm Progress Group (incl Prairie Farmer	Disney	Rural Press (Austrailia)	$57 million
Electronic Musician, Mix, Club Industry	Cardinal Business Media	Primedia	$45 million
Spin	Bob Guccione Jr and partners	Miller Publishing	$40 million
Six tennis, sailing, ski consumer magazines including Tennis	New York Times Co.	Miller Publishing	$35 million

Source: Jeff Garigliano, "Top 10 Deals of 1997," Folio via MediaCentral, Top 10 Magazine Deals of 1997, on Web site at www.mediacentral.com/Magazines/Folio/980101/news54.htm/737896, accessed January 1, 1998.

Meigher Communications (launched in 1994 by former Time Inc. executive Chris Meigher) have been acquiring.

One trend has been the lessening of head-to-head competition in some categories of magazines aimed at identical markets, just as multiple newspapers under competing ownerships became uneconomical for all the players. For example, there are 295 periodicals that describe themselves at being aimed at the automotive audience. But the two major consumer magazines, Car & Driver (long published by Ziff-Davis) and Road & Track (once part of by CBS Publishing), are now published under the Hachette-Filipacchi label. Similar consolidation has occurred in other consumer categories: Ski and Skiing magazines, which are both part of Times Mirror; and Popular Photography (formerly Ziff-Davis) and American Photo (once CBS), which are both part of Hachette-Filipacchi (Modern Photography has disappeared). Competition remains strong in these areas, however: In 1998, there were 45 automotive periodicals with more than 200,000 circulation from 28 different publishers.[27]

A phenomenon of the 1990s that was not prevalent in the past was the appearance of venture capitalists and specialized investment funds for purchasing and operating magazines. In the past, mutual funds might have invested in publicly owned companies that published magazines. But their goal was to share in the growth of those companies in the form of increased value of the investment. This changed est consumer and business publications, however, makes multimagazine houses all the more necessary for the future.

But even a cursory knowledge of magazine publishing history demonstrates that, as the aforementioned short list suggests, as many groups go as come. Curtis, which once include the *Saturday Evening Post*, and Fawcett are gone. A Macfadden descendent survives, as do Hearst, Meredith, McGraw-Hill and Time.

On the other hand, Triangle Publications, the publishing powerhouse built by Walter Annenberg in the 1950s and anchored by *TV Guide*, has been divested into pieces owned by several companies. Broadcaster CBS, whose portfolio in the 1970s included *Woman's Day*, *Road & Track* and *Field and Stream*, sold off its magazines. Ziff-Davis is still a substantial publisher specializing in computer publications. But in the 1980s, it sold off the magazines it had owned and built up for decades: including *Car and Driver*, *Modern Bride* and *Popular Photography*. They are now with Times Mirror (*Skiing*), Primedia (*Modern Bride*) or Hachette-Filipacchi (*Popular Photography*).

The day of the mass circulation magazine is ending. The largest magazines of 1997 all have smaller circulations than in 1980. The five largest magazines of 1980—*TV Guide*, *Reader's Digest*, *National Geographic*, *Better Homes & Gardens*, *Woman's Day*—sold 15 million fewer copies per issue, or nearly 25% less, in 1997.

With the risk still high and the entry cost substantial, especially for small players, new mass circulation magazines will be a rarity in the field. Publishers will have to rely on good profits yielded by relatively small revenue from several publications for company or division viability.

FOREIGN PUBLISHERS IN U.S. MARKET

The United States has been an attractive market for investment by publishers from other countries. It provides a massive, unified audience that largely speaks a single language. It has an economy that allocates a greater share of its spending on advertising (about 2% of GDP) than anywhere else in the world. It has been a relatively stable economy. The content of the publishing business is protected by the First Amendment and the business environment is far less regulated than in Europe, where both union- and government-imposed work rules tend to be larger factors.

For these reasons, and probably others that pertain to individual companies, foreign ownership of U.S. publishers is far greater than U.S. ownership abroad.

Although the entry of the foreigners has involved buying up some going magazines, they have also committed funds to the start-up of new publications. The following are some of these ventures:

• Reed-Elsevier is owned jointly by two European companies, the British Reed International and the Netherlands' Elsevier. Reed-Elsevier publishes more than 1,100 scientific and medical journals. Its major U.S. subsidiary, Cahners Publishing, includes trade journals as varied as *Control Engineering*, *Travel Weekly*, *Restaurants & Institutions* and *Broadcasting & Cable*. It also published more than 1,000 scientific and technical journals in the United States and aboard. However, in 1996, Reed-Elsevier sold the consumer magazines it picked up over the years, including *American Baby* and *Modern Bride*.

Guide, Reader's Digest, National Geographic, Better Homes & Gardens, Woman's Day—sold 15 million fewer copies per issue, or nearly 25% less, in 1997.

With the risk still high and the entry cost substantial, especially for small players, new mass circulation magazines will be a rarity in the field. Publishers will have to rely on good profits yielded by relatively small revenue from several publications for company or division viability.

FOREIGN PUBLISHERS IN U.S. MARKET

The United States has been an attractive market for investment by publishers from other countries. It provides a massive, unified audience that largely speaks a single language. It has an economy that allocates a greater share of its spending on advertising (about 2% of GDP) than anywhere else in the world. It has been a relatively stable economy. The content of the publishing business is protected by the First Amendment and the business environment is far less regulated than in Europe, where both union- and government-imposed work rules tend to be larger factors.

For these reasons, and probably others that pertain to individual companies, foreign ownership of U.S. publishers is far greater than U.S. ownership abroad.

Although the entry of the foreigners has involved buying up some going magazines, they have also committed funds to the start-up of new publications. The following are some of these ventures:

• Reed-Elsevier is owned jointly by two European companies, the British Reed International and the Netherlands' Elsevier. Reed-Elsevier publishes more than 1,100 scientific and medical journals. Its major U.S. subsidiary, Cahners Publishing, includes trade journals as varied as *Control Engineering, Travel Weekly, Restaurants & Institutions* and *Broadcasting & Cable*. It also published more than 1,000 scientific and technical journals in the United States and aboard. However, in 1996, Reed-Elsevier sold the consumer magazines it picked up over the years, including *American Baby* and *Modern Bride*.

• Paris-based Hachette-Filipacchi (itself a subsidiary of Lagardere Groupe) was the largest foreign publisher of consumer magazines in the United States in 1998. Daniel Filipacchi gained prominence in the U.S. market with an abortive attempt to revive the venerable *Look*, which had been killed by Cowles Communications in 1971. He fell far short of his goal and suspended publication in 1979 after about a year's effort. Filipacchi had previously acquired Popular Publications, Inc., a group that included *Argosy, Camera 35* and *Railroad*. Its 1998 holdings included *Woman's Day, Elle, Elle Decor, Home, Metropolitan Home, Mirabella, Audio, Car Stereo Review, Premiere, Video, Family Life* (acquired from Rolling Stone founder Jann Wenner in March 1995) and a high profile political magazine start-up, *George*.

• Bertelsmann, through its Gruner & Jahr subsidiary, is Germany's largest publisher (*Stern, Brigitte*). In the 1970s, it expanded to the United States to publish Geo, a slick picture magazine not unlike *National Geographic*. In April 1978, the company also purchased Parents' Magazine Enterprises, publisher of the 1.6 million circulation monthly *Parents'*, as well as *Children's Digest, Humpty Dumpty* and others. *Geo* did not survive. *Children's Digest* et al., were sold to Children's Better Health Institute. And, despite acquiring *McCall's* and *Family Circle*, Gruner & Jahr has not become a major publisher in the United States (However, see Chapters 2 and 5 for details of Bertelsmann's role in booking publishing and recorded music.)

• Canada's Thomson Corporation may be nicknamed the "stealth" player for its low profile role with its subsidiaries. Although selling off much of its newspaper and magazine ventures for redeployment into electronic information services, Thomson remained, in 1998, a major foreign-based owner of U.S. trade magazines. Among them is the Medical Economics group, which included 13 periodicals with more than an aggregate of 1 million circulation. It's Jane's Information Group includes Jane's *Defence Weekly*.

• United News & Media is the British media holding company for the national newspapers *Daily Express, Daily Star* and *Sunday Express*, as well as substantial broadcast interests. It crossed to the United States in 1983 with the purchase of Gralla and Miller Freeman, publisher of medical and computer periodicals. It has since expended its U.S. magazine holdings considerably, buying groups of publications that include titles such as *Videography, Golf Retailer* and *Keyboard* (as in music, not computers).

• In a highly unusual instance of a Pacific Rim country expanding into the U.S. print media, in 1996 Softbank, Japan's largest software distributor, acquired Ziff-Davis, known for its computer magazines. Softbank also bought the largest trade show in the United States, the Comdex. In 1998, however, to raise some cash, Softbank sold 29% of Ziff-Davis to the public.

On the other hand, Britain's Associated Newspapers Group, which took an interest in *Esquire* in 1977 and seemed poised for more, sold *Esquire* in 1978 and has retreated from U.S. shores. The Economist Group, part of Britain's Pearson, in 1981 started printing its flagship financial weekly *The Economist* in the United States. In 1998 it had 278,000 circulation, but it has not greatly expanded its presence. Harlequin Enterprises, the Canadian publisher best known for its romance novels, tried to start a magazine publishing group in the United States with its acquisition of the Laufer Company, publisher of *Tiger Beat*. But it divested these properties and is itself part of Canada's Torstar Corporation. Finally, News Corp., the global Australian-based media giant, acquired some of the largest and most prominent U.S. magazines, including *TV Guide*. But ultimately News Corp. decided these were not strategic properties and, in 1997 and 1998, sold virtually all of its U.S. magazines except the supermarket tabloid, *Star*.

So far, the presence of the foreign publishers is rather small. Even the sizable Spanish-speaking constituency has not seen the expansion of Latin America's publishers into the U.S. market.

U.S. VENTURES ABROAD

Few U.S. publishers have been active in other parts of the world. Reader's Digest publishes about 39 international editions in 15 languages. (*Canadian Reader's Digest* is a separate entity.) Each is locally edited under general supervision from U.S. headquarters. These international editions have a combined circulation of about 12 million.

Hearst has long been involved in overseas publishing, directly and through the licensing of its titles to local publishers. It claims to be the world's largest publisher of monthly magazines, with 95 international editions in addition to its U.S. titles. Hearst is most actively involved in the United Kingdom, where it publishes nine monthly magazines, primarily local versions of such U.S. titles as *Cosmopolitan* and *Good Housekeeping*. In the United Kingdom it publishers through its subsidiary, the National Magazine Company Limited. In most other countries, it licenses its titles to local publishers. Although the look of *Cosmopolitan* in Brazil, published by Editoria Abril, has a familiar look, like most of Hearst's titles abroad it uses mostly indigenous editorial material.

Condé Nast is also active in international publishing, with both licencing and foreign subsidiaries. Condé Nast, like Hearst, also publishes a few titles overseas that do not have U.S. counterparts.

Time and *Newsweek* both have extensive editions aimed at English-speaking audiences in Latin America, Asia and Europe. They are substantially different editorially from the domestic editions, with sales of about 1 million copies per issue. Neither corporate parent, Time Warner or the Washington Post Co., has substantial ownership in magazines abroad.

Overall, it is safe to judge that in publishing the foreign presence in the United States is more visible than the U.S. presence in any foreign market. In general, it appears that there are few synergies that can be brought to bear in global publishing, especially between languages and cultures. Whereas the world's consumers are increasingly cosmopolitan, cultural and linguistic differences remain significant barriers to would-be global media companies. There are successful exceptions, but the truth of the matter is that very few French magazines, Italian novels or U.S.-made situation comedy TV shows survive the transition to another language and culture.[29]

MAGAZINES AND NEW MEDIA

The magazine business suffered a dramatic erosion of its share of media advertising when television entered the marketplace. Magazine share dropped from 13% in 1945 to 9% by 1950 and did not bottom out until it hit 5.2% in 1975. However, since then, magazines have resisted further erosion in its advertising market share, holding at 5.3% in 1997.[30]

One way in which publishers have co-opted newer media and information technologies has been by creating magazines addressed to audiences for newer media. For example, one of the largest magazines and most successful consumer magazines owes its being to television. With *TV Guide*, Walter Annenberg accurately foresaw the opportunity the young industry provided for a localized guide for television program schedules and, increasingly, the culture of televison. Other publishers have created cable guides.

An earlier discussion noted that the proliferation of both consumer and trade magazines has been targeted to hobbyists and professional users and purchasers of computers and new video equipment. These offerings have come from both entrepreneurs and the large group publishers. In 1998, there were 383 consumer and trade publications oriented around computing. They ranged from the quarterly *HP OmniGo World*, "an independent publication for users of the HP OmniGo organizer," published by Thaddeus Publications of Fairfield, Iowa, to the 1.2 million circulation *PC Magazine*, started by Ziff-Davis in 1982. About 150 periodicals exist to cover television or video. These ranged from titles such as *Soap Opera News* (a weekly started in 1997 by a small Florida company) to *Digital Home Entertainment* (from the CurtCo Freedom group) to technical trade magazines like *CCTV Applications & Technology* (from Burke Publishing).

Like *TV Guide*, many other publications take advantage of interests created by video and theatrical film: including *Sports Illustrated* (Time Warner), the new *ESPN Sports* (Disney) and *Soap Opera Digest* (Primedia). The growing attention paid to the World Wide Web spawned a slew of magazines, some of which lasted only a few years, such as *Internet Guide*. Still, in 1998, there were 15 periodicals aimed at Web users and advertisers wishing to reach them. They included *Internet World*, from Mecklermedia, a company largely spawned by the Internet. In one paradox, Microsoft, known as a software company, created *Slate*, initially as a subscription online "magazine," followed by its introduction as a traditional paper-based version. Ebay, an online auction site, which had 5.6 million registered users in 1999, created a traditional print magazine to help this community with tips on buying and selling online. It was being published by Krause Publications, which had a list of 35 periodicals such as *Old Car* and *Stamps*.

Thus, hard copy has proven to be robust, fueled by new media interests and the resulting magazine titles and their publishers.

Publishers Seek to Capitalize on Content Expertise

In addition to seeking opportunities in magazine publishing, since the 1980s many publishers have looked for ways to leverage their editorial strengths and advertising base to use the developing media formats: in cable programing and networks, computer games, video cassette programs and Web sites. Time Warner cloned its *E! Entertainment* magazine into a cable network, then sold its interest to a joint venture in which Comcast is a majority owner.[31]

The 1982 edition of *Who Owns the Media?* suggested the hopes and expectations of publishers at that time:

> Meredith Corp. announced formation of its own video "publishing" unit. Again, with content inspired by articles in its magazines, such as *Better Homes & Gardens*, Meredith expected to deliver programming to cable operators via satellite and also sell programs on cassette and disc. In addition, Meredith was looking forward to using interactive cable systems when (and if) they become widespread, to develop programming and advertising that could take advantage of that capability. In the meantime, Meredith has been participating with CompuServe, Inc. . . . in providing supplementary editorial content from recent issues of its magazines "online" to subscribers of CompuServe's data base system.[32]

Hearst, CBS, Playboy, McGraw-Hill, in addition to Meredith, are among those that at one time or another actively pursued similar opportunities. The results have been mixed. Playboy has had success in extending its brand to cable TV as well as a subscription Internet site. Still, in 1997, Playboy revenues from all forms of video programming still amounted to just over half as much as from its flagship magazine.

In many cases, publishers entered joint ventures with partners that brought other types of specialization, either in production or distribution. For example, Hearst and American Broadcasting Cos. initiated several ventures as early as 1981 to produce and supply women's programming for cable television. Hearst, on its part, was expected to provide programming ideas from its women's magazines, which include *Good Housekeeping, Harper's Bazaar* and *Cosmopolitan*. ABC would provide production and cable networking expertise. As it turned out, the venture's largest success was the ESPN sports networks, with 20% owned by Hearst and the remainer owned by Disney (ABC's parent as of 1997). Hearst also has minority shares in A&E, a cable network co-owned by ABC and NBC; Lifetime, co-owned with ABC; and New England Cable News, co-owned with MediaOne. However, after some early miscues, by 1998 little to none of the programming on any of these networks have branded identity with Hearst magazines.

Many of the larger publishers had great hopes for cable and video extensions of their titles in the early 1980s. For the most part, tie-ins with their magazine editorial material has been minimal. Successes have been more in the nature of conventional business investments, such as Hearst with its interests in cable networks, or Time with its early investment in cable and later through its Warner and Turner Broadcasting mergers and acquisitions.

On the Web

Magazine publishers have set up Web sites in prodigious numbers. By the start of 1999, 23 of the 50 largest magazines had their own Web sites, including those of Time Warner, Hearst and Meredith. The Web has given added exposure to many smaller, independent publishers who have a new avenue for promotion, exposure and even revenue. One example is *E/The Environmental Magazine*, a 50,000 circulation bimonthly published by the Earth Action Network. *Indy Car & Championship Racing* magazine is published by ICR Publications and has 39,000 print subscribers, but it also has its own Web site with an online subscription.

Few magazines were directly covering their expenses from their Web sites in 1998. For example, the Playboy Online unit reported revenue of $3 million in the first half of 1998. That was nearly twice the revenue from the same period in 1997. But the operation lost $2.2 million, reflecting the considerable up-front cost of building and staffing a Web site. Still, Playboy was one of only a handful that actually had paying subscribers.[33] See Chapter 7 for a more detailed discussion of the online business and its relation to traditional media companies.

SUMMARY AND DISCUSSION

The traditional magazine seems to be in no immediate danger of being overwhelmed by electronic technologies. The magazine industry is diverse, dynamic and responsive to change. Through the 1980s and 1990s, it held its own among advertisers and

in overall circulation. Like book publishing, it is a field with relatively low capital
entry barriers so long as the publisher is not trying to start a mass circulation consumer publication. Magazine publishing (like book publishing), utilizes outside services for virtually its entire physical production and distribution process, unlike most
newspapers, which tend to own their own presses and control their own delivery.
Indeed, it may be argued that this guaranteed access to a distribution channel has
been the most important single factor in maintaining diversity and dynamism.

The fact that there were nearly 12,000 different magazine titles published by
thousands of firms, however, does not accurately reflect the degree of competition or
concentration in the industry. Almost by definition, the objective of each magazine
is to create its own unique sphere by catering to a distinct audience segment. *Motor-
cycle Product News* does not compete with *Time* or *College and Research Libraries*. *PC
Week* and *InfoWorld* magazines do battle for many of the same advertisers, but they
are not in direct competition with *Abdominal Imaging* or *Prairie Farmer*. Magazines
and books are perhaps the best examples of monopolistic competition: There are
many similar products, but each one is perceived as being different enough from the
others to create its own unique market. The distinction may be by geography
(*Philadelphia, Southern Living, Fishing in Maryland*), specialized content (*Popular Photography, Insurance Marketing*), demographics (*Town & Country, Modern Romances,
Seventeen*), intellectual level (*Harper's, Marvel* comics, *New Yorker*), generalized content (*People, TV Guide, Better Homes & Gardens*) or other designations.

Although it may be argued that newspapers do not compete with one another in
different cities, daily newspapers all tend to provide the same function for a single
mass audience each day. While a fire in Cincinnati and a budget hearing in San Jose
are reported only locally, any given paper across the country on a given day will have
much the same national and international news, similar types of local stories and
advertising. Few magazines have such similarities.

It is for this reason, perhaps, that group ownership of magazines is seldom raised
when discussion turns to media concentration. It is hard to make an antitrust case
that Hachette-Filipacchi's purchase of both *Car & Drive* and *Road and Track* gives
that magazine an unfair advantage over other magazines, or even over advertisers
that might include General Motors or Goodyear. Nor does the fact that Times Mirror publishes *Popular Science* and *Outdoor Life* have any impact on the free flow of
ideas through these or other magazines.

Moreover, many magazines also face competition from thousands of newsletters,
such as "Old House Journal" or "Kiplinger's." Whereas many of these cost far more
than magazines and are thus directed to special business audiences, they do serve as
an easier-entry format than magazines in which a publisher may provide information
for a distinct market. Newsletters tend to be supported 100% by circulation revenue
and thus can serve many diverse audiences that are too small to support an adver-
tising-backed publication.

The nature of the market is such that competition is restricted to a great extent
by the limited audience for most publications. The first publisher to discover a market niche, either in a trade or the consumer area, has an edge in reaching those
interested in that subject. Sometimes there is room for a second or third publication.

In the case of fads, such as the sudden discovery of Internet, several magazines may hit the market at once, but the size of the market—both the limited advertising base or the potential universe of subscribers—may not economically be able to support all the entries.

Except for the largest mass circulation magazines, publishers are very aware of the limited resources of their advertisers. Bobit Publishing Co.'s *School Bus Fleet* may be the only vehicle for advertisers that wish to reach that market. But the many small suppliers who advertise in the periodical would have to cut down on their space or stop advertising altogether if the publisher exercised its "monopoly" position to raise rates with abandon. At the same time, most special interest publishers have a limited universe of potential advertisers and cannot afford to lose too many. It is the limited advertising and audience that makes the first entry often the only one to survive. Perhaps typical is *Call Center Magazine*, started by Telecom Library in 1988. Its niche is "Information on using technology to sell, service & keep your customers." With total controlled circulation of 34,000 and many of its advertisers small companies with employees numbered in the dozens, it is not a niche that is ripe for extensive direct competition.

In most cases, magazines are started to fill a niche that no one else has noticed or that was felt to be too small. Although an individual may not consider it worthwhile to run a business publication with a potential free circulation of 5,000, a group that specializes in such periodicals may start or acquire such a magazine at an early stage and use its management and marketing skills to make it a profitable operation.

For the future, the Internet holds more in opportunities and threats for magazine publishers than video ever did. Web sites are much more about graphics and editorial content, whereas video has a far greater element of production values in which magazines had no particular skills. Chapter 7 covers the developments in online publishing. Magazines might eventually see a decline in their audience share and even advertising should online become both culturally ingrained and technically more user friendly. But, whereas newspapers could face a major loss in revenue if they do not hold on to their highly profitable classified advertising, there is no similar chunk of magazine-type advertising revenue that is so amenable to going online. Online may be a threat to incumbent publishers, but any inroads are likely to be slower and more readily counteracted than with their newspaper cousins.

Perhaps one telling factor that bodes well for the continued robust competition in the magazine business is the continuing relevance of the conclusion from the 1982 edition of *Who Owns the Media?*:

> Magazine publishing is an easy entry field and this brings into it a profusion of new products each year. The tendency is for successful publications to be purchased by multiple title publishers, or for the success of one title to provide the resources for the publisher to start or acquire additional publications and thus become a group. Despite the high mortality rate and the competition from other media, the growth in additional magazine titles shows no sign of letting up. In addition, a single magazine with even a small, but perhaps influential audience (in a specialized field), can be a very effective voice, even when published by a company that owns no other magazines. Along with books, magazines provide society with a broad range of information, education and entertainment.[34]

NOTES

1. 1950: *Ayer Directory of Publications*, annual (Bala Cynwyd, PA: Ayer Press). 1998: *Oxbridge Directories of Print Media and Catalogs on CD-ROM*, third quarter, 1998. The precise number is slippery. A search of the Oxbridge database initially found 11,829 titles that qualified, but the search initially omitted magazines published at irregular intervals, such as 10 times or 14 times annually. On the other hand, little in this chapter would be effected by an under- or overcount of even a few dozen at this magnitude of a universe.

2. See Jean-Louis Servan-Schreiber, *The Power to Inform* (New York: McGraw-Hill, 1974), pp. 36–38.

3. Among the histories of magazines, all from the 1960s, are James L. C. Ford, *Magazines for Millions* (Carbondale, IL: Southern Illinois University Press, 1969); Frank Luther Mott, *A History of American Magazines*, 5 vols. (Cambridge, MA: Harvard University Press, 1968); Theodore Peterson, *Magazines in the Twentieth Century* (Champaign-Urbana, IL: University of Illinois Press, 1964); and John Tebbel, *The American Magazine: A Compact History* (New York: Hawthorn Books, 1969).

4. Calculated from Publishers Information Bureau gross advertising revenue, cited in Benjamin M. Compaine, et al., *Who Owns the Media? Concentration of Ownership in the Mass Communications Industry* (White Plains, NY: Knowledge Industry Publications, Inc.), p. 149. 1997 data from *Advertising Age*, "Ad Age Data Place—6/15/98: Top 300 Magazines by Gross Revenue," June 15, 1998, pp. S-1ff. Also see Web site at www.adage.com/dataplace/archives/dp230.html.

5. Carolyn Kitch, "The American Magazine Business: An Overview," in Alan Wells and Ernest Hakanen (eds.), *Mass Media & Society* (Greenwich, CT: Ablex Publishing Corp., 1997), Chapter 7.

6. Ibid.

7. 1980: Compaine, et al., *Who Owns the Media?*, p. 150. 1997: Magazine Publishers of America, "Circulation for A.B.C. Magazines by Circulation Size Groups for Second Half of 1997," and *Oxbridge Directories of Print Media*, 1998.

8. From Benjamin M. Compaine, *The Business of Consumer Magazines* (White Plains, NY: Knowledge Industry Publications, Inc., 1982), p. 29; prices from Communications Industry Forecast, p. 294. CPI data from U.S. Statistical Abstract, 1997, online, Table 752, p. 487.

9. "Magazine Advertising Cost Analysis" (New York: Magazine Publishers of America), F.S. 230.

10. G. Bruce Knecht, "How Magazines Make It to Stores—and Why They Soon May Not," *Wall Street Journal*, February 26, 1998, p. 1.

11. Ibid.

12. Ibid.

13. Rolf Maurer, "Distribution Dilemmas, Retail Rewards," *Folio*, January 1, 1998, on Web site at www.mediacentral.com/Folio/.

14. Knecht, p. 1.

15. Ibid.

16. Ibid.

17. Ibid.

18. U.S. Bureau of the Census, Census of Manufacturers, 1977, Table 7; 1992 Census of Manufacturers report MC92-S-2, "Concentration Ratios in Manufacturing," on Web site at www.census.gov/mcd/mancen/download/mc92cr.sum.

19. Compaine, *Who Owns the Media?*, p. 157.

20. But as the 1981 figure, this too is subject to discrepancies with reality. Just as it may undercount groups because of the self-imposed requirement for circulation auditing (most magazines simply self-report circulation or use the U.S. Postal Service annual "sworn" reporting statement), there may be a small overcount. This is due to the situations where holding company subsidiaries are identified as the publishing group. For example, Fairchild Publications is listed as the publisher of *Footwear News* and *W*, and there is a separate count for *Discover* and *FamilyPC*, listed as Disney Magazines. However, as Fairchild at the time was owned by Disney, they were counted as one group of the 210 reported earlier. But other, more obscure subsidiaries of parent companies may not have been weeded out in this compilation.

21. Compaine, *Who Owns the Media?*, p. 159.
22. Samir A. Husni, "Influences on the Survival of New Consumer Magazines," *Journal of Media Economics* 1.1 (Spring 1988), pp. 39–49.
23. *Media Decisions*, June 1978, p. 46.
24. Cheryl Arvidson, "Brill: Content Magazine Helps Journalists Hold Themselves Accountable," The Freedom Forum Online, at http://www.freedomforum.org/professional/1998/7/30brill.asp.
25. Patrick M. Reilly, "Disney Launches Magazine to Rival Sports Illustrated," *Wall Street Journal*, May 6, 1997.
26. Felicity Barringer with Geraldine Fabricant, "Tina Brown Edits Her Career to Match the Zeitgeist," *New York Times*, accessed at Web CRL www.nytimes.com/yr/mo/day/news/financial/tinabrown-media.html. July 13, 1998.
27. Search of *Oxbridge Directories of Print Media and Catalogs on CD-ROM*, third quarter, 1998.
28. Jeff Garigliano, "Top 10 Deals of 1997," *Folio* via MediaCentral, Top 10 Magazine Deals of 1997, on Web site at www.mediacentral.com/Magazines/Folio/980101/news54.htm/737896, accessed January 1, 1998.
29. See Benjamin M. Compaine, "The Future of Media Companies in the International Arena," Case note, Instituto De Superioress De La Empresa, Barcelona, Spain, on Web site at www.shore.net/~bcompain/valencia.htm.
30. McCann-Erickson data in *Facts About Newspapers, 1998*, Newspaper Association of America, 1998.
31. "Comcast, ABC Form Venture to Acquire Major Interest in E! Entertainment Television," Press Release from Comcast Corporation, January 28, 1997.
32. Compaine, *Who Owns the Media?*, p. 183.
33. U.S. Securities and Exchange Commission, Form 10-Q for Playboy Enterprises Inc. filed on August 12, 1998. Playboy reported 26,000 subscribers to a premium portion of its site, at $60 annually.

4

The Television Industries:
Broadcast, Cable, and Satellite

Douglas Gomery

In 1999, American Telephone and Telegraph (AT&T) (as well known as any name in corporate America) suddenly became the largest player in cable television, an arena for which it was not known. AT&T entered cable with its acquisition of Tele-Communications, Inc. (TCI) just months earlier, and offered more than $56 billion to acquire MediaOne, catapulting it to the top of the cable industry. This was the biggest deal in media history.

Although the play-by-play of the AT&T–MediaOne deal may not have long-term consequences, it is nonetheless instructive in identifying the shifting base of new and old players and their goals in the merging video and telephony arena. The chain of events began when Comcast offered nearly $50 billion to acquire the larger MediaOne. MediaOne itself was largely the combination of several small cable franchises acquired by regional telephone operator USWest, which then added Continental Cablevision. In 1998, USWest spun off MediaOne into a separate company, having apparently decided that the cable and telephone businesses were not a good fit.

A month later, AT&T topped Comcast's offer. Comcast attempted several approaches to raise its own offer, including the possibility of partnering with Microsoft and America Online (AOL). Microsoft had an interest in promoting its operating software in the new generation of "smart" cable boxes. AOL wanted to guarantee high speed access for its online service. But none of these deals with Comcast came together. Instead, Microsoft, which had previously made a $1 billion investment in Comcast, made a deal worth $5 billion to supply AT&T's cable operation with digital set-top boxes. And AOL struck an agreement with direct broadcast satellite (DBS) provider DirecTV to use that satellite-to-home service as a high speed pipeline for its Internet service.

Thus, in the 1990s, AT&T (still thought of as a long distance phone company) became cable's dominant player, with direct access to one third of all cable customers, plus one third more through joint agreements. AT&T would become the dominant cable player in 18 of the top 20 media markets in the United States. At the same time, it became a potential, but still unrealized, competitor to provide local exchange service in the same territory.

These and other players knew that the stakes in the TV industry in the United States were high. Nearly 98% of U.S. households had television sets. Cable was growing and so was DBS direct to home satellite TV service. Broadcast, cable and DBS were the technologies that comprised the television industry. Home video, which delivered primarily motion pictures, and the production of TV programs by the Hollywood studios, are discussed with movies in Chapter 6. Pay television, such as HBO and Showtime, is also best understood as a delivery of motion pictures, and thus is also treated in Chapter 6 as an extension of the Hollywood cinema industry.

TRENDS IN THE VIDEO BUSINESS

Although overall audience levels have declined, the four major television broadcast networks—Disney's ABC, General Electric's NBC, CBS and News Corporation's Fox—still accounted for more than half of prime time television viewing in 1999. But outside prime time, the broadcast networks were losing badly to the plethora of niche cable services. Broadcast television viewership over 24 hours a day, 7 days a week decreased from a 64 share in mid-1997 to a 61 share in mid-1998. This continued a long-term trend, while basic cable posted its highest ever prime time audience levels, according to the Cable Advertising Bureau and Nielsen Ratings. During the 1997–1998 television season, the four major networks accounted for a combined 55% share of prime time viewing among all television households (as compared to 59% in the previous year and as high as 90% at their peak); UPN and WB, the two newest networks, achieved a combined 9% share of prime time viewing.

Still, broadcasting was a profitable business, and so the number of commercial and noncommercial broadcast television stations increased to 1,583 in 1998 from 1,561 in 1997. Advertising revenues for the six broadcast networks reached $15.2 billion in 1997. Broadcasters sold slightly more advance commercial time for the 1998–1999 season (over $6.4 billion) than was sold for the 1997–1998 season (nearly $6.3 billion). In comparison, far more cable programming networks split $5.7 billion in advertising revenue in 1997, an increase of 16% over 1996. Households subscribing to cable indicated they still watched the broadcast networks even if they subscribed to cable—a combined 58% share of all day viewing in the 1996–1997 television season.

In 1999, according to A. C. Nielsen estimates, 67.7 million households subscribed to cable in 68% of homes with television. More than 97% of cable customers had access to 30 or more channels, and 60% had 54 or more channels. As seen in Table 4.1, most homes in the mid-1990s could get more than 30 channels, a 50% increase from about 20 channels in the early 1980s, and 500% greater than the 5 channels in the early 1970s.

Consider the changes wrought during the 1990s:

- The infrared remote control gave users the capability to randomly access channel 42 as easily as channel 3, evening the playing field between VHF, UHF and cable-only channels.
- UHF stations, on cable, have the same technical quality as VHF have had, and so that long-held UHF picture inferiority disappeared.

TABLE 4.1
Homes by Number of TV Channels Able to Receive

	1	2–3	4–6	7–10	11–20	21–30	30+
Early 1950s	32%	36%	11%	21%	—	—	—
Early 1960s	3	18	55	24	—	—	—
Early 1970s	1	12	42	35	9%	1%	—
Early 1980s	—	3	25	40	27	5	—
Early 1990s	—	—	4	9	18	7	62%
Late 1990s	—	—	—	1<	1<	1	97

Source: Ed Papazian (ed.), *TV Dimensions '97* (New York: Media Dynamics, Inc., 1997), p. 28. Late 1990s, "Systems and Subscribers by System Channel Capacity," from NCTA on Web site at www.ncta.com/glance. html, accessed July 1, 1999.

- Advertisers ran many of the same commercials on cable networks as on broadcast network. And, indeed, advertising became as pervasive on cable programming as on broadcast.
- DBS, in about 7% of households in 1998, proved a real, if not fully interchangeable, competitor to cable.
- Long gone are the days when the typical household had access to only three choices on television. In 1983, the average home still had only 14 television channels. By 1999, that number had expanded to 50 or more channels per home.
- In the 1980s, NBC, ABC, CBS and PBS defined the TV universe. No more. Although watching TV remained the favorite pastime of most Americans, because of the explosion of cable and satellite, choices typically number in the dozens—with the set on more than 8 hours per day.[1]

The news from the TV business and its changing ownership made headlines, as when in 1995, for example, the Walt Disney Corporation bought Capital Cities/ABC for more than $17 billion. Two of the world's largest and most famous companies, General Electric with its NBC unit and Microsoft with its joint ventures with NBC, owned large portions of the TV world. This made the industry seem more concentrated. As the 1990s began, two scholars concluded that "an examination of concentration ratios indicates that high levels of concentration exist in most of the [media] industry segments."[2]

The TV industry's growing concentration deserves close attention. Are the top broadcast companies owned by a smaller number of groups? How does the increase in the number of broadcast networks balance against consolidation in ownership of chains of local stations? For cable, AT&T created a formidable cable leader with access to two thirds of households in the United States—either directly or though joint deals. For DBS, DirecTV controlled about 90% of the revenues in 1998.[3]

Broadcast enterprises (TV and radio) (as seen in Table 4.2) represented some of the best known companies in the nation. Not only are they well known as an NBC or Disney, but also are part of some of the nation's most influential media companies such as the New York Times Co. and the Washington Post Companies. Even when a viewer is watching a television station owned by Scripps, Belo, Lin, Young, Pulitzer, Raycom or Chronicle, and does not know it, they are plugging into what many pundits consider as the most influential and pervasive mass medium in history.[4]

TABLE 4.2
Broadcast Revenues of Media Largest Companies, 1995–1997

Company	1997 (in millions)	1996 (in millions)	1995 (in millions)	1997 Media % of Total Revenue	1996 Media % of Total Revenue	1995 % of Total Revenue
1. CBS	$4,839	3,390.0	3,483.0	88.6	78.2	79.6
2. NBC (GE)	4,803	4,940.0	3,659.0	93.2	94.5	93.4
3. ABC (Walt Disney)	4,572	4,005.0	4,177.0	66.2	61.1	67.2
4. News Corporation	2,730	2,500.0	1,580.0	49.2	62.4	53.7
5. Tribune	927	681.0	630.0	39.2	32.3	31.2
6. Gannett	704	641.5	523.8	15.7	15.2	13.1
7. Cox	650	391.0	354.0	19.6	12.7	13.0
8. A. H. Belo	537	333.4	322.6	43.1	40.4	43.9
9. Sinclair	517	326.0	273.5	100.0	86.1	100.0
10. Univision	460	370.3	321.3	100.0	100.0	100.0
11. BHC Commun*	444	446.3	454.7	100.0	100.0	100.0
12. Viacom	422	390.3	385.5	15.7	16.2	19.0
13. Hearst	422	368.0	285.0	14.9	14.3	11.3
14. Washington Post	338	335.2	306.0	18.8	19.6	19.3
15. E. W. Scripps	331	349.6	320.3	30.1	29.9	29.2
16. Lin Television	292	273.4	217.2	100.0	100.0	100.0
17. Raycom Media	286	200.0	187.0	100.0	97.3	97.2
18. Young Broadcasting	264	261.5	245.8	100.0	100.0	100.0
19. Pulitzer Publishing	227	208.5	188.0	38.8	39.0	39.8
20. Chronicle Publishing	148	147.0	131.0	32.8	31.5	24.5

*Formerly Chris-Craft Industries.
Source: *Advertising Age*, August 17, 1998, August 18, 1997, August 19, 1996, accessed July 12, 1999, on Web site at adage.com/dataplace/100_LEADING_MEDIA_COMPANIES.html.

Table 4.2 shows that in some cases the broadcast holdings are essentially the entire business of the company. Lin, Young and BHC Communications are examples. In other cases, broadcasting is a relatively small part of the media group, such as Gannett, Hearst and Viacom. Many other companies fall in between. Thus, there is no consistent profile of the structure of a broadcasting enterprise.

In 1996, a typical 30-second national commercial cost more than $268,000 to air. The average network prime time hour contained 8 minutes of commercials, and the average non-prime time hour contained 13 minutes. All this added up to more than $44 billion per year spent by advertisers on TV in 1997, as seen in Table 4.3.[5]

Although advertising expenditures on television have continued to climb, there is a pronounced shift toward cable. Whereas absolute expenditures on network and spot broadcast categories have flattened, expenditures on cable networks picked up in 1994 and accelerated in 1997. During the 1990s, cable TV networks offered thousands of advertising slots. Cable empowered the television set to become the great video jukebox. The rapid increase in subscribers, the explosion of free and pay-per-view channels and rate deregulation all provided the cable industry with an aura of growth. Whereas even the most popular cable networks enjoyed only a fraction of the audience ratings of the broadcast networks, the portfolio of channels from Tele-

TABLE 4.3
Television's Volume of Advertising (in millions)

	Total	Cable	Network	Spot	Local
1997	$44,519	$7,626	$13,020	$9,999	$11,436
1996	42,484	4,472	13,081	9,803	10,944
1995	37,828	3,535	11,600	9,119	9,985
1994	35,391	2,671	11,600	9,120	9,986
1993	30,584	1,970	10,209	7,800	9,029
1992	29,409	1,685	10,249	7,551	8,554
1991	27,402	1,521	8,933	7,110	7,985
1990	28,405	1,393	9,383	7,788	8,252
1985	21,287	989	8,060	6,004	5,714
1980	11,488	72	5,130	3,269	2,967

Sources: Robert J. Coen, "Ad Spending Tops $175 Billion During Robust '96." *Advertising Age*, May 17, 1997, p. 20; Standard and Poor's Industry Surveys, "Publishing," February 6, 1997, p. 2; McCann-Erickson data from Web site at www.tvb.org/tvfacts, accesssed July 12, 1999.

Communications, Comcast, Time Warner and others began to aggregate view numbers approaching the broadcast networks. Cable's efficiency and target ability added value to an ad campaign. But the sheer number of channels and the microscopic audiences they typically attracted made it a different advertising vehicle than broadcasting.

By the mid-1990s, cable reached 67% of all homes in the United States, and even more (81%) among households with annual incomes of $60,000 or more. Cable targeted more like radio (see Chapter 5) than over-the-air TV, as most subscribers had from 40 to 50 viewing options. So adding to the revenue base of advertising were cable subscription fees, which totaled over $25 billion in 1998. DBS added several billion more. But, before analyzing who owns all this television, it would be useful to review its history and in particular how programs are produced, distributed and presented to the public.[6]

TELEVISION IN THE UNITED STATES: A BRIEF HISTORY

In the context of media history, television's tenure has been brief: a mere half century. There were technical television experiments as early as the late 1920s, and the Federal Communications Commission (FCC) allocated channels before World War II, but the industry as a mass medium did not commence until after that war. The innovation of television broadcasting in the United States began with an FCC order in late 1945 reinstating pre-World War II broadcast TV standards, and its system of 13 channel allocations. The Commission postponed a decision on a color standard and began programming in black-and-white imagery and FM-generated sound using the National Television System Committee's 525 scanning lines at 30 frames per second, which the FCC adopted in 1941. This was still the standard in the 1990s.

The late 1940s saw stations go on the air and TV network programming—by NBC, CBS and ABC—began. But FCC engineers reported that a co-channel interference needed to be resolved. To viewers in Princeton, New Jersey, for example, the signal of channel 2 in New York and channel 2 in Washington, DC created a Venetian blind pattern of horizontal bars when viewed. So, in 1948, the Commission issued a notice to freeze the allocation process. It was not until 1952 that this Freeze was lifted by the Sixth Report and Order. The Order allocated VHF spectrum to channels 2 to 13 and UHF spectrum to channels 14 to 83. The whole of pre-Freeze TV consisted of 108 stations, principally in selected large cities. Although it may be difficult to imagine today, there existed considerable doubt—until the Freeze ended—about the exact form and precise impact of broadcast television's future. Would advertising-supported radio networks take control? Would Hollywood own and operate TV networks? Would television be distributed into movie theaters? Would there be pay TV?[7]

Once the Freeze was lifted, entrepreneurs of all sorts rushed in, and by 1960 there were some 450 stations on the air. The radio networks, led by NBC and CBS, carried the day as radio profits subsidized the innovation of their owned and operated television stations in the largest cities in the United States. In small cities, owners affiliated with NBC and CBS first, and then the ABC and DuMont networks. The number of homes with TV sets grew from a few million in 1950 to nearly 60 million by 1960, covering most of the United States. Thereafter, growth in sets in homes simply matched the increase in households. VHF stations became profitable as the United States fell in love with TV along with (or because of) Lucy.[8]

But VHF did not cover the whole nation. After the Freeze, the FCC added UHF channels. With an inferior signal and lack of UHF tuner equipped TV sets, UHF stations rarely made money. To address the latter problem, Congress enacted the All Channel Receiver Act of 1962. By 1964, all new TV sets had to be built to receive both VHF and UHF. Thus, whereas only 10% of TV sets could receive UHF signals in 1963, well over half were equipped five years later and virtually all were by the 1980s.[9] The FCC also extended UHF's power and antenna height. Ironically, only the proliferation of cable in the 1980s truly solved the UHF problem, as all broadcast channels became functionally equal on cable.

Rationale for Broadcast Regulation

Broadcasting historically has been far more heavily regulated than any other medium discussed in this book, with the possible exception of cable. Under the Communications Act of 1934, the FCC is charged with making effective use of spectrum space by means of allocation to broadcasting and other services. This is performed with the public interest, convenience or necessity as the key, although undefined, guiding principle. In practice, this breaks down into several more specific factors explaining why the FCC regulates broadcasting, and why concern over concentration is a prime aspect of that regulation.

Spectrum Scarcity

The prime rationale for government's role in broadcasting has long been the technical limitation of usable spectrum space. Potential use of the spectrum depends on priorities and needs at any given time and on technical discoveries impinging on its efficient use. Spectrum that is serviceable for broadcasting is limited, because only certain areas have characteristics conducive to broadcasting and other services compete for, and have been assigned, some of that same space. The result is insufficient space for all who wish to broadcast, and thus only some can be allowed to do so if any are to be heard.

This in itself would not imply government regulation. Congress could have adopted a market mechanism early on. For example, exacerbating any technical limits on spectrum availability was the huge demand created by the government's policy of giving it without cost. Free goods tend to be in shorter supply than goods with a price. But Congress specifically retained ownership of spectrum as a public resource, and thus services using a portion of the spectrum have to be licensed for given periods of time while specifically giving up any vested interest in any part of the spectrum. Such a system obviated the normal pricing mechanism as a means of market control, and required some choice among applicants wishing to broadcast. Under this approach, a broadcast license is thus a limited privilege—the right to make use of a specific frequency assignment for a specified period (usually three years, until 1981 when Congress extended radio licenses to seven years and television licenses to five, with both extended to eight years under the Telecommunications Act of 1996), with an expectation of renewal baring major problems.

Localism

Although expressed in different ways over the years, the FCC has clearly held that the "best" broadcast station is locally owned and operated. Such ownership was deemed in the public interest as it would presumably be closer to local needs and concerns, and thus the station would more adequately reflect and project that community than some absentee-owned operation or central network. Such a policy strongly affected such basic decisions as television allocations (e.g., the 1952 Sixth Report and Order), wherein the need to provide as many local TV channels as possible led directly to the intermixture phenomenon of combining UHF and UHF stations in direct competition. Thus, a fairly consistent public social policy was developed at as vast an economic cost as has been deemed politically acceptable. But "in practice, localism is futile because it is much more profitable for stations to affiliate with a network or provide syndicated material distributed by satellite or even landlines, thus giving up most of their practical control over programming than to produce or select their own programs."[10] Further, because of localism, few markets had more than three television channels, which limits the formation of additional national networks with the potential benefit of greater diversity.

Public Interest

The FCC regulates broadcasting, beginning with the essential licensing process itself, "in the public interest, convenience, and necessity," the undefined standard on which the Communications Act of 1934 (and its 1927 predecessor and its 1996 successor) is built. In the 1960s and 1970s, such regulation of cable (but not licensing) was an extension of the need to promote broadcasting as a free service, and hence in the public interest. Virtually all FCC decisions and court reviews of those decisions have been decided on varied interpretations of just what the public interest requirement was at any given time. As but one example, the FCC's 1965 "Policy Statement on Comparative Broadcast Hearings" declared it in the public interest that seven factors be taken into account when two or more applicants for the same facility were being considered for a license: diversification of control of the media,[11] full-time participation in station operation by owners, proposed program service, past broadcast record, efficient use of frequency, character of the applicant and "other factors."[12]

Structure Affecting Diversity of Content

Concerned with promoting diversity of content to a public with sundry interests, the FCC has followed an unwritten but fairly clear policy of seeking to modify the ownership of broadcasting facilities as a means of effecting changes in content. In the volumes of FCC hearings and reports on questions of ownership, a key and constant element is use of the term "diversity." It is repeatedly asserted that diversity of media control is in the public interest, not just because such diversity presumably prevents undue concentration of media editorial and economic clout, but because such ownership will be more likely to provide a broader variety of content choices to the public. Whereas the economics of commercial broadcasting often mitigate against such a process, the fact remains that the FCC still follows a process of seeking content diversity through ownership diversity. Typical of this approach by both the FCC and its Appeals Court "watchdog" was the agreement when then FCC Chairman Ferris and Appeals Court Judge Bazelon specifically noted that the key to diversity in the industry was "structural" regulation of the media.[13] A major rationale for regular investigations of network operations by both Congress and the FCC is recognition of the fact that as networks provide programming for virtually all television stations—even the independents, most of whose reruns are syndicated off-network productions—some degree of control over their operations is essential if government-fostered "improvements" in the level of programming were to have any effect whatsoever. As becomes evident, however, even this rationale was being questioned by the 1980s in the face of the new technological innovation and developing competition.

Requirement to Regulate Monopoly

Both the 1927 (Section 13) and the 1934 (Section 313 as amended) acts specifically applied antitrust laws to the field of broadcasting, calling for revocation of any station license from an owner accused of monopolistic activities in the industry. If any such license was so revoked, the FCC was further directed to refuse any future construction permits or license applications from that party. Just as these laws constrained the FCC, the Sherman (1890) and Clayton (1910) Acts direct the Antitrust Division of the Department of Justice. As the two governmental agencies most concerned with monopoly in broadcasting, the FCC and the Department of Justice have "acted sometimes in tandem sometimes at cross purposes and sometimes independently,"[14] partially owing to their differing "triggering" concerns. Whereas the Justice Department looks for undue economic concentration, the FCC is interested in diversifying the public's sources of entertainment and information. In 1978, the Federal Trade Commission (FTC) joined the fray in its investigation of overall mass media ownership. In a two-day symposium, the FTC gathered and later published a collection of papers assessing concentration in print and broadcast media.[15] A policy option report subsequently circulated within the agency, but it was never publicly released.

The FCC has typically acted either with a policy-oriented rule making or an ad hoc decision on specific situations. The Department of Justice has more options: It can and has taken part in FCC rule making or ad hoc decision-making procedures as an interested party, it can actively petition the FCC to undertake some specific action or it can file an antitrust suit in the courts. Both agencies have been strongly affected in the past by political aims and pressures of the administration in power as well as by Congress. Both, but especially the Justice Department, can and have acted behind the scenes to pressure business or the other agency to its will without specific action. Justice is somewhat limited in initiating actions by the legal tradition of primary jurisdiction, which basically says that those seeking redress must first seek action from the regulatory agency in question (here, the FCC) before proceeding directly to the courts. Thus, in several of the discussions that follow, note that the Antitrust Division first sought action from the Commission and only after that took more direct action.

Numerical Limits on Multiple Ownership

The first numerical restriction on broadcast ownership came in 1940 when ownership was limited to three television stations and up to six FM stations. In 1944, as a compromise to an NBC petition for a limit of seven TV stations to any one owner, the FCC increased the TV limit to five stations. No limit was suggested for AM broadcasting, but in rejection of CBS's attempt to acquire KQW in San Jose as its eighth owned and operated station, the FCC created a defacto limit of seven stations to be held by any one AM station owner.[16]

The Commission first considered a cohesive policy of multiple broadcasting ownership limitation in 1948. The rules finally adopted in November 1953 applied numerical limits of seven AM, seven FM, and five television stations, dropping earlier consideration of such variables as minority control, number of people served, etc. This was the first actual rule affecting AM control. With further consideration of the problems of UHF television then becoming apparent, the Commission increased the limit on television ownership to seven stations, no more than five of which could be VHF. This final (September 1954) adjustment of the rules was upheld in a 1956 Supreme Court decision.[17]

Not until the early 1980s was serious disagreement heard on these long-accepted rules. (Indeed, only in the late 1970s had any single group owner first held the 21-station maximum of AM, FM and TV stations.) It had become increasingly apparent that an arbitrary limit on number of stations was not an effective way of limiting single-owner access to a large portion of the nation's population (i.e., the three networks). Combined with this was a feeling that ownership limits, if any, should be applied equally across broadcasting, cable and newer media. The growing potential for competition to broadcasting resulted in fresh examination of old rules written in a far simpler time.[18]

THE ROLE OF NETWORKS

Whether for over-the air or cable outlets, national and regional networks exist to interconnect stations for common and simultaneous distribution of programs and advertising. The network acts as something of a broker between local stations or cable systems, program producers and advertisers. From radio days to the present, basic issues of public policy concern about networks have remained, generally speaking, those of excessive domination of advertising, programming and local affiliate stations. These were historically operationalized into four policy objectives that have and continue to guide government regulation:

1) To make available the highest quality programming, especially in news and public affairs.
2) To provide for diversity in the sources of those program, and control over the selection of programs by industry gatekeepers.
3) To minimize economic market power by any industry institution.
4) To encourage minority and specialized content rather than wasteful duplication of the lowest common denominator broadcast content.[19]

The increase in the number of national broadcast networks from three to six since 1986, as well as the abundance of cable-only networks, has substantially lessened the need for the FCC or other agencies to concern themselves with remedies to these issues. In many respects, they have largely been achieved.

Development of Network Regulation

First the Radio Act of 1927 (Section 4h) and then the Communications Act of 1934 (Section 303i) gave the FRC/ FCC authority to make special regulations applicable to stations engaged in chain (or network) broadcasting. Few such regulations emerged until the FCC undertook the first detailed analysis of the role and impact of networks in the chain broadcasting investigation of 1938–1941.

The expansion of television in the 1990s led to various congressional investigations, especially into the potential monopoly role of networks. Catalysts for the probes included the decline of the Dumont television network, the weakness of ABC as a distant third in television networking, the merger of ABC with Paramount Theaters Inc. in 1951 and the general problems of UHF, including the clear lack of network interest in affiliating with such stations. Frustration was widely expressed over the changes occurring in broadcast and the dominant role of networks, which to many observers seemed to make allocations and other issues difficult to resolve.

The massive *Network Broadcasting* report in 1957 focused on the measurement of network concentration and control, such as affiliation practices, option time, advertising rates and station compensation arrangements.[20] Among the report's recommendations were a ban on option time, a curb on station ownership, separating networks' front station representation and a general loosening of network control over talent.[21]

While the FCC considered the recommendations of the network study, another staff began a detailed analysis of network programming methods, problems and trends. Reports from this investigation appeared throughout the first half of the 1960s. The FCC began to consider specific rules to limit network control of prime time programming.

Network Regulation in the 1970s and Early 1980s

Two attempts by the FCC to curtail network power were the Prime Time Access Rule and the financial interest and syndication rules. The Prime Time Access Rule (PTAR) took effect at the beginning of the Fall 1971 program season. Networks were limited to three hours nightly of prime time programming (effectively a half hour reduction in the existing pattern). The FCC hoped thereby to increase local program production at best, but to diversify program production sources at least. The basic result was a glut of popular syndicated game shows. The rules were phased entirely in 1996.[22]

The financial rules were implemented about the same time. They essentially prohibited the networks from having a financial interest in the programming other than news and from domestically syndicating any programs. The intent here too was to curb network power over independent producers and to encourage quality programming. They resulted in little apparent change in programming, but did help create new wealth among Hollywood studios and some independent producers. The rules were effectively ended by the FCC, nudged by the courts, in 1995.[23]

In 1972, the Justice Department's Antitrust Division entered the fray with antitrust suits against all three national networks, aimed at further divorcing them from control, ownership and syndication rights to prime time programming. With stops and starts, they were settled with Consent Decrees in 1976 with NBC and 1980 with ABC and CBS. The agreements limited network activity in some areas of programming and in their relation with program producers and syndication.

Other studies of the networks followed. Most telling was one issued in 1980 by Stanley Besen and Thomas Krattenmaker. Given a substantially free hand to design their study, they broadened the mandate and in the process dramatically changed the course of some 40 years of FCC study on "the network problem." The new study looked at networks in the context of changing technology & the oncoming competition, since realized, from cable, home video, satellite systems, various forms of pay television and the like. These free-market advocates concluded that the broadcast TV business was no longer seen as a self-contained unit of limited competition, but rather as merely one form of input to home receivers.[24]

Balanced against the three networks were affiliates. With ownership limited to five, then seven stations into the 1980s, station owners were a fragmented industry with little individual bargaining power with the networks. Central to the investigation of networks over the years has been the degree of freedom accorded to local station network affiliates. The controlling factor has been the Commission's spectrum allocation decisions to provide local stations to as many communities as possible—thus creating about 70 of the top 100 markets with access to only three commercial VHF channels, and only about 15 markets with more than three VHF channels. More than anything else, this has limited the number of networks to three, as affiliation with UHF channels was avoided until cable became widespread. For decades, entry to network affiliation status was thus limited because there can be but one entry per network in a given market. Except in markets with more than three VHF channels, a "bilateral oligopoly" existed where neither networks nor stations had much flexibility (e.g., changing affiliations, etc.). It was a paradox that in markets with fewer than three VHF channels, the smaller markets actually had the upperhand in network relations because one of the networks had to take a secondary affiliation, with but few of its programs being carried in a shared station arrangement.

Of special concern to regulators in the years spanning from the 1960s to the 1980s was the control networks exercised over the form and structure of the TV programming industry. Prime time viewing options for the majority of the national audience are provided by broadcast networks. Other viewing hours are also dominated by networks in that affiliates use network programs about 65% of their total broadcast time, and independent stations make heavy use of syndicated off-network material originally programmed by a network. Over the years, several trends lead to this situation.

In the final analysis, however, networks succeeded because, given the constraints of allocation, stations simply found it more profitable to affiliate than to go independent. As long as that was true, it was unlikely that market pressures could create substantial change in the dominating role of networks.

One such source has been the independent production community in Hollywood, generally divided into the *majors*, which are part of theatrical film firms, and the *independents*, which usually rent production facilities from others. Although producers have been accused of being a rather tight group, there is in fact easy entry to the production circle. Pricing is affected by the ability of the networks to produce their own programming if costs become too high. Moreover, the power of the producers is limited because they do not control first-run distribution, which is handled by the networks.[25]

The packagers felt constrained with only three markets for their product. But, with the rise of three newer networks, as well as cable networks and a slowly increasing market of stations for syndicated products (both off-network and first-run), the packagers have found greater opportunity, despite the end of PTAR and Fin-Syn rules. Network decisions on how long a series played on a network are important to the potential syndication life of that series off-network, for if there are not enough episodes, then syndicators cannot sell the material to local stations for typical "stripping" (running five days a week) for a minimum of several months at a time. Few series break even, let alone make money on network runs. Network payments do not usually cover the cost of production, so syndication is an important source of profits for producers. Network decisions on series length thus have a direct impact on the profits of program packagers. But with more networks, it has been possible for shows that are dropped by one network to be picked up by another, or to continue in the syndication market. (Perhaps the most visible example of this was Paramount's *Star Trek*, which had a longer life in first-run syndication than it did for the network.)

The innovation of TV had come with ownership limits. But by the late 1980s, regulatory deregulation had taken hold and so the FCC lessened upper limits. For example, late in 1985, the Commission increased the number of stations one entity could own from 7 to 12 stations.

Telecommunications Act of 1996

The 1996 Telecommunications Act also eliminated the long-standing restrictions on broadcast network ownership of cable systems. (Earlier FCC rule making, congressional action, as well as the 1996 Telecommunications Act removed restrictions that had prevented telephone companies from acquiring or creating a cable system operation.) The Act removed many of the ownership limits of broadcast stations. It removed the numeral cap on the number of stations, replacing it with language that an individual, company or corporation could own broadcast television stations that reached up to 35% of households in the United States, with UHF stations counting half their actual reach for this limitation calculation.[26]

The Act also removed the long-standing ban on joint radio–broadcast TV ownership in the same market. As the Commission interpreted the 1996 Act, it extended broadcast licenses to eight years to facilitate competition; under previous rules, TV stations had to renew their broadcast licenses every five years. The reasoning was that the lengthened license term would reduce the burden to broadcasters, and allow the competitive marketplace to operate more efficiently.

The Courts also did their part. For example, in 1997, the Supreme Court voted 5–4 to uphold a broadcaster-favored regulation requiring cable systems to carry local TV stations, even if those stations offer little more than home shopping or religious programming.

The Differing Network Strategies

The broadcast networks have long dominated the television industry, under similar economics but based on different strategies. Until its sale to General Electric Co., NBC sought to exploit a manufacturing linkage to its parent company, TV set manufacturer Radio Corporation of America. (DuMont, another early TV set maker, tried but failed to establish a network in the early 1990s, hampered by a lack of station assignments in major cities). CBS and ABC spun off television networks and station ownership from their respective radio operations and sought to exploit programming advantages. At first advertisers supported television by sponsoring entire programs, such as the *Kraft Music Hall* or *The Colgate Comedy Hour*. In the mid-1950s, the Hollywood film industry entered television production, releasing huge feature film libraries to create *The Late Show*, as well as producing westerns and detective shows such as *Cheyenne* and *77 Sunset Strip*. Hollywood supplied such popular programs that the networks began selling time to advertisers in minute blocks, in the same manner advertisers bought pages or half pages in newspapers and magazines. By the early 1960s, the NBC and CBS networks vied for the top of the ratings. ABC did not gain full parity until the 1970s. It was then that the U.S. Department of Justice launched its investigation of the monopoly practices of the networks and negotiated rules banning the networks from syndicating their own hit programs.

The mid-1970s represented the peak of the influence of network broadcast television. Viewers and advertisers had little other choice. Affiliates, networks and their stockholders shared in the profit and growth. More independent stations went on the air to offer an alternative. Throughout this era of network ascendency, TV increasingly became a major part of the daily lives of Americans (as can be seen from Table 4.4).

Cable TV

The hours of set use grew steadily as did the number of channels available. Cable was providing more reasons for keeping the TV set turned on. With the widespread availability of easy-to-use remote controls during the 1980s, channel "surfing" became a new approach to TV use. Indeed, with the innovation of the remote control and cable TV, the growth of audiences watching network programming began to fall as a proportion of all viewing. Yet, total viewing increased when factoring in cable channels.

Cable TV has been around almost as long as broadcast TV. Cable television originated as a service to households in mountainous or geographically remote areas where reception of over-the-air television signals was poor or nonexistent. "Community antennas" were erected on nearby mountain tops, and homes were connected to these towers to receive local broadcast signals. By the late 1950s, community antenna TV (CATV) operators began to take advantage of their ability to pick up additional broadcast signals from hundreds of miles away, and add them to the package of retransmitted network programs. By 1962, almost 800 cable systems serving 850,000 subscribers were in business. Not surprisingly, local broadcasters opposed local cable operators importing distant signals, viewing this as competition. They

TABLE 4.4
Average Weekly Television Viewing, Selected Years, 1950–1997

	Weekly Set Usage Per Home	Channels Available Per Home	Channels Viewed Weekly	Time Spent Per Channel Weekly
1950	32.5 Hours	2.9	2.8	11.6 Hours
1960	36.5	5.9	4.2	8.7
1970	42.0	7.4	4.5	9.3
1980	46.5	10.2	5.6	8.3
1990	48.5	27.2	8.8	5.5
1997	50.0	43.0	10.3	4.9

Source: Ed Papazian (ed.), *TV Dimensions '97* (New York: Media Dynamics, Inc., 1997), p. 21.

pressured the FCC to expand its jurisdiction and place restrictions on the ability of cable systems to import distant television signals. This action had the effect of slowing the development of cable during the 1960s.[27]

Regulation of Cable Ownership

Although the cable industry had to contend with a period of increased regulation from the FCC, backed by the courts, few of these regulations addressed ownership. Various policies determined what signals the cable operators had to carry and what they could not. For a time, they were limited to what Hollywood movies they could run (very new and very old films, but not those in between—the very films that had become popular as "Movie of the Week" fare for the broadcast networks).

The FCC did adopt rules prohibiting television networks and telephone companies from owning cable and restricted owners of broadcast stations to owning cable franchises in markets other than their television markets. In the 1960s, the FCC did initiate some queries on cable ownership issues, but overall devote little attention to effects of horizontal concentration or vertical integration in the cable industry. There were no limits on the size of local cable systems on the aggregation of local systems into multiple system operators (MSOs). There were no restrictions on combining program ownership and cable ownership. In fact, the incentive for cable operators to make cable subscription more attractive by investing in programming was considered a healthy alternative to the broadcast oligopoly.

The regulation of cable, favored if not actively encouraged, by various broadcast interests peaked in 1966 with the FCC's highly restrictive Second Report and Order,[28] upheld by the Supreme Court in 1968 in the *Southwestern Cable* case.[29] By 1978, the FCC was undoing much of its previous regulation and in 1984 Congress enacted the Cable Communications Act, which substantially eliminated most of the old restrictions on cable systems. Control over rates continued to be an issue and 1992 legislation resulted in some cable systems having to modestly lower rates. But the 1996 Telecommunications Act effectively eliminated most rate regulation by 1999.

Under the 1992 cable legislation, the FCC did determine limits for affecting both horizontal and vertical consolidation in the cable industry. A single entity was limited to control of cable systems that passed no more than 30% of all homes passed by cable (35% under some conditions of minority ownership). They are further restricted to programming a maximum of 40% of their channels with programming bought from affiliated companies (i.e., those in which the cable operator has at least a 5% interest).[30]

Although cable systems grew slowly during the period of maximum regulation, the beginning of relaxation of regulation in the late 1970s coincided with cable's pioneering of satellite distribution technology. Combined, they helped fuel a pronounced growth of channels available to consumers and thus to a substantial increase in cable subscribers. In 1975, cable switched from terrestrial microwave and even cassette distribution of its movies to a national satellite distribution system. Pay services, in general, and HBO, in particular, created interest in cable for households that already could get a full array of quality broadcast TV signals.

Satellites changed the cable business dramatically and profoundly, paving the way for the explosive growth of program networks. Following HBO, Ted Turner used satellite distribution to offer WTBS, the independent TV UHF television station he owned in Atlanta. It programmed sports, off-network re-runs and movies to cable customers across the United States, and became the first "superstation." Other networks that existed only on cable, such as ESPN and BET, also turned to satellite for distribution. As the 1980s began, nearly 15 million households were cable subscribers.[31]

Cable system entrepreneurs rode the wave of this change, cobbling together multiple systems or MSOs. For example, in 1976, TCI had 500,000 total subscribers. Two decades later, TCI included more than 16 million subscribers (or about one quarter of all cable subscribers) nationally. In addition, TCI, through its Liberty Media affiliate, also held ownership stakes in a multitude of cable networks. Time Warner built on its HBO innovation by acquiring and building a system of cable operations. These two lead the way to the modern multiple system operations defining the cable business of the 1990s. By 1990, cable TV had penetrated more than 50% of households in the United States; more than two thirds had cable 10 years later.

Changes in the Broadcast TV Network Landscape

The three broadcast networks—CBS, NBC and ABC—continued their domination of television through the mid-1980s. But major changes were about to shake the cozy club:

- The original owners of all three networks sold out: RCA sold NBC to General Electric; ABC let Capital Cities acquire it; CBS was sold to Loews, Inc.
- In 1986, the first serious challenge to the networks in 30 years appeared when News Corporation launched its Fox network. The eventual success of Fox seemed to embolden other motion picture studios to start their own networks.
- In 1995 came the United Paramount Network (UPN), a joint undertaking from Viacom's Paramount studio and Chris-Craft (a major owner of local stations) and the WB—the Warner Bros. Network, which is part of Time Warner. Both, like Fox before them, allied with former independent TV stations.
- In 1998, Paxson Communications, owner of more than 50 stations, launched PaxNet, the seventh national broadcast TV network.
- The number of cable program networks increased from 28 in 1980 to 74 by the decade's end. By 1998, the number of national cable video networks had grown to more than 170, supplemented by dozens of regional networks. In 1998, over 57% of all cable subscribers were receiving 54 channels or more.

The cable industry exists under a structural paradox, much like their newspaper cousins. Although there are numerous cable companies nationally, with a handful of exceptions, each local cable system operator is a monopoly provider. Thus, there are few structural forces to govern the price cable operators charge their customers. In 1989, Congress's General Accounting Office issued a report finding that basic cable

TV rates had risen about 29% over the previous two years, while overall rates (including pay channels) were up by 14%.[32] Public interest groups protested. In response to perceived weak on service amid hefty price increases in 1992 Congress passed the Cable Television Consumer Protection and Competition Act, which required new service standards, such as answering telephone calls in a timely manner; required program providers to make their channels available to alternative distribution services, such as wireless cable or multichannel multipoint distribution systems (MMDS) (see later); and required the ownership limits described earlier.

In the most far-reaching portions of the 1992 Act, Congress vested the FCC with the responsibility of controlling subscriber fees and launched a series of complex proceedings and rules that rolled back rates for some systems for several years. Cable systems were subject to rate regulation in areas that lacked "effective competition." The Act also reopened the long-standing "must carry" controversy. Broadcasters won the right to negotiate to be paid for their signal, and the broadcasters took cable TV channel space. From this strategy, ABC launched ESPN2, NBC started MSNBC and Fox began FX.

The cable operators lobbied to undo the 1992 law and could claim some success with the Telecommunications Act of 1996. It relaxed the 1992 regulatory regime, promising operators more flexibility in packing their channels and pricing their services. The Telecommunications Act fully exempted small systems (those with fewer than 50,000 subscribers and no ties to large MSOs), and for all other cable television systems removed price caps in three years for all types of service except "basic tier," which included over-the-air local channels and public TV local channels. Cable companies in small towns and rural areas were relieved of cap regulation in 1996.[33]

The enactment of the telecommunications reform law freed cable companies to further innovate. Among the MSOs that entered local telephone, long distance and Internet service provider business were MediaOne, Time Warner, Cablevision System and @Home, a joint venture of TCI, Cox Communications, Comcast and venture capital firm Kleiner, Perkins, Caufield and Byers. Cable networks also developed World Wide Web sites, including ESPN Sports Zone, Discovery Online and CNN Interactive. Indeed, behind the passage of the Telecommunications Act of 1996 was the assumption that technological innovation and new market entrants would lead to lower prices and better service without direct governmental requirements and rule-making. Telephone companies could and would provide cable service, and cable companies could and would provide telephone service. The implementation of this experiment was taking longer than the optimists. Most importantly for ownership, the 1996 Act also kicked off a wave of acquisitions and mergers, as players jockeyed for position in the merging markets.

TV in Flux

In response to cable's growth, in the 1990s the major broadcast TV networks tried to establish unique brand identities to help them stand apart from the crowd and stem the decline in viewership. Each network used air time, worth millions of dollars, for self-promotions. NBC pioneered the practice of branding individual nights of television. Based on then current shows, Saturday was tagged "Thrillogy" to highlight *The Pretender* and *Profiler*; Thursday became "Must See TV," based on *Seinfeld, Friends* and *ER*. ABC picked up on the practice, labeling Friday night programming "TGIF." And Fox trumpeted *The Simpsons* and *King of the Hill* as "Non-Stop Fox." The major networks increasingly used "seamless programming," abandoning the title sequences and commercial breaks that had traditionally separated shows. NBC researchers claimed these branding practices have sharply cut audience losses between programs, and helped stem the tide of viewers discovering new cable TV networks.[34]

On the cable side, by the early 1990s, entrepreneurs had introduced a vast array of cable channels, with the most popular fully or partially owned by one of the major cable MSOs or another powerful media company. Table 4.5, identifying many of the cable network and their MSO investors, is a partial and static list, needing to be updated on almost a weekly basis.[35] With a rare exception, these networks are part

TABLE 4.5
Major Cable MSO Ownership in National Video Programming Services, 1998

Programming Service	Year Started	MSO Interests (%)
Action Pay-Per-View	1990	TCI (35)
American Movie Classics	1984	Cablevision (75)
Animal Planet	1996	TCI (49), Cox (25)
BBC America	1998	TCI (25), Cox (12)
Black Entertainment Network	1980	TCI (35)
BET Movies	1997	TCI (81)
The Box Worldwide	1985	TCI (78)
Bravo	1985	Cablevision (75)
The Cartoon Network	1992	Time Warner (100)
Cinemax	1980	Time Warner (100)
CNN	1980	Time Warner (100)
CNNfn	1995	Time Warner (100)
CNN Headline News	1982	Time Warner (100)
CNN/SI	1996	Time Warner (100)
Comedy Central	1991	Time Warner (100)
Court TV	1991	TCI (50) Time Warner (50)
Discovery Channel	1985	TCI (49) Cox (25)
E! Entertainment	1990	Comcast (40) MediaOne (10) TCI (10)
Encore	1991	TCI (100)
FiT TV	1993	TCI (50)
Fox Sports Net	1996	TCI (25) Cablevision (37)
Fox Sports World	1997	TCI (50)
FX	1994	TCI (50)
Golf Channel	1995	Comcast (43) MediaOne (14)
Home Box Office (HBO)	1972	Time Warner (100)
HBO 2	1975	Time Warner (100)
HBO 3	1993	Time Warner (100)
HBO Family	1996	Time Warner (100)
Home Shopping Network	1985	TCI (19)
Independent Film Channel	1994	Cablevision (75)
MoreMax (Cinemax2)	1991	Time Warner (100)

(Continued)

TABLE 4.5 (*Continued*)

Programming Service	Year Started	MSO Interests (%)
MuchMusic USA	1994	Cablevision (75)
Odyssey Channel	1973	TCI (32)
Outdoor Life Network	1995	Cox (33), TCI (17) Comcast (8) MediaOne (8)
Ovation: The Arts Network	1996	Time Warner (4)
Prevue Channel	1988	TCI (44)
PIN (Product Information Net)	1994	Cox (45)
QVC	1986	Comcast (57), TCI (43)
Romance Classics	1997	Cablevision (75)
Sci-Fi Channel	1992	TCI (19)
Speedvision	1995	Cox (33), TCI (17) Comcast (8) MediaOne (8)
Starz!	1994	TCI (100)
Starz!2	1996	TCI (100)
Style	(1998)	Comcast (40), MediaOne (10) TCI (10)
TBS	1976	Time Warner (100)
Telemundo	1987	TCI (50)
TLC (The Learning Channel)	1980	TCI (49) Cox (25)
TNT (Turner Network Television)	1998	Time Warner (100)
Travel Channel	1987	TCI (49) Cox (25)
Turner Classic Movies	1994	Time Warner (100)

Sources: National Cable Television Association, National Video Services, Cable Television Developments, Spring 1998, at 27–97; TCI Web site at www.tci.com. Eben Shapiro and John Lippman, "Murdoch Sells TV Guide to an Affiliate of TCI," *Wall Street Journal*, June 12, 1998, p. B1. Comcast Web site at www.comcast.com. Cox Web site at www.cox.com. Various 10-K Reports at www.sec.com.

of companies with diverse media holdings. Table 4.6 lists the top media companies by the revenues just from cable TV. (See also Table 4.20 for the largest cable networks and their owners.)

These "cable" companies abound with familiar and some less familiar names. Indeed, by most rankings, AT&T (now owner of the TCI cable holdings), Time Warner and Disney ranked as the largest media corporations in the United States. Table 4.6 does provide some expected and perhaps less expected outcomes, including:

- More than half (16) of the 25 companies in 1997 derived substantially all of their revenue from cable. TCI and MediaOne were absorbed by AT&T, and there have been other mergers since then, but other substantial players, such as Adelphia and Charter, continued to concentrate in cable only.
- Among the cable holdings of multimedia firms, most showed over the 1995–1997 period that cable revenues were an increasingly greater proportion of total revenue. Disney, Viacom and especially News Corporation were in this category. This may reflect either acquisition or new business (News Corporation's case), or simply that the cable business was growing faster than other media segments held by these companies.
- In other cases (Time Warner, Cox and NBC among them), cable's share of overall revenue was relatively steady, growing at about the same rate as their other businesses.

These may be a useful trends to track for insights into changes in the structure of the cable industry.

TABLE 4.6
Top 25 Media Companies by Cable TV Revenues

Company	Cable 1997 (in millions)	Cable 1996 (in millions)	Cable 1995 (in millions)	1997 % Media Revenue	1996 % Media Revenue	1995 % Media Revenue
1. Time Warner	$10,063	$9,000.0	$7,654.0	75.6%	75.9%	75.3%
2. Tele-Communications	6,429	5,954.0	4,878.0	100.0	100.0	100.0
3. Viacom, Inc.	2,273	2,013.7	1,647.2	84.3	83.8	81.0
4. U S West Media Group	2,323	1,726.0	1,657.4	100.0	100.0	100.0
5. Comcast Corporation	2,073	1,871.1	1,719.9	100.0	100.0	100.0
6. Walt Disney Co.	1,950	1,690.0	1,205.1	28.3	25.8	19.4
7. Cablevision System	1,949	1,315.1	1,078.1	100.0	100.0	100.0
8. Cox Enterprises	1,610	1,460.3	1,286.2	48.6	47.5	47.1
9. News Corp.	1,200	520	20	21.6	11.5	0.5
10. USA Network	796	591.5	500.0	100.0	100.0	100.0
11. Discovery Communications	756	557.0	448.5	100.0	100.0	100.0
12. InterMedia	565	276.7	205.6	565	100.0	100.0
13. Adelphia Communications	515	472.8	403.6	100.0	100.0	100.0
14. Charter Communications	494	412.9	338.8	98.8	97.9	100.0
15. Marcus Cable	479	431.3	401.5	100.0	100.0	100.0
16. Century Communications	459	368.5	331.3	100.0	100.0	100.0
17. Lenfest Group	449	397.3	266.2	100.0	100.0	100.0
18. Prime Cable	424	397	NA	100.0	100.0	NA
19. Lifetime Television	398	257.0	212.0	100.0	100.0	100.0
20. NBC TV	350	290.0	260.0	6.8	5.5	6.6
21. A&E Television Networks	349	303.8	273.6	100.0	100.0	100.0
22. TCA Cable	308	253.3	190.7	100.0	100.0	100.0
23. CBS	302	249.6	213.8	5.5	100.0	100.0
24. Falcon Cable	271	251	151	100.0	100.0	100.0
25. Washington Post	257	229.7	194.0	14.3	13.5	12.3

NA: Not available.

Sources: 1996 and 1995: "100 Leading Companies by Media Revenue," *Advertising Age*, August 18, 1997, p. S5. 1997: From Web site at :adage.com/dataplace/archives/dp232.html, from *Advertising Age*, August 18, 1998, accessed July 15, 1999. Figures are net revenue from advertising supported media only.

THE BASICS OF THE TELEVISION BUSINESS

Television is today, as it was in the beginning, dominated by large corporations, usually divided as broadcast, cable or DBS operations. But the basic operations remain the same, and are taken up later.[36]

The television industry over its short history has continued in flux, but its basics of operation have remained remarkably constant. First programs must be produced; viewers watch programs not technology. Once made, then the programming must be distributed, which is traditionally done by national networks. The final step is presentation to the viewer—by local broadcast stations, by local cable franchises or by DBS operators. Simply put, broadcasting from a tower offered a method of presentation for a half century. Delivery by wire—a cable—added a second. Beaming directly from a satellite created a third. Others include physical distribution on videotape or disc, and still others that are addressed in Chapter 6. But all these means of presentation require programs to be produced and then distributed.

Production

TV programs come from a variety of sources, but the major one is the Hollywood studios (see Chapter 7). These fill prime time and syndication's off-peak hours, as well as create most soap operas and game shows. Prime time in the evening has long remained the focus—the crucial period for the most expensive to be presented. Although prime time accounted for 22% of the hours programmed by a major network, it accounted for nearly half its advertising revenues. Yet with prime time programs regularly shown twice (the first run and re-run), prime time shows totaled only 38% of all program costs, thus providing a healthy margin of profit. In contrast, sports represented less than one tenth of a typical network's programming time, and whereas sports pulled in twice that amount in advertising revenues (20%), it accounted for 37% of programming costs and so proved less profitable than re-runable Hollywood studio-created fare.

The key change in production in the 1990s was more production directly under network control. From 1970 to 1993, the financial interest and syndication rules limited network production to sports and news because they could not retain the "after network" rights from their valuable hits. With the phasing out of this policy, a greater proportion of prime time comedies and dramas were being produced under the aegis of broadcast networks.[37]

The value of vertical control of program production was seen with News Corporation's ownership of both a movie studio, Twentieth Century-Fox, and direct ownership of the Fox TV network. Rupert Murdoch, CEO and controlling stockholder of News Corporation, had come to the United States to create what no one had in 30 years: a TV network that could effectively compete with ABC, NBC and CBS. Disney's 1995 purchase of ABC solidified vertical integration as a key concept in program production. The strategic value of a Hollywood–network vertical integration has its proponents, but its potential drawbacks as well. It is explored further in Chapter 9.

Vertical integration was much of the force behind Time Warner's WB network and Viacom/Chris-Craft's United Paramount Network (UPN). Vertical integration means the prime time productions are made by the networks. By the late 1990s, even

NBC and CBS—with no direct studio links—were making their own shows by renting Hollywood facilities. For the 1997–1998 TV season, for example, NBC had a financial interest in half its shows, up from one third two years earlier. Those two networks negotiated for—and got—ownership participation with the studios if the network accepted the studio's show for network schedule.[38]

By 1999, there were few "independent" producers left in Hollywood. It took deep pockets to create and sustain high risk prime time productions. The major Hollywood studios and the networks were among the few who could. A rare exception was Hallmark Cards, Inc., long a participant in TV production through its fabled *Hallmark Hall of Fame* series (started in 1952 on NBC). In 1994, Hallmark, a private company, purchased the assets in independent producer Robert Halmi and backed his production of miniseries and TV movies. By 1999, the Halmis had produced some 300 hours of TV for Hallmark, accepting small profits on the routine TV fare. Halmi budgeted for a loss on miniseries in the United States, expecting to make his profits through syndication abroad. For example, the 1998 miniseries *Merlin* cost NBC $12 million, even though it cost the company $28 million to produce. The producer reasoned the revenues from abroad would more than make up the difference. For its part, NBC may have calculated that until it developed its syndication skills, booking risk-free, inexpensive-to-rent productions from Hallmark made more sense than producing through NBC productions division. *Merlin* ranked as the highest rated miniseries in Germany, Spain and England, and Halmi and Hallmark's strategy proved successful yet again.[39]

Sports, the second most popular TV fare, worked differently because neither Hollywood nor the networks controlled its production. TV had to negotiate with powerful, monopoly sports leagues and pay billions of dollars in fees. The networks were willing to do this because sports worked so well at attracting young male viewers whom advertisers coveted. Every new deal with the National Basketball Association (NBA), National Football League (NFL), Major League Baseball and the National Collegiate Athletic Association (NCAA) seemed to set records.[40]

The major TV corporations in the 1990s began to seriously embrace sports as a source of programming and began to purchase teams. The Walt Disney Company owned both cable's all-sports channel ESPN and Major League Baseball's Anaheim Angels; News Corporation owned both the Fox Sports cable network and Major League Baseball's Los Angeles Dodgers; Time Warner owned TBS and TNT, which regularly cablecast sports, and the Atlanta Braves baseball team. Owning sports franchises became yet another avenue for vertical integration. The high cost of broadcast rights helped drive advertising rates to levels competitive with leading entertainment programs. However, in 1997, only ABC's *Monday Night Football*, at $360,000 for a 30-second advertisement, was among the 10 most expensive regularly scheduled programs. The comparison of advertising rates for the top broadcast television shows in 1997 can be seen in Table 4.7.[41]

Ratings and Revenue

The late 1990s saw an anomaly: Although broadcast network ratings were falling, their costs for prime time programs and sports were increasing. Even as their absolute attractiveness shrunk, the broadcast networks still offered the sole means by which

TABLE 4.7
Top 10 Broadcast Television Shows by Advertising Rates in 1997

Show and Network	Cost, 30-Second Ad
1. Seinfeld (NBC)	$575,000
2. ER (NBC)	560,000
3. Friends (NBC)	410,000
4. Veronica's Closet (NBC)	400,000
5. Monday Night Football (ABC)	360,000
6. Home Improvement (ABC)	350,000
7. Union Square (NBC)	310,000
8. The X-Files (Fox)	275,000
9. The Drew Carey Show (ABC)	275,000
10. Frasier (NBC)	275,000

Source: *Advertising Age*, September 1997, p. 1.

to reach a broad national audience, and so could charge advertisers a premium try-ing to reach a mass audience. NBC in 1998, for example, trying to offset the $13 mil-lion it contracted to pay for each future *ER* episode, charged $650,000 per 30-sec-ond advertising spot for what was then the number one show in prime time. ABC, CBS and Fox, the winners of a multiyear agreement with the NFL, even asked their affiliates to give back time that the network could then sell—an historical break from the traverse that had been the way the business had operated since its incep-tion during the late 1940s.[42]

Although the four network share of audience fell below two thirds of the average prime time audience, advertising rates that were paid to the big broadcast networks rose faster than inflation. Top shows regularly raised advertising rates about 15% annually even as audiences shrank. But individual cable networks were small and fragmented. Broadcast networks alone could deliver to advertisers what was left of the mass audience. Despite all the change, the mass audience still looked to the broadcast networks for much of their viewing, and cable still served as the alterna-tive for much of the audience most of the time. Based on this new economics of sup-ply and demand, advertisers paid a premium for that special TV product—first-run prime time fare. Simply put, if a new movie was opening, or a cosmetics company was introducing a new fragrance, their advertising agencies often paid the $500,000 for a 30-second spot on a top-rated show because it alone could reach one third of the audience that might be tempted to go to that new movie or try that new fra-grance.[43]

The networks (and their affiliate stations) also create profit from non-prime time programming: from news and late night fare in particular. The networks generate their greatest profit margins from relatively cheap late night programming, followed by daytime soaps and news. But, in terms of absolute amounts of profits, prime time is so large in terms of the audience and advertising revenues that its absolute profits overwhelm all other day parts.

For decades, critics of television programming called for more news and public affairs. News production (long a loss leader to evoke good relations with the FCC) became a profit center in the 1990s, particularly with the highly profitable news magazine shows such as *60 Minutes* and *20/20*. By the late 1990s, news magazines accounted for more than 10 hours per week in prime time on NBC, CBS and ABC. NBC's *Dateline* was scheduled four different nights a week in the 1998–99 TV season. Whereas the trend toward more vertical integration usually focused on the relation between Hollywood and the networks, the networks had long produced and distributed the nightly evening news, late night and early morning shows. The difference is that news shows only gathered a single run, whereas certain successful Hollywood fare seemed to be able to be shown over again.[44]

Networks and Distribution

To produce one show, and then present it only in a single market is not nearly as financially attractive as distributing the same show through a network to the entire country (and beyond, through syndication). These are economies of scale at work. The actual physical distribution in the 1980s has been by satellite; the actual terms varied by market size as negotiated in affiliation contracts. Because of the considerable economies of scale involved, the networks became the bottleneck of the TV business. With the greater profitability available of running network programming, local programming became less attractive to station owners, with the exception of local news. The networks, through their hold on distribution, were the key to the equation that formed, and continues to hold, the core TV business.[45]

For mass advertisers such as McDonalds, Ford, MCIWorldcom and Sears, there is simply no cost-effective alternative to the networks. Network TV remains the only place advertisers can reach big groups of people quickly. In 1997, NBC led with the most programming with 99 hours, followed by CBS with 86 hours, ABC with 84.5 hours, Fox with 41 hours, WB with 16 hours and UPN with 10 hours per week. The "Big Four" had nearly complete penetration across the United States, with UPN following at 94%, and WB the weakest at 86%.[46]

Cable networks in the 1990s surely proliferated, but none regularly drew any more than 1% or 2% of the possible TV audience. In 1997, the Big Four networks reported more than $21 billion in operating revenues, up 13% from 1996. Cable promised more original programming, but sports predominated in cable ratings precisely because it was original.

With network affiliation, local stations had neither the need nor the motivation to do much in the way of original local programming except news. Local news became highly profitable, particularly in the larger markets.

The economics of networks has attracted many. Barry Diller, who helped make the Fox network a force by the mid-1990s, repositioned the most popular cable network, USA Network, in the image of a traditional broadcast network. He saw that as a cable network, USA could regularly hope for an average rating of 2%, as compared to ratings five to six times that figure for a broadcast network. USA copied Fox: It allied with Hollywood's Universal's TV operation and then began to buy stations. With a base of owned and operated stations (just as the major networks had done for decades), USA Network could guarantee advertisers it could reach more than one quarter of the population.[47]

Observers may wish to track three network trends of the 1990s into the 21st century:

- First, will the new networks continue to catch up to the former Big Three (NBC, CBS and ABC) plus Fox? In 1998, Fox pushed ABC to fourth place in a key February sweeps race. It was the first time one of the former Big Three had been beaten by Fox. Will UPN and the WB perform as well?[48]
- Second, will the networks continue to flex their muscles by reversing a decades old policy of affiliates receiving compensation for playing network shows? Will they begin to charge a fee for some programs, as cable channels have long been doing? In 1999, the Fox network unilaterally reclaimed for itself more than 30% of the advertising time then being sold by local affiliate stations in prime time. This was projected to add between $50 and $100 million to the Fox network.[49]
- Finally, will competition become more serious from non-English-language networks—particularly Spanish-language networks? Indicators of this trend were the undertakings of Univision and Telemundo Miami and Los Angeles in 1998. That year, the top-rated broadcast TV station in Miami during the February sweeps was WLTV-TV, owned by the Univision network. Whereas nationwide Univision and Telemundo were regularly being watched by about only one eighth the number of viewers of the English-language networks, there are fewer of them to compete for the growing Hispanic population in the United States.[50]

Syndication

Networking has never been the sole means of distribution. There is a syndication process whereby the programs are sold market by market, exclusively to individual stations. These may be former network reruns, as well as original programming. Among the latter are game shows such as *Jeopardy*, and talks shows like *The Oprah Winfrey Show*. These are popular but do not possess the reach—and thus the advertising rates—of the top network programs (as can be seen comparing Table 4.8 to Table 4.7).

TABLE 4.8
Cost of 30-Second Equivalent National Advertisement: Syndicated TV Shows, 1996

Program and Rank	Type of Program	Cost
1. Home Improvement	off-network	$136,000
2. Seinfeld	off-network	105,000
3. Entertainment Tonight	first run	101,000
4. Mad About You	off-network	92,000
5. Wheel of Fortune	first run	85,000
6. The Simpsons	off-network	85,000
7. Jeopardy	first run	83,000
8. Star Trek: Deep Space Nine	first run	77,000
9. Access Hollywood	first run	71,000
10. The Oprah Winfrey Show	first run	69,000

Source: *Advertising Age*, January 13, 1997, p. S5.

In 1999 there were 17 major syndicators in the United States. All but 2 of these were subsidiaries of other media companies. The only syndicator that could be truly called an "independent" at the time was Carsey-Warner. Its shows included *The Cosby Show*, *Cybill* and *Roseanne*. Because the most popular prime time programs were consistently coming from the major Hollywood studios (see Chapter 6), syndication is as much an extension of Hollywood as of television. Yet with the lifting of the financial interest and syndication rules during the early 1990s, the networks—long shut out of syndication—started becoming major players as well. CBS acquired King World in 1999, thereby leapfrogging to the top of the syndication marketplace. At the time, King World provided the *The Oprah Winfrey Show*, *Jeopardy!* and *Wheel of Fortune*. In 1997, King World had given Winfrey options to purchase two million King World common shares as part of a financial package for a new contract. Winfrey's show, estimates indicated, generated more than $260 million per year in revenue.[51]

Syndicated programs can be large revenue producers. *Jeopardy!* and *Wheel of Fortune* each drew $125 million in annual licensing fees. Rebroadcast or local versions of both shows generated healthy revenues in the international market. Indeed, King World's key to success centered on keeping their franchises fresh by collaborating closely with their international partners to produce a well-researched attractive product, and creating customized promotional advertisements for international licensees. It was this well-honed package the apparently justified the $2.5 billion in stock CBS paid. It also made Winfrey, holder of those King World options, one of CBS' largest stockholders.[52]

Presentation to the Public

It is at the local level (i.e., over-the air, through a cable subscription or DBS contract) that viewers watch TV programs. Stations owned and operated by a network would show all network offerings. The vast majority of stations have affiliate agreements with a network, which means they may, but need not, broadcast all of their network's programming. They may replace a low rated network offering with a locally produced but more likely syndicated program. More often than not, it is over some controversial program that a station owner preempts a network show. For example, in 1997, when the lead character declared herself a lesbian in ABC's sitcom *Ellen*, some affiliate stations refused to carry that episode or subsequent *Ellen* episodes in which she told friends and relatives about her sexual orientation.[53]

Free broadcast TV is, of course, not free. Viewers pay with their time to watch, or ignore, commercials. Advertisers pay with cash. There are three types of advertising: national, regional spot (in selected markets) and purely local (in a single market). National advertising rates are established weekly by audience estimates made weekly by A. C. Nielsen. But, for local markets (or collections of local markets), estimates of audiences are only done in specific months, called sweeps, when the all shows are rated, and then spot and local advertising rates are set for the following months. Consequently, networks help their affiliates (and owned and operated stations) by offering more specials and episodes of their most popular shows during sweeps—in particular during November, February and May.[54]

The top advertisers on television have long been major brand companies such as Proctor & Gamble, major automobile companies such as General Motors and Ford and brand name product creators like Kellogg and Unilever. All seek to craft packages of television advertising to reach and influence potential customers. Candy, fast food, medicine, soap, cereal, toy, soft drink and coffee marketers typically allocate three quarters to nearly all their advertising budgets to television.[55]

Although broadcast stations and networks took in the greater amount of advertising dollars, cable and DBS advertising was growing more rapidly. Proctor & Gamble and General Motors are the leading advertisers on cable TV (as seen in Table 4.9). But the preponderance of ad support still goes to the broadcast networks (as seen in Table 4.10).

One of the critical unresolved problems for advertisers in the late 1990s was to gain some sense of who was watching their advertisements; channel surfing was playing havoc with conventional measurement techniques. As the number of channels has risen, the average time spent watching any single channel has dropped. Most viewers focus on a handful of channels, typically about 10, but surf among them. A

TABLE 4.9
The Top Advertisers on Cable Television, 1995–1997

Advertiser	1997 Spending (in millions)	1996 Spending (in millions)	1995 Spending (in millions)
1. Proctor & Gamble	$238.7	$201.2	$177.6
2. General Motors	174.8	116.6	90.0
3. Time Warner	105.7	94.0	45.0
4. Phillip Morris	100.8	74.9	64.6
5. Kellogg Co.	86.8	61.2	50.8
6. Diageo	84.1	61.6	N.A.
7. Unilever	76.9	62.6	45.4
8. Johnson & Johnson	76.3	64.4	40.7
9. Mattel	74.6	44.7	32.8
10. Chrysler Corp.	68.0	51.5	42.8

Sources: *Advertising Age*, April 14, 1997, p. S28; September 28, 1998, on Web site at adage.com/dataplace/archives/dp256.html, accessed July 15, 1999.

TABLE 4.10
Trends in TV Advertising Revenues (in millions)

	ABC/CBS/NBC	Fox	WB/UPN	Ad-Supported Cable Nets	Barter Syndication
1990	$ 8,750	$ 360	—	$1,375	$1,250
1991	8,332	515	—	1,625	1,340
1992	8,908	675	—	1,915	1,410
1993	8,742	805	—	2,175	1,560
1994	9,300	985	—	2,370	1,710
1995	10,040	1,130	95	2,655	1,800

Source: Ed Papazian (ed.), *TV Dimensions '96* (New York: Media Dynamics, Inc., 1996), p. 32.

typical network affiliate garnered eight to nine hours of watching per week per adult in the household for its network fare and local news. Pay cable channels, when purchased, were on about half that amount of time per week, followed by basic cable television channels, averaging about two and half hours per adult per week. No one can be sure how these relative viewing patterns might change, but the concept of the niche audience should continue to define the nature, shape and economics of watching TV.[56]

The TV industry is best characterized by ever-fragmenting audiences. In particular, cable television channels never sought a mass audience, but instead targeted and sold "demographic clusters" to advertisers. According to the demographics, men watched Comedy Central and ESPN, and women regularly landed atop the audience tabulations for Lifetime and the Family Channel. Advertisers then chose those clusters containing persons to whom they targeted their products. For example, The Nashville Network (TNN) built up a weekend block of motor sports programming attractive to men from age 18 to 49. TNN (CBS owned) attracted advertisers—from soft drink and beer bottlers to auto and tire makers—seeking to sell their wares to young, male car enthusiasts. To appreciate how specialized the TV world has become, consider that only one eighth of all men from age 18 to 49 need to watch ABC's *Monday Night Football* to make it one of the top 10 rated programs each Fall. Meanwhile, UPN countered with a Monday night line-up of male-oriented comedies (i.e., *Guys Like Us, Desmond Pfeiffer, Malcolm & Eddie*) for the other young males opting not to watch pro football.[57]

With the Spanish-speaking U.S. population on track to surpass African Americans as the nation's largest minority group, advertisers were re-evaluating niche advertising. Studies regularly showed that different ethnic groups watched different TV shows. One such study highlighted the disparity by Black and White households. Whereas *Seinfeld* was the top-rated show among Whites, it ranked 54th among African Americans. In contrast, Fox's *Living Single* came in second with Black audiences, but ranked 115th in White households.[58]

This system of specialization led to a proliferation of channels, as shown in Table 4.11. Between 1990 and 1996 alone, the number of basic channels available to MSOs more than doubled to 139. This was a sevenfold increase from 1980, when cable was starting to expand into many major cities. The number of pay channels has not been as dramatic, but has been split between the flat rate channels and the newer pay-per-view channels that depend on more advanced technology. The choices continue to grow as does the capacity of cable systems.[59]

Models for Cable Network Formation

There have been two basic models for successful start-up and distribution of a cable network. Although putting together the idea and some programming for a niche network may be relatively easy (at least compared to a broadcast network), the key to success is getting enough cable systems to carry the programming. Despite the substantial increase in the channel capacity of cable systems, there are few systems that have room to carry everything. DBS systems, on the other hand, using more

TABLE 4.11
National Cable TV Networks by Type of Service, 1990–1998

	Basic	Premium	Pay-Per-View
1980	19	8	0
1985	41	9	4
1990	65	5	5
1991	67	7	4
1992	71	8	4
1993	80	9	7
1994	94	20	8
1995	104	21	8
1996	126	18	7
1997	131	14	6
1998	139	18	10

Source: National Cable Television Association, from NCTA estimates and "Directory of Cable Networks," on Web site at www.ncta.com/glance.html, accessed July 16, 1999.

advanced digital systems, have been able to offer subscribers more viewing options (at a price) than the most advanced operational cable system in 1999.

One model has been the entrepreneur or small company putting together a channel. The other has been an existing MSO and/or studio offering a service. But either way, the start-ups have found they must create an incentive—in the form of an ownership position—of one or more MSOs in the network. A typical example is the Golf Channel, launched in 1995. Although founded by a media entrepreneur along with golf legend Arnold Palmer, its investors included major MSOs Comcast, MediaOne and Cablevision Systems.[60]

The second scenario is that of start-ups by the established players. Among them are Time Warner's Comedy Central, CNN spin-offs CNNfn and CNN/SI and AT&T-owned premium services Encore and Starz! But even they need other MSOs to find a spot for them in their channel line-up. Hence the investment pattern seen in Table 4.5 of networks such as Fox Sports Net, BBC America and E! Entertainment.

A new pattern that emerged in the late 1990s, perhaps signaling a relative maturing of the cable industry, has been networks started as spin-offs of already successful networks. This includes the Disney-created ESPN2; Viacom's TV Land, which came from the success of Nick at Nite; and CNN's sports, financial and Spanish-language variations of its all-news formula. Niche economics meant relatively small audiences, but with very low costs, so these offerings continued to be economically attractive.[61]

BROADCAST TV'S MAJOR PLAYERS

Table 4.12 lists the top 20 markets based on the number of households, covering more than two of every five households in the United States. Economies of scale are critical in the television industry. It is cheaper to operate a collection of stations (per station)

TABLE 4.12
Location of the Top 20 TV Markets

Market and Rank	TV Households
1. New York City	6,812,540
2. Los Angeles	5,135,140
3. Chicago	3,164,150
4. Philadelphia	2,667,520
5. San Francisco-Oakland-San Jose	2,368,970
6. Boston	2,186,100
7. Dallas-Ft. Worth	1,959,680
8. Washington, DC	1,965,160
9. Detroit	1,846,950
10. Atlanta	1,772,130
11. Houston	1,665,550
12. Seattle-Tacoma	1,548,200
13. Cleveland	1,475,820
14. Tampa-St. Petersburg-Sarasota	1,463,090
15. Minneapolis-St. Paul	1,457,130
16. Miami-Ft. Lauderdale	1,418,940
17. Phoenix	1,343,040
18. Denver	1,230,440
19. Pittsburgh	1,136,230
20. Sacramento-Stockton-Medesto	1,131,300

Source: *Broadcasting and Cable Yearbook 1999*, p. C-8.

than a single operation. Television stations in the top markets are thus almost always owned in groups. The urban-based ownership enables these leading groups (seen in Table 4.13) to efficiently reach large audiences, and thus serve as the basis of the major networks. Smaller groups such as Tribune, Gannett, Chris-Craft and Belo have been critical for the establishment of the newer WB and UPN networks. Indeed, among the top 12 station owners, only the Belo chain is not part owner of a network.[62]

All chains concentrate on major cities, grouping to reach the biggest possible audiences. The networks own the maximum allowable number of stations that just gets them under the current ownership limits of 35% of TV households. As seen in Table 4.14, these owners all were part of major media conglomerates. The top 20 listing, compiled from *Broadcasting & Cable* magazine, finds broadcast TV station ownership nearly always the basis of a major media conglomerate.

In sum, according to a survey produced by *Broadcasting & Cable* magazine, the nation's top 25 TV station groups, including all the networks, own or control 36% of all the commercial TV stations in the United States, up from 33% in 1997 and 25% 1996. As of April 1998, the top 25 groups, whose membership controlled or owned 432 of the nation's 1,202 commercial TV stations, nearly all in the top 10 markets. Chiefly responsible for this growing concentration is the 1996 Telecommunications Act where before the passage of that law broadcast station owners were limited to 14 television stations and coverage of no more than one quarter of the nation's TV households. The Telecommunications Act of 1996 eliminated the numerical cap, and lifted the coverage cap limit to 35%.[63]

TABLE 4.13
Top 25 Station Groups

1. **Fox Television Stations Inc.**
(subsidiary of News Corp. Ltd.)
FOX
1999 S. Bundy Drive
Los Angeles, CA 90025
Phone: (310) 584-2000
Web site: fox.com
Executives: K. Rupert Murdoch, chairman, News Corp./Fox Entertainment Group Inc.;
Mitchell Stern, chairman, Fox TV Stations
23 stations/40.6% of U.S./34.5% per FCC
Other media interests: Fox Television Network; Fox Filmed Entertainment (Fox Television Studios,
20th Century Fox, Twentieth Television; cable channels Fox News Channel, 50% of FX (buying
remainder), 34% of Outdoor Life and 33% of Golf Channel; 50% of Fox/Liberty (sports) Networks
and Fox Sports Net (buying remaining 50%); 49.5% of Fox Family Worldwide (Fox Family Channel,
Fox Kids Network); *New York Post*, TV Guide

2. **CBS Television Station Group**
CBS
51 W. 52nd Street
New York, NY 10019
Phone: (212) 975-4321
Fax: (212) 975-4516
Web site: cbs.com
Executives: Mel Karmazin, president, CBS Corp.; Jonathan Klein, president, TV group
15 stations/33.7% of U.S./32.8% per FCC
Other media interests: CBS Television Network; 83% of Infinity Broadcasting Corp. (about 160
radio stations, TDI Worldwide Inc. [outdoor advertising]); CBS Radio; Eyemark Entertainment; CBS
Broadcast International; cable channels Nashville Network, Home Teams Sports, Country Music Tele-
vision; CBS New Media; 30% of CBS TeleNoticias; buying King World Productions

3. **Paxson Communications Corp.**
PAX
601 Clearwater Park Road
West Palm Beach, FL 33401
Phone: (561) 659-4122
Fax: (561) 659-4754
Web site: pax.net
Executives: Lowell W. "Bud" Paxson, chairman, Paxson Communications Corp.; Jon Jay Hoker,
president, TV group
49 stations/58% of U.S./29% per FCC
Other media interests: Pax TV network; two radio stations

4. **Tribune Broadcasting Co.**
TRB
435 N. Michigan Avenue
Suite 1900
Chicago, IL 60611
Phone: (312) 222-3333
Fax: (312) 329-0611
Web site: tribune.com
Executives: John W. Madigan, president, Tribune Co.; Dennis J. FitzSimons, broadcasting president
20 stations/37.5% of U.S./27% per FCC
Other media interests: Four radio stations; Tribune Entertainment Co.; superstation WGN; Tribune
Media Services; cable channels CLTV News in Chicago, 50% of Central Florida News 13; 33% of
Qwest Broadcasting LLC; 25%of WB Television Network; 50% of Knight-Ridder/Tribune Information
Services; four newspapers. Online holdings include 20% of Digital City Inc., 16% of CareerPath.com;
8% of iVillage Inc., 4% of Excite Inc., 2% of America Online

(Continued)

TABLE 4.13 (*Continued*)

5. **NBC Inc.**
(subsidiary of General Electric Co.)
GE
30 Rockefeller Plaza
New York, NY 10112
Phone: (212) 664-4444
Fax: (212) 664-4085
Web site: nbc.com
Executives: John F. Welch Jr., chairman, GE; Robert C. Wright, president, NBC; Patrick T. Wallace, president, TV group
13 stations/28% of U.S./26.6% per FCC
Other media interests: NBC Television Network; cable channels CNBC and MSNBC (with Microsoft Inc.); joint venture member in A&E Television Networks (with ABC Inc. and Hearst-Argyle Television Inc.); CNBC Europe and other broadcasting and cable networks in Europe and Asia; buying 15% of ValueVision International (home shopping) Network. Online interests include MSNBC.com, NBC Online Ventures, NBC SuperNet (with Microsoft) VideoSeeker, InterView, 60% of Snap!, buying 6% of Intertainer

6. **ABC Inc.**
(subsidiary of Walt Disney Co.)
DIS
77 W. 66th Street
New York, NY 10023
Phone: (212) 456-7777
Fax: (212) 456-6850
Web site: abc.go.com
Executives: Michael D. Eisner, chairman, Disney; Steven M. Bornstein, president, ABC Inc.; Robert F. Callahan, president, broadcasting operations
10 stations/24.2% of U.S./24% per FCC
Other media interests: ABC Television Network; 35 radio stations; ABC Radio Networks; Buena Vista Television (distribution); Disney/ABC Cable Networks, including Disney Channel, Toon Disney, 80% of ESPN, 50% of Lifetime Television, 39.5% of E! Entertainment Television, partner in A&E Television Networks (with NBC Inc. and Hearst-Argyle Television Inc.); Walt Disney Television International; Fairchild Publications (including *W, Women's Wear Daily* and *Jane*). Online holdings include ABC Multimedia Group, ABC.com, ABCNews.com, 43% of Infoseek

7. **United Television Inc./Chris-Craft Industries Inc.**
UTVI
132 S. Rodeo Drive, 4th Floor
Beverly Hills, CA 90212
Phone: (310) 281-4844
Fax: (310) 281-5870
Executives: Herbert J. Siegel, president, CCI; Evan C. Thomson, president, United TV/executive vice president, CCI
10 stations/21.7% of U.S./18.8% per FCC
Other media interests: 50% of UPN (joint venture with Viacom Inc.)

8. **Gannett Broadcasting**
GCI
1100 Wilson Boulevard
Arlington, VA 22209
Phone: (703) 284-6760
Fax: (703) 247-3114
Web site: gannett.com
Executives: John J. Curley, chairman, Gannett Co. Inc.; Cecil L. Walker, president, broadcasting
21 stations/17.3% of U.S./17.2% per FCC
Other media interests: Multimedia Cablevision Co.; about 90 newspapers, including *USA Today*. Online interests include Gannett New Media, USA Today Online, New Century Network

(*Continued*)

TABLE 4.13 (*Continued*)

9. **Hearst-Argyle Television Inc.**
HTV
888 7th Avenue
New York, NY 10106
Phone: (212) 887-6800
Fax: (212) 887-6875
Web site: hearstcorp.com/feat21.html
Executives: Frank A. Bennack Jr., president, Hearst Corp.; John G. Conomikes, president, H-A Television; vice president, Hearst
32 stations/17.6% of U.S./16.1% per FCC
Other media interests: Seven radio stations; Hearst-Argyle Television Productions; Hearst Entertainment and Syndication, Hearst New Media and Technology (stake in Netscape, 50% of Women.com Networks). Parent owns 50% of Lifetime Television, New England Cable News (with MediaOne); TVA (Brazilian pay TV company, with ABC Inc.), 20% of ESPN and partner in A&E Television Networks (with NBC Inc. and ABC); 12 newspapers; 16 consumer magazines, including *Esquire, Town & Country, Good Housekeeping, Harper's Bazaar*; book publishing (William Morrow & Co., Avon Books)

10. **USA Broadcasting Inc.**
USAI
152 W. 57th Street
New York, NY 10019
Phone: (212) 314-7200
Fax: (212) 314-7309
Executives: Barry Diller, chairman, USA Networks Inc.; Jon Miller, president, USA Broadcasting
13 stations/30.9% of U.S./15.5% per FCC
Other media interests: 49% of KPST (TV) San Francisco and 45% of KTVJ(TV) Denver, WHSL(TV) St. Louis and WTMW(TV) Washington; option to buy 45% of WJYS(TV) Chicago. Parent owns Home Shopping Network; Studios USA; cable networks USA Network and Sci-Fi Channel; Ticketmaster. Online interests include Ticketmaster Online-CitySearch Inc.; is buying Lycos (Internet portal)

11. **Sinclair Broadcast Group Inc.**
SBGI
2000 W. 41st Street
Baltimore, MD 21211
Phone: (410) 467-5005
Fax: (410) 467-5043
Web site: sbgi.net
Executives: David D. Smith, president, TV;
56 stations/24.4% of U.S./14.2% per FCC
Other media interests: About 50 radio stations

12. **Paramount Stations Group Inc.**
(subsidiary of Viacom Inc.)
VIAB
5555 Melrose Avenue
Los Angeles, CA 90038
Phone: (323) 956-8100
Fax: (323) 862-0121
Web site: paramount.com/hometv.html
Executives: Sumner M. Redstone, president, Viacom; Anthony Cassara, president, Paramount Stations Group
19 stations/25.6% of U.S./13.6% per FCC
Other media interests: UPN (joint venture with Chris-Craft Television Inc.); Paramount Domestic Television. Parent owns cable networks MTV, Showtime and a stake in Comedy Central; Paramount Pictures; 80% of Spelling Entertainment; book publisher Simon & Schuster; Blockbuster Video; movie theaters with more than 1,000 screens. Online holdings include Imagine Radio, Red Rocket

(*Continued*)

225

TABLE 4.13 *(Continued)*

13. **Univision Communications Inc.**
    UVN
    1999 Avenue of the Stars
    Suite 3050
    Los Angeles, CA 90067
    Phone: (310) 556-7676
    Fax: (310) 556-7615
    Web site: univision.net
    Executives: A. Jerrold Perenchio, chairman, Univision; Thomas Arnost, Michael Wortsman, co-presidents, television group
    13 stations/27.1% of U.S./13.5% per FCC
    Other media interests: Spanish-language Univision Network; cable channel Galavision

14. **A. H. Belo Corp.**
    BLC
    400 S. Record Street
    Dallas, TX 75202
    Phone: (214) 977-6606
    Fax: (214) 977-2030
    Executives: Robert W. Decherd, president, Belo; 9% owner Ward L. Huey Jr., president, broadcasting division/vice chairman, Belo
    22 stations/13.6% of U.S./13.4% per FCC
    Other media interests: Two radio stations; cable channels Northwest Cable News, TXCN; six daily newspapers. Online holdings include dallasnews.com.

15. **Telemundo Group Inc.**
    (subsidiary of Sony Pictures Entertainment and AT&T Corp.'s Liberty Media Corp.)
    PRIVATE
    2290 W. 8th Avenue
    Hialeah, FL 33010
    Phone: (305) 884-8200
    Fax: (305) 889-7980
    Executives: Peter Tortorici, president; Roland A. Hernandez, CEO, Telemundo
    8 stations/21.4% of U.S./10.7% per FCC
    Other media interests: Spanish-language Telemundo network

16. **Cox Broadcasting Inc.**
    PRIVATE
    1400 Lake Hearn Drive NE
    Atlanta, GA 30318
    Phone: (404) 843-5000
    Fax: (404) 843-5280
    Web site: cimedia.com/business/aboutcim/coxglance.html
    Executives: David Easterly, president, Cox Enterprises Inc.; Nicholas Trigony, president, broadcasting
    11 stations/9.8% of U.S./9.6% per FCC
    Other media interests: Parent owns/is buying 59 radio stations; owns 18 cable systems and cable channels, including 50% of Spanish-language Gems Television, 24.6% of Discovery Communications Inc. and 10.4% of E! Entertainment Television; 10% of Primestar

17. **Young Broadcasting Inc.**
    YBTVA
    599 Lexington Avenue
    New York, NY 10022
    Phone: (212) 754-7070
    Fax: (212) 758-1229
    Web site: wric.com/young.html
    Executives: J. Vincent Young, chairman; Deborah A. McDermott, executive vice president, operations
    13 stations/9.1% of U.S./9% per FCC
    No other media interests

(Continued)

TABLE 4.13 *(Continued)*

18. **E. W. Scripps Co.**
SSP
312 Walnut Street
Suite 2300
Cincinnati, OH 45201
Phone: (513) 977-3000
Fax: (513) 977-3728
Web site: scripps.com
Executives: William R. Burleigh, president, Scripps; Paul "Frank" Gardner, senior vice president, broadcasting
10 stations/9.9% of U.S./8.05% per FCC
Other media interests: Scripps Productions; cable channels Home & Garden TV and the Food Network, and a stake in SportSouth; Scripps Media; 19 newspapers

19. **Hicks, Muse, Tate & Furst Inc.**
Private (Lin and Sunrise chains)
200 Crescent Court, Suite 1600
Dallas, TX 75201
Phone: (214) 740-7300
Fax: (214) 740-7313
Executives: Thomas O. Hicks, chairman
Note: Hicks Muse owns 80% of LIN Television Corp. and about 87% of Sunrise Television Corp.
29 stations/10.4% of U.S./8.01% per FCC

20. **Shop at Home Inc.**
SATH
5388 Hickory Hollow Parkway
Nashville, TN 37230
Phone: (615) 263-8000
Fax: (615) 263-8084
Web site: shopathomeonline.com
Executives: Kent E. Lillie, president, Shop at Home; Everit A. Herter, executive vice president, affiliate relations
6 stations/15.4% of U.S./7.7% per FCC
Other media interests: Internet shopping

21. **Post-Newsweek Stations Inc.**
(subsidiary of Washington Post Co.)
WPO
3 Constitution Plaza
Hartford, CT 06103
Phone: (860) 493-6530
Fax: (860) 493-2490
Web site: washpostco.com
Executives: Donald E. Graham, chairman, the Washington Post Company; G. William Ryan, president, Post-Newsweek Stations
6 stations/7.2% of U.S./7.2% per FCC
Other media interests: Parent owns CableOne Inc.; Pro Am Sports System (sports network); *Newsweek* magazine; 24 daily and weekly newspapers, including the *Washington Post*, and 50% of *International Herald Tribune*. Online holdings include newseek.com.

22. **Raycom Media Inc.**
PRIVATE
RSA Tower
201 Monroe Street
Montgomery, AL 36104
Phone: (334) 206-1400
Fax: (334) 206-1555
Web site: raycomsports.com/media.html

(Continued)

TABLE 4.13 *(Continued)*

22. **Raycom Media Inc.** *(Continued)*
    Executives: John Hayes, president, Raycom Media; Wayne Daugherty, John Llewellyn, Jeff Rosser, TV
    group vice presidents
    30 stations/ 8.8% of U.S./ 6.6% per FCC
    Other media interests: Two radio stations; Raycom Sports (marketing and production)

23. **Meredith Broadcast Group**
    MDP
    1716 Locust Street
    Des Moines, IA 50309
    Phone: (515) 284-3348
    Fax: (515) 284-2393
    Web site: meredith.com
    Executives: William T. Kerr, chairman, Meredith Corp.; John Loughlin, president, broadcast group
    11 stations/7.8% of U.S./6.3% per FCC
    Other media interests: parent owns 20 magazines, including *Better Homes and Gardens* and *Ladies'
    Home Journal*; book publishers Meredith and Ortho books

24. **Media General Broadcast Group**
    MEGA
    100 N. Tampa Street, Suite 3150
    Tampa, FL 33602
    Phone: (813) 225-4600
    Fax: (813) 225-4601
    Web site: media-general.com
    Executives: J. Stewart Bryan III, president, Media General Inc.; James Zimmerman, president, broad-
    cast group
    13 stations/5.3% of U.S./4.4% per FCC
    Other media interests: parent owns Media General Cable; 21 newspapers; 40% of *Denver Post*; online
    holdings include 18% of Hoover's Online

25. **Clear Channel Communications**
    CCU
    200 Concord Plaza, Suite 600
    San Antonio, TX 78216
    Phone: (210) 822-2828
    Fax: (210) 822-2299
    Web site: clearchannel.com
    Executives: L. Lowry Mays, chairman, Clear Channel; William R. "Rip" Riordan, COO, Clear Chan-
    nel Television/executive vice president, Clear Channel Communications
    18 stations/7% of U.S./4.2% per FCC
    Other media interests: 454 radio stations and radio networks in nine states including Premiere (after
    merger with Jacor Communications Inc. is completed); 70 radio stations in foreign countries; about
    220,000 outdoor faces; 29% of Spanish-language radio station owner Heftel Broadcasting Corp.

Source: Elizabeth A. Rathbun, "Fox is Leader of the TV Pack," *Broadcasting & Cable*, April 19, 1999, pp.
39–58.

After the passage of the 1996 Act, the broadcast VHF and UHF television stations were owned by fewer parties. Local marketing agreements further enabled
groups to operate a second station in many markets. A wave of consolidation quickly followed passage of the 1996 Act, as Fox purchased New World's stations, CBS
and Westinghouse blended their array of TV stations and Multimedia folded its stations into the Gannett TV Group. In 1997, group ownership reached another all-
time high, with the number of group-owned TV stations rising from 898 in 1995 to
1,006 in 1997. In the top 100 markets, group-owned stations increased from 547 in

TABLE 4.14
Parent Companies of the Leading Broadcast Television Operations, 1997

Parent Corporation	Broadcast (Non-cable) TV Holdings
1. Time Warner	WB Television Network, Warner Bros. studio
2. Walt Disney	Stations group, ABC TV network, Disney studio
3. News Corporation	Stations group, Twentieth Century-Fox studio
4. Viacom, Inc.	Stations group, UPN network, Paramount studio, Spelling Entertainment Group
5. TCI	None
6. Sony	Sony Pictures Entertainment studio, partial ownership of Telemundo network
7. General Electric	Station group, NBC network
8. Westinghouse	Station group, CBS network
9. Gannett	Station group
10. General Motors (Hughes Electronics)	None
11. Comcast	None
12. Seagram	Universal TV studio, part ownership of Networks, Inc.
13. Hearst	Station group, syndication unit
14. McGraw-Hill	Station group
15. US West Media Group	None
16. New York Times Co.	Stations group, production service
17. Tribune Co.	Stations group, production and syndication
18. Washington Post Co.	Stations group
19. Cox Enterprises	Stations group
20. Bloomberg	Syndicated long and short form financial programing

Source: "25 Top Media Groups," *Broadcasting & Cable*, July 7, 1997, pp. 22–28.

1995 to 633 in 1997. Significantly, this increase occurred primarily among UHF stations, which with the growth of cable had become "equal" to viewers and so more valuable. Not only did group ownership of broadcast TV stations expand in absolute numbers, the percentage increased as well, from 1995 to 1997, reaching an all-time high (to that point) of 81% in the top 100 largest markets. Group owners in the top 100 markets owned nearly all VHF stations (some 93%), and increased their ownership of UHF Top 100 market stations from 62% to 73%, breaking all records. There were also fewer group owners in all markets, a decline from 210 in 1995 to 184 in 1997. This decline of 26 groups took place despite the fact that some 40 new groups came into existence in this dramatic two-year period. This simply accelerated a 25-year trend where group TV station ownership grew.[64]

In sum, these networks hardly control all broadcast television stations, but nonetheless economies of scale in this industry dictate that they can and will dominate over-the-air television in the major urban centers of the United States where most Americans live. They deliver the programs watched by most, and define what broadcast television is—the most used medium in history. Since the late 1950s, all have acquired their biggest draws—outside sports—from Hollywood studios (see Chapter 6), and so once the FCC eliminated rules of program ownership, Hollywood entities have either acquired networks (e.g., the Disney takeover of ABC) or started their own (as Twentieth Century-Fox did with Fox; the Warner Bros. studio, owned by Time Warner, did with the WB; and Paramount Pictures, owned by Viacom, did with UPN). With all the changes in the 1990s, the longtime networks continued to dominate, but they also served to inspire competition. The networks, as owners of a substantial number of owned and operated stations, are discussed first by non-Hollywood-affiliated companies, which is the older strategy, and then by vertical integration with a major Hollywood studio, which is the key trend of the late 20th century. This new strategy, led by News Corporation's Fox unit, takes advantage of complete vertical integration of production, distribution and presentation. Finally, two pretenders, aspiring to become true national broadcast networks in the 1990s, are discussed.[65]

The Old Network Strategy

In 1999, **NBC** led the way with old network, nonvertical strategy, backed by parent General Electric (GE), one of the largest companies in the world. NBC represented a small division of one of the world's largest manufacturers. In addition to the NBC television network and a series of owned and operated broadcast television stations, GE also owned part interest in cable networks CNBC, Bravo, American Movie Classics, Bravo, Arts and Entertainment and MSNBC—the latter in an alliance with Microsoft. But to the public, NBC remained a fabled broadcast TV network, and it was home to such hits as *ER*, *Seinfeld* and *Friends*. In 1997, Robert Wright asserted that NBC made in excess of $1 billion in earnings from all its TV enterprises—broadcast and cable alike.[66]

General Electric's investment began in 1986 when it purchased NBC. To symbolize this takeover, CEO Jack Welch announced that he was changing the name of the landmark RCA Building at 30 Rockefeller Center to the GE Building. Unhappy network staffers feared the Peacock Network would be "morphed" into just another cog in the GE corporate machine. Even NBC's own late night star, David Letterman, dared to take on-air jabs at Welch and his boys from the Fairfield, Connecticut, GE headquarters. Yet these fears seemed to have been for nought. Robert C. Wright, the GE-trained lawyer chosen by Welch to run NBC, transformed the company into the powerhouse of the TV business by deftly expanding NBC beyond broadcasting into cable, new media and global television, creating a diversified media company with strong prospects for growth and driving the "new" NBC to greater revenues and earnings.[67]

Wright reported in GE's annual report in 1998 that NBC had registered its sixth consecutive year of double-digit gains in earnings. Driving NBC's financial performance were record earnings and profits at NBC television stations and at the cable networks CNBC and MSNBC. These gains more than offset cost increases for prime time programming on the NBC television network. The NBC television network finished the 1997–1998 TV season as America's most-watched network for the third year in a row, placing first in the prized adult age 18 to 49 demographic category by a 34% margin. For the third consecutive season, it had five or more of the nation's top-rated prime time shows; and led by *The Tonight Show with Jay Leno*, its late night programs continued to win their respective time periods. *Late Night with Conan O'Brien* registered the highest ratings in its five-year history. CNBC cemented its position as a leader in business television when it finalized an alliance with

---

PROFILE: General Electric Company

Basic Data:
Headquarters: Fairfield, CT
Web site: www.ge.com
CEO in 1999: John F. Welch, Jr.
1998 Sales (in millions): $100,469
1998 Net Profits (in millions): $9,296
1998 Assets (in millions): $355,935
Rank in 1998 Forbes 500—Sales: 5

Market Holdings:
Broadcast Television: NBC television network, NBC owned and operated broadcast televi-sion stations (WNBC-New York, KNBC-Los Angeles, WMAQ-Chicago, WCAU-Philadel-phia, and WRC-Washington, DC, among others).

Cable Television: Cable TV networks including CNBC, MSNBC (in partnership with Microsoft), CNBC-Asia, NBC-Asia, Super Channel (United Kingdom), CNBC-Europe, canal de Noticias NBC (South America), part ownership in AMC, Bravo, and SportsChannel regional networks through a quarter interest in Rainbow Programming Holdings with Cablevision Systems as well as shares in Arts & Entertainment, The History Channel, and Court TV.

Other Interests: GE Aircraft Engines, GE Appliances, GE Capital Fleet Services, GE Electri-cal Distribution & Manufacturing, GE Power Systems, GE Information Services, GE Light-ing Division, GE Medical Services, GE Plastics, GE Transportation Systems, General Elec-tric Capital Services, GE Capital Commercial Real Estate Financing, GE Capital Mortgage Services, General Electric Capital Aviation Services, General Electric Capital Railcar Ser-vices, General Electric Investment Corporation, General Electric International Operations.

Significant Events:
1986: Acquires RCA, including NBC, for $6.4 billion
1996: GE is continuing to grow, with operations in more than 100 countries around the world, with 250 manufacturing plants in 26 different nations, employing some 239,000 people.
1996: As new television season starts, NBC owns a financial interest in nearly two thirds of the network shows.
1997: NBC teams with Dow Jones to form global television and Internet partnership in line with GE's corporate global strategy.
1998: Business Week decalres General Electric's CEO Jack Welch America's Number One corporate manager.
1998: General Electric passses $100 billion in revenues.
1998: NBC finsihes season in May 1998 as number one network in ratings.
1999: NBC becomes the first broadcast television network to team with a home shopping channnel, Value Vision.

Dow Jones in early 1998, which by providing access to the editorial resources of the *Wall Street Journal* strengthened CNBC in Europe, Asia and the United States. Advertising revenue increased 36%, and distribution rose 7% to 68 million sub-scribers. Ratings for CNBC's daytime business news programming grew 59%, with prime time audiences up 75%. After two years of operation, MSNBC, the 24-hour cable and Internet news service co-owned by NBC and Microsoft, was reaching more than 46 million cable households and had commitments in place to reach 60 million by the year 2001. Advertising sales and subscriber fees more than doubled in 1998. The channel's companion Web site, MSNBC on the Internet, was ranked the number one news site on the World Wide Web throughout 1998.[68]

Indeed, through the mid-1990s, NBC dominated in TV entertainment and sports, all because Wright, the ultimate GE insider, did exactly what Jack Welch wanted—he imported GE's hard-driving culture to NBC. Welch noted this irony: "People say, Jack, how can you be at NBC, you don't know anything about dramas or comedies. . . . Well, I can't build a jet engine, either. I can't build a turbine. Our job at GE is to deal with resources—human and financial. The idea of getting great talent, giving them all the support in the world, and letting them run is the whole management philosophy of GE, whether it's in turbines, engines, or a network."[69]

Led by Wright and Welch, NBC was run the "GE way"—thinking strategically, globally and in the long term. Speed and simplicity are praised; bureaucracy is decried. Wright had moved into the new cable businesses to create a hedge against the decline of TV broadcasting. Whereas the network owned and operated TV stations still represent the bulk of NBC's revenues and profits, that business is in a long, slow, seemingly inexorable decline. In 1986, broadcasting had 92% of viewers; in 1999, it had 67% of viewers. When the Big Three TV networks changed hands in the mid-1980s, the conventional wisdom was that NBC got a rotten deal. While ABC was sold to Capital Cities, a broadcasting company, and CBS went to Laurence Tisch, who promised to rebuild, NBC wound up with the "light bulb" people. However, Wright turned out to be the "right" man. A protégé of Welch, Wright had proven himself in GE's plastics and housewares divisions, and even gotten media experience when he spent three years in Atlanta as president of Cox Cable in the early 1980s. Although Wright had never worked in broadcasting, he was hardly the TV neophyte his critics wanted to believe.[70]

Wright pushed a two-pronged strategy: Cut costs and find ways to get into cable. Far from getting credit early on for his cable strategy, Wright took a beating in the early 1990s when NBC's prime time ratings tumbled. To make matters worse, the collapse came just as the TV advertising market fell into its worst slump in two decades. NBC's profits plummeted from a peak of $603 million in 1989 to just $204 million in 1992. Still, cost-cutting and investing in cable paid off in the long run. NBC prospered, and by 1996, had nine of the top 20 shows on broadcast TV. And cable has paid off as viewers surf their way to more alternatives. Wright's plan also has pushed into long-term investments in Europe and Asia: CNBC Asia, CNBC Europe, NBC Europe and NBC Asia.[71]

It did not hurt that Jack Welch loves television. Welch had a fax machine installed in his home as soon as GE bought NBC so that every morning before breakfast he could read the overnight Nielsen ratings for his new acquisition. These daily report cards are just one of the things Welch likes about television. GE bought NBC in 1986 because the company wanted a cash flow stream at a time when its manufacturing businesses were coming under pressure. Welch figured NBC should be thought of as a core part of GE's information businesses, which in 1996 accounted for $11 billion of the company's estimated $79 billion in revenues. In 1995, NBC alone brought in 5.6% of GE's revenues and 7.6% of its profits. Welch takes a special interest in the network, and in 1997 never missed *Seinfeld*, *Frasier* and *Law and Order*. Jack Welch is the ultimate couch potato—owning his own network.[72]

To hedge for all future shows Wright demanded a stake in ownership. In 1997, he claimed NBC's goal was to have half ownership stake in its full prime time schedule by 1998. Equity stakes lead to syndication profits, but it also assured NBC of control over shows it pitches, influencing the writing and directing. A far bigger problem lay with MSNBC, where Wright and company were still trying to develop the Internet side. Wright and Welch willingly invested in NBC's future. In March 1997, NBC completed its $2.3 billion deal with the Olympics, giving the network exclusive U.S. television rights in 2004, 2006 and 2008. He also pursued cost-cutting. For news, NBC began to use local news feeds to fuel CNBC and MSNBC, and sent out one-person "crews" (i.e., instead of teams) to cover stories. And Welch and Wright continued to bet on cable TV, and so by the close of 1997, NBC stood second (only to TCI) in cable network ownership.[73]

But not everything Welch and Wright touched turned to gold. International deals proved tricky. For example, in 1997 NBC's Azteca venture hit rock bottom. This alliance between NBC and Mexico's Television Azteca dissolved, and both networks blamed each other for the breakdown. In 1994, NBC and Azteca agreed that NBC would manage and provide programming expertise to the upstart Mexican network in exchange for $7 million and a chance to expand its identity abroad. NBC said Azteca broke its contract by refusing to honor an option NBC wanted to exercise to buy 1% of Azteca shares and by failing to pay more than $5 million due for technical assistance and programming. Azteca said it filed a lawsuit alleging that NBC should not be allowed to buy any shares because it did not provide services that were part of the deal.[74]

As NBC approached 2000, it was expanding into new and different directions, led by its pioneering (for a broadcast TV network) move to sell products directly to the public through a partial ownership in Value Vision home shopping cable network. Welch and Wright's stated goal was to turn viewers into direct consumers. In 1999, Value Vision ranked a distant third, behind Comcast's QVC (in 67 million households in 1999) and USA Networks' the Home Shopping Network (in 53 million homes). Yet, with all this expansion, and deep pockets, NBC also cut positions. For example, in September 1998, NBC announced that it would cut 4% of its workforce, or 250 jobs. After a thorough review, Wright, with Jack Welch's blessing, cut people from every division to raise profits on a continual basis.[75]

CBS represented the other old-line, traditional TV network. It became part of the Westinghouse Electric Corporation in November 1995 in a $5.4 billion deal that brought the network and its owned and operated stations with the Group W television stations. Two years later, in December 1997, Westinghouse transformed itself officially to CBS, Inc. The CBS Corporation emerged as a stand-alone media company as chairman Michael Jordan rang the opening bell of the New York Stock Exchange, and Bill Cosby, who had a prime time television program on CBS television network, bought the first 1,500 shares of the "new" company. The remaining Westinghouse corporate industrial businesses—nuclear power, government services and manufacturing process controls—were sold, and CBS became solely a media company in 1998.* CBS programming chief Mel Karmazin planned to have CBS as the top network with the top owned and operated TV stations in the United States.[76]

---

*As we go to press, in late 1999 Viacom proposed to acquire CBS. The deal, when and if finalized, would formally combine the two companies sometime during the spring of 1999. See Douglas Gomery, "The Company That Would Be King," *American Journalism Review*, December, 1999, page 66.

PROFILE: CBS Corporation

Basic Data:
Headquarters: New York City
Web sites: www.cbs.com
CEO in 1999: Mel Karmazin
1998 Sales (in millions): $6,805
1998 Net Profits (in millions): –$12
1998 Assets (in millions): $20,139
Rank in 1998 Forbes 500—Sales: 228

Market Holdings:
Broadcast Television: CBS television network, CBS owned and operated television stations (including WCBS-New York, KCBS-Los Angeles, WBBM-Chicago, KYW-Philadelphia, KPIX-San Francisco, WBZ-Boston, WFOR-Miami and KDKA-Pittsburgh, among others); owner of King World Syndication.
Cable Television: The Nashville Network, Country Music Television.
Radio: CBS radio network, CBS radio owned and operated stations (including WCBS-New York, WBZ-Boston and KDKA-Pittsburgh, among others).
Film & Television: Joint venture in Twentieth Century-Fox Home Entertainment.

Significant Events:
1993: New management team, led by former PepsiCo executive Michael Jordan, took and began to transform the company.
1994: Sells electrical distribution and control business to car parts maker Eaton.
1995: Acquires CBS from Loews, Inc. for $5.4 billion and combines Group W Westinghouse owned 5 television broadcast and 18 radio stations with CBS owned and operated units.
1996: Sells Knoll Group furniture maker and defense electronics unit for combined $3.5 billion.
1996: Buys Telenoticias, a 24-hour news channel seen in 22 Spanish-speaking countries.
June 1996: Acquires Infinity Broadcasting, major radio company, for $4 billion.
1997: Buys cable's The Nashville Network and Country Music TV for $1.55 billion, and thus expands into cable programming.
1997: Former Infinity Radio CEO Mel Karmazin takes charge of radio and television, and a year later he would replaces Michael Jordan as CBS's CEO.
1997: Acquires American Radio Systems chain for $2.6 billion, bring CBS radio owned stations to number 175.
1997: On December 1, 1997, the Westinghouse Electric Corporation becomes CBS Corporation and moves headquarters from Pittsburgh to New York City, and sells last of industrial assets.
1998: CBS conceeds deaft and sells its money losing cable TV network Eye of people to Discovery Commuications, Inc.
1999: CBS sells to Viacom.

Radio (see Chapter 5) would rank alongside television as the defining mass media structure of the new CBS. Jordan decided that CBS would not try to be a pure conglomerate of many unrelated parts, but a media conglomerate that would dominate broadcast radio and television, and hopefully the newer mass media as well. This transformation began when Jordan left PepsiCo in 1993 to head Westinghouse, and then decided to be a buyer of broadcasting, starting with the 1995 purchase of CBS. Radio and then cable TV acquisitions came next. Jordan expected to be either number one or two in every major radio market in the United States (at least those where CBS had stations). By the close of 1997, Jordan had bought or sold some $25 billion worth of companies on the theory that specialization is where company strategy should go, in the manner of General Electric. Jordan could not make the power generating business grow. Because it was falling further behind the competition, Jordan sold out. Westinghouse was no more; CBS was a radio and television conglomerate as it had for more than a half century.[77]

Still CBS struggled as TV network pundits considered its prime time audiences "too old"; the network did not attract adults from age 18 to 49 that were Madison Avenue's favorite targets. The network brass were smart enough not to mess with proven hits like 60 Minutes and Touched by an Angel. Both remained the cornerstones of the CBS broadcast TV schedule. Indeed, 60 Minutes had finished in the top 10 more often than Dallas, Cheers, I Love Lucy or Gunsmoke. But CBS was slow to get into cable TV; it was mid-1997 when CBS took some of the monies from the sale of Westinghouse's assets to buy Gaylord Entertainment for an estimated $1.5 billion for Gaylord's two cable channels, The Nashville Network and Country Music Television. The new CBS aggressively pushed anywhere and everywhere. For example, in April 1997, CBS began to target Latin America-bound airline passengers as its CBS TeleNoticias aired monthly programming blocks in English and Spanish on United Airlines flights to Latin America from Miami and New York. The airline had approached CBS after surveys of its overseas passengers showed quality in-flight programming would draw more customers.[78]

CBS took the strategy of not going after the young, but after the Baby Boomers. Through the late 1990s, every eight seconds a Baby Boomer turned 50; Bill Clinton, Dolly Parton and millions born during the prosperity of the late 1940s and early 1950s were CBS's targets. This demographic "pig in the python" continued to buy, and so advertisers continued to seek to reach them. CBS bet on leading the way by branding itself as the network of choice for the Boomers. Demographers have long warned that the Baby Boom has changed everything it has touched, but for as long as network TV has been around, advertising credo has dictated to seek out only 18- to 49-year-olds; avoid those over 50. According to the theory, after age 50, people become too set in their ways and it makes no sense to try to persuade them to try something new.[79]

CBS executives foresee a prime time audience embracing a safe, simpler world populated by their own. Historically, this experiment signaled the end of an era. A generation ago, in 1970, CBS set off the age of TV programing for the urban, hip 18- to 35-year-old consumers, canceling long popular shows and acknowledging the Baby Boom generation had grown up. Through the 1960s, CBS led the ratings wars with its rural hits, such as The Beverly Hillbillies and Petticoat Junction, which drew audiences who had grown up in the Great Depression and wanted their stories on the tube to portray nostalgia for simpler times. In 1970, CBS's owner William Paley pulled the plug. CBS consultants told Paley that the Baby Boomers were redefining marketing practices. Off went Hee Haw and Green Acres, and on came All in the Family and The Mary Tyler Moore Show. Rural was out; New York and Minneapolis were in. Older faces were replaced by Mary and the "Meathead."

In the mid-1990s, CBS changed course to become more associated with American Association of Retired Persons (AARP) than Music Television (MTV). Unexpected hits such as *Touched by an Angel*, which has already spawned a spin-off called *Promised Land*, provided examples of the "new" CBS. *60 Minutes*, the ultimate in over-50 demographics, beat back a charge by an unabashedly hip *Dateline*, and regained its status as the premiere magazine program on television. But age was not the lone demographic group CBS was re-targeting. In March 1997, it invested $100 million to acquire 22% of SportsLine USA, which offers Internet sports scores and video clips. Here the CBS target was male viewers, both young and old.[80]

As 1998 began, CBS agreed to pay $500 million per year for four years for the rights to air the professional football games of the American Football Conference. CBS brass allocated what they figure will be the necessary millions of dollars from projected cash flows generated by its recently acquired Nashville Network and Country Music Television cable networks. Indeed, through these recent acquisitions, history has come full circle. Over the 1980s and 1990s, TNN proved profitable with its niche older audience, one in part generated by re-running former CBS hits such as *Dallas*. All these corporate maneuvers aimed at the Baby Boom generation took the "new" CBS down a path that it hoped would make the company more profits.

In some matters, CBS played it as safely and traditionally as its rivals. The new CBS bought more broadcast TV stations; in 1998, it acquired a Dallas-Fort Worth station for $485 million in stock, giving CBS a presence in the nation's seventh largest television market. CBS also began to play the Internet, whereby it acquired sizable stakes in two sites in exchange for promotion on its television, radio and outdoor advertising properties. For $100 million in investment and promotion, CBS got 35% of Hollywood.com, and a 50% stake in Storerunner.com, a site that scans other Web sites for bargains for shoppers. The two Internet deals followed a pattern CBS has used successfully in two previous transactions, trading advertising time and lending its powerful name for stakes in start-up companies. So far the strategy has paid off handsomely. CBS's two other Internet partners, CBS Market-watch.com and Sportsline USA Inc., sold shares to the public, inflating CBS's stake in those two new companies to more than $500 million. And, as already analyzed, CBS agreed to buy the leading television syndicator King World for $2.5 billion in stock.[81]

Yet, like NBC, the CBS corporation looked for ways to cut costs in the 1990s. During the fall 1998, for example, Mel Karmazin announced News Division job cuts of 7%, thus reducing the budget for news by 10%. About 120 persons lost their jobs. It also struck a deal with its affiliates about the same time to shift about $50 million annually to the network to help pay for the new NFL contract singed during January 1998. Affiliates gave up part of their annual cash payment plus some advertising time. With CBS having the least presence on cable and no studio base like its rivals, Mel Karmazin (having replaced Michael Jordan) will continually need to "re-invent" the company. Thus, few were surprised in May 1999 when CBS, aiming to package more comprehensive advertising deals, agreed to buy Outdoor Systems, Inc., a billboard company, for $6.5 billion in stock plus $1.8 billion in taking over debt (for a total purchase price of $8.3 billion). With this important deal, CBS could offer potential advertisers radio, TV and billboard advertising packages.[82]

The New Network World: Part of Hollywood

Fox, a part of Rupert Murdoch's News Corporation, led the way into broadcast TV network vertical integration with Hollywood. After a decade, Fox showed some maturity as a network and growing brand recognition with its appeal to the hip, young adult audience. Indeed, Fox's Sunday night presented as good as popular television had to offer, with the *Simpsons* and the *X-Files*. During the final week of January 1997, the Fox network achieved a rare win for the week based on its first telecast of a Super Bowl, finishing the week with a 14.5 rating and 23 share. The synergy with the studio seemed to be paying off. So did owner Rupert Murdoch's billions spent on professional football.[83]

Like him or not, Rupert Murdoch forever changed the face of broadcast network television. When Murdoch announced Fox's initial offering as *The Joan Rivers Show*, skeptics howled and called him insane. But with *The Simpsons*, *X- Files* and NFL football, the Fox network became a player, consistently nipping at the heels of the Big Three.

He invested boldly. In 1997, for example, Murdoch realized he needed to acquire even more attractive programming and so bought the Los Angeles Dodgers baseball team. Dodgers' President Peter O'Malley, who announced the agreement, lauded Murdoch and company: "I believe Fox Group will be an outstanding owner of the Dodgers." O'Malley, who agreed to remain as Dodgers president, pointed out that "their support of Major League Baseball and their commitment to the community is extraordinary." But as the 1990s ended, Fox's schedule looked like its major network rivals—save for the lack of a national news organization. Murdoch did hire Roger Ailes, formerly of CNBC and before that of the Reagan White House, to create a 24-hour-a-day cable rival to CNN. Murdoch figured that Fox needed to differentiate its news, calling CNN (owned by Time Warner) "too liberal."[84]

But as the 1990s ended, Murdoch turned to a global strategy, with the Fox television network as one key part. Although Fox certainly had its impact in the United States, News Corporation's Star TV satellite service claimed it regularly reached 220 million Asians. Murdoch saw global TV expansion at News Corporation's core. Murdoch's world presence simply could not be avoided: beginning satellite services in Japan and Latin America, adding services in Asia and Europe, and buying Manchester United, the British football team. Murdoch saw two global news channels: Fox News and the British-based Sky News.[85]

But, Murdoch had problems too. In the mid-1990s, while barely surviving an FCC inquiry aimed at stripping him of his TV stations, Murdoch underwent surgery. At age 70, he began to think about a successor, and announced a series of more responsible positions for his son Lachlan, the official heir apparent. As 2000 approached, Rupert Murdoch announced he had no immediate plans to step down, or to sell his controlling interest in News Corporation. But, he did want the investment world to know Lachlan would take over the global news and entertainment empire some time after 2000.

Lachlan Murdoch will have a hard act to follow. Rupert Murdoch surely played the role as the bold leader in the communications industry. Former CBS executive Howard Stringer has called Murdoch the leader of a new "Napoleonic era" of com-

---

PROFILE: The News Corporation Limited

Basic Data:
Headquarters: Sydney, Australia
Web site: N/A
CEO in 1997: Rupert Murdoch
1997 Revenues (in millions): $11,264
1997 Net Income (in millions): $564
1997 Assets (in millions): $30,832
Rank in 1998 Forbes International 500: 217

Market Holdings:
Broadcast Television: Fox Broadcasting Company (television network), Fox television stations, Inc. (owned and operated TV stations including WNYW-New York, KTTV-Los Angeles, KRIV-Houston, WFLD-Chicago, KDAF-Dallas and WTTG-Washington, DC, among others), Heritage Media, New World Entertainment (television stations and program production),
Cable Television: FX cable network, Fox news cable channel, Kids International, International Family Channel network, 15 regional sports cable channels.
Film & Television: Twentieth Century-Fox studio, Fox Video Company, Fox Broadcasting Company, Twentieth Century-Fox Home Entertainment, BSkyN, the Sky Channel satellite service in Europe, STAR TV in Asia, JSkyB in Japan satellite television, Canal FOX in Europe, Sky Entertainment Services in Latin America, VOX and DF1 television in Germany.
Music: small music company.
Publishing: magazines including joint deal with *TV Guide*, and *Good Food*; newspapers, including the *Boston Herald*, the *New York Post*, the *Sun* (London, England), the *News of the World* (London, England), the *Times* (London, England); HarperCollins book publishing.
Other Interests: CineBooks, Inc. (Computer systems), Los Angeles Dodgers (Major Leaguer baseball), 100 daily and weekly newspapers in Australia, Ansett Transport industries

Significant Events:
1985: Rupert Murdoch buys Twentieth Century-Fox studio; establishes in the United States.
1986: Begins Fox television network.
1989: Starts Sky television and becomes a major force in TV in Europe.
1993: Acquires 64% of START TV in Asia.
1994: Spends $1.6 for rights to broadcast National Football League games.
1997: Acquires the 80% of New World Communications group not already owned for about $2.5 billion in securties, and with the new 10 television stations News Corporation becomes largest owner of TV stations in the United States.
1997: Agrees to buy Los Angeles Dodgers baseball team for $350 million.
1997: Agrees to buy International Family Channel cable network for $1.9 million.
1997: Rupert Murdoch's son James named president of News American Digital publishing, a new unit that will consolidate all of News Corporation's electronic pushing operations.
1998: Spins off Fox Group as IPO to raise cash for investment.

---

munications. Murdoch added to his image when he told reporters: "The only good regulator is a dead regulator." But Murdoch was a skilled businessperson. When the Fox network was hot, he sliced off the Fox Group from News Corporation (including television production, distribution and presentation) and sold it to the public at a premium. He retained control, of course. During Spring 1999, Liberty Media Group Chairman John Malone became one of the largest shareholders in News Corporation through two transactions valued at $2.1 billion. Combined, the two deals gave Malone about a 7.5% stake in News Corporation, making him the largest shareholder after Capital Group Inc., which then owned about 8.5%, and the Murdoch family, which owned about 33% of the company—enough to retain controlling interest.[86]

ABC, owned by the Walt Disney Corporation, is not only a famous TV network, but also owns TV stations in major cities across the United States. It was assumed that Disney, one of Hollywood's most successful companies, would revitalize ABC. But this did not prove to be the case; instead, the other assets in that mega-deal—cable's ESPN, A&E and Lifetime networks—did far better. So, in August 1997, ABC made headlines, not with promised new hit shows, but by firing some 200 staffers. Instead of battling NBC and CBS for the top spot in the network ratings war, ABC was forced to fight off Fox for fourth place. Disney's famed synergy was simply not working for ABC. Only the owned and operated stations continued to do well.[87]

The failure was not from a lack of trying. The poor ABC network performance was tarnishing Michael Eisner's otherwise legendary record as the "savior" of the Walt Disney Corporation. Thus, beginning in the Fall 1997 TV season, ABC launched a dozen new series, replacing every 8:00 pm show. This shakeup also launched ABC's increased reliance on its Burbank-based parent as the number of Disney produced shows more than doubled. Eisner even brought back a revamped *Wonderful World of Disney*, which he hosted. Disney stores displayed advertisements for the new ABC shows in their windows. The network received some help when the movie studio granted it an exclusive for a mid-sweeps presentation of *The Lion King*. Despite such moves, ABC slid further behind both NBC and CBS.[88]

Overall, the Disney company continued to do well enough so that Eisner remained Wall Street's darling—at least through 1999. In February 1997, for example, stockholders at the Disney annual meeting approved an extension of Eisner's contract, allowing him to collect $300 million in stock and salary over the next decade. Eisner correctly noted that because he had taken over as chief executive in 1984, the value of Disney stock had soared from $2 billion to $50 billion. Dozens of picketers outside the meeting accused Disney and Eisner of exploiting foreign workers while fattening the bottom line and their salaries. One protestor calculated: "It would take a Haitian 16.8 years to earn Eisner's hourly income of $9,783." Indeed, since its acquisition of ABC, Disney had spent two years on damage control, best symbolized by the celebrated hiring and firing of super Hollywood agent Michael Ovitz.[89]

In the past, Disney had synergy success as theatrical features led to millions of sales of home video, visits to theme parks and sales of action figures. The process of building up a TV network required more than appearances by ABC soap opera stars signing autographs at Disney theme parks. Eisner and Ovitz became deeply involved in choosing the shows for the network, and neither seemed to know what young adults desired in network TV offerings. In 1999, Eisner was still trying, and failing, with ABC. Eisner would not give up on attempted synergy. For example, he successfully launched *ESPN Magazine*, based on its cable networks, and targeted the same audience of Time Warner's *Sports Illustrated*. The magazine adopted the sometimes cheeky style of ESPN's nightly Sports Center newscast, with "style, wit, and attitude," and exploited the Disney-owned baseball team, the Anaheim Angels, and the Disney-owned professional

---

PROFILE: The Walt Disney Company

Basic Data:
Headquarters: Burbank, CA
Web site: www.disney.com
CEO in 1997: Michael D. Eisner
1998 Sales (in millions): $23,226
1998 Net Profits (in millions): $1,717
1998 Assets (in millions): $43,537
Rank in 1998 Forbes 500—Sales: 46

Market Holdings:
Broadcast Television: ABC Television Network, ABC owned and operated stations (e.g., WABC-New York City, KABC-Los Angeles, WLS-Chicago).
Cable Television: Ownership of networks: ESPN Networks, part owner of Arts & Entertainment & The History Channel, part owner of Lifetime, Toon Disney as well as TV networks in Europe and Japan.
Film & Television: Hollywood Pictures, Touchstone Pictures, Walt Disney Pictures, Miramax studio, Walt Disney Television, Buena Vista Pictures Distribution, Buena Vista Home Video.
Music: Walt Disney Music Company, Hollywood Records.
Radio: ABC Radio networks, ABC owned and operated stations (e.g., WRQX-FM-Washington, DC, WABC-AM-New York City, WMAL-AM-Washington, DC).
Publishing: Disney Publishing Group
Theme Parks: Disneyland (California), Walt Disney World (Florida), EuroDisney (Paris, France), Tokyo Disneyland; Disney–MGM Studio park.
Other Interests: The Mighty Ducks (National Hockey League), Anaheim Angels (Major league baseball), Disney retail stores, Broadway plays such as "The Lion King," Disney Cruise Line, Disney Vacation Clubs.

Significant Events:
1995: The Disney Channel becomes available in the United Kingdom.
1996: Acquires 25% interest of the California Angels baseball team and takes on the role of managing general partner.
1996: Buys Capital Cities/ABC television network and stations and cable TV interests.
1996: Disney World celebrates its 25th anniversary.
1997: Michael Eisner's contract with Disney is extended to 2006.
1997: Fifteen million southern Baptists threaten to boycott the Walt Disney Company, however, boycott is virtually impossible because Disney ownership is so broad.
1997: CEO Michael Eisner exercises 7.3 million of his stock options worth more than a half billion dollars.
1998: Michael Eisner pushing memoir, *Work in Progress* (Random House).
1998: Disney acqiures 43% stake in Web portal Infoseek.

---

hockey team, The Mighty Ducks. The question for the 21st century remained: Could Eisner ever do the same for the ABC television network?[90]

The **WB**, which is owned primarily by Time Warner, functioned like ABC, owned and fed by one of the largest media companies in the world. But unlike ABC, no one expected the WB to deliver vast audiences, and from 1995 through 1999, it did not. The WB scrambled just to catch up with Fox. Also consider that the WB did not start as a broad-based network, but as one that was niche driven from the beginning. The WB took direct aim at 18 to 49 year olds with children in the home. Thus, one of its earliest hits was *Dawson's Creek*, a coming of age drama. Time Warner figured it would lose money, and through 1999, no profits had been made.[91]

Again synergy between a Hollywood studio and a TV network remained key to the WB's future. But other problems remained as it struggled to match the ratings of ABC, CBS or NBC. For example, distribution never blanketed the United States through broadcast affiliations. And, so in April 1998, betting that viewers did not care whether they saw their favorite shows on cable or over-the-air, the WB signed a first of its kind distribution deal with TCI cable (later part of AT&T) to fill in smaller markets where no WB broadcast affiliate existed. This would expand the WB's reach from about 90% of homes in the United States to a number closer to what NBC, ABC and CBS regu-

---

PROFILE: Time Warner Inc.

Basic Data:
Headquarters: New York, NY
Web site: www.pathfinder.com
CEO in 1999: Gerald M. Levin
1998 Sales (in millions): $14,582
1998 Net Profits (in millions): $168
1998 Assets (in millions): $31,640
Rank in 1998 Forbes 500—Sales: 102

Major Holdings:
Broadcast Television: The WB Network.
Cable MSO's: Time Warner Cable with clustered MSOs in New York City, Tampa Bay, Milwaukee, St. Louis, Houston and Raleigh & Durham, NC.
Cable Networks: Turner Broadcasting (includes CNN, TNT & TBS), HBO, Cinemax, CNNSI (combining cable network and *Sports Illustrated* magazine), Turner Classic Movies, The Cartoon Network.
Film & Television: Warner Bros. Studio, WB Television (producing such shows as *ER* and *Friends*), Lorimar Television (syndicating such shows as *Dallas*), Quincy Jones Entertainment (producer of *Fresh Prince of Bel Air*), Warner Home Video, HBO Pictures, New Line Cinema movie studio, Fine Line Features movie distribution.
Magazines: Fortune, People, Sports Illustrated, Time, Weight Watchers, Asiaweek, Money, Entertainment Weekly, Mad Magazine, Life.
Music: Atlantic Recording Group, Warner Bros Records, Ivy Hill Corp. Elektra Entertainment, plus other labels.
Publishing: Warner Books, Little, Brown book publishers, Time-Life books, Book-of-the-Month-Club, History Book Club.
Other Interests: DC Comics, Six Flags entertainment and theme parks, Atlanta Hawks (Professional basketball), Atlanta Braves (Major League baseball).

Significant Events:
1989: Time and Warner merge.
1996: The FTC reaches a settlement with Time Warner allowing its $6.2 billion merger with Turner Broadcasting.
1997: CEO Gerald M. Levin orders companywide budget cuts of 3% to 5% to boost lagging stock price.
1997: Time Warner posts $30 million profit, with revenues reporting to climb 25% to nearly $6 billion, led by its cable TV MSOs and networks.
August 1997: Time Warner cable begins to sell and trade to custer MSOs to help lower $17 billion debt.

larly accessed. Along with Time Warner's own cable MSO, this meant many small town viewers saw the WB only on cable or through DBS.[92]

Hits from studio synergy were slow in coming. *Buffy the Vampire Slayer* was its first, but the show's average rating placed it outside the top 100 shows for broadcast TV's prime time. But with the bar lowered, *Buffy* (and later *Dawson's Creek*) had a chance to stay on the schedule. In 1990, nearly 50 shows regularly reached at least one quarter of the audience; by 1999, the number could be counted on one hand. The WB stayed with *Buffy* because it hoped (as happened with Fox's *The X-Files*) the show would eventually become a brand for the WB in the public's mind. Instead of heralding high ratings, WB researchers noted that *Buffy* serviced a niche, frequently winning its time period in New York and Los Angeles among men between age 18 and 40.[93]

One of the key principles of a network was to own and operate a group of stations so as to insure a base audience for network programming. Time Warner, as big as it is, owned no broadcast television stations. Thus, early on, the WB effected a partnership with the fourth largest group of broadcast TV stations, those owned by the Tribune Company of Chicago. In March 1997, Tribune boosted its share of the ownership in the WB to 21.9%, and ran the WB on its nearly 20 stations. With tribune's superstation WGN, the WB spread across the nation and its shows were often shown twice on cable, once through a local affiliate as well as on WGN.[94]

As with ABC and Fox, the question of synergy creating profits remained unanswered. Time Warner, and its partner the Tribune company, surely had the deep pockets necessary to keep losing money. But eventually, sometime after 2000, a decision will have to be made, or at least major adjustments will have to be set in place. Time Warner and Disney represented the two largest media conglomerates in the world in 1999. Could they effect profit making in other media into network TV success?[95]

UPN, which is owned by Viacom, offered the final example of studio broadcast TV network synergy. Viacom owned Paramount Pictures, and sought to use its studio to craft the United Paramount Network. With such well-known franchises as Paramount Television, MTV, Nickelodeon, VH1, Nick at Nite, Showtime and The Movie Channel, as well as newer brands such as TV Land, Sundance Channel, M2: Music Television, United Paramount Network (UPN) and the Paramount Channel in the United Kingdom, Viacom ranked as one of the most prominent and prolific content factories in the world. In the most direct manner, Paramount's evergreen *Star Trek* franchise launched the UPN in 1995 both with frequent re-runs of the original series as well as the premier of a new version called *Star Trek: Voyager*.[96]

Viacom also offered up a television group—one of the largest television broadcasting groups in the United States by reach, covering more than one quarter of all U.S. households. Many of the top markets were represented: WPSG, Philadelphia; WSBK, Boston; WDCA, Washington, DC; KTXA, Dallas-Ft. Worth; WKBD, Detroit; WUPA, Atlanta; KTXH, Houston; KSTW, Seattle; WTOG, Tampa; WBFS, Miami; WGNT, Norfolk; WUPL, New Orleans; KMAX, Sacramento; WNDY, Indianapolis; WWHO, Columbus; WNPA-TV, Pittsburgh; and KAUT-TV, Oklahoma City. Still UPN needed to scramble to make sure it had affiliates in New York and Los Angeles. Sumner Redstone, CEO and chief stockholder of Viacom,

---

PROFILE: Viacom, Inc.

Basic Data:
Headquarters: New York, NY
Web site: www.viacom.com
CEO in 1997: Sumner M. Redstone
1998 Revenues (in millions): $12,096
1998 Net Profits (in millions): $–48
1998 Assets (in millions): $23,613
Rank in 1998 Forbes 500—Sales: 130

Market Holdings:
Broadcast Television: Partner in UPN television network, owner and operator of broadcast television stations in Philadelphia, Boston, Washington, DC, Dallas, Detroit, Atlanta, Houston, Seattle, Tampa, Miami, New Orleans and Indianapolis, among others.
Cable Television: Owner of cable networks, including MTV, M2, VH-1, Nickelodeon, Nike at Nite, Showtime, The Movie Channel, The Paramount Channel (UK), Comedy Central.
Film & Television: Paramount Pictures Corporation (major Hollywood studio), National Amusements movie theater chain (with screens in 11 countries), Famous Players theater chain in Canada, Blockbuster Entertainment Group (home video), Blockbuster Pictures Holding Corporation (investments in films), Spelling Entertainment Group (television producer), Republic Entertainment (film and TV producer and distributor), Paramount Home Video, Worldvision Enterprises (television syndicator), Viacom International, United International Pictures.
Music: Blockbuster Music (retailer of music), Famous Music.
Publishing: Simon & Schuster, Prentice-Hall, Macmillan Publishing USA, Schimer Books, Charles Scribner's Sons, Thorndike Press, Twayne Publishers, Pocket Books, Allyn & Bacon, Ginn books, MTV Books.
Other Interests: Viacom retail stores; Virgin Interactive Entertainment; Paramount Parks: Kings Island, outside Cincinnati, OH, Kings Dominion, near Richmond, VA, Paramount's Carowinds, near Charlotte, NC, and Raging Waters, near San Jose, CA, among others.

Significant Events:
1970: Viacom created as FCC rules that CBS can no longer syndicate operations.
1987: Sumner Redstone's National Amusements, Inc. of Dedham, MA buys controlling interest of Viacom, Inc. for $3.4 billion.
1996: Launches new cable network—TV Land.
1996: Sumner M. Redstone fires Paramount Pictures boss Frank Biondi and takes over.
1996: Creates M2: Music Television, a new "freeform" music television cable channel.
1997: Sells USA Cable networks to Seagram Ltd. for $1.7 billion.

---

allied with Chris-Craft Industries, whose stations were located in these markets as well as in Philadelphia, San Francisco and Boston; the plan was only missing Chicago (market three) in TV's top 10 households.[97]

Backed by Redstone, UPN executives have declared they alone are in it for the long haul and are prepared to spend $1 billion to make a profitable prime time operation. Losses came regularly, and even with the fully amortized Paramount programming, there seemed no end in sight. In the end, UPN sought to best the WB, and prove Fox had a rival. The UPN network, like the WB, attracted younger viewers, whereas CBS and Fox were beginning to see their audiences age. According to one study done in late 1997, CBS had the oldest audiences, with the median over age

52. NBC and ABC followed—far behind—at median age 40, with Fox at age 33, UPN at age 32 and WB at age 24 on the median. The rivalry between WB and UPN was real and competitive for young viewers.[98]

The rivalry also was fierce for affiliations. For example, in 1998, five Sinclair Television Group stations—judging UPN was losing out to the WB—dis-affiliated with UPN and signed with the WB. Sinclair bet for the long run and signed for 10 years. In a statement, Sinclair said WB guaranteed Sinclair will receive compensation of $64 million for the first eight years; the deep pockets of Time Warner spoke louder than those of Viacom. In addition, Sinclair's WFBC-TV in Greenville, South Carolina, agreed to switch once its affiliation agreement was up. This affiliate jockeying will be a continued feature of the UPN and WB rivalry after 2000.[99]

New Networks—The Pretenders

Whereas the WB and UPN should still be labeled experiments in 1999, the impact of the success of Fox has spurred others to try to join the ranks of the major broadcast television networks. These "experiments" are so early in their history that it is impossible to tell if they will survive. Yet their very genius underscores the continuing potential of profitability of a network, and the health of broadcast television. Their attempts also underscore the lower barriers to entry of the broadcast TV market. It was some 30 years after the 1955 demise of Dumont that Fox was started. During the dozen or so years after Fox's success, four more came along. In addition to the UPN and WB, the USA Network and PaxNet were facing difficult futures.

The USA Network started with the stations of the Home Shopping Network, Inc. (along with partner Silver King Broadcasting), reaching nearly one third of households in the United States. Then former Fox executive Barry Diller teamed up with mighty Seagram Company of Montreal, Canada, (see Chapter 6)—owner of Hollywood's Universal studio—to turn cable's USA Network into the next WB or UPN. The publicity surrounding this new network focused on Diller's latest bid to return to the front lines of TV broadcasting in the United States. Diller and his associates reasoned they could synergize Universal's television production plus their stations to fashion a success where UPN and the WB failed.[100]

PaxNet was up and running on the final day of August 1998, based on re-runs such as *Flipper* and *The Love Boat*. This was no synergy play, but an extension of Lowell "Bud" Paxson's ownership of TV stations in top media markets such as WPXN channel 31 in New York City, KPXN channel 30 in Los Angeles, WCFC channel 38 in Chicago, WPPX channel 61 in Philadelphia, KKPX channel 65 in San Francisco, WPXP channel 60 in Boston and WPXW channel 66 in Washington, DC. Paxson Communications Corporation had grown into one of the largest collections of broadcast television stations in the United States by selling its radio stations (to Clear Channel Communication for nearly $700 million), and pouring that money into broadcast television station acquisition. As noted earlier, the FCC counted UHF stations as only "half," and Paxson acquired UHF stations that covered more than half the U.S. population, but officially they were counted as less than the 35% FCC upper bound. Still its New York City station cost Paxson more than $250 million.[101]

BROADCAST TV MINOR COMPANIES

The networks define the major players of the broadcast television industry in 1999. They presented the programming that TV viewers watched most, and they owned vast collections of stations. Minor companies are defined as those having no network connections other than being affiliates of one of these networks. These affiliated chains of stations may reach large audiences, but are dependent on a network, and can and did switch network affiliations as it may advantage these owners. Table 4.15 lists a dozen of the larger "minor" chains—companies ranging from media conglomerates like Cox and Young Broadcasting, which both owned little other than broadcast television stations in 1999. Even Young Broadcasting, with its Los Angeles KCAL-TV (purchased in 1995 for $368 million) plus six ABC affiliates, four CBS affiliates and one NBC affiliate, was no tiny operation. But, would such single line broadcasters be able to survive as the 21st century commenced?[102]

Stand-alone broadcast TV station groups became rarer in the 1990s. More typical were groups of TV stations owned by media conglomerates with their economic power vested in other fields (mostly newspapers; see Chapter 1). For example, newspaper powerhouse Gannett, in the mid-1990s, owned 18 television stations, all affiliated with NBC, ABC or CBS. Here is a newspaper company with a strong position in the television business. Also in the top 20 were Belo, known for the *Dallas Morning News* and other newspapers; Cox Broadcasting, a private company known for its newspaper the *Atlanta Constitution*; the Hearst-Argyle Group, known for Hearst's magazines; E. W. Scripps Co., known for the *Cincinnati Post* newspaper; the New York Times Company, known for its heralded flagship newspaper; and Post-Newsweek Stations, also known as a division of the company that publishes the *Washington Post*.[103]

TABLE 4.15
Rank Order of Important Minor Television Broadcasting Companies

Name	Address	FCC Penetration (percentage of homes reached)*	Real Penetration (percentage of homes reached)
Cox	Atlanta	9.5%	11.4%
Hearst-Argyle Television	New York	9.2	11.6
Young Broadcasting	New York	9.0	9.1
E. W. Scripps	Cincinnati	8.7	10.4
Sinclair Broadcast Group	Baltimore	8.2	14.2
Post-Newsweek Stations	Hartford, CT	7.1	7.1
Meredith	Des Moines, IA	6.2	7.6
Granite Broadcasting	New York	5.9	7.7
Raycom Media	Montgomery, AL	5.6	6.4
Pulitzer Broadcasting	St. Louis	5.2	5.5
Media General	Richmond, VA	4.7	5.3
Allbritton Communications	Washington, DC	4.2	4.3

*where UHF reach counts as half in FCC calculations.
Source: "25 Top TV Groups," *Broadcasting & Cable*, June 30, 1997, pp. 36–41.

Take the New York Times Company as a typical example. This media giant may be considered a "newspaper" company, but it makes millions from television as well. Here is a massive media conglomerate with $2.6 billion in revenues in 1996, and assets (in 1996) of even more at $3.5 billion. Yet the company had enough of a presence in the electronic media that *Broadcasting & Cable* magazine, in July 1997, ranked the New York Times Company as the 16th largest media group in its electronic media oriented ranking because of its ownership of six television and two radio stations. WQXR-FM and WQEW-AM get the bulk of the publicity, being in the same city as the famous newspaper, but television stations in Huntsville, Alabama; Scranton, Pennsylvania; Memphis, Tennessee; and Norfolk, Virginia; among others, throw off millions of dollars in profits each year. The New York Times Company is acquiring as well. In July 1996, it added two NBC affiliates, KFOR-TV of Oklahoma City and WHO-TV of Des Moines, Iowa, to its TV empire.[104]

In *Broadcasting & Cable Yearbooks* of the late 1990s, under "Group Ownership," there are two dozen pages of listings of TV station owners. The network powerhouse ABC starts the listing, but the first page in 1998 included All American TV, Inc. (San Dimas, California, with 10 stations in small communities in Alabama, Georgia, Illinois, Mississippi, Missouri, New Mexico, Oklahoma and Tennessee). Although single (or two) station owners are rare, they do exist. For example, in the middle is the Journal Company, publisher of the *Milwaukee Journal-Sentinel* newspaper, which started WTMJ-TV as a pioneer in the 1940s and still owns this NBC affiliate in this top 30 market. In 1998 the Journal Company also owned KTNV-TV of Las Vegas as its only TV holding.[105]

None of these small operations simply stand still and wait for the networks to buy them out. As noted in the previous analysis about urban markets, the networks really do not want to own stations in small markets. Therefore, companies like the Ackerley Group will continue, so long as the FCC ownership rules and basic TV economics do not fundamentally change. Ackerley controls affiliates in Utica, Binghamton, Syracuse and Rochester, New York. Syracuse's WIXT (channel 9) became a regional TV hub that piped programming to three sister ABC network affiliates in upstate New York and consolidated most of those stations' business functions. Here is small time broadcast group owner's equivalent of cable clustering analyzed later. The Ackerley Group, WIXT's owner, minimized costs by using a central digital broadcasting system, and therefore boosted profits. WIXT became the regional hub for WUTR (channel 20) in Utica, WIVT (channel 34) in Binghamton and Rochester station WOKR (channel 13)—all affiliates of the ABC network—handling accounting, creative services and technical operations for all the stations in the group. Ackerley invested more than $2 million to install the digital system and linked the four stations with fiber optic cable. Each station will maintain a local sales and community affairs staff plus local news operation, but some news programming with a wide regional interest, like a story about Syracuse University sports, will be carried on all the stations in the cluster. Ackerley, a publicly traded company based in Seattle, owns 13 TV stations in New York and California, plus four radio stations, outdoor advertising business and the NBA's Seattle Supersonics basketball team. In March and April 1999, the Ackerley Group purchased WOKR-TV, the ABC affiliate in Rochester, New York; KMTR-TV, the NBC affiliate in Eugene, Oregon; and KCOY-TV, the CBS affiliate in Santa Maria, California.

WOKR joined WIXT in Syracuse, WUTR in Utica and WIVT in Binghamton, and KMTR joined KMTZ in Coos Bay, Oregon, KMTX in Roseburg, Oregon, KVIQ in Eureka, California and KFTY in Santa Rosa, California. The Television Broadcasting segment owns, or operates under management agreements, 13 stations in California, New York, Washington, Oregon and Alaska. The strategy became to own stations in contiguous markets in order to realize operating efficiencies. In 1998, the company's revenues mounted to more than a quarter of a billion dollars, and it thrived in the world of TV's giant network-owned television operations.[106]

THE CABLE TV MARKET

In 1999, most Americans watched television either through cable (85%), or through a direct to home satellite service, or "wireless" cable (the remaining 15%). Through 1998, the number of cable subscribers continued to grow, reaching 65.4 million as of June 1998—up about 2% in a single year. The total number of cable alternative subscribers also grew—principally DBS—from 9.5 million as of June 1997 to 11.2 million as of June 1998, an increase of over 18%. Thus, in February 1996, President Clinton signed the new telecommunications law that promised de-regulation would lead to vigorous competition and lower rates. The reality is that since then, cable TV rates have increased more than four times faster than inflation. According to the government's most recent figures, cable TV prices rose 7.9% for the 12 months ending in March 1998. General inflation was just 1.4% during the same time period.[107]

The 1996 Telecommunications Act placed the FCC in charge of monitoring rate increases, but gave it a weak stick. Critics from both sides of the aisle agree the Commission has not done an adequate job holding the line. But the FCC should not be blamed. The two leading substitutes (direct broadcast satellites and delivery through local telephone wires) that were expected to rival cable for the consumer's affections, provide real competition and thus lead to lower prices have proven impotent threats. The local telephone companies have largely passed on cable, and instead placed their corporate bets on the Internet. These phone executives learned TV was a whole different business, requiring management skills that were not in their portfolio.

In the 1990s, cable nearly always represented a monopoly. There existed a limited number of additional cable overbuilds in 1998. In communities where the incumbent cable operators face such competition, they respond in a variety of ways, including lowering prices, adding channels at the same monthly rate, improving customer service or adding new services such as interactive programming. The average cable monthly fee has long passed the $1 a day, approaching $40 per month, and Americans have begun to notice. TV used to be "free;" now cable operators openly talk of separating out popular networks (like ESPN) and charging $1 to $4 a la carte per month for that set of sports channels alone. If all those pay channels and pay-per-view events and bills for other choices cable TV offers are added in, this can frequently mean a three-figure monthly bill.[108]

Still the average cable customer was paying more. At the end of 1998, the FCC reported that cable rates rose more than four times the rate of inflation. According to the Labor Department's Bureau of Labor Statistics, between June 1997 and June 1998, cable prices rose 7.3% as compared to a 1.7% increase in the Consumer Price Index used to measure general price changes. A portion of these rate increases is attributable to capital expenditures for the upgrading of cable facilities (up 21% over 1996), an increased number of channels and nonvideo services offered and increased programming costs (license fees increased by 18.4% and programming expenses increased by 20.9%, reported the FCC).[109]

In addition, as cable and DBS charged a monthly fee, cable TV owners gained two streams of revenue. All cable and DBS viewers paid to gain access, and then "paid" again through indirect advertising costs tacked on to the products and services they purchased. Basic cable networks (also shown on DBS) as a group generated about 60% of their revenues from advertising and 40% from license fees paid. As can be seen in Table 4.16, the monies flowing into cable TV grew substantially over the 1990s. Although not shown in the table, so did those flowing to DBS.[110]

Yet, in the 1990s, the cable industry continued to grow in terms of subscriber penetration, channel capacity, the number of programming services available, revenues, audience ratings and expenditures on programming. The cable industry remained healthy financially, which enabled it to invest in improved facilities, either through upgrades or rebuilding. As a result, as the 1990s ended, there continued to be increases in channel capacity, the deployment of digital transmissions that provided better picture quality and the initiation of nonvideo services, such as Internet access. All these improvements meant that cable's more than 65 million subscribers (as of June 1998) had improved channel capacity (some systems, such as Comcast's Orange County, California, system offered more than 120 video channels), and increased audience ratings (nonpremium cable viewership rose from a 38 share at the end of June 1997 to a 41 share at the end of June 1998). Cable system owners in the 1990s formed regional clusters. In 1998, the FCC reported some 117 clusters of systems serving at least 100,000 subscribers. Although the number of clusters declined, the trend for clusters to increase in size continued, and these clustered systems accounted for more than half the nation's cable subscribers.[111]

TABLE 4.16
Cable TV Fees, 1990–1997 (in millions)

	Basic Networks Carriage Fees	Basic Networks Advertising	Premium Channels Carriage Fees	Total
1990	1,100	1,802	1,968	4,870
1991	1,321	2,046	1,939	5,306
1992	1,503	2,339	1,971	5,813
1993	1,935	2,778	2,141	6,854
1994	2,228	3,345	2,412	7,985
1995	2,683	4,036	2,817	9,536
1996	3,121	4,876	3,112	11,109
1997*	3,500	5,850	3,394	12,744

*estimate

Sources: *Veronis, Suhler and Associates Communications Industry Forecast*, 9th ed., July 1995, p. 164; *Veronis, Suhler and Associates Communications Industry Forecast*, 11th ed., July 1997, p. 185.

Upgrading cable systems continued in 1998. For example, Comcast's digital service began to offer customers over 175 digital and analog channels, including 75 to 85 analog channels, 24 premium digital, 30 to 40 digital pay-per-view channels and 40 audio music channels. Partner MediaOne's digital service offered approximately 189 channels, including up to 77 analog, 72 digital video channels and 40 digital music channels. For another example, Cablevision Systems in 1998 began to offer over 100 channels in some of its service areas. As such, average channel capacity for cable systems continued to increase. In August 1997, year-end average cable system analog channel capacity reached 78 channels; by year-end 1998, it was up to 90 channels.[112]

Using Kagan date, the FCC calculated that in 1997 the cable industry invested a total of about $6.8 billion on the construction of plant and equipment, a 21% increase over the $5.6 billion spent in 1996. Expenditures in 1997 included approximately $960 million for maintenance, $700 million for new builds, $1.65 billion for rebuilds, $2 billion for upgrades and $1.46 billion for converters/inventory. Most of the expenditures were for system upgrades and rebuilds. Since 1995, expenditures for the improvement of existing plants has increased approximately 20% each year. In 1995, operators spent $2.5 billion on upgrades and rebuilds combined, whereas in 1996 $3 billion was spent and in 1997 $3.7 billion was spent. In order to offer customers the advanced, two-way services, such as telephony and cable-only Internet access, cable operators must make their systems two-way activated. In 1997, many of the large MSOs spent as much as half a billion dollars each on capital expenditures. For example, by the end of 1998 Cox spent $3.3 billion over five years to upgrade its infrastructure to deploy new services to subscribers. Capital expenditures in 1997 alone for Cox were $708 million. In 1996 and 1997, Comcast spent $800 million to upgrade most of its cable systems nationwide. In 1997, TCI's cable group spent $538 million, as compared to $1,834 million and $1,591 million during 1996 and 1995, respectively. TCI indicated to the FCC, prior to its decision to potentially merge with AT&T, that it planned to spend $1.8 billion between 1998 and 2000 to complete its upgrade program to increase channel capacity, provide high speed data and offer pay-per-view video, but does not include plans for voice telephony.[113]

According to Warren Publishing, cable systems with a capacity of 30 or more channels accounted for 83% of cable systems in October 1997. This represents 8,260 systems nationwide. The percentage of systems with channel capacities of 54 or more channels accounted for 19% of cable systems in October 1997, or 1,886 systems. In October 1998, cable systems with a capacity of 30 or more channels accounted for 85% of cable systems, or 8,328 systems. Cable systems with channel capacities of 54 or more channels accounted for 21% of cable systems in October 1998, or 2,040 systems. In October 1997, 98% of all subscribers were served by systems with capacities of 30 or more channels. Moreover, 58% of all subscribers were served by systems with capacities of 54 or more channels in October 1997. In October 1998, 99% of all subscribers were served by systems with capacities of 30 or more channels and 62% of all subscribers were served by systems with capacities of 54 or more channels in October 1998.[114]

Capacity led to the ability to carry more networks. Cable followed the principles of networking. The number of satellite delivered programming networks increased in 1998 from 172 in 1997 to 245 in 1998. And these were vertically integrated. In 1998,

cable MSOs, either individually or collectively, owned half of 78 national programming services, particularly the most popular ones. Sports programming was offered on
29 regional sports networks, many owned at least in part by MSOs. The number of
regional and local news networks continued to grow, with 25 news services currently
competing with local broadcast stations and national cable networks such as CNN.
At the end of 1998, the FCC reported from Nielsen Television data, that in 1997 the
number of basic cable networks increased by 5, from 126 to 131. The number of premium networks decreased from 18 to 14, but increased by 6 channels during the first
half of 1998, to reach 20 total premium networks. The number of pay-per-view networks remained constant at about 8. (Both premium and pay-per-view channels are
discussed in Chapter 6 because they primarily show movies.)[115]

At the end of 1998, the FCC reported (again using Kagan data) that annual cable
industry total revenue grew 10% in 1997 to reach $30.8 billion. By the end of 1997,
revenue per subscriber grew 8% to $480 per subscriber per year, or $40 per subscriber
per month. Advertising revenues retained by MSOs increased almost 16% in 1997
from $1.7 billion in annual revenue in 1996 to $1.9 billion in 1997. Premium tier
revenues and home shopping revenues grew the least in 1997. Annual revenue from
pay tiers remained constant at about $5 billion per annum. Revenue from home
shopping services was also constant in the late 1990s at about $150 million.[116]

Mergers continued strongly in the late 1990s. The average system size increased
26.5% from an average 79,322 subscribers per system in 1996 to an average 100,353
subscribers per system in 1997. Between January and June 1998, the average number
of subscribers per system transaction was 405,366, a half-year increase of over 300%.
The total number of subscribers affected by system transactions in 1997 increased
43.4% from approximately 8 million subscribers in 1996 to approximately 11 million
subscribers in 1997.[117]

In sum, from the 1970s to the 1990s, cable TV grew rapidly over the years, as
shown in Table 4.17, with the number of franchises increasing from nearly 2,500 in
1970 to well over 11,000 in 1997. This growth slowed in the 1990s, as cable TV has
matured as an industry. Attractive programming fueled this growth. As seen in
Tables 4.18 and 4.19, the leading cable TV networks are ranked by their number of
subscribers; all are familiar to TV fans of the 1990s. These figures, from 71 million
on down, offer the universes that each of the cable networks can reach, in the same
manner that 97 million households with television sets can receive a broadcast network. All the top 20 cable networks are now familiar names, signifying niches of particular interest from ESPN and sports to CNN and news.

CABLE OWNERSHIP

Because of growth and mergers, the leading cable operations (whether MSO or networks) are part of the most important and biggest media companies (as can be seen
in Table 4.20), which provides their parent companies. Although some have no
direct cable holding, all have some operations that appear on local cable systems. For
example, the Sony Hollywood studio (see Chapter 6) makes television programs

TABLE 4.17
Growth of Cable TV Franchises

	Number of Systems
1970	2,490
1975	3,506
1980	4,225
1985	6,600
1990	9,575
1991	10,704
1992	11,035
1993	11,108
1994	11,214
1995	11,351
1997	10,950
1998	10,845

Note: The change in the number of systems operating each year is determined by three factors: 1) New systems that began operation during the year. 2) Older systems coming to the attention of *Television & Cable Factbook* for the first time and therefore included in the total for the first time. 3) The splitting or combining of systems by operators.

Sources: Alan B. Albarron, *Media Economics* (Ames: Iowa State University Press, 1996), p. 93, on Web site at www.ncta.com/glance.html, accessed July 1, 1999.

TABLE 4.18
The Top 20 Cable Networks and Their Owners, 1998

Cable Network	Owner(s)	Households with Access
1. Discovery Channel	TCI, Cox, Newhouse	75,300,000
2. TBS	Time Warner	75,000,000
3. C-SPAN	Major MSOs	74,100,000
4. Fox Family Channel	News Corp	73,000,000
5. ESPN	Disney	73,000,000
6. CNN	Time Warner	73,000,000
7. Lifetime	Disney, Hearst	72,500,000
8. TNT	Time Warner	72,400,000
9. A&E	Disney, Hearst, NBC	72,000,000
10. The Weather Channel	Landmark Communications	71,600,000
11. CNN Headline News	Time Warner	69,800,000
12. USA Network	Seagram	69,677,000
13. MTV	Viacom	69,400,000
14. AMC	NBC, Cablevision	69,000,000
15. The Learning Channel	TCI, Cox, Newhouse	67,500,000
16. QVC	Comcast, TCI	67,412,000
17. Nickelodeon	Viacom	67,000,000
18. TNT	Time Warner	66,600,000
19. VH1	Viacom	64,500,000
20. CNBC	NBC, Dow Jones	64,000,000

Source: National Cable Television Association, on Web site at www.ncta.com/glance.html, accessed July 1, 1999.

TABLE 4.19

Top 10 Programming Services by Subscribership & Ownership

(Rank—Network—Number of Subscribers, in millions—Ownership Interest)

 1. TBS—74.4—Time Warner
 2. ESPN—73.8—Disney
 3. Discovery Channel—73.7—TCI, Cox, Newhouse
 4. USA Network—73.7—TCI, Seagram
 5. CNN—73.7—Time Warner
 6. C-SPAN—73.3—underwritten by major cable MSOs
 7. TNT—73.1—Time Warner
 8. Nickelodeon/Nick at Nite—72.6—Viacom
 9. Fox Family Channel—71.8—News Corproation
10. A&E—71.7—Disney, Hearst, NBC

Notes: In addition to cable, other services such as MMDS (wireless cable) and DBS (direct broadcast satellite) distribute these signals. Superstations are not included in this ranking.

Source: Paul Kagan Associates, "Cable Program Investor," August 14, 1998, p. 11.

TABLE 4.20

Parent Companies of the Top Cable Television Operations

Name and Rank	Cable Holdings
1. Time Warner	MSOs, CNN: Headline News, CNN/SI, CNN Airport, CNNfn, HBO, Cinemax, TNT, TBS, the Cartoon Network, Turner Classic Movies (TCM) and portions of BET, networks
2. Walt Disney	ESPN, ESPN2, ESPNEWS, and Disney Channel, and shares of A&E, the History Channel, Lifetime Television networks
3. News Corporation	The Family Channel, fx, Fox Sports, Fox news networks
4. Viacom	MTV, Showtime, Sundance, TV Land, The Movie Channel, Nickelodeon, VH-1, Comedy Central networks
5. TCI	MSOs, shares of Bravo, Home Team Sports, BET, AMC, Fox Sports, the Learning Channel, the Travel Channel, QVC, Starz!, Encore, Discovery, and numerous regional sports networks
6. Sony	No Holdings
7. General Electric	MSNBC, CNBC, and partial shares of AMC, Bravo, A&E, the History Channel, the Independent Film Channel and regional sports networks
8. Westinghouse	The Nashville Network, Country Music Television, Eye on People networks
9. Gannett	No Holdings
10. General Motors' Hughes	No Holdings
11. Comcast Corporation	MSOs, QVC, E!, Outdoor Life and sports regional networks
12. Seagram	Partial ownership of USA Networks
13. Hearst	Interests in Lifetime, A&E, History, New England Cable News networks
14. McGraw-Hill	No Holdings
15. US West Media Group	MSOs, Outdoor Life network
16. New York Times	No Holdings
17. Tribune	Superstation WGN, ChicagoLand 24-hour local news networks
18. Washington Post	MSOs
19. Cox Enterprises	MSOs, portions of Outdoor Life and Discovery networks
20. Bloomberg	No Holdings

Source: "25 Top Media Groups," *Broadcasting and Cable*, July 7, 1997, pp. 22–28.

TABLE 4.21
Television as Part of Global Top Media Corporations

Company	TV Industries Owned
1. Time Warner	Production, Broadcast, Cable, DBS
2. Walt Disney	Production, Broadcast, Cable
3. Bertelsmann AG	European Production, Broadcast, Cable, DBS
4. News Corp.	Production, Broadcast, Cable, DBS
5. Viacom*	Production, Broadcast, Cable
6. Sony Entertainment	Production, Broadcast, Cable
7. AT&T Broadband & Internet Services	Cable
8. Seagram's Universal Studios	Production, Broadcast, Cable
9. CBS*	Production, Broadcast, Cable
10. Comcast	Cable
11. Cox Enterprises	Production, Cable, DBS
12. General Electric's NBC	Production, Broadcast, Cable
13. Gannett	Broadcast
14. Globo Organization	Non-U.S. television production, broadcast & cable
15. Pearson	European Production, Broadcast
16. EMI	No television
17. CLT/UFA	European Production, Broadcast
18. United News & Media	European Production, Broadcast
19. Fuji Television Network	Asain Production, Cable
20. Cablevision Systems	Cable

*prior to CBS merger.
Source: "The Global 50," Variety, August 23–29, 1999, pp. A47–A58.

through its Columbia Television unit, and these shows are part of the programming from NBC down to TBS to the Family Channel. The others are typically owners of television stations but are known for some other media enterprise—such as McGraw-Hill, a major magazine and book publisher (see Chapter 2) with TV stations, and the New York Times, a major newspaper publisher (see Chapter 1) that also owns TV stations.[118]

In sum, as can be seen from these tables, these are parts of some of the biggest companies in the media business in the United States. Table 4.21 was complied by Variety magazine at the start of Fall 1997. This shows the globalization of the television business, both broadcast and cable, in the United States. Only Britain's EMI and Rank companies do not have some ownership presence in television.

Yet cable begins basically as a monopoly. The cable television franchise provides a classic example of a media monopoly. The core of the cable television operation, where the programming meets its customers, is the basic local franchise. And cable television franchises are monopolies (except in rare cases of so-called overbuilding, where two cable systems are built covering the same area) for their legally defined area. That monopoly forms the economic power of the cable television business, through government protection. Once one owner obtained a legal franchise, for a defined period of time no competitor can arise to challenge the franchise holder. To take advantage of significant economies of operation, corporations collect franchises under one corporate umbrella, creating a multiple system operator (MSO), where a number of cable franchises are collected together under a common owner and reap significant economies of scale. An MSO can have a single accounting department, a single sales force, a single repair division, for example, and spread these and other fundamental costs across the various franchises, and thus have a lower per franchise cost with constant revenues and hence higher profits. In the 1990s, a handful of cable television's MSOs controlled the vast amount of cable systems and hence monopolized the cable television business.[119]

The top multiple system operators are shown in Table 4.22 and June 1997 is a typical indication of the trend of the late 1990s. The key point is that the leading companies—here TCI (in 1998 taken over by AT&T) and Time Warner—dominated by a wide margin, followed by the US West Media Group, Comcast, Cox and Cablevision Systems. With cable in two thirds of the households in the United States, TCI was the clear leader in 1997 with about one in four subscribers. Time Warner was second with nearly the same. By 1999, AT&T would own TCI, and be in a contest with Comcast to take over what had been the US West Media group, by then labeled MediaOne. The names may have been different, but the concentration of power in the MSOs was even more pronounced—all based on the typical cable legal monopoly.[120]

The prizes these MSOs sought were the cable ownership in the suburbs of America's biggest cities. The top 10 biggest cable systems are expectedly found in or around major urban areas such as New York City, Chicago and Los Angeles, and owned by the leading cable companies such as TCI, Time Warner, MediaOne, Comcast, Cablevision Systems and Cox Communications. The top 700 (of 10,000) systems captured half of all customers, and were owned by these major MSOs. Economic logic dictated that such local monopolists will ultimately combine because it becomes possible to economize with economies of scale. As mergers take place, these and other fixed costs can and are amortized over larger revenue bases. Simply put, this means greater profits, a classic case of scale economies. The original cable wildcatters, who erected a large antenna to bring in distant signals, cashed out rather than try to continue to compete. In short, the fragmented cable industry (with sim-

TABLE 4.22
Top MSOs and Households Reached

Name and Rank	Address	Subscribers (in millions)	Homes Passed	Basic Penetration
1. AT&T Broadband & Internet Services	Denver, CO	16.2	25.0	65%
2. Time Warner Cable	Stanford, CT	12.9	21.0	61%
3. Comcast	Philadelphia	5.4	7.6	61%
4. Cox	Atlanta	5.1	7.4	69%
5. Adelphia	Coudersport, PA	4.9	7.6	65%
6. Charter	St. Louis	3.9	6.1	64%
7. Cablevision Systems	Woodbury, NY	3.4	5.1	67%
8. Falcon	Los Angeles	1.1	1.8	63%
9. Insight Communications	New York City	1.0	1.6	64%
10. Jones Intercable	Engelwood, CO	1.0	1.6	63%

Source: "Top MSOs Own 90% of Subs," *Broadcasting & Cable*, May 24, 1999, pp. 34–44.

ilar corporate nameplates like Cablevision Industries, Cablevision Systems and Continental Cablevision) gave way to a handful of corporate giants named AT&T and Time Warner.[121]

CABLE TV'S "BIG THREE"

AT&T fundamentally restructured the cable MSO industry in 1998 and 1999 when it first took over TCI and then MediaOne to envelop more than one third of all cable customers. AT&T's offer to purchase MediaOne represented at the time the biggest unsolicited bid for any company to that date in U.S. history. AT&T spent a record $4,900 per subscriber, about 50% more than the typical price per subscriber among recent acquisitions. In less than a year, AT&T grew from having no presence in cable TV to become the largest company in cable history, having amassed a concentration of power in the mass media that has not been seen since the late 1930s when NBC and CBS controlled radio.[122]

The implications of the AT&T record acquisitions were important and numerous. AT&T acquired access to roughly 35% of the nation's cable customers or about 22 million households. AT&T Chairman C. Michael Armstrong avoided a costly, drawn-out bidding war for MediaOne by crafting a multifaceted agreement with both Comcast and Microsoft. And he promised AT&T would not sit still, continuing its quest to fashion deals so as to further dominate the cable, telephone and Internet worlds past the year 2000. Armstrong bet that the 21st century would be a world of "bundled digital communications" without separate local telephone, long distance, cable and Internet providing companies. AT&T would supply all four needs through one digital wire. This would attract millions of new customers, and Armstrong figured AT&T's revenue increases would need to be measured in the billions of dollars.[123]

Whereas MediaOne may not be a familiar name as a cable company, it is better understood as the cable holdings of Baby Bell US West (formally the US West Media Group), which came to power after a 1996 deal in which US West purchased Continental Cablevision for $5.3 billion. Under the agreement, Continental added 4.2 million customers in 20 states to US West Media Group's already sizable holdings of 2.9 million cable customers in 33 states. The US West Media Group, with headquarters in Denver, instantly became a $4 billion cable giant; at the time, Continental, based in Boston, was the nation's third largest MSO. But the combining of the two companies into the US West Media Group did not go well. Continental Cablevision's founder Amos B. Hosteller, Jr. quit rather than move to Denver; Hosteller had founded the company and run it from Boston for 30 years. His experienced management team left with him, so US West Media Group started as a major player with limited experience in managing cable systems. The hoped-for synergy between cable TV and telephone voice and data services seemed far off in the future.[124]

One move was obvious. It was no surprise when US West in late October 1997 spun off US West Media Group. The US West Media Group became MediaOne

Group. It was this company in flux—with 5 million customers in 20 states—that attracted Michael Armstrong as an easy and simple (but expensive) means to add to AT&T's already sizable cable empire.[125]

That empire was based on a 1998 deal whereby AT&T acquired TCI, then the largest cable MSO in the United States (it had been throughout the 1990s). Surely the FCC's approval of the AT&T purchase of TCI in February 1999 ranked before the AT&T acquisition of MediaOne as the most important deal in cable TV history. The $57 billion transaction united the leading long distance telephone company with the leading MSO. By March 1999, days before the announcement of the MediaOne deal, AT&T formally announced the TCI deal was complete, ahead of schedule. TCI, with nearly 11 million customers and approximately 18 million homes passed, was but an AT&T division, which it called AT&T Broadcast & Internet Services. The acquisition of TCI gave AT&T for the first time a direct "broadband" connection to millions of customers' homes on lines that the company owned and operated. By weaving TCI's powerful, broadband cable network with AT&T's Worldwide Intelligent Network, AT&T began company plans to deliver integrated telephony, entertainment and high speed Internet access services and a host of new communications capabilities to customers. Michael Armstrong appointed Leo J. Hindrey, Jr., former president of TCI, as head of AT&T's Broadband & Internet Services division, headquartered in Denver, Colorado.

For the full year 1998, the TCI Group had revenues of approximately $6 billion, 32,000 employees and approximately 191,600 share owners. In 1998, AT&T had revenues of $53.2 billion, assets of $60 billion, 3.2 million shareholders and about 107,800 employees. Separately, TCI combined Liberty Media Group, its programming arm, and TCI Ventures Group, its technology investment unit, to form the new Liberty Media Group. The new Liberty Media Group was issued separate tracking stock, and although Liberty Media will be a 100% owned subsidiary of AT&T, it will be accounted for as an equity investment. Under the tracking stock arrangement, all of Liberty Media's earnings (or losses) will be excluded from the earnings available to the AT&T common shareowner, and it will be primarily managed and governed by a separate operating board under CEO (and the person most responsible for building TCI) John Malone.[126]

AT&T also acquired valuable TCI shares in multiple in program suppliers—from Black Entertainment Network to the Discovery Channel, from the Travel Channel to the Learning Channel, from QVC networks to the Home Shopping networks, from Starz! to Encore, from Court TV to Encore. Although TCI rarely owned all of these ventures, it had a key voice in their operation. Second, TCI also had led the way in clustering, so that, for example, nearly all cable TV systems in the San Francisco Bay area were controlled by one firm, and operations costs were far lower per subscriber than if these same sized systems were scattered across the United States. The Bay area's 1.5 million cable TV customers used the same 1-800 number to schedule installation and complain about power outages. TCI saved millions of dollars annually with these and other economies of scale.[127]

John Malone deserves credit (or damnation) for the development of TCI. More people have probably heard of NBC's founder David Sarnoff or CBS's originator

William S. Paley, yet John Malone deserves to join their company. He took cable from CATV in 1973 to the merger with AT&T. When Malone negotiated the selling of TCI to AT&T, he became AT&T's largest single stockholder with a 1.5% share. And Malone retained control over Liberty Media Group, TCI's arm for cable programming with everything from big stakes in the Discovery Networks (49%), QVC (43%), USA Networks (21%), Fox Sports (50%), BET (34%), Telemundo (25%), among others. (This is the same John Malone, discussed earlier, who then negotiated a deal with News Corporation to become that company's third largest shareholder.)[128]

Malone's career reflects the rise of TCI. Born March 7, 1941, in Milford, Connecticut, Malone was trained as a scientist, earning a Bachelor of Science in Electrical Engineering and Economics at Yale, a Master of Science in Industrial Management from Johns Hopkins and a PhD in Operations Research from Johns Hopkins in 1967. He began his career in 1963 at Bell Telephone Laboratories in economic planning and research, but moved toward management by taking a position at McKinsey & Company, a consulting firm. In 1970 he moved to become Vice President at General Instrument Corporation, and then to Jerrold Electronics, a general instrument subsidiary where he was president. Here he came into contact with the emerging cable TV business, joining TCI in 1973 with founder Robert Magness. From 1973 through 1996, Malone purchased more cable systems than any person in history, and fashioned TCI into the clear industry leader. In 1996, Malone began to phase out of the day-to-day operations, selecting Leo Hindery, Jr. as his successor.[129]

Hindery represented a new generation of cable leaders. Hindery came to TCI as an MBA-trained executive, as part of one of Malone's many deals during the 1970s and 1980s. Hindery founded InterMedia Partners in 1988 and in time fashioned his own mini-TCI, serving more than 930,000 subscribers in the Southeast. He then sold out to join Malone. As they prepared to sell out in 1997, Malone and Hindery were running an enterprise with revenues approaching $10 billion per annum, with assets on the books of more than $30 billion. Yet the mid-1990s were not good years for TCI because the company was not growing by the leaps and bounds of the 1980s. Malone and Hindery tried to counterpunch, but no clear dominant strategy emerged as 1997 ended. Investments in telephony and the Internet seemed to be going nowhere, only absorbing vast amounts of money away from the bottom line. The promised 500 channel information superhighway seemed a long way in the future. The proposed, and much heralded, 1993 merger with Bell Atlantic continued to haunt them. It was no wonder that Malone jumped at the chance to sell out to AT&T, while retaining control of Liberty Media Group; Hindrey sought to run AT&T Broadband & Internet Services.[130]

Time Warner ranked, in 1999, just behind AT&T as the largest cable MSO. Time Warner had only about half AT&T's customer base, but with 13 million this was no small company. The two were partners in many deals, so it was sometimes difficult to separate them. For example, in Texas they formed two 50-50 joint ventures in Houston; Kansas City Cable Partners was another 50-50 venture co-managed by several hundred thousand customers. Across the nation they seemed forever swapping systems, always seeking the optimal cluster. TCI had swapped cable systems in central and northern Florida serving about 200,000 customers for Time Warner's 170,000 customers in Avalon, New Jersey, and Bucks County, Pennsylvania. TCI had traded nearly 100,000 customers in systems in Portland, Biddeford and Wells, Maine, and Racine, Wisconsin, for Time Warner's equal number in Champagne, Urbana, DeKalb, Rochelle and Danville, Illinois. Subscribers in TCI's Schenectady, Amsterdam and Central Square, New York, systems were swapped for Time Warner customers in Cannonsburg, Pennsylvania, St. Louis and Sheridan, Wyoming. By the late 1990s, Time Warner was concentrating on clustering in and around New York City, Tampa, Florida, Raleigh, North Carolina, Charlotte, North Carolina, Austin, Texas, Los Angeles, Milwaukee and Rochester, New York.[131]

Time Warner was similar to AT&T in its vast vertical control of programming. As analyzed in Chapter 6, it controlled pay movie channels HBO and Cinemax. But Time Warner was also the parent of news leader CNN, entertainment attractions' TBS—the SuperStation, TNT, the Cartoon Network and Comedy Central, as well as specialized channels such as BET and QVC. And these Time Warner cable networks were doing well in 1999. For example, TNT was reaching more than 70 million homes through cable and satellite delivery with its movies and sports programming, and had passed Seagram's USA Network as the most watched on cable TV in terms of both total households and of the key age 18 to 49 demographic group that is so vital to advertisers. Launched to 17.6 million households in 1988, which was the largest launch in cable TV history, TNT started as a movie network, and then in 1989 acquired rights to NBA basketball. In 1998, its re-running of NBC's hit *ER* attracted record audiences. TNT also drew high ratings with its original made-for-cable movies.[132]

Internationally CNN was the most popular channel. But all the alphabet soup of Time Warner cable programming was available nearly everywhere on the planet. But this should not mean that there is a seamless international oligopoly. The giants often fought. In July 1997, for example, after much struggle Time Warner cable finally agreed to carry the new Fox News channel, owned by Ted Turner's rival Rupert Murdoch. Time Warner agreed only as part of a deal that gave Murdoch valuable access to Time Warner MSOs around the United States, and Time Warner in turn would gain access to Murdoch's vast network of international satellite television systems in Latin America, China and elsewhere. Under the agreement, New York's Mayor Rudolph Giuliani, who had earlier tried to intervene on Murdoch's behalf, would turn over one of the five cable channels the city now controls for educational programming to Time Warner, which would then provide that channel to the Fox news channel. This only came after months of bitter accusations, which spilled out into the main stream press through the coverage of this "local" story by the *New York Times*. Time Warner as a programmer rarely sat still. When it converted TBS from Superstation (an over-the-air independent channel beamed to systems outside Atlanta, its home market) to a basic cable channel, it added a second stream of income by charging cable operators. The estimated new revenue would generate an additional $100 million in cash flow for Time Warner by 2000.[133]

The goal on the end was to add services, charge customers more and increase revenues. For example, late in August 1997, Time Warner announced it would begin to add 14 channels in New York City systems during the fall 1997. The new services are part of a $400 million network upgrade in Manhattan, Queens and Brooklyn over four years. The new channels include a package of 11 programming services ranging from sports to arts, called MetroChoice, which the company will sell for $1.95 per month for customers who take its basic and standard service. The company also will provide, at no extra cost, the new movie channel Starz, and HBO 2 and Cinemax 2 to customers who already receive HBO and Cinemax. Thirty networks vied for three slots as part of a $400 million high tech upgrade of Time Warner's 1.1 million subscriber New York cable system. For a glut of new cable channels struggling to survive, a slot in New York, with its influential audience of media buyers, critics and advertisers, was an incomparably invaluable asset. Executives from Viacom, Disney and dozens of other aspirants made pilgrimages to New York City to make elaborate pitches to Time Warner's Gerald Levin. Such pitching will continue as there are more networks vying for too few real slots. Only expensive upgrades to fiber optics, which will happen slowly because of great expense, will change that. Such bargaining power added profits and economic muscle to Time Warner's synergistic use of its cable MSOs and cable programming channels.[134]

In March 1999, **Comcast Corporation** sought to become a player in cable TV (i.e., a true rival equal to AT&T and Time Warner) by taking over MediaOne Group Inc. in an all stock deal valued at about $50 billion. As analyzed earlier, Comcast lost that deal, but did firmly entrench itself as the third leading MSO. This climaxed a five-year acquisition spree by Comcast, beginning in 1994 with the purchase of QVC, the shopping channel ($1.4 billion). In the process, Comcast absorbed both Jones Intercable, Prime Communications and E. W. Scripps' cable systems, as well as parts of the AT&T–MediaOne merger. Brian Roberts ran the ever-expanding Comcast, and his father, Ralph Roberts (Comcast's founder), remained as Chairman of the Board. Here was a rare example of a family enterprise that remained in the family. The Roberts only shared that ownership control with the Microsoft corporation, which in 1997 infused $1 billion in cash into Comcast in exchange for an 11% share of the company. This was Microsoft's biggest outside investment ever and was meant to reinvent the controversial software giant; it also meant that Comcast would be the most closely watched of cable's top MSOs in 1999 as the site for interactive cable TV modem experiments.[135]

Comcast Cable, long based in Philadelphia, will remain a key cable MSO power based on cable's ultimate cluster—stretching from Philadelphia to Baltimore to the suburbs of Washington, DC. Comcast was also vertically integrated, with SportsNet, a 24-hour regional sports network with a customer base of roughly 2.5 million viewers in the Philadelphia region, an outgrowth of a company investment in the Philadelphia Flyers professional hockey team, and the Philadelphia 76ers professional basketball team. It was anchored by airing of these teams' games, as well as those of the Philadelphia Phillies baseball team. In late September 1997, Comcast's successful shopping channel, QVC, began to telecast from its new state-of-the-art facility, Studio Park, which allowed the electronic retailer to expand and refresh the product offerings. Also in September 1997, Comcast launched digital TV to customers in portions of the company's Orange County, California, cable system, and areas of Comcast's Philadelphia market. Finally, Comcast was a leader in cable's expansion as an Internet provider through Comcast@Home.[136]

In late October 1997, it was announced that Brian Roberts had gained a controlling number of Comcast shares. These were passed on to him by Ralph Roberts, the company's founder and Chairman of the Board. The deal gave Brian Roberts a majority of the voting power in the family holding company, Sural Corporation, which controlled 82% of the Comcast voting power. Ralph Roberts would continue in his position as chairman; Brian Roberts would take on more responsibility as president. From headquarters in downtown Philadelphia, in 1969 Comcast ranked 369th on the *Fortune* 500 listing. There was also Comcast Cellular with 762,000 customers in Pennsylvania, New Jersey and Delaware, and two key indoor sports arenas in Philadelphia: the CoreStates Center and CoreStates Spectrum. There was no doubt the Roberts had built a regional media empire; but, had it been a mistake to let AT&T outbid it for MediaOne? Would the Roberts be satisfied as a regional powerhouse? Would AT&T or Time Warner's superior system holdings and programming assets overwhelm Comcast?[137]

TWO LONGTIME CABLE PRETENDERS

AT&T, Time Warner and Comcast ranked as the Big Three in the cable MSO business in 1999. Together they controlled more than half of all the customers subscribing to cable TV in 1999. The remainder of the top 10 controlled about one third as many. The Big Three also owned shares in nearly all the important cable TV networks. They exemplified vertical integration. But there existed, at the time, two pretenders who by copying the AT&T, Time Warner and Comcast model, sought to challenge them. Neither entry was as big or as vertically integrated, but these companies did have programming interests and MSO size advantages. A long list of small MSOs still exemplified cable's past of Mom-and-Pop system operators. But, Cox and Cablevision Systems are about equal in size, and with a major merger could challenge.

Cox Communications, Inc., collecting cable MSOs, cable programming and future broadband applications, was controlled by Cox Enterprises, an extension of its newspaper and television empire. So, like Time Warner, Cox was a diversified media company. This privately held company was like Comcast in that it was family owned. But Cox Enterprises was far more famous for its other media products, including a score of daily newspapers (led by its flagship the *Atlanta Constitution*), a dozen broadcast TV stations and more than 20 radio stations. Diversification spread beyond the media as Cox controlled Manheim Auctions, the world's largest auto auction company. Cox Enterprises was organized in 1968, but the company dated back to 1898 when founder James M. Cox acquired his first newspaper in Dayton, Ohio. By 1999, annual Cox Enterprises' gross revenues tallied nearly $5 billion per annum, making it one of the largest private companies in the United States.[138]

With its purchase of TCA Cable in 1999 for $3.26 billion in cash and stock plus the assumption of $736 million in debt, Cox added 883,000 subscribers to its collection of cable systems totaling about five million subscribers. Cox then moved to number four. Cox was set to trade systems so as to cluster and cut costs. In 1999, most of Cox's systems were scattered. Its network holdings were not among the biggest that the Big Three controlled. Cox owned shares of cable programmers, including the Speedvision Network (automotive, marine and aviation-related programming), GEMS Television (Spanish-language programming targeted at women outside the United States), the Outdoor Life Network, the Product Information Network (for Infomercial distribution), the Discovery networks (the Discovery Channel, the Learning Channel, Animal Planet and other ancillary businesses), the Viewer's Choice pay-per-view service and the Sunshine Network offering regional sports programming in Florida.[139]

Cox Communication bet that the future growth lay in upgrading its systems into an advanced broadband network of coaxial and fiber optic lines. It would start in Hampton Roads, Virginia, Omaha, Nebraska, New Orleans, Phoenix, San Diego and Orange County, California. Its Orange County operation was the nation's first cable system delivering the complete full-service package of analog and digital cable television, local and long distance telephone, and high speed Internet access, all over a single network. Will technical innovation be enough so that Cox will not be overwhelmed by AT&T and company? Or will Cox have to partner with one or more of the giants?[140]

Cablevision Systems ranked an equal to Cox in the cable business, but was much smaller overall. Although located in 19 states, its MSO concentration was found in the New York City suburbs. Headquartered in Long Island, New York, Charles Dolan organized Cablevision Systems in 1973 as he correctly figured that the maximum profits in cable MSO ownership and operation lay in the suburbs. He focused on Long Island's Nassau and Suffolk counties, as well as Fairfield, Connecticut, northern New Jersey, and Westchester County, New York, even though these regions received as many over-the-air television stations as any sector of the United States. Suburbanites wanted more, Dolan reasoned, and they had the discretionary income to pay for additional TV channels.

Dolan also reasoned that he needed a wealthy partner to fund Cablevision Systems' expansion. In 1988, Dolan made a major move and took on General Electric's NBC as a minority partner. General Electric had recently purchased NBC, and prior to that had helped Dolan finance the expansion of Cablevision Systems. Funded by GE, Cablevision Systems and NBC moved into cable network programming in a major way, building American Movie Classics and Bravo. These are its cable programming success stories. Cablevision Systems and NBC also controlled sports programming in the New York City region, owning not only Madison Square Garden and its cable programming outlet, but also basketball's Knicks and hockey's Rangers. Finally, there was the innovative local 24-hour local news on cable TV begun in 1986 as News 12 Long Island. With prize winning series on breast cancer, drug abuse and Alzheimer's disease, a brand image was established. During election campaigns, News 12 Long Island regularly staged candidate debates and gained a sizable suburban audience.[141]

But whereas Cablevision Systems accomplishments were considerable, and ownership extensive, it was far closer to Cox in subscribers held, and far behind the Big

Three. The question for the future lay with expansion possibilities. Would Cablevision Systems continue (funded by General Electric) along the lines of Comcast (as regional power), seek to expand nationally like AT&T, or take some other road? In 1999, all that was certain about Cablevision Systems was that it was set to go broadband to seek more revenues by offering Internet access. Like other cable entrepreneurs, Dolan promised 500 channels, movies on demand and interactive video entertainment and information.[142]

SMALLER CABLE MSOs

After AT&T's TCI, Time Warner, Comcast, Cox and Cablevision Systems, there are smaller MSOs, just one fifth the size of an AT&T, and more likely one tenth the size of a top MSO. "Minor" MSOs are those over 275,000 customers. The discussion begins with analysis of Adelphia and Charter because, as of 1999, these two seemed poised to join the previous five to form a "Big Seven." But this is only a guess, because deals and mergers were underway—inspired by the fear of falling further behind AT&T.[143]

Adelphia Communications Corporation had begun as a pioneer cable company, located in Coudersport, Pennsylvania, and slowly grew over the years as a pure MSO. And, in April 1999, Adelphia announced it was purchasing Harron's cable systems for $1.17 billion. In March 1999, Adelphia announced it was buying Century Communications Corporation for $3.6 billion in cash and stock, creating an MSO equal to Cox and Cablevision Systems MSOs, which then stood at five million customers. Prior to this merger (at the end of 1998 and the beginning of 1999), Adelphia had acquired three smaller cable MSOs, and so along with the Century deal, doubled the size of the company. The Rigas family was seeking to stay close to the Big Three purely as an MSO, forging their medium-sized family-owned operation into an MSO power. As 1999 ended, the questions remained unanswered. Would Adelphia sell out? Would it further expand? Did its spree of takeovers mean that the 21st century would begin with all small cable MSOs selling?[144]

Charter Communications had almost matched Adelphia's acquisitions spree by 1999. But if there had to be a bet on one cable company that might challenge the Big Three, it would be Charter. This company was backed by Paul Allen's wealth, which he had accumulated as a founder of Microsoft. Allen, with no ties to cable before April 1998, spent $3 billion to acquire Marcus Cable, then one of the top 10 MSOs. Marcus' franchise areas were primarily in Alabama, Indiana, California, Wisconsin and Texas. Three months later, in July 1998, Allen announced the acquisition of Charter Communications, another top 10 MSO, for $4.5 billion. Charter's primary locations were in California, Alabama and Texas. Nearly a year later, in May 1999, Allen purchased Fanch Communications, a Denver cable company, in a deal valued at just over $2 billion, and Falcon Cable TV, for another $2 million in cash and stock plus the taking over of $1.6 billion in debt. As May 1999 ended, Allen named the collection Charter, and suddenly his accumulated operations were collectively serving more than five million cable subscribers. Charter thus matched Cox, Cablevision

Systems and Adelphia as the fourth largest cable MSO. No one believed Allen was finished, and Cox, Cablevision Systems and Adelphia were not sitting still. Who would grow? Who would stay put? Who would sell out? No one was sure.[145]

Smaller operations were simply trying to survive. These typically had started as pioneer CATV operations during cable's early days, and hung on with original (usually family) ownership. They had not sold out as of early 1999, but ranked as candidates for acquisition by one of the seven major companies already analyzed. See Table 4.23 for examples of smaller systems.

TCA Cable TV, headquartered in Tyler, Texas, represented one of the bigger minor companies, with nearly 900,000 subscribers at the start of 1999. Like nearly all minor operators, TCA concentrated on small town America—in TCA's case, communities in Arkansas, Louisiana and Texas. A generation before, in 1981, the late cable pioneer Robert M. Rogers merged a dozen or so small MSOs into TCA. In 1999, the average TCA system had about 11,000 subscribers, yet the 75 or so systems added to annual revenues of $308 million, net income of $38 million and assets of $721 million. These figures represented rounding errors for AT&T, but did rank TCA among cable's elite. The problem was, as 1999 ended, how to simply survive in the new world dominated by AT&T. TCA joined rather than fight, and so went into joint deals with AT&T broadband. It rarely took on debt, but financed upgrading its systems for Internet access through current cash flow. Would these conservative measures ensure survival? That is doubtful. A better bet would be for TCA and smaller companies to cooperate as effective divisions of an AT&T based on joint deals.[146]

Massillon Cable TV was far smaller than TCA, ranking in 1998 as the 73rd top MSO with 45,000 subscribers. Here was a private, family-owned operation, a seeming anachronism in the world of daily mergers. Massillon Cable was more reminiscent of cable's past than its present and future. It had two systems in Massillon and Wooster, Ohio. Richard W. Gessner and his family run the company and own a majority share of its stock. They acquired the original franchise for Massillon in 1966 and they established cable TV in Wooster in 1967. They stuck with these two systems, and followed industry operational trends. Thus, by 1999, Gessner was building a hybrid fiber optical coaxial network for Massillon and Wooster. The new converter boxes also included an interactive program guide and WorldGate, a program

TABLE 4.23
Ranked Order of Important Minor MSOs

Name and Rank by Subscribership	Address	Subscribers	Homes Passed	Basic Penetration Rate
Cable One	Phoenix	735,000	1,000,000	74%
Mediacom	Middletown, NY	725,000	1,045,000	69%
Bresnan Communication*	White Plaines, NY	658,000	967,000	68%
MultiMedia Cablevision	Wichita, Kansas	515,500	835,500	62%
Fanch Communications*	Denver	503,000	755,000	67%
Service Electric Cable TV	Mahanoy, PA	293,000	409,000	72%

*Before taken over by Charter Communications
Source: "25 Top MSOs," *Broadcasting & Cable*, June 16, 1997, pp. 40, 42.

that provided Internet service. Massillon did maintain a Web site, but it is impossible to be sure if it will survive. Surely Massillon Cable will be a test case.[147]

Eagle Communications, ranked as the 96th top MSO with 13,000 subscribers as of March 1998, provided at least one option—diversify in small town America, in communities that AT&T simply would not find profitable enough to consider. Located in Hays, Kansas, in the western third of the state, under President and Chief Operating Officer Robert E. Schmidt, the company owned and operated seven cable systems in 1999. Flagship operations were Hays (population 18,000) and Goodland (population 5,000). Eagle simply extended its media operations, which had focused on radio stations in western Kansas, Missouri and Nebraska. Eagle knew the local market, and figured the big players would not be able to or care to compete for such small profits. As with other tight oligopolies (e.g., music analyzed in Chapter 5), there was room on the edges for small operations. This will continue in small towns for cable as the 21st century begins.[148]

PURE CABLE PROGRAMMERS

As demonstrated earlier, the common advantage the larger MSOs have was monopoly control of thousands of customers who had no alternative for cable TV than the local franchisee. Based on this monopoly control, the MSOs analyzed acquired more systems, and thus exploited sizable economies of scale. These MSOs also clustered, and again took advantage of cost savings. The final advantage they possessed was vertical control of programming by owning (or sharing in the ownership) popular programming. But two important companies reasoned that this last advantage—control of programming—was enough to maximize profits from investments in cable TV. Michael Eisner of Disney, Rupert Murdoch of News Corporation and Sumner Redstone of Viacom passed on MSO ownership, and played the cable game strictly though programming. (Indeed, Viacom had owned systems, but sold them, to focus on its programming strategy.) News Corporation, Disney and Viacom were analyzed earlier as owners of Fox, ABC and UPN broadcast networks. Here the focus is on their cable programming strategy.

Disney and Viacom took the cable programming strategy by focusing on sports and music. Viacom concentrated on music's MTV and Nickelodeon and Disney purchased ESPN in 1995 as part of its acquisition of ABC/Capital Cities. No better or more successful programming strategy can be found than ESPN. In September 1979, as cable television reached but 14 million homes, ESPN arrived to offer advertisers and sports fanatics a network far more specialized that ABC, CBS or NBC. A year after the first cablecast, ESPN was available 24 hours a day. Beginning in early 1982, ESPN began making huge strides as it signed with the National Basketball Association for 40 regular season and 10 playoff games. So, in August 1983, ESPN topped WTBS as the largest cable network in the United States, reaching over 27 million homes, available in all 50 states. The network even started to turn in profits. Another turning point came in 1987 when ESPN signed rights to televise 13 NFL games. The league was convinced because ESPN by then reached half of all cable homes, and was the first cable network to do so. In 1989, ESPN International debuted, and early in the 1990s, ESPN started cable casting Major League Baseball. By 1995, when Disney acquired it as part of its acquisition of ABC/Capital Cities, ESPN had diversified with a radio network, a second cable network (ESPN2 or to its fans the deuce), an Internet site, SportsZone and its own sports award show, the ESPY's. Disney, in turn, fashioned ESPN into four networks, adding the acquired Classic Sports Network and ESPNews, and launched the *ESPN Magazine*. All products and services were aimed at men, particularly young men.[149]

In response to ESPN's successes, with a three-year string of investments, Rupert Murdoch turned the Fox Entertainment into a partial owner of all but four of the nation's 23 regional sports networks. Fox thus could offer advertisers a set of regional packages that almost matched the national reach of ESPN. Thus, if an advertiser sought an audience of young men, the advertisers could go to ESPN or buy the Fox regional package. To advertisers, Murdoch offered one-stop shopping for most of the sports teams in three major professional sports—an alterative to ESPN for advertisers who wanted to buy into baseball, hockey and NBA basketball. Ad this to Fox's exclusive contract for the NFC professional football plus ownership of Los Angeles Dodgers baseball, this sports strategy gave Disney and Fox a powerful strategy for operating in cable TV. MSOs, even those as powerful as AT&T, needed Disney and Fox programming. Here was a powerful alternative to starting with the monopoly owner that rested in cable systems. But News Corporation was also intertwined with the major MSOs. For example, Liberty Media Group has long been a Murdoch partner, helping Murdoch launch his regional sports strategy. And with Liberty having investments in other cable companies, as owning 10% of the cable leader Time Warner, and in programming services like the Discovery Network, in which Cox and other cable companies also own a stake, this meant that Liberty (formally owned by AT&T) was a partner with Fox.[150]

The programming side represented profitability as long as the player controlled top programming exclusively. In 1996, for example, the Walt Disney Company's ESPN made $550 million, generating more profit than either the NBC, ABC or CBS networks, according to a study done by the Wall Street firm Schroder Wertheim & Co. (In fact, Time Warner's HBO, CNN and TNT, Viacom's MTV and Nickelodeon all made more money than CBS did in 1996.) As late as the mid-1980s, a cable network that could make more profits than a major broadcast TV network would have been unthinkable. But as cable penetration rates have grown, and cable rates have risen so fast, and advertising revenues have risen, cable networks of the 1990s added millions of dollars to the bottom lines of their corporate owners. These profit statements glowed, and Viacom, News Corporation and Disney executives and owners figured that, rather than invest the necessary billions in cable upgrades and acquisitions, they would simply play the programming game, based on ownership of a Hollywood studio and of key cable programming channels. Indeed, cable's top companies—AT&T and Time Warner—were betting on both sides of the cable equation: MSO's monopoly basis and cable programming's beach head monopoly power.[151]

The best measure of this is in the escalating prices being paid for existing networks. For example, the USA Network and the Sci Fi networks regularly draw audience shares measured in one or two percentage points. But, in September 1997, Seagram was willing to pay more than $1.7 billion for them. Established cable networks are not easily duplicated because the increase in "shelf space" promised with the "coming" of 500 channels never came to be—always remaining somewhere in the future. Wall Street analysts figured that buying an existing cable TV network was best seen as a "real estate play," nailing down a slot in a limited universe. There seems to be a limit on the number of players in any one niche, such as BET for African Americans or Lifetime for females. (In 2000, a second female target cable channel called Oxygen, is due to come online, and it will test if two of this genre can survive.)

To further appreciate and measure the economic power of the entrenched cable networks requires a look at how successful they are at passing along price increases. Early in 1998, the National Football League renegotiated it contracts with cable TV's ESPN as part of an $18 billion set of deals. Owner Walt Disney Company planned a 20% increase in ESPN fees because of the power of this network and it was far easier to extract increases through increases to MSOs than to charge more in advertising rates. ESPN agreed to pay $600 million per year for eight years, two and half times the previous rate, for NFL football games on Sunday nights. If the increase were spread evenly over the homes presently with cable TV, each would have to pay about $4.65 a year for ESPN alone. The average cable bill would rise by 1.5% per annum. After adding in other cost increases, a 10% to 20% rate increase will be passed onto customers within the current industry framework of oligopoly power.[152]

A CABLE TV ALTERNATIVE

Cable TV did so well in the 1980s and 1990s that entrepreneurs sought alternative delivery systems. One true alternative did arise: direct to home satellite service, or as it is more commonly known DBS. Use of satellites to deliver programming directly to the home was given form in 1980 by the Communications Satellite Corporation, which applied in December 1980 to the FCC for permission to design and launch a DBS system to reach the rural United States. This would be the first of a number of proposals filed with the FCC in the early 1980s when the potential for DBS seemed bright. None succeeded during the 1980s; indeed, at one time, DBS was mocked as standing for "Don't Be Silly." This first era crested when in 1984 United Satellite Communications began operation using a Canadian satellite, funded by the Prudential Insurance Company. But this venture signed up only 10,000 subscribers; in 1985 it closed up shop, nearly $50 million in debt. Through the later 1980s and into the early 1990s, the only "working" DBS system was to bootleg cable and network distribution systems. Rural (and rich) Americans bought a professional 9-meter dish, and took in the signals being transported to cable systems and between broadcast networks and their affiliates. In response, networks began to scramble their signals.[153]

But, in the 1980s, satellite to home service did not represent the only alternative to cable TV. For two decades the Baby Bells seemed set to innovate a cable alternative. They already had wires into homes; they were already upgrading these systems;

they were seeking to expand their markets. And they had deep pockets—through the 1980s nearly six times as much revenue per annum as the biggest MSO. This innovation never came to be; as of 1999, the entry by the Baby Bells into cable TV was tentative at best. Consider the example where middle western Baby Bell Ameritech introduced cable TV service in Chicago suburbs to present an alternative to TCI. By 1999, Ameritech New Media had either acquired or started only 87 cable systems, serving but 200,000 subscribers. At that time, AT&T, not the Baby Bells, was leading the telephone industry into cable. And AT&T needed to acquire cable systems in order to bridge that last mile, and offer enough bandwidth of services of telephony, mass entertainment and the Internet.[154]

A second alterative in the 1980s also seemed promising, but never panned out. Multichannel Multipoint Distribution Service (MMDS) or wireless cable also could be found in limited areas. Only one million households signed up. MMDS never had offered a comparable number of services, and so the wireless cable industry's total revenues maximized at less than a half billion dollars per annum. In 1998, Standard & Poor's lowered the debt rating on all wireless cable companies to CCC+, and Heartland Wireless, a large wireless operator, to D, stating that wireless cable never was or would be a viable competitor. In 1998, CAI Wireless and Heartland Wireless, two of the nation's largest, filed for bankruptcy.[155]

Even the deep-pocketed Baby Bells tried and failed with MMDS. For example, in November 1997, BellSouth launched a digital version of this microwave service in New Orleans, offering more than 160 channels. This roll out promised superior technology—based on a new Zenith wireless box converter—to bring digital before cable (or for that matter broadcasters) came up to speed with digital television. New Orleans seemed ripe for such an experiment because of its flat terrain, which is a necessity for line of sight microwave signals. Yet success was not achieved.[156]

A third possible alternative did not come along until the late 1990s. Electric utilities also have wires into the home, and during 1998 and 1999, several electric utilities announced and rolled out cable-like services. In particular, Tacoma City Light began offering cable service in Tacoma, Washington. In Maryland, Virginia and Washington, DC, PEPCO has formed a joint venture with RCN, named Starpower, to offer video, telephone and Internet services in the Washington, DC area. But this just offered a tentative beginning, and the electric utilities faced all the significant barriers to entry that had already defeated the Baby Bells and MMDS companies. Unless some technical or regulatory change entered the equation and reduced these barriers, it is unlikely that electric utilities will offer more than limited alternatives in selected areas.[157]

DBS

The second era of DBS innovation commenced in July 1994, when DirecTV, backed by the deep pockets of Hughes and its owner General Motors, began selling dozens of channels that could be accessed through an easy-to-install pizza-sized dish. Within a couple of years, four million, mostly rural, Americans had signed up; one study found that early adopters cut their video cassette renting by 70%, and instead watched movies on DBS—a classic case of the substitution effect. Because this analysis showed that about 34% of VCR households account for about 75% of total tapes rented, the introduction of DBS was successfully off and running. The 1990s class of DBS services permitted households to receive digitally compressed signals, up to 200 per customer. Without digital compression, only 32 channels would come through, and DBS (as it was during the failed innovative attempts in the 1980s) would not be perceived as a product equal to cable, but more like MMDS and its limited channels. DBS expanded choice with the full complement of the various cable services, but also by offering additional sports feeds and pay-per-view movies.[158]

At first, cable operators did not fear the new DBS. Innovation had failed in the past; only rural Americans without access to cable systems signed up. But later suburbanites began to sign up, and by June 1998, DBS counted 7.2 million subscribers, representing 9.4% of all "multichannel video" subscribers. That is, cable had about seven of eight multichannel video customers, DBS had 10%, and all the others took away the rest. The FCC reported, late in 1998, that 2.2 million of the 3.6 million net new cable, Baby Bell, MMDS and electric utility video subscribers in 1998, or almost two thirds, chose DBS. Consumers continued to report that the biggest drawbacks of DBS service were the difficulties associated with the provision of local broadcast signals and the up-front cost of equipment and installation. But Congress seemed to be addressing the former problem as 1999 ended, and as for the latter, prices continued to fall.[159]

Table 4.24 lists the top four DBS companies in the United States in 1997. But with DirecTV's purchase of first USSB, and then PrimeStar, the DBS industry in 1999 stood at two firms: DirecTV, which is large with the vast majority of the customers, and Echostar, which was struggling to simply stay in business. It would seem to be a safe bet that DirecTV would emerge sometime after 2000 as the lone DBS alternative.[160]

In 1999, **DirecTV** ranked well atop the DBS industry, with about 90% of the business. Beginning in 1994, Los Angeles-based Hughes built on its experience as a manufacturer of communications satellites. DirecTV served as a natural extension of Hughes' existing business. DirecTV enlisted manufacturer Thomson of France to develop the 18-inch dishes and receivers in return for an exclusive contract to man-

TABLE 4.24
The Top DBS Companies (in millions)

Company	1998	1997	1996 Revenues	1995 Revenues
DIRECTV	$3,500.0*	$1,663.2	$912.0	$313.0
PrimeStar	**	$1,097.0	720.0	350.0
US Satellite Broadcasting	**	$456.6	292.0	108.0
EchoStar	$400.0*	$358.8	211.4	163.9

*author's estimates from company reports
**taken over by DIRECTV
Sources: *Advertising Age*, August 18, 1997, p. S5; *Advertising Age*, August 18, 1998, p. S5.

ufacture and sell the first million. Congress then helped. In the 1992 cable act it required cable programmers to charge equitable rates to DBS as a way to boost an alternative to cable. DirecTV did so well that Hughes began selling off its military contractor and electronics supplier divisions and focus exclusively on commercial satellite operations. Still, by the close of 1997, DirecTV had posted more than $300 million in losses, and it did not begin to show profits until 1999.[161]

DirecTV had become a profitable powerhouse, and the only true alternative to cable. At first DirecTV had competition, but USSB of St. Paul, Minnesota, a unit of Hubbard Broadcasting, shared transponders since 1994, and sold to DirecTV in 1998. In January 1999, DirecTV took over PrimeStar Partners, owned by the leaders of the cable industry, in a deal valued at $1.82 billion in cash and stock. Only EchoStar remained. DirecTV had sought to become a monopoly in the fashion that cable systems had long been for most customers, and succeeded. In 1999, DirecTV became DBS's virtual monopoly, and the nation's third largest multichannel video provider, only behind AT&T and Time Warner. PrimeStar's departure signaled that its cable owners, which formed PrimeStar to stake a position in DBS, were confident enough in cable to abandon DBS to DirecTV. Cable owners were confident that their stakes in key programmers would place DBS at a competitive disadvantage.[162]

DirecTV focused on differentiating its product from cable. In 1999, DirecTV took direct aim at TV's sports junkies (i.e., young male viewers), offering exclusive delivery of all of the men's NCCA basketball tournament games up to the Final Four, and all of the out-of-market NFL games. DirecTV also continued to aim to woo movie fans by offering channel after channel of pay-per-view films. To make installation easier, it began to subcontract with Bell Atlantic and even small nonmajor cable companies (e.g., Austin, Texas-based Classic Cable, Chicago-based Anderson-Eliason Cable Group and Sikeston, Missouri-based Galaxy Telecom). DirecTV also has jumped on the Internet bandwagon by offering a satellite-delivered high speed Internet access service with a telephone return path. This service allows up to a 400 kbps downstream connection, which is slower than cable modems, but is more than seven times faster than analog telephone modems. This service was available independent of DBS service or, with DirecDUO, a dual-functioning DBS antenna, consumers can receive both video programming and DirecPC services. In 1999, DirecTV signed with AOL to provide that service via satellite.[163]

DirecTV also partnered with Hollywood. In December 1997, for example, DirecTV signed with Time Warner to produce MTV-like fare exclusively for DirecTV. Late in 1997 it was also announced that DirecTV would begin to air original TV movies and series made by such Hollywood producers and directors as Francis Ford Coppola and John Landis. The 184 hours of fresh TV movies and series began to run on DirecTV during the summer 1998 as pay-per-view programming costing subscribers $2.99 for two-hour blocks for such fare as a remake of *Dr. Jekyll and Mr. Hyde* by Francis Ford Coppola's American Zoetrope company. Like HBO, Showtime, TNT and other major cable networks did since the 1980s, DirecTV seemed determined to boost its brand by producing or acquiring unique, high quality programming, hoping in the long run to become a programming brand of choice.[164]

But, in the short run, it had been the 1999 purchase of PrimeStar Partners that sealed DirecTV's near monopoly position. PrimeStar, formed by the leading MSOs, led by TCI and Time Warner, was created simply to prevent DirecTV from taking over. PrimeStar struggled for five years, and then with cable operators satisfied that DBS would not create more than one serious rival, they sold out. In 1994, the situation looked very different because PrimeStar had been up and running for weeks before DirecTV's June 1994 launch. With its cable partners, there is no lack of programming. But by 1997, business was so bad (in part because operators never push PrimeStar) that the partners sought to sell out to News Corporation. But that deal, and others, fizzled. So did a 1997 national marketing campaign to promote its new, more potent 225-channel, high power service. In the end, TCI sold to AT&T. This cable giant, however, did not want PrimeStar Partners, which was sold to DirecTV.[165]

EchoStar Communications Corporation remained the sole competitor for DirecTV. Always underfunded compared to Hughes, EchoStar's founder Charles Ergen, a Tennessee-bred entrepreneur, sought to counterpunch his bigger and better financed rival as best as he could. Lower prices and "free" installation tempted some. But on the programming side, DirecTV always came up with superior offerings because programmers wanted to distribute through the DBS system with the vast majority of the customers. Ergen continued to try new strategies, but fell further behind. He pleaded with Congress for help, and marginally remained in business in 1999. In the long run, unless Congress does something or an antitrust action is taken, it seems likely that EchoStar will not survive. The DBS industry that seemed to offer cable customers several choices in 1994 will soon be reduced to one choice.[166]

TELEVISION'S OWNERSHIP FUTURE

By 1999, the 1996 Telecommunications Act had not delivered its promised greater competition, greater choice and lower prices for TV service. The broadcast network oligopoly had expanded, but the bottleneck of a few networks continued. In cable, with the domination of AT&T and a few cable MSOs (nearly all operating legal franchise monopolies), the industry had gotten more rather than less concentrated. And DBS had effectively been reduced to a single company. The Baby Bells, MMDS or electric utilities failed to offer competition. Most Americans lived in areas with a small number of broadcast stations, and about one quarter of all households stuck with them. In multichannel video, people could choose from the local cable monopoly or DirecTV. This duopoly was better than what had existed in 1990, but only because it was not a monopoly. Would anything change this situation? Two factors, technical change and government intervention, seemed to offer hope.[167]

Technical Change

Better images through digital television might offer some hope to break the oligopolistic deadlock in the TV industry. But it looked as if when these sharper pictures came to the home, they would be supplied by existing enterprises. DirecTV led the way, although in 1999 few had purchased the digital TV set needed to actually see the superior pictures. The cost of a digital set in 1999 was a minimum of $5,000, or about 20 times that paid for a similarly sized analog set. Given the history of the electronics industry, no one figured these high prices would last, but according to most predictions it would be at least a decade before a majority of households owned a digital TV set. As was the case with VCRs and computers, the price would need to fall well under $1,000 before digital TV can expect to become a mass medium in the home.[168]

In 1999 the cable industry was still working to upgrade its systems, so that it had the required extra capacity. Plans varied. In 1998, the FCC reported that TCI executives, when surveyed, stated that they figured digital video would present a widely appealing product that would achieve high penetration among its customers. By the time AT&T acquired TCI, there were 500,000 customers able to access digital TV, the vast majority without the needed sets. AT&T's Michael Armstrong publicly repeated the same optimism, but privately did not order TCI's upgrading to speed up. By the end of 1998, Cox was marketing its digital product in all nine of its major cluster markets, led by Orange County, California, where it had achieved 10% penetration on a 252,000 subscriber system. As of August 1998, Comcast was offering digital service in Sacramento, Philadelphia, Baltimore, parts of Middlesex, Union and Essex Counties in New York, New Jersey and Indianapolis. In May 1998, Time Warner began testing digital cable in its Austin, Texas, system. It should be well after 2000 before the majority of cable customers can and will be able to see digital pictures.[169]

Although cable was on its own as to the speed and commitment to digital, broadcast stations were required to convert or lose their licenses. In April 1996, the FCC granted broadcasters licenses for digital television because they promised to begin to telecast advanced television. The starting date was November 1, 1998, with only a few thousand sets in people's homes. The FCC plan only demanded that, by the turn of the century, residents of the nation's 10 largest markets be able to watch digital TV. (Some smaller city stations also planned to convert as well.) In 1999, the Paul Kagan forecast organization extrapolated from this, and projected that only 1 in 40 would have a digital TV by 2001, one quarter of households will have come on board by 2005, and still half the nation will still be watching "old fashioned TV" in 2009. So, on a determined schedule, all broadcast stations will convert by 2010. If that date of completion comes and goes without stations meeting their obligations, then the FCC will more than likely extend the "drop dead" date, and the process of transformation will be extended. Because the broadcasters kept their guaranteed licenses—for free—only greater profits will drive them to convert.[170]

The other heralded technical change that might disrupt the TV oligopoly has been the impact of the Internet. As millions began to use the Internet on a regular basis at home, entrepreneurs sought to introduce technologies to offer the Internet through the television set using set-top box and a program such as WebTV. In 1998, the FCC reported that access to the Internet over cable generally has become easier, and that service (using cable wires to transmit Internet material) will come to be an expected cable service in the future. This would simply represent a new market for current oligopolists. But the acceptance of service like WebTV seems more doubtful. WebTV Plus offered programming not available to regular viewers and required additional equipment such as a personal computer with a television tuner add-on card and an up-to-date version of Windows. TV seems to be an entertainment system, whereas the Internet is an information provider. The marriage of these two separate functions will require at least a generation of learning to re-think the use of both.[171]

Despite the increase in interest in Internet video, the medium is not seen as a direct competitor to traditional video services at this time. Currently, Internet video is used primarily for news, sports clips and other brief video excerpts because of the inferior quality of the picture and the need for viewers to have the proper software and hardware. Webcasters hope that streaming will eventually improve so that they can offer movies, sports and television shows, but industry observers believe video streaming is unlikely to compete with traditional video media in the foreseeable future. We are talking about fundamental change in media use, and that process (i.e., the coming of movies or the use of the PC) requires a generation. The *Wall Street Journal* headlined the right question: "When a TV Joins a PC, Will Anybody Be Watching?"[172]

Antitrust Concerns

Technological hopes aside, we have seen three parts of the TV industry. The broadcast networks and their affiliates have long operated as an oligopoly, collectively working through their trade association the National Association of Broadcasters. But today the broadcast networks' oligopoly power has lessened because they form just a part of the cable TV universe. Most people watch the broadcast networks through cable delivery rather than through broadcasting. Thus, the key question in 1999 was: Can cable operators acting alone or acting together exercise market power in the purchase of video programming? This upstream market tends to be regional or national because programmers attempted to develop networks much broader than the local cable franchise area. Observation during the 1990s indicated that MSOs had an incentive to coordinate their decisions in the upstream market for the purchase of programming on a national or regional level. The more concentrated the market, the more likely that buyers will possess some market power (or "monopsony" power). The MSO source of power will continue.

Vertical integration, or the extent to which programming services are affiliated with cable operators, will also continue. MSOs will continue to seek to control the flow and price of valued inputs through exclusive distribution contracts or monopsonistic pressure, and in turn to deter entry and competition in the marketplace, and limit the diversity of cable programming, thereby reducing the number of voices available to the public. In the 1990s, the number of both vertically and nonvertically integrated national satellite-delivered programming services increased significantly. In 1998, of the 245 national satellite-delivered programming services identified, the FCC found that some 39% were vertically integrated with at least one MSO, about the same as in 1997. That this seems stable masks that new entrants, such as the Golf Channel analyzed earlier, were offset by more vertical integration.

Looking at the situation from the MSO side, cable MSOs, either individually or collectively, owned 50% or more of 78 national programming services, up from 47% in 1996. MSOs simply took control in the most popular services, so that in 1998, in terms of prime time ratings, 9 of the top 15 video programming services were vertically integrated.

Vertical integration in national cable programming continues to involve principally the largest cable system operators. Ownership interests in each of the 95 vertically integrated services were held by any one of seven of the nation's eight largest cable MSOs. Many of these programming services were jointly held by multiple MSOs. In 1998, TCI, the largest MSO, held ownership interests in 28% (67 of 242) of all national programming services. Time Warner, the nation's second largest MSO, held ownership interests in 12% (30 of 240) of all national programming services. This, the FCC correctly identified, constituted a key portion and source of the huge company's power.[173]

As of the mid-1998, the FCC also noted the following horizontal relations. AT&T's TCI had a 10% ownership interest in Time Warner, Inc. and all of its subsidiaries, including a 10% ownership interest in Time Warner Cable and a 10% ownership interest in Time Warner/Turner programming services. MediaOne, later acquired by AT&T, had a 25% ownership interest in Time Warner Entertainment, L.P., which included a 25% ownership interest in Time Warner Cable. Furthermore, Comcast Corporation had acquired Jones Intercable, then the nation's eighth largest MSO with 1.5 million subscribers—and so on. The major cable companies work together in joint deals, thus expanding their collective power and raising barriers to entry.[174]

Downstream local markets for the delivery of programming also remained highly concentrated with cable at 85.3%; DBS at 12.1%; MMDS at 1.3%; and special systems for multiple family dwellings, usually apartments or condominiums at 1.2%. While DBS continued its expansionary trend of gaining new subscribers, the market share of cable decreased from 87% in June 1997 to 85% in June 1998. Using the market shares for each technology, the estimate of the Hersfindahl–Hirschmann Index (HHI) is 7,015, a decrease from the HHI of 7,567 for 1997. Nevertheless, an HHI of 7,015 remained several times greater than the 1,800 threshold at which a market may be considered "highly concentrated."[175]

Clustering, a process by which MSOs consolidated system ownership within separate geographical regions, added to the anticompetitive effects in the 1990s. Whereas clustering provided a means of reducing costs, and attracting more advertising, clustering also significantly raised barriers to entry to potential overbuilders. As already noted, in the 1990s, MSOs continued to undertake system mergers, acquisitions, divestitures, swaps and joint ventures to maximize regional "clusters" of contiguous cable systems. During 1997, there were more than 100 such cable transactions with a total market value of approximately $22.2 billion involving approximately 11 million subscribers. A similar pattern continued in 1998. This tendency toward larger clusters reflected ever greater economies of scale. Between 1996 and 1997, the FCC found that the number of clusters and subscribers in the two smallest size categories (100,000–199,000 and 200,000–299,000 subscribers) decreased, and in the largest size category (over 500,000 subscribers), the number of clusters increased by 60% and the number of subscribers increased by 54%. TCI, for example, aggressively pursued clustering, and so at the end of 1996 in the Chicago metropolitan area, there were five cable operators with large subscriber bases: TCI, Time Warner, MediaOne, Jones and Multimedia, in addition to Ameritech, Prime and Triax. Since September 1997, TCI has announced a number of swaps and acquisitions through which it has gained control of the systems previously owned by Time Warner, MediaOne, Jones and Multimedia that would allow TCI to control more than 90% of the Chicago metropolitan market.[176]

System-for-system "swaps," or trades, enable MSOs to increase their regional clusters while minimizing financial outlays and avoiding capital gains taxes. Here again, TCI led the way. In the 1990s, the largest proposed system-for-system swaps were between TCI and Time Warner, TCI and MediaOne, TCI and MultiMedia, and TCI and Insight. In 1998 alone, TCI agreed to swap some of its systems in Florida, Hawaii, Maine, New York, Ohio, Texas, Illinois, Oregon, Missouri, New Jersey, Pennsylvania, Florida, Wisconsin and Georgia, involving more than one million customers.[177]

Cable and broadcast oligopoly concentration, however, pale in comparison to the monopoly problem of DBS. When in 1999 DirecTV bought up the last of its serious competition, this new TV industry, which was supposed to lead to a more competitive marketplace, simply added a single service to the already oligopolistic market. That the oligopoly has long been a problem has been identified in the work of Sylvia M. Chan-Olmsted. These forms of concentration have led her to conclude that the cable business was moderately concentrated to the same degree as broadcast television, only growing more concentrated. Chan-Olmsted saw a path toward more and more concentration. Her study was done before the 1996 Telecommunications Act and the resulting mergers, but based on her analysis of the 1992 cable act more concentration is certain. And DBS is adding to this concentration problem.[178]

Rising DBS prices should be expected. The power of the entrenched industry can be seen in its continual ability to raise prices to customers. In one 1996 survey for systems in and around Washington, DC, it was found that rates were going up from 7% to 15% per annum, well beyond the inflation rate of 3%. Spiraling price increases began in the late 1980s. Responding in October 1992, Congress, over President George Bush's veto, passed a law designed to restrain rate increases. The FCC issued regulations and hired 160 new employees in an effort that promised to cut customer's prices by an average of 17%. Prices fell for a time, but then the industry realized there was no real competition from the Baby Bells. It began to exercise its monopoly power and prices were pushed up once again. Double-digit price increases became the norm, signaling how little was the impact of the telephone companies' promised cable service, and of the small reality of direct to home from satellite offerings.[179]

The outcomes of oligopolistic corporate behavior depends on how many firms there are, how big they are in relation to each other, past corporate histories and sometimes the whims of individual owners. When they cooperate, they act like a monopolist; yet cooperation comes only with a handful of issues, such as expanding the marketplace possibilities for all or keeping out new and powerful competitors. Oligopolists work together to fashion positive governmental policies toward their industry, and thus to keep out potential competitors. Nothing unites a media oligopoly more than a threat from the outside. Simply put, oligopolists tend to seek and agree on an informal set a rules for "competition," restricting the game of profit maximizing to themselves. Oligopoly will define the ownership of TV into the future.[180]

NOTES

1. James Walker and Douglas Ferguson, *The Broadcast Television Industry* (New York: Allyn & Bacon, 1998), pp. 121–134; Patrick R. Parsons and Robert M. Frieden, *The Cable and Satellite Television Industries* (New York: Allyn & Bacon, 1998), pp. 1–11.

2. Alan B. Albarran and John Dimmick, "Concentration and Economics of Multiformity in the Communication Industries," *Journal of Media Economics* 9.4 (1996), pp. 41–50.

3. See *Broadcasting & Cable* magazine's review of "Top 25 Television Groups," April 19, 1999, pp. 38–58; Christopher Farrell and Richard A. Melcher, "The Lofty Price of Getting Hitched," *Business Week*, December 8, 1997, pp. 36–37; Albarran and Dimmick, pp. 41–50; Robert W. McChesney, *Corporate Media and the Threat to Democracy* (New York: Seven Stories Press, 1997). Data on recent mergers from Securities Data Corporation as cited in Leslie Wayne, "Wave of Mergers Is Recasting Face of Business in U.S.," *New York Times*, January 19, 1998, pp. A1, A13.

4. This corporate data is entered consistently for the end of 1997, and will be out of date as you read this. For special situations we have updated through 1998–1999. For the history of any company, see *Hoover's Guide to Media Companies* (Austin, TX: Hoover's Business Press, 1996). Even better, for a contemporary capsule of the company, see Hoover's Web site at www.hoovers.com. Know that for detail—without charge—one needs to consult the Web site of the U.S. Security and Exchange Commission, known as EDGAR, at www.sec.gov.

5. A fine yearly summary of TV usage can be found in the annual editions of Edward Papazian's *Television Dimensions*, from Media Dynamics, Inc., New York City. See, for example, Edward Papazian (ed.), *Television Dimensions '97* (New York: Media Dynamics, Inc., 1997), pp. 17–40. For current comparative statistics among broadcast, cable and satellite delivered TV, see also the Web site of cable television advertising bureau at www.cabletvadbureau.com.

6. Douglas Gomery, "The Centrality of Media Economics," *Journal of Communication* 43.3 (Summer 1993), pp. 190–198.

7. This history is drawn from Andrew F. Inglis, *Behind the Tube: A History of Broadcasting Technology and Business* (Boston: Focal Press, 1990), particularly Chapters 4 (monochrome television) and 5 (color TV); and Walker and Ferguson, particularly Chapters 1, 2 and 6.

8. Referring, of course, to one of the first successful situation comedies in the 1950s, "I Love Lucy."

9. See Compaine, et al., *Who Owns the Media?* 2nd ed. (White Plains, NY: Knowledge Industry Publications, 1983), p. 306.

10. B. Owen, *Economics and Freedom of Expression: Media Structure and the First Amendment* (Cambridge, MA: Ballinger, 1975), p. 111.

11. For one analysis see J. Busterna, "Diversity of Ownership as a Criterion in FCC Licensing Since 1965," *Journal of Broadcasting* 20 (Winter 1976), pp. 101–110.

12. FCC, "Policy Statement on Comparative Broadcast Hearings," 1 FCC 2d 393, pp. 329–338.

13. *Broadcasting* (February 5, 1979). Both men spoke at a symposium on the future of networks at UCLA.

14. W. Baer, et al., *Concentration of Mass Media: Assessing the State of Current Knowledge* (Santa Monica, CA: Rand Corp Publication R-1584-NSF, September 1974), p. 10.

15. Federal Trade Commission, Bureau of Competition, *Proceedings of the Symposium on Media Concentration*, 2 Vols. (Washington, DC: Government Printing Office, December 1978).

16. H. H. Howard, "Multiple Broadcast Ownership: Regulatory History," *Federal Communications Bar Journal* 27.1 (1974), pp. 1–70 (pp. 8–18 cover much of the following section).

17. *United States v. Storer Broadcasting Corp.* 351 US 192 (1956). These regulations were never waived, a rare thing in FCC ownership policy.
18. FCC, Network Inquiry Special Staff. *New Television Networks: Entry, Jurisdiction, Ownership and Regulation* (Washington, DC: Government Printing Office, 1980), Vol. 1, pp. 437–440.
19. W. G. Manning and B. Owen, "Television Rivalry and Network Power," *Public Policy* 24 (Winter 1976), pp. 55–56.
20. U.S. House of Representatives, Committee on Interstate and Foreign Commerce, *Network Broadcasting*, Report . . . 85th Cong. 2d Sess., House Report 1297 (January 27, 1958).
21. *Broadcasting* (September 30, 1957), p. 31.
22. M. I. Hamburg and S. N. Brotman, *Communications Law and Practice* (New York: Law Journal Seminars-Press, 1996), §3.09[1].
23. Ibid., §3.09[4].
24. S. M. Besen and T. G. Krattenmaker, "Regulating Network Television: Dubious Premises and Doubtful Solutions," *Regulation* (May/June 1981), pp. 27–34.
25. B. M. Owens, et al., *Television Economics* (Lexington, MA: Lexington Books, 1974), p. 19.
26. See Doug Halonen, "Historic Rewrite Finally Passes," *Electronic Media*, February 5, 1996, pp. 1, 54; and Patricia Aufderheide, *Communications Policy and the Public Interest: The Telecommunications Act of 1996* (New York: Guilford Press, 1999).
27. The history of cable TV in the United States is the subject of Chapter 1 of Robert W. Crandall and Harold Furchgott-Roth, *Cable TV: Regulation or Competition?* (Washington, DC: The Brookings Institution, 1996), pp. 1–23. For the official industry version see the Web site of the National Cable Television Association at www.ncta.com.
28. See S. M. Besen and R. W. Crandall, "The Deregulation of Cable Television," in T. G. Krattenmaker, *Telecommunications Law and Policy*, 2nd ed. (Durham, NC: Carolina Academic Press, 1998), pp. 509–522.
29. *United States v. Southwestern Cable Co.*, 392 U.S. 157 (1968).
30. FCC, "Horizontal and Vertical Ownership Limits for Cable Television," MM Docket No. 92-264, 1993 FCC LEXIS 5406 (1993), as found in Krattenmaker, pp. 639–648. Enforcement of the 30% rule for cable ownership was still not being enforced in 1999, pending resolution of a Federal District Court ruling that such limits were unconstitutional. (*Daniels Cablevision v. United States*, No. 92-2292, D.D.C., released September 16, 1993). The vertical ownership limits were upheld by the Court.
31. See Robert G. Picard (ed.), *The Cable Networks Handbook* (Riverside, CA: Carpelan Publishing, 1993) for a host of examples of the growth of the alphabet soup on new cable channels.
32. See U.S. General Accounting Office, *Telecommunications: National Survey of Cable Television Rates and Services* (1989); "GAO on Cable," *Broadcasting*, August 7, 1989, p. 30.
33. Mike Mills, "Telecommunications Bill Passed," *Washington Post*, February 2, 1996, pp. A1, A15.
34. For a fine survey of the important programs in the history of cable TV before the middle of 1997, see the staff produced "10 Shows That Made Cable," *Electronic Media*, July 21, 1997, pp. 33, 36–43. Data on spending comes from the National Cable Television Association's extensive Web site at www.ncta.com.
35. For an earlier list, see David Waterman and Andrew A. Weiss, *Vertical Integration in Cable Television* (Cambridge: MIT Press, 1997), pp. 24–32. See Paul Kagan Associates' yearly reports, in this case: "Economics of Basic Cable Networks" for ownership surveys and the NCTA Web site for up-to-the-minute data at www.ncta.com.
36. See "Top 20 Cable Networks" found on the NCTA Web site at www.ncta.com.
37. Walker and Ferguson, pp. 33, 58, 79–80.
38. Jenny Hontz and Cynthia Littleton, "Webs Making Their Own Way," *Variety*, July 14–20, 1997, pp. 25, 29.
39. Kyle Pope, "Big Spender," *Wall Street Journal*, May 21, 1999, pp. A1, A6. Our essay is about ownership of TV in the United States, but certainly there are implications and interactions with TV elsewhere in the world as examined in Manual Alvarado's "Selling Television," in Albert Morin (ed.), *Film Policy: International, National, and Regional Perspectives* (London: Routledge, 1996), pp. 62–71.

40. See "Impact of Sports Programming Costs on Cable television Rates," GAO Report, RCED-99-136, June 1999.

41. Kyle Pope and Stefan Fatsis, "NBC, Turner Sports May See Less Profit Showing More Games in New NBA Pact," *Wall Street Journal*, November 12, 1997, p. B9; Stefan Fatsis and Kyle Pope, "TV Networks Rush to Splurge on NFL Deals," *Wall Street Journal*, December 12, 1997, pp. B1, B8. See also Web site at www.wsj.com.

42. Ronald Grover, "If These Shows Are Hits, Why Do They Cost So Much?," *Business Week*, April 13, 1998, p. 36.

43. Mike Reynolds, "TNT, Nick Take '97 Ratings Crowns," *Cable World*, January 5, 1998, pp. 1, 26. See Web site at www.cableworld.com.

44. Douglas Gomery, "Media Ownership: Concepts and Principles," in Alison Alexander, James Owers and Rodney Carveth (eds.) *Media Economics* (Hillsdale, NJ: Lawrence Erlbaum Associates, 1998), pp. 45–52; Kyle Pope, "How Many TV Newsmagazines Are Too Many?," *Wall Street Journal*, May 30, 1997, pp. B1, B2. See also Web site at www.wsj.com.

45. Advantages are also generated by cable TV networks as well explained in Waterman and Weiss, pp. 58–61, 74–75.

46. Kyle Pope, "Why TV Ad Prices Are Rising Even as Viewership Is Falling," *Wall Street Journal*, May 12, 1997, p. B1; Kyle Pope, "Networks Sell Themselves as Broadcast Brands," *Wall Street Journal*, April 2, 1997, pp. B1, B6. See also Web site at www.wsj.com.

47. Indeed, one "dirty secret" of the TV business is that for decades while the networks themselves showed little profit, their "owned and operated" stations—fed by the very same networks—regularly generated profit margins of 50% or better. In 1997, even Fox's owned and operated stations were able—for the first time—to generate $1 billion in revenues, with half that flowing directly to the bottom line.

48. Diane Mergimas, "Networks Brainstorm for New Income Sources," *Electronic Media*, February 23, 1998, pp. 1, 31; Kyle Pope, "Fox Pushes ABC to Bottom in 'Sweeps' Ratings," *Wall Street Journal*, March 6, 1998, p. B2; Steve McClellen, "Nets Are Big 4's Weakest Link," *Broadcasting & Cable*, March 2, 1998, p. 4. See also Web site at www.wsj.com.

49. Kyle Pope, "ABC Official Urges Sweeping Change, Such as Fees for Some Network Fare," *Wall Street Journal*, April 7, 1998, p. B9. See also Web site at www.wsj.com.

50. See Web site at www.univision.net.

51. Joe Schlosser, "View From the Top," *Broadcasting & Cable*, January 18, 1999, pp. 36–74; Steve McClellan, "King Brothers To Split . . . Stock, That Is," *Broadcasting & Cable*, December 8, 1997, p. 70; Kyle Pope, "The Talk of TV: Oprah Stays, King World Pays," *Wall Street Journal*, September 16, 1997, pp. B1, B14. See also Web site at www.wsj.com.

52. Kyle Pope, "In CBS-King Deal, Keep an Eye on the Players," *Wall Street Journal*, April 2, 1999, p. B1; Seth Lubove, "Oprah, Barbra, and Roseanne," *Forbes*, November 3, 1997, pp. 42–43; Greg Spring, "It's Still Oprah's World, For Now," *Electronic Media*, September 22, 1997, pp. 1A, 26.

53. James Walker and Douglas Ferguson, *The Broadcast Television Industry* (New York: Allyn & Bacon, 1998), pp. 58–61, 114–119.

54. See Mark Christensen and Cameron Stauth, *The Sweeps* (New York: William Morrow, 1984), as a vivid detailed description of a trend that changed little as the 20th century ended.

55. For up-to-date reports of who is spending what on TV advertising, see *Advertising Age*'s Web site at www.adage.com.

56. Douglas Gomery, "Dinosaurs Who Refuse to Die," *American Journalism Review*, March 1995, p. 44. See Web site at http:// www.ajr.org.

57. "TV's Changing Demographics," *Electronic Media*, April 20, 1998, pp. 22–32.

58. Ronald Grover, "Must See TV for Left Handed Men Under 30," *Business Week*, December 14, 1998, p. 104.

59. Edward Papazian (ed.), *Television Dimensions '97* (New York: Media Dynamics, Inc., 1997), pp. 107–124.

60. "Inside TGC," on Web site at www.thegolfchannel.com/navigation/frameset/insideindex.htm, accessed July 12, 1999.

61. For more on *TV Land*, see Web site at http:// www.nike-at-nite.com; on parent company Viacom, see Web site at www.viacom.com, as well as Chapter 7.

62. See Belo 1998 Annual Report, p. 10—found at Web site at www.belo.com.

63. Sara Brown, "The Big Get Bigger," *Broadcasting & Cable*, April 6, 1998, pp. 8–9.

64. Herbert H. Howard, "The 1996 Telecommunications Act and TV Station Ownership: One Year Later," *Journal of Media Economics* 11.3 (1998), pp. 21–32.

65. This was not so much different from the listing *Broadcasting & Cable* magazine published in 1993 when Capital Cities/ABC was first, CBS second, NBC third, Tribune fourth, Fox fifth, Home Shopping Network sixth and Chris-Craft seventh. See "Top Television Groups," *Broadcasting & Cable*, March 22, 1993, pp. 29–30.

66. Diane Mermigas, "Robert Wright Q & A: Challenges of a New Age," *Electronic Media*, May 12, 1997, pp. 1, 12.

67. Steve McClellan, "Another Banner Year (Financially) for NBC," *Broadcasting & Cable*, December 15, 1997, pp. 80–81.

68. The annual reports for General Electric and the information therein are all contained on Web site at www.ge.com.

69. See Thomas F. O'Boyle, *At Any Cost: Jack Welch, General Electric, and the Pursuit of Power* (New York: Knopf, 1998).

70. Kyle Pope, "Tuning in to the Hard Truths," *Wall Street Journal*, April 19, 1999, pp. B1, B4. For more on Welch's philosophy, see the corporate Web page at www.ge.com.

71. For the latest fare on NBC—as well as MSNBC and CNBC—see Web site at www.nbc.com.

72. Marc Gunther and Henry Goldblatt, "How GE Made NBC No. 1," *Fortune*, February 3, 1997, found on Web site at www.ge.com.

73. Diane Mermigas, "NBC Looks Beyond Prime Time for Profits," *Electronic Media*, May 12, 1997, p. 13; Kyle Pope, "Shut Out by NFL, NBC Pays Big to Keep 'ER'," *Wall Street Journal*, January 15, 1998, pp. B1, B6; Douglas Gomery, "Gunfight at the All-News Corral," *American Journalism Review*, December 1997, p. 50. See also Web sites at www.wsj.com and www.ajr.org.

74. "Dow Jones, GE's NBC Agree on Plan to Consolidate TV Channels Overseas," *Wall Street Journal*, December 9, 1997, p. B6. See also Web site at www.wsj.com.

75. Kyle Pope, "NBC Is Expected to Unveil Cuts Up to 250 Jobs," *Wall Street Journal*, September 17, 1998, p. B22. See also Web site at www.wsj.com.

76. Steve McClellan, "Mel Karmazin Makes (and Accepts) No Excuses." *Broadcasting & Cable*, November 17, 1997, pp. 28–30, 40. See also the interview with Karmazin in the same issue pp. 35–36, 38–39.

77. Bernard Wysocki, Jr., "In the New Mergers, Conglomerates Are Out, Being No. 1 Is in," *Wall Street Journal* (December 31, 1997), pp. A1, A12. See also Web site at www.wsj.com.

78. Kyle Pope, "Tuning in to the Hard Truths," *Wall Street Journal*, April 19, 1999, pp. B1, B4; Douglas Gomery, "Time for a New Look for '60 Minutes,'" *American Journalism Review*, March 1996, p. 48. See Web site at www.ajr.org.

79. Kyle Pope and Timothy Aeppel, "CBS Shake-Up Now Has to Play a Tough Crowd," *Wall Street Journal*, May 27, 1997, pp. B1, B8. See also Web site at www.wsj.com.

80. Stephen Baker, "The Coming Sparks at Westinghouse," *Business Week*, June 9, 1997, pp. 36–37.

81. For the latest on CBS programming—for the national network and for the owned and operated stations—see Web site at www.cbs.com.

82. Sally Beatty, "CBS's Infinity Agrees to Buy Billboard Firm, *Wall Street Journal*, May 28, 1999, p. A3; Ronald Grover and Richard Siklos, "CBS," *Business Week*, April 5, 1999, pp. 75–82; Kyle Pope, "CBS to Shift $50 Million from Affiliates to Help Pay Bill for NFL Broadcasts," *Wall Street Journal*, June 1, 1998, p. B6; Eben Shapiro, "CBS Considers Cost Cutting Measures as Programming Expenses Skyrocket," *Wall Street Journal*, August 26, 1998, p. B2. See also Web site at www.wsj.com.

83. For the latest on Fox television, see Web site at www.fox.com.

84. Kyle Pope, "Tuning in to the Hard Truths," *Wall Street Journal*, April 19, 1999, pp. B1, B4; Michael Schneider, "Fox Turns 10; In the Very Beginning, Few Shared Fox Vision," *Electronic Media*, April 21, 1997, pp. 1, 20.

85. Douglas Gomery, "A Very High-Impact Player," *American Journalism Review*, July/August, 1996, p. 52. See Web site at www.ajr.org.
86. John Lippman, "News Corp. to Spin Off 20% of Fox in IPO," *Wall Street Journal*, June 30, 1998, p. A9; Lynette Rice, "10 Years from Wannabe to Big Four," *Broadcasting & Cable*, September 22, 1997, pp. 36–38.
87. Bruce Orwall, "Reviving the Not-So-Wonderful World of Disney," *Wall Street Journal*, September 24, 1998, p. B9; Mike Reynolds, "Disney Doing Digital, ESPN Going Regional," *Cable World*, December 15, 1997, pp. 1, 66; see Web site at www.cableworld.com.
88. Kyle Pope, "Tuning in to the Hard Truths," *Wall Street Journal*, April 19, 1999, pp. B1, B4.
89. Bruce Orwall and Kyle Pope, "Disney, ABC Promised 'Synergy' in Merger: So, What Happened?," *Wall Street Journal*, May 16, 1997, pp. A1, A9; Diane Mermigas, "Mouse Has Its Hands Full with ABC," *Electronic Media*, May 12, 1997, p. 16. See Web site at www.wsj.com.
90. Orwall and Pope, "Disney, ABC Promised 'Synergy,'" pp. A1, A9; Bruce Orwall, "Disney to Launch Sports TV Network for California," *Wall Street Journal*, December 11, 1997, p. B10. See Web site at www.wsj.com.
91. See Web site at www.timewarner.com.
92. Kyle Pope, "Time Warner's WB Network Signs Novel Distribution Accord with TCI," *Wall Street Journal*, April 30, 1998, p. B5.
93. Lynette Rice and Steve McClellan, "The WB Gets New Legs," *Broadcasting & Cable*, August 11, 1997, pp. 20–24.
94. Elizabeth A. Rathburn, "Tribune's Renaissance," *Broadcasting & Cable*, July 8, 1996, pp. 4, 8–9.
95. Kyle Pope, "Limping 'Buffy' Gets a Lift From WB," *Wall Street Journal*, May 14, 1997, pp. B1, B11; "Time Warner Unit Plans to Eliminate 23% of Staff Positions," *Wall Street Journal*, May 1, 1998, p. B4; Leslie Cauley and Patricia M. Reilly, "CNN and Time Are Facing a Bumpy Road to Synergy," *Wall Street Journal*, August 14, 1998, p. B1, B4; Eben Shapiro, "Time Warner Builds Internet Superstore," *Wall Street Journal*, September 14, 1998, pp. B1, B4. For the latest information, see Time Warner's Web site at www.timewarner.com.
96. See Web site at www.viacom.com.
97. Information from official Viacom source at Web site at www.viacom.com.
98. Larry Collette and Barry R. Litman, "The Peculiar Economics of New Broadcast Entry: The Case of United Paramount and Warner Bros.," *Journal of Media Economics* 10.4 (1997), pp. 3–22.
99. Michael Schneider, "Fox, CBS Get Older; WB, UPN Younger," *Electronic Media*, December 15, 1997, pp. 1A, 30; Jon Lafayette, "Sinclair Switching 6 Stations," *Electronic Media*, December 15, 1997, pp. 1, 61; Steve McClellan, "Sinclair Dips into $1 Billion Purse for Max Media," *Broadcasting & Cable*, December 8, 1997, p. 16.
100. Robert La Franco, "The Diller Option," *Forbes*, December 28, 1998, pp. 51, 53; Eben Shapiro, "Will Barry Diller Be a Winner on the Web?," *Wall Street Journal*, October 20, 1998, pp. B1, B4; Diane Mermigas, "Patching Together a TV Giant; $4.1 Billion Diller Deal," *Electronic Media*, October 27, 1997, pp. 1, 45; Eben Shapiro and Bruce Orwall, "Diller and Universal Team Up to Build Television Titan," *Wall Street Journal*, October 21, 1997, pp. B1, B6; Eben Shapiro, "With USA Network Up for Grabs, Heat Is on Its Chief," *Wall Street Journal*, August 4, 1997, pp. B1, B6. For more on how this experiment unfolds, see Web site at www.seagram.com.
101. Steve McClellan, "Bud Paxson Sets His Sights to Be Lucky Number 7," *Broadcasting & Cable*, June 30, 1997, pp. 42–45; Kyle Pope, "New Network Has Faith in Family, Infomercials," *Wall Street Journal*, December 18, 1997, pp. B1, B8; Kyle Pope, "From Near Outcast to Toast of TV Land," *Wall Street Journal*, April 22, 1997, pp. B1, B10.
102. Jon Lafayette, "Young Broadcasting Sets Up War Chest," *Electronic Media*, December 22–29, 1997, p. 32.
103. See "Multi-Station Ownership," in *TV Datatrak*, first quarter 1997, Published quarterly by Media Market Resources, Inc., New York City, pp. 115–137.
104. Floyd Morris, "New York Times Co. Posts A 60 Percent Rise in New Income," *New York Times*, February 6, 1997, p. D9; "Top 25 Media Groups," *Broadcasting & Cable*, July 7, 1997, p. 26; Adam

Bryant, "The New York Times Co. Reports Improved Results for 3d Quarter," *New York Times*, October 17, 1997, p. C6.

105. This analysis is from the *1998 Broadcasting & Cable Yearbook* (Washington, DC), pp. A-2–A-27.
106. See Web site at www.ackerley.com.
107. FCC, *In the Matter of Annual Assessment of the Status of Competition in Markets for the Delivery of Video Programming*, Fifth Annual Report. Adopted: December 17, 1998. Released: December 23, 1998. On Web site at www.fcc.gov, pp. 4–5.
108. Ibid., p. 4.
109. Ibid., p. 5.
110. Parsons and Frieden, pp. 68–114, 225–229.
111. FCC, "In the Matter of Annual Assessment," pp. 6, 8.
112. Ibid., p. 12.
113. Ibid., pp. 21–24.
114. Ibid., pp. 12–13.
115. Ibid., pp. 9, 14.
116. Ibid., pp. 17–18.
117. Ibid., p. 25.
118. For the latest fare—TV and otherwise—to come from the Sony production lot, see Web site at www.sony.com.
119. Parsons and Frieden, pp. 195–237; Waterman and Weiss, pp. 152–157.
120. Indeed, the diffusion is so great that Heicon Corporation, the 50th largest MSO in the United States in 1997, according to the National Cable Television Association, has but 115,000 subscribers. Most systems are small with less than 1,000 subscribers, with three quarters of the systems in the United States in 1997 with 1,000 or less subscribers. See the NCTA Web site for the latest information and rankings at www.ncta.com.
121. See "Top 50 DMA Ranked by Percentage of Cable Penetration," in *Broadcasting & Cable Yearbook*, 1997, and *TV Datatrak*, first quarter 1997, published quarterly by Media Market Resources, Inc., New York City, pp. 7–9.
122. Peter Elstrom, Richard Siklos, Roger Crockett, Catherine Yang and Amy Barrett, "AT&T: What Victory Means," *Business Week*, May 17, 1999, pp. 34–36.
123. Rebecca Blumenstein and Leslie Cauley, "Ma Bell's Plan Is to Serve Up TV, Phone Via Cable," *Wall Street Journal*, May 6, 1999, pp. B1, B11; "As Worlds Collide, AT&T Grabs a Power Seat," *Wall Street Journal*, May 6, 1999, p. B1; Scott Wooley, "A Two Front War," *Forbes*, May 31, 1999, p. 55; Allan Sloan, "AT&T Media One Soap Opera Has Just About Everything," *Washington Post*, May 11, 1999, p. E3; Leslie Cauley and Rebecca Blumenstain, "Comcast, in AT&T Accord, Abandons MediaOne Bid," *Wall Street Journal*, May 5, 1999, pp. A3, A8.
124. Leslie Cauley, "U S West Takes Over a Huge Cable Firm, Then Angers Its Brass," *Wall Street Journal*, August 29, 1997, pp. A1, A6; "USWMG's Lillis Takes Stock," *Multichannel News*, September 15, 1997, pp. 1, 54; Leslie Cauley and Mark Robichaux, "US West Media to Pay $5.3 Billion to Buy Continental Cablevision," *Wall Street Journal*, February 28, 1996, pp. A3, A4.
125. Steven Lipin, "U S. West to Split into Two Companies," *Wall Street Journal*, October 27, 1997, pp. A3, A6; Kent Gibbons, "U S West Will Split Cable, Phone," *Multichannel News*, November 3, 1997, pp. 1, 59. See Web sites at www.wsj.com and www.multichannel.com.
126. Stephanie N. Mehta and John Simons, "Justice Clears AT&T Acquisition of TCI," *Wall Street Journal*, December 31, 1998, p. A3; Rebecca Blumenstein and Gregory Zuckerman, "AT&T Prepares Massive Bond Offering," *Wall Street Journal*, March 18, 1999, p. A3. From information issued by AT&T on its Web site at www.att.com.
127. K. C. Neel, "TCI Cuts Deals with Century, MediaOne, Multimedia," *Cable World*, December 15, 1997, p. 7. See Web site at cableworld.com.
128. Ronald Grover, "Malone," *Business Week*, October 5, 1998, pp. 118, 122.
129. To catch the bottom line oriented flavor of Hindery's management philosophy, read his candid interview with Jim McConville in "Digital Blast From TCI's Hindery," *Electronic Media*, September 1, 1997, pp. 1, 18.

130. John M. Higgins, "TCI Faces Sinking Sub Numbers," *Broadcasting & Cable*, June 30, 1997, pp. 8, 10; Mark Robichaux, "Malone Says TCI Push into Phones, Internet Isn't Working for Now," *Wall Street Journal*, January 1, 1997, pp. A1, A3; Price Colman, "John Sie: All the Right Movies," *Broadcasting & Cable*, November 24, 1997, pp. 28–31.

131. John M. Higgins, "Time Warner Reconnects," *Broadcasting & Cable*, December 8, 1997, pp. 36–37, 40; Kent Gibbons and Joe Estrella, "Summer of Love Continues; TCI, Time Warner Ink Deals for 2M+ Subs," *Multichannel News*, September 8, 1997, pp. 1, 63; John M. Higgins, "TCI, Time Warner Cut $2.2B System Deals," *Broadcasting & Cable*, September 8, 1997, p. 11; Kim Mitchell, "More Moves at TCI," *Cable World*, September 8, 1997, p. 43. For the latest deals, see Web site at www.multichannel.com.

132. Ray Richmond, "TNT Leads Cable Boom," *Variety*, July 21–27, 1997, pp. 17–18. It should be remembered that Professional Wresting does well in the cable TV ratings. For example, as reported in *Broadcasting & Cable* on page 60 in its September 1, 1997 issue, TNT's professional wrestling wholly owned show "World Championship Wrestling," finished number 1 and number 2 in the ratings that week.

133. John M. Higgins, "Time Warner Reconnects," *Broadcasting & Cable*, December 8, 1997, pp. 36–37, 40.

134. Waterman and Weiss, pp. 165–169; Parsons and Freiden, pp. 194–201.

135. For the most recent financial and corporate happenings at Comcast, see its extensive Web site at www.comcast.com.

136. Kent Gibbons, "Comcast, Cablevision Post Steady Gains," *Multichannel News*, November 17, 1997, p. 46; Diane Mermigas, "Bill Gates Drops a Cool $1 Billion as Microsoft Goes Cable," *Electronic Media*, June 16, 1997, pp. 1, 36.

137. For the latest on Comcast, consult its extensive Web site, which incudes, a vast array of financial data at www.comcast.com.

138. See Web site at www.cox.com.

139. Leslie Cauley, "Cox to Buy TCA's Cable for $3.26 Billion," *Wall Street Journal*, May 12, 1999, pp. A3, A4.

140. See the Web site at www.cox.com.

141. Kent Gibbons, "Comcast, Cablevision Post Steady Gains," *Multichannel News*, November 17, 1997, p. 46; Marianne Paskowski, "Dolan's Mother of All Clusters," *Multichannel News*, June 16, 1997, p. 56; R. Thomas Umstead and Joe Estrella, "Dolan's Super Cluster," *Multichannel News*, June 9, 1997, pp. 1, 70. See Web site at www.multichannel.com.

142. Marianne Paskowski and Kent Gibbons, "After a Busy Year, Dolan's Eye Next Moves," *Multichannel News*, December 1, 1997, pp. 1, 142–143, 145. See Web site at www.multichannel.com.

143. For an analysis as of 1995—as clustering was beginning—see Sylvia Chan-Olmsted, "Market Competition of Cable Television: Reexamining Its Horizontal Mergers and Industry Competition," *Journal of Media Economics* 9.2 (1996), pp. 25–41.

144. Leslie Cauley, "Latest Adelphia Deal to Make It No. 4 Cable-TV Firm; Accord to Buy Family-Owned Harron for $820 Million Cheered by Wall Street," *Wall Street Journal*, April 13, 1999, p. B4; Leslie Cauley, "Adelphia Will Buy Century in $3.6 Billion Deal," *Wall Street Journal*, March 8, 1999, pp. A3, A4; Leslie Cauley, "Adelphia Is Buying FrontierVision in $1 Billion Deal," *Wall Street Journal*, February 24, 1999, p. B8. See corporate Web site at www.adelphia.net.

145. Leslie Cauley, "Charter to Buy Yet Another Cable Firm," *Wall Street Journal*, May 27, 1999, pp. A3, A8; Leslie Cauley and Kara Swisher, "Billionaire Allen to Buy Marcus Cable," *Wall Street Journal*, April 6, 1998, p. A3; John M. Higgins, "Allen's Big Buy Not His Last," *Broadcasting & Cable*, August 3, 1998, p. 6.

146. By the March 1998 National Cable Television Association ranking, as well as the April 1998 ranking by *Broadcasting & Cable* magazine, it is 16th. See its Web page at www.tca-cable.com.

147. Massillon Cable is small that only bits and pieces can be found on its operations. See Web site at ww.multichannel.com and www.cableworld.com.

148. See Web site at www.eaglecom.net.

149. Jeff Jensen, "Stakes Rising in Cable TV's Sports Battle," *Advertising Age*, April 13, 1998, pp. S14–S15. See Web site at www.adage.com. See also Alan Schwartz, "The Show Must Go On," *P.O.V.*, February 1998, pp. 66–74; Marc Spiegler, "Betting on Web Sports," *American Demographics*, May 1996, p. 24.

150. See Web sites at www.newscorp.com and www.att.com.

151. Kent Gibbons, "Viacom's Cable Nets Post Solid Quarter," *Multichannel News*, November 3, 1997, p. 42. See Web site at www.multichannel.com.

152. Leslie Cauley, "ESPN's New Football Deal Is Expected to Boost Rates for Cable TV Nest Year," *Wall Street Journal*, January 16, 1998, p. B6; Stefan Fatsis, "For Pro Football, Giant TV Pacts May Carry a Price," *Wall Street Journal*, January 15, 1998, p. B6. See Web site at www.wsj.com.

153. We dealt with MMDS earlier. We also note that during the 1970s, once HBO determined that there was money to be made with alternatives to broadcast network television, entrepreneurs looked for ways to program pay TV movies. First came subscription TV, from a base of a single channel system first approved by the FCC in 1968. The first STV system went on the air in 1977. Yet STV never really got off the ground, and through the early 1980s, as the United States was wired and the alternative of home video was innovated, STV never developed as an true alternative at all. In May 1983, the FCC approved MMDS or "wireless" cable—formally multichannel multipoint distribution service. But as already noted, MMDS has made little dent in the marketplace.

154. Bryan Gruley, "It's the Phone Man at the Door—and He Has a Deal on Cable TV," *Wall Street Journal*, September 22, 1997, pp. A1, A14; "Ameritech Lands Another Franchise," *Cable World*, March 10, 1997, p. 104; Monica Hogan, "TCI, Ameritech Battle in Arlington Heights," *Multichannel News*, December 8, 1997, p. 69; Lee Hall, "Ameritech Cable on Tough Road," *Electronic Media*, August 11, 1997, pp. 1, 28; Parsons and Freiden, pp. 124–134. See Web site at www.wsj.com.

155. FCC, *In the Matter of Annual Assessment*, pp. 6, 54–55; Andrew Kreig, "Wireless Cable: Connecting to the Future," *Multichannel News*, June 23, 1997, p. 53. For current updates, see Web site at www.multichannel.com.

156. Leslie Cauley, "BellSouth Plans Wireless Cable in New Orleans," *Wall Street Journal*, November 19, 1997, p. B12; Jim Barthold, "BellSouth Launches Digital MMDS in New Orleans with Zenith Boxes," *Cable World*, November 24, 1997, p. 8. See Web site at www.wsj.com.

157. FCC, *In the Matter of Annual Assessment*, p. 8.

158. Parsons and Frieden, pp. 147–151; Robert N. Wold, "United States DBS History: A Long Road to Success," *Via Satellite*, September 1996, pp. 32–34, 36, 38, 40, 42, 44.

159. FCC, *In the Matter of Annual Assessment*, pp. 4–6, 41–42.

160. Robert N. Wold, "The DBS/DTH Road Show," *Via Satellite*, May 1996, pp. 46, 48, 50, 52, 54.

161. Frederic M. Biddle and Joann S. Lublin, "Hughes to Tap Smith as Chief and Chairman," *Wall Street Journal*, October 20, 1997, pp. A3, A6. See Web site at www.wsj.com.

162. Douglas Gomery, "The Making of a Satellite Behemoth," *American Journalism Review*, May 1999, p. 82.

162. FCC, *In the Matter of Annual Assessment*, pp. 49–51.

164. See the Web site at www.directv.com and Alan Breznick, "New From DirecTV: A Lot of First-Run Movies, Series," *Cable World*, November 17, 1997, pp. 1, 46: Frederic M. Biddle and Leslie Cauley, "DirecTV Seeks New Partners, Fresh Programs," *Wall Street Journal*, December 17, 1997, pp. B1, B8; Price Colman, "No Laurel Resting for DirecTV's Hartenstein," *Broadcasting & Cable*, November 3, 1997, pp. 52–53.

165. Alan Breznick, "PrimeStar Delays High-Power Service," *Cable World*, November 17, 1997, pp. 12, 42; Alan Breznick, "TCI, Cox May Back Away From Marketing Primestar," *Cable World*, November 24, 1997, pp. 1, 53.

166. FCC, *In the Matter of Annual Assessment*, pp. 50–51; Alan Breznick, "The Dish on PrimeStar, EchoStar: High-Power Plans, New Offers," *Cable World*, July 28, 1997, pp. 1, 53; Mark Robichaux and John Lippman, "EchoStar Sues News Corporation, Seeks $5 Billion," *Wall Street Journal*, May 12, 1997, p. B6.

167. Parsons and Frieden, pp. 125–134.

168. See Michael Dupagne, "Exploring the Characteristics of Potential High-Definition Television Adapters," *Journal of Media Economics* 12.1 (1999), pp. 35–50.

169. FCC, *In the Matter of Annual Assessment*, pp. 30–31.

170. The reporting on the coming of the broadcast digital age was been extensive. The best survey at the time of the initial digital broadcasts, November 1, 1998, can be found in Catherine Yang et al., "Digital Day," *Business Week*, October 26, 1998, pp. 144–158. See also FCC, *In the Matter of Annual Assessment*, pp. 63–65.

171. FCC, *In the Matter of Annual Assessment*, pp. 7–8, 33–36.

172. For a review of the state of the Internet and TV, see Ibid., pp. 67–68. See also Jim Barthold, "Launching Digital: Lots of Q's, But Few A's," *Cable World*, December 8, 1997, pp. 130, 132; Matt Stump, "Gearing Up for Digital," *Cable World*, December 1, 1997, p. 106; G. Christian Hill and Jeffrey A. Trachenberg, "When a TV Joins a PC, Will Anybody Be Watching?" *Wall Street Journal*, April 3, 1996, pp. B1, B6. George Mannes, "Lost Horizon," *Video Review*, April 1992, pp. 23–26, nicely contrasts the past "blue sky" predictions of the future of TV with the cold reality of what actually happened.

173. FCC, *In the Matter of Annual Assessment*, pp. 94–96.

174. Ibid., p. 96. See also Martin Peers, "Giants Chow Down Indies," *Variety*, September 15–21, 1997, pp. 31, 33.

175. FCC, *In the Matter of Annual Assessment*, pp. 80-8, C-1–C-3.

176. Ibid., pp. 89–90.

177. Ibid., p. 91.

178. Sylvia M. Chan-Olmsted, "Market Concentration for Cable Television: Re-examining Its Horizontal Mergers and Industry Concentration," *Journal of Media Economics* 9.2 (1996), pp. 25–41.

179. Cable World Staff, "MSOs Map 1998 Rate Hikes," *Cable World*, December 8, 1997, pp. 1, 150; Paul Fahri, "Cable TV Rates Going Up Sharply," *Washington Post*, May 18, 1996, pp. A1, A9; Chris McConnell, "FCC Zeros in on Cable Competition," *Broadcasting & Cable*, December 15, 1997, p. 16; John M. Higgins, "Cable Ramps Up Rates," *Broadcasting & Cable*, December 8, 1997, pp. 6–7.

180. Douglas Gomery, "Media Ownership: Concepts and Principles," in Alison Alexander, James Owers and Rodney Carveth (eds.) *Media Economics* (Hillsdale, NJ: Lawrence Erlbaum Associates, 1998), pp. 45–52.

5

Radio Broadcasting and the Music Industry

Douglas Gomery

In May 1999, the music industry of listening seemed to being turned upside down when MTV announced it was acquiring Sonicnet music services on the Internet. This symbolized a tidal wave of Internet music providers that would define the next century and compete with the radio and music store retailers. Michael Ovitz (who tried to re-craft Disney and was fired by Michael Eisner; see Chapter 6) was helping to create checkout.com, a company on the Internet that would, in part, sell compact discs (CDs) online. Ovitz, like many other entrepreneurs, heralded the Internet as the next revolution in American entertainment, a chance for artists to present music directly to the public without going through a larger company like Disney.

But radio corporations did not sit still as online music took away their business. In 1999, radio's biggest company, Hicks Muse's Chancellor Broadcasting, announced the formation of three Internet divisions to tender radio's sounds to the public over the World Wide Web. Chancellor's AM/FM division would seek to build a network of portals tied to the company's near 500 stations. Chancellor had ceeded the Internet turf to broadcast.com, but it would challenge Ovitz's notion that artists could use the Internet to sing and make music directly to their fans.[1]

Why all the fuss? Because music making and listening was and will continue to represent an important and universal popular art form. People listen, and most are fans of one musical artist or another. Indeed, as the 20th century ended country crossover diva Patsy Cline had been dead for 27 years, but still lived through her recordings and play on the radio—as fans young and old to discovered and re-discovered her unique stylings. Radio choices are numerous in major cities, playing the hits of today as well as the greats of the past. And, of course, people can purchase music at retail stores or increasing online.[2]

Radio and the music recording industries have been symbiotically linked since the middle of the 20th century. They share trade press in *Radio & Records*. They offer continuous streams of music, but yet do not overlap in ownership; radio has one set of owners and the music industry has another. The music industry has long remained in the hands of few major companies—consolidated from six to five in 1998—but the radio industry underwent significant consolidation after the February 1996 passage of the Telecommunications Act. Not since the 1940s has radio been so concentrated in the hands of so few owners.[3]

RADIO BROADCASTING IN THE 1990S

Radio has long been a ubiquitous mass medium, in nearly every home, automobile and portable Walkman player. In the 1990s, the average household had access to more than five radios. During a typical week, radio broadcasting reaches nearly all possible listeners, at least for a few moments, with the average person listening more than three hours per week. Radio broadcasting reaches all types of persons (and is measured as persons because households, like television, make no sense as a basic unit). Advertisers target different ethnic groups (Blacks, Hispanics and others), age groups (young, middle-aged and old), income classes (e.g., the well-off listen to more news/talk format than others) and genders. Adult contemporary sounds worked best for those from 25 to 34 years old and all-news radio found its audience almost exclusively in the over 35 years old crowd. Album-oriented rock was aimed at teenagers; their college-aged cousins seemed to prefer classic rock and contemporary hits radio. Country looked to an older audience, as did easy listening and nostalgia with its big band sounds. In the 1990s, radio reached about three in four adults each day, with the elderly being the least likely to listen (about two in three). During the week, most people listen at some point, usually at rush hour, radio's prime time.[4]

As the 1990s ended, the share of FM was about 80%. Although FM's share of total listening to listed stations has continued to rise, it has slowed. The most listened-to stations were FM stations in New York City and Los Angeles, which are the top two radio markets in the United States. The rock spectrum (from album-oriented rock to classic rock to new rock to progressive rock) continued to attract the most listeners and did so by a considerable margin. The next most popular format was country (11.51%), Black/urban (11.02%) and news/talk (10.34%). Of these top four format categories, only Black/urban seemed to be growing at the time. Rock, at about 14.6% of the radio audience, seemed to be constant, despite some stations shifting from one flavor of rock to another. Country's position continued to erode, although not as seriously as news/talk (country peaked in Spring 1993 with 13.8% of all listening to listed stations). However, whereas country's losses appear to be easing somewhat, news/talk's have accelerated. The news/talk format was down to 10.3%. News/talk suffered on both AM and FM. The category's of AM listening was down 41.2% as the century ended; even FM news/talk slipped to below 2% of all listening.[5]

Conversely, two struggling formats appeared to be on the rebound as the century ended. Adult contemporary and contemporary hits radio (CHR) appeared to have reinvented themselves with the emergence of several subcategories (i.e., rhythmic CHR and modern adult contemporary stations). Oldies and classic hits, which peaked in 1995, slipped to about 7% of all listening. However, they remained at a higher level than was met during the early 1990s. Hispanic proved to be another growing format, moving to eighth overall by 1999. Religious stations, as well as gospel stations, posted increases, both on AM and FM. Jazz and classical radio remained radio's least popular, both with about 2% of the audience.[6]

These radio formats attracted advertisers. In 1996, according to the Radio Advertising Bureau, total advertising for the radio industry rose 8%, following an 8% increase the year before, an 11% gain in 1994 and a 10% gain in 1993—to figures approaching and then surpassing $3 billion per annum just for national advertising, with spot and local adding even more. As long as the U.S. economy was doing well, radio advertising spending continued to grow. Radio remained important because it functioned as the bastion of local advertising, which still accounts for more than three quarters of the total spent.[7]

The current success of radio, a technology innovated in the 1920s, may seem paradoxical in the age of computers and the World Wide Web, but ease of access certainly provides the necessary precondition. Literally, everyone has a radio; across the United States in the late 1990s there were some 600 million radios in use, including the nearly 150 million in automobiles. Most everyone listens at some point in the week, and the typical listener (e.g., in a car on the way to and from work, or at home relaxing or seeking the latest weather information) tunes in every day. The radio is easy to use, everywhere, cheap to procure, portable and filed with choices. And unlike books, magazines, television and film, radio does not demand full attention while in use.[8]

Thanks to federal deregulation, which began for radio in the early 1980s, the number of radio stations on the air in the United States has steadily grown—from roughly 10,500 in 1985 to more than 12,000 in 1997. Of these, more than 10,000 air advertising and are profit motivated, and nearly 2,000 are noncommercial, often affiliated with National Public Radio network, and allied with some type of educational organization. The Telecommunications Act of 1996 freed commercial owners (and potential owners) of radio stations to acquire more and group them in large chains. Thus, whereas these new groups hardly own all the stations, they do garner a greater share of revenues, approaching half. The new radio chain (or group) entrepreneurs seek to "cream skim" and buy only the most profitable stations, and thus the chain average profit rates are higher. They also seek the stations in the biggest media markets where the potential advertising spending is the highest. In the top 20 media markets, a handful of radio stations (usually chain owned) holds more than half the revenues generated from advertising.[9]

Radio as an industry remained "free" because advertisers continued to pay the freight, seeking to target their messages to specific groups who listen to certain musical and talk formats on certain stations. Most advertisers perceive radio as a cheaper means than television and newspapers. Listener levels are measured by Arbitron, Inc., a company that surveys people to determine which stations they listen to, how often and for how long. This then gets translated into demographic surveys that stations use to sell advertising at certain prices. Rates are generally highest to advertise during drive time in the morning or afternoon, because the audience is "captured" with no alternative, and for audiences in the 18–49 age group and of high income. The average station gets most from local and spot advertising by national brands. Some network advertising is done as well.[10]

THE MUSIC INDUSTRY IN THE 1990S

The radio musical format is tied to styles of music and the production, distribution and sales of the music industry. Radio's popularity spiked vast music sales. In 1996, the dollar value of annual domestic shipments of prerecorded music reached $12.5 billion. This came in the form of compact discs (CDs), CD singles, audio cassettes, cassette singles, long-playing vinyl records, vinyl singles and music videos shipped to record retailers and other accounts. Their numbers total over one billion units—precisely 1.14 billion in 1996. The $12.5 billion year-end value (calculated at suggested list price) for all audio and music video product reflected 15 consecutive years of positive growth for the industry.[11]

The International Federation of the Phonographic industry pegged world music sales for 1997 at around $40 billion, of which the United States represents about 34%, followed by Japan, the European nations and then other less wealthy countries. The global picture is becoming increasingly important. RIAA midyear statistics for 1998 showed U.S. shipments up almost 12%, and all indications since then show many retailers will finish the year with comparable statistics up over 1997.[12]

The Recording Association of America (hereafter RIAA)—the trade group of the "Big Five" companies—noted in 1999 that recorded music is the world's universal form of communication. It touches every person of every culture on the globe to the tune of $38.1 billion annually, and the U.S. recording industry accounts for fully one third of that world market. It employs thousands of people, including singers, musicians, producers, sound engineers, record promoters and retail salespersons. In its continuing effort to remain the premier source for comprehensive data and information on the recording industry, the RIAA compiles, analyzes and reports on data concerning the volume of shipments and the value of all formats of recorded music shipped into all market channels. It identifies trends in music, while also constructing consumer profiles based on exhaustive, ongoing tracking of consumers across the United States.[13]

Consolidation in both the retail and wholesale sector continued: Camelot bought The Wall and Spec's Music and then got purchased themselves by Trans World. Wherehouse bought Blockbuster Music; CDNOW and Music Boulevard merged; Bertelsmann bought a chunk of barnesandnoble.com. The net effect of the last few years is that for most mainstream labels, 80% of sales are generated by about 10 accounts: Alliance, Target, Anderson (Wal-Mart), Tower, Best Buy, Trans World Entertainment, Handleman, Valley Media, Musicland, Wherehouse/Blockbuster. By 1999, there existed but 10 major accounts, half of which are specialty stores. The number of store locations that these 10 companies represent stabilized as most unprofitable locations were shuttered so those that are left were generally experiencing good sales.

But at the level of the production and distribution of music, if the union of 1998 PolyGram and Universal was any indication, the concentration of economic power would rest with a handful of companies. Only Time Warner is headquartered in the United States. EMI is British, Seagram Canadian, Bertelsmann German and Sony Japanese. All are among the largest corporations in the media business, indeed in all of the corporate world. The music industry is truly international in its ownership even if the country that still dominates sales is the United States.[14]

Virtually every music industry panel discussion during the late 1990s included executives waxing euphoric over the tremendous possibilities the Internet offered. It was possible to more effectively market directly to the consumer; to revive out-of-print titles; and to offer unique events, like celebrity chats, to millions of consumers at once. This is pretty exciting stuff. But consider the reality. In 1994, CDNOW was one of the first companies to begin offering CDs for sale on the Internet. Other companies soon followed suit: CDNOW, Music Boulevard, and Tower, plus Amazon.com, barnesandnoble.com, Blockbuster, Camelot, Hastings, TransWorld, Kmart and Wherehouse online. Of even greater importance is the entry of companies such as Sony, BMG and Warner Music Group into direct-to-the-consumer sales via their Web sites. And there were a number of artists such as Prince and Sara McLaughlin who built their own sites, and sold as well as promoted from them. Toss in a few companies like NetRadio, who had positioned themselves as Internet broadcasters with "buy" buttons on the screen, and in 1999 it started to look like everyone saw online music retailing as part of their revenue stream. Current hits sold at a lower rate online, whereas older music (i.e., catalog titles) sold more. Most online companies reported about 60% of their sales in catalog business, and retail shops had long reported catalog sales at 40%. Second, almost everything sold online was a CD, whereas cassettes still sold briskly in retail shops. Finally, about half of the online companies accepted international orders, and of those that do, about 40% of their shipments went overseas.

Internet bandwidth, hardware and software limitations and cable modem penetration remained barriers to significant growth. The beginning of the 21st century will continue to be defined by a great deal of experimentation; new economic models, such as pay for play, will be tested. The definition of what constitutes an album will be tested. The definition in the past had come from the limitations of what the physical carrier could hold. In an online world that limitation becomes less important. Because the marketplace is more song driven than ever (witness the success of compilations), artists and consumers might show interest in deciding how many cuts they want to compile as an "album."

In an online environment, label branding has not been shown to be particularly effective with consumers. Why should a consumer have to remember what label Jewel is on? Bertelsmann (or BMG) recognized that in 1998 by moving to acquire a piece of barnesandnoble.com. In contrast, retailers with brick-and-mortar locations have an advantage as they launch Internet locations because they have already established identities with consumers. Amazon, CDNOW and Music Boulevard have all had to pay enormous sums of money for portal positioning in a bid for Internet market share. The value of those portal agreements will become less important as a consumer's favorite local store goes online. New musical acts will continue to emerge in whatever forum. So the major will remain major. The Big Five will continue to hold vast catalogs of past artists' music, and these "oldies" will continue to make up some 40% of all music sold. For example, Patsy Cline, who died in 1963, was one of Universal's top-selling artists based on past hits and newly discovered material.[15]

Technologically, the 1990s was the decade of the compact disc. In 1996 that meant a staggering 778.9 million sold, generating nearly $10 billion in sales. Although music companies continue to produce and distribute every genre of music in the cassette format in 1997, the cassette format experienced a 17% decline from 1996 when "only" 225 million were shipped. The demand for music videos continued to grow. By these and many other measures, noted later, the selling of recorded music certainly represents a healthy and important mass media industry.[16]

Despite these differences, radio and music sales will remain symbiotically linked. Radio broadcasting and music recording industries will continue to be intertwined, and so an examination of the music industry serves as the basis for the second half of this chapter and the analysis of ownership with the radio industry.[17]

RADIO'S HISTORY AND BASICS

Radio broadcasting as a mass medium goes back to the 1920s, but the radio of today—with its diverse musical formats—did not begin until the late 1950s, prompted by the coming of television to seek an alternative role in society. This "new" format-driven radio industry was defined by the rise of the disc jockey as the star and the format, which is the combination of music played. In the process, these pioneers created an entirely new form of entertainment symbiotically linked to popular music, geared to specific demographics and tied to commuting to and from work or school. Radio broadcasting went from a sequential series of programs to an ongoing stream of consciousness of music and talk. People no longer tuned for specific events, but just tuned in.

By the mid-1950s, the "new" radio had made its deal with television, and assumed a new role in the mass media matrix. "Your Hit Parade" as a weekly variety show was replaced by top 40 rock with its limited playlist of tunes broadcast over and over again. As formats proliferated, stations innovated new wrinkles. Over time came country, urban contemporary and easy listening. In the end what happened, as survey after survey indicated, was that different audiences sought out and stuck to "their" sound, and then once the station learned what its audience was, it began to "sell" that audience to advertisers who cultivated that particular age, sex, income and/or education group. Over time, radio researchers learned that listeners, for example, to news and soft rock were more likely than not to be married, and listeners to top 40 and album rock were not likely to be married. Rock listeners seemed to move a lot and listeners to news radio were likely to have lived in their home for a relatively long time. Album rock listeners watched less television, whereas top 40 listeners did watch at lot of television. By the mid-1980s, the National Association of Broadcasters (NAB) had spread this money making formulae to its member stations.[18]

Different types of pop music formats came and went. Forms of nonmusical programming were tried, and evolved into all various combinations of news and talk. The coming and going of program cycles fascinated all industry watchers. There were, of course, other parts to radio broadcasting besides the programming, but the business itself was unusually focused on its own content. Looking back over four decades, there has been no other for-profit enterprise in which the whole organization talked so much about what station played what combination of music, or let Rush Limbaugh loose instead.[19]

By the mid-1990s, many argued that radio had become too formulaic. Country radio aimed, not so much at Garth Brooks fans, as at "adults 18–34 who listened on their way to and from work," and more females than males. Artists who did not fit that pattern of attraction were simply not played. For example, top 40 became contemporary hits radio, and abandoned the teenagers who had years ago helped to create it. A complete listing of these format formulae was out of data as soon as the computer was turned off. Editions of the *Broadcasting & Cable Yearbook* of the late 1990s contained more than 75—starting with adult album alternative (AAA), moving on to urban contemporary, variety (four or more formats), Vietnamese and finally "women." In between there is music by country of origin, genre, past and present, by mixture such as full service and news and talk. This publication, aiming to miss no one, even lists "other" as programming strategy.[20]

Music remains at the core of what radio plays, but music companies do not advertise directly or pay for this. No member of the Big Five music companies surveyed paid as do advertisers. Yet the link remained vital. In 1997, nearly half of those surveyed, despite all the MTV hype, revealed that radio helped them select what they chose to purchase as their new compact disc. The same results were reported in the 1970s, and the 1960s, and even the late 1950s. Elvis started this, and in 1964 the Beatles made it a permanent part of the radio–music axis. Radio stations needed music as a supplier of programming.[21]

The problem was that, by the late 1990s, programming for radio became more complicated because mainstream pop music had fractured into dance hits, rap music, new rock hits and more. During the late 1950s and early 1960s, top 40 aimed to be broad based in its appeal, but that meant it was not as efficient a targeting mechanism for advertisers. And as top 40's audience aged, their tastes changed; top 40 became adult contemporary, pop music for the over 35 crowd (its lite version for the even older). Progressive and album-oriented stations seemed to seek out college aged and younger listeners. Age was now in the mix and so race and income and other "demographics" soon followed; so this added urban contemporary and rap music, Hispanic and Christian stations.[22]

Targeting audiences continued the game as the 1990s ended, and the weapon of choice was the FM band. *The Broadcasting & Cable Yearbook* of 1997 listed 140 radio markets, from New York City to Montgomery, Alabama, and *Duncan's Radio Market Guide* listed 174 radio markets. For both, New York City—and its vast suburbs in New Jersey, Connecticut and New York State—ranked number one with more than 14 million potential listeners in the late 1990s. At the other end, Montgomery, Alabama, offered the potential advertiser just 263,200 possible listeners. So in terms of station popularity, New York City contained the top 14 stations by population reached, with market 2, Los Angeles, making up the rest of the top 20. Potential audience reach was the key variable. In sum, markets 91 though 140 just about equaled New York City in terms of possible listeners. Thus, radio surely driven by the FM revolution with its limited signal range, had become more of a suburban medium, led by stations in and around New York, Los Angeles, Chicago, San Francisco, Philadelphia, Detroit, Dallas, Houston, Boston and Washington, DC—the fabled top 10.[23]

The sale of advertising has provided the revenues for broadcast radio since the 1920s and so the audiences sought by radio programming have been driven by crafting a "product" to sell to advertisers—on a national, regional and local basis. To customers it seemed free. In the mid-1920s, networks developed, first NBC, then CBS, then Mutual and then ABC. These networks continued after the music format revolution, but gradually lessened in their importance. Only CBS and ABC continued as the 20th century ended.[24]

Radio began on the AM dial, and it was not until the 1940s that FM radio, the dominant modulation medium today, came into being. The FM signal is technologically superior to AM, but here (as usual) economic power mattered more. So it was not until the 1960s that FM began to overtake AM as the band most listened to by audiences. By 1983, the number of authorized FM stations on the air in the United States first surpassed the number of AM stations on the air, and stereo helped even more (as seen in Table 5.1).[25]

Radio provided sounds for relaxation, often serving as accompaniment at work in an office, as a source for information up to the minute from an all-news station, and companionship as people drive to and from work. Radio functioned for the individual, was not demanding, was aurally encompassing and was open ended. Listeners dial hopped to maintain their own fantasy through the music they loved.[26]

Radio broadcasting used to be TV's down home cousin—no more. Suddenly TV had a serious rival. Indeed, by the late 1990s, radio proved effective for TV stations and networks to promote upcoming shows, particularly new network shows and changing local newscasts. One report for 1998 found that TV broadcasters and cable networks and systems spent nearly $160 million on national radio in 1997, placing radio near the top of where TV spent its advertising dollars. When local and regional spending must also be considered, the linkage between TV and radio is obvious.[27]

Radio proved important because of its local domination. A collection of popular stations in a city could mean millions of dollars in advertising. In 1997, for example, CBS controlled more than one third of all advertising dollars poured into radio in Boston, one half in Philadelphia, one fifth in Washington/Baltimore, one fifth in San Francisco, one quarter in St. Louis and Los Angeles and one third in Dallas/Ft. Worth and one third in Detroit. Wall Street analysts recognized this, and solidly supported the mergers that led to Hicks Muse, CBS and Clear Channel, the largest col-

TABLE 5.1
The Slow Rise of AM and Rapid Rise of FM, Selected Years, 1970–1997

Year End	AM Stations	FM Stations	Total
1997	4,812	5,488	10,300
1990	4,897	4,392	9,379
1985	4,718	3,875	8,593
1980	4,589	3,282	7,871
1970	4,323	2,916	6,519

Sources: Vincent M. Ditingo, *The Remaking of Radio* (Boston: Focal Press, 1995), p. 61; and *Broadcasting & Cable*, October 13, 1997, p. 67.

lections of radio stations in history, and a redefinition of the radio industry in the United States during the 1990s.[28]

Through the 1980s, radio broadcasting had been more decentralized and thus considered a monopolistically competitive industry. That is, there were many stations offering closely competitive "products" (i.e., formats), particularly in major markets. These were substitutes for one another. There might be several country stations, and although not exactly the same, research showed that the average person switched among but a score of stations. Further, each substitutable station in the market sought to differentiate their on-air product in the mind of the listener by way of different combinations of music, different disc jockeys and personalities and different marketing tactics. And FCC rule demanded decentralized ownership. But, as analyzed in the following section, the ownership rules were relaxed, and chains developed collections of stations numbering in the hundreds. With this concentration of ownership, decisions of formats were made within the same group, and so the economics of monopolistic competition disappeared, and radio broadcasting became a classic oligopoly—particularly within bigger markets.[29]

We can measure the new world of radio and the rise of monopoly power by looking at the increases in station selling prices. Studies have found that the number of transactions increased dramatically as the duopoly rules were eliminated. Prices doubled, and the sale of KRTH-FM in Los Angeles set a record at $110 million for access to the vital Los Angeles market. These, in turn, added financial barriers of entry to the radio business, and the industry must be judged as surging toward oligopoly status in line music, movies and television. Still, basic operations remained local, with a station producing the programming, distributing it by tower to a local area. Concentration of ownership did not lead to a re-birth of networking. Unlike television, for example, where production is done in Hollywood and then distributed by stations, for radio the programming is based on music and personalities and remained local as chain managers figured the best collection of formats market by market.[30]

During the 1990s, music stations in particular cut back on any original news gathering and instead plugged into services such as "Metro Networks" and "Shadow Broadcast Services." What the stations get for their outpouring is a bare bones newscasts, a handful of local headlines, not all that different from the other score of stations in the market subscribing to the same service. Most, to be honest, simply clipped and summarized the morning newspaper, with no beat reporters to call their own. Only talk and news formatted stations bothered to hire reporters of their own. Most all news stations existed in only the top media markets, and even they have small news staffs, such as WTOP-AM in Washington, DC, which serves the capital with eight staff reporters.[31]

In selected major markets, the all-news format usually ranked consistently among the top-rated stations. In 1997, New York City had three, but the national total is fewer than four dozen. CBS owned one quarter of these stations. Few outside New York can support more than one, although many have tried to increase that total. Washington, DC once had three, but only one survived into the mid-1990s. And, this one rarely cracks the top 10 in ratings, although it does well financially because its audience ranks above average in terms of buying power. In New York City, for example, WINS-AM finished sixth in the ratings, in a highly fractured market, but second in advertising dollars taken in at nearly $30 million per annum. The audiences for all news are cumulative because they listen in 15-minute blocks and the stations simply repeat the cycle three or four times per hour.[32]

Talk radio of the 1990s was led by Rush Limbaugh. Since 1990, Limbaugh increased the number of stations onto talk format from 400 in 1990 to more than 1,100 by the mid-1990s. Limbaugh was clearly the star—on more than 600 stations and earning more than $30 million per annum for his syndicator. With the cost of national network transmission dropping by more than half as satellite time fell in the 1980s and early 1990s, syndicators and radio networks alike look for the next Limbaugh. Yet talk controversy can cause problems. For example, in March 1997, WILM-AM radio in Wilmington, Delaware, had become so uncomfortable with Rush Limbaugh's confrontational broadcast style, that he was dropped after six years. This was the first time Rush was dropped from a top 100 market for programming reasons. An increasing number of local advertisers were reluctant to have their spots aired during Limbaugh's program.[33]

In sum, country and rock music defined radio's top attractions during the late 1990s. Other musical forms became the exceptions, even in major markets. At the lower end of the popularity came limited interest formats like classical music. Classical stations struggled to survive, barely hanging on. The exception was high income areas. In the suburbs of Washington, DC, for example, there were many listeners to WGMS-FM (for Good Music Station), a commercial formatted classical station, which was then the top-rated classical station in the United States with some $8 million in revenues per annum. WGMS-FM's average listener was 52 years old and earned $72,500, then twice the national average. But, in toto, classical stations reached but 3% of the radio audience. In 1997, about 460 stations (of the more than 12,000 stations) could be called classically music formatted, with 40 as profit seeking commercial stations and the rest (420) noncommercial.[34]

Religious stations combined talk and music by secular principles. An estimated 20 million listeners nationwide, when surveyed, state they regularly tune to some form of religious radio. Since 1990, this format expanded from 1,000 to more than 1,500 stations, making it the fourth ranking format behind country, news/talk and adult contemporary music. Religious programming on television may gain a higher profile, but the radio dial is littered with religious choice. One third of these stations operate as nonprofit on the AM dial and subscribe contributions—like passing the plate—among listeners. Profit seeking religious stations also seek contributions.[35]

Selected cultural groups also represent targeted audiences. As Black Americans grow richer, they are one class that is reached by urban contemporary sounds. And in the 1980s, as an experiment, AM stations switched to Spanish-oriented music and talk and saw their ratings climb. The format then made it across to the FM dial and to every major Hispanic market in the United States (i.e., major cities in the North and West, as well as a band of cities across the South) so that by the mid-1990s there were at least one and usually two FM Hispanic target stations. The number grew to more than 420 stations in the mid-1990s.[36]

TABLE 5.2
Number of U.S. Radio Stations by Format, Selected Years, 1989–1996

Format	1989	1994	1996
Country	2,320	2,591	2,537
Adult Contemporary	1,954	1,452	1,379
News/Talk	398	1,094	1,225
Religious	668	846	875
Golden Oldies	701	756	775
Standard/Big Band	456	356	383
Classic Rock	126	342	426
Top 40	733	337	304
Album Oriented	305	306	366
Spanish	208	293	326
Urban Contemporary	188	241	260
Soft Contemporary	167	175	165
Easy Listening	294	136	112
Alternative/Progressive	27	113	138
Full Service	27	84	41
Variety	74	67	59
Ethnic	37	60	58
All News	38	57	64
Black/Rhthym and Blues	84	53	51
Classical	50	44	42
Jazz	28	24	60
Business	39	12	15
Total	8,922	9,439	9,661

Sources: *Veronis, Suhler and Associates Communications Industry Forecast*, 9th ed., July 1995, p. 127; *Veronis, Suhler and Associates Communications Industry Forecast*, 11th ed., July 1997, p. 140.

There are many formats (as can be seen in Table 5.2). However, most people listen regularly to five or less stations. Thus, whereas African American press and television remain blips on any media radar screen, in radio Black formats often rank in the top 10. In Washington, DC, the urban contemporary format (read Black middle-class youth) is often tops as it is in any city with a sizable African American population. That does not mean Whites do not listen or that White "crossover" acts are not aired. To hit a middle-class audience, the urban contemporary radio stations often target one third of the audience as White middle-class youth. If they were to simply add Black middle class to black poor, it would make their total audience less attractive to advertisers, who want an audience that not only wants to buy but has the money to buy. Radio audience research does indicate that a Black audience is usually a loyal one, whereas the White population is more fickle and more fragmented.[37]

In sum, programming aside, what drives radio as a business is what music attracts, and what audiences advertisers wish to target. As seen in Table 5.3, this works well and on a national level, where radio's share of advertising is about $1 in $12 spent. In accumulation, as seen in Table 5.4, this has been rising as the population grows and the economy expands.

This means that major corporations have spent millions on radio. Sears, AT&T, General Motors, Chrysler, News Corporation (for Fox TV), MCI, Tandy (for Radio

TABLE 5.3
Radio's Share of Advertising

	Percent of Advertising Dollars
1998	7.3%
1997	7.2
1996	7.0
1995	7.0
1994	7.1
1993	6.8
1992	6.8
1991	6.8
1990	6.7

Source: Standard and Poor's Industry Reports, 1999, "Publishing,"
found on Web site at www.netadvantage.standpoor.com.

TABLE 5.4
Radio's History of Advertising Revenues, 1981–1996 (in millions)

	Network	National Spot	Local	Total
1996	$465	$2,093	$9,854	$12,412
1995	426	1,920	9,124	11,470
1994	411	1,867	8,374	10,652
1993	407	1,629	7,532	9,568
1992	377	1,479	6,899	8,755
1991	440	1,575	6,578	8,591
1990	433	1,626	6,780	8,839
1989	427	1,530	6,463	8,420
1988	382	1,402	6,109	7,893
1987	371	1,315	5,605	7,292
1986	380	1,333	5,313	7,026
1985	329	1,319	4,912	6,563
1984	388	1,184	4,412	5,884
1983	254	1,023	3,739	5,015
1982	218	909	3,365	4,492
1981	196	854	3,007	4,057

Source: Radio Advertising Bureau analysis (1981–present) from Ernst Young, Radio Expenditure Reports, Miller Kaplan & Arase and Hungerford Aldrin Nichols & Carter.

Shack), Sunsource Health Products (for Ginsana) and Philip Morris (for Maxwell House Coffee and Miller Beer) regularly ranked as top advertisers on radio. They aimed at those people listening to FM stations in their cars (as can be seen in Table 5.5).[38]

Advertisers relish the reach and frequency of radio because they know it reaches three quarters of all customers on an average day, and nearly all Americans on a weekly basis. This data is from a Spring 1996 survey analyzed by the Radio Advertising Bureau (RAB), and applied to all persons age 12 and older, and indicated the highest radio audiences were composed of women from age 18 to 64 (i.e., those who

TABLE 5.5
Shares of Radio Listening, By AM versus FM & By Location (In percent)

Year	By Station Band		By Location		
	AM Stations	FM Stations	At Home	In Automobiles	Total out of Home
1990	23.1%	76.9%	45.2%	25.7%	54.8%
1991	23.6	76.4	44.4	27.2	55.6
1992	21.9	78.1	44.4	27.3	55.6
1993	22.1	77.9	43.1	29.0	56.9
1994	20.5	79.5	41.2	29.7	58.8
1995	21.1	78.9	40.5	30.6	59.5
1996	20.0	80.0	39.1	30.8	60.9
1997*	19.5	80.5	38.2	31.4	61.8

* = estimate

Sources: The Veronis, Suhler and Associates Communications Industry Forecast, Ninth edition, July 1995, p. 131; The Veronis, Suhler and Associates Communications Industry Forecast, Eleventh edition, July 1997, p. 140.

surely make most of the buying decisions in the United States). And all surveys in 1999 indicated that radio advertising revenues seemed to be headed up.[39]

THE FCC

A radio station needs a broadcast license from the Federal Communications Commission (FCC) to operate. In February 1996, President Clinton signed into law the Telecommunications Act of 1996, which directed the FCC to revise its rules, to eliminate the national multiple radio ownership rule and to relax the local ownership rule. In an order adopted in March 1996, the FCC implemented these provisions. The Commission then followed with a report examining how these changes effected the radio industry using data from March 1996 through November 1997, which suggested significant changes had occurred in both ownership and performance.[40]

By the mid-1990s, the radio broadcasting industry had been largely deregulated, particularly relating to the number of stations an entity may own. The national limits of 7 AM and 7 FM total seemed quaint by 1997. The 1996 Telecommunications Act took away most all restrictions. In particular, prior to 1992, no single group or individual could own more than one AM or one FM in a single market—known as the duopoly rule. This was designed in the early days of radio regulation (in the Communications Act of 1934) to prevent concentration of ownership in a single local market. But the Telecommunications Act of 1996 loosened ownership restrictions far more. For example, in markets with 45 or more commercial stations, a single company may own up to 8 stations with no more than 5 as AM or FM. If the market has from 30 to 44 commercial radio stations, then the total number one owner can acquire drops to 7, with a maximum of 4 in the same class of AM or FM. For smaller markets with from 15 to 29 radio stations, the total "cap" (permitted absolute amount) drops to 6, with 4 of any one modulation. Finally, in markets with less than 14 commercial radio stations, the top total that any one company can own is 5, with no more than 3 as AM or FM (up to half the stations in the market). The FCC also extended the length of the license period.[41]

The Telecommunications Act of 1996 set off the greatest merger wave in history. CBS took over Infinity Broadcasting; Hicks Muse, a Dallas investment firm, acquired more than 400 stations. In a telling metaphor, Infinity's founder, Mel Karmazin, noted: "It's like combining two ocean front properties." He meant that the new empire would not be some mom-and-pop collection of rural stations in small towns, but would own 7 outlets in New York City, 6 in Los Angeles, 10 in Chicago, 8 in San Francisco and 4 in Washington, DC. In the top 10 markets, the new CBS radio combo, had it been in place in 1995, would have commanded nearly one third of all radio broadcasting advertising revenues in the United States.[42]

For its study the FCC found that at the national level, approximately 2.5% more commercial radio stations had started broadcasting during the period under review, that is, from March 1996 to November 1997. However, the number of owners of commercial radio stations had declined by 11.7% primarily due to mergers between existing owners. The result of these mergers changed the ranking and composition of the top radio station owners. At a local level, the FCC found that there had been a downward trend in the number of radio station owners in Arbitron Metro markets. Further, the top owners in each Metro market generally accounted for an increasing share of the total radio advertising revenues in these markets. However, there does not appear to be any downward trend in the variety of radio formats available to consumers in these markets. Acquiring radio companies appeared to have pursued format diversification, rather than dominating a format.[43]

At the industry level, publicly traded companies whose primary business is radio broadcasting experienced robust financial performance. Although their profit margins varied, this depended largely on how much debt they took on to effect their mergers and acquisitions. Despite high debt loads, the FCC found, their financial health was good, which was reflected in stock returns better than those of the typical Standard & Poor's 500 company. The market's valuation of radio companies suggested that the stock market foresaw future earnings growth in the radio industry.

The Telecommunications Act of 1996 opened expansion, according to the FCC, because provisions first required that the Commission eliminate any provisions that limited the number of AM and FM stations that one entity could own or control on a nationwide basis. Still there continued to be rules capping ownership within each market.

Looking at the particulars, the FCC found that since the passage and implementation of the Act, there has been an increase of about 2.5% in the number of commercial radio stations. As of November 1997, there were over 10,470 commercial radio stations in the United States. Of these, about 54% (5,656) were FM stations and 46% (4,819) were AM stations. All the growth in stations since passage of the 1996 Act had been in FM stations. Whereas the number of radio stations has grown, the number of radio owners has declined by 11.7%. As of November 1997, there were 4,507 owners of radio stations across the United States.

The decline in the number of owners reflected the consolidation of the radio industry that was the result of a tremendous amount of trading in radio stations. The FCC calculated that in the first year of the Telecommunications Act, 2,066 radio stations changed owners (about 20% of the total number of stations). In contrast, in the 12-month period prior to the Act, some 988 radio stations changed owners. As a result of this trading activity, the FCC observed that there are now 32 radio station owners with over 20 stations. Consequently, there has been a significant increase in the number of large group owners since March 1996. Further, there have been changes in the composition of the top 50 radio group owners, reflecting mergers between companies that were among the top 50 radio owners. Thus, the decline in the number of owners of radio stations nationally reflects mergers or acquisitions between existing owners that has resulted in more large radio group owners.

Traditionally, one measure of diversity of concern for the FCC has been the number of independent owners of radio stations in a local market. The FCC calculated that a decline in the number of radio owners nationally reflected a general trend across markets, and was not simply the result of consolidations in a few large or small markets. A second dimension of diversity concerned program diversity as reflected, at least in part, by the number of distinct radio formats available in each market. The FCC found that diversity by this measure did suffer with the wave of mergers. Finally, a standard measure of economic concentration is the Herfindahl–Hirschman Index (HHI). The FCC calculated the HHI for each radio market using radio station revenues and noted that as the size of the market decreased, HHIs generally increased. This, the FCC analysts concluded, suggested there was a general trend toward increased economic concentration across markets. In other words, fewer owners generally earned a larger percentage of the revenue in their market.

This trend of fewer owners generally earning a larger percentage of market revenue is further emphasized by looking at the revenue share of the top four owners in the market (i.e., the four-firm concentration ratio). The FCC calculated that the revenue share had generally risen across markets. By November 1997, the top four radio owners generally accounted for about 90% of their market's total revenues.

Rather than concentrating on particular formats, these owners chose to operate stations with a variety of formats, which allowed them to appeal to more advertisers, and in particular to advertisers who want to reach a variety of audiences. If advertisers could purchase all the different types of radio advertising they needed from just one owner, then they could each save the cost of contracting with additional owners.

Finally, the FCC used Standard & Poor's (S&P) Compustat database to obtain financial information on all publicly traded companies whose primary SIC code, or industry classification, was radio broadcasting (SIC 4832). Using this criteria, commission staffers collected quarterly data and calculated financial ratios for 18 companies representing over 700 stations, and more than 33% of total reported radio industry revenues. Thus, most of the companies included on its list were larger group owners, and therefore may not reflect the performance of smaller owners (i.e., owners of two or fewer stations). To give perspective to the calculated financial ratios, commission staffers calculated similar ratios for the S&P 500 companies, and then compared the median value of the calculated financial ratios for radio companies to the median value of the same ratios for the S&P 500 companies. They used the median, rather than the average, as financial ratios are rarely normally distributed and it is important that outliers (i.e., unusually high or low values) do not distort the analysis. They used the S&P 500 companies to create the benchmark financial ratios because the S&P 500 is typically thought of representing the "market." Thus, this reflects an effort to create benchmarks based on a broad swath of companies.

With the aforementioned presumptions in mind, the FCC staffers analyzed the financial health of the radio industry as of 1997. By various measures, the FCC staff found radio companies grossing more than the typical public company. Although not generating the same level of cash flows to interest expense as other companies, radio companies were generating enough cash flow to meet their interest obligations. The FCC found that radio companies were better off than the typical S&P 500 firm. Altogether, the FCC calculated that the radio industry was enjoying robust health and excellent future prospects; radio company stocks were doing relatively well. Such an interpretation is consistent with reported evidence in *Broadcasting & Cable* magazine. Over 1997, the *Bloomberg/Broadcast & Cable* radio index was up 107%, and the S&P 500 index was up 31%. Clearly, investors viewed the Telecommunications Act's relaxation of radio ownership limits as improving the future prospects of the radio industry because much of this price appreciation was properly ascribed by industry observers to the radio industry's drive toward consolidation. Thus, following the FCC's lead, the next section considers the major consolidations of radio ownership and analyzes how the consolidation took place, and what business strategies resulted.

RADIO'S MAJOR CORPORATIONS

Although local radio stations air to a local audience, it has long been known that there are sizable economies of scale in radio, with chains defining the industry to limits set by government. It was not until the Telecommunications Act of 1996 that chains could grow to vast empires. That consolidation is the central theme of this section. In 1997 the top 10 of 1996 shrunk to the top 6 by the end of 1997 (as seen in Table 5.6). These dominant players defined the bulk of the listenership in the United States (as seen in Table 5.11). The shrinkage of concentration and listenership was even greater in 1998. And (as seen later in Table 5.10) these radio holdings were often, but not always, part of larger media conglomerates.

By Fall 1998, the top media groups were led by a Big Three: Hicks Muse, CBS and Clear Channel. Disney's ABC and Cox followed.

Because radio operates locally, the discussion centers on one market, Washington, DC, which provides a vivid example of the new ownership in a top 10 market. Through the mid-1990s, change in ownership was the order of the day. Hicks Muse's Evergreen, and CBS—both members of radio's new majors—moved into the nation's capital to take over stations in a populous and well-off market. Thanks to strong Washington demographics, although the market was eighth in population

TABLE 5.6
Top 10 Media Companies Ranked by Radio Revenues (1995 base)

Name and Rank	Radio Revenue in Millions			Radio as % of Company's Media		
	1997	1996	1995	1997	1996	1995
1. CBS Corp.	$1,187.0	$933.5	$880.3	21.7%	21.5%	20.4%
2. Evergreen Media Corporation***	*	438.6	248.1	*	100.0	100.0
3. Walt Disney Company	450.0	420.0	406.0	6.5	6.4	6.5
4. Clear Channel Communications	402.9	320.4	270.0	48.9	49.5	45.5
5. American Radio Systems****	374.1	322.4	194.7	100.0	100.0	100.0
6. Jacor Communications*****	503.4	315.4	290.7	94.9	92.1	92.3
7. Capstar Broadcasting***	570.0	249.3	**	100.0	100.0	**
8. SFX Broadcasting***	*	234.5	190.4	*	100.0	100.0
9. Chancellor Broadcasting***	548.9	231.2	185.3	100.0	100.0	100.0
10. Cox Enterprises	199.6	191.0	123.6	6.0	6.2	4.5

*No longer separate company in 1997.
**Not a separate company in 1995.
***In 1999, a part of Hicks Muse's AM/FM group (see Table 5.7).
****In 1999, a part of CBS's Infinity Broadcasting group (see Table 5.7).
*****In 1999, a part of Clear Channel Communications group (see Table 5.7).
Sources: *Advertising Age*, August 18, 1997, p. S5; *Advertising Age*, August 18, 1997, p. S10.

TABLE 5.7
The 10 Top Radio Groups Ranked by Revenues

Radio Group	Headquarters Location	Estimated 1998 Revenue (in millions)	Number of Stations
1. Hicks Muse's AM–FM	Dallas	$1,857	460
2. CBS's Infinity Broadcasting	New York City	$1,668	163
3. Clear Channel Communications	San Antonio, TX	$1,223	484
4. Disney's ABC Radio	Dallas	$355	43
5. Entercom Communications	Bala Cynwyd, PA	$311	85
6. Cox Radio	Atlanta	$284	58
7. Hispanic Radio	Dallas	$187	42
8. Cumulus Media	Milwaukee	$175	248
9. Citadel Communications	Las Vegas, NV	$165	118
10. Susquehanna Radio	York, PA	$163	26

Source: "Radio Control: Top 25 Claim 19% of Stations," *Broadcasting & Cable*, August 30, 1999, pp. 26–32.

reached, it was sixth in advertising dollars spent. The Washington radio community had not seen such an "invasion" since the early days of radio when NBC and CBS established major outlets in the nation's capital. After the dust cleared, eight stations controlled by Hicks Muse and Westinghouse/CBS accounted for more than one third of all advertising dollars (and nearly that in listener share). Indeed, eight companies controlled about 90% of the total ratings and revenues.[44]

In the hit 1988 movie *Working Girl*, an aspiring Wall Street tycoon played by Melanie Griffith hatches a plan to help a company gain a foothold in broadcasting,

TABLE 5.8
Top 10 Media Companies by Radio Revenues, 1996 and 1997

	Radio Revenue (in millions)		Radio as % of Company's Media	
	1997	1996	1997	1996
1. CBS Corporation	$1,187.0	$554.0	21.7%	12.4%
2. Capstar*	570.0	249.3	100.0	100.0
3. Chancellor Media	548.9	231.3	100.0	1000.0
4. Jacor Communications	503.4	223.8	94.9	89.2
5. Walt Disney	450.0	420.0	6.5	6.5
6. Clear Channel	402.9	340.7	48.9	47.8
7. American Radio Systems**	374.1	322.4	100.0	100.0
8. Cox Enterprises	199.6	191.0	6.0	6.2
9. Sinclair	66.6	40.0	12.9	10.6
10. Tribune	65.5	64.2	2.8	3.0

*Owned by Hicks Muse in 1999.
**Owned by CBS in 1999.
Source: *Advertising Age*, August 17, 1998, p. S10.

TABLE 5.9
The 25 Top Media Groups and their Radio Holdings

1. Time Warner Inc.—No Radio
2. The Walt Disney Company—ABC Radio Network, AM & FM stations
3. Sony—No Radio
4. Viacom*—No Radio
5. News Corporation—No Radio
6. Tele-Communications, Inc.**—No Radio
7. Seagram—No Radio
8. CBS—AM & FM stations, CBS Network
9. General Electric's NBC—No Radio
10. Cox Enterprises—AM & FM stations
11. Comcast Corporation—No Radio
12. Gannett—No Radio
13. Hearst Corporation—No Radio
14. McGraw-Hill Companies—No Radio
15. New York Times—Two radio stations

*Prior to proposed CBS Viacom merger of September 1999
**Prior to 1998 merger with AT&T
Source: "25 Top Media Groups," *Broadcasting & Cable*, September 7, 1998, pp. 26–34.

through radio. Yet all seasoned Wall Streeters put her down: "Radio is small potatoes." But this "working girl" was prophetic, and later after Congress shed decades-old rules, more than one quarter of the commercial radio stations changed hands in deals worth an estimated $25 billion. By late 1997, Westinghouse/CBS and Hicks Muse's group controlled roughly half the radio advertising in the top five markets in the United States (i.e., New York, Los Angeles, Chicago, San Francisco and

Philadelphia). Trading was so heavy that one station, KYCW in Seattle, had four owners between January 1996 and October 1997. The motivation is to group advertising buying and thus increase radio's revenue side; the "new" radio took dead aim at television and newspaper's share of the advertising pie.[45]

Muse, Tate & Furst, Inc. (hereafter simply Hicks Muse), an investment company unknown to the radio business in 1995, by the 1990s had more stations (in excess of 400) than at any point since radio was innovated in the United States. The deals came along with startling speed. In February 1997, the largest radio group was formed through two deals worth more than $1.6 billion. The combined company, to be called Chancellor Media Corporation, was put together by Hicks Muse, and later that month Hicks Muse acquired Evergreen and the rush was on. Next came the purchase of 10 radio properties owned by Viacom Inc. for $1.075 billion, bringing Hicks Muse to notice with a combined enterprise of 103 radio stations in 21 markets with aggregate net revenues of more than $700 million and an enterprise value of about $5 billion.*

In April 1997, Evergreen grabbed up Gannett's last five radio stations (WGCI-AM and WGCI-FM in Chicago, KHKS-FM in Dallas and KKBQ-AM and KKBQ-FM in Houston) for $340 million, and sold WPNT-FM and WLUP-FM in Chicago and KDFC-FM in San Francisco to Bonneville International Corporation for $205 million. They did the latter to make sure the company could not be judged by the U.S. Department of Justice as being too strong in any one place. In 1999, there was even talk that Hicks Muse and Clear Channel Communication might get together, but as of mid-1999, no such mega-deal had taken place. But, if it did—with Clear Channel's acquisition of Jacor—the result would constitute the greatest concentration of radio stations in U.S. history.[46]

In late 1998, Chancellor Media Corporation announced it would stop acquisitions as it digested August 1998's $3.9 billion merger with sister company Capstar Broadcasting. This August 1998 merger established Hicks Muse as the number one owner in radio history. From August 1998 on, the game was maximizing revenues from these combined properties—by offering national sponsors national deals including regional advertising in "clusters." By 1999, Thomas Hicks had cut 24 separate deals in two years, cresting a portfolio that Wall Street valued at between $16 billion and $24 billion. Chancellor Media (110 radio stations) plus Capstar Broadcasting (355 radio stations) gave Hicks Muse its dominant 465 radio stations.[47]

In March 1999, Thomas Hicks announced plans to drop the purchase of Lin television stations. He let go top management. The heavy debt taken on to build the company did not seem to be paying off; he seemed to be cashing in. (This was long expected because Hicks Muse is an investment company by origin.) But despite this uncertainty, Hicks Muse maintained more stations than CBS and Clear Channel, but about the same amount of revenue. All had estimated annual revenues for 1999 in the $2.5 billion range. The cash flow thrown off was about the same at $1 billion

---

*As we go to press, in late 1999 Hicks, Muse proposed to sell its radio holdings to Clear Channel Communications, Inc. The deal, when and if finalized, would formally combine the two companies sometime during the spring of 2000.

per annum. Hicks Muse debt, at $7.5 billion, was twice that of Clear Channel, and fifty times that of CBS radio's Infinity division.[48]

Based in Dallas, Texas, and run principally by Thomas O. Hicks, Hicks Muse by mid-1997 had 5 stations in New York City, 5 in Los Angeles, 8 in Chicago, 10 in San Francisco, 8 in Philadelphia, 7 in Detroit, 2 in Dallas, 8 in Washington, DC, 2 in Houston and 3 in Boston. He would continue to buy more. Hicks Muse owned radio down to Jackson, Tennessee (media market 257), as well as television stations, wireless television operations in Argentina and Mexico, Muzak franchises and cable television operations for hospitals. Hicks Muse would invest in whatever it figured would make money (i.e., hotels and real estate). Ghirardelli Chocolate, Chef Boyardee and Stetson hats were controlled by Hicks Muse. In 1994, when federal deregulation opened up radio, Hicks Muse purchased two stations in Sacramento and built up from there.[49]

At the time the annual *Broadcasting & Cable* report on radio ownership came out in July 1997, Hicks Muse also had acquired Katz Media Group for $155 million in cash plus $128 million in assumed debt. Katz was a leading seller of radio (and television) national spot advertising. Katz sold advertising time on behalf of 2,000 local radio stations and 340 television stations, and in its section of the radio world raked in more than half of the $1.5 billion market for targeted national advertising on local stations. Hicks Muse, Cox, NBC and ABC were broadcasters in the "rep" business. Further, Hicks Muse formed a national radio network. It hired David Kantor, then the president of ABC Radio Networks, to run what would be called "AMFM Radio Networks."[50]

But Hicks Muse's biggest deal took place in late August 1997 with the purchase of SFX Broadcasting's 71 stations (a former radio top 10 group owner) for $1.2 billion in cash. The deal gave Hicks Muse some 413 stations, although the company was trading so fast no one was sure of the exact number. Whatever the precise holdings, revenues were guaranteed to have made Hicks Muse the first billion dollar (in terms of revenues) radio owner.

SFX itself had been a powerhouse, based in New York City, with stations in Dallas and Houston as well as Pittsburgh (market 20), Indianapolis (market 36), Charlotte, North Carolina (market 37), Hartford, Connecticut (market 42) and Richmond, Virginia (market 56).[51]

This SFX deal caught the eye of the U.S. Department of Justice, which began to investigate. As a result, Hicks Muse stopped radio acquisitions and began to cooperate with the Department of Justice, announcing it would sell 11 stations before the end of 1997. These stations were in Connecticut and New York: WEFX-FM, licensed to Norwalk, Connecticut; WKHL-FM, licensed to Stamford, Connecticut; WRKI-FM, licensed to Brookfield, Connecticut; WAXB-FM, licensed to Patterson, New York; WPUT-AM, licensed to Brewster, New York; WFAS-AM/FM, licensed to White Plains, New York; and WZZN-FM, licensed to Mt. Kisko, New York.[52]

In early November 1997, the U.S. government moved to try to block part of the Hicks Muse–SFX merger. In a complaint filed in U.S. District Court in New York, the department alleged that the deal with SFX to buy four Long Island stations would result in local businesses paying higher radio advertising prices, which would ultimately be passed on to consumers. The government alleged this deal would create a dominant Long Island radio group with more than 65% of the local radio advertising market. The outcome of the case, if it goes to trial, will lie on the definition of the whole of the advertising market, and the identification of effective substitutes for radio listening.[53]

But Hicks Muse always had other investments. In September 1997, in a $100 million deal, Hicks Muse purchased the OmniAmerica Group to construct radio and TV transmission. In November 1997, Hicks Muse moved internationally. With Ernesto Moya, a leading member of the Mexican business community, it established an exclusive relationship under which Evaluacion y Manejo de Empresas, a Mexico City-based firm, would invest in Mexican industrial companies. This seemed to be heading Hicks Muse, which since its formation in 1989 had completed more than 100 deals with an aggregate capital value in excess of $25 billion ($7 billion in media), to acquire and invest in TV and radio properties throughout Latin America, Caribbean, Spain and Portugal. Radio in these areas is still highly fragmented. Hicks Muse took positions such as partnering in Venevision, the largest producer of Spanish-language programming in South America, and also with the Univision network. The world of media seemed to be the next battlefield for the mightiest force in U.S. radio. Yet its commitment into the 21st century looked to be 50–50 at best. Thomas Hicks considered whether he and his firm ought to cash in or try to milk profits from its 400+ radio stations through skilled management of costs and adapting economies of scale.[54]

CBS owned far fewer radio stations than Hicks Muse, but its 161 stations earned just as much in revenues, and about half the CBS profit in 1999.* With stations in the top 10 market, CBS, led by CEO and founder of Infinity radio Mel Karmazin, represented a contrast to Hicks Muse. It was a media company with a very profitable radio division, not held for speculation, but functioning at the heart of the corporation's strategy for the future.[55]

In the 1990s, CBS played the radio strategy of buying and operating stations in only the biggest U.S. markets. (Hicks Muse concentrated on medium- to small-sized cities.) Thus CBS had a larger revenue base. When the Westinghouse Electric Corporation acquired CBS in November 1995 for $5.4 billion, the creation of this radio conglomerate became a core part of the broader Westinghouse strategy; in December 1997, the corporation was officially renamed CBS. The new CBS then sold off all remaining nonmedia assets. New CEO Michael Jordan, decided to sell off units where his company might not be able to achieve number one status in the marketplace. His strategy was not to be a conglomerate of many unrelated parts, but a media company that would dominate broadcast radio and broadcast television.

And, when Mel Karmazin succeeded Jordan in 1998, he concentrated on squeezing maximum profits from the CBS radio group. As of the end of 1998, CBS owned 161 stations in 34 markets, laying claim to 9 of the top 16 top billers and controlling about 1 in 9 of advertising spending for radio.[56]

---

*As we go to press, in late 1999 Viacom proposed to acquire CBS. The deal, when and if finalized, would formally combine the two companies sometime during the spring of 2000. See Douglas Gomery, "The Company That Would Be King," *American Journalism Review*, December 1999, p. 66.

PROFILE: CBS Corporation

Basic Data:
Headquarters: New York City
Web sites: www.cbs.com
CEO in 1999: Mel Karmazin
1998 Sales (in millions): $6,805
1998 Net Profits (in millions): –$12
1998 Assets (in millions): $20,139
Rank in 1998 Forbes 500—Sales: 228

Market Holdings:
Broadcast Television: CBS television network, CBS owned and operated television stations
   (including WCBS-New York, KCBS-Los Angeles, WBBM-Chicago, KYW-Philadelphia,
   KPIX-San Francisco, WBZ-Boston, WFOR-Miami and KDKA-Pittsburgh, among others);
   owner of King World Syndication.
Cable Television: The Nashville Network, Country Music Television.
Radio: CBS radio network, CBS radio owned and operated stations (including WCBS-New
   York, WBZ-Boston and KDKA-Pittsburgh, among others).
Film & Television: Joint venture in Twentieth Century-Fox Home Entertainment.

Significant Events:
1993: New management team, led by former PepsiCo executive Michael Jordan, took and
   began to transform the company.
1994: Sells electrical distribution and control business to car parts maker Eaton.
1995: Acquires CBS from Loews, Inc. for $5.4 billion and combines Group W Westinghouse
   owned 5 television broadcast and 18 radio stations with CBS owned and operated units.
1996: Sells Knoll Group furniture maker and defense electronics unit for combined $3.5 billion.
1996: Buys Telenoticias, a 24-hour news channel seen in 22 Spanish-speaking countries.
June 1996: Acquires Infinity Broadcasting, major radio company, for $4 billion.
1997: Buys cable's The Nashville Network and Country Music TV for $1.55 billion, and thus
   expands ito cable programming.
1997: Former Infinity Radio CEO Mel Karmazin takes charge of radio and television, and a
   year later he would replaced Michael Jordan as CBS's CEO.
1997: Acquires American Radio Systems chain for $2.6 billion, bringing CBS radio owned
   stations to number 175.
1997: On December 1, 1997, Westinghouse Electric Corporation becomes CBS Corporation
   and moves headquarters from Pittsburgh to New York City, and sells last of industrial
   assets.
1998: CBS conceeds defeat and sells its money losing cable TV network Eye of People to
   Discovery Commuications, Inc.
1999: CBS sells to Viacom.

CBS' radio ownership strategy was to dominate as many of the nation's biggest media markets as possible. Under Mel Karmazin, CBS not only owned the flagship station in New York, WCBS-FM, but also six more stations in the largest media market in the United States, New York City. As the 1990s ended, the breadth of ownership in the largest markets in the U.S. was impressive: eight radio stations in Los Angeles (media market 2), seven in Chicago (media market 3), eight in San Francisco (media market 4), five in Philadelphia (media market 5), six in Detroit (media market 6), six in Dallas (media market 7), five in Washington, DC (media market 8), five in Houston (media market 9), and four in Boston (media market 10). In the

TABLE 5.10
CBS Radio Stations, 1997

Atlanta: WAOK-AM, WVEE-FM & WZGC-FM
Austin: KJCE-AM, KAMX-FM & KKMJ-FM
Baltimore: WBGR-AM, WBMD-AM, WCAO-AM, WJFK-AM, WLIF-FM, WOCT-FM, WQSR-FM,
     WWMX-FM & WXYV-FM
Boston: WBZ-AM, WEEI-AM, WNFT-AM, WRKO-AM, WAAF-FM, WODS-FM, WBCN-FM,
     WBMX-FM, WEGQ-FM, & WZLX-FM
Buffalo: WECK-AM, WJYE-FM, WLCE-FM & WYRK-FM
Charlotte-Gastonia-Rock Hill: WFNZ-AM, WGIV-AM, WBAV-FM, WNKS-FM, WPEG-FM, WSOC-FM
     & WSSS-FM
Chicago: WMAQ-AM, WSCR-AM, WBBM-AM & FM, WCKG-FM, WJMK-FM, WUSN-FM & WXRT-
     FM
Cincinnati: WGRR-FM, WKRQ-FM & WMMA-FM
Dallas-Ft. Worth: KHVN-AM, KOOO-AM, KRLD-AM, KLUV-FM, KOAI-FM, KRBV-FM,
     KVIL-FM & KYNG-FM
Detroit: WWJ-AM, WXYT-AM, WKRK-FM, WOMC-FM, WVMV-FM & WYCD-FM
Fresno: KMJ-AM, KOQO-AM & FM, KKDJ-FM, KNAX-FM, KSKS-FM & KVSR-FM
Hartford: WTIC-AM & FM, WRCH-FM & WZMX-FM
Houston: KXYZ-AM, KIKK-AM & FM & KILT-AM & FM
Kansas City: KOWW-AM, WDAF-AM, KBEQ-FM, KFKF-FM, KMXV-FM, KUDL-FM & KYYS-FM
Killeen-Temple, TX: KKIK-FM
Las Vegas: KXNO-AM, KXNT-AM, KLUC-FM, KMXB-FM, KMZQ-FM & KXTE-FM
Los Angeles: KFWB-AM, KNX-AM, KRLA-AM, KCBS-FM, KLSX-FM, KROQ-FM, KRTH-FM &
     KTWV-FM
Minneapolis-St. Paul: WCCO-AM & WLTE-FM
Monterey-Salinas-Santa Cruz: KLUE-FM
New York: WFAN-AM, WINS-AM, WCBS-AM & FM, WNEW-FM & WXRK-FM
Philadelphia: KYW-AM, WIP-AM, WPHT-AM, WOGL-FM & WYSP-FM
Pittsburgh, PA: KDKA-AM, WBZZ-FM, WDSY-FM & WZPT-FM
Portland, OR: KUPL-AM & FM, KBBT-FM, KINK-FM, KKJZ-FM & KUFO-FM
Portsmouth-Dover, NH: WMYF-AM & WZNN-AM
Riverside-San Bernardino: KFRG-FM
Rochester: WCMF-FM, WPXY-FM, WRMM-FM & WZNE-FM
Sacramento: KCTC-AM, KHTK-AM, KQPT-AM, KNCI-FM, KRAK-FM, KSFM-FM,
     KYMX-FM & KZZO-FM
San Francisco: KBRG-FM, KCBS-AM, KFRC-AM & FM, KYCY-AM & FM, KITS-FM & KLLC-FM
San Jose: KEZR-FM, KOME-FM & KUFX-FM
St. Louis: KFNS-AM, KMOX-AM, KEZK-FM, KSD-FM & KYKY-FM
Seattle-Tacoma: KRPM-AM, KBKS-FM, KMPS-FM, KYCW-FM & KZOK-FM
Tampa-St. Petersburg-Clearwater: WQYK-AM & FM
Washington, D.C.: WPGC-AM & FM, WARW-FM, WHFS-FM & WJFK-FM
West Palm Beach-Boca Raton: WEAT-FM & WIRK-FM
Worcester, MA: WWTM-AM

Source: Radio & Records Web site at www.rronline.com.

next 10, CBS held strong radio positions in Atlanta (media market 12), Minneapolis (media market 16), St. Louis (media market 17), and Baltimore (media market 19). (See Table 5.7.) All this added up to an equal status as Hick Muse, but accomplished in a far different manner.[57]

CBS also acquired the Westwood One radio network, which merged with its own CBS network. Named for the Westwood neighborhood in Los Angeles by founder Norman J. Pattiz in 1974, Westwood One took off when Pattiz hired local disc jockey (DJ) Casey Kasem to host a countdown pop music program. Pattiz "networked" this program to hundreds of radio stations across the United States. By the early 1990s, there were five Westwood One radio networks—Westwood One, NBC's The Source, NBC Talknet, NBC Radio Network and Mutual. These offered such feeds as "MTV News," "Bright AC," "The Oldies Channel," "Country Countdown," "Money Magazine Business Report," "Science Update" and the regular broadcasts of Dr. Joyce Brothers, Don Criqui and Larry King. Westwood One's growth accelerated because it had acquired two of the more fabled network properties in radio history: Mutual (for $37 million in December 1985 from Amway) and NBC (for $50 million in 1987 from General Electric). The building up of CBS meant the combination of network radio's past giants into one network force.[58]

But Jordan had also consummated one of the biggest mergers in radio industry. In September 1997, he signed to buy American Radio Systems Corporation for $1.6 billion. Boston-based American Radio, then the nation's fifth largest radio company, owned 98 stations. This single deal brought Westinghouse's total radio holdings to 175, and was the core of bringing CBS to equal status with Hicks Muse.[59]

Here was the supplementation of CBS's big city strategy. By acquiring American Radio, CBS added five stations in San Francisco (market 4) and seven in Boston (market 10), plus a slew of stations in medium-sized cities like Cincinnati (media market 25), Sacramento, California (media market 28), Buffalo, New York (media market 40) and Las Vegas (media market 45). Thus, at the time of the merger, whereas American Radio owned more stations than CBS (104 vs. 74), they reached less than half of Westinghouse's listeners. Still, in its 1996 radio ownership listing, *Broadcasting & Cable* placed American Radio Systems in seventh place and moving up with the completion of the August 1996 purchase of EZ Communications for $655 million. At the time, the EZ deal (small by 1997 standards) ranked as the second largest in radio history. The EZ purchase did symbolize what was to come: Owner and founder Art Keller, who had begun with one station in 1967 in suburban Washington, DC, decided to "cash in" rather than try (with 23 stations) to compete with the new radio powers.[60]

Clear Channel Communications, Inc., based in San Antonio, Texas, ranked third behind Hicks Muse and CBS, but was the only other major radio company in their league. Clear Channel took a compromise road, owning big city stations like CBS, but also owning radio in smaller markets as well. As the 1990s ended, Clear Channel owned stations in the top U.S. markets: three in New York City (market 1), three in Los Angeles (market 2), three in Chicago (market 3), two in San Francisco (market 4), five in Dallas (market 7), eight in Houston (market 9). Yet Clear Channel was still best thought of as a force in small and medium markets in communities such as Grand Rapids, Michigan (media market 66), and El Paso, Texas (media market 69). (See Table 5.11.) Like Hicks Muse and CBS, Clear Channel owns and operates television stations. But, unlike its competitors, Clear Channel had also expanded abroad, acquiring radio stations in Australia, New Zealand and the Czech Republic. Clear Channel's most significant move, however, was its 1998 acquisition of Jacor group.[61]

The Jacor purchase was so big that, in April 1999, the U.S. Department of Justice would approve the announced $4.4 billion deal only if Clear Channel sold 18 sta-

TABLE 5.11
Clear Chanel Communications Radio Stations, 1997

Austin: KFON-AM, KEYI-FM, KHFI-FM & KPEZ-FM
Cleveland: WERE-AM, WENZ-FM & WNCX-FM
Columbia, SC: WOIC-AM, WARQ-FM, WMFX-FM & WWDM-FM
Cookeville, TN: WHUB-AM, WPTN-AM, WGIC-FM & WGSQ-FM
El Paso, TX: KHEY-AM & FM & KPRR-FM
Ft. Myers-Naples: WKII-AM, WCKT-FM, WOLZ-FM, WQNU-FM & WXRM-FM
Grand Rapids: WTKG-AM, WOOD-AM & FM, WBCT-FM, WCUZ-FM & WVTI-FM
Greensboro-Winston Salem-High Point: WSJS-AM, WTQR-FM & WXRA-FM
Houston-Galveston: KPRC-AM, KSEV-AM, KJOJ-AM & FM, KBXX-FM & KMJQ-FM
Jackson, MS: WOAD-AM, WKXI-AM & FM & WJMI-FM
Jacksonville: WNZS-AM, WZNZ-AM, WFSJ-FM, WPLA-FM, WROO-FM & WTLK-FM
Key West, FL: WKRY-FM
Lancaster, PA: WLAN-AM & FM
Little Rock: KDDK-FM, KMJX-FM, KMVK-FM, KOLL-FM & KSSN-FM
Louisville: WHAS-AM, WKJK-AM, WWKY-AM, WAMZ-FM, WQMF-FM & WTFX-FM
Marathon, FL: WAVK-FM
Memphis: KWAM-AM, WDIA-AM, WREC-AM, KJMS-FM, WEGR-FM, WHRK-FM &WRXQ-FM
Miami-Ft. Lauderdale: WFTL-AM, WINZ-AM, WIOD-AM, WBGG-FM, WHYI-FM, WLVE-FM, WPLL-
    FM & WZTA-FM
Milwaukee: WOKY-AM, WKKV-FM, WMIL-FM & WZTR-FM
Mobile: WNTM-AM, WKSJ-AM & FM, WDWG-FM, WMXC-FM & WRKH-FM
New Haven, CT: WAVZ-AM, WELI-AM & WKCI-FM
New Orleans: WODT-AM, WYLD-AM & FM, KHOM-FM, KKND-FM, WNOE-FM & WQUE-FM
Norfolk: WJCD-FM, WMYK-FM, WOWI-FM & WSVY-FM
Oklahoma City: KEBC-AM, KTOK-AM, KJYO-FM, KNRX-FM, KTST-FM & KXXY-FM
Orlando: WQTM-AM, WWNZ-AM, WJRR-FM, WMGF-FM, WSHE-FM & WTKS-FM
Panama City, FL: WDIZ-AM, WFSY-FM, WPAP-FM, WPBH-FM & WSHF-FM
Pensacola, FL: WTKX-FM & WYCL-FM
Plantation Key, FL: WFKZ-FM
Providence, RI: WWBB-FM & WWRX-FM
Raleigh-Durham: WDUR-AM, WFXC-FM, WFXK-FM, WQOK-FM & WZZU-FM
Reading, PA: WRAW-AM & WRFY-FM
Richmond: WRNL-AM, WRVA-AM, WTVR-AM & FM, WRVQ-FM & WRXL-FM
San Antonio: KTKR-AM, WOAI-AM, KAJA-FM & KQXT-FM
Springfield, MA: WHYN-AM & FM
Tallahassee, FL: WNLS-AM, WJZT-FM, WSNI-FM, WTNT-FM & WXSR-FM
Tampa: WHNZ-AM, WZTM-AM, WMTX-AM & FM, WRBQ-AM & FM, WHPT-FM, WKES-FM &
    WSJT-FM
Tulsa: KAKC-AM, KQLL-AM & FM, KMOD-FM, KOAS-FM & KQSY-FM
West Palm Beach-Boca Raton: WBZT-AM, WEAT-AM, WKGR-FM & WOLL-FM

Source: Radio & Records Web site at www.rronline.com.

tions. The Department determined the original deal had reduced competition in the advertising markets of Cleveland and Dayton, Ohio, Louisville, Kentucky, and Tampa, Florida. (The radio mergers and acquisitions market was so fluid at this point that independent analysts announced they figured the Clear Channel merger should have been properly valued at $6.4 billion.) The merger was finally consummated in 1999, and the employees at Jacor, then headquartered in Covington, Kentucky, were finally absorbed into Clear Channel. The 20-year-old Jacor company's CEO Randy

Michaels was named President of the combined company's 450 U.S. radio stations. "This merger is going to allow us to wreak havoc in new and interesting ways," Michaels told Gavin, admitting that doubling the number of stations will require "some reorganization" in his staffing. "Ultimately, it's the blending of the people, the assets, and the balance sheets that's going to make us the winner," he said. "No one in this business or anywhere else knows radio like Randy. I'm confident he'll be a huge force in taking all 450 radio stations to their peak," said Clear Channel President Mark Mays. "I'm also glad I don't have to compete against him anymore." And what about further acquisitions? "Four hundred and fifty is just a stepping stone to 1,000," Michaels quipped in 1999.[62]

The acquisition of Jacor moved Clear Channel more outside the top 10 metro markets of the United States, with the exception of adding a couple of outlets in Los Angeles. Jacor added strong positions in medium-sized cities such as Denver (media market 23, with nine stations), Cincinnati (media market 25, with eight stations) and Columbus, Ohio (media market 32, with seven stations). Salt Lake City, Utah; Rochester, New York; Louisville, Kentucky; Jacksonville, Florida; Toledo, Ohio; Lexington, Kentucky, and Boise, Idaho were also populated by Jacor—now Clear Channel—stations.[63]

Like its rivals, Jacor sought to cluster station ownership, so it spread costs across several stations and sold advertising in the same market to compete directly and effectively with metropolitan newspapers and television stations, but with better targeting. Jacor had so much success in Cincinnati, its home base, that in 1997 the U.S. federal government forced Jacor to sell a station rather than risk a formal complaint. In Cincinnati, spreading through southern Ohio and into northern Kentucky, Jacor's seven area radio stations plus its television station, the ABC affiliate WKRC, were heard or seen by 1.2 million people, whereas the leading newspaper, the *Cincinnati Enquirer*, had a daily circulation of "only" 200,000. As the 1990s ended, this clustering formed a clear trend by Hicks Muse, CBS and Clear Channel to dominate and extract more profits from the cities where they pushed up against the limit permitted by federal ownership policy. They saw the competition not as other radio stations per se, but television and newspapers that also offered extended reach to advertisers.[64]

And the case of Jacor offered another important trend in the changing radio business. Indeed, starting from early 1995, Jacor went from a bit player in the radio business to a rising star; it just did not expand as fast as Hicks Muse, CBS or Clear Channel. Starting with 26 stations in 1995, in 18 months Jacor had moved into 32 markets with nearly 150 stations. Thus, symbolically, from January 1996 to June 1997, Jacor fully participated in the buying binge—yet remained relatively behind. Only the extremely aggressive survived the merger mania of the late 1990s.[65]

To Clear Channel, the purchase of Jacor was one important deal among many. Although earlier Clear Channel deals paled in comparison, in the history of the radio industry they were surely of consequence. During Summer 1997, Clear Channel acquired Paxson Communications Corporation's 46 radio stations for nearly $700 million. As part of the deal, Clear Channel paid $33 million for two FM and two AM stations in West Palm Beach, Florida, which Paxson was then in the process of purchasing from American Radio Systems Corporation. Paxson, a top 20 radio

TABLE 5.12
Jacor Radio Stations, 1997

Atlanta: WGST-AM & FM, WKLS-FM & WPCH-FM
Baltimore: WPOC-FM
Casper, WY: KTWO-AM & KMGW-FM
Cedar Rapids, IA: KXIC-AM, WMT-AM, KKRQ-FM & WMT-FM
Charleston, SC: WEZL-FM, WRFQ-FM, WSUY-FM & WXLY-FM
Cheyenne, WY: KGAB-AM, KIGN-FM, KLEN-FM & KOLZ-FM
Cincinnati: WKRC-AM, WLW-AM, WEBN-FM, WOFX-FM & WWNK-FM
Cleveland: WKNR-AM, WTAM-AM, WGAR-FM, WLTF-FM, WMJI-FM & WMMS-FM
Boise, ID: KIDO-AM, KFXD-AM, KARO-FM, KCIX-FM, KLTB-FM & KXLT-FM
Columbus, OH: WFII-AM, WLOH-AM, WTVN-AM, WAZU-FM, WCOL-FM,WHOK-FM,
    WHQK-FM,WLVQ-FM, WNCI-FM & WZAZ-FM
Dallas-Ft. Worth: KDMX-FM & KEGL-FM
Dayton: WONE-AM, WBTT-FM, WLQT-FM, WMMX-FM, WTUE-FM & WXEG-FM
Denver: KHOW-AM, KOA-AM, KTLK-AM, KBCO-FM, KBPI-FM, KHIH-FM & KRFX-FM
Des Moines: WHO-AM & KLYF-FM
Findlay, OH: WHMQ-FM
Fort Collins, CO: KCOL-AM & KPAW-FM
Greeley, CO: KGLL-FM
Houston-Galveston: KHMX-FM & KTBZ-FM
Idaho Falls, ID: KID-AM & FM
Jacksonville: WJGR-AM, WZAZ-AM, WJBT-FM, WQIK-FM & WSOL-FM
Las Vegas: KBGO-FM, KFMS-FM, KSNE-FM & KWNR-FM
Lexington, KY: WLAP-AM, WTKT-AM, WKQQ-FM, WLKT-FM, WMXL-FM & WWYC-FM
Lima, OH: WIMA-AM, WBUK-FM & WIMT-FM
Los Angeles: KIIS-AM & FM
Louisville: WFIA-AM, WDJX-FM, WLRS-FM, WSFR-FM & WVEZ-FM
Macomb, IL: WLRB-AM
Marion, OH: WMRN-AM & FM & WDIF-FM
Minneapolis-St. Paul: KSGS-AM & KMJZ-FM
Munfordville, KY: WLOC-AM & WMCC-FM
Ottawa, OH: WQTL-FM
Phoenix: KHTC-FM & KZZP-FM
Pocatello, ID: KWIK-AM & KPKY-FM
Portland, OR: KEX-AM, KOTK-AM, KKCW-FM & KKRZ-FM
Rochester, NY: WHAM-AM, WHTK-AM, WMAX-FM, WMHX-FM, WNVE-FM, WRCD-FM
    & WVOR-FM
Salt Lake City: KALL-AM, KFAM-AM, KISN-AM, KKAT-FM, KODJ-FM, KURR-FM & KZHT-FM
San Diego: KOGO-AM, KPOP-AM, KSDO-AM, XTRA-AM & FM, KGB-FM, KHTS-FM,
    KIOZ-FM, KKBH-FM, KKLQ-FM, KMCG-FM & KXGL-FM
San Jose: KSJO-FM
San Luis Obispo, CA: KBAI-AM
Sandusky, OH: WLEC-AM & WCPZ-FM
Santa Barbara, CA: KIST-AM, KQSB-AM, KSBL-FM & KTYD-FM
Sarasota-Bradenton: WAMR-AM, WSPB-AM, WCTQ-FM, WSRZ-FM & WYNF-FM
Sebring, FL: WITS-AM, WJCM-AM & WYMR-FM
St. Louis: KATZ-AM & FM, KMJM-FM & WCBW-FM
Tampa: WDAE-AM, WFLA-AM, WAKS-FM, WDUV-FM, WFLZ-FM, WTBT-FM & WXTB-FM
Toledo: WCWA-AM, WSPD-AM, WIOT-FM, WRVF-FM & WVKS-FM
Twin Falls, ID: KLIX-AM & FM & KEZJ-FM
Washington Court House, OH: WOFR-AM & WCHO-FM
Youngstown-Warren: WNIO-AM, WKBN-AM & FM & WNCD-FM

Source: Radio & Records Web site at www.rronline.com.

owner at the time of the deal, was moving to television (see Chapter 4), and delivered not only control of the Miami radio market (market 11, nine stations), but also a sizable presence in Tampa (media market 21), Orlando (media market 38), West Palm Beach (media market 49), Jacksonville (media market 53), Lakeland (media market 104), Pensacola (media market 125), Tallahassee (media market 167) and Panama City (media market 224). (Paxson's only other holdings were in media market 44, Nashville.)[66]

The Walt Disney Company with its 1996 merger with ABC became a relative radio giant. But its radio holdings were smaller in number than those of Hicks Muse, CBS or Clear Channel. Disney offered a significant presence, however, because overall it ranked as the largest media conglomerate in the world. Michael Eisner and his management team kept a significant position in radio, keeping these assets rather than selling them off as it did with the newspapers it acquired from ABC/Capital Cities. Although Disney had the resources to become a larger radio power, it had chosen not to expand.

When in July 1996 Disney acquired Capital Cities/ABC, the headlines blared about synergy of a Hollywood studio and a television network. This deal vaulted Disney onto the list of major radio companies. There was a flagship station in New York City, WABC-AM, and significant holdings in top 10 markets: in media market two, Los Angeles (three stations); in market three, Chicago (two stations); in market four, San Francisco (two stations); in market six Detroit (three stations); in market seven Dallas (two stations); in market eight Washington, DC (three stations). (See Table 5.13.) Whereas many of these in the top 10 radio markets represented old-line AM stations, they continued to reach large audiences. Because of this top 10 market strategy, with about two dozen stations, Disney operated more like CBS, than like Hicks Muse or Clear Channel.

Still Disney took obvious opportunities to use synergy. In September 1997, Disney built on the ESPN brand when ESPN radio obtained exclusive rights for Major League Baseball for five years. The prior year, ABC Radio Networks announced a national roll out of Radio Disney, a live radio network for families and children under age 12. The network's format included the top 40-style playlist for children and several short-form features each hour. Radio Disney had made its debut in

TABLE 5.13
Disney/ABC Radio Stations, 1997

Atlanta: WDWD-AM, WKHX-FM & WYAY-FM
Chicago: WLS-AM & WXCD-FM
Dallas-Ft. Worth: WBAP-AM & KSCS-FM
Detroit: WJR-AM, WDRQ-FM & WPLT-FM
Los Angeles: KABC-AM, KTZN-AM & KLOS-FM
Minneapolis-St. Paul: KDIZ-AM, KEGE-FM, KQRS-FM, KXXP-FM, KXXR-FM & KXXU-FM
New York: WABC-AM & WPLJ-FM
San Francisco: KDIA-AM, KGO-AM & KSFO-AM
Seattle: KKDZ-AM
Washington, DC: WMAL-AM, WJZW-FM & WRQX-FM

Source: Radio & Records Web site at www.rronline.com.

PROFILE: The Walt Disney Company

Basic Data:
Headquarters: Burbank, CA
Web site: www.disney.com
CEO in 1997: Michael D. Eisner
1998 Sales (in millions): $23,226
1998 Net Profits (in millions): $1,717
1998 Assets (in millions): $43,537
Rank in 1998 Forbes 500—Sales: 46

Market Holdings:
Broadcast Television: ABC Television Network, ABC owned and operated stations (e.g., WABC-New York City, KABC-Los Angeles, WLS-Chicago).
Cable Television: Ownership of networks: ESPN Networks, part owner of Arts & Entertainment & The History Channel, part owner of Lifetime, Toon Disney as well as TV networks in Europe and Japan.
Film & Television: Hollywood Pictures, Touchstone Pictures, Walt Disney Pictures, Miramax studio, Walt Disney Television, Buena Vista Pictures Distribution, Buena Vista Home Video.
Music: Walt Disney Music Company, Hollywood Records.
Radio: ABC Radio networks, ABC owned and operated stations (e.g., WRQX-FM-Washington, DC, WABC-AM-New York City, WMAL-AM-Washington, DC).
Publishing: Disney Publishing Group.
Theme Parks: Disneyland (California), Walt Disney World (Florida), EuroDisney (Paris, France), Tokyo Disneyland; Disney-MGM Studio park.
Other Interests: The Mighty Ducks (National Hockey League), Anaheim Angels (Major league baseball), Disney retail stores, Broadway plays such as "The Lion King;", Disney Cruise Line, Disney Vacation Clubs.

Significant Events:
1995: The Disney Channel becomes available in the United Kingdom.
1996: Acquires 25% interest of the California Angels baseball team and takes on the role of managing general partner.
1996: Buys Capital Cities/ABC television network and stations and cable TV interests.
1996: Disney World celebrates its 25th anniversary.
1997: Michael Eisner's contract with Disney is extended to 2006.
1997: Fifteen million southern Baptists threaten to boycott the Walt Disney Company, however boycott is virtually impossible because Disney ownership is so broad.
1997: CEO Michael Eisner exercises 7.3 million of his stock options worth more than a half billion dollars.
1998: Micael Eisner pushing memoir, *Work in Progress* (Random House).
1998: Disney acqiures 43% stake in Web portal Infoseek.

November 1996 in four markets: Atlanta, Minneapolis, Salt Lake City and Birmingham, and seemed to tap into a small, but lucrative, market to build through synergy on the fabled Disney brand of family entertainment. Again, like CBS, Disney still built radio networks.[67]

And although a relatively small division at Disney, Disney management, led by Michael Eisner, certainly recognized radio's contribution to Disney profit accumulation. For example, Children's Broadcasting Corporation would no longer distribute its Aahs World Radio programming after January 1998, because Disney was pushing its children's network. At its peak, Aahs reached approximately 40% of the country, but Disney denied it forced stations to jettison the alternative in favor of its own children's radio. Still, this seemed to be the case to an outsider. Will Disney continue to remain "small potatoes" in radio after 2000? No one can be sure, but paying close attention to this decision will tell much about the direction Disney will take as a media conglomerate, and if Disney sells, will change the ownership structure of the U.S. radio industry.[68]

Cox, like Disney, represented a diverse media corporation far more famous for other operations. Its sizable radio division was based in Atlanta, Georgia, but the public focused on its newspaper operations, best known for the *Atlanta Constitution*. This Sunbelt company also had interest in broadcast television and cable (see Chapter 6). But as seen in the tables, Cox also had a substantial number of radio stations, with four in market two, Los Angeles, and clusters in Atlanta and Orlando.[69]

And like Disney, Cox sat out the radio merger frenzy of the mid-1990s, but still saw strong increases in revenues from radio. Still Cox moved a bit. In September 1997, for example, Cox and the privately held Homewood Partners and WEDA Limited agreed to start a small FM station in Homewood, Alabama, to serve the nearby Birmingham market. Also that month, Cox acquired three Texas stations in San Antonio, from KISS Radio of San Antonio Limited, an affiliate of Rusk Corporation, for $30 million. For $250 million, Cox Radio also acquired NewCity Communications. But despite Cox's relative radio power, it fell behind Hick Muse, CBS and Clear Channel.[70] But it did own powerful clusters of stations in Atlanta, Miami, Tampa, Orlando, San Antonio and Birmingham.[71]

But Cox, like Disney, concentrated on expansion in other areas. It expanded and upgraded its cable television MSOs via an advanced broadband network of coaxial and fiber optic to more customers. Cox partnered with Sprint, TCI and Comcast to offer personal communications services. Cox@Home, its high speed Internet service, debuted in Orange County in December 1996. Cox Digital Telephone, a residential telephone service, was launched in Orange County in September 1997 and in Omaha in December 1997.

RADIO'S MINOR COMPANIES

The aforementioned top radio groups represent the biggest companies in an ever-consolidating radio industry. They seem to point to a continuing trend of consolidation as the radio industry continues to adapt to the looser FCC ownership caps set in place in 1996. No one knows how far this consolidation will go. So media conglomerates like McGraw-Hill Companies (see Chapter 2), the New York Times Company (see Chapter 1) and the Tribune Company (see Chapter 4) continued to hold on to and operate radio station groups, awaiting radio industry's shake out from merger and acquisitions. All of these companies got involved with radio years ago, and simply chose to take a wait-and-see attitude on their relatively small holdings.

The aforementioned radio owners are recognizable because of the fame achieved by other divisions. Many other minor companies were not as recognizable. In 1998, these smaller companies followed as top 10 players: Entercom, Heftel, Emmis, Cumulus and Susquehanna. All seemed to be in play in the 1990s, as management and ownership figured out if they were large enough to deal with Hicks Muse, CBS or Clear Channel, or if they should seek their own mergers, or cash in and invest the millions elsewhere.

The choice would be difficult. Entercom, based in Bala Cynwyd, Pennsylvania, had revenues of about $200 million and 41 stations, and Heftel, based in Dallas, had 39 stations. Cumulus, based in Milwaukee, had 207 stations, but all in small markets. And Susquehanna, based in York, Pennsylvania, had 14 stations. Moreover, the 20th largest radio group in 1998, the Tribune Company of Chicago, had radio revenues barely besting $50 million. This seemed small when compared to the $3 billion per annum taken in by Hicks Muse, CBS and Clear Channel.[72]

Nobody knows what these minor radio powers will do in the future, but in 1999 they were still important, albeit minor, players in the radio business. It is impossible to profile all of them, but it is worth five case studies to consider the options.

Emmis Broadcasting Corporation ranked as the sixth largest owner of radio stations in terms of reach in 1999. Based in Indianapolis, Indiana, Emmis followed the CBS and Disney strategy through ownership of a few stations in major markets: three stations in New York City, one station in Los Angeles, one station in Chicago, four stations in St. Louis and three stations in Indianapolis. Emmis' strategy also included defending its Indiana home base and the two Indiana radio networks, Network Indiana and AgriAmerica Network. Realistically, however, Emmis remained vulnerable.[73]

Bonneville International Corporation of Salt Lake City was controlled by the Mormon Church. It owned and operated WDBZ-FM in New York City, radio's largest market, plus an FM station in Los Angeles, the nation's number two market. Bonneville also has multiple presences in Chicago (media market three), San Francisco (media market four), Dallas (media market seven), Washington, DC (media market eight) and Houston (media market nine). Thus, Bonneville had holdings in major markets just like CBS, Disney and Emmis, but on a scale much closer to that of Emmis. Bonneville was very different in that its president was also the President of the Church of the Latter Day Saints. Bonneville did not seem to be a candidate for a merger so long as the Church figured its mission helped in religious activity.[74]

Citadel Broadcasting Corporation, based in Big Fork, Montana, followed the Hicks Muse model with stations in medium and smaller markets, led by Providence, Rhode Island, and Allentown, Pennsylvania. In 1997, Citadel required ownership of five times more stations than Bonneville to reach the same audience. Could it hold out based on audiences reached by nine stations in Wilkes Barre, Pennsylvania (media market 62), eight in Albuquerque, New Mexico (media market 71) or four in Spokane, Washington (media market 87)? Because Citadel owned nothing but radio, it was a throwback to an earlier era when successful small town entrepreneurs could expand in the business they know best and without taking advantage of economies of scale and other organizational strictures. It seemed to be a logical candidate for a merger.[75]

Spanish Broadcasting System, Inc., based in New York City, owned radio stations in a handful of markets, led by New York City, Los Angeles, Chicago and Miami. But it represented a niche giant, with a concentration of stations aimed at the growing Hispanic population. Safely in the hands of Raul Alacon, Jr., who owned controlling interest in 1999, Spanish Broadcasting functioned for advertisers seeking to reach the Hispanic market. Because other radio groups did not possess any expertise in this niche play, Spanish Broadcasting seemed safe.[76]

Radio One seemed to be a case similar to Spanish broadcasting. Minority-owned Radio One was doing very well with its niche service. Indeed, Radio One had a 28% increase on same-station revenues, and a 43% increase in broadcast cash flow as 1999 commenced—about double the industry average. Its launch as a public company in May 1999 saw share prices start at $24 and close at $34.625. At that price, Radio One was valued by the market at $600 million, making it the most valuable African American-owned company in the United States. (Cable TV's BET was larger but private in 1999.) Still Radio One remained a family-owned operation. President William Liggins and his mother, CEO Catherine E. Hughes, controlled more than half the stock even after the initial public offering. (Hughes co-founded Radio One in 1980.) With some 26 radio stations in the nation's top 19 African American markets, the focus was on Washington, DC, and Richmond, Baltimore, Philadelphia, Atlanta, Detroit, St. Louis and Cleveland. Radio One's announced goal in 1999 was by the early part of the 21st century to own radio stations in the nation's top 30 African American markets.[77]

But stubborn single station owners did hang on during the radio merger frenzy of the late 1990s. No clustering here, simply a struggle to survive. There is no reason to list them all here (see the *Radio & Records* Web site at www.rronline.com), but one example, WRNR-FM of Washington, DC illustrates the frustrations of operating as a single and independent company in a world of radio consolidation. Jack Einstein is a throwback to the days when the FCC restricted ownership of radio. His WRNR-FM (for Rock And Roll), based in Annapolis, Maryland, sought to simply survive as the bigger consolidated companies took over the Washington, DC market. He had no advantages of scale economies to reduce costs, nor could he sell a whole set of stations and formats to big advertisers. There was temptation to cash out, as Einstein did in 1987 to Duchossois Communications Company. But he could not resist the lure of running a radio station and programming vintage and progressive rock. So with a "group" of three stations all in the Washington, DC market, he sought narrow formats and played on. (His son was the featured disc jockey.)

This operation was valued in 1999 at just $2.0 million. Einstein surely added diversity to the radio world, but no one is sure how long these independents can keep going.[78]

RADIO'S OWNERSHIP AND FUTURE

The consolidation of the radio business will likely continue, and only small stations operating at small profit margins in small markets will survive as single niche owners. Past FCC rules are now gone and, during the 1990s, a revolution in radio ownership commenced. The U.S. Department of Justice will continue to impose antitrust tests—such as a maximum share of the total advertising in a market—but that should not stop the movement toward a tight oligopoly.

Indeed the 1990s saw the consolidation of the radio industry. In 1997, there were nearly 900 deals worth nearly $10 billion. Thus, as early as the close of 1997, radio's top 15 players were pulling in about one third of all advertising sales. Mergers will lead to greater efficiency and lure advertisers looking for bigger reach.[79]

The U.S. Department of Justice should remain an important player as well. Since the FCC has lifted its ownership limits, it has been up to the U.S. Department of Justice to judge if a merger violated the antitrust laws. Prior to the Telecommunications Act of 1996, ownership was so limited as to make Department of Justice consideration unnecessary. During the late 1990s, the Department of Justice negotiated a number of consent decrees: in Cincinnati, Jacor agreed to sell and thus saw its share of the advertising dollars fall from 53% to 46%; and CBS, as a result of its Infinity merger, in nine separate markets agreed to divest stations. When the new administration is inaugurated in January 2001, it will surely re-formulate this Justice Department intervention.[80]

This consolidation will place a bigger burden on public radio. Through the 1990s, the federal government has provided between $200 million and $300 million per year for the Corporation for Public Broadcasting, with about $50 million of this each year scheduled for National Public Radio (NPR). Despite all the promises of Republicans to "zero out" the allotment from the federal treasury, the amount is scheduled to rise by the year 2000. Although the audiences for public radio are small relative to their broadcast cousins, the shows have a loyal and vocal constituency who urged their members of Congress to maintain and increase federal funding. Consequently, the nation's 694 public radio stations will continue to gain funding from the federal treasury, as well as state and local governments, foundation grants and viewer contributions.[81]

It will also place continued pressure on the FCC to create more stations. In February 1999, the FCC issued its "Microradio Proposal," voting to issue a Notice of Proposed Rule Making to establish a low power, or "microradio," service that could add hundreds of FM stations to an already crowded FM band. The Notice of Proposed Rulemaking specifically proposed to license new 1,000 watt and 100 watt low power FM radio stations and set up a third microradio class for 1–10 watt stations. The National Association of Broadcasters lobby opposed it, as National Association of Broadcasters (NAB) president and CEO Eddie Fritts noted that if fully implemented this proposal would add as many as 4,000 low power stations. Fitts noted that there were already nearly 12,500 radio stations (3,500 of them added since 1980), and argued that they already provided a rich array of local news, sports, entertainment and public service programming.[82]

In contrast, musicians, colleges and community activists praised the microradio proposal. William Kennard, Chair of the FCC in 1999, also saw expanding this low power segment as opening up radio ownership to minorities, small business, women and niche communities. By April 1999, the FCC had received more than 13,000 inquiries in the four months since its proposal. Independent bands wrote in, as did religious broadcasters looking for more outlets. Applicants included the city of Atlanta, so it could broadcast traffic and weather and city council meetings; churches to broadcast sermons to the elderly; a blind man in Nashville to broadcast to his fellow visually impaired; and former radio pirates coming up from underground. Yet if the proposal goes through after 2000, it could dramatically expand ownership of broadcast radio.[83]

The future also depended on Internet radio. In 1999, the Web portal Yahoo! initiated a radio service called Yahoo! Radio with 10 tracks of audio. Other search engines seemed to be more than willing to follow. This convergence of the radio and the Internet ultimately depended on listeners flocking to even more niche-driven programming than radio had delivered for five decades. Experiments abounded. Spinnner.com offered 175,000 songs on 120 channels in formats from surf to gumbo, from funk to gospel. Ads were displayed visually on the computer screen and within the audio—the latter at about 90 seconds per hour so as to differentiate from broadcast radio. MTV also started an Internet service. Stations could also be accessed directly as listed on www.radio-directory.com. This process of innovation was in flux in 1999.[84]

Delivery by satellite was also in flux. Innovators were trying to start up national broadcasting services from satellites to offer a similar all-through-the-U.S. service. In 1999, CD Radio stood as the leader and used a two-inch dish attached to the rear of an automobile window or to a window at home. For 100 channels, the cost after installation was announced to be about $10 per month. The possibility of widespread adaptation was given a boost in 1999 when automobile makers Ford and General Motors announced they would offer CD Radio in new cars from Ford and XM Satellite Radio (owned partially by Clear Channel) in future General Motors cars. It was not clear, however, if one or both would succeed.[85]

There was also the issue of new radio technology. In 1999, a revolutionary new radio receiver went on the market called the Blaupunkt DigiCeiver. According to Blaupunkt, this offered the first truly digital AM/FM radio ever made. At the heart of this new radio was a specialized computer, digitizing "programs." Although so-called digital radios had been sold for years, these did not process the signal in the digital domain, and the signal path remained pure analog from antenna to speaker. The DigiCeiver technology developed by Blaupunkt operated in a manner analogous to digital audio, but at much higher frequencies. Just as analog sound waves are converted into the bits and bytes of digital audio data, the DigiCeiver converts analog radio frequency signals into digital data. Once this is done, digital software is used to produce high quality stereo sound, to reduce interference and distortion, to decode and extract information contained in the RDS subcarrier, and to provide a high level of digital control over the functioning of the analog front end circuitry. The DigiCeiver eliminates a whole range of conventional radio circuits, replacing them with software code that can be reprogrammed as needed to change operating parameters, to fine tune performance or to accommodate new features.[86]

Finally, after 2000, radio will have to deal with changing demographics. During the 1990s, most diversity issues centered around African Americans and Hispanics, but Asian Americans will need to be addressed as well, because these populations are

expected to double by 2020. Research has shown all are avid and regular r
teners. Immigrants to the United States during the 1990s—from the Phillippi...,
Vietnam, China and India—will also add to the diversity issue: But what is the best
way to reach these peoples? Because they are younger than the U.S. norm (median
age of 31 vs. 43 for all races in the United States) and better educated (about 42%
have college degrees vs. 25% of the population of the United States as a whole),
they earn one quarter more than the norm. In 1999, according to Department of
Commerce data, there were 305 radio stations owned by minorities: 164 by African
Americans, 134 by Hispanics, 5 by Asians and 2 by Native Americans. Although
the number declined from that of the earlier 1990s, at 3 percent overall, this is much
higher than the one half of 1% figure of the late 1970s. If microradio is implemented, then diversity of ownership will increase.[87]

Even the majors realize their inability to reach nonmainstream audiences. Clear
Channel announced early in 1999 that they would spin off nine stations to African
American buyers (led by Radio One and Blue Chip Broadcasting) and to the His-
panic-owned Mega Communications as part of $230 million in deals so that the
FCC would approve the purchase of Jacor. Clear Channel, as of February 1999, came
in at 470 stations in 107 markets, just surpassing Hicks Muse's 465 stations. This
meant there was a virtual dead heat in regard to the number of stations, but it also
meant the first step in the FCC trying to diversify radio ownership during an era best
characterized by consolidation and acquisitions.[88]

THE MUSIC INDUSTRY: TODAY AND YESTERDAY

Radio provided exposure to new music, and the multibillion dollar music industry
sold it to fans in increasing numbers. Music sales tripled from $4 billion in 1985 to
more than $12 billion by 1994. By the close of the 1990s, one estimate placed the
U.S. music market at about one third of $40 billion world music sales. Executives
from one of the industry majors told the press that more than half of Warner Music
Group's sales came in the United States, the rest from around the world. The industry worked to gain hits in the United States, yet would crossover sell around the
world as well. In the late 1990s, for example, Sony's Celine Dion sold more than 9
million copies of her album, "Falling Into You," in the United States, and a remarkable 14 million more outside the United States. Until mid-1998, when Seagram
acquired PolyGram in a historical $10 billion deal, six vast companies dominated
sales; thereafter, the Big Six became the "Big Five," always able to maintain significant barriers to entry to keep $7 of every $8 spent on CDs and audio cassettes.[89]

The tight oligopoly shrunk, but its basic operating principles remained constant.
Through the 1990s the majors contested for market share. The *Wall Street Journal*,
for example, estimated that from January 1997 to May 1997 Universal Music
Group's share of current album sales jumped to second place from last place a year
earlier. Warner still ranked first at 17.3%, Universal next at 14.9%, EMI third at
13.5%, BMG fourth at 13.2%, PolyGram fifth at 11.8% and a slumping Sony in
sixth place at 11.6%. Independents (i.e., nonmembers of the Big Six) altogether

totaled the rest. The aforementioned six dominated, as they captured all the top-selling album spots for 1996 (as seen in Table 5.14).[90]

SoundScan, the company that tabulated sales, stated that sales rose 10% in 1998 to a record 710 million units. Through December 13, 1998, the combination of Polygram (12.9%) and Universal (at 10.9%) as the "new" Universal led the way with 23.8% of all sales. Sony followed at 17.4% market share for sales in the United States, followed by Warner at 17.3%, BMG at 14.1% and EMI at 14.0%. Everything from Sony's *Titanic* soundtrack to new heartthrob "boy groups" like BMG's 'N Sync plus a stream of Rap hits (for the first time ever in 1998 rap albums matched country in sales), underscored how the White world had embraced and showcased the urban poetry and music called Rap. In sum, the Big Five still sold about seven of every eight CDs, despite the presence of hundreds of independents fighting for that other unit.[91]

The stars of the oligopolists seemed everywhere. The Recording Industry Association of America (RIAA) awarded Gold and Platinum Awards to Pink Floyd's "The Wall" and Billy Joel's "Greatest Hits Volume I and II," as the best-selling double albums in RIAA history. At the 22 million and 18 million marks, respectively, they trailed Michael Jackson's "Thriller" at 25 million, and the Eagles' "Their Greatest Hits 1971–1975" at 24 million. Barbra Streisand's 1994 double album, "The Concert," was certified double Platinum, marking her 11th career multi-Platinum album.

TABLE 5.14
The Top 10 Best-Selling Newly Recorded Albums of 1996

---

1. **"Jagged Little Pill" by Alanis Morissette**, released in 1995, with sales by the close of 1996 at 7.4 million, for her angry rock ballads for Warner Music Group. Estimates placed her world sales—by the close of 1996—at more than 24 million units sold. So, as of early in 1997, "Jagged Little Pill" was the best-selling debut album in history. This album, *Forbes* estimated, contributed more than $200 million in revenues to Warner Music Group.
2. **"Falling Into You," by Celine Dion**, released by Song Music Group in 1996, with sales by the close of 1996 at 6.1 million. By the close of 1996, Dion had sold an estimated 50 million records.
3. **"The Score," by the Fugees** (a Haitian American hip-hop trio that seemed to defy category and some called rap and rhythm and blues influenced as well) released by Sony Music Group in 1996, with sales by the close of 1996 at 4.5 million.
4. **"Tragic Kingdom," by No Doubt**, a ska-influenced pop band, released in 1995, with sales by the close of 1996 at 4.4 million. This album was released in late 1995 by the California-based band with an upbeat pop sound that crossed over to a variety of radio formats and got a significant boost from radio. By the end of 1996 it was in first place for several weeks.
5. **"Daydream," by Mariah Carey**, released in 1995 by Sony, with sales by the close of 1996 at 3.1 million.
6. **"All Eyez on Me," by 2Pac**, released in 1996, with sales by the close of 1996 at 3.0 million for gritty rap music.
7. **"Load," by Metallica**, released in 1996, with sales by the close of 1996 at 3.0 million.
8. **"Secrets," by Toni Braxton**, released in 1996, with sales by the close of 1996 at 2.9 million.
9. **"The Woman in Me," by Shania Twain**, with sales by the close of 1996 at 2.8 million. This country star released this album in 1995 by PolyGram's Mercury record label. In 1996, she was the top selling country artist, male or female or group.
10. **"What's the Story Morning Glory," by Oasis**, released in 1995, with sales by the close of 1996 at 2.6 million. This British group reminded many of the Beatles.

Source: Peter Newcomb, "The Music Never Stopped," *Forbes*, March 24, 1997, pp. 90–95.

In 1999, Streisand was the female artist with the most multi-Platinum albums, with Madonna coming in a close second with 10.[92]

The star system was operable in all portions of the music business—even the classical market. For example, Polygram Classics, and its London, Deutsche Grammophon and Philips labels, were absorbed into Universal Music Group in 1998. Polygram's "The Three Tenors in Concert" (Jose Carreras, Placido Domingo and Luciano Pavarotti), over the decade of the 1990s, achieved more than two million sales worldwide. Tenor Andrea Bocelli's "Romanza," also on PolyGram, was released September 1997 and sold 14 million worldwide in one year! The success came because Polygram was able to convince nonclassical music fans to purchase just this one album. But pop music sold far more albums. The Spice Girls' debut album, "Spice," hit the five million mark, becoming the best-selling single album release in 1997. Puff Daddy & The Family's "No Way Out" certified double-Platinum. These artists needed one of the Big Five to distribute their work to the public, and they signed the stars and then collected on their sales.[93]

In March 1999, the RIAA released its annual demographic survey of 3,051 music purchasers in the United States. "Several interesting profiles emerged in 1998, including the boom in R&B and Gospel, as well as the sharp decline in Rock sales," said Hilary Rosen, RIAA President and CEO. "Demographic shifts also continued with women out buying men for the second year, and a drop in purchases among 15 to 29 year-olds, contrasted by significant growth among those age 35 and older."[94]

In February 1998, the RIAA released its annual year-end shipments statistics, which revealed the size of the U.S. music recording industry in 1998 to be $13.7 billion. Rock and country maintained their decade-long domination of the market, although rock continued to decline, dropping from 32.5% in 1997 to 25.7% in 1998. The absence of hits from established rock artists; the continued decline of the rock subgenre, alternative (down from 11% to 9%); and the shrinkage of buyers in the 20 to 24 age bracket, once a stronghold for rock, proved contributing factors to rock's decline. With 14.1% of the market, country remained stable and was able to maintain its second-place market position. Meanwhile, the hot genres of 1998 were rhythm and blues (R&B), gospel and soundtracks. R&B's growth (from 11.2% in 1997 to 12.8% in 1998) came mainly in the 35+ age group, who bought albums by Lauryn Hill, Brian McKnight, Levert, Sweat & Gill, Erykah Badu, Jon B. and Janet Jackson. Gospel surged from 4.5% in 1997 to 6.3% in 1998, showing the greatest market growth of any genre due to the crossover success of a number of gospel/Christian artists who appeal to R&B, pop, country and rock fans (e.g., Kirk Franklin's "The Nu Nation Project," which certified Platinum; Lee Ann Rimes' "You Light Up My Life"; DC Talk's "Super Natural"; and Point of Grace's "Steady On"). Blockbuster movie soundtracks (e.g., from *City of Angels, The Wedding Singer, Armageddon, Hope Floats* and the *Titanic*) propelled this genre's growth from 1.2% in 1997 to 1.7% in 1998.[95]

Continuing the trend from 1997, women accounted for a higher percentage of units purchased than men (51.3% vs. 48.7%). Women over age 30 accounted for the largest share of purchases, and their genres of choice proved to be pop and country

(65% and 60%, respectively). This increase in buying among older women can be attributed to the Titanic "phenomenon," along with the success of artists such as Celine Dion, Shania Twain, Jewel, Sarah McLachlan, Sheryl Crow and Mariah Carey. Conversely, men under age 30 outpaced their older counterparts; rock dominated their purchases, followed by a combination of R&B and rap (62% and 51%, respectively). In fact, consumers over age 30 were the only demographic to show any growth. Consumers age 35 and older accounted for 39% of the units purchased in 1998, as compared to 22.1% 10 years ago. In 1998, 12% of all purchases were made by those age 50 and older, as compared to just 6% 10 years ago. Country and pop dominated the music choices made by these mature consumers, accounting for 51% and 53%, respectively. Likewise, the drop off in the proportion of purchases accounted for by 15- to 24-year-olds (32.2% in 1996 vs. 28% in 1998), once the mainstay of the market, continued.

In 1998, tape and record clubs were out, and the Internet was in and growing rapidly. By the mid-1990s, compact discs sold well-over two thirds of the marketplace (68.4%). Full-length audio cassettes continued in second place, experiencing a slow but steady decrease. Although the cassette share declined significantly, the format remained a cost-effective, portable alternative to CDs for a host of applications. Singles and vinyl records sold in small numbers. Most shoppers still used record stores, but more were turning to the local Wal-Mart or the Internet.[96]

Radio exposed these and other artists and musical forms, yet radio did not take up the promotional function until the 1950s—three decades after radio commenced as a commercial enterprise. Before 1950, nearly every sound from radio was live. The musical recording industry pre-dated the 20th century, but the high fidelity sounds that drove multimillion record sales did not commence until after World War II (first on 78 rpm discs and then on 33$\frac{1}{3}$ and 45 rpm discs). The late 1940s was a period of important innovation; the 1950s was a period of great sales, starting with Elvis. The 33$\frac{1}{3}$ rpm long-playing record became the album; the 45 rpm record became the single and inspired the first radio format: top 40. The latter symbiotically linked the music and radio broadcasting industries.[97]

The next great advance took place in the late 1950s when it became possible to record and reproduce multiple channels of sounds (at first simply two channels of stereo). Coupled with the rise of FM radio, two tracks quickly gave way to multi-tracks. In the 1970s, audio tape cassettes came along and began to eat away at the 33$\frac{1}{3}$ rpm long-playing records because of their ease of use. For the first time, the music could be carried "anywhere," and Sony's Walkman became ubiquitous. During the 1970s and 1980s, scientists went one step further and introduced digital sound. The prior system was analog, which allowed hiss and extraneous sounds to mingle with the music. Digital breaks the sound down into bit components, eliminates extraneous sounds and then plays a purer, cleaner sound (although it was often sampled and so missing some of the richness of the analog system). The music industry released digital sound by way of compact discs (CDs), and by the mid-1990s, the CD nearly eliminated the long-playing 33$\frac{1}{3}$ record. CDs were the medium of choice, audio cassettes were the medium of convenience and sound purists preferred the medium of the 33$\frac{1}{3}$ record.[98]

The music business has been effected by economics as well as technical change. The prosperity of the 1950s, coupled with the youth market and the innovation of rock 'n' roll music, spurred sales growth. By the late 1950s, yearly revenues exceeded half a billion dollars. With the rise of the Baby Boom in the mid to late 1960s, the industry took off and prospered as measured in billions of dollars of sales and billion of albums and singles sold. The United States has long been the center of the world's recorded music business and, until the 1980s, the major companies were based in the United States. Then foreign companies bought up U.S. companies, such that by 1997 only one, Time Warner, was based in the United States (although all concentrated their sales in the United States).

MUSIC INDUSTRY BASICS

From the 1950s through the 1990s, six major music companies dominated. But in mid-1998, Seagram, owner of the Universal Music Group, purchased PolyGram for more than $10 billion and squeezed the Big Six down to the Big Five. Consolidation was also taking place in both the retail and wholesale sectors. For example, Camelot bought The Wall and Spec's Music and then Trans World absorbed Camelot. Wherehouse bought Blockbuster Music; CDNOW and Music Boulevard merged; Bertelsmann bought a chunk of barnesandnoble.com. The net effect for the Big Five and their dozens of labels was that 80% of sales was generated by about 10 accounts: Alliance, Target, Wal-Mart, Tower, Best Buy, Trans World Entertainment, Handleman, Valley Media, Musicland and Blockbuster. The number of store locations that these 10 companies represented stabilized as most unprofitable locations were closed during the late 1990s. And the CD (which debuted in 1983) accounted for more than three quarters of their sales. Tables 5.15 and Table 5.16 summarizes the state of the industry in the late 1990s.

Tables 5.17 and 5.18 show that young people buy music, and for all the talk of the Internet, they still buy it at music stores. Table 5.19 reveals that rock music is still the most popular genre of music. Table 5.20 illustrates that the members of the Big Six, which still defined the industry prior to Seagram's purchase of Polygram in mid-1998, ranked among the biggest media companies in the world. Table 5.20 proves that the music industry is indeed global, with companies located all around the world.

Yet the process of creating a CD has changed little during the 1990s. Table 5.21 shows that many people and operations are involved in getting a compact disc to the marketplace. The next section briefly describes this process. It also discusses the Big Five who dominated the music recording industry.

Production of an album is where the music industry started. Artists made recordings and then millions of copies were manufactured. Here the process was similar to Hollywood movie making in that artists made their music "independently," but to sell their wares around the world required a contract for distribution from one of the Big Five. The Big Five could maximize exposure and thus maximize possible sales. So, in 1999, the Big Five controlled the copyrighted music, not only the musical

TABLE 5.15
Demand for Recordings, 1990–1997 (Millions of units shipped)

	LPs	CD albums	Cassette Albums	Total Units Shipped**
1990	11.7	286.5	442.2	865.7
1991	4.8	333.3	360.1	801.0
1992	2.3	407.5	366.4	895.5
1993	1.2	495.4	339.5	955.6
1994	1.9	662.1	345.4	1,122.7
1995	2.2	722.9	272.6	1,112.7
1996	2.9	778.9	225.3	1,137.2
1997*	3.2	840.0	200.0	1,137.2

*estimate
**vinyl singles, LPs, CD albums, cassette albums, cassette singles, CD singles, and music videos
Source: *Veronis, Suhler and Associates Communications Industry Forecast*, 11th ed., July 1997, p. 229.

TABLE 5.16
Values of Recordings Shipped ($ millions)

	Cassette Albums	CD Albums	LPs	Singles	Music Videos	Total
1998	1,413.5	11,418.0	27.4	329.4	535.2	13,723.5
1997	1,517.4	9,911.8	36.7	440.5	318.2	12,236.8
1996	1,905.1	9,939.3	37.6	401.1	238.1	12,533.8
1995	2,303.9	9,375.7	24.6	394.2	221.8	12,320.3
1994	2,980.8	8,459.7	12.1	374.1	229.3	12,068.0
1993	2,913.5	6,510.2	10.0	391.8	211.0	10,046.6
1992	3,113.3	5,324.2	9.0	406.1	153.4	9,024.0
1991	3,016.2	4,340.1	31.3	329.0	117.5	7,834.2
1990	3,468.9	3,453.8	83.0	362.0	173.4	7,541.1

Source: Standard and Poor's Industry Reports, "Movies & Home Entertainment Survey," 1999, found on Web site at www.netadvantage.standardpoor.com.

TABLE 5.17
Shares of Recorded Music: Unit Sales by Age Group, 1990–1996

	Age 10–19	Age 20–24	Age 25–34	Age 35–44	Age 45+
1990	25.9%	16.5%	27.8%	18.0%	11.8%
1991	26.3	17.9	27.0	16.5	12.5
1992	26.8	16.1	26.0	18.3	12.9
1993	25.3	15.1	25.1	19.6	14.8
1994	24.7	15.4	24.4	19.4	16.1
1995	25.1	15.3	24.4	18.3	16.1
1996	25.1	15.0	23.9	20.2	15.1

Sources: *Veronis, Suhler and Associates Communications Industry Forecast*, 9th ed., July 1995, p. 201; *Veronis, Suhler and Associates Communications Industry Forecast*, 11th ed., July 1997, p. 222.

TABLE 5.18
Shares of Recorded Music: Unit Sales by Outlet, 1990–1996

	Record Stores	Other Stores	Tape/Record Clubs	Mail Order
1990	69.8%	18.5%	8.9%	2.5%
1991	62.1	23.4	11.1	3.0
1992	60.0	24.9	11.4	3.2
1993	56.2	26.1	12.9	3.8
1994	53.3	26.7	15.1	3.4
1995	52.0	28.2	14.3	4.0
1996	49.9	31.5	14.3	2.9

Sources: *Veronis, Suhler and Associates Communications Industry Forecast*, 9th ed., July 1995, p. 202; 11th ed., July 1997, p. 226.

TABLE 5.19
Shares of Recorded Music: Unit Sales by Genre, 1990–1996

	Rock	Country	Pop	Rhythm & Blues	Rap	Classical	Jazz	Gospel	Other*
1990	36.1%	9.6%	13.7%	11.6%	8.5%	3.15	4.8%	2.5%	8.8%
1991	34.8	12.8	12.1	9.9	10.0	3.2	4.0	3.8	7.5
1992	31.6	17.4	11.5	9.8	8.6	3.7	3.8	2.8	8.6
1993	30.2	18.7	11.9	10.6	9.2	3.3	3.1	3.2	7.7
1994	35.1	16.3	10.3	9.6	7.9	3.7	3.0	3.3	8.5
1995	33.5	16.7	10.1	11.3	6.7	2.9	3.0	3.1	10.1
1996	32.6	14.7	9.3	12.1	8.9	3.4	3.3	4.3	8.2

*Other includes soundtracks, children's music, oldies, new age, and additional genres that do not fit into the categories listed.

Sources: *Veronis, Suhler and Associates Communications Industry Forecast*, 9th ed., July 1995, p. 202; 11th ed., July 1997, pp. 224–225.

TABLE 5.20
Music as Part of Global Top Media Corporations

Company*	Holdings
1. Time Warner	Warner Music and other labels, member Big Five
2. Walt Disney	Disney Music and other labels
3. Bertelsmann AG *BMG*	RCA and other labels, member Big Five
4. News Corporation	Small Music division
5. Viacom	No music
6. Sony Entertainment	Columbia Music, member Big Five
7. AT&T Broadband & Internet Services	No music
8. Seagram's Universal Studios	MCA, Decca and others labels, member Big Five
9. CBS	No music
10. Comcast	No music
11. Cox Enterprises	No music
12. General Electric's NBC	No music
13. Gannett	No music
14. Globo Organization	No music
15. Pearson	No music
15. EMI	Capitol and other labels, member Big Five

Source: "The Global 50," *Variety*, August 23–29, 1999, pp. A47–A56.

TABLE 5.21
Manufacturing and Distribution Cost of CDs, 1996

	Cost to the Record Label to Create DC
Disc and Package	$1.10
Recording Costs	.30
Producer Costs	.35
Songwriter Costs	.65
Performer Costs	.80
Managers and Lawyers	.20
Artist Pensions	.10
Music Video Production Costs	.25
Advertising and Promotion	.65
Distribution	1.15
Amortizing New Artist Development	1.40
Other	.85
Operating Profit and Executive Salaries	2.00
Cost to Produce and Distribute CD	**$9.80**
Retailer's Rent	.75
Retailer's Labor Costs	.90
Other Retail Costs	.95
Total Cost of CD to Retailer	**$12.40**
Retail Price to Customer	**$11.99–$15.99**

Source: *Washington Post*, February 15, 1996, p. F1.

recordings themselves, but also their published form. Complex agreements insured that creators were protected and gained small, but steady, royalties in most cases (i.e., massive checks if the music on CD sold millions). Guilds and unions protected the "independent" artists, yet deals for royalties varied, depending on the power of the star. If the company deemed a star worthy, then it would pay not only a bonus to sign, but a high royalty and the costs of production and marketing, satisfied to reap the rewards from its distribution fee. Otherwise the artist was charged, against future royalties, for all the expenses of producing an album. The Big Five majors took no chances, and so promoted heavily. Promotion was primarily through radio, but also by sending their stars out on tour, and having them make a video for MTV, CMT, BET or some other cable TV musical showcase.[99]

Realistically, the odds of success even in the best cases were long. Most new performers must sell between 500,000 and 1,000,000 copies to begin to gain any payback above their advance. The Big Five all maintained staffs of talent scouts who frequented clubs to find the next Alanis Morissette or Garth Brooks. They listened to demo after demo. In the era when the music retailing business had become fully computerized, down to the smallest store in the smallest town, the selection of talent remained an art. One factor remained necessary, but not sufficient to become a star—a contract with one of the "Big Five."[100]

Distribution lacks the excitement of producing new talent and is not as visible to the public as a chain of music retail stores, but remains the core source of the power of the Big Five. The majors were defined by their domination of distribution around the world. Here is where the globalism created a barrier to challengers. Small, even regional, labels could not afford to create worldwide distribution networks, and so distributed only within defined territories. Musicians might sign with smaller labels first, but they always aspire to move to one of the Big Five in order to maximize their sales. Management experts worked to extract economies of scale of distribution. They might have to guess which album to promote most heavily, but typically spread their promotional monies evenly because they were unable to decipher which was more likely to "break out."[101]

The key to distribution power has always been the economies of scale of the first copy. It costs a great deal to make the first record, and then very little relatively speaking to reproduce it for whatever markets in which it can be sold. The majors exhibited vertical integration of production and distribution. This made entry by true independents (not so-called independent labels that distribute through the Big Five) very difficult. High and consistent volume of sales gave the majors the dominant share of economic power. Then they can take advantage of marketing campaigns that cost a great deal, but spread over many outlets really cost very little per exposure to potential buyers.

An independent cannot match these marketing efforts. Small labels cannot keep up a consistent cash flow to support such distribution systems and in time face a financial crisis that forces them to sell to a member of the Big Five. These companies can handle delinquent accounts and have the lawyers to pursue deadbeats. They have the trade association, the RIAA, based in Washington, DC, to lobby the government for favorable rules and to collectively pursue pirates. Retail chains, anxious to maintain a constant flow of profits that only come with hits, are more willing to stock the music of the Big Five than to take a chance on unproven independents that may not last. The majors can discount to a retail chain and ask for display space. That the advantages lay with the dominant firms is obvious after a look at any sales chart.

The other key variable is promotion. Radio, and its cable TV cousins—MTV, VH-1, CMT and the like—regularly played Big Five CDs and videos to introduce music to fans in whatever venue they desired. Since radio stations, as already analyzed, were not always owned by the Big Five, the relation between promotion and the Big Five has been difficult since the "payola" scandal days of the late 1950s. Yet, after 2000, with new radio owners and the lessening of the power of MTV, it seems that radio group owners would take cash to play certain albums. The Big Five would pay for an hour's worth of time, and then program the stations with its music, as a sort of radio version of an infomercial. These "showcases" would disclose their music company sponsors right up front. This new trend was led by Mel Karmazin, and began with country music divisions in Nashville. One 1998 report had EMI paying $1 million an hour for showcasing Garth Brooks' newest album. This is a direct result of the radio mergers. Nearly half the stations had new owners who were hungry to prove the worthiness of their deals, and they were not tied to radio's past problems and traditions. Such new synergies among radio and music will be a key focus in the 21st century.[102]

Selling is where fans express their choices with dollars. Into the 1990s, the bulk of music products on compact disc or audio cassette were purchased at specialized retail stores such as Tower or Blockbuster Music, or general discount stores such as Wal-Mart, Kmart and Target. Radio and cable television's VH-1 and MTV, both owned by Viacom, introduce the new sounds. At the selling end, was an open industry with much entry and exit. Almost any retailer, even grocery and convenience stores, was able to sell compact discs. Thus, the business is highly competitive and volatile. As sales of music stagnated in the mid-1990s, specialized record stores found it hard to compete against the discounters like Wal-Mart; and many stores closed when the Internet became a new way for purchasing recorded music.[103]

Consider the case of the Musicland Stores Corporation. In the early 1990s, Musicland expanded and ran up debt. Even though its Sam Goody stores were among the most noted in the industry, competition proved still and Musicland closed scores of locations during the mid-1990s. They retained more than 1,000 shops in all but one U.S. state, plus locations in Puerto Rico, the Virgin Islands and the United Kingdom. Musicland was, at that time, the biggest music retailer in the United States (whether under the name On Cue, Media Play or Sam Goody). Yet when the economy expanded during the late 1990s, sales increased to nearly $2 billion per annum from Sam Goody stores, Media Play Outlets and On Cue shops (in 1999, these totaled 1,300 locations). The Big Five could easily absorb the ups and downs of the economy, and have other divisions help cover debt costs, but a smaller retailer had to operate in a far more volatile marketplace.[104]

In 1999, Musicland completed agreements with its senior credit lenders for a $50 million term loan that provided additional financing. In exchange for the loan, Musicland granted the lenders warrants equal to 5% of the company's stock. The retailer also obtained other agreements necessary to relieve its financial burdens, such as an amendment to its revolving credit agreement that provided long-term relief from restrictive financial covenants, amendments to real estate loans relating to three Media Play stores and a distribution facility and lien waivers from subordinated debt holders. The company warned that it would need cooperation from the Big Five in the form of normal credit terms. To counter the growing presence of the Internet, Musicland started four Web sites of its own. Sales in shopping malls still accounted for 90% of Musicland's sales in 1999, and management figured this social experience would continue even as online shopping expanded.[105]

One would think that selling music could be protected by ownership by a giant conglomerate. But even music retail chains that functioned as part of vast media conglomerates seemed to have no special advantage in recorded music retailing. Viacom never could make Blockbuster Music Inc. very profitable. Cross-promotions with Viacom-owned MTV did not help. In 1993, Viacom had acquired Blockbuster for its video stores as an extension for vertical integration of movies from its Paramount movie studio (see Chapter 4). In the mid-1990s, Viacom extended Blockbuster into music sales. But this move did not seem to work, and profits proved far less than comparable investments in cable TV networks or its start-up UPN broadcast network.

PROFILE: Viacom, Inc.

Basic Data:
Headquarters: New York, NY
Web site: www.viacom.com
CEO in 1997: Sumner M. Redstone
1998 Revenues (in millions): $12,096
1998 Net Profits (in millions): $–48
1998 Assets (in millions): $23,613
Rank in 1998 Forbes 500—Sales: 130

Market Holdings:
Broadcast Television: Partner in UPN television network, owner and operator of broadcast television stations in Philadelphia, Boston, Washington, DC, Dallas, Detroit, Atlanta, Houston, Seattle, Tampa, Miami, New Orleans and Indianapolis, among others.
Cable Television: Owner of cable networks, including MTV, M2, VH-1, Nickelodeon, Nike At Nite, Showtime, The Movie Channel, The Paramount Channel (UK), Comedy Central.
Film & Television: Paramount Pictures Corporation (major Hollywood studio), National Amusements movie theater chain (with screens in 11 countries), Famous Players theater chain in Canada, Blockbuster Entertainment Group (home video), Blockbuster Pictures Holding Corporation (investments in films), Spelling Entertainment Group (television producer), Republic Entertainment (film and TV producer and distributor), Paramount Home Video, Worldvision Enterprises (television syndicator), Viacom International, United International Pictures.
Music: Blockbuster Music (retailer of music), Famous Music.
Publishing: Simon & Schuster, Prentice-Hall, Macmillan Publishing U.S., Schimer Books, Charles Scribner's Sons, Thorndike Press, Twayne Publishers, Pocket Books, Allyn & Bacon, Ginn books, MTV Books.
Other Interests: Viacom retail stores, Virgin Interactive Entertainment, Paramount Parks: Kings Island outside Cincinnati, OH; Kings Dominion, near Richmond, VA; Carowinds near Charlotte, NC; and Raging Waters, near San Jose, CA.

Significant Events:
1970: Viacom created as FCC rules that CBS can no longer syndicate operations.
1987: Sumner Redstone's National Amusements, Inc. of Dedham, MA, buys controlling interest of Viacom, Inc. for $3.4 billion.
1996: Launches new cable network—TV Land.
1996: Sumner M. Redstone fires Paramount Pictures boss Frank Biondi and takes over.
1996: Creates M2: Music Television, a new "freeform" music television cable channel.
1997: Sells U.S. Cable networks to Seagram Ltd. for $1.7 billion.

Executives at Musicland and Blockbuster—and all other ailing record store chains and independent stores—first pointed to giant discounter Wal-Mart as the competitor with all the advantages, able to extract discounts from the members of the Big Five, and to sell in bulk so that the pennies made one sale at a time mounted into millions of dollars profit. Wal-Mart only drew the line on what music it would carry, refusing to sell albums with the industry's "Parental Advisory—Explicit Lyrics" stickers, mostly albums by rappers and rhythm and blues artists. Wal-Mart had so much clout that it even could demand changes in album cover art such as adding a bikini over the nude photograph on White Zombi's "Super-sexy Swingin' Sounds" album. As the single largest seller of pop music in the United States, the

Big Five even redesigned cover art for albums it shipped *only* to Wal-Mart. Wal-Mart was so influential that, by the late 1990s, it would ask and get the Big Five to remove "offensive" cuts and eliminate select lyrics from albums before Wal-Mart would sell them. Wal-Mart labeled these "edited" and "clean" albums. In the late 1990s, Wal-Mart's more than 2,000 U.S. stores sold about 1 in 12 albums.[106]

But at least it is possible to gain access to information about the overall corporate activities of Wal-Mart and Viacom. One important music retailer in the 1990s, with estimates well in excess of $1 billion sales annually, was Tower Records, part of the private MTS Corporation. MTS, as a private corporation, was not required to report any data about its operations. *Forbes* ranked it as one of the top 200 private companies in the United States; guesstimates indicate that Tower Records employed more than 7,000 persons, and regularly made profits measured in the millions of dollars. But MTS remained illusive, and so sales rankings cannot be calculated for Tower without the necessary data.[107]

The Internet also offered an ever-changing situation, but during the late 1990s, "booksellers" like Borders and Amazon.com (see Chapter 2), and pure Internet music retailers (led by CD Now), accumulated more sales. The Internet, examined later, surely heralded the most publicity in 1999, but was still in a significant transitional phase making it impossible to analyze its precise impact. Consider the case of Amy Nye Wolf, former Goldman, Sachs analyst, who started a chain of airport kiosks called AltiTunes. In 1995, the AltiTunes located at Newark Airport sold some $300,000 of music in its first year. Success and growth were uneven, but by 1999 Wolf's company was also in train stations (e.g., Grand Central in New York City in 1998). The idea was to be there for the spur of the moment purchase by a few thousand of the more than half million travelers who daily passed through. TrainTunes will be judged as the 21st century opens as to whether this "new" means of sales will be able to generate long-term profits and make its place in the U.S. music selling business.[108]

MUSIC'S MARKET STRUCTURE—THE BIG FIVE

But whatever the sales venue, most of the music the vendor sold came from the Big Five. Through volatility of sales, their production and distribution oligopoly held. The innovation of the CD and the Internet did not lessen its collective—it seemed to actually increase it. The only real question each year concerned who ranked where in terms of sales. The following paragraphs examine the Big Five in their order of ranking as of 1999 (realizing these rankings change yearly).[109]

Seagram's Universal Music Group stood atop the music business in 1999 because of its purchase of Polygram. Even as late as 1997, the Universal Music Group languished near the bottom of the rankings. New owner Seagram, led by dominant stockholder Edgar Bronfman Jr, looked to move up, and it did so in one bold and swift move. As the 1990s ended, the Universal Music Group (in its previous life known as the MCA Music Group) included labels MCA, Geffen, Uptown, GRP and Decca. Its stars included Counting Crows, Nirvana, Bobby Brown, Vince Gill, Reba McIntyre, George Strait, Mary J. Blige and the Wallflowers.[110]

PROFILE: The Seagram Company Ltd.

Basic Data:
Headquarters: Montreal, Canada
Web site: www.seagram.com
CEO in 1997: Edgar M. Bronfman, Jr.
1997 Revenues (in millions): $11,752
1997 Net Income (in millions): $502
1997 Assets (in millions): $21,628
Rank in 1998 Forbes International 500: 207

Market Holdings:
Cable Television: Partner (along with TCI) with Home Shopping Network, and partner USA
    Networks, Inc. (includes USA cable network and Sci-Fi cable network), as well as televi-
    sion production and broadcast television stations under Silver King division.
Film & Television: Universal Studios, Inc., Universal Studios Enterprises, Universal Studios
    Home Entertainment Group, Cinema International Corporation, Sony Cineplex movie the-
    ater chain (in partnership with Sony entertainment), Brillstein-Grey Entertainment (film pro-
    ducer), Universal Studios New Media Group, equity owner in HBO Asia, Telecine of Brazil,
    Cinecanal in Latin America, Showtime in Australia and Star Channel in Japan.
Music: Universal Studios Music Entertainment Group, Geffen Records, MCA Records, GRP
    Recording Company, Interscope Records, Hip-O Records, Decca Records, Motown Records
Theme Parks: Universal Studios Tour, Yosemite Concession Services, Universal Studios Tour
    Florida.
Other Interests: The Tropicana Beverage Group (fruit juices), The Seagram Beverage Group,
    Seagram Chateau & Estate Wines Company, Chivas Regal Scotch Whiskey, Absolut
    Vodka, Captain Morgan Original Spice Rum, Mumm and Perrier-Jouet Champaigns,
    Sandman Ports and Sheriies, Tessera premium wines, Spencer Gifts

Significant Events:
1995: Acquires 80% interest in entertainment giant MCA Inc. for $5.7 billion with former
    owner Matsushita Electric Industrial Company, Ltd. of Japan retaining 20%.
1996: MCA, Inc. renamed Universal Studios, Inc. (all film and TV operations plus Spencer Gifts).
1996: Sells MCA's Putnam Berkley book publishing group for $300 million.
1997: Sells 30 million shares of Time Warner to Merrill Lynch & Company for $1.4 billion,
    leaving 26.8 million shares still owned.
1997: Buys independent film producer October Films.
1997: Purchases Viacom, Inc.'s half interest in USA cable networks for $1.7 billion.
1997: Allies with Home Shopping Network, Inc. For television combination to be called USA
    Networks, Inc. to expand in cable and broadcast television under Barry Diller.

The Seagram Company had purchased controlling interest in 1995 and Bronfman, heir to a billion dollar Canadian liquor and juice seller, assumed control before
his 40th birthday. He took Seagram in a new direction toward entertainment. At the
point of the sale, the Universal Music Group ranked as the second largest portion of
the entertainment company, after film and television production and distribution
with revenues at $1.4 billion, and cash flow at $200 million. Wall Streeters valued
the Universal Music Group—if it were a stand-alone enterprise—at $2.75 billion at
the time of the sale.[111]

Through the late 1990s Bronfman began to reshape the Universal Music Group.
For example, in 1996, after weeks of negotiations the Universal Music Group
acquired half interest in Interscope Records, one of the hottest and most controver-

sial (for "gangsta" rap) labels of the 1990s. Time Warner wanted out; Bronfman was willing to share the risk to the tune of $200 million in cash. He then hired Doug Morris, formerly of Warner, to run the Universal Music Group. Bronfman sought to change the MCA music division's image, which insiders nicknamed the "Music Cemetery of America" Group. At that point, the top sellers were deceased artists such as Patsy Cline, who sold a predictable 750,000 units per year. The Interscope purchase represented a major break with the past.[112]

Yet Bronfman inherited numerous problems. Geffen Records, the once high flying MCA label, had cooled down. Founder David Geffen exited. David Simone, formerly of PolyGram, was brought in to revive the label. Based in West Hollywood, California, Geffen had done well in the past with acts like Nirvana and Guns N' Roses. At the cutting edge during the 1980s (based on releases by such stars as Elton John, Donna Summer, Aerosmith and Guns N' Roses), by the late 1990s Geffen was only generating about 2% of the total sales of the Universal Music Group. Its replacement for the Universal Music Group had become the Def Jam label—absorbed in the PolyGram merger. Could both or either be built up to power the new Universal Music Group?[113]

But these two attempts at revitalization proved small adjustments in the total integration of Polygram NV into the Universal Music Group. PolyGram NV was a division of Philips Electronics NV based in the Netherlands. PolyGram's labels included Motown, A&M, Island, Mercury, Polydor and Deutsche Grammophon. Stars included Bryan Adams, Bon Jovi, Sheryl Crow, Shania Twain, Sting, U2, Elton John, Soundgarden and Salt-n-Pepa. Change commenced in November 1998 when Brofmann decided to fire Danny Goldberg from PolyGram's Mercury Group and hire Doug Morris to create a new management team. He started atop as the combined revenues of Universal and PolyGram meant that the "new" Universal Music Group had about one quarter of the music sales as 1999 commenced. Seagram became the new leader of the Big Five.[114]

Morris sought to follow the Clive Davis model, which placed the bulk of expenses for production and promotion on to fewer stars. By early 1999, his Universal Music Group fired several thousand Polygram employees to cut costs, and therefore boosted profits instantly. By 2000, Seagram's restructuring would become the largest in music recording history. But by cutting costs Universal risked issuing fewer future albums. As a result, its 25% market share would surely drop unless Morris and company recorded some very popular new acts.[115]

PolyGram added considerable assets. In the mid-1990s, Alan Levy came to PolyGram. Based in London, he signed and developed such artists as Boyz II Men and the Cranberries. He promoted Sheryl Crow, Jon Bon Jovi and Melissa Etheridge to stardom. He made Mercury Nashville soar as he recorded and promoted country siren Shania Twain. Twain was the highest debuting solo female artist of her day and her second album, "The Women in Me," redefined the female country performer. Her songs sounded more like pop than country, which appealed to executives looking for crossover categories that fit in to changing radio formats. Could PolyGram's considerable assets maintain the Universal Music Group's lead? That was the most important question for the recorded music market leader of 1999.[116]

The Warner Music Group did well with its music division in the mid-1990s, and ranked second behind Seagram. Warner's Music functioned as a division of the vast, multinational media conglomerate, Time Warner, the sole member of the Big Five headquartered in the United States. (Seagram's headquarters was in Montreal, Canada, but its Universal Music Group worked out of Los Angeles.) Warner labels included Warner Brothers, Reprise, Giant, Sire, Elektra, Atlantic, Atco, Curb and Rhino, as well as 24 other labels. Its stars included Metalica, R.E.M., Eric Clapton, Green Day and Madonna. Clearly, Warner's most successful operation was its Atlantic label, which alone sold 1 of every 11 albums in 1997. Its own reports suggested that in 1998 about $1 in $5 flowing into Time Warner came from its music division, as did one in four dollars of profits.[117]

PROFILE: Time Warner Inc.

Basic Data:
Headquarters: New York, NY
Web site: www.pathfinder.com
CEO in 1999: Gerald M. Levin
1998 Sales (in millions): $14,582
1998 Net Profits (in millions): $168
1998 Assets (in millions): $31,640
Rank in 1998 Forbes 500—Sales: 102

Major Holdings:
Broadcast Television: The WB Network.
Cable MSO's: Time Warner Cable with clustered MSOs in New York City, Tampa Bay, Milwaukee, St. Louis, Houston and Raleigh & Duhram, NC.
Cable Networks: Turner Broadcasting (includes CNN, TNT & TBS), HBO, Cinemax, CNNSI (combining cable network and *Sports Illustrated* magazine), Turner Classic Movies, The Cartoon Network.
Film & Television: Warner Bros. Studio, WB Television (producing such shows as *ER* and *Friends*), Lorimar Television (syndicating such shows as *Dallas*), Quincy Jones Entertainment (producer of *Fresh Prince of Bel Air*), Warner Home Video, HBO Pictures, New Line Cinema movie studio, Fine Line Features movie distribution.
Magazines: *Fortune, People, Sports Illustrated, Time, Weight Watchers, Asiaweek, Money, Entertainment Weekly, Mad Magazine, Life.*
Music: Atlantic Recording Group, Warner Bros Records, Ivy Hill Corp. Elektra Entertainment, plus other labels.
Publishing: Warner Books, Little, Brown book publishers, Time-Life books, Book-of-the-Month-Club, History Book Club.
Other Interests: DC Comics, Six Flags Entertainment and Theme Parks, Atlanta Hawks (Professional basketball), Atlanta Braves (Major League baseball).

Significant Events:
1989: Time and Warner merge.
1996: The FTC reaches a settlement with Time Warner allowing its $6.2 billion merger with Turner Broadcasting.
1997: CEO Gerald M. Levin orders company-wide budget cuts of 3% to 5% to boost lagging stock prices.
1997: Time Warner posts $30 million profit, with revenues reporting to climb 25% to nearly $6 billion, led by its cable TV MSOs and networks.
August 1997: Time Warner cable begins to sell and trade to custer MSOs to help lower $17 billion debt.

Still Warner was a company in turmoil, not because it was not doing well but because it was not doing as well as before. In July 1994, Warner Music group stood atop the music business, then accounting for almost one quarter of all retail music sales in the United States, by far the largest share of the Big Six. In 1994, the Warner Music Group had sales of $3.3 billion worldwide. The company reported that the revenue contributions broke down with direct U.S. sales accounting for one quarter of the $3.3 billion in revenues, direct international sales accounting for 37%, sales through the Columbia House Record Club (half owned with fellow Big Five member Sony Music) for 15%, manufacturing around the world for others at 12% and sheet music sales and rights fees at 10% of total music group revenues. By 1998, under longtime film studio head Robert Daly and his aide-de-camp Terry Semel, Warner Music took a distinct "back seat" to the Universal Music Group—and even behind Sony, which on the strength of the *Titanic* sound track and the popularity of Celine Dion, had a very productive 1998.[118]

Parts of the Warner Music Group, such as Warner/Chappell Music Publishing, remained leaders. Valued by some insiders at a half billion dollars based on its extensive copyright list (e.g., Cole Porter, Rodgers & Hart and Madonna, as well as "Happy Birthday"), Warner/Chappell generated an estimated $100 million in operating profit alone, based on revenues of $500 million, and was growing at a healthy 10% per annum. In the 1990s, music publishing emerged as one of the more profitable and stable segments of the music business as copyright owners like the Warner Music Group received royalties from all formats, from all new sales outlets.[119]

Even as the Warner Music Group moved past $4 billion in annual sales, all the headlines focused on suits and complaints by jettisoned executives Mo Ostin and Lenny Waronker. Interscope drew complaints from anti-Rap protestors who condemned songs such as "Cop Killer" and artists like Tupac Shakur, and was eventually sold to the Universal Music Group. Doug Morris, who had been hired to boost Warner Music Group sales, lasted just about a year. Despite this turmoil, the momentum and size of Warner Music Group was indisputable; the *Wall Street Journal* noted that before the Universal and PolyGram merger, Warner was the largest and most powerful music company in the business by virtue of acts like Hootie & the Blowfish, Alanis Morissette, Jewel, Duncan Sheik, Sugar Ray and Aaliyah.[120]

But few insiders figured that Warner would stay on top over the new Universal Music Group. The promised synergy had never spread through and from Warner's music group. Artists hesitated to sign, and those who did (e.g., R.E.M., for a reported $80 million) saw subsequent albums turn in sales measured in the hundreds of thousands, not millions. The late 1990s were transitional years for Warner Music. New acts such as Prodigy, Third Eye Blind and Sugar Ray had done well, but no one seemed to think Alanis Morissette and Fleetwood Mac would continue. Warner needed new acts, and whether or not it would sign any remained an open question.[121]

The Sony Music Group did consistently well during the 1990s. As of early 1998, for example, the Sony Music Group had pushed ahead of rival Warner, as well as BMG and EMI (at least for recently released albums, according to SoundScan). Its

1998 music revenues came to $6 billion, with operating profits of $700 million. Its labels were doing very well—with Columbia (Bob Dylan, Mariah Carey, Will Smith, Barbra Streisand), Epic (Michael Jackson, Pearl Jam, Billy Joel), 550 Music (Celine Dion, Ben Folds Five) and Work Group (Fiona Apple, Jamiroquai) leading the way. President of the division, Thomas Mottola, had ridden the wave of new stars. Rankings would fluctuate, but profits could be built on simply being a member of the Big Five and then having a good year. Mottola's wife, Mariah Carey, was a key, but so was the distribution of the soundtrack for *Titanic*. In 1998, Mottola's $1 million payment for the soundtrack looked like a magical investment. Mottola had the same management team through the 1990s, and kept his job by signing Celine Dion and then assembling her "My Heart Will Go On," which went on to sell more than 26 million units worldwide.[122]

In 1999, Sony Music Group included American Recordings, Columbia, Epic, 57 Records, 550 Music, Harmony Records, Legacy Recordings, Razor Sharp, Relativity Recordings, Shotput Records, Sony Music Soundtrax, Red Ink, Stonecreek Recordings, Untertainment, The WORK Group and Sony Wonder (a children's/family unit). Artists spanned the musical spectrum, with Lauryn Hill, Michael Bolton, Gloria Estefan, Rage Against the Machine, Dixie Chicks, Savage Garden, and Mary Chapin Carpenter. Sony Music International added labels (e.g., Soho Square, Dance Pool, Mambo, Rubenstein, Dragnet, and Squatt) and artists (e.g., Julio Iglesias, Ricky Martin, Vicente Fernandez, Alejandro Fernandez, Oasis, Jamiroquai, Sade, Roberto Carlos, Daniela Mercury, Shakira, Tina Arena, Harlem Yu, Ana Gabriel, Claudio Baglioni, Jean Jacques Goldman, and Meja). Sony Classical included the labels Arc of Light, Masterworks, Sony Broadway, Sony Classical, SEON, and Vivarte, and the artists Isaac Stern, Placido Domingo, Yo-Yo Ma, Jane Eaglen, Tan Dun, Esa-Pekka Salonen, Midori, Hilary Hahn, Murray Perahia, Angelika Kirschlager, Richard Danielpour, Juilliard Quartet, Ying Huang and Joshua Bell. The SW Networks provided audio entertainment news and services to over 1,000 affiliated radio stations in 10 format-specific news networks for contemporary hits radio (CHR), alternative, country, urban, Adult Contemporary, modern AC, talk, and classic/album rock. Sony/ATV Music Publishing was a worldwide music publishing venture with copyrights and catalogues by the Beatles, Bob Dylan, Babyface, Pearl Jam, Joni Mitchell, Jimi Hendrix, Lloyd Price, LL Cool J, Willie Nelson, Brooks & Dunn, Leonard Cohen and Roger Miller. Sony Disc Manufacturing produced CDs, CD-ROMs, DVDs, MiniDiscs and audio cassettes from facilities in Terre Haute, Indiana, Pitman, New Jersey, Springfield, Oregon, and Carrollton, Georgia.[123]

As 1998 closed, Sony's Celine Dion's "Let's Talk about Love" and the *Titanic* soundtrack had each sold more than 19 million units. Mariah Carey's "Butterfly" had sold 8 million units, Oasis' "Be Here Now" 7 million units, followed by Barbra Streisand's "Higher Ground," Dion's "Falling Into You," and the *Men in Black* soundtrack at 4 million units each. Other multimillion selling 1998 releases included albums by Fiona Apple, Bone Thugs-N-Harmony, Michael Jackson, Jamiroquai, Ricky Martin, Pearl Jam, Will Smith, Wham! and the soundtrack from *My Best Friend's Wedding*. Debut and developing artists selling more than 500,000 units during the year included Savage Garden, Meja, Monica Naranjo, Jimmy Ray, Finley Quaye, Wes, Alejandro Fernandez, Fiona Apple, Ben Folds Five, Ginuwine, Amanda Marshall, Maxwell and Uncle Sam.

Sony expanded its roster throughout Asia with a cooperative arrangement in China to develop a Chinese-language repertoire, and new signings including Cantopop star Leon Lai and Taiwanese superstar Jeff Chang. Sony Classical enjoyed phenomenal success albums by Yo-Yo Ma and Itzhak Perlman. New signings included *Titanic* composer James Horner, tenor Marcelo Alvarez, violinist Eileen Ivers and baritone Jubilant Sykes.[124]

PROFILE: Sony Corporation

Basic Data:
Headquarters: Tokyo, Japan
Web site: www.sony.com
CEO in 1997: Norio Ohga
1997 Revenues (in millions): $55,058
1997 Net Income (in millions): $1810
1997 Assets (in millions): $48,490
Rank in 1998 Forbes International 500: 18

Market Holdings:
Broadcast Television: Partner in Telemundo Group, Inc., Hispanic broadcaster.
Cable TV: None.
Film & Television: Sony Pictures Entertainment, Columbia Pictures Entertainment, Tri-Star Motion Pictures Company, Triumph Releasing Corporation, Columbia Tri-Star television production and distribution, Columbia Tri-Star Home Video, Sony Pictures Studio and the Culver City Studios.
Music: Sony Music International, Epic Records Group, Tri-Star Music Group, Barris Music.
Publishing: None.
Other Interests: Electronic and electrical equipment manufacture, including a full range of mass market and professional audio and video equipment as well as semi-conductors, cathode ray tubes, home video game software, computers, and telephone and telecommunications equipment, insurance and financing interests.

Significant Events:
1988: Buys CBS records for $2 billion.
1989: Buys Columbia pictures from Coca-Cola for $4.9 billion.
1994: Founder Akio Morita resigns after brain hemorrhage.
1996: Releases feature film *Jerry McGuire*, and sparks recovery of film division, which dominates the movie summer season of 1997 with movie hits such as *My Best Friend's Wedding* and *Air Force One*.
1997: Kicks off *Men in Black* movie promotion with expansive tie-in to Ray-Ban sunglasses.
1997: Consumer electronics division reports 82% increase in operating profits for fiscal year ending March 31, 1997.
1997: Partners with investment banker Blackstone Group to invest in manufacturing electronics for the "digital revolution."
1997: With partners pays $539 million for 65% of Telemundo Group, Inc., Hispanic broadcaster, and becomes managing partner.
1999: Cuts 17,000 jobs (10% of the workforce) and closes 15 manufacturing plants.

Sony Music, a division of giant Sony electronics company of Japan, entered the music recording business with the 1998 purchase of CBS Records for $2 billion in cash. When the deal was announced, CBS was the world's largest and most successful record company, with 6,000 employees worldwide and profits at an all time high.[125]

But Sony was never able to synergize the music division with electronics manufacturing—still this failure was not from a lack of trying. In April 1997, Sony tapped Howard Stringer to lead synergy. This former CBS executive oversaw Sony Retail Entertainment and Sony Online Ventures. Stringer, who reported directly to Sony Corporation President Nobuyuki Idei, was to try to fashion other synergies. But, by 1999, his efforts reaped mediocre rewards at best. The Sony MiniDisc never became a mass medium. And in 1997 Sony unveiled a Web site for its latest promotional tool. But Sationsony.com simply fell further behind Amazon.com. By the late 1990s, the Sony Music Group was laying off these staffers. Sony Music stressed that it was pushing forward with Sony Signatures Music, to make money from music-associated merchandising. Products included full lines of clothing to assorted lava lamps. For example, there were 22 accounts for the group Kiss alone, including apparel, comic books and action figures, each generating about $5 million. New star Celine Dion gave hope, and in 1998 she came through. Evidently, the star system would continue to drive this industry. Still the best way to position Sony within the Internet world remained a concern for the 21st century.[126]

The EMI Group PLC was also trying to move up in the rankings. The EMI Group had been, until 1996, a division of Thorn EMI PLC (formally Electrical and Music Instruments), a vast British media and manufacturing conglomerate. Thorn had started in the lighting business, and then went into television set and home appliance manufacture. Thorn looked for entertainment to sell its radios, TV sets and record players, and so developed a music division. In time, Thorn's EMI division acquired Capitol Records, and made millions of dollars in profits from sales of records by the Beatles and Pink Floyd. Indeed, even though the Beatles quit recording in 1969, they remained the company's biggest seller until 1979, accounting for fully one quarter of company sales through the 1980s. In 1996, Thorn spun off EMI Group PLC, and thereafter struggled at the bottom of the music oligopoly rankings, making pretax profits of just one half billion dollars in the fiscal year ending March 31, 1998.[127]

In 1999, EMI prepared for a new era. Under the leadership of Sir Colin Southgate for two decades, in March 1999 the EMI board selected one of its own, Eric Nicoli, to lead the company into the next century. Nicoli, formerly head of United Biscuits (known for its Keebler line of cookies), announced he would take EMI in a new direction, away from lavish deals of the past. Still more than most, EMI relied on key acts (e.g., Garth Brooks, the Rolling Stones and Janet Jackson). EMI was set to deal with the new world of marketing by the Internet.[128]

EMI Music owned important labels like Capitol, EMI, Liberty, Chrysalis, Virgin, SBK, Curb and EMI. Stars included the Bonnie Raitt, Smashing Pumpkins, Deanna Carter and Arrested Development. EMI Group PLC also represented a rare instance among the Big Five by vertically integrating and operating a retailing division called

HMV retail stores. Even before new management took over in 1999, in 1997 EMI began restructuring its musical arms under Ken Berry. Charles Koppelman was out. Southgate stressed that this was a positive move toward reaching the leadership in global marketing in an integrated fashion. It was in the United States that EMI seemed to have trouble maintaining sales. Berry moved to sign David Bowie to a deal promising a minimum of $2 million per year. Operating from a base in Los Angeles (the Koppelman administration had worked from offices in New York City), Berry faced a mixed fiscal picture. The whole EMI Group, which encompassed all EMI labels plus music publishing plus the HMV retail chain, was making money, but a large chunk came through retailing. Only EMI Latin as a record label seemed to be growing with vigor.[129]

There was a problem because one artist, Garth Brooks, was at the core of EMI. In November 1997 Brooks showed his muscle when he and EMI Group PLC's Nashville division announced the long-awaited album "Sevens" would be released two days before Thanksgiving. Brooks had been withholding "Sevens" for months because he was unhappy with the terms EMI Group PLC proposed for its distribution, promotion and release. In the end, EMI Group PLC surrendered, going as far as to replace the head of Capitol Nashville per Brooks' demand and agreeing to promote "Sevens" beyond country radio. It worked—"Sevens" set records for sales.

Brooks more than any musical act of the 1990s showed that big stars still drove the business, and when they were on top, they could play hard ball by demanding and getting what they wanted. Brooks knew that EMI Group PLC was desperate to get "Sevens" in the stores before Christmas 1997 when the Big Five companies pulled in 40% of their annual revenues. Brooks, whose dazzling stage shows and populist albums made him a favorite in the 1990s, needed and got a hit. Wal-Mart alone ordered 1.4 million copies of "Sevens," pushing total sales since commencing his professional career in 1989 near the mythical 100 million sold.[130]

The Bertelsmann Music Group (BMG) is the least known of the Big Five. It is a division of a privately held German company with well-known labels (e.g., RCA, Arista, Zoo and Windam Hill) and stars (e.g., Whitney Houston, ZZ Top, TLC, Kenny G., Crash Test Dummies, Ace of Base and Toni Braxton). The Bertelsmann Music Group entered the music business in 1986 by purchasing the RCA Victor Company.[131]

Bertelsmann AG, the parent company, in 1999 ranked as a $14.7 billion worldwide media enterprise with four major divisions: entertainment, book (see Chapter 2), newspaper and magazine publishing and printing and manufacturing operations. It made claims of ranking right behind Disney and Time Warner as the largest media company in the world. With headquarters in Germany, but with the music group headquartered in New York City, media operations included music, television, film, video, interactive entertainment and direct marketing, as well as compact disc and cassette manufacturing. BMG Entertainment North America oversees all of BMG Entertainment's businesses in the United States, including recorded music, music publishing, direct marketing, merchandising and online. Under President and CEO Strauss Zelnick, the company was home to some of the best-known names in the entertainment business (e.g., the Dave Matthews Band, Annie Lennox, Alan Jackson, George Winston and Clint Black). Its joint venture with LaFace Records introduced TLC, the biggest-selling female group of all time.

Bertelsmann's offices were headquartered in Gutersloh, Germany, a town of less than 100,000. This meant senior management worked far from the music hot spots. Yet while Time Warner, Disney and Rupert Murdoch gathered all the headlines, Bertelsmann matched their billions of dollars in revenues each year. Quietly, Reinhard Mohn and family ran the show, controlling a trust that owned 69% of the voting stock. This is why this company, with but 11% of stock publicly traded, was in effect the world's largest private media company.[132]

Its record of accomplishment, however, was impressive. Consider the case of Arista Records, one of the world's most successful record labels, having launched and nurtured the careers of numerous artists (i.e., Sweden's Ace of Base, the U.K.'s Annie Lennox and Canada's Crash Test Dummies). During its history, Arista has recorded such legendary performers as Carly Simon, Aretha Franklin, Barry Manilow and the Grateful Dead, and produced two of the most successful movie soundtracks of all time, *The Bodyguard* and *Waiting to Exhale*. Based in New York City, Arista was founded in 1975 by Clive Davis. Arista Nashville is the country music division established in 1989. Under President Tim DuBois, the label has built a superstar roster that includes Alan Jackson, Brooks & Dunn, Pam Tillis, The Tractors and BlackHawk. Arista Records had a higher percentage of albums turn gold than any other label. In 1998, Arista alone sold more than $420 million, making it the largest sales year in the labels's history since its founding in 1974. The year 1998 also represented the sixth straight increase in sales. In that year, Arista released, through parent BMG, 35 albums and nabbed a combined 71 slots on the charts—singles and albums that contained those singles—led by Usher, next, Sarah McLachlan and Monica. Industry watchers speculated that $42 million came to the company as profit by focusing on a few artists. Davis used the old fashioned strategy of breaking singles on radio, and then leveraging album sales from that air play. BMG paid Davis for his expertise handsomely at an estimated $12 million per annum.[133]

New York-based RCA Records has a long and distinguished history. In 1997 it was the home to Bruce Hornsby, SWV, La Bouche, Chantay Savage and The Verve Pipe. A successful joint venture with Loud Records produced hits from Wu-Tang Clan, Mobb Deep, Raekwon and Delinquent Habits. RCA's nearly century-old musical legacy included the complete works of Elvis Presley, and country's Alabama. Clint Black, Martina McBride, Aaron Tippin, K. T. Oslin, Mindy McCready and Lonestar, among others, have recorded for RCA. A sister company, BNA Records, was created in 1991 with flagship artists Lorrie Morgan and John Anderson.

By 1997, the Windham Hill Group had established itself as the premier label in contemporary adult instrumental music, as well as other adult-oriented genres (i.e., jazz and folk). Some of its most prominent artists are George Winston, Jim Brickman, Michael Hedges, Janis Ian and Liz Story. Windham Hill is also well known for its seasonal albums and conceptual samplers, and includes the Private Music label, which features a number of world-class artists such as Etta James, Taj Mahal and Toots Thielemans.

Under the leadership of Senior Vice President and General Manager Gary Newman, BMG Special Products creates customized theme and artist-based music compilations for use by a host of companies in direct marketing, premium and incentive program activities. BMG Special Products' clients include Reader's Digest, Seagrams, Avon Products, Nestle, Shell Oil, The Smithsonian, Kellogg's and IBM. BMG Distribution stocked more than 11,000 music and video selections and ships half a million units daily to retailers around the United States. Along with handling every aspect of positioning music, video and CD-ROM releases at retail, BMG Distribution was responsible to its labels for marketing, sales, fulfillment, credit and collection.

In 1999, BMG Direct moved to bolster its position in the Christian music market by acquiring the Word Family Record and Tape Club, which is the oldest Christian music club. The Word club, which is believed to have 130,000 members, will be integrated into the Sound and Spirit Christian Music Club run by BMG Direct. As part of the deal, Word Entertainment will continue to license music and video product to BMG's various clubs on a nonexclusive basis. BMG also operated BMG Music Service, BMG Classical Music Service and the BMG Jazz Club.

Established in 1987, New York-based BMG Music Publishing has become one of the top groups worldwide and is considered to be the world's fastest growing music publishing company. Under the leadership of President Nicholas Firth, this division made more than 127 music publishing acquisitions in 12 countries and by 1997 held the rights to more than 700,000 songs (including the catalogs of the Beach Boys, B.B. King and Barry Manilow).[134]

Management was stable during the 1990s. In September 1994, the 37-year-old former movie studio executive Strauss Zelnick took over BMG Entertainment. He quickly cut costs as only a Harvard-trained business school and law school graduate could do. He fired label heads, save Clive Davis, and sold off such operations as the Imago record label. But cutting is one thing; finding new talent is another. He struggled to find new artists. In 1997, although BMG ranked last in sales in the rock market, overall sales were growing at a double-digit clip—principally because of Arista, where Clive Davis had hits from Whitney Houston, Toni Braxton and Kenny G. Davis' joint venture with producer Babyface's LaFace records alone brought BMG $400 million in annual sales.[135]

THE MUSIC INDUSTRY'S MINOR COMPANIES

Yet the Big Five did not control everything. Like their counterparts in the motion picture industry, the Big Five regularly took in $7 of every $8 spent on recorded music. There thus existed some room on the margins for minor companies. There literally existed thousands of pretenders seeking to replace PolyGram as the sixth member of the oligopoly. One of the most visible attempts in the mid-1990s was made by the Walt Disney Company. In July 1997, Disney agreed to buy independent label Mammoth Records in a move to gain a foothold in the music business. At $25 million, this was a small transaction by Disney standards, and would add to Disney's Hollywood Records, a division that never seemed to become a true multitalent, multigenre record label. Since 1988, when Disney created Hollywood Records, it had signed talent from rappers to alternative rockers. Yet by 1997, Hollywood Records had not broken a single act, and losses had mounted to more than $100 million. Disney then tried to build a stable of specialty labels, each focused on single musical genre; Mammoth was to be the alternative rock imprint. Disney also created a Nashville division aimed at the country market, plus Walt Disney Records, which covered children's music.[136]

There was no doubt that the Disney experience was a sour one, with Hollywood Records unable to generate a single hit. Over time it also had trouble attracting new talent. As Disney spent millions throughout the 1990s, its lack of success produced an embarrassing hole in the company's media portfolio and a dent in its reputation as a company that succeeded in anything it tried. Even its movie soundtracks proved to be a big disappointment through the 1990s. Only the obvious tie-ins to animated features like *The Lion King* did substantial business. After 2000, Disney will undoubtedly keep trying to sign new talent, and further test the synergistic power of its film and television operations.[137]

News Corporation, like Disney, was another multibillion media conglomerate that was unable to become the sixth member of the recorded music oligopoly. Late in 1996, Murdoch appointed his son James to try to create a music division of substance, leveraging the News, Inc.'s powerful positions in television, film, books and other media. James Murdoch announced that he would move slowly, developing acts in-house, and would not try to instantly build up a new division equal to Universal Music Group. Mushroom Records and Festival Records were the beginning. But, will Rupert Murdoch back this effort to create the equivalent of the Fox TV network, which became a powerful player in a few years?[138]

It should come as no surprise that former Big Five executives often try to mount their own companies. For example, in 1996, six months after being dismissed as head of MCA Music, Al Teller raised $20 million from Wall Street and founded Red Ant Records. One month later, Teller sold Red Ant to Alliance Entertainment Corporation, the largest independent distributor of music, for $40 million and became Alliance's new co-chief executive officer. Alliance bet that Teller could use his contacts and experience to vault Alliance into the big leagues. Like all who came before him, Teller failed. He cut deals with nontraditional outlets such as Barnes & Noble; he allied with Microsoft to sell music on an Internet site, Music Central, But, before 1999, Alliance filed for bankruptcy and put Red Ant up for sale. Teller could not make a go of it even when Alliance peaked at $700 million in annual revenues.[139]

This Red Ant experience has been repeated time and again. This grim reality, however, did not seem to dampen the enthusiasm of potential entrances. Hundreds

---

PROFILE: The News Corporation Limited

Basic Data:
Headquarters: Sydney, Australia
Web site: N/A
CEO in 1997: Rupert Murdoch
1997 Revenues (in millions): $11,264
1997 Net Income (in millions): $564
1997 Assets (in millions): $30,832
Rank in 1998 Forbes International 500: 217

Market Holdings:
Broadcast Television: Fox Broadcasting Company (television network), Fox television stations, Inc. (owned and operated TV stations including WNYW-New York, KTTV-Los Angeles, KRIV-Houston, WFLD-Chicago, KDAF-Dallas and WTTG-Washington, DC, among others), Heritage Media, New World Entertainment (television stations and program production)
Cable Television: FX cable network, Fox news cable channel, Kids International, International Family Channel network, 15 regional sports cable channels.
Film & Television: Twentieth Century-Fox studio, Fox Video Company, Fox Broadcasting Company, Twentieth Century-Fox Home Entertainment, BSkyN, the Sky Channel satellite service in Europe, STAR TV in Asia, JSkyB in Japan satellite television, Canal FOX in Europe, Sky Entertainment Services in Latin America, VOX and DF1 television in Germany.
Music: small music company.
Publishing: magazines, including joint deal with *TV Guide*, and *Good Food*; newspapers, including the *Boston Herald*, the *New York Post*, the *Sun* (London, England), the *News of the World* (London, England), the *Times* (London, England); HarperCollins book publishing.
Other Interests: CineBooks, Inc. (Computer systems), Los Angeles Dodgers (Major League baseball), 100 daily and weekly newspapers in Australia, Ansett Transport industries.

Significant Events:
1985: Rupert Murdoch buys Twentieth Century-Fox studio; establishes in the United States.
1986: Begins Fox television network.
1989: Starts Sky television and becomes a major force in TV in Europe.
1993: Acquires 64% of START TV in Asia.
1994: Spends $1.6 for rights to broadcast National Football League games.
1997: Acquires the 80% of New World Communications group not already owned for about $2.5 billion in securities, and with the new 10 television stations News Corporation becomes largest owner of TV stations in the United States.
1997: Agrees to buy Los Angeles Dodgers baseball team for $350 million.
1997: Agrees to buy International Family Channel cable network for $1.9 million.
1999: Rupert Murdoch's son James named president of News American Digital publishing, a new unit that will consolidate all of News Corporation's electronic pushing operations.
1998: Spins off Fox Group as IPO to raise cash for investment.

---

of small-time independents were seeking a niche, trying to break out, and then ended up being purchased by a member of the Big Five. Goldmine magazine annually lists nearly 50 pages of such independents; the following are a few typical examples (starting at the beginning of the alphabet):

Aaron Avenue Records, based in Arlington, Texas, exemplified a regional niche independent, only recording bands from and selling to fans in North Central Texas.

Acoustic Disc, based in San Rafael, California, was an independent that specializes in acoustic music.

Alligator Records, of Chicago, Illinois, recorded blues and sold by mail order and the Internet.

Arrival Records, of Plymouth, Minnesota, recorded and sold inspirational music for the Christian market.

Art Monk Construction, based in Falls Church, Virginia, in the Washington, DC suburbs, put out music by its friends that he considered better than most other music available. Monk raised money from a professional football career.

Audio Outings, based in Asheville, North Carolina, made albums for children to try to help them develop their imaginations and make parenting easier. Its top seller was not a musician, but psychologist Bett Sanders.

AVI Entertainment, of Santa Monica, California, functioned as a classic rock reissuer—selling the work of Slim Harpo, the Standells, Chocolate Watch Band, Lightin' Slim, Lazy Lester, Silas Hogan and Lonesome Sundown.

Big Boss Records, of Valdosta, Georgia, specialized in hip-hop and rhythm and blues music and released its first album in May 1996.

There are literally hundreds of others—probably less than 1,000—but no complete list is available. In the end, because making compact discs is relatively cheap, many will try. But because of their power of distribution and promotion and marketing is so advantageous, the Big Five will surely continue to dominate.[140]

The most profitable and permanent niche for independents is re-issuing music. The biggest player here is Reader's Digest Music, which does not do its own recording, but re-issues collections of music. Founded in 1960, using the lists of customers for direct sales of books and other merchandise, Reader's Digest aims at an older audience and has been famous for its sales of collections of Glenn Miller and Benny Goodman. By the late 1990s, its oldies albums were focusing on collections of Neil Diamond, Linda Ronstandt, and the Mamas & the Papas. Reader's Digest began to seek crossover albums, trying the likes of Ella Fitzgerald, Sheryl Crow, Kenny Rogers, Floyd Cramer and Judy Collins. All these albums have been assembled from 15,000 master recordings it had licensed from the Big Five. Its music sales around the world have long been considerable at nearly a half a billion dollars per year, but exact figures are hard to recover because they are buried within the direct sales in the company reports. It has also sold 140,000 of the three compact disc collection of the recordings of Pasty Cline.[141]

Sometimes bands act as their own music companies. For example, in its 10 year existence, Windspread Panic (with Southern rock inspirations, long instrumental jams and a beat to dance to) never had a video on MTV or cracked the *Billboard* top 200, but this six-member unit by 1999 had sold 140,000 copies of its 1991 release. Touring and word of mouth via the Internet helped sell out the Fox Theater in Atlanta in 1998, and led to sales of several thousand albums. This might be small potatoes to the Big Five, but it surely meant life for this band. Moreover, Space Wrangler, Everyday, Ain't Life Grand, Bombs and Butterflies and Light Fuse Get Away have also sold between 100,000 and 200,000 albums by 1999. This proves that one eighth of all sales of music in the United States is up for grabs.[142]

THE OLIGOPOLY AND THE FUTURE OF MUSIC

...... Big Five make up a varied, international lot, dominating the music business throughly and completely. Successful independents, such as Motown, invariably are acquired by one of the Big Five. It is estimated that they control nearly 90% of all the revenues gathered each year. The majors block new entrants and control the contracts and distribution of virtually all the major music stars in the world. It is a tricky balance to collude yet not to tread or risk antitrust potential decrees such as those that spilt production and distribution from exhibition in the movie business in the late 1940s. The fact that Edgar Bronfman Jr. would in 1998 pay more than $10 billion for one of the oligopolists to gain access to the world market (estimated at $30 billion per year) would seem to prove the long-term viability of the music industry. Bronfman and company figured that they could capture the bulk of the sales by the Internet and become even richer. Here was a strong oligopoly, able to maintain barriers to entry to protect their dominant market positions.[143]

The Big Five work together through the RIAA (based in Washington, and founded in 1952 to protect the property interests of its member clients) to resist proposed government restrictions, fight piracy and struggle against tariffs and trade restrictions abroad. The RIAA's awards—gold, platinum and multi-platinum records—gain the vast proportion of publicity, but economic issues are paramount. Consider that, for example, half the association's employees work in the antipiracy division. In 1997, for example, its lawyers filed suits against music archive sites on the World Wide Web that offer full-length copyrighted recordings. RIAA's sound recordings represent a powerful contribution to the U.S. balance of trade. The RIAA helped the Big Five move into China. It also battled cheap copies that flooded the world from the Netherlands, Germany and Sweden—more than 100 million illegal CDs per annum.[144]

The Internet   *see charts at end of book.*

Virtually every music industry panel discussion of the Internet as the 1990s closed included executives waxing euphoric over its tremendous possibilities. One could more effectively market directly to the consumer; one could revive out-of-print titles; one could offer unique events, like celebrity chats, to millions of potential consumers at once. In 1994, CDNOW pioneered offering CDs for sale on the Internet. Other companies soon followed suit: Music Boulevard, Tower, Amazon.com, barnesandnoble.com, Blockbuster, Camelot, Hastings, TransWorld, Kmart and Wherehouse. Of even greater importance was the entry of Sony, BMG and Warner Music Group. Even noted artists, such as Prince and Sara McLaughlin, mounted their own sites that sell as well as promote. Toss in a few companies like NetRadio, which positioned itself as an Internet broadcaster, who also have "buy" buttons on the screen, and it starts to look like everyone sees online music retailing as part of their revenue stream. When AOL in 1999 purchased two Internet music firms—Spinner Networks and Nullsoft, for a total of $400 million—no analysis could ignore Internet sales as simply another experiment.[145]

The beginning of the 21st century will be defined by a great deal of experimentation. Old paradigms will be tested. For example, is radio or television going to be the applicable strategy for handling musical content? New economic models, like pay for play, are going to be tested. What makes for an album will be up for grabs. In the past the definition came from the limitations of what the physical carrier could hold. In an online world, that limitation becomes less important. Because the marketplace is more song driven than ever (witness the success of compilations), there will be an environment in which artists and consumers show interest in deciding how many cuts they want to compile as an album. In an online environment, label branding has not been shown to be particularly effective with consumers. Why should a consumer have to remember what label Jewel is on? BMG has already recognized that, moving to acquire a piece of barnesandnoble.com.

The change started in 1995 when the Big Five began to post information from their catalogs online. In the mid-1990s, there was much hype surrounding the Internet. The truth is that most companies had yet to determine how the Internet would work save as a publicity vehicle. Everyone had a Web site; no one made any profits. The music retailers developed Web sites as an extension of mail order and telephone ordering. But, translating the retail shopping experience—particularly browsing and impulse buys—was yet to be achieved. Questions remained: How would returns be handled? How could credit card security be guaranteed? How could a promotion be run? How can delivery costs be allocated? The consumer was stuck between the familiar trip to a Tower Music store, and the prospect of ordering through CDNOW. Some sites let people download a sample, or in the case of EMI's Capitol Records, an entire song. How else can customers learn of new music to buy aside from radio and MTV?

It looks like the Big Five will cooperate until a permanent solution is found. In May 1999, Seagram's Universal Music Group and Bertelsmann's BMG Entertainment announced a joint venture called GetMusic.com, an Internet Web site aimed at promoting the labels' artists and selling CDs online. Most everyone recognizes that the Internet and digital music distribution is where the industry is headed, and the fact that these two giants were pooling their resources in a future-oriented venture might lead one to further domination by the Big Five.

Yet one big problem remained. MP3, a program that allows customers to download music, struck fear at the executive and ownership level of the Big Five. MP3 was free, unsecured and becoming very popular. It was the free part that proved most frightening; with music being exchanged for free on the Internet, huge revenue streams are becoming dried up. As technology companies like Microsoft, IBM, AT&T and Liquid Audio battle to devise solutions to prevent this from happening.[146]

The RIAA insisted in 1999 that MP3 was simply a means to violate copyright and downloading using MP3 from the Internet was simply stealing. MP3 is an abbreviation for MPEG-1, Layer-3. It compresses audio files into a format available for playback on any MP3 compatible devise, either stored on a computer's hard drive or on a portable system. MP3 enabled computer users to share music, rapidly, easily and simply. The RIAA was mad because it offered a way for independents to get around the distribution system imposed by the Big Five. In an effort to protect their oligopoly, the RIAA in December 1998 organized to standardize and control Internet distribution. Universal Music Group and BMG in May 1999 became the first two to declare plans for distribution over the Internet. Working with Intertrust Technologies Corporation and its Digibox technology, the Universal Music Group hoped to develop a pirate proof software for distribution ready for use before 2000. BMG and Universal set up a joint venture called GetMusic. Sony then followed suit working with Microsoft.[147]

GetMusic.com may signal that the industry will move to compete against MP3 with real products, not rhetoric. After all, an Internet Web site from a record label is bound to promote (or at least favor) its own records. This leaves consumers at the mercy of the strength of the company's roster, which ebbs and flows with the trends. This is the reason that, traditionally, record companies do not have their own radio stations. If a radio station began to factor in "label" as a major attribute of a record, its competition would likely "mop up" that radio station. Today, "label" is largely irrelevant to the consumer. However, Universal's massive 25% share of the market and BMG's 17% means that together they have 42% of the talent pool. With close to half of the talent pool, they can begin to provide a robust consumer experience. GetMusic.com just might be that experience if they team up with a broadband portal like America Online or Yahoo!/Broadcast.com? This remained a key problem in 1999.[148]

The Web in 1999 was a site for price wars. Once Wal-Mart entered cyberspace, it began to undercut retailers and cyber competitors by offering such hits as Toni Braxton's "Secrets" and George Strait's "Clear Blue Skys" at $11.88 (including shipping and handling)—far cheaper than what one might pay anywhere else. By mid-1997, Wal-Mart was hawking some 40,000 products online. Tower Records, Camelot and Newbury were also online by the mid-1997, but they offered less choice than Wal-Mart and sold at higher prices. Virtual music stores such as CDNOW and Music Boulevard could not match Wal-Mart's low prices either, and it seems that Wal-Mart will run smaller competitors out of business.[149]

Promotion is the other key. Several independent hip-hop labels, many without the funding to participate in priority placement programs at traditional retail, are selling directly to consumers via the Internet. In addition, some independent labels are using the Internet to sell their most controversial releases, which are often shut out of larger retail stores because of their violent themes and racy lyrics. For example, Sacramento, California-based Black Market Records used the Internet to sell the latest rap release from Anerae Brown, whose records are X-Rated. Brown's album had a difficult time getting manufactured and sold in the United States, because it was allegedly recorded from his prison cell. The rapper is serving a life sentence for murder. Another label, AWOL Recordings, is using the Internet to protest the imprisonment of rapper C-Bo, who was jailed because he violated a condition of his parole that required him not to glorify the gangsta lifestyle. The AWOL site posts a statement from the rapper's lawyer that claims C-Bo's jail sentence is a violation of his First Amendment rights. The brand equity of some streetwise hip-hop labels has resulted in fan sites that are devoted, not to the artists, but to the labels. Death Row and No Limit are two examples of labels that have fan-created Web sites devoted to the hip-hop lifestyle preached by its artists. Hip-hop lifestyle programming is flourishing on the Internet. Improvements in streaming technology, along with wider deployment of broadband Web connections, are giving rise to an unprecedented amount of choice for hip-hop fans.[150]

In April 1999, the hot race to establish a de facto digital download standard has gotten even hotter as leading technology companies Microsoft and RealNetworks jockey for mind and market share in this emerging space. The stakes are high. A new report by Forrester Research predicts that digital music downloading will add $1.1 billion to the U.S. music industry by 2003. About 34% of consumers say they are interested in purchasing digitally delivered music, according to the Forrester study, which surveyed about 6,700 online consumers. Forrester senior analyst Mark Hardie estimated that MP3 will continue to dominate the download technology over legitimate download offerings, but MP3 piracy will give way to legitimate technology by 2002. Efforts at establishing an industry-approved download effort should fully catch on with consumers by 2003. There is likely to be chaos among consumers over the next few years, as several competing download systems continue to emerge alongside ongoing growth of piracy in the unprotected MP3 format.[151]

But the Web can be used for other variations of music distribution and sales. Consider Musicmaker.com, a Web site that lets music fans create customized CDs. The dream here is no music store, only cyberspace sales. Instead of selling the album the artist and distributor has produced, manipulation of the mouse leads to precisely the album the customer wants. In 1999, more than 150,000 songs were stored digitally and then company software let the customer do the rest. The cost is real (vs. the promises of MP3 alternatives) in 1999 at $9.95 for the first five songs and $1 a track after that, plus a shipping charge. But Musicmaker.com did not have the cooperation of the Big Five and it offered mostly independent productions by unknown artists. Musicmaker comes with a "Watermark" so it is possible to track stolen songs. Finally, it takes hours to download a single album using telephone lines.

CDNOW and N2K (owner of Music Boulevard) merged in March 1999 to create a powerhouse Web music seller—to rival Amazon.com, which began to sell music in late 1998. Each of the Big Five will establish a successful Web site in the manner of a record club and shopping mall outlet. Or, will some other solution will evolve?[152]

Tracking Sales   —See photocopy notes.

With all the attendant publicity surrounding the Internet and World Wide Web, a far more influential change came in the manner of accurately counting what was selling. In 1991, SoundScan introduced reliable sales data charting. Prior to 1991, ranking of top album sales were based on telephone surveys of record store employees. SoundScan changed that to point of purchase computer recording of data, as the scanner bar code information on each unit was fed to a central computer in Hartsdale, New York. Suddenly 30 years of imprecise hunches were replaced by hard information. The rumor that male clerks failed to report sales of albums they did not like was the stuff of industry legend. SoundScan proved a boon to independent labels, and to the rap and country genres. It established the power of Wal-Mart as music's top retailer.[153]

SoundScan sells data to the Big Five and *Billboard*. By the late 1990s, it stood at the very heart of the music business. SoundScan demonstrated, contrary to long-held myth, that albums did not generally start at a low position in the *Billboard* carts and then climb up, but through publicity and star power often started near the top. Sound-Scan demonstrated that being number one on the charts was actually a trivial accomplishment because for some weeks an album with only 150,000 in sales topped the charts and in other weeks 350,000 sales were needed. By 1997, the cry among the Big Five was that SoundScan was too powerful in an industry where the Internet and new song styles were constantly refitting the popularity of certain performers.[154]

SoundScan enabled the industry to more clearly target its audience. For example, in August 1997, the RIAA released the results of an inaugural effort to gather net shipments data on Hispanic music in the United States. During the first six months of 1997, nearly 20 million total units of Hispanic product (compact discs, audio cassettes and music videos) entered the market with a list value of $213.2 million—a jump of 22.8% in units and 25.1% in dollars compared to 1996 midyear figures. Compact discs jumped from 9.2 million units to 11.2 million units in 1997 for a 21% increase. The value of these shipments (at suggested list price) increased 24.2% over the previous period. Audio cassettes showed a similar pattern of growth: units went from 6.6 million to 8.3 million, a 25% midyear jump. The value of cassette shipments grew 27% from $52.5 million at the first half of 1996 to $66.8 million in 1997. In 1996, 36 million units of Hispanic music were shipped into the market valued at $392 million. This survey reported solid numbers on what the industry had long figured only anecdotally. With its enormous crossover appeal, many specialized types of Hispanic music (i.e., Tejano, Salsa, Samba, Mexican R&B, etc.) are flourishing. Music is clearly part of the dynamic mix of Hispanic magazines, television and radio programming that has become a vital part of our culture.[155]

The Future

SoundScan was a technology that fundamentally changed the business in the 1990s. The industry remained stable, however, so true experimentation took place only at the margins. For example, in late 1997, Sony Music planned to sell Mariah Carey's new album as a package set—with both a compact disc and an audio cassette together. This packaging experiment comes as audio cassettes were losing favor with customers. (The music companies are happy because the average $16 compact disc provides far more profit than the $11 audio cassette. Still the audio cassette format was hardly dead, accounting for $2 billion of the industry total of $12 billion in sales. And prerecorded tapes predominate overseas.) Carey's "Butterfly" set would sell for a suggested retail price of $24.98; though in the retail world of discounting it would sell for closer to $20. If sold separately, the compact disc would sell for a suggested retail price of $17.98, and the audio cassette for a suggested retail price of $10.98. This will be a much looked at experiment considering that Carey was Sony's biggest seller of the 1990s and her previous album sold some seven million units (one quarter in tape format). Industry surveys indicate that only half of customers buy exclusively in compact disc format, and only one in five have a compact disc player in their car. This figure puts tapes at one quarter of sales, and this trend will probably be slow to go away unless there is a rise in the automobile installations of CD players.[156]

In 1999, for example, Sony's electronic's division announced a new CD player called a Super Audio CD. This would seek to overcome the "problem" that audio fans had complained of since the innovation of the compact disc in 1982, that is, a lack of warmth that the best analog systems could and still do produce. Using a direct stream digital system, the Super CD Player could match the smooth sound waves in a way that the older CDs could only approximate. Whereas in 1999 the first models sold for $4,000, these were meant to capture the audiophiles. After 2000, the price should fall, and Sony is betting that fans will replace their older CD sets. Because it is comparable with the older CD, there exists no problem for playing the estimated 12 billion CDs sold since 1982.[157]

But the older means of selling music, cassettes and vinyl, have not simply vanished as CDs have taken over. The cassette became popular in the 1960s and 1970s after 8-track tapes failed. And whereas its sound quality has never been up to CD quality, cassettes are cheap and easy to use. Repeated efforts in the 1990s failed to supplant the cassette with better sounding digital tapes, and with no easy and cheap way to record on a CD, there looks to be a market for cassettes well into the next century. Vinyl also continued to sell in small numbers, because of the warmth that collectors valued. This market will be specialized, but it will survive because collectors prize valued albums as much for their sound quality as for their cover art.[158]

New technologies will surely come, yet in the end it is the concentration of power in the Big Five that must stand as the central issue of concern for the music industry of the future. Will the Big Five continue its domination and make entry as an independent difficult? Concentration has long persisted. It seems as if nothing short of a Web revolution will break up the Big Five as the 21st century commences. The music industry is as tight and powerful oligopoly as exists in any media business analyzed in this book, and it should and will remain that way well into the next century.[159]

NOTES

1. Lisa Napoli, "MTV Is Buying Two Services from TCI Music," *New York Times*, May 21, 1999, p. C8; Andrew Pollack, "Ovitz Helps Form Online Entertainment Venture," *New York Times*, May 21, 1999, p. C8; Carlos Tejada, "Chancellor Media to Form Two Web Units and Seek Partners," *Wall Street Journal*, May 20, 1999, p. B2.
2. For current information, see various Web sites noted later, plus *The M Street Journal*. *Broadcasting & Cable* used to cover radio extensively, but by 1999 had conceded the trade press market to *Radio & Records*, which offers the best data from Web site at rronline.com.
3. This vital link is well documented in Geoffrey P. Hull, *The Recording Industry* (New York: Allyn & Bacon, 1998), pp. 95–105.
4. See, e.g., John Meriel, "Adult Contemporary Sings a Happy Tune," *Broadcasting & Cable*, July 27, 1998, p. 35. For a description of various formats, see "There's A Radio Format for Everybody," found on the Radio Advertising Bureau (RAB) Web site at www.rab.com.

5. This portrait is from Duncan's Web site at www.duncanradio.com—first created by Jim Duncan as an outgrowth from his *Duncan's Radio Market Guide*. Through the later quarter of the 20th century, this guide has functioned as a vital source on radio revenues and marketing information. Duncan—in print and now online—presents market-by-market analyses of revenue histories and projections, particularly for advertising agencies as they craft multimedia campaigns. See also Chuck Taylor, "Country Radio Leads in Listeners," *Billboard*, May 24, 1997, pp. 51–52; Donna Petrozzello, "Country Format Is Radio's Favorite," *Broadcasting & Cable*, March 10, 1997, pp. 53–54.

6. See several Web sites for information on all radio stations in United States and their formats: www.airwaves.com, www.radioinfo.com, www.radio-directory.com. For state association, see Web site at www.broadcast.net, which also includes equipment sellers. The *Radio & Records* Web site (www.rronline) contains a detailed listings of all owners, large and small; this is a huge file. The Arbitron's companysite at www.arbitron.com and contains much recent information on listening trends and format trends.

7. Steve McClellan, "Ad Spending to Inch Up in '99," *Broadcasting and Cable*, December 14, 1998, p. 35.

8. Elizabeth A. Rathburn, "Radio Still Going Strong," *Broadcasting & Cable*, October 19, 1998, p. 58.

9. Standard & Poor's Industry Surveys, "Broadcasting & Cable," June 26, 1997, pp. 1, 5, 8, 16.

10. Ibid., pp. 16–17.

11. For the history of any company, see *Hoover's Guide to Media Companies* (Austin, TX: Hoover's Business Press, 1996). For a contemporary capsule of the company, see Hoover's Web site at www.hoovers.com. Know that for detail—without charge—one needs to consult the Web site of the U.S. Security and Exchange Commission, known as EDGAR, at www.sec.gov. Seek out the most recent annual report and most recent 10-K report.

12. See Erich Boehm and Adam Sandler, "$39 Bil Strikes Solid Chord for Music Biz," *Variety*, May 3–9, 1999, pp. 34, 99; and see also National Association of Record Merchandisers Web site at www.narm.com.

13. See Web site at www.riaa.com for further statistics about the music industry.

14. See the rankings of international corporations in *Forbes*, July 28, 1997, and *Business Week*, July 7, 1997, to verify the international importance of the music industry. All the aforementioned firms are detailed save the privately owned Bertelsmann. Time Warner, Sony, Seagram (including after 1998 PolyGram] and EMI are all in the top 500 largest public corporations in the world.

15. Patrick M. Reilly, "Music Album Sales Continue to Grow, Fueled by New Artists of Varying Genres," *Wall Street Journal*, July 10, 1997, p. B5.

16. The RIAA hired the accounting and research firm Coopers & Lybrand to compile the year-end figures, based on quarterly reports from RIAA member companies. These numbers represent shipping data from companies that distribute 90% of the prerecorded music in the United States. To calculate unit shipments and dollar values for the remaining 10%, Coopers & Lybrand uses actual retail sales data from SoundScan to estimate industry shipments by nonreporting companies.

    Together, the data reflects the level of wholesale activity for the entire industry. When reviewing these numbers, remember that they represent the quantity of product shipped to retailers, record clubs and direct and special markets, minus any returns for credit on unsold product. The dollar value of these shipments is calculated at suggested list price. See the RIAA Web site at www.riaa.com.

17. Let me note at this point that recognizing that in the end the theory and method one utilizes determines the form of the answers one obtains, it is important to be up front with the terms of economic analysis we use later. Restricting ourselves to ownership questions, and simply seeking to understand the actions and effects of key institutions, we choose to employ the industrial organization economics methodology, which seeks to explain the basic workings of a media industry as well as set up possibilities of comparing it to other industries and judging how well the industry is operating. We recognize that there are other approaches, but this chapter is not a survey of all methods of media economics, but rather an analysis of an emerging field within media studies. See Douglas Gomery, "The Centrality of Media Economics," *Journal of Communication* 43.3 (Summer 1993), pp. 190–198.

18. Geoffrey P. Hull, *The Recording Industry* (New York: Allyn & Bacon, 1998), pp. 97–101; David T. McFarland, *Future Radio Programming Strategies: Cultivating Listenership in the Digital Age*, 2nd ed. (Hillsdale, NJ: Lawrence Erlbaum Associates, 1997), pp. 63–74.

19. The history of radio since the innovation of top 40 rock format in the 1950s can be found in photographs in the second half of B. Eric Rhodes, *A Pictorial History of Radio's First 75 Years* (West Palm Beach, FL: Streamline Press, 1996). The history of "Modern Radio" is neatly summarized in Chapter 3 (pp. 47–72) of Edward Jay Whetmore, *The Magic Medium: An Introduction to Radio in America* (Belmont, CA: Wadsworth, 1981).

20. *The Broadcasting & Cable Yearbook—1997* (Washington, DC: Broadcasting & Cable, 1997), p. B-626.

21. The pioneering sociological work of Paul Hirsch remains crucial. See, for example, this representative article: "Production and Distribution Roles among Cultural Organizations," *Social Research* 45 (1978), pp. 315–330. Hirsch's work ought to be updated to reflect changes in the industry and population. In 1997, radio was avoiding teenagers and looking for the 25 to 34 year olds that advertisers most covert. See Steve Knopper, "Most Radio Stations Aren't Targeting Teens," *Billboard*, March 22, 1997, pp. 1, 92.

22. Recent trends in format appeal is summarized in McFarland, pp. 74–83.

23. James H. Duncan, Jr., "Radio's Biggest Signals . . . ," *Duncan's Radio Comments*, January 1997, issue No. 17; James H, Duncan, Jr., *Duncan's Radio Market Guide* (Cincinnati, OH: Duncan's American Radio, Inc., 1997), pp. 10–12; *The Broadcasting & Cable Yearbook—1997*, p. B-705.

24. See, e.g., Dick Rosse, "How Sweet It Was," *Broadcasting and Cable*, April 19, 1999, pp. 74–76, for a contemporary look back at the Mutual radio network.

25. Geoffrey P. Hull, "Radio and Records: Top 40 and the Ghost of Todd Stortz," *Feedback*, 38.1 (Summer 1997), pp. 15–19.

26. C. Archer, "Are Consultants Running Everything?," *Radio & Records*, September 15, 1995, p. 82; McFarland, pp. 27–36.

27. John Meril, "Television Looks to Radio for Fall Campaigns," *Broadcasting & Cable*, August 17, 1998, p. 65.

28. Bill McConnell, "FCC Eyes Radio Ad Domination," *Broadcasting & Cable*, August 24, 1998, p. 18; Elizabeth A. Rathbun, "Station-Rich Owners Get Richer," *Broadcasting & Cable*, August 11, 1997, pp. 31–32; Donna Petrozzello, "Radio's Time Is Now," *Broadcasting & Cable*, March 17, 1997, pp. 60, 62. Marc Schiffman's "Rock Panels Discuss Consolidation Issues," *Billboard*, November 1, 1997, p. 88, neatly tells of the problems of rock stations in the new world of major media powerhouse corporations.

29. For the case of radio as a monopolistically competitive industry, see Gomery, "The Centrality of Media Economics," pp. 190–198.

30. For analysis of changes in the radio industry, see the *Journal of Radio Studies*; e.g., Shane's "Modern Radio Formats: Trends and Possibilities," *Journal of Radio Studies* 3 (1995–1996), pp. 3–9. See its Web site at www2.okstate.edu/journal_of_radio_studies.

31. Marc Fisher, "No News Is . . . Much Cheaper," *Washington Post*, February 11, 1997, p. C7.

32. Robin D. Schatz, "All News, Almost All Profit, All the Time," *New York Times*, June 24, 1996, p. D7.

33. Michael Oneal, "Everybody's Talkin' at Us," *Business Week*, May 22, 1995, pp. 104–105, 108.

34. Marc Fisher, "Dumbing Down Dvorak," *Washington Post*, May 25, 1997, pp. G1, G6–G7.

35. Caryle Murphy, "They're Finding God on the Radio Dial," *Washington Post*, May 27, 1997, pp. A1, A8.

36. See Godfrey Ashley, *Future Sell: Radio's Niche Marketing Revolution* (Boston: Focal Press, 1997); Donna Petrozzello, "Spanish Radio Coming into Its Own," *Broadcasting & Cable*, January 9, 1995, p. 49.

37. Marc Fisher, "Colors of the Radio Spectrum," *Washington Post*, December 3, 1996, pp. E1, E7.

38. See "Radio's Top National Advertisers—1995," found on the Radio Advertising Bureau's Web page at www.rab.com.

39. See "Radio Reaches 77 Percent of All Customers Every Day . . . And 95 Percent Every Week," and "Radio Ad Revenues Up 11 Percent in July; Record Setting Growth Trend Continues," both found on the Radio Advertising Bureau's Web site at www.rab.com.

40. Federal Communications Commission, Mass media Bureau, Policy and Rules Division, "Review of the Radio Industry, 1997," MM Docket No. 98-35, issued March 13, 1998 as part of 1998 Biennial Regulatory Review.

41. Alan B. Albarran, *Media Economics: Understating Markets, Industries, and Concepts* (Ames, IA: Iowa State University Press, 1996), pp. 67–68.

42. James H. Duncan, Jr., "Dealing with the Porcupine . . . The World of Radio After Deregulation," *Duncan's Radio Comments*, March 1996, issue no. 15.

43. This FCC report used publicly available information gathered from BIA Publications' MasterAccess Radio Analyzer database and Standard & Poor's Computstat database to examine changes in the radio industry between March 1996 and November 1997.

44. Marc Fisher, "Colors of the Radio Spectrum," *Washington Post*, December 3, 1996, pp. E1, E7; Paul Fahri, "For Radio Stations, Does Big Mean Bland?," *Washington Post*, "Washington Business," July 1, 1996, p. 5.

45. Eben Shipiro, "A Wave of Buyouts Has Radio Industry Beaming with Success," *Wall Street Journal*, September 18, 1997, pp. A1, A6.

46. Elizabeth Rathbun, "Chancellor, Clear Channel Deal Likely, *Broadcasting & Cable*, March 8, 1999, p. 40; Brian Steinberg, "Robust Results Are Expected at Radio Firms," *Wall Street Journal*, July 13, 1998, p. B8A; Elizabeth A. Rathbun and Donna Petrozzello, "Hicks's Sticks Hit 267," *Broadcasting & Cable*, February 24, 1997, pp. 6, 8.

47. Elizabeth Rathburn and John M. Higgins, "Hicks Loses Appetite," *Broadcasting & Cable*, January 25, 1999, pp. 3, 128; Elizabeth Rathburn, "Chancellor Settling Down, *Broadcasting & Cable*, November 16, 1998, p. 55.

48. Carlos Tejada, "Investor Puts Plans for media Empire on Hold," *Wall Street Journal*, March 16, 1999, pp. B1, B6; Stephanie Anderson Forest and Richard Siklos, "Hicks: Behind the About Face," *Business Week*, February 15, 1999, pp. 58, 60.

49. "Thomas Hicks Follows the Radio-TV Muse," *Broadcasting & Cable*, June 23, 1997, pp. 38–42.

50. Steve McClellan, "Chancellor Creates Radio Network," *Broadcasting & Cable*, September 29, 1997, p. 64; Steve McClellan, "Chancellor Buys Katz Media Group," *Broadcasting & Cable*, July 21, 1997, pp. 53–54; John Lippman, "Evergreen Media, Chancellor to Buy Katz Media Group," *Wall Street Journal*, July 15, 1997, p. B3.

51. Elizabeth A. Rathbun, "Hicks Tops 400," *Broadcasting & Cable*, August 25, 1997, pp. 6, 10.

52. Elizabeth A. Rathbun, "CapStar/SFX Merger detailed," *Broadcasting & Cable*, September 1, 1997, p. 40; "Hicks, Muse Commits Capital for Purchases of Food Companies," *Wall Street Journal*, September 23, 1997, p. B16.

53. Chris McConnell, "Justice Puts Brakes on SFX, Chancellor," *Broadcasting & Cable*, November 10, 1997, p. 16.

54. "Hicks Muse Tackles Towers," *Broadcasting & Cable*, September 8, 1997, p. 46; Brian Garrity, "Strategic Focus of Private Equity Buyers Highlighted in Third Quarter," *Mergers & Acquisitions Report*, October 27, 1997, p. 2; "Hicks, Muse Sets Latin Media Venture," *New York Times*, December 17, 1997, p. D10.

55. Richard Siklos, "Reinventing CBS," *Business Week*, April 5, 1999, pp. 74–82.

56. Elizabeth Rathburn, "CBS Keeping Close Hold on Infinity Spin Off," *Broadcasting & Cable*, November 23, 1998, p. 29; Brian Steinberg, "Robust Results Are Expected at Radio Firms," *Wall Street Journal*, July 13, 1998, p. B8A.

57. Paul Fahri, "Justice Dept. Clears Westinghouse Purchase of Infinity," *Washington Post*, November 13, 1996, p. E1; James H. Duncan, Jr., "A Second Generation Enters the Radio Industry," *Duncan's Radio Comments*, June 1996, issue no. 16, pp. 1–4.

58. Elizabeth A. Rathbun, "CBS, ABC: Two Roads to Radio," *Broadcasting & Cable*, September 15, 1997, pp. 73–74.

59. Mark Landler, "Westinghouse to Acquire 98 Radio Stations," *New York Times*, September 20, 1997, pp. 27, 30; Stephen Baker, "The Coming Sparks at Westinghouse," *Business Week*, June 9, 1997, pp. 36–37.

60. Paul Fahri, "EZ Communications Sold for $655 Million," *Washington Post*, August 6, 1996, pp. D1, D2; Elizabeth A. Rathbun, "ARS Thinks Bigger Is Better, Buys EZ," *Broadcasting & Cable*, August 12, 1996, pp. 52–53.

61. Kathy Chen, "Broadcasters Blast New Scrutiny of Radio Deals," *Wall Street Journal*, April 7, 1999, pp. B1, B4; Brian Steinberg, "Robust Results Are Expected at Radio Firms," *Wall Street Journal*, July 13, 1998, p. B8A; Elizabeth A. Rathbun, "Clear Channel Tops 100," *Broadcasting & Cable*, June 10, 1996, pp. 27–28.

62. See Alejandro Bodipo-Memba, "Clear Channel Communications Wins Bidding for Jacor Communications, Inc.," *Wall Street Journal*, October 9, 1998, p. B9; and "Michaels President of Clear Channel Radio," by Tony Sanders, May 1999—from Web site at www.Garvin.com.

63. Steinberg, "Robust Results," p. B8A.

64. Andrea Adelson, "Jacor a Rising Star Among Radio Networks," *New York Times*, June 23, 1997, p. D6.

65. Donna Petrozzello, "Jacor in a Rush," *Broadcasting & Cable*, March 24, 1997, p. 51.

66. Karen Blumenthal, "Clear Channel Agrees to Buy Billboard Firm," *Wall Street Journal*, October 24, 1997, p. A3; Donna Petrozzello, "Paxson Sells Radio Holdings to Clear Channel for $693M," *Broadcasting & Cable*, June 30, 1997, p. 46; Elizabeth A. Rathbun, "Texas Size: Clear Channel Builds a Broadcast Dynasty," *Broadcasting & Cable*, October 7, 1996, pp. 56–59.

67. John Merli, "ESPN Radio Steps Up to the Plate," *Broadcasting & Cable*, October 20, 1997, pp. 53–54; Donna Petrozzello, "ABC Says Kids Listen as Much as Adults," *Broadcasting & Cable*, June 30, 1997, p. 65; Donna Petrozzello, "Network Radio Ratings Fall in Fall," *Broadcasting & Cable*, March 17, 1997, pp. 62–63.

68. Elizabeth A. Rathbun, "CBS, ABC: Two Roads to Radio," *Broadcasting & Cable*, September 15, 1997, pp. 73–74.

69. Steinberg, "Robust Results," p. B8A.

70. See Good News from Cox," *Broadcasting & Cable*, August 18, 1997, p. 34; and Standard & Poor's Industry Surveys, "Broadcasting & Cable," June 26, 1997, p. 8.

71. See Cox corporate Web site at www.cox.com.

72. Elizabeth A. Rathburn, "Some So-So on Sign-ergy," *Broadcasting and Cable*, October 12, 1998, pp. 6–7.

73. Steinberg, "Robust Results," p. B8A and information from Web site at www.rronline.com.

74. See Web site at www.rronline.com.

75. Ibid.

76. Ibid.

77. Media in Washington, DC, headquarters of Radio One cover this thriving business in some detail as in Jerry Knight, "Strong Demand Lifts Radio One Stock IPO," *Washington Post*, May 7, 1999, pp. E1, E3, and Jerry Knight, "Black Broadcasting Firm Readies Unusual Pair of IPOs," *Washington Post*, March 29, 1999, "Washington Business," p. 7. See also Elizabeth A. Rathburn, "Radio One Reaches Out with IPO," *Broadcasting and Cable*, March 22, 1999, p. 36, and information from Web site at www.rronline.com.

78. Steven Ginsberg, "Einstein Thinks He Has the Equation at WRNR-FM," *Washington Post*, "Washington Business," September 23, 1996, p. 14.

79. Kathy Chen, "Broadcasters Blast New Scrutiny of Radio Deals," *Wall Street Journal*, April 7, 1999, pp. B1, B4; "Industry Snapshot," *Investor's Business Daily*, December 8, 1997, p. A1; Jill Goldsmith, "Radio Companies to Play Happy Tune, Reporting Rise in Same Station Revenue," *Wall Street Journal*, July 11, 1997, p. B10; "Radio Reordered," *Broadcasting & Cable*, July 1, 1996, pp. 27–34; "Radio's Top 25 Groups," *Broadcasting*, November 16, 1992, pp. 55–56.

80. Joel I. Klein, "DOJ Analysis of Radio Mergers," presented at ANA Hotel in Washington, DC, February 19, 1997, a statement from the Acting Assistant Attorney General of the United States in charge of the Antitrust Division, 18 pages mimeo. See also Donna Petrozzello, "Justice Looks at Rochester Radio," *Broadcasting & Cable*, September 9, 1996, p. 10; Elizabeth A. Rathbun, "Justice Caps Radio Ownership," *Broadcasting & Cable*, August 12, 1996, p. 9.

81. Paul Fahri, "Public Broadcasting Close to Getting More U.S. Funds," *Washington Post*, October 9, 1997, pp. C1–C2; Andrea Adelson, "A Wider Public for Noncommercial Radio," *New York Times*, February 10, 1997, p. D8.

82. For current status of this proposal, see Web site at www.fcc.gov.

83. Bill McConnell, "Big Flap Over Small Stations," *Broadcasting and Cable*, April 19, 1999, pp. 26–36; Kathy Chen, "Battle of the Airwaves," *Wall Street Journal*, March 22, 1999, pp. B1, B4.

84. Kara Swisher and Evan Ramsted, "Yahoo! Holds Talks on Acquiring Broadcast.com, Boosting Shares," *Wall Street Journal*, March 23, 1999, p. A3; Paul M. Scherer, "Satellite Broadcaster CD Radio Expected to Announce Investment of $200 Million," *Wall Street Journal*, November 16, 1998, p. B7. Radio stations began in 1998 broadcasting on the Web. Many were in 1999, but this situation was changing so fast that it is impossible midway through the year to denote what the ultimate trend will be, so we recommend these Web site information sources. See Radio & Records online Web site at www.rronline.com. More information is available from the Web site at www.billboard.com—for all the various charts, all the way back through the 1950s. See also Web site at www.directionsinmusic.com for analysis of sources to acquire music, from the Internet sales, off the Web directly and from copying radio stations.

85. Gregory L. White and John Lippman, "Satellite Radio Gets a Lift from Ford and GM," *Wall Street Journal*, June 16, 1999, pp. B1, B6.

86. For more information about DigiCeiver technology, visit Blaupunkt's Web site at www.blaupunkt.com.

87. John Merli, "Asian Americans Fastest Growing Group," *Broadcasting & Cable*, November 9, 1998, p. 49; Bill McConnell, "Few and Far Between," *Broadcasting & Cable*, October 5, 1998, pp. 28–34; Chris McConnell, "Minority Ownership: A Not Much Progress Report," *Broadcasting & Cable*, July 20, 1998, p. 7.

88. Elizabeth Rathburn, "Clear Channel, Jacor Spin Offs," *Broadcasting & Cable*, February 15, 1999, p. 14.

89. See P. J. Alexander, "Entry Barriers, Release Behavior, and Multi-Product Firms in the Music Recording Industry," *Review of Industrial Organization* 9 (1994), pp. 85–98. There are any number of guides to entering and making it in the music business. As good as most, and better than many as the 20th century ended, is Dick Weissman, *The Music Business: Career Opportunities and Self-Defense*, 2nd rev. ed. (New York: Three Rivers Press, 1997), which undoubtedly will be updated about the year 2001.

90. Descriptions abound for the music business. One of the best because of its international perspective is Robert Burnett, *The Global Jukebox* (London: Routledge, 1996). There are numerous guides of how to break into the music business and one of the best is Weissman, *The Music Business*. See also Patrick M. Reilly, "Universal Music Charts a Comeback with Hot Artists," *Wall Street Journal*, May 29, 1997, p. B4.

91. Patrick M. Reilly, "Recorded Music Industry Belts Out an Improved Year," *Wall Street Journal*, December 23, 1998, p. B4.

92. Byran Reesman, "The State of the Music Industry 1997," *Goldmine*, pp. 122–123, 126–127.

93. RIAA's Gold and Platinum Awards Program was instituted in 1958, and in 1997 Gold awards represent manufacturer sales of 500,000 units, one million units for Platinum, and Multi-Platinum status is awarded to product that has sold over two million units. This information is regularly reported in *Billboard*—including its Web site at www.billboard.com—and on the World Wide Web site of the RIAA at www.riaa.com.

94. These 1998 statistics were found on Web site at www.riaa.com.

95. These 1998 statistics were found on Web site at www.riaa.com and were compiled by Taylor Nelson Sofres Intersearch (previously Chilton Research Services) from a monthly national telephone survey. (TNS Intersearch surveys 3,051 music buyers each year.) Data from the monthly survey, tabulated annually and semi-annually, is weighted by age and sex, and then projected to reflect the U.S. population age 10 and over. The reliability of the data is +1.7% at a 95% confidence level. See an earlier survey—Don Jeffery, "Music-Buying Habits Detailed in RIAA Study," *Billboard*, April 19, 1997, pp. 8, 103—for contrast.

96. As previously, these 1998 statistics were found on Web site at www.riaa.com.

97. See Andre Millard, *America on Record: A History of Recorded Sound* (New York: Cambridge University Press, 1995), for more on this history.

98. For more information, see R. Serge Denisoff, *Solid Gold: The Popular Record Industry* (New Brunswick, NJ: Transaction Books, 1975); and Sidney Shemel and M. William Krasilovsky, *The Business of Music* (New York: Billboard Publications, 1995).

99. Geoffrey P. Hull, *The Recording Industry* (New York: Allyn & Bacon, 1998), pp. 78–94, details with skill the functions and impact of this part of the music business.

100. Peter Newcomb, "The Music Never Stopped," *Forbes*, March 24, 1997, pp. 90–95; Jeffrey A. Trachenberg, "Haunting the Clubs with Warner's Ace Talent Scout," *Wall Street Journal*, August 7, 1996, pp. B1, B2.

101. Hull, pp. 27–45.

102. Patrick M. Reilly, "Radio's New Spin on an Oldie: Pay for Play," *Wall Street Journal*, March 16, 1998, pp. B1, B8.

103. Greg Jaffe, "No Hits, No MTV, Just Worshipful Fans," *Wall Street Journal*, February 17, 1999, pp. B1, B4; Jeffrey A. Trachtenberg and Eben Shapiro, "Record Store Shakeout Rocks Music Industry," *Wall Street Journal*, February 26, 1996, pp. B1, B8.

104. Ed Christian, "Musicland Shows Improvement in 3rd Quarter," *Billboard*, November 8, 1997, pp. 63, 65; Ed Christian, "Musicland Decreases Its Losses for First Quarter," *Billboard*, May 3, 1997, p. 6; Musicland Says Most Suppliers Agree to Defer Debt and to Keep on Shipping," *Wall Street Journal*, February 14, 1997, p. B6.

105. Scott Scholten, "Musicland Plans to Do Better Than Forecasts," *Wall Street Journal*, June 1, 1999, p. B9B.

106. Emily Nelson, "Logistics Whiz Rises at Wal-Mart," *Wall Street Journal*, March 11, 1999, pp. B1, B8; Neil Strauss, "Wal-Mart's CD Standards Are Changing Pop Music," *New York Times*, November 12, 1996, pp. A1, C12.

107. On the difficulties of private company data acquisition, see Steve Kichen and Tina Russo McCarthy, "Wall Street? No, Thanks," *Forbes*, December 1, 1997, pp. 180–262.

108. Colleen Mastony, "Turbulant Takeoff," *Forbes*, May 3, 1999, p. 94.

109. Ed Christian, "WEA Regains No. 1 in Album Market Share for '97," *Billboard*, October 18, 1997, pp. 55–56, 62, offers a comprehensive report as 1997 ended. Regular reports can be found in the middle month (about the 18th or 19th) of January, April, July and October in *Billboard*—online on Web site at www.billboard.com—from SoundScan compiled information.

110. Don Jeffrey, "Universal Revenue, Profit Up Sharply," *Billboard*, August 23, 1997, p. 6; Larry LeBlanc, "Universal Music Enjoys Sales Surge," *Billboard*, March 29, 1997, p. 54; Don Jeffrey, "Sony Universal: '96 Ends Up," *Billboard*, February 23, 1997, p. 53.

111. Laura Landro and Eben Shapiro, "Seagram Will Trade DuPont for MCA Inc," *Wall Street Journal*, April 7, 1995, pp. A1, A11; Michael Oneal and Ronald Grover, "The Mogul," *Business Week*, April 24, 1995, pp. 122–125; Rita Koselka and Randall Lane, "What Matsushita Left on the Table," *Forbes*, July 3, 1995, pp. 46–48; Paula Dwyer, Margaret Dawson and Dexter Roberts, "The New Music Biz," *Business Week*, January 15, 1996, pp. 48–51; Patrick M. Reilly, "Can Music Giant BMG Change Its Tune?," *Wall Street Journal*, March 10, 1997, p. B4; Standard & Poor's Industry Surveys, "Music & Home Entertainment," February 27, 1997, p. 11.

112. Reilly, "Universal Music Charts a Comeback with Hot Artists," p. B4; Geraldine Frabrikant, "MCA Agrees to Buy Stake in Interscope Record Label," *New York Times*, February 22, 1996, p. D4.

113. Reilly, "Recorded Music Industry Belts Out an Improved Year," p. B4; Patrick M. Reilly, "Geffen Records Turns to David Simone of PolyGram to Pump Up the Volume," *Wall Street Journal*, October 3, 1997, p. B5.

114. Patrick M. Reilly, "A Fallen Mogul Plots Another Comeback," *Wall Street Journal*, January 19, 1999, pp. B1, B10; Charles Goldsmith, "PolyGram Reports Profit Skid of 86 percent for the First Half," *Wall Street Journal*, July 23, 1998, p. B11; "PolyGram's Earnings in 1996 Slumped 18 Percent on Poor Record Sales," *Wall Street Journal*, February 13, 1997, p. B12; Paula Dwyer, Margaret

Dawson and Dexter Roberts, "The New Music Biz," *Business Week*, January 15, 1996, pp. 48–51; Standard & Poor's Industry Surveys, "Music & Home Entertainment," February 27, 1997, p. 10.

115. Adam Sandler, "Dirge Playing at U," *Variety*, January 25–31, 1999, p. 38.

116. Adam Sandler, "PolyGram Gives Goldberg Power Boost," *Variety*, September 22–28, 1997, pp. 30, 67; Patrick M. Reilly, "PolyGram to Reorganize Management at Its Lagging U.S. Music Operations," *Wall Street Journal*, August 1, 1997, p. B2; Shawnee Smith, "George Jackson Named Motown President/CEO," *Billboard*, November 8, 1997, pp. 1, 99; Melinda Newman, "Motown Under Umbrella of New Mercury Group," *Billboard*, September 27, 1997, pp. 1, 107; Patrick M. Reilly, "Motown Head Harrell Quits, Ending Tempestuous Tenure at PolyGram Unit," *Wall Street Journal*, August 12, 1997, p. B7; Jeff Clark-Meads, "PolyGram Reaps Gains from Restructuring," *Billboard*, August 2, 1997, pp. 6, 97.

117. Patrick M. Reilly, "Record Industry Rallied in Quarter as Unit Sales of Albums Climbed 9 Percent," *Wall Street Journal*, April 3, 1997, p. B9A; Standard & Poor's Industry Surveys, "Music & Home Entertainment," February 27, 1997, p. 10; Dwyer, Dawson and Roberts, pp. 48–51. See also www.pathfinder.com, the company's Web site, and the published annual report for 1998.

118. The company's condensed annual report for 1998 can be found as *The Time Warner Factbook, 1998*, see pp. 12–13.

119. Jeffrey A. Trachtenberg, "Time Warner Music Unit Considers Selling a Stake in Its Publishing Arm," *Wall Street Journal*, February 13, 1997, p. B12; Mark Landler, "The War for Warner: You're On, Mr. Fuchs," *New York Times*, June 25, 1995, pp. F1, F12.

120. Eben Shapiro and John Lippman, "Film Flops, Dated Tunes Bedevil Warner Co-chairmen," *Wall Street Journal*, December 4, 1997, pp. B1, B10; Patrick M. Reilly, "Dissonance in a Music Industry Alliance," *Wall Street Journal*, April 10, 1997, pp. B1, B17; Eben Shapiro, "Time Warner to Set Standards to Handle Controversial Music," *Wall Street Journal*, May 19, 1995, p. B12; Patrick M. Reilly, "Time Warner's Atlantic Looks Likely to Top Charts as No. 1 Record Label," *Wall Street Journal*, December 1, 1997, p. B8; Eben Shapiro and John Lippman, "Film Flops, Dated Tunes Bedevil Warner Co-chairmen," *Wall Street Journal*, December 4, 1997, pp. B1, B10; Jeffrey A. Trachtenberg, "Music Chiefs at Warner Try for Harmony," *Wall Street Journal*, November 20, 1995, pp. B1, B7; Jeffrey A. Trachtenberg, "Management Turns at Warner Music; Will Its Success?," *Wall Street Journal*, June 23, 1995, p. B4; Jeffrey A. Trachtenberg, "Music Chiefs at Warner Try for Harmony," *Wall Street Journal*, November 20, 1995, pp. B1, B7; Jeffrey A. Trachtenberg, "Management Turns at Warner Music; Will Its Success?" *Wall Street Journal*, June 23, 1995, p. B4.

121. Mark Robichaux, "Time Warner Posts $30 Million Profit, Bouncing Back from Year Earlier Loss," *Wall Street Journal*, July 17, 1997, p. B10; Robert La Franco, "Synergy; Now What?, *Forbes*, October 20, 1997, p. 184; Patrick M. Reilly, "Nancy Berry to Run Virgin Records, While Quartararo Is Expected to Leave," *Wall Street Journal*, September 22, 1997, p. B6; Geraldine Fabrikant, "At Time Warner, Music of a Slower Tempo," *New York Times*, July 14, 1997, pp. D1, D10; Richard Harrington, "1996 Turned Down the Volume on Record Sales," *Washington Post*, January 8, 1997, p. C7; Craig Rosen, "Phil Quartararo Moves into Key Warner Position, *Billboard*, November 25, 1997, pp. 1, 93; Craig Rosen, "WMG Assesses Its Future," *Billboard*, August 30, 1997, pp. 1, 97; Don Jeffrey, "Warner Music Revenue, Profit Down in 1st Qrt.," *Billboard*, April 26, 1997, pp. 1, 91.

122. Reilly, "Recorded Music Industry Belts Out an Improved Year," p. B4; Patrick M. Reilly, "Sony Music Has Upbeat Tune as Label Turns Around," *Wall Street Journal*, February 23, 1998, p. B4.

123. See Web site at www.sony.com.

124. See Sony annual report online at Ibid.

125. Standard & Poor's Industry Surveys, "Music & Home Entertainment," February 27, 1997, p. 10; Dwyer, Dawson and Roberts, pp. 48–51.

126. Don Jeffrey, "Sony Music Layoffs Touch Epic, Columbia, Distrib," *Billboard*, October 4, 1997, p. 7; Brett Atwood, "Sony Adds Muscle to Its Internet, ECD Efforts," *Billboard*, June 21, 1997, pp. 1, 82; Don Kaplan, "Sony Arm Spins Artists into Brands," *Billboard*, April 5, 1997, pp. 59–60; Don Jeffrey, "Sony, Universal: '96 Ends Up," *Billboard*, February 22, 1997, p. 53.

127. Gautam Naik, "EMI Pretax Profit for Year Fell 19% to $502.5 Million," *Wall Street Journal*, May 28, 1998, p. B7.

128. Adam Sandler, "EMI Bakes New Plans with Nicoli," *Variety*, March 15–21, 1999, p. 24.

129. Adam Sandler, "Success Trumpets EMI Latin," *Variety*, April 19–25, 1999, pp. 24, 62; Patrick M. Reilly, "EMI Seeks Aide at Bertelsmann's Arista to Head North American Operations," *Wall Street Journal*, December 18, 1997, p. B6; Adam White and Jeff Clark-Meads, "EMI Music Overhauls Its N. American Operations, *Billboard*, June 7, 1997, pp. 1, 94; Jeff Clark-Meads, "EMI Upbeat on Global Biz," *Billboard*, March 8, 1997, pp. 1, 8; Adam Sandler, "EMI's Healthy Taste of Berry," *Variety*, June 2–8, 1997, p. 20; Enrich Boehm, "Bowie Inks 15-Year EMI Pact," *Variety*, May 26–June 1, 1997, p. 20; Reilly, "Recorded Music Industry Belts Out an Improved Year," p. B4; Patrick M. Reilly, "EMI Reports Net Fell 24 Percent, Cites U.S. Units," *Wall Street Journal*, May 28, 1997, p. B6; Dwyer, Dawson and Roberts, pp. 48–51; Standard & Poor's Industry Surveys, "Music & Home Entertainment," February 27, 1997, p. 10; Mark Landler, "EMI Finally Advances into Multimedia," *New York Times*, May 23, 1995, p. D4.

130. Patrick M. Reilly, "EMI, Hogtied, Finds Out You Don't Mess with Garth," *Wall Street Journal*, November 5, 1997, pp. B1, B19; Reilly, "Nancy Berry to Run Virgin Records," p. B6; Richard Harrington, "1996 Turned Down the Volume on Record Sales," *Washington Post*, January 8, 1997, p. C7. For more on Brooks' impressive sales records as of late 1997, read Saviano, "Garth's on Fire," pp. 22–25.

131. Dwyer, Dawson and Roberts, pp. 48–51; Standard & Poor's Industry Surveys, "Music & Home Entertainment," February 27, 1997, p. 10.

132. Jim Milliot, "Strong Year Pushes Total BDD Revenues Close to $700 Million," *Publisher's Weekly*, August 28, 1995, p. 26; John Templeton, "Bertelsmann: When Being a Giant Isn't Enough," *Business Week*, November 12, 1990, pp. 72–74; "The Global Power Elite," *Forbes*, July 28, 1997, pp. 150, 190.

133. Adam Sandler, "Arista's Alchemy," *Variety*, February 8–14, 1999, p. 30.

134. Rosanna Tamberg, "Bertelsmann Music Club Unit in Canada Claims Unfair Actions by Warner Music," *Wall Street Journal*, December 1, 1997, p. B6; "Bertelsmann Gets Bigger," *Business Week*, April 15, 1996, p. 65; "Ich Bin ein Amerikaner," *The Economist*, June 18, 1994, pp. 69–71.

135. Patrick M. Reilly, "Can Music Giant BMG Change Its Tune?," *Wall Street Journal*, March 10, 1997, pp. B1, B4; Jeffrey A. Trachtenberg, "Bertelsmann AG Names Zelnick President of Unit," *Wall Street Journal*, September 14, 1994, p. B10; Adam Sandler, "BMG Waltzes Under Strauss," *Variety*, July 28–August 3, 1997, pp. 24, 72.

136. Bruce Orwall, "Disney Nears Pact to Buy Mammoth in Attempt to Boost Its Music Business," *Wall Street Journal*, July 21, 1997, p. B7; Adam Sandler, "Disney's Mammoth Deal," *Variety*, July 28–August 3, 1997, p. 24; Trip Gabrile, "The Corporate Wooing and Winning of Mammoth Records," *New York Times*, July 28, 1997, p. D7.

137. Bruce Orwall, "At Walt Disney, Record Label Hits Sour Note," *Wall Street Journal*, May 21, 1997, pp. B1, B11; Craig Rosen, "Disney Plans to Raise Its in Music Biz," *Billboard*, August 2, 1997, pp. 1, 103.

138. Patrick M. Reilly, "News Corp. Readies Expansion in Music," *Wall Street Journal*, December 5, 1996, p. B12.

139. Patrick M. Reilly, "Alliance Entertainment Seeks Protection From Creditors, Pointing Up Music Woes," *Wall Street Journal*, July 15, 1997, p. B3; Patrick M. Reilly, "Alliance Entertainment Is Betting on New Music Man," *Wall Street Journal*, October 24, 1996, p. B8.

140. Supplement to *Goldmine*, May 10, 1996: "Annual Indie Directory," pp. 1–48. Updated every May.

141. Irv Lichtman, "Reader's Digest Music, Warner Resound Link," *Billboard*, September 13, 1997, pp. 7, 103.

142. Greg Jaffe, "No Hits, No MTV, Just Worshipful Fans," *Wall Street Journal*, February 17, 1999, pp. B1, B4.

143. Richard Siklos, "Can Record Labels Get Back Their Rhythm?," *Business Week*, July 27, 1998, pp. 52–53.

144. Robert S. Greenberger and Craig S. Smith, "CD Piracy Flourishes in China, and West Supplies the Equipment," *Wall Street Journal*, April 24, 1997, pp. A1, A13; Linton Weeks, "Turning Up the Power," *Washington Post*, July 30, 1997, pp. C1, C2. See RIAA Web site at www.riaa.com.

145. Thomas E. Weber, "AOL to Buy Two Internet Music Firms in Sock Deals Valued at $400 Million," *Wall Street Journal*, June 2, 1999, p. B6.

146. Adam Sandler, "Drumbeat Grows for Digital," *Variety*, April 19–25, 1999, pp. 24, 62.

147. Adam Sandler, "Now Sony Does Windows, Too," *Variety*, May 17–23, 1999, pp. 31, 82.

148. Ron Cadet, "GetMusic.com Brings BMG & Universal to Retail Fore," from Web site at www.Garvin.com.

149. Don Jeffrey and Brett Atwood, "Price War on the Web?," *Billboard*, June 14, 1997, pp. 1, 95.

150. Brett Attwood, "Sites + Sounds," Billboard online, April 20, 1999.

151. As of early May 1999, see Eben Shapiro, "Seagram's Universal Music Sets Up Partnership to Sell Music on the Web," *Wall Street Journal*, May 4, 1999, p. B12; Kara Swisher, "New Software Turns PCS into Jukeboxes," *Wall Street Journal*, May 3, 1999, p. B6. This debate, struggle and innovation about a standard and effective technology for distribution will continue into the 21st century, and this book will be far out of date as you read it. To best keep up with its permutations, see the RIAA Web site at www.riaa.com and the Web site of Radio & Records for a trade press perspective at www.rronline.com.

152. Andrea Peterson, "Two Web Sellers of CDs, Tapes Plan to Be a Duet," *Wall Street Journal*, March 17, 1999, pp. B1, B4; Reese, "Sites + Sounds," December 22, 1998.

153. Tom McCourt and Eric Rothenbuhler, "SoundScan and the Consolidation of Control in the Popular Music Industry," *Media, Culture & Society* 19.2 (April 1997), pp. 201–218, offers the best account of the changes wrought by SoundScan as of the late 1990s.

154. Andrew Ross Sorkin, "SoundScan Makes Business of Counting Hits," *New York Times*, August 11, 1997, p. B5.

155. As reported on the Web site of the RIAA at www.riaa.com.

156. Patrick M. Reilly, "Sony to Package New Carey Album as CD/Tape Set," *Wall Street Journal*, August 29, 1997, p. B2; Mike Shalett, "Writing Off the Cassette: A Big Mistake," *Billboard*, September 6, 1997, p. 5; Brett Atwood, "Music CD-ROMs, Once Promising, Showing Decline," *Billboard*, May 3, 1997, pp. 1, 59.

157. Peter Landers, "Sony Announces New CD Player with Better Sound," *Wall Street Journal*, April 7, 1999, p. B4.

158. Walter S. Mossberg, "Sony Again Attempts to Sell Its Mini-CD, Focusing on Recording," *Wall Street Journal*, May 28, 1998, p. B1.

159. Burnett, *The Global Jukebox*.

6

The Hollywood Film Industry: Theatrical Exhibition, Pay TV, and Home Video

Douglas Gomery

The cinema century ended on May 19, 1999, with the premiere of George Lucas's much-awaited *Star Wars: Episode I—The Phantom Menace*. More than one month before its premiere (22 years after Lucas' original *Star Wars* opened) fans began to line up. For his $115 million cost, producer and director George Lucas took 90% of the money Twentieth Century-Fox collected from box office revenues, after a distribution fee. Toy maker Hasbro paid Lucas a quarter of a billion dollars in licensing fees plus stock options; PepsiCo agreed to spend $2 billion to promote *Episode I—The Phantom Menace* and two future sequels along with its soft drinks. Pepsi guaranteed at 3,000 screens across the United States that it would sell toys and other merchandise in the lobby. (Indeed, even before the movie premiered, retailers reported selling out of the new toys and action figures.) Collectors stood in line for hours in order to buy action figures of the movie's villain, Darth Maul, and Wall Street bid up the prices of Hasbro stock. That this motion picture defined popular entertainment for the early Summer 1999 is testament to the power of Hollywood motion pictures.[1]

Star Wars: Episode I—The Phantom Menace opened to record first day ticket sales of $28.5 million, as buyers lined up at theaters, and overwhelmed the telephone and Internet circuits. The record was hardly news; the only question was how long the revenue would keep flowing in. The latest edition of *Star Wars* represented the economic power of Hollywood. With distribution by one of the Big Six studios, there was no way (even with its $100 million+ cost) that *Star Wars: Episode I—The Phantom Menace* would not make vast profits. Theater owners signed to play it for months; pay TV longed for its video release; home video retailers knew that it would make them profits sometime in 2000. By then, the Big Six will have turned to another myth capturing entertainment shaping motion picture event.[2]

Nothing better than the creation and release of *Star Wars: Episode I—The Phantom Menace* symbolized the continuing importance and economic power of the major studios of the Hollywood movie industry. George Lucas alone could not distribute his epic; he needed Twentieth Century-Fox. He also needed pay TV networks and home video retailers to capture the expected multiple streams of revenues. Prior to 1950, movie theaters provided the lone source of revenues. Then came additional revenues from re-showings on broadcast television; then Hollywood added multiple venues on cable TV; finally, it got a significant boost from home video rental and sales. Indeed, by the mid-1990s, domestic box office in the United States and Canada ranked but the equivalent, in the average stream of revenues, of domestic and foreign home video sales and rentals, the equivalent of foreign theatrical rentals. Domestic and foreign pay TV ranked next, with domestic broadcast and basic cable farther behind.[3]

Here is classic price discrimination—releasing a film so as to maximize the revenues from each separate "window." Basically, this meant that the Big Six released films in the following order: theaters, home video, pay-per-view, pay cable and finally, broadcast and basic cable television. Each window in this sequence was an exclusive. A new window opened only when all value of the previous window had been captured. Customers knew that if they waited, then the cost they paid at that window would be lower than the prior one. Home video also allows customers to view the film whenever they desire. If they wait long enough, then they could purchase a blank tape and copy it from free over-the-air broadcast television. It is no wonder that, in 1999, whereas theatrical premieres drew the most publicity, most of the monies paid came from home video purchase or rental.

But with all this additional money pouring into the system, only six major studios gathered the bulk of it. Whatever the venue (theatrical, cable TV or home video), the locus of the production and distribution of most of the films people saw continued to be Hollywood in general, and the major studios in particular. In a profile of former Hollywood agent Michael Ovitz, Lynn Hirschberg of the *New York Times* put it best: "Hollywood is a small community—there are only six big movie studios, four big TV networks, and three big talent agencies. (The people who own and run these organizations) talk to one another every day. They confide, they feud, they forgive, they do business together, they vacation together."[4]

In 1999, the Hollywood film industry remained a closed oligopoly of the Big Six: (in alphabetical order) Disney (owned by the Walt Disney Corporation), Paramount Pictures (owned by Viacom), Sony Pictures (owned by Sony), Twentieth Century-Fox (owned by News Corporation), Universal Pictures (owned by Seagram) and Warner Bros. (owned by Time Warner). All competed to produce and release the top hits, but all cooperated to make sure the game remained among themselves. Who was on top which year varied, but only the Big Six premiered possible blockbuster hits in multiplex theaters during the 1990s—and surely will well into the future.[5]

And audiences of film fans in the United States seemed to love the system. The 1990s surely ranked as a "Golden Age" of interest in movie watching. Since 1988, attendance had increased 35%, whereas the population rose 11%. Worldwide business at the box office also remained quite healthy, with Paramount and Fox's co-production *Titanic* by the close of 1998 having grossed more than $1.8 billion in tickets worldwide. In 1998 two of the Big Six, Viacom's Paramount Pictures and Disney, exceeded $1 billion in world box office revenues. Twentieth Century-Fox, Sony and Warner Bros. gathered in about three quarters of a billion dollars each. Seagram's

Universal Pictures trailed, but was far ahead of MGM or DreamWorks SKG, two operations that were struggling to expand the ranks of the Big Six.[6]

Although this meant higher revenues—surging into the billions if all the multiple sources of revenues were counted—expectedly, the costs of producing that precious first negative also grew. In the late 1990s, the average motion picture cost neared $60 million, and inflated to more than $80 million if marketing and publicity costs, primarily television advertising, were added in. (See Table 6.1.) And this was an average, so *Titanic* alone cost more than $200 million just to fashion the first negative. So when counting box office revenues, many Hollywood films appear to have "lost" money. But, in the long run, even much-heralded box office losers like *Speed 2* and *The Postman* would eventually see revenues exceed costs after studio executives added in all the multiple streams and waited long enough.[7]

Because of this long-term profitability, the Big Six studios retained a growing appetite for hot new talents. By the late 1990s, newcomers Gwyneth Paltrow and Ben Affleck, as well as proven box office winners like Jim Carrey and Tom Cruise, could command $20 million a picture. This is where the role of the agent came in; they negotiated on behalf of their clients. An agent's job was to try to maximize salary and participation in profits. The star system was always run this way, certainly since it was developed as a cornerstone of the Hollywood film industry by Charlie Chaplin and Mary Pickford more than 75 years earlier. Agents came about during the 1950s as manipulating tax laws offered advantages to freelancing actors and actresses who were no longer under sole contract to one studio.[8]

The Big Six constantly desired to pay stars less money, while always recognizing that stars stood at the core of what made them money. The well-publicized struggles among actors (and their agents) versus the studios masked the reality that the Big Six were constantly profitable and never threatened. Business in Hollywood through the 1990s was getting better. Indeed, 1998 was a record year for going to the movies. By the end of 1998, *Titanic* alone had grossed some $600 million in the United States from theater patrons alone. So popular was *Titanic* that it was still collecting theatrical revenues even as it was being released on video. The $7 billion collected in theaters in the

TABLE 6.1
MPAA Average Negative Cost

	Average Production Cost Per Feature (in millions)	Average Advertising Cost Per Feature (in millions)
1998	$52.7	$25.3
1997	$53.4	$22.3
1996	$39.8	$19.8
1995	$36.4	$17.7
1994	$34.2	$16.1
1993	$29.9	$14.1
1992	$28.9	$13.5
1991	$26.1	$12.1
1990	$26.8	$12.0

Source: Motion Picture Association of America Web site at www.mpaa.org.

United States and Canada set a record, some 9% greater than the year before. Attendance also jumped more than 5% to nearly 1.5 billion tickets sold.[9]

In the 1990s, Hollywood's big problem was how to top *Titanic*. Hollywood tried to assimilate the lessons of the recent past, and different members of the Big Six came to different managerial conclusions. William Mechanic, who held the title of chairman of filmed entertainment at Twentieth Century-Fox, took the lesson from *Titanic* to be "proceed with caution." Formerly the top video executive at Disney, but a relative newcomer to the front lines of the movie business, Mechanic had more than survived the success of co-producing *Titanic* but also experienced the box office failure of *Speed 2*. So he decreed there would be no more $100 million extravaganzas. Every 1999 Fox release would be aimed at a specific demographic group, with the hope that one or two would gain the momentum to reach a wider audience. In contrast, Disney's 1998 studio chief, Joe Roth, came to the opposite conclusion. Having formerly occupied Mechanic's post at Fox, Roth had observed many cyclical swings over the years, and figured *Titanic* signaled an ever-increasing interest in big budget movies. He would counterprogram, and seek the next *Titanic* mega-hit. This simply signaled the long-term cyclical trend of Hollywood blockbuster tradition: program and counterprogram.[10]

The common theme, since the mid-1970s, was the search for the new blockbuster. Backed by massive fusillades of television advertising, Twentieth Century-Fox's *Independence Day*, the unexpected mega-hit of Summer 1996, reinforced this strategy when it became Hollywood's first billion dollar blockbuster. *Independence Day* demonstrated more convincingly than ever that the Big Six studios' apparent ability to create action-oriented, special-effects-laden entertainments that would seize the imagination of audiences worldwide, spew forth vast revenues not only at the box office and television in its multiple forms, but also from music theme track albums, theme park rides and myriad other tie-ins (particularly toys).

Consider 1997

The cinema business in the late 1990s was seasonal. The Big Six could not guarantee a hit, only make sure the public was exposed to it and could positively vote its preferences. So in Summer 1997, predictably just before the Memorial Day weekend, the Big Six launched one potential blockbuster after another. Warner Bros., led for almost two decades by the imperiously self-confident team of Robert Daly and Terry Semel, started with a formula comedy called *Father's Day*, starring Billy Crystal and Robin Williams, and the fourth iteration of their *Batman* franchise called *Batman and Robin*. Hoping for a respectable opening weekend of about $12 million, *Father's Day* instead debuted to a tepid $8.8 million, and led to a paltry $36.4 million theatrical gross worldwide. *Batman and Robin*, sadly for Warner, opened to the weakest box office numbers of any *Batman* sequel. Disney's animated entry, *Hercules*, did respectable business, but its audience was disappointing when compared with its triumphant predecessor, *The Lion King*. Twentieth Century-Fox trotted out a big disaster picture called *Volcano*. And Universal, with the ever-dependable Steven Spielberg, delivered yet another major hit in *Jurassic Park: The Lost World*.

But as the Summer 1997 sped on, if Spielberg had mastered the formula, his rivals had not. It was Twentieth Century-Fox's sequel, *Speed 2: Cruise Control*, that provided the most devastating evidence. The first *Speed*, released in 1996, cost a mere $37 million but grossed $125 million in the United States alone. Confident that it had uncovered a new franchise, Fox poured some $140 million into the sequel, even though Keanu Reeves, who had co-starred with Sandra Bullock in the original, had bowed out to be replaced by Jason Patric. Opening amid an extravagant promotional television blitz, *Speed 2* registered a respectable $16.2 million at 2,600 theaters, but then sank as a result of negative word of mouth. The film ultimately would gross a mere $48.6 million in the United States, partially recouped with $105.2 million overseas. The failure of *Speed 2* came as a particular shock because it contradicted the notion that special effects movies were the new opiate of the mass market. When *Twister* became a big hit in 1996, executives at the Big Six studios figured that digital magic could compensate for the absence of credible story and big stars. Not so for *Speed 2*, which featured arguably the most expensive special effects stunt yet attempted. Audiences would supposedly be riveted by the sight of a giant cruise ship smashing into a coastal resort, literally sailing through the middle of town. The Big Six began to re-think the practice of spending millions on special effects, and turned to the star system (with the exception of George Lucas' much anticipated prequel to *Star Wars*).[11]

So the summer started with a record number of films being set for screens, all costing more than $100 million to make and publicize. Warner Bros.' expensive comedy *Father's Day* never took off. And, so after grossing but $23 million domestically, it disappeared, hoping to make up the gap in pay TV and home video. Traditionally, a low first-run domestic theatrical figure means that revenues from other sources will most likely be low as well. Warner's *Batman and Robin*, the fourth in the highly profitable series, and *Conspiracy Theory*, a thriller starring Julia Roberts and Mel Gibson, were also expensive 1997 disappointments.

Sequels sometimes work to guarantee a good theatrical opening, but not in every case; big stars only give the studio a chance, not a guarantee. And there always are surprises. Twentieth Century-Fox may have lost millions on the sequel *Speed 2: Cruise Control*, but it made millions on *The Full Monty*, which cost only $3 million. Sony finished as Hollywood's leader in 1997 solely on the strength of three summer hits: *Men in Black*, a science fiction comedy (unexpected); *Air Force One*, starring Harrison Ford (expected); and *My Best Friend's Wedding*, a romantic comedy starring Julia Roberts (unexpected). In short, Summer 1997 was typical, with a handful of big winners, a couple of surprises and some that seemed to be winners (with big stars, pre-sold scripts and vast special effects), and yet domestic grosses amounted to less than $100 million (i.e., the cut-off level of success for a blockbuster). As can be seen from Table 6.2, all this adds up to billions of dollars at the box office. And the billions of dollars bet each summer (and Christmas) is increasing, leading to intense competition. This system also guarantees larger than normal profits for the Big Six as long as they are able to keep new companies from entering into this prescribed game of blockbuster making.

Summer 1997 also was one of rumor of what might be ahead. *Speed 2* and *Batman and Robin* both had approached $150 million in cost, and there was a growing buzz

TABLE 6.2
Domestic Theatrical Movie Industry Profile

	Box Office Gross (in billions)	Admissions (in millions)	Average Admission Price
1998	$6.9	1,480.7	$4.69
1997	$6.4	1,387.7	$4.59
1996	$5.9	1,338.6	$4.42
1995	$5.5	1,262.6	$4.35
1994	$5.4	1,291.7	$4.18
1993	$5.2	1,244.0	$4.14
1992	$4.8	1,173.2	$4.15
1991	$4.8	1,140.6	$4.21
1990	$5.0	1,188.6	$4.23

Source: Motion Picture Association of America Web Site at www.mpaa.org.

about James Cameron's delayed *Titanic* project, then still shooting in Mexico. It was on track to become cinema's most expensive epic, and was scheduled to be the centerpiece of Twentieth Century-Fox's 1997 summer. Just at the time when insiders were concluding that there would be no surprise hits, along came Sony's *Men in Black*. With TV's Will Smith in the lead, *Men in Black* seemed to have a narrow audience. Early tracking studies (i.e., the name for audience research) suggested a strong "want-to-see" for only young men. But Sony executives remained skeptical because the film lacked a major star, told a comic book-like story, and in an era when movies ran well past two hours, *Men in Black* clocked in at just 90 minutes, including credits. But this seemingly risky investment generated $51 million at the box office during its initial Independence Day weekend. By mid-July 1997 it had already grossed close to $140 million, and was being heralded as the hit of the summer. Sony, which had been down on its luck, was suddenly the hot new studio in town. The lesson is clear: No one can ever truly predict a blockbuster.[12]

Indeed, the defining moment of 1997 occurred not during the summer season, but in December when Twentieth Century-Fox (with last minute partner Paramount) delivered a much-delayed, much-maligned *Titanic*. Costing between $220 million and $240 million (depending on which accounting methods used), *Titanic* was considered too long, too expensive and too accident prone. But by year's end, it already had grossed $134 million, on its way to a worldwide record. The very executives who had earlier scaled back their spending and their expectations were now even more perplexed. Final numbers revealed that the industry had rolled up an impressive 8.3% gain in total box office, the highest jump of the decade. Moreover, admissions had climbed to 1.31 billion, the loftiest level since 1966. Thus, in the end, despite two decades of dire predictions that theatrical exhibition would be dead by 1997, box office grosses in the United States continued to rise to nearly $6 billion, up a healthy 8%. In 1997 an unprecedented 21 feature films passed the $100 million mark in domestic grosses, led by Universal's *The Lost World: Jurassic Park* with $382 million and Sony's *Men in Black* with $300 million. Sony and Twentieth Century-Fox passed the $1 billion mark in domestic revenues. Disney ranked as the top studio outside the United States for the second year in a row, clocking receipts of close to $1.3 billion, an industry record. The rankings for 1997 can be found in Table 6.3. The winners in 1997 were Sony, Disney (including Miramax), Universal and Time Warner's New Line. Warner Bros. and Twentieth Century-Fox saw declining box office revenues in 1997, and Paramount simply tred water.[13]

In the end, the Big Six remained firmly in place, and even as new releases were being hammered into place, there always existed an optimism based on the fact they and they alone were members of an exclusive club where long-term failure was almost impossible. Summer would lead to fall when Big Six executives could launch their more artistically ambitious projects. But they knew summer, like Christmas, meant go-for-broke when the big movie-going audiences were out there with wallets in hand. Summer was blockbuster time. Most of the movies that would be released in Summer had been in the works for years. All desired to make the next *Titanic*.

The Big Six Oligopoly and Merger Mania

Indeed, a new Warner was created by the $15 billion consolidation of Time and Warner, bringing this Hollywood studio into the center of the largest media company in the world. In 1993, Viacom acquired Paramount studios, Twentieth Century-Fox studio expanded from Murdoch's original 1986 takeover, and Sony took Columbia Pictures and reorganized it into Sony Entertainment. Halfway through the decade, Canadian liquor giant Seagram bought MCA, and renamed it Universal studio. This merger mania was driven by vast profits that are available from owning a member of the Big Six. New owners wanted want in.

Yet with all these mergers, the structure of the industry has changed little. These six Hollywood operations—Warner, Paramount, Twentieth Century-Fox, Sony, Disney and Universal—still define the world's dominant motion picture makers and distributors. Many fans look back to the 1930s and 1940s as the Golden Age of movies, but in fact the 1990s were when the Big Six achieved their greatest power and

TABLE 6.3
Domestic Box Office Market Shares, 1997

Corporate Parent, Studio	No. of Releases	Gross (in millions)	Market Share
Sony	38	$1,271.1	20.4%
Disney	34	890.7	14.3
Viacom, Paramount	27	734.9	11.8
Time Warner, Warner Bros.	27	680.3	10.9
News Corp., Twentieth Century-Fox	20	651.3	10.4
Seagram, Universal	13	613.3	9.9
Disney, Miramax	33	421.0	6.7
Time Warner, New Line	31	389.6	6.2
MGM	13	158.5	2.5
Others	163	429.7	6.9
TOTAL	399	$6,240.4	6.3

Source: Leonard Klady, "H'wood's B. O. Blast," *Variety*, January 5–11, 1998, p. 96.

profitability. Others tried to enter without success; although the DreamWorks SKG experiment continues as of mid-1999. Through the 1980s and 1990s indeed MGM virtually had dropped out, unable to match the power of the "Big Six."[14]

Each of the Big Six studios used a different business strategy, reflecting the personality of the studio chief as well as the financial condition and strategic objectives of the parent company:

- **Disney** represented the well-oiled machine, fashioning almost paramilitary operations, but succeeding less as the 1990s ended. Michael Eisner tried to continue his amazing streak of making Disney's profits grow.
- **Paramount** co-claimed *Titanic*, but invested less than Twentieth Century-Fox, reflecting an overall policy pursuing less riskier films as deemed by Sumner Redstone.
- **Sony** was still seeking to make its grand experiment of marrying a movie studio and an electronics maker consistently profitable. But, the combination was not working and its Japanese owners looked for and tested new business strategies.
- **Twentieth Century-Fox** laid greater claim to *Titanic* than co-investor Paramount, but still Murdoch's concentration seemed to be on the Fox network rather than feature film making.
- **Universal**, owned since only the mid-1990s by Seagram, evidenced a certain skittishness as Edgar Bronfman Jr. set in place and then tinkered with a new management; he was constantly trying to re-invent a new diversified media conglomerate.
- **Warner Bros.** was a studio seemingly caught in a downward spiral, faced a palpable crisis as Robert Daly and Terry Semel, the longest tenured Hollywood executives, cobbled together a program of potential blockbusters.

Strategies came and went. During the 1990s, this six-member oligopoly retained tight and firm control. Two scholars looked at the position in 1994 and concluded that "an examination of concentration ratios indicates that high levels of concentration exist in most of the (media) industry segments," including motion pictures.[15]

The Motion Picture Association of America (MPAA) deals with common concerns, from rating films to smoothing the way for international distribution, to protecting valuable copyrights around the world. Whereas critics of the film industry usually focus only on the MPAA's ratings system, its longtime head, Jack Valenti, earns his $1 million a year salary by helping the oligopolists expand revenues from around the world. Valenti can more often be found abroad, far from his home office at 16th and "I" Street in Washington, DC. One poll ranked the MPAA as the 18th most powerful lobby in Washington, DC as 1997 ended. Although Valenti's total association budget ($60 million per annum it is estimated) would make and market but a single modest blockbuster, the Big Six know it is money well spent to protect their turf and expand their markets.[16]

Through the MPAA, the Big Six cooperate on common issues, which then frees them to pursue the development of the blockbusters that set in motion such a vast array of profit-making deals. The familiar names of the companies found in Table 6.4 attest to the worldwide attractiveness of the modern movie blockbuster and its economic power.

TABLE 6.4
All-Time Top 25 Films at U.S. Box Offices

Feature Film	Company	Release Year	Rentals
Star Wars	Twentieth Century-Fox	1977	$270,918,000
E.T.—The Extraterrestrial	Universal	1982	$228,168,939
Jurassic Park	Universal	1993	$212,953,417
Return of the Jedi	Twentieth Century-Fox	1983	$191,648,000
Independence Day	Twentieth Century-Fox	1996	$177,190,000
The Empire Strikes Back	Twentieth Century-Fox	1980	$173,814,000
The Lion King	Disney	1994	$173,057,366
Forrest Gump	Paramount	1994	$156,000,000
Batman	Warner Bros.	1989	$150,500,000
Home Alone	Twentieth Century-Fox	1990	$140,099,000
Twister	Warner Bros.	1996	$133,464,330
Ghostbusters	Sony's Columbia	1984	$132,720,000
The Lost World	Universal	1997	$130,086,760
Jaws	Universal	1975	$129,549,325
Raiders of the Lost Ark	Paramount	1981	$115,598,000
Indiana Jones and the Last Crusade	Paramount	1989	$115,500,000
Men in Black	Sony	1997	$114,110,497
Terminator 2	Sony's TriStar	1991	$112,500,000
Aladdin	Disney	1992	$111,740,683
Mrs. Doubtfire	Twentieth Century-Fox	1993	$111,000,000
Indiana Jones and the Temple of Doom	Paramount	1984	$109,000,000
Beverly Hills Cop	Paramount	1984	$108,000,000
Back to the Future	Universal	1985	$105,496,267
Batman Forever	Warner Bros.	1995	$105,000,000
Home Alone 2	Twentieth Century-Fox	1991	$103,377,614

Source: "All-Time Top Film Rentals," *Variety*, October 13–19, 1997, p. 30.

The revenue flows seemed endless. For example, because of its fabulously successful theatrical re-release in February and March 1997, Fox's *Star Wars* trilogy regained its crown as the top grossing set of films. Add in the moneys from foreign revenues, pay TV, home video and broadcast TV unreelings, as well as merchandising tie ins, and *Star Wars* stood in 1999 as a multibillion dollar property, fully amortized, with millions more expected in the future from re-releases.[17]

With all the monies generated from a film over the course of its life, the true cost of a film is rarely known. As part of the 1999 open trial of former Disney executive Jeffrey Katzenberg verses his former boss Michael Eisner, an internal Disney company memo was revealed showing 10 ways that a Disney accountant hid cost data so as not to reveal the data necessary to pay Katzenberg any more than was necessary under his percentage of the profits deal. An agent may negotiate a good deal, but the Big Six were skilled at making sure that they paid out as little as possible. They publicize these "cost figures," which "prove" that the vast majority of feature films "lose" money, when the actual data would reveal just the opposite conclusion: Few ever lose money in the long run.[18]

The Big Six use their "cost data" to argue for cost-cutting and producer restraint. They argue they simply cannot "afford to pay" what the stars or their agents seek.

Indeed, during the 1990s, the Big Six seemed to be doing a good job of keeping agents and their star clients' demands in check; it was the costs of special effects that seemed to be "out of control." The third expensive variable, pre-sold stories, also remained in check. It seems that the next crisis may come when a screenwriter demands and gets $3 or $4 million for one script, and the executives go on the record as "outraged!"[19]

In order to maximize profits, the studios joined together, cooperating to the point of co-producing expensive feature films (e.g., Twentieth Century-Fox and Paramount's co-financing of *Titanic*). These studios are not worried about losing money in the long run; they expend enormous effort to craft theatrical hits so that the revenues will be as high as possible, all the while trying to keep costs as low as possible. This trend began when Universal's Lew Wasserman pioneered the blockbuster strategy with the June 1995 release of *Jaws*.

A SHORT INDUSTRY HISTORY

Remarkably, the handful of companies that define Hollywood have been around since the Great Depression. They have weathered world wars, rested through recessions, innovated wide screen and color technologies and struggled with the coming of over-the-air and cable television and the diffusion of home video. These factors, plus a host of other technological, social and economic changes in life in the United States—from suburbanization to changing roles of men and women—have not shaken Hollywood's hold. The studios actually have gotten more powerful.

A 1990s list of the major Hollywood corporations looks remarkably similar to an inventory of the 1930s film institutions. Drops outs come only under extraordinary circumstances. Consider the case of RKO. In 1928, the Radio Corporation of America and the Keith-Albee-Orpheum theater chain merged to create Radio Keith Orpheum. RKO survived on the margin through the 1930s and 1940s, but was taken out of the movie-making business during the mid-1950s by its new owner, eccentric billionaire Howard Hughes.

The modern movie industry oligopoly began after World War I with the rise of a collection of studios located in and around Hollywood. Whereas in 1999 only Paramount Pictures still had a Hollywood address, the locus of production and distribution decision making was still centered in southern California—in Burbank, Universal City, Culver City or Westwood. *Variety* has accurately noted that, by the late 1990s, "as an aggregate, entertainment production has become L.A. County's no. 1 industry, replacing aerospace."[20]

The coming of sound solidified Hollywood's control over the world cinema market, and moved the film industry into the studio era. Film making, film distribution and film exhibition were owned and dominated by five corporations: Paramount Pictures, Loew's (parent company for the more famous MGM), Fox Film (later Twentieth Century-Fox), Warner Bros. and RKO. These five corporations ruled Hollywood during the 1930s and 1940s, and operated around the world as fully vertically integrated business enterprises. This Big Five owned the most important movie theaters in the United States. By controlling picture palaces in all of America's downtowns, they took in three quarters of the average box office take. Only after they granted their own theaters first run and soaked up as much of the box office grosses as possible, did they then permit smaller, independently owned theaters to scramble for the remaining bookings—sometimes months, or even years, after a film's premiere.[21]

Paramount Pictures long represented the most profitable and powerful Hollywood company. More than any other member of the Big Five during the "Golden Age," Paramount relied on its chain of more than 1,000 theaters to maintain its corporate might, holding dominion throughout the heartland of the United States from Chicago to New Orleans. Not surprisingly, a former Chicago theater man, Barney Balaban, stood at the top of this corporate colossus. This trained accountant set up Hollywood studios as modern business enterprises, hiring more lawyers and MBAs than movie stars. Balaban was the first CEO to require his signature for all significant corporate expenditures, whether it was for a wig for Bing Crosby or a new popcorn machine for a theater in Omaha. Balaban's conservative corporate strategy made him a darling of Wall Street, and in 1946 Paramount earned a record $40 million profit, a figure that would stand unmatched for two decades.

Metro-Goldwyn-Mayer (MGM) ranked right behind Paramount. From a purely business perspective, MGM functioned as a successful unit within the larger enterprise of Loew's, Inc. A fully integrated movie company, Loew's owned a movie studio, a network for international distribution, and a highly profitable theater chain centered in the five boroughs of New York City. Indeed, Loew's management, led by Nicholas M. Schenck, ran the company as if it were a chain of movie houses supplied with MGM's films. In Culver City, California, a suburb of Los Angeles, MGM had a complete movie factory with 27 sound stages on 168 acres, processed 150,000 feet of film each day, and contained more than 15,000 items to be used in movie after movie. (By the late 1990s, the Culver studio was home to Sony Entertainment.)

Twentieth Century-Fox ranked behind Paramount and MGM. Although the Great Depression did not prove kind to the fortunes of Fox, after it merged with Twentieth Century Pictures in 1935, the new management of Joseph M. Schenck and Darryl F. Zanuck made Twentieth Century-Fox into a Hollywood powerhouse. Studio boss Darryl F. Zanuck surely earned more public notoriety than CEO Joseph M. Schenck, but it was Schenck who kept the theater chain humming as it presented Fox features, shorts and newsreels. Zanuck set the image of the authoritative studio boss, frequently bellowing to all subordinates and sycophants: "Don't say yes until I've finish talking!"

Warner Bros. (always abbreviated unless referring to the four men themselves) was the family-run operation among the major movie studios. Eldest brother Harry was president, middle brother Abe supervised distribution and baby brother Jack headed the studio in Burbank, California. The innovation of sound put the company on the map, as did ownership of nearly every major movie place in the middle Atlantic region and its pioneering of gangster films. Yet the 1930s and 1940s never proved very profitable for this studio; regular prosperity really did not come until the 1970s when Steven J. Ross (discussed later) fashioned the modern-day Warner Communications.

Radio-Keith-Orpheum (or RKO) was formed so that RCA could market its sound equipment, and the Keith-Albee-Orpheum vaudeville theaters could be converted into movie houses. Although the studio created many memorable films— such as *Citizen Kane* and the Astaire–Rogers musicals—the crown jewel of RKO profitability only came from the animation features and shorts it distributed for Disney between 1937 to 1954. The feature-length *Snow White and the Seven Dwarfs* proved an unexpected hit in 1938; *Pinnochio* and *Fantasia* followed. In the mid- and late 1950s, when Disney hit it big in television and theme parks, RKO went out of business as a movie producer.

The Big Five tolerated some competition. Universal Pictures, Columbia Pictures and United Artists constituted the Studio Era's "Little Three" because each depended on the Big Five for access to the top theaters in the United States. Universal played only a marginal role during the 1930s and 1940s, surviving on low budget comedies from Abbott and Costello, weekly serials (i.e., *Flash Gordon* and *Jungle Jim*), and cheaply made Woody the Woodpecker cartoons. Columbia rested squarely on the shoulders of the owners the Cohn brothers, Harry and Jack, a true two-executive operation. United Artists barely stayed in business during the 1930s and 1940s, and later, during the 1950s and 1960s, ranked as a studio power.

The suburbanization of America and the coming of television shook the film industry to it roots. Yet seven of these eight operations survived. After RKO's fall, it remained the "Big Eight" through the 1950s and 1960s when the Walt Disney operation replaced RKO. But the 1950s and 1960s were not without struggle. MGM almost went out of business, and eventually combined forces with United Artists. MGM/UA never did very well, and its joint failure to adjust to the new world of television set up the Big Six—Warner, Paramount, Fox, Columbia (later bought by and renamed Sony), Universal and Disney.

Warner Bros. began its transition into what today is Time Warner when in July 1956 founding brothers, Harry and Abe Warner, sold their shares to a syndicate headed by Boston banker Serge Semenenko and New York investment banker Charles Allen. The new owners cut ties to the past, and quickly embraced television production with the pioneering series *77 Sunset Strip* and *Maverick*. But during the remainder of the 1950s and into the 1960s, Warner the movie company struggled, its balance sheet moved into the red. In July 1969, Kinney National Services, Inc., a New York conglomerate engaged in parking lots, car rental, construction and funeral homes, purchased Warners. Steven J. Ross, son-in-law of Kinney's founder, took charge and would shape the modern Warner Bros. In 1989, Ross merged Warner with Time, and the modern Time Warner conglomerate was born.

Paramount Pictures began to change in 1949 when Barney Balaban, under pressure from the U.S. Supreme Court's 1948 divorcement and divestiture order, split his empire in half. Paramount Pictures retained ownership of the production and distribution arms; a new theater company emerged as United Paramount Theaters under former Balaban aide, Leonard Goldenson. In time, Goldenson purchased ABC television and began his own empire. Throughout the 1950s, Paramount Pictures followed a fiscally conservative strategy, and slowly fell further behind the competition. During the Fall of 1966, a giant conglomerate, Charles Bluhdorn's Gulf + Western

Industries, acquired Paramount. Bluhdorn installed himself as Paramount's president and hired former press agent Martin Davis to run things in New York and former actor Robert Evans to revitalize the studio in California. In the mid-1980s the hits flowed from the Melrose Avenue studio: the *Star Trek* films, the Eddie Murphy films, and even television spin-offs such as *The Untouchables* (1987). In 1989, Gulf + Western dropped that awkward corporate title and became Paramount Communications. In 1993 it was purchased by National Amusements, which enveloped Paramount into its Viacom division.

Twentieth Century-Fox began its transition to a new era in 1951 when it signed its court-ordered consent decree to spin off its theaters. Generally, during the 1950s, Twentieth Century-Fox did well (most notably with CinemaScope) under the guidance of Spyros Skouras. When longtime studio boss Darryl F. Zanuck resigned in 1956 to enter independent production, the company was strong. Skouras tried out a number of replacements (most notably Buddy Adler), but none could match Zanuck's record; soon Fox began to lose money. To help prop up the balance sheet, Skouras sold part of the famed back lot to Alcoa to be developed into Century City; he was the first to tender movies to the TV networks for prime time showings, commencing with NBC's *Saturday Night at the Movies* in 1963. In 1970, Twentieth Century-Fox lost a record $77 million, and a corporate struggle ensued. The company was on the verge of declaring bankruptcy. Luckily, there were several hits already in the pipeline, including *Patton* (1970) and *M*A*S*H* (1970). So, in 1977, Fox was ready to fully exploit *Star Wars* and make the move back to the top of the Hollywood studio hierarchy. In 1985, News Corporation acquired Twentieth Century-Fox.

Sony had its origins as Columbia Pictures. The new Columbia began in 1951 when brothers Harry and Jack Cohn established a Screen Gems subsidiary to produce television series, and brought in producer-directors Sam Spiegel, David Lean, Elia Kazan, Otto Preminger and Fred Zinnemann to create such hits as *From Here to Eternity* (1953), *On the Waterfront* (1955), *The Caine Mutiny* (1954) and *The Bridge on the River Kwai* (1957). The Cohn brothers ruled until their deaths in 1956 (Jack) and 1958 (Harry), and then former assistants Abe Schneider and Leo Jaffe succeeded them. In the 1960s, prosperity continued with *Lawrence of Arabia* (1962), *A Man for All Seasons* (1966), *In Cold Blood* (1967), *Oliver!* (1968) and *Funny Girl* (1968). The 1970s were not kind to Columbia; the studio lost $30 million in 1971. Cost-cutting became the order of the day. In 1972, Columbia sold its studio lot, and moved in to share operations at Warner's Burbank studio. Columbia remained a viable entity, and sold out in 1980 to Coca-Cola. Coke's experience was a disaster, and it sold to Sony.

Universal was only a marginally profitable movie company during the 1930s and 1940s. When the company was sold in 1952 to the Decca music company, Edward Muhl became head of production and looked for independent deals. Notably, James Stewart came on board to create a number of fine Westerns, all directed by Anthony Mann (i.e., *Winchester 73*, 1950, and *Bend of the River*, 1952). But in 1958, Universal's fortunes took a turn into the red; a year later, the MCA talent agency acquired the Universal back lot, and three years later, the whole company. Under government pressure of an antimonopoly suit, MCA spun off its talent agency and moved into the movie (and TV) business full time.

Disney rose to the status of a major as Walt Disney used television to promote his expanding motion picture operations. But with his death in 1966, the company languished under his heirs. It was not until 1984 when Michael Eisner was brought in that Disney prospered. Eisner brought a rich base of executive experience to Disney. Certainly he learned his strategies from his experience at Paramount during the 1970s under Barry Diller. At Disney, Eisner had help from studio boss Jeffrey Katzenberg. Eisner and Katzenberg added new "brand names"—Touchstone and Hollywood Pictures—and hits poured out. In 1987, *Three Men and a Baby* pushed beyond $100 million in domestic box office take, making it the first Disney film to pass that vaulted mark. And *Three Men and a Baby* represented a quintessential example of the new Disney; its stars, Ted Danson and Tom Selleck, came from the world of television, which kept its production budget well below the industry average.

The Wasserman Era

As Hollywood adapted to the TV era, Lew Wasserman of Universal led the way. Beginning as an agent, Wasserman moved into independent television and film production when he took over Universal in 1962. During the following two decades, Wasserman showed the film industry how to use a flexible system of production and distribution, deal with television, and in the process re-invented itself. Four achievements rank Wasserman as the leading executive of his age:

1) Wasserman initiated independent production, based in Hollywood. As an agent he "sold" his clients as corporate properties, and turned MCA into the leading independent producer of radio, television and film. James Stewart and Alfred Hitchcock allied with Universal as "independents," able to package their own projects, yet always dependent on the studio for distribution and release.[22]

2) Wasserman accumulated a library of film titles, which he then sold to broadcast TV, pay TV and then exploited again as the home video era commenced. He even bought a film library from Paramount, and so initiated a new era in which studios prospered by milking long-term value from their libraries of older films (and TV shows).

3) Wasserman pioneered movies made for television, even as Universal produced and syndicated half-hour and hour-long broadcast television shows. With TV movies, Universal became the largest network supplier of network broadcast television programming, reaching a crest in 1977 with *Roots*, the most popular TV show of its era.

4) With his broadcast TV base providing the dependable profit streams, Wasserman returned to the feature film and pioneered the blockbuster motion picture, dominating an era from the pioneering exploitation of *Jaws* (1975) through the then record setting *E.T.: The Extraterrestrial* (1982).[23]

Wasserman's final innovation in business practice would, through the late 1970s, fundamentally re-define feature film making. He coupled mass saturated advertising on prime time television with simultaneous bookings in new shopping mall cineplexes across the United States with the release of *Jaws* in 1975. The film created a sensation and with it Universal initiated the era of blockbuster feature films, forever altering the Hollywood film making and distribution landscape. Advertising on television became the key to turning a feature film into a blockbuster, enabling the studio distributor to earn millions from "ancillary rights."[24]

Jaws was not the first film sold by and through broadcast television, but its million dollar success proved that strategy was the one that would re-define Hollywood. The Wasserman-led Universal money-making machine reached it climax and closure with *E.T.* in 1982, bringing the company that was languishing two decades earlier revenues that needed to be measured in the billions of dollars.[25]

By June 1975, six companies had come to hold hegemony over the creation and distribution of movies throughout the world. The Big Six prospered through movies, as well as prime time TV shows. Since the end of World War II, they survived the forced selling of their theater chains, the advent of cable and pay television and later the home video revolution. During the 1980s, new owners paid billions of dollars for the right to own one of these studios. For example, in 1981, Twentieth Century-Fox was purchased by Denver oilman Marvin Davis; four years later he sold the company to the Australian Rupert Murdoch, who combined it with the chain of six big city independent television stations that he had acquired from Metromedia Television. The new Twentieth Century-Fox made and showed films and other fare on its new Fox television network.[26]

As analyzed later, Sony took over Columbia, Seagram acquired Universal, Viacom merged with Paramount and Time joined with Warner. Thus, everyone but Disney took on new owners. Still year in, year out, they controlled between 80% and 90% of the expanding movie business in the United States and a bit less in the rest of the world. Every few years a couple of bold pretenders—during the 1980s Orion Pictures and New World—emerged to challenge, but none survived past creating a few modest hits. Although as the 1990s were ending, DreamWorks SKG was mounting a serious challenge. In the real Hollywood industry, the dozens of independent producers have no choice but to distribute their films through one of the six major studios if they wish to maximize their return on investment, and if they want the largest possible audience to see their work. (See Table 6.5.)[27]

By the late 1990s, the majors' power was derived, as it had been since the 1920s, from their unique ability to distribute films worldwide. At considerable expense, all maintain offices in more than a dozen cities in North America (and up to 50 overseas), where their representatives are in constant contact with the heads of the dom-

TABLE 6.5
Total Releases: Hollywood Movie Companies

	Rated Movies by MPAA	Total Movies Released
1998	661	509
1997	673	510
1996	713	471
1995	697	411
1994	635	453
1993	605	462

Source: Motion Picture Association of America Web site at www.mpaa.org.

inant theater chains. A studio's "hit parade" record at the box office is what impels theater owners (a conservative lot with most of their assets invested in real estate) to consistently rent its products. Most movies people think of in the United States are funneled through Hollywood's Big Six (as seen in Table 6.5). Thus, as much as the history of the Hollywood film industry has changed, it has remained the same.

Modern Hollywood commenced in the mid-1970s as the industry fashioned the blockbuster strategy to turn television into a friend, not a foe. Through the final quarter of the 20th century, the oligopoly learned to generate billions of dollars in profits from creations that may start with a feature film, but then go on to touch all forms of mass media (i.e., from radio advertising to music sound tracks, from novelization of film stories to magazines discussing the latest cinematic trends, from presentation of television to entertainment sites galore on the World Wide Web). Each movie aspired to become a theatrical smash hit, because if it does then it may be turned into a "product line"—including toys, theme park rides, T-shirts and McDonald's campaigns. An endless array of licensed tie-ins generate additional millions.[28]

The blockbuster strategy led to escalating costs of production and distribution. Indeed, the average cost of production in 1997 jumped, but this time by 34% to more than $53 million. And it was not just *Titanic* (production cost at least $200 million) or *Batman and Robin* (production cost $125–$150 million), but such pedestrian fare as *The Postman* and *Starship Troopers*, which cost nearly $100 million to produce. Over 10 years, Jack Valenti reported that costs rose 166%; actors and actresses fees were credited first, with routine pay checks of $15 million per film, and in some cases $25 million. (Director James Cameron made an estimated $100 million on *Titanic*.) It is no wonder that the studios had independent divisions (read, low budget), because for the price of one *Titanic* they could pick up a dozen small features; some of these turned out to be Academy Award winners (*Good Will Hunting*, *The Full Monty* and *Shine*). When asked if Warners would now—after the enormous success of *Titanic*—be willing to make a $200 million movie, Robert Daly replied, "Not on purpose."[29]

OPERATING THE HOLLYWOOD OLIGOPOLY

The cycle of feature film creation runs through the power in distribution of the Big Six. A feature film that will be seen around the world must be "green lighted" or "picked up" by one of this group. The following paragraphs describe and analyze this process.

Production is the initial phase. Some production companies work directly as units of the Big Six, but more often than not the producer is an affiliated "independent" company—formed by a star, director or producer through an agent. Most feature films, after a script has been fashioned, start shooting on location, often with considerable help and subsidy by a local government that has wooed the production to theoretically boost the local economy. After some weeks of location shooting, production then finishes up in a Hollywood studio. All the states, and many of the cities, during the 1990s ran bureaus to lure film making companies to their locales to spend monies on local talent, lodging and food. Some states and cities have even financed small studio developments to tempt film makers. For example, in Summer 1997, actor Tim Reid, with considerable subsidies from the state of Virginia, built a small studio complex for $11 million in Petersburg, including a 15,000-square-foot sound stage, a postproduction editing facility and a 15-acre "back lot" with a three-block urban street standing set. Virginia also exempted Reid and his fellow film professionals from state sales taxes to lure them to buy equipment and services in Virginia. In addition, the state waived hotel taxes for film crews staying more than 30 days. These incentives are offered in nearly every U.S. state—as well as the service of closing streets, bridges and public buildings in order that filming can go on.[30]

A small number of productions begin without a studio "green light," just the hope that they will be picked up. But this is risky, and requires a wealthy individual or corporation to "take a flyer." Yet, in 1999, enough risk lovers existed that each of the Big Six had established "independent film" divisions to distribute a small number of pick-ups each year. These independent distributing divisions, led by Disney's Miramax, loved to find small budget films that had a sellable "cutting edge." But, as with the furor surrounding Miramax's widely successful *Pulp Fiction*, there was risk to calculate and deal with when going further than general movie going tastes would allow.

The Big Six also expanded their means of generating sources for potential blockbusters, and further added to their venues to exploit hit movies. For example, consider their movement to sponsor and milk Broadway plays. Disney pioneered this effort with *The Lion King*, and Universal Pictures mounted *Jekyll & Hyde* on Broadway knowing it would later be made into a movie. Twentieth Century-Fox staged a version of *The Full Monty*, and Warner looked to put on *Batman* to keep it in the public eye and inspire another sequel. Hollywood has long bought rights and then filmed original Broadway successes. By the early 1990s, the studios and their parent corporations were regularly funding productions based on material from their extensive library of films and literary rights. By 1999, they stood as top Broadway producers, reaping profits from past hits.[31]

Distribution never gets much attention, but insiders recognize its importance. Whereas Hollywood publicity focuses on the production of films (i.e., its stars, stories and special effects), distribution has always been a key to corporate longevity. Indeed, worldwide distribution has been the basis of Hollywood's power. More than any other mass media business, the Hollywood film industry proved the advantages of globalizing—with its considerable power from economies of scale—long before the term *global media* was ever invented.[32]

The stakes here can best be seen in comparative spending on advertising to promote pictures—principally on television. Consider that in 1998 overall domestic advertising spending for motion pictures rose 9% to $2 billion, according to a study by Competitive Media Reporting, a nationally recognized tracker of advertising spending. Individually, Universal Pictures spent nearly $200 million to advertise its 15 motion picture releases in 1998, an increase of 43% from the year before (the largest advertising spending jump among the Big Six). However, Universal's domestic advertising spending—on three more films than in 1997—placed it but fourth overall, according

to Competitive Media Reporting. Universal had a new owner and it increased advertising and promotion spending to get off to a good start. Sony, on the other hand, grew
conservative, despite the considerable monies spent on *Godzilla*, which was supposed
to be its Summer 1998 blockbuster. In fact, Sony fell to sixth in advertising spending,
although its 32 1998 releases exceeded what each of the other majors released. Disney
led the way with $323 million (up 10%), followed by Warner Bros. at $268 million (up
31%), Paramount at $199 million (down 10%), Universal also at $199 million (up
43%) and—in fifth, ahead of Sony—came Twentieth Century-Fox at $159 million
(down 12%). But what appears as market strategy difference simply reflects studios trying to project the most efficient use of monies to promote current product, and giving
them an enormous advantage over all pretenders.

The MPAA reported in March 1999 that average promotion costs per feature had
increased 13% in 1998 to $25.3 million. But the spending on advertising did not
completely correlate with box office success. For example, Disney, the top studio in
1998 advertising spending, released 22 pictures (2 more than in 1997) and also had
the top box office market share with $1.1 billion. Second place in market share was
Paramount, which released 13 pictures and had box office of $1.1 billion, but was
third in ad spending. The advertising ranking for movie studios did not completely
parallel the spending for their corporate parents, which spent advertising dollars on
a wide range of media products beyond just theatrical releases. Competitive Media
Reporting recorded advertising expenditures for the top five media companies. Disney led the way with $470 million, followed by Time Warner at $413 million. This
made sense because these two were generally ranked as the two largest media companies in the world. This monetary power of promotion was one important advantage in the race to maintain barriers to entry and to corporate longevity.[33]

Only in the rare cases does Hollywood miss out on more than half the business.
At considerable expense, the Hollywood majors maintain offices around the globe,
where their representatives are in constant contact with the heads of the dominant
theater chains, pay TV outlets and home video retailers. Hollywood's regular production of hit films provides a strong incentive for foreign theater, pay TV and home
video companies to consistently deal with them rather than an independent. This
has led to joint deals with foreign companies to build theaters in Britain, Australia,
Germany, Spain and France, and to run cable TV networks all over the world.
Through all these new technologies of presentation, the Hollywood Big Six have
stood at the center of profit maximizing strategies, much to the chagrin of foreign
policymakers who seek to protect their native culture industries.

During the 1990s, the global theatrical market expanded significantly. Once the
monies had been committed to the promotion of a film blockbuster event, it made
sense to amortize that cost worldwide. The major Hollywood companies pioneered
the selling of their products around the world, beginning in the days after World
War I. By the mid-1990s, the Big Six were taking in an estimated $5 billion in
rentals worldwide, which is what they kept after sharing box office take with
exhibitors. Yet foreign revenues come more in the form of payments for pay TV and
rentals and sales for home video. There was also a trend to upgrade cinemas abroad,
modeling them after the mega-plexes being built in the United States. With the

emancipation of state control television broadcasting and the wiring of cable and the spread of satellite services, the vehicles for distribution were more in place in the 1990s. Homes in Europe, for example, acquired VCRs at almost the same rate as in the United States. Rupert Murdoch was aware of this trend because he came to Hollywood from abroad.[34]

Presentation—often misleadingly referred to as theatrical exhibition—starts with the premiere weekend release of the 150 or so potential Hollywood blockbusters. The aforementioned millions of dollars spent on TV advertising focuses the public's attention on the film. A strong first weekend, the theory goes, will lead to positive "word of mouth," and then increasing revenues on down the line for pay TV and home video.

Indeed, it was the aftermarket, or the streams of income from pay TV and home video, that gave the Big Six one of their most sizable advantages. They alone could milk a hit through years of revenues, after the initial major cost. Competitors had to wait and hope. The majors already had streams of revenue constantly being generated from sources initiated years before.[35]

A series of windows of presentation became formalized in the 1990s. For feature films, the process began in theaters, and then went "downstream" to the former "ancillary" markets of pay TV and home video. There are rare exceptions. A handful of films each year fail in U.S. theaters but are able to garner significant box office returns in video. However, such cases are the exceptions. In the vast majority of cases, the theater remains the "voting booth," where the return on the $60 million investment for the average theatrical feature is determined. A theatrical blockbuster guarantees millions of additional dollars from the home video and pay television arenas. That is why the major Hollywood companies work so hard to craft a hit in the theaters. Once they have a proven commodity there, the rest of the way is usually smooth sailing.[36]

Interestingly, the continuing importance of theaters became more "obvious" during the 1990s. Consider that at the beginning of the 1980s, a number of serious pundits, including the multinational consulting firm Arthur D. Little, Inc., studied the film industry, and predicted there probably would be no need for movie theaters by 1990. Everybody could (and would) stay home, and view Hollywood's best through pay TV and home video. Instead, going out to the movies has remained a viable leisure-time activity. Few predicted that more screens would be added, creating more than 30,000 available screens in the United States. Theatrical release in the 1990s required more theater screens so Hollywood could take full advantage of the economies of scale from television advertising to fashion a hit that would pay for itself through pay TV and home video. Because the cost of marketing a feature film can often exceed $30 million, if it is spread over more theaters, marketing costs per theater per film can remain relatively low. The economies of scale of television advertising of theatrical features provides the foundation of the multiplex, and the creation blockbusters.

One of the key innovations in the film business was overnight data generation. It is important to know when and if a blockbuster is being voted in. A. C. Nielsen's Entertainment Data, Inc., founded as the blockbuster era commenced, by the late

1990s was functioning as an integral part of the motion picture distribution and exhibition community. Entertainment Data innovated the collection and dissemination of the box office data by creating a centralized computer reporting service. By 1997, Entertainment Data was collecting data from approximately 32,000 screens—indoor and drive-in—based in the United States, Canada, the United Kingdom, Germany, Spain and France. After number crunching, its products and services not only included daily box office reports, but also instant analysis of trends. Its weekend box office results defined success and failure every Monday morning, as well as influenced future multimillion dollar marketing campaigns. Its reports ranged from estimates of the size of the annual box office take in Peoria, Illinois, to the average opening weekend gross for R-rated action pictures released during the summer. Big Six executives poured over this data and analysis from their offices in Los Angeles and New York.[37]

To maximize revenues from all venues, the major studios have long worked together to enforce a system of classic price discrimination. The process was simple a generation ago. Features opened with big premieres and publicity. Then they played off from first run to second run to third run and so forth. The number of runs denoted the segments of the differentiation that came from what economists called price discrimination. The coming of television simply added runs at the end, but these runs were more profitable than the earlier ones.[38]

If there is a secret, it is that the Big Six have expanded the markets that generate monies to pay off these costs. The Hollywood movie industry produces "theatrical" films that first show up in 30,000 U.S. multiplexes and thousands more around the world. Here is where the publicity is generated concerning which film is a hit and which one is a bust. But the money really comes later, when the film appears on pay TV, is sold or rented for home video, and later is shown on basic cable TV and on broadcast TV. And then there is video. Home video matured as a market outside the United States during the 1990s, but still lagged rental fever in the United States. The figures are impressive. In 1996, Americans spent an average of $133 per annum renting video. Wherever the source, video numbers had grown impressive. For example, Twentieth Century-Fox sold 15 million copies of its blockbuster *Independence Day* outside the United States, adding more than $200 million wholesale to the revenue stream with this single title.[39]

Horizonal and Vertical Integration

The Big Six have long possessed a host of other advantages that enabled them to maintain their considerable economic power and keep out the competition. For example, cross-subsidization enabled a Hollywood Big Six conglomerate—with interests in a number of media markets—to extract profits from one thriving area to prop up another less financially successful area. Single-line corporations do not have this luxury and so aspiring Hollywood operations invariably fail. Second, reciprocity enables members of the Big Six to choose to whom they will sell and then only deal with those companies that cooperate with other units of the media conglomerate. For example, Seagram's Universal Pictures might not sell movies to Time Warner's HBO unless Time Warner's cable franchises book Universal's (partially owned) U.S. television network.

In the end, these forces have led the Big Six to integrate horizontally and vertically. They have generated considerable profits from a wide spectrum of mass media enterprises, including theme parks (Seagram and Disney, in particular), recorded music (Seagram, Sony and Time Warner, as discussed in Chapter 5) and television production (all, as discussed in Chapter 4). Each helped the movie division. Movies inspired theme park rides, prescribed film scores and songs supplied hits for the music divisions, and television supplied pre-sold stars and stories. And make no mistake about it, the major Hollywood companies will continue to be the big winners with this horizontal diversification. Consider that Disney, Paramount, Warners, Universal, Sony and Twentieth Century-Fox "instantly" became the defining producers in home video in the 1990s.[40]

Vertically, during the 1980s and 1990s, the Big Six built up considerable power by spending millions to acquire interests in movie theater chains, cable television systems, over-the-air television stations, TV networks and home video operations such as Blockbuster Video. All figured that controlling the markets "downstream" was vital for the long-term survival and prosperity of any dominating Hollywood operation. The Big Six wanted to be there, as full participants, when customers handed over their money.

While NBC and CBS struggled in the 1990s to throw off the days of the financial interest and syndication restrictions, and produce their own shows, the new model in late 1990s Hollywood was to own a network. Disney had ABC, Twentieth Century-Fox had the Fox network, Time Warner had the WB, Viacom had UPN and Universal was in the process of creating the USA Network. Thus, the production of prime time television was clearly in the hands of these eight companies (i.e., the Big Six, plus CBS and NBC). DreamWorks SKG was making an attempt, as were a handful of independents, but it was Hollywood and its new network partners who were in control.[41]

Two economic motivations lead the chief executive officers of the major Hollywood companies to spend millions to secure vertical control. First, vertical integration enables a company to take full advantage of reductions in costs associated with only having to "sell" to another part of the same company. Sony can, thus, take a Sony movie or book it into one of its many Loews multiplexes. Time Warner can offer a Warner Bros. movie directly to subsidiary HBO, and show it to the millions of households that subscribe to a Time Warner cable system, and then tender sales through Warner's video arm. This can be coordinated without a fleet of salespeople to drum up business. The positive effects of vertical integration can be debated, but they do exist and do help create barriers to entry to the Big Six.[42]

More important, however, is the issue of market control. A vertically integrated company need not worry about being shut out of one of those key ancillary markets. Indeed, one of the majors would rather work with a known "rival" than see a new competitor arise. So, despite the merger talks of 1989, Paramount and Time Warner continued to jointly own and operate a vast theater circuit that gave both a strong, dependable position in key cities (principally Los Angeles), guaranteeing that their movies would receive the best possible opening in their jointly owned chain. Indeed today's "theatrical window," despite talk of the impact of cable television and home video, remains the most important venue to create the blockbusters that can be exploited in other media. However, the vertical stream extends far past traditional theaters and video outlets. In 1995, Disney stunned the world by purchasing ABC/Capital Cities. There were many reasons for this acquisition, but the most significant was Disney's control over access to a major over-the-air TV network and to cable TV outlets. Vertical integration has extended to all forms of movie presentation, principally pay TV and home video (discussed later).[43]

All these advanatages added up to a huge and almost predictable flow of revenues (as seen in Table 6.6). Whatever additional new television technologies appear in the future, the business of the Hollywood major studios will continue to seek top dollar charges for seeing the film as early as possible, whereas less fervent fans can wait and see it for a few cents on basic cable TV or "free" broadcast television. Starting with a theatrical showing, then home video, pay cable, cable television, network television, local over-the-air television and any other possible venues that come along in the forthcoming years, the object of this price discrimination will continue to be to get as much revenue as possible from a product.

These principles and practices have led the Big Six of the 1990s to robust economic health, and a staus of powerful and rich multinational corporations. To appreciate how important they have become in the world in 1997, see Table 6.7. The Big Six form the cores of the globalization of the mass media. They are numbers one, two, four, five, six and nine. In July 1997, *Business Week* produced its Global 1000, and the Walt Disney Company ranked 28th worldwide, Sony 74th, Time Warner 105th, Seagram 231st, News Corporation 234th and Viacom 334th. And in their respective countries of origin, they ranked among the biggest of all companies. News Corporation ranked 3rd in Australia, Seagram 3rd in Canada and Sony 10th in Japan. For the other three, based in the United States and comparing with only multinationals based in the United States, the Walt Disney Company ranked 18th, Time Warner 60th and Viacom 158th. Finally, it is instructive to note that Sony was the 4th largest foreign-owned presence in the United States, Seagram was 18th and News Corporation was 28th. Here is globalization and economic power of the highest order.[44]

Thus the Hollywood film industry in the 1990s is involved in more than just the film business. Although their film divisions may focus on the creation of feature films, the vast accumulation of profits comes from presentation on television. During the final quarter of the 20th century, Hollywood embraced and used television to considerable advantage. It also provided spill over profits for nearly every division of media conglomerates. But television never threatened the oligopoly power of the Big Six. An understanding of the Hollywood film industry requires a look at the oligopoly.

THE OLIGOPOLISTS: THE HOLLYWOOD MAJORS

As previously noted, six vertically integrated operations represent Hollywood: Time Warner's Warner Bros. studio, Disney, News Corporation's Twentieth Century-Fox studio, Sony's Columbia, Viacom's Paramount studio and Seagram's Universal stu-

TABLE 6.6
Movie Distributor Revenues (in millions)

Year	Domestic Home Video	Foreign Home Video	Total Home Video	Domestic Theatrical Exhibition	Foreign Theatrical Exhibition	Total Theatrical Exhibition	Domestic Television	Foreign Television	Total Television
1990	$2,759	$2,296	$5,055	$2,283	$2,100	$4,383	$1,641	$1,415	$3,056
1991	3,009	2,616	5,625	2,292	2,017	4,309	1,781	1,450	3,232
1992	3,494	2,852	6,346	2,397	2,044	4,441	1,887	1,460	3,347
1993	3,850	3,166	7,016	2,597	2,250	4,847	2,019	1,580	3,599
1994	4,343	3,504	7,827	2,610	2,260	4,870	2,142	1,615	3,757
1995	4,330	3,760	8,090	2,660	2,260	4,920	2,320	1,960	4,280
1996	4,535	4,105	8,640	2,885	2,455	5,340	2,515	2,185	4,700
1997*	4,920	4,460	9,380	2,845	2,550	5,395	2,670	2,330	5,000

*Estimate.
Sources: Veronis, Suhler and Associates Communications Industry Forecast, 9th ed., July 1995, pp. 196–197; 11th ed., July 1997, pp. 216–217.

TABLE 6.7
Film as Part of the Global Top 50 Media Corporations

Company and Rank	Film Interests
1. Time Warner	Warner Bros., member Big Six
2. Walt Disney	Releases under Disney, Hollywood Pictures, Miramax and Touchstone, member Big Six
3. Bertelsmann AG	No film interests
4. News Corporation	Twentieth Century-Fox, member Big Six
5. Viacom	Paramount Pictures, member Big Six
6. Sony Entertainment	Sony Entertainment and Columbia Pictures, member Big Six
7. AT&T Broadband & Internet Services	No film interests
8. Seagram's Universal Studios	Universal Studios, member Big Six
9. CBS	No film interests
10. Comcast	No film interests
11. Cox Enterprises	No film interests
12. General Elecric's NBC	No film interests
13. Gannett	No film interests
14. Globo Organization	Started independent film production in 1998
15. Pearson	No film interests

Source: "The Global 50," *Variety*, August 23–29, 1999, pp. A47–A56.

dios. As seen in Table 6.8, this advertising struggle is part of the contest for market share, which changes virtually every season. They are discussed in alphabetical order, and the reader is urged to consult the current data for which is "up" and which is "down" at any one point in time.[45]

Disney is part of the vast Walt Disney Corporation. This, one of the world's largest media companies, led by CEO Michael Eisner for nearly two decades, is best understood as a well-oiled machine, fashioning films in an almost paramilitary manner. Whether under the brand of mainstream Hollywood Pictures, or Touchstone Pictures, or specialized "independent" fare from the Miramax division, during the 1990s Disney led the way as a major Hollywood power. Michael Eisner had begun re-crafting the company in 1984 and climaxed Disney's ascension to the top of the media world with the $19 billion takeover of Capital Cities/ABC on the last day of July 1995. Until late in the 1990s Eisner made the Disney balance sheets glow. Indeed,

TABLE 6.8
Domestic Box Office Market Shares of Big Six (%)

Corporation	1993	1994	1995	1996	1997	1998
Disney	19.2	23.1	22.5	25.2	21.0	21.9
Twentieth Century-Fox	10.7	9.4	7.6	12.5	11.2	10.6
Paramount	9.3	13.9	10.0	12.6	11.8	15.8
Sony	18.5	9.2	12.8	11.1	20.4	10.9
Universal	13.9	12.5	12.5	8.4	9.9	5.5
Warner	21.9	22.3	22.9	20.7	17.1	18.7

Source: Standard and Poor's Industry Survey, "Movies & Home Entertainment," May 20, 1999, pp. 1–2, found on Web site at www.netadvantage.standardpoor.com.

from mid-1985 through late 1990 the company broke profit records for more than 20 straight quarters. Operating margins regularly increased; cash flow swelled the company's coffers. Indeed, through the final sixth of the 20th century the Disney company, with its ever increasing profits, came to represent Hollywood's quintessential business success story.[46]

During the 1990s, Disney became so successful that Eisner tapped into outside financing for feature films. Through Silver Screen's limited partnerships, doctors and dentists and other well-off investors were able to "get into the movie game" by pur-

---

PROFILE: The Walt Disney Company

Basic Data:
Headquarters: Burbank, California
Web site: www.disney.com
CEO in 1997: Michael D. Eisner
1998 Sales (in millions): $23,226
1998 Net Profits (in millions): $1,717
1998 Assets (in millions): $43,537
Rank in 1998 Forbes 500—Sales: 46

Market Holdings:
Broadcast Television: ABC Television Network, ABC owned and operated stations (for example, WABC-New York City, KABC-Los Angeles, WLS-Chicago).
Cable Television: Ownership of networks: ESPN Networks, part owner of Arts & Entertainment & The History Channel, part owner of Lifetime, Toon Disney as well as TV networks in Europe and Japan.
Film & Television: Hollywood Pictures, Touchstone Pictures, Walt Disney Pictures, Miramax studio, Walt Disney Television, Buena Vista Pictures Distribution, Buena Vista Home Video.
Music: Walt Disney Music Company, Hollywood Records.
Radio: ABC Radio networks, ABC owned and operated stations (for example, WRQX-FM-Washington, DC, WABC-AM-New York City, WMAL-AM-Washington, DC).
Publishing: Disney Publishing Group.
Theme Parks: Disneyland (California), Walt Disney World (Florida), EuroDisney (Paris, France), Tokyo Disneyland; Disney-MGM Studio park.
Other Interests: The Mighty Ducks (National Hockey League), Anaheim Angels (Major League Baseball), Disney retail stores, Broadway plays such as *The Lion King*, Disney Cruise Line, Disney Vacation Clubs.

Significant Events:
1995: The Disney Channel becomes available in the United Kingdom.
1996: Acquires twenty-five percent interest of the California Angels baseball team and takes on the role of managing general partner.
1996: Buys Capital Cities/ABC television network and stations and cable TV interests.
1996: Disney World celebrates its twenty-fifth anniversary.
1997: Michael Eisner's contract with Disney is extended to 2006.
1997: Fifteen million Southern Baptists threaten to boycott the Walt Disney Company, however boycott is virtually impossible because Disney ownership is so broad.
1997: CEO Michael Eisner exercises 7.3 million of his stock options worth more than a half billion dollars.
1998: Michael Eisner pushing memoir, *Work in Progress* (Random House).
1998: Disney acquires 43% stake in web portal Infoseek.

chasing $10,000 shares of future Disney "blockbusters." E. F. Hutton's vast network of brokers quickly sold these offerings and millions poured in at lower-than-market rates of interest. Eisner knew these investors shouldered most of the risk, and he tempted more than 140,000 "partners" for a total of $1 billion to be used for Disney film making.[47]

Eisner pioneered serious exploitation of home video. At first, Disney simply repackaged past animation classics, generating revenues that flowed directly to the corporate bottom line. A new era for home video commenced in 1987 when *Lady and the Tramp* generated more than $2 million in orders before a single copy was shipped. When renting tapes still generated 90% of the dollars, Eisner placed *Bambi* and *Fantasia* into "video sell through" so every family could buy and own a copy. Starting with *The Little Mermaid* in 1989, new animated "classics" poured from the Disney shop: *Beauty and the Beast* (1991), *Aladdin* (1992), *The Lion King* (1994), *Pocahontas* (1995), *Toy Story* (1995), and *The Hunchback of Notre Dame* (1996).

Disney set industry records as it sold Baby Boomers and their children animated videotapes. In 1993, for instance, *Aladdin* sold 10.6 million copies in its first three days on the shelf, en route to an astonishing 24 million sold (a record at the time). In 1994, Disney re-issued *Snow White and the Seven Dwarfs*, which surpassed the *Aladdin* totals, and generated $300 million in home video revenues—a significant boost to the growing corporate profitability. This success and new moneys pushed Eisner to make more deals and alliances. For example, in February 1997, he announced a 10-movie deal with Pixar and stated that Disney would buy a small stake in Pixar Animation Studios, joint producer of *Toy Story*. The two companies signed a 10-year, five-film production deal. Disney and Pixar are 50/50 partners in the feature films and any related products. In January 1997, the Walt Disney Company began airing its animated films on the newly acquired ABC-TV network. By releasing such theatrical blockbusters as *Toy Story* and *Pocahontas* to broadcast TV, Disney leveraged benefits from one part of the company to another—achieving successful synergy.[48]

By the late 1990s, Disney stockholders were satisfied and so granted Eisner a new contract entitling him to $300 million in stock and salary over the next decade. Since Eisner had taken over as CEO in 1984, the value of Disney stock had soared from a collective worth of $2 billion to a staggering $50 billion. Shareholders rejected resolutions requiring Disney to more strongly police foreign workplaces and to examine pay policies to link them to job performance. Dozens of picketers outside the meeting accused Disney of exploiting foreign workers while fattening the wallets of top executives. One critic noted that it would take a Haitian worker 16.8 years to earn Eisner's hourly income of $9,783. It looks as if Eisner will run Disney well into the 21st century.[49]

Yet this success did not come without controversy. Eisner took risks, including "green lighting" films for adults through its Miramax division. Since acquiring Miramax in 1993 for $80 million, Eisner increased its releases from about 20 to 30 per annum, and domestic grosses rose from $146 million in 1993 to nearly $400 million in 1997. Eisner was proud of the Miramax brand; it gave Disney a new movie niche—intelligent, hip cinema with an edge. Corporate critics pointed out that this "edge" included excessive violence, rampant drug use, and unnecessarily graphic sex scenes. But, by 1999, this division alone was producing $125 million in pre-tax profits![50]

Here again Eisner set a key trend of the 1990s. Miramax's success encouraged Time Warner to pump monies into its niche brand, New Line, and Universal acquired October Films. Sony established a "classics" division, and Fox created Searchlight. All of these were aimed at an educated, film buff audience. There was a turning point in 1996 when Miramax, with *The English Patient* and *Sling Blade*, swept the Academy Awards. Suddenly, Miramax was not just a respectable way to move a new brand, and not just a distributor of edgy fare. It was at the core of what Eisner boasted as the proper strategy to run a modern media conglomerate—that is, provide something for all audiences—and was honored by its industry at the same time.[51]

In 1998, the Disney film group achieved four major hits: *Mulan*, Disney's 36th full-length animated feature, which reinforced the company's preeminent position in animated films with a domestic box office of $121 million. Touchstone's *Armageddon*, which was released in July, went on to earn nearly $500 million at the worldwide box office, setting a new mark as the highest grossing live action movie ever released by the company. *Good Will Hunting*, in addition to winning Academy Awards for best supporting actor (Robin Williams) and best screenplay (Matt Damon and Ben Affleck), became Miramax's all-time box office champ with $138 million grossed in theaters across the United States and Canada alone. Along with *Scream 2*, which grossed $101 million at the U.S. and Canadian box offices, *Good Will Hunting* catapulted Miramax to its best year ever.[52]

Disney's movie operations were not uncovering and producing the next *Titanic*, but the studio was keeping costs at bay and generating decent profits from its film group. In 1998, Disney chopped more than $500 million in costs out of what was a $1.5 billion budget in the previous year alone, reducing film production to fewer than 20 movies from more than 30 per annum during the early 1990s; the non-Miramax operations of three film labels—Disney, Touchstone, and Hollywood Pictures—were combined into one. As a result, the studio dropped to about a dozen development executives, and planned to acquire about 100 (down from 200) scripts a year. The studio also cut back on lavish premieres, and other perks (e.g., they denied Adam Sandler's request for a private jet to a European press tour for *The Waterboy*).

Instead of trying for more hits, Disney wanted to make sure that more profit from fewer hits made its way directly to the bottom line. In 1998, for example, Disney briefly halted production on a science fiction film called *Bicentennial Man* when its projected budget rose beyond $100 million; this latest "Robin Williams film" only got back on track when the producer trimmed the expected cost to $90 million. But later, when the budget again crept upward, Disney made a deal with Sony to split the costs and profits, which cut Disney's commitment to less than $50 million.[53]

By 1999, Disney seemed to be a company in transition. Eisner terminated dozens of animators, who through the early 1990s had been among the hottest corporate "talent." Eisner told those whose contracts were up for renewal that they could take a pay cut of as much as 25% or leave. In April 1999, the company reported a 41% drop in earning for the most recent quarter (as compared to the same quarter in 1998).

Although no one disagreed that the company still possessed one of the great brand names in the movie (and entertainment) business, the glow of earnings increases seemed over as the century ended. Disney management blamed investments in cruise ships, a set of new arcades called Disney Quest, the opening of a series of ESPN restaurants, new programming for cable's Disney Channel, and weak movie performance. Profits were down and no one had a formula for easy recovery. And Disney could not turn around the ABC television network. The overflowing moneys from home video seemed to be completely milked. Eisner and company had a new challenge.[54]

Paramount Pictures is part of the National Amusements conglomerate, which in turn owns Viacom, Inc., which in turn includes Paramount as one of its divisions. Unlike Disney, where no one shareholder controls the company, Sumner Redstone effectively controls National Amusements, Inc. And although he operates a conservative company, his Paramount movie studio did take one of the 1990s biggest risks with *Titanic*. Paramount split the costs with Fox, proving once again that one megablockbuster could make the corporate bottom line glow like few other mass media investments in the United States.

In 1993, Viacom, Inc. took over Paramount in a bitter public battle. Since then, Redstone has sought to meld Paramount into his vast diversified corporate empire, which includes TV networks such as MTV, The Movie Channel, Showtime, and the United Paramount broadcast TV network (see Chapter 5), and book publishing with Simon & Schuster (see Chapter 3). During the struggle for Paramount, Redstone even acquired video rental leader Blockbuster as a logical extension—vertical integration—of the revenue generation of Paramount's movies.[55]

Redstone dominated "his" movie studio, owning controlling interest in the company, and for a time placed himself in charge of "green lighting" new movies. By 1995, Redstone had passed his National Amusements theater chain to his daughter so he could concentrate on the production side after he fired movie studio boss Frank Biondi. The trade paper *Variety* properly called Redstone "the vicar of Viacom." Redstone himself bragged that the first thing he ordered after acquiring Paramount was a 25% cut in the number of features Paramount "green lighted" each year.

Redstone's track record atop Paramount Pictures is mixed. He is too conservative, and seems to prefer established "cash cows" such as cable's MTV. Although the synergies with Blockbuster Video seem "obvious," it took until 1999 for them to be realized. Redstone took on $9 billion in debt to finance the acquisition of Paramount, and this constantly dragged down earnings reports. To lessen debt, Redstone blinked in negotiations and, by Wall Street calculations, "gave away" his share of the U.S. cable networks to former partner Seagram in order to retire $1.7 billion of the debt.[56]

Still, as 1998 ended, Paramount was launching a Classics division to battle against Miramax. This division was funded by the millions being thrown off by *Titanic*. Paramount Classics started small in 1999, at the bottom of a list headed by Disney's Miramax, Fox Searchlight, and Sony Classics. This meant that all of the Big Six had stakes in "independent" divisions.[57]

Redstone got lucky with *Titanic*. James Cameron's movie epic was supposed to sink under its $200 million cost, its three-hour length, its lack of big stars, and an ending that everyone knew ahead of time. Yet, within a year, *Titanic* became the all-

---

PROFILE: Viacom, Inc.

Basic Data:
Headquarters: New York, New York
Web site: www.viacom.com
CEO in 1997: Sumner M. Redstone
1998 Revenues (in millions): $12,096
1998 Net Profits (in millions): negative $48 million
1998 Assets (in millions): $23,613
Rank in 1998 Forbes 500—Sales: 130

Market Holdings:
Broadcast Television: Partner in UPN television network, owner and operator of broadcast television stations in Philadelphia, Boston, Washington, DC, Dallas, Detroit, Atlanta, Houston, Seattle, Tampa, Miami, New Orleans, and Indianapolis, among others.
Cable Television: Owner of cable networks including MTV, M2, VH-1, Nickelodeon, Nike At Nite, Showtime, The Movie Channel, The Paramount Channel (U.K.), Comedy Central.
Film & Television: Paramount Pictures Corporation (major Hollywood studio), National Amusements movie theater chain (with screens in eleven countries), Famous Players theater chain in Canada, Blockbuster Entertainment Group (home video), Blockbuster Pictures Holding Corporation (investments in films), Spelling Entertainment Group (television producer), Republic Entertainment (film and TV producer and distributor), Paramount Home Video, Worldvision Enterprises (television syndicator), Viacom International, United International Pictures.
Music: Blockbuster Music (retailer of music), Famous Music.
Publishing: Simon & Schuster, Prentice Hall, Macmillan Publishing USA, Schimer Books, Charles Scribner's Sons, Thorndike Press, Twayne Publishers, Pocket Books, Allyn & Bacon, Ginn books, MTV Books.
Other Interests: Viacom retail stores, Virgin Interactive Entertainment, Paramount Parks as Kings Island outside Cincinnati, Ohio, Kings Dominion, near Richmond, Virginia, Paramount's Carowinds near Charlotte, North Carolina, and Raging Waters, near San Jose, California, among others.

Significant Events:
1970: Viacom created as FCC rules that CBS can no longer own syndication operations.
1987: Sumner Redstone's National Amusements, Inc. of Dedham, Massachusetts buys controlling interest of Viacom, Inc. for $3.4 billion.
1996: Launches new cable network—TV Land.
1996: Sumner M. Redstone fires Paramount Pictures boss Frank Biondi and takes over.
1996: Creates M2: Music Television, a new "freeform"music television cable channel.
1997: Sells U.S. Cable networks to Seagram Ltd. for $1.7 billion.
1999: Buys CBS.

---

time record motion picture theatrical grosser. Paramount, which took on the North American rights (passing the rest of the world to Twentieth Century-Fox, the film's original studio), made out extraordinarily well, and sold the television rights to NBC for a record $30 million. NBC acquired the exclusive rights for broadcast television to show *Titanic* five times in five years, beginning in 2000. This deal was done even before the film had finished in theaters.[58]

Overall, during the late 1990s, Paramount's box office stagnated, masked by the success of *Titanic*. But Paramount did not do as poorly as Warner Bros. Redstone was so conservative that he systematically demanded all expensive projects have financial partners, and so he lost out on maximizing revenues with "hot" properties. During 1998, Paramount fully financed only 7 of its 17 features. According to the second-guessers, Paramount should have owned all rights to hits like *Face Off*, instead of settling for half the action. The studio also developed the 1998 hit *Saving Private Ryan*, but nonetheless ended up splitting the deal with DreamWorks SKG. The rationale for this policy, as implemented by president of production Sherry Lansing, was to follow Redstone's dictum to make the studio's dollars go further and reduce its risk. For *Titanic*, Redstone capped Paramount's investment at $65 million. Redstone preferred consistent profits, rather than ride the ups and downs of blockbuster film making. Simply put, Redstone hated risk.[59]

Sony Pictures, owned by one of the largest electronics manufacturers in the world, merged with Columbia Pictures in 1989 to conduct a long-term experiment: Could it marry a movie studio with a maker of mass entertainment? Through the 1980s, former owner Coca Cola tried to synergize marketing skills with movie making. That experiment did not work. Through the 1990s, Sony's vast success as an innovator and seller of Walkmen, Trinitron TV sets, and everything else that was good in mass electronics also failed to carryover. Neither Coke nor Sony had any comparative advantage in Hollywood movie making, and the results showed.[60]

Sony acquired not only an ongoing movie and television studio, but an extensive library of nearly 3,000 movies and 23,000 television episodes. However, through the early 1990s, Sony was unable to turn this Hollywood studio into a money making operation, even through synergies from its ownership of one of music's Big Six (see Chapter 5). And Sony's attempt to use movies to help sell Sony VCRs never worked out; in November 1994, Sony wrote off nearly $3 billion. Thereafter, Sony simply turned to operating a movie studio. By 1997, its investment paid off when it finished as the top grossing studio in Hollywood. Hits included *Jerry Maguire*, *My Best Friend's Wedding*, *Men in Black*, and *Air Force One*. Still critics focused on the heavily publicized 1998 failure of *Godzilla*, which had every possible merchandising tie-in and a record TV advertising budget, but could not bring fans into theaters after the first couple of weekends.[61]

The faceless (and publicity shy) Sony corporate executives in Tokyo could not find a studio head who could turn out regular hits. Initially, Sony spent $700 million to acquire the services of studio executives Jon Peters and Peter Guber. But with no hits, Peters left in May 1991 and Guber in September 1994. Successor Mark Canton left in September 1996 before anyone realized he had engineered a comeback. In 1997, Sony reached $1 billion in North American revenue from box office in record time, only the second studio—after Disney in 1996—to reach $1 billion. Canton had "green lighted" Sony's turn around.[62]

Yet Canton's successor, John Calley, basked in the glory of Canton's movies. Calley inherited *Jerry McGuire*, and counted up Sony's earning from the record 1997 summer. Here seemed positive proof that simply staying in the Big Six would, in the long run, mean vast profits for some manager. (To be sure, neither Canton nor Calley were perfect. When Canton trumpeted a three-picture acting plus producing deal with actress Alicia Silverstone, soon after she vaulted to fame in the 1995 hit *Clueless*, Calley had to live with the dud *Excess Baggage* that the deal produced.)

PROFILE: Sony Corporation

Basic Data:
Headquarters: Tokyo, Japan
Web site: www.sony.com
CEO in 1997: Norio Ohga
1997 Revenues (in millions): $55,058
1997 Net Income (in millions): $1,810
1997 Assets (in millions): $48,490
Rank in 1998 Forbes International 500: 18

Market Holdings:
Broadcast Television: Partner in Telemundo Group, Inc., Hispanic broadcaster.
Cable TV: None.
Film & Television: Sony Pictures Entertainment, Columbia Pictures Entertainment, Tri-Star Motion Pictures Company, Triumph Releasing Corporation, Columbia Tri-Star television production and distribution, Columbia Tri-Star Home Video, Sony Pictures Studio and the Culver City Studios.
Music: Sony Music International, Epic Records Group, Tri-Star Music Group, Barris Music.
Publishing: None.
Other Interests: Electronic and electrical equipment manufacture including a full range of mass market and professional audio and video equipment as well as semi-conductors, cathode ray tubes, home video game software, computers, and telephone and telecommunications equipment, insurance and financing interests.

Significant Events:
1988: Buys CBS records for $2 billion.
1989: Buys Columbia pictures from Coca-Cola for $4.9 billion.
1994: Founder Akio Morita resigns after brain hemorrhage.
1996: Releases feature film *Jerry McGuire*, and sparks recovery of film division which dominates the movie summer season of 1997 with movie hits such as *My Best Friend's Wedding* and *Air Force One*.
1997: Kicks off *Men in Black* movie promotion with expansive tie-in to Ray-Ban sunglasses.
1997: Consumer electronics division reports 82% increase in operating profits for fiscal year ending 31 March 1997.
1997: Partners with investment banker Blackstone Group to invest in manufacturing electronics for the "digital revolution."
1997: With partners pays $539 million for 65% of Telemundo Group, Inc., Hispanic broadcaster, and becomes managing partner.
1999: Cuts 17,000 jobs (10% of the work force), and closes 15 manufacturing plants and reorganizes a software company.

Although there was a great deal of talk about the Japanese takeover of Hollywood (Matsushita bought MCA/Universal Studios a few months later), looking back in retrospect, Japanese owners did best when they hired U.S. managers and tried to operate as a mainstream profit maximizing Big Six motion picture studio.[63]

Sony did establish one trend, that is, re-vertically integrating with the theatrical side. In September 1997, Sony's Loews Theater Exhibition Group chain of theaters merged with the Cineplex Odeon chain of theaters (partially owned by Seagram, itself owner of Universal Pictures). At the time, this created the second largest movie exhibition company in North America—with 2,600 screens in 460 locations in the United States and Canada. This represented the re-consolidation of the movie exhibition side of the cinema business with a member of the Big Six. The chain would promote Sony (and Universal) products and see if that might lead to greater profits. As is analyzed later, this experiment set off a wave of theatrical consolidation, but did not spark much in the way of more re-vertical integration.[64]

The late 1990s saw other changes at Sony. Calley, with Tokyo's blessing, collapsed its TriStar Pictures into its Columbia Pictures brand. It shut down specialized Triumph Films and stuck with Sony Classics as its single specialized "independent" brand. Whereas Calley still planned to release the same number of movies per annum, more would be lower budget "focused" films aimed at teenagers, or films "picked up" from independent producers. With fewer full-time producers on the lot, Tokyo would like lower costs, and Calley would consolidate his power. Calley also began to work more closely with Howard Stringer, who had been hired to head Sony's "new media ventures." Stringer reported directly to Sony president Nobuyuki Idei in Tokyo, who showed his interest by opening a new U.S. headquarters in New York City in order to keep a closer watch on media and technology trends, and to keep tighter control of its U.S. operations. The Sony experiment is still a work in progress.[65]

Twentieth Century-Fox was a core part of News Corporation, an international media empire owned by Rupert Murdoch. Murdoch was and is a risk taker. There is no better example than his massive bet on *Titanic*, the greatest success in movie history. Murdoch is more remembered for his Fox television network, but his success in movie making has been just as crucial to News Corporation's long-term bottom line.[66]

Titanic—a cooperative venture between Twentieth Century Fox and Paramount Pictures—was originally budgeted for $100 million, but doubled to $200 million as the movie scheduled for premiere during the summer 1997, but slipped to a Christmas 1997 premiere. Fox planned to produce *Titanic* alone, but when it early on deemed that production costs were soaring well past $100 million, Murdoch looked for a partner. As noted above, Sumner Redstone signed on—so long as his side of the investment went no higher than $65 million. In exchange Fox gave Paramount full domestic box office rights, retaining everything else for itself. Murdoch has always been the most global of the Hollywood film studio owners, as might be expected for one who grew up in Australia, and was educated at Oxford University in England. The *Titanic* phenomenon doubled studio profits. And with the new *Star Wars* picture due out in May 1999, and two more scheduled during the next century, Twentieth Century-Fox stood atop the Hollywood Big Six rankings. Losses from *Volcano* and *Speed 2* were easily forgotten.[67]

But *Titanic*'s success raised Fox's expectations unrealistically. Throughout spring 1998, the behavior of the senior executives at Fox was akin to that of a weekend gambler who, having finally hit the jackpot, determined never again to blow the winnings. Despite *Titanic*, no one really wanted to take another risk. When Jan De Bont, the Dutch-born former cinematographer responsible for directing *Twister* and *Speed*, pitched a science fiction western to be called *Ghost Riders in the Sky*, Fox executives turned him down because it seemed risky and would cost in excess of $100 million. In 1998, Twentieth Century-Fox began to cut the number of production deals on the lot by more than 40%. Murdoch slashed the budget for *X-Men*, a production based on the Marvel Comics series about mutant superheroes, from $100

PROFILE: The News Corporation Limited

Basic Data:
Headquarters: Sydney, Australia
Web site: N/A
CEO in 1997: Rupert Murdoch
1997 Revenues (in millions): $11,264
1997 Net Income (in millions): $564
1997 Assets (in millions): $30,832
Rank in 1998 Forbes International 500: 217

Market Holdings:
Broadcast Television: Fox Broadcasting Company (television network), Fox television stations, Inc. (owned and operated TV stations including WNYW-New York, KTTV-Los Angeles, KRIV-Houston, WFLD-Chicago, KDAF-Dallas and WTTG-Washington, DC, among
others), Heritage Media, New World Entertainment (television stations and program production).
Cable Television: FX cable network, Fox news cable channel, Kids International, Internation-
al Family Channel network, 15 regional sports cable channels.
Film & Television: Twentieth Century Fox-studio, Fox Video Company, Fox Broadcasting
Company, Twentieth Century-Fox Home Entertainment, BSkyN, the Sky Channel satellite
service in Europe, STAR TV in Asia, JSkyB in Japan satellite television, Canal FOX in
Europe, Sky Entertainment Services in Latin America, VOX and DF1 television in Germany.
Music: small music company.
Publishing: magazines, including joint deal with *TV Guide*, and *Good Food*; newspapers,
including *The Boston Herald*, *The New York Post*, *The Sun* (London, England), *The News of
the World* (London, England), *The Times* (London, England); HarperCollins book publishing.
Other Interests: CineBooks, Inc. (Computer systems), Los Angeles Dodgers (Major League
Baseball), 100 daily and weekly newspapers in Australia, Ansett Transport Industries.

Significant Events:
1985: Rupert Murdoch buys Twentieth Century-Fox studio; establishes in the United States.
1986: Begins Fox television network.
1989: Starts Sky television and becomes a major force in TV in Europe.
1993: Acquires 64% of Sky TV in Asia.
1994: Spends $1.6 for rights to broadcast National Football League games.
1997: Acquires the 80% of New World Communications group not already owned for about
$2.5 billion in securties, and with the new 10 television stations News Corporation
becomes largest owner of TV stations in the United States.
1997: Agrees to buy Los Angeles Dodgers baseball team for $350 million.
1997: Agrees to buy International Family Channel cable network for $1.9 million.
1997: Rupert Murdoch's son James named president of News American Digital publishing, a
new unit that will consolidate all of News Corporation's electronic pushing operations.
1998: Spins off Fox Group as IPO to raise cash for investment.

million to $65 million by shaving expensive stunts and effects. Murdoch was a busi-
nessman, and sometimes his conservative instincts took over. Fox's slate held less
event-style pictures, skewing more heavily toward demographically targeted pictures
like *Hope Floats*, *Ever After*, and *How Stella Got Her Groove Back*, which were aimed
at specific demographic groups and were less costly to make and promote.[68]

Titanic traumatized Fox with more than issues of cost. Every studio boss feels a
sense of panic when a project goes over budget, but *Titanic* represented a new expe-

rience for Hollywood. Its costs had spun wildly out of control and the whole town had followed it obsessively. The largest of the Hollywood trade papers, *Daily Variety*, even developed a logo depicting a sinking ship for its "*Titanic* Watch" stories. To this day, no one will confirm the film's ultimate cost, partly due to normal studio obfuscation and partly due to legitimate differences over accounting. Although Murdoch never commented publicly about the *Titanic* ordeal, his reaction was vividly reflected in terms of his policy decisions. He looked more to his favorite business model: carefully controlling the global distribution.[69]

Murdoch sought synergies. A late 1990s project was to fashion the hit Fox TV show, *The X-Files*, into a hit feature film. Here the Fox worldwide pipeline could work its magic. There had been very few successful precedents for this sort of an exercise, whereby an ongoing TV show would be expanded into a movie. Certainly the success of Paramount's *Star Trek* movies was a positive sign. But there were a few built-in problems with *The X-Files*. One was the creator of the show, Chris Carter, who believed his TV series represented not just good storytelling, but high art. Carter intended to write the script and have one of his key TV directors shoot the movie. The editing, scoring, and other facets of the movie would also be done by the show's existing TV staff. The Fox movie executives bit their lips and kept quiet because they knew Carter represented an important franchise to Fox TV. The movie proved a hit, and surely Fox will try to milk it as Paramount has done with *Star Trek* for many years.[70]

Murdoch also picked up independent films, and attempted to turn them into hits. Returns could be considerable. The *Wall Street Journal* reported in 1998 that *The Brothers McMullen*, made for $300,000, earned $10 million at the box office in the United States. But it would have never made this success without Twentieth Century-Fox's Searchlight division picking it up and distributing it. More typical were high side, lower budget films like Fox's *There's Something about Mary*, which cost $23 million and grossed nearly $200 million by the end of 1998.[71]

Former CBS executive Howard Stringer called Murdoch the leader of a new "Napoleonic era" of communications. Murdoch told reporters: "The only good regulator is a dead regulator." And Murdoch is always on the look out to enhance his company's image. In 1997, for example, Murdoch offered candidates a total of one hour of free time on election eve as well as 10 one-minute "position statements," all to be broadcast in prime time on Fox. Thus, whereas former network anchors Walter Cronkite and John Chancellor had to spend two more months lobbying ABC, CBS, and NBC to match Murdoch's offer, he already had taken the high road. Surely no one can doubt that Murdoch is a skilled player in the changing world of mass communications with a clear vision for the future: a media empire, embracing all technologies and content forms, dominating mass media markets covering the entire planet, with movies as one of the centerpieces if that global pipeline strategy.[72]

In the end, Murdoch wants to pass his company to his children. In February 1997, his daughter Elisabeth became the general manager of Sky TV, fueling speculation that she would take over when her father retires. In April 1997, he appointed his son, Lachlan, to assume overall corporate responsibility of News Corporation's publishing units. If Murdoch succeeds, he will be the rare corporate creator to be able to pass his legacy to his children. He and Sumner Redstone have that in common.[73]

Universal Pictures has been owned since 1995 by Seagram Limited of Montreal, Canada, and, like Sony, has been conducting an experiment: Can the heir to a fortune in one area re-invent the company as a movie (and, in Seagram's case, also music) media conglomerate? In the late 1990s, Edgar Bronfman Jr. put into place several management teams as he shaped the future direction of the company. He was an outsider who bought in, and then had to prove he could actually run a media conglomerate. Seagram will see if it can do a better job with Universal into the next century.[74]

Seagram was serious about building up its entertainment side. So, in July 1998, Seagram sold its Tropicana juice business to Pepsico for $3.3 billion cash. The sale price was nearly triple the $1.2 billion Seagram paid Beatrice for Tropicana a decade earlier. This

---

PROFILE: The Seagram Company Ltd.

Basic Data:
Headquarters: Montreal, Canada
Web site: www.seagram.com
CEO in 1997: Edgar M. Bronfman, Jr.
1997 Revenues (in millions): $11,752
1997 Net Income (in millions): $502
1997 Assets (in millions): $21,628
Rank in 1998 Forbes International 500: 207

Market Holdings:
Cable Television: Partner (along with TCI) with Home Shopping Network, and partner USA Networks, Inc. (Includes USA cable network and Sci-Fi cable network) as well as television production and broadcast television stations under Silver King division.
Film & Television: Universal Studios, Inc., Universal Studios Enterprises, Universal Studios Home Entertainment Group, Cinema International Corporation, Sony Cineplex movie theater chain (in partnership with Sony entertainment), Brillstein-Grey Entertainment (film producer), Universal Studios New Media Group, equity owner in HBO Asia, Telecine of Brazil, Cinecanal in Latin America, Showtime in Australia, and Star Channel in Japan.
Music: Universal Studios Music Entertainment Group, Geffen Records, MCA Records, GRP Recording Company, Interscope Records, Hip-O Records, Decca Records, Motown Records.
Theme Parks: Universal Studios Tour, Yosemite Concession Services, Universal Studios Tour Florida.
Other Interests: The Tropicana Beverage Group (fruit juices), The Seagram Beverage Group, Seagram Chateau & Estate Wines Company, Chivas Regal Scotch Whiskey, Absolut Vodka, Captain Morgan Original Spice Rum, Mumm and Perrier-Jouet Champaigns, Sandman Ports and Sherries, Tessera permium wines, Spencer Gifts.

Significant Events:
1995: Acquires 80% interest in entertainment giant MCA Inc. for $5.7 billion with former owner Matsushita Electric Industrial Company, Ltd. of Japan retaining 20%.
1996: MCA, Inc. renamed Universal Studios, Inc. (all film and TV operations plus Spencer Gifts).
1996: Sells MCA's Putnam Berkley book publishing group for $300 million.
1997: Sells 30 million shares of Time Warner to Merrill Lynch & Company for $1.4 billion, leaving 26.8 million shares still owned.
1997: Buys independent film producer October Films.
1997: Purchases Viacom, Inc.'s half interest in USA cable networks for $1.7 billion.
1997: Allies with Home Shopping Network, Inc. for television combination to be called USA Networks, Inc. to expand in cable and broadcast television under Barry Diller.

need for cash began in early 1995 when Seagram purchased MCA and renamed it Universal in order to diversify it away from liquor and other beverages. And although Bronfman and his father had long owned stock in other major media companies, through the late 1990s they were fully committed to Universal; they sold off the last of the media investments, a stake in Time Warner for $1.4 billion in cash. Bronfman made it his full-time job to re-invent Universal in general, and the film studio in particular.[75]

Bronfman first cut costs. For example, he let the Zucker brothers' production deal lapse because such deals typically cost a studio between $1 and $2 million a year to cover an office, a development executive, phones, faxes, messengers, photocopying, and assistants. Write offs were made on movies invested by the previous owners, and when during spring 1997, Bronfman said goodbye to Steven Spielberg, he lost a valuable asset, distributing such blockbusters as *The Lost World: Jurassic Park*. Spielberg moved to his own studio-in-making DreamWorks SKG.

To prepare for life without Spielberg, Bronfman hired Frank Biondi, Jr., from Paramount, and former agent Ron Meyer. They began to sign up big name talent, from director Penny Marshall to actor Sylvester Stallone. Bronfman and his executives announced an expansion of production, to double studio output to 24 films by the year 2000. Bronfman also bought October Films, to become Universal's equivalent of Miramax. October, famous by the mid-1990s for such art house favorites as *Secrets & Lies* and *Breaking the Waves*, would release an additional 20 films a year. To help finance all this, Bronfman turned to Citicorp for a $1.1 billion line of credit. But as 1998 ended, Universal's film division was reporting losses, and Meyer was placed in complete charge. Bronfman and Meyer tried to play catch up.

The trend looked good as summer 1999 commenced. Bronfman and Meyer were able to score two hits by releasing them just before and just after the new *Star Wars* film. First came *The Mummy*, which quickly reached blockbuster status, achieving within a month the needed $100 million in theatrical revenues. Then came *Notting Hill*, which did even better. By the mid-summer 1999, Universal had vaulted to third place in current rankings among the Big Six. Still, this would not be the first major studio to go hot and then languish again under new management. Because Universal was a member of the Big Six, it would survive and then most likely thrive. There was no more closely watched studio than Universal; no one knew what would happen into the next century.[76]

Warner Bros., part of the Time Warner media colossus, commenced with the Time plus Warner merger in 1990. As the world's largest media company, Warner Bros. has had a long, profitable record. But, as the 1990s ended, its short-term prospects were uncertain. This was not because of a new owner, but because of the nonadaptability of two of Hollywood's longest tenured studio executives, Robert Daly and Terry Semel. But in 1999 they were fired, and the Warners studio set out to re-invent itself.

Time Warner was created as a major Hollywood studio and music company, Warner Communications, and a leading publisher, Time, Inc., merged. The Warner Bros.' studio produced a vast array of motion pictures that would then play on its cable television systems with its HBO and other networks. In addition, each year Time Warner also sold millions of music cassettes and compact discs, home videos, magazines, and books—all hoping to synergize with Warner's movies. Structurally, Time Warner was organized into four divisions: film and TV entertainment, music, publishing, and cable TV.[77]

The force behind the merger was Warner Communication CEO Steven J. Ross. The merger was advertised as a combination of equals, and at first, Ross and J. Richard Monro of Time, Inc. were listed as co-CEOs. But this "sharing of power" proved shortlived; within a year, Ross stood alone atop Time Warner. But Ross died in December 1992, and thus did not live to see the fruits of the merger. The actual day-to-day running of Time Warner fell to Ross' protégé, Gerald M. Levin. It has been hard going for Levin because of the debt taken on from the merger.[78]

PROFILE: Time Warner Inc.

Basic Data:
Headquarters: New York, N.Y.
Web site: www.pathfinder.com
CEO in 1999: Gerald M. Levin
1998 Sales (in millions): $14,582
1998 Net Profits (in millions): $168
1998 Assets (in millions): $31,640
Rank in 1998 Forbes 500—Sales: 102

Major Holdings:
Broadcast Television: The WB Network.
Cable MSO's: Time Warner Cable with clustered MSOs in New York City, Tampa Bay, Milwaukee, St. Louis, Houston, and Raleigh & Duhram, North Carolina.
Cable Networks: Turner Broadcasting (includes CNN, TNT & TBS), HBO, Cinemax, CNNSI (combining cable network and Sports Illustrated magazine), Turner Classic Movies, The Cartoon Network.
Film & Television: Warner Bros. Studio, WB Television (producing such shows as *ER*, and *Friends*), Lorimar Television (syndicating such shows as *Dallas*), Quincy Jones Entertainment (producer of *Fresh Prince of Bel Air*), Warner Home Video, HBO Pictures, New Line Cinema movie studio, Fine Line Features movie distribution.
Magazines: Fortune, People, Sports Illustrated, Time, Weight Watchers, Asiaweek, Money, Entertainment Weekly, Mad Magazine, Life.
Music: Atlantic Recording Group, Warner Bros. Records, Ivy Hill Corp., Elektra Entertainment plus other labels.
Publishing: Warner Books, Little Brown book publishers, Time-Life books, Book-of-the-Month-Club, History Book Club.
Other Interests: DC Comics, Six Flags Entertainment and Theme Parks, Atlanta Hawks (Professional Basketball), Atlanta Braves (Major League Baseball).

Significant Events:
1989: Time and Warner merge.
1996: The Federal Trade Commission reaches a settlement with Time Warner allowing its $6.2 billion merger with Turner Broadcasting.
1997: CEO Gerald M. Levin orders company wide budget cuts of 3 to 5% to boost lagging stock price.
1997: Time Warner posts $30 million profit, with revenues reporting to climb 25% to nearly $6 billion, led by its cable TV MSOs and networks.
August 1997: Time Warner cable begins to sell and trade to custer MSOs to help lower $17 billion debt.

Warner had done well as a movie studio until the mid-1990s. The years after that proved weaker in sales. *Batman and Robin*, the fourth in the series over eight years, did not do well. The 1989 original cost $40 million to make, and added $27.5 million in marketing costs. For this the domestic box office revenues plus international box office (outside the United States and Canada) plus reported home video revenues added to more than $500 million. So with pay TV and home video outside the United States, there was a healthy profit. But each sequel, *Batman Returns* in 1992 and *Batman Forever* in 1995, did not match that figure and despite millions of dollars in revenues, their costs had soured past $100 million. But although the profits were lower, they were at least predictable. Add in the continuation of the sales of everything from T-shirts to Batman cookie jars to Halloween costumes, all sold through Warner Bros. retail stores, and sizable synergy continued.[79]

Yet Levin was looking for more, and knew it took years to realign a studio. For example, he sought to speed up the process of "green lighting." Consider *The Incredible Mr. Limpet*, a special effects laden Warner Bros. project based on the 1964 Don Knotts comedy about a man who becomes a fish. Through the final years of the 1990s, Jim Carrey was rumored as the likely star of the re-make, with Steve Oedekerk, a top screenwriter who has directed such films as *Ace Ventura: When Nature Calls*, as director. But the negotiations over who should be paid what amount stalled the project. Oedekerk and Warner Bros. clashed because the studio wanted the film to be made for about $100 million, and Oedekerk insisted on more spectacular and expensive special effects technology that would drive the cost up to about $130 million. As 1998 ended, it looked like the project would never be made, despite the fact that Warner Bros. already had spent several million dollars developing it. Levin was frustrated by Daly and Semel's management, which led to their termination.

Warner had two hits, *Analyze This* and *The Matrix*, in 1999. Most observers believed the studio had long relied on a tight cohort of directors and producers—best exemplified by Clint Eastwood to the movie going public. The mediocre years of the late 1990s pushed Daly and Semel to go beyond this group, and to try new directors and producers. But no one knew how long Levin would give them to re-invent Warner Bros.[80]

Their time frame seemed to be getting shorter. In 1997, Levin ordered companywide budget cuts from 3% to 5% over three years in his struggle to pay down Time Warner's $18 billion debt. He cut salaries and perks. He cut the fleet of corporate aircraft, did away with glossy quarterly reports for shareholders, and reduced the number of copy machines. At the movie studio based in Burbank, re-invention began.[81]

The studio began to seriously exploit Warner's library of past titles—including short subject Looney Tunes starring Bugs Bunny, Daffy Duck, and Elmer Fudd, among others—in grand style. Time Warner Consumer Products Chief Dan Romanelli candidly admitted that the total revenues of sales related to merchandising related to simply the Looney Tunes figures had reached an astonishing $3.5 billion, underscoring the 1990s vital link between movie making and merchandising. In 1994, according to one source, worldwide retail sales of all licensed merchandising surpassed the $100 billion mark for the first time. Warner wanted to match Disney—for example, Disney's tie-in with Burger King for *Toy Story* in 1995 was reported to be worth $45 million.[82]

THE HOLLYWOOD FILM INDUSTRY

Warner also led the way with product placement, whereby the studio sold companies a place in an upcoming feature film. For example, for Christmas 1998, the Warner comedy release *You've Got Mail* integrated this placement all the way to the title—based on the familiar America On Line (AOL) copyrighted Internet greeting. AOL was practically a co-star with Tom Hanks and Meg Ryan. The movie featured frequent shots of the AOL logo, its sign off screen, and its "instant messaging" template. Director-writer Nora Ephron and AOL executives worked closely together, and so the line of television with advertising versus movies without advertising blurred as Warner's bottom line increased. It was logical when Warner's new motion picture marketing executive in 1998 was hired directly from McDonald's.[83]

Yet the failure of *Mad City* and *Father's Day* alerted industry insiders to Warner's studio slump. As Daly and Semel neared and passed the age of traditional retirement, industry watchers began to whisper that new studio blood was needed. Critics pointed out that the Warner share of the domestic box office had constantly fallen from a crest 20% share in 1992. And new management began as the twentieth century ended.[84]

In the end, the responsibility lay with CEO Gerald Levin. Even *Fortune*, a magazine owned by Time Warner, suggested that the CEO had a dangerous predilection for "risking his own neck." As the new century approached, having survived 10 turbulent years since helping to engineer the merger of Time Inc. and Warner, Levin certainly deserved some sort of special trophy as the ultimate survivor. His empire showed a fivefold increase from the level at which it was stagnating five years before. Many mocked Levin's lack of "charisma," and all praised his long-term strategy of complete media diversification. Levin might not be as famous as his vice president, Ted Turner, or rival bosses such as Michael Eisner, but no one person has created a more powerful global media company.[85]

THE PRETENDERS: DREAMWORKS SKG AND MGM

With the riches in the power of the Big Six, there will always be pretenders trying to make the oligopoly bigger. From 1993 on, there was no more watched attempt than that by Steven Spielberg, David Geffen, and Jeffrey Katzenberg to fashion a major with DreamWorks SKG. (Note: S = Spielberg, K = Katzenberg, G = Geffen.) Closely held by the three and a few wealthy supporters (such as Microsoft's Paul Allen to the tune of $500 million), DreamWorks SKG would try to do what no entity had done since the late 1920s—add to the corporate lineup of the major studios.[86]

In September 1997, DreamWorks SKG released its first feature film, *The Peacemaker*, starring George Clooney and Nichole Kidman. In its first crucial weekend, *The Peacemaker* grossed a modest $12.5 million in U.S. and Canadian theaters, and went onto be come a modest hit at best. Its much anticipated animated feature rumored to be based on the life of Moses, the *Prince of Egypt* (produced by Katzenberg of Disney animated fame), did not come out until late 1998. Neither was a hit. Only Spielberg's *Saving Private Ryan* helped.[87]

DreamWorks SKG was competing for the fabled seventh spot in the Hollywood industrial pantheon with MGM/UA. Both its MGM, and its United Artist's division, were part of Kirk Kerkorian's Tracinda private corporation, a billion-dollar private holding company most famous for its building of the MGM Grand casino in Las Vegas. The 1990s had not been kind to either MGM or UA. Kerkorian desperately tried to ape the Big Six by turning United Artists into a speciality label. But what MGM/UA needed were blockbuster hits on a regular basis, which was something the company in all its incarnations in the 1970s, 1980s, and 1990s had rarely achieved.[88]

Desperately in November 1997, MGM (through its parent company Tracinda Corporation) filed for a $200 million stock offering to raise money. Kerkorian took one third of the stock, bringing his investment to $1 billion. The stock offering received tepid response from Wall Street, signaling what serious investors thought of Kerkorian's new attempt to revitalize MGM/UA. And when it came, for example, to discussing salary with Sharon Stone in 1998, MGM/UA management had to pass on her demand for $15 million to do a sequel to the 1992 hit *Basic Instinct*. The studio could not take such a big risk, and without taking such risks the great blockbuster that might bring MGM/UA back to its former glory will never be made and exploited. Clearly, MGM/UA was teetering toward bankruptcy again, most likely to be sold out to and absorbed by a member of the Big Six.[89]

THEATRICAL EXHIBITION

All theatrical films start their life on a screen in a multiplex. These multiplexes are organized as chains to take advantage of the economies of scale of operation, and it is important to negotiate discounts on items sold at their concession stands. The theater chains can keep all the moneys from selling popcorn and the like, but they share the box office revenues with whichever of the Big Six was distributing the film. Whereas the Big Six control nearly all of production and distribution, they do not even come close to owning every movie screen in every multiplex in the United States (as seen in Table 6.9). Indeed, there are only two chains affiliated with the Big Six: Sony and Universal's Loews Cineplex chain and Viacom's National Amusements chain. These two cases are analyzed next, and then the independent chains, which dominated theatrical screens around the United States, are discussed.[90]

Loews Cineplex came about through a merger where Sony's Loews Theater Exhibition Group chain of theaters acquired the Cineplex Odeon chain of theaters (based in Toronto, Canada, and partially owned by Seagram). The combined entity at the time was re-named Loews Cineplex Entertainment, based in New York City, and controlled 2,600 screens in 460 locations in the United States and Canada. Expectations were high, with annual revenues hoped to be in excess of $1 billion. With vast concentration of screens in key cities such as Washington, DC, New York, and Chicago, Loews Cineplex in 1999 was 51% owned by Sony, 26% owned by Seagram's Universal Studios, and the remainder was traded publicly. The hope was that Loews Cineplex could open Sony and Universal feature films in a way to maximize revenues down through the other multiple venues. This surely had worked for the

TABLE 6.9
Largest Theater Chains, 1998

Chain	Number of Locations	Screens
Regal	727	5,347
Carmike	540	2,720
Cineplex	460	2,600
AMC	226	2,117
Cinemark USA	193	1,754
General Cinema	189	1,059
Viacom (National Amusements)	118	1,072

Source: *Wall Street Journal*, January 20, 1998, p. A3.

major Hollywood studios during the 1930s and 1940s, but whether this vertical integration would prove a viable strategy at present remained an open question.[91]

National Amusements formed a small portion of Viacom. Indeed, in 1993 during the frenzy when Redstone acquired Paramount, there was no mention of jettisoning "his" theatrical chain. Yet through the 1990s, Redstone did not participate in the mergers and expansion of rival chains, or build many new multiplexes in the United States. He instead looked to the United Kingdom, Mexico, and South America for theatrical expansion. He also placed his daughter Shari Redstone as head of the theater chain. He then began to train her as his father had trained him. Shari Redstone, a 1979 graduate of Boston University law school, started a career in criminal law, but soon switched to corporate concerns and joined the family business. She seemed to be the logical heir to the Redstone fortune when her father finally retires.[92]

Independent Chains

But the majority of the ownership of the theatrical side of the movie business was not with vertically integrated Hollywood affiliated companies. During the 1990s, outsiders took over this portion of the business. For example, in early 1998, two of the leading U.S. investment companies—Hicks Muse, Tate & Furst, Inc., and Kohlberg Kravis Roberts & Company (KKR)—poured vast sums into Tennessee-based Regal Cinemas Companies to fashion a chain of theaters that at one point (with all pending deals) summed to 5,347 screens in 727 locations in 35 states. Not all portions of the deal were finalized, but still Regal during the late 1990s came to symbolize the new life of theatrical exhibition into vast independent chains. Regal led the way to challenge the Hollywood strategy of vertical integration. The Big Six had to deal with Regal to optimally place their films; Regal needed the Big Six to supply product. This classic bilateral oligopoly would become the poker game to end all poker games—all theaters sought to hold onto portions of the riches thrown off by successful blockbusters.[93]

The establishment of independent chains had its origin with the forced break-up of Hollywood's longtime vertical control. During the 1920s through the 1940s, the major Hollywood companies had owned the most important theaters and dominated exhibition. The possibility of new entrants came about only because of the much-heralded antitrust case settled in 1948, *U.S. v. Paramount*. The U.S. Supreme Court ordered the divorcement and divestiture of Hollywood's theatrical chains, and so forced the Big Five to sell off their theater chains. New entrants entered; the Hollywood-controlled chains were sold and reconfigured. And from all this came the basis of new chains of cinemas, which then built multiplexes, first in shopping centers and then in shopping malls.[94]

Consider General Cinema, which is still a powerful player 50 years later. When Phillip Smith built his first drive-in outside Detroit in 1935, the downtown movie palaces owned by Paramount controlled all booking of films into the Detroit area. A drive-in was the only way Smith could enter the market because Paramount simply did not care. But in 1949, once Paramount signed a court-imposed consent decree, Detroit became an open market for the movie exhibition. Smith expanded, opening drive-in after drive-in, booking first-run films, and admitting children free as long as their parents paid full fare. Smith was one of the leaders who sought the whole suburban family, emphasized tempting profitable concession stands, and made his mark in the exhibition side of the formerly closed film business.

Philip Smith died in 1961 just as the drive-in industry reached its zenith. His son, Richard Smith, then 36 years old and a Harvard MBA graduate, moved General Cinema into the new suburban shopping centers that were being built across the United States. By the late 1960s, General Cinema, as the company had been renamed, owned nearly 100 shopping center theaters, the largest collection in the United States at that time. By 1967, General Cinema was earning a record $2 million in profits on more than $40 million in revenues from 150 theaters. By 1970, the number of theaters topped 200, with all the new ones having two or more screens. General Cinema doubled these numbers by 1975 as it disappeared from the original drive-in business; Smith realized that the shopping mall cinema would thereafter define movie going in the United States. With acres of free parking, and easy access by federally sponsored highways, the shopping mall grew to accommodate the majority of the nation's indoor screens, and became the locus of Hollywood's attention. The son had taken the company down a path his father never saw.[95]

Yet futurists predicted Smith and his competition were traveling down a road headed for a dead end. They predicted the end of "going out to the movies." Sure, fans would venture out on occasion to watch their favorites, but the burgeoning set of television options at home—led by pay TV and home video—would kill the theatrical movie show. The image of the movie fan, they predicted, would shift from the darkened theater to the home equipped with cable television, a video cassette recorder, a satellite dish, and a giant 50-inch screen. This seemed a simple and straightforward application of the economic principle of the substitution effect. The innovation and popularity of the mega-plex—with free parking, dozens of new movie choices, concession stands the size of small restaurants, and arcades of games and extra fun—halted such speculation. The melancholy scenario of a stagnant theater industry, with little growth and change because of television, never came true. In fact, through the final quarter of the 20th century, there has been renewed interest and more growth than at any time in the history of cinema. The 1990s turned out to be the "Golden Age" of theatrical exhibition.

The move to the multiplex cinema (and the opening of thousands of new screens, as seen in Table 6.10) caused a fundamental change in release of films. As late as the early 1970s, Hollywood feature films used to be released regularly throughout the year, with the big hits saved for Christmas. In the world of the shopping mall, the summer, defined as beginning at Memorial Day and ending with the Labor Day weekend, denoted the season when the Hollywood majors unleash their hits. By the late 1990s, the summer movie season accounted for nearly 50% of the domestic box office take. New films opened in clusters each weekend as the Big Six sought to position their offerings to become the next blockbuster. The exhibition business remained a core social activity for the young. The bulk of admissions came from persons under 40, with the majority being teens, but an urban-based, college-educated audience of adults into their forties continued to be faithful to theaters.

Concession stands in the mega-complexes regularly produced millions of dollars in profits. Buckets of popcorn sometimes cost more than $5, and soft drinks were almost as much. Candy was dispensed in as large or small amounts as demanded. Summer action films sold the most popcorn; contemplative romance comedies sold the least. Popcorn remained tops in consumption, providing nearly half of all concession stand sales, despite the introduction of everything from cappuccino to enchiladas.[96]

All this money led to more screens in mall-plexes for consumers to choose from, particularly in major cities. With more screens per complex (pushing the average into the twenties) all chains carefully researched and selected new sites. As the exhibition industry moved through the late 1990s, the national total of available screens passed 30,000, a nearly 25% increase since 1991. And each new screen was more profitable than the one it replaced, because economies of scale reduced per screen operating costs, and with revenues growing from 4% or 5% per annum, profits increased. The 1990s could be characterized as a "building boom" for theaters, even as TV provides more outlets to see films after their theatrical premieres.[97]

Regal Cinema Companies stood atop the cinema exhibition world with nearly 4,000 screens. The rise of Regal Cinemas offers one of the most remarkable stories of a new entrant. During the 1990s, this Knoxville, Tennessee-based circuit grew from a single twin theater in Titusville, Florida, to the world's largest theater chain. There were 3,672

TABLE 6.10
Motion Picture Screens, USA

	Drive-In Screens	Indoor Screens	Total Screens
1998	746	33,440	34,186
1997	815	30,825	31,640
1996	826	28,864	29,690
1995	847	26,958	27,805
1994	885	25,701	26,586
1993	850	24,887	25,737
1992	872	24,233	25,105
1991	908	23,662	24,570
1990	915	22,774	23,689

Source: Motion Picture Association of America Web site at www.mpaa.org.

screens in 406 locations in 30 states as 1999 commenced under founder and CEO Michael L. Campbell, with clusters of mega-plexes in Kentucky, Tennessee, and North Carolina. In November 1989, Campbell started Regal, and by 1993 he had 315 screens before his company went public. He then went on an acquisitions spree. In 1994, he acquired National Theaters, then the Litchfield chain, then took over Neighborhood Entertainment, Georgia State Theaters, and the Cobb circuit. By 1998, annual revenues totaled more than $700 million, with numerous plans on the drawing board for even further expansion. *Forbes* estimated that its profit rate average for 1992 through 1997—before the mega-merger—was an impressive 14%, with $310 million in sales in 1997, and a market value over $1 billion. This company's short history offers proof that the theater exhibition side is not the oligopoly—far different in its ownership and operation than the Hollywood production and distribution side has long been.[98]

In retrospect, it is obvious why Regal caught the eye of Hicks Muse and KKR investment bankers. It was able to create profits from small town cinemas through skilled management without taking on excess debt. Indeed, before the Hicks Muse and KKR deal, Regal had one tenth of the debt of Carmike and one eighth that of AMC. Regal was an aggressive company. For example, in June 1997, it opened the Brandywine Town Center Cinema 16 and Fun Scape in Wilmington, Delaware. The area's largest cinema complex, along with the 90,000 square foot FunScape, contained all amenities of the late 1990s: stadium style seating, wall-to-wall screens, digital sound, high back seats, computerized ticketing, and a cafe Del Moro serving gourmet coffees, teas, and baked goods. The FunScape featured a food court, a children's play area with giant stuffed toys, an interactive CD-ROM room, batting cages, bumper cars, a 19th-century style carousel, and a host of other amusement park-like attractions.[99]

Carmike (a chain of theaters, also not affiliated with Hollywood) ranked second as the 1990s ended, and along with Regal followed a business strategy of seeking to monopolize exhibition in small towns and medium-sized cities across the United States. In 1999, Carmike Cinemas of Columbus, Georgia, had more than 500 theater complexes with some 2,837 screens. It ranked second to Regal with operations in 36 states all through the South and Middle America. Wall Street praised Carmike's profitability, yet the company did not exist until 1982, when Carl Patrick bought the Martin Theater chain of Georgia and renamed it for his two sons, Carl, Jr. and Mike. Initially, the company operated only in the South, but as it grew it moved into all areas of the nation, into more than half of the 50 states. Some labeled it the Wal-Mart of the movies, and so few were surprised when in 1997 Carmike formed a joint venture with Wal-Mart itself to develop family fun centers to be called "Hollywood Connections."[100]

By the close of the 1990s, Carmike's cinemas were frequently the only show in town. By operating primarily in media markets with less than 200,000 persons, Carmike avoided head-to-head competition with the entrenched Loews Cineplex, National Amusements, and AMC. Michael Patrick installed a pioneering computer system that enabled a handful of managers to operate the whole chain. Wall Streeters praised this cost cutting. Slowly and inexorably through the 1980s, Carmike grew by 50 or so screens a year; the Patricks retained about three quarters of the company voting stock, and thus effective control. By 1988, there were more than 600 screens in 216 complexes in 135 cities, and "suddenly" Carmike was the biggest chain in the Sunbelt, and fifth in the United States. Carmike played hard ball with the Big Six, and the Patricks boldly told the *Wall Street Journal* in 1995 that "Either You Play Carmike or Blockbuster." The Big Six recognized Carmike's power and often bowed to the Patricks' demands.[101]

AMC Entertainment, Inc. (AMC) was no newcomer, but a pioneer in collecting a number of different sized screens in one multiplex. There was a large auditorium (possible 400 seats) to play and milk the current blockbuster, and then a series of sur-rounding auditoria of a couple hundred seats to play whatever else the chain had booked. Based in Kansas City, Missouri, its history stretched back to the pioneering days of movies in the mall. Originating from the small independent Durwood chain, AMC expanded during the 1950s first with drive-ins, then in 1963 it opened the first pre-planned twinned screened cinema, the Parkway One, with 400 seats; the Parkway Two had 300 seats. But they had a common ticket booth and a single con-cession stand. The Parkway cost around $400,000, and was closely observed within the industry as a pioneering test case. Profits exceeded all expectations, and so by 1969 AMC opened a six-plex. Then gradually through the 1970s, its multiplexes had 8, 10, 12, and then more screens. By the time the newly named AMC went pub-lic in 1983, it owned some 700 screens in toto, scattered around the Midwest. Still controlled by the Durwood family, AMC has never stopped growing, but only seemed the laggard as compared to Regal and Carmike.[102]

In 1997, AMC management fostered a plan to convert all its 14 to 16 average company complexes into modern 30-screen minimum complexes—requiring more than a half a billion dollars in new investment. When the AMC Grand Cinema com-plex opened in Dallas, Texas, in May 1995, skeptics questioned this corporate logic. How could a 24-screen complex become profitable in a former industrial area of ware-houses and vacant lots? Two years later, the complex was attracting 3 million patrons per year, and so the Durwoods, buoyed by their Dallas success, built 60 new mega-complexes at a cost of $30 million each within two years. AMC executives proudly issued press releases pointing to company data that indicated that these new com-plexes drew one third more patrons than the industry per screen average. And thanks to better popcorn sales, revenues averaged 10% more than the industry average.[103]

Unlike Regal and Carmike, AMC deliberately clustered its cinemas in major mar-kets, often facing off against Loews Cineplex in Los Angeles, Houston, Dallas, Den-ver, St. Louis, Kansas City, Tampa, and Washington, DC. It purposely left the small-er cities to Regal and Carmike. AMC tried a brand loyalty with its "frequent guest" program, which with regular attendance can lead to prizes as well as credit card advance ordering. In July 1997, restaurant chain Planet Hollywood and AMC announced the formation of a joint venture to develop, own, and operate a set of movie and restaurant complexes under the brand name "Planet Movies by AMC."[104]

In April 1999, AMC became the first theater chain to charge in excess of $8.00 for admission to regular evening shows in Los Angeles. AMC raised its top ticket price in well-off areas from $7.75 to $8.50—in Santa Monica, in Century City, and in Woodland Hills. The 2,600 screen chain was expected to look to this case, and then if it worked, raise ticket prices at other locations across the country. In early

1999, AMC was charging $8.50, and surprisingly, Southern California ticket prices have always lagged behind those in New York City. At $9.50 per adult, Loews Cineplex's Sony Lincoln Square on Manhattan's Upper West Side early in 1999 ranked as the nation's most expensive regular format movie ticket. The Big Six, whose theatrical income is a percentage of box office sales, welcomed news from their backyard, noting that it was unusual for AMC to take the lead in a price hike.

Cinemark USA ranked below Regal, Carmike, and AMC in screens owned in 1999. Its key strategies included discounting and expansion into non-U.S. markets. Established in 1984 by Lee Roy Mitchell, this exhibition veteran selectively bought up small circuits, and so by the mid-1990s Cinemark USA owned more than 1,700 screens in half the states, with the most in Texas. Mitchell's strategy was based on discounting. He ran "dollar" second-run cinemas against pay TV and home video. In 1987, it became the first chain to build a discount seven-screen multiplex in Corpus Christi, Texas. He also expanded into Central and South America, principally Mexico, Argentina, Peru, and Brazil. He and his wife Tandy Mitchell operate from their Dallas, Texas, headquarters. Their first investment, Consolidated Theaters of Salt Lake City, has expanded into a force not only in the United States, but also in Latin America.[105]

CG Theaters, the new name for General Cinema, was by 1999 "only" the sixth largest chain. General Cinema had not expanded as fast as a Regal or Loews Cineplex, but this Newton, Massachusetts-based company was highly profitable, and was moderately expanding—taking on Carmike and Cinemark in the South and Southwest, and Cinemark USA and National Amusements in Mexico and Argentina. The company also in 1997 announced a deal with actor and entrepreneur Robert Redford to fashion a specialized chain—Sundance Cinemas—devoted to independent films. Finally, CG Cinemas had been the leader, in the late 1990s, pioneering the "upscale" theater experience. It called this "Premium Theater," all for record price tickets (in 1999, $12 to $15), but offering extra amenities such as special seating, special and limited access, and a first-class allied full service restaurant that serves dinner before the movie and dessert and coffee after it. The success of the "Premium" concept will not be evident until the first years of the next century.[106]

United Artists Theatre Circuit (UA), represented a sizable chain in 1999, but one most observers figured would be sold in the near future. Few doubted that it would soon be folded into one of the chains analyzed here. Hicks Muse tried to add the United Artists Theatre Group to Regal in 1998, but this $300 million deal fell through. Based in suburban Denver, UA in early 1998 had Merrill Lynch Capital Partners as its majority shareholder. Although the company does not herald its unprofitability, it lost $87 million in 1995, $67.5 million in 1996, and $13 million during the first half of 1997. During the 1960s, UA followed AMC in pioneering multiplexing, but with a half a billion dollars of debt on its books in the 1990s and no prospect for making money, most observers look for it to be sold. Still, early in 1999, with more than 2,000 screens worldwide, UA remained a presence in half the U.S. states and in Latin America as well.[107]

Hoyts Cinemas, based in Australia, noticed all this activity on the theatrical side in the United States and so set up shop in 1986. By 1999, Hoyts owned and operated 1,542 screens worldwide, with 945 in the United States. Regal and Carmike were basing their expansions in the South, so Hoyts invaded the Northeast. Australia is still Hoyts' core (with one screen in six down under), but the new Hoyts was also building cineplexes in Argentina, Austria, Chile, Germany, Mexico, and New Zealand. It has been a pioneer in stadium seating auditoria in the United States (Solomon Pond Cinema 15 in Berlin, Massachusetts, is its first stadium-style theater) and looked to export this new seating pattern elsewhere in the world.[108]

Theatrical Pretenders

Although the aforementioned nine companies owned about three quarters of all screens in the United States, there was still room for smaller chains to seek a niche, and then build on that basis. For example, Edwards Theater Circuits, Inc., based in Newport Beach, California, in 1999 had 775 screens in California. James Edwards, at at 90 years old, bought his first theater in 1930 for $1,000, and presented Howard Hughes' pioneer sound film, *Hell's Angels*. Thereafter, he struggled as an independent operator, unaffiliated with a major Hollywood studio, until the Paramount decrees opened possibilities. Still he retained true to his Southern California roots. He played conservatively, and so the Edwards chain stood as a debt-free company. Edwards was adding new complexes with greater leg room, stadium style seating, larger screens, freshly made pizza, candy by the pound, and a powerful set of digital sound systems. This was not one of the top nine chains in terms of number of screens or revenues, but it was a model company according to Wall Street experts because of its above average profitability.[109]

Wall Streeters also appreciated that Edwards did not back down from stronger rivals when they invaded its territory. In 1997, on one side of a two-lane road in Ontario, California, stood the giant Ontario Mills shopping mall and an AMC 30-plex. Challenged, Edwards opened a 22-screen mega-plex across the street. Both were filled because they played current hits on a half dozen screens, and so fans could arrive at almost any time and see their favorites from start to finish. Both AMC and Edwards recognized 1990s theatrical fundamentals: the intersection of two nearby freeways, I-10 and I-15, and the booming populations of nearby San Bernardino, Riverside, Redlands, and Pomona.[110]

Edwards also led the way—with Hoyts and Regal—in building mammoth complexes with luxury seats and stadium-styled auditoria. By 1999, there were more than 2,000 new mega-complexes nationwide. This trend will surely play itself out in the next century, resulting in some sort of downturn.[111]

Circuits smaller than Edwards needed to carve out another niche. For example, the Clearview Cinema Group sought to mix art films and children's fare. Clearview, based in Madison, New Jersey, shunned the typical blockbuster action adventure films, and instead tried to find fare for senior citizens, empty nesters, and parents with small children who did not approve of violence or sex in the movies. Clearview targeted selected affluent suburban communities, starting in New Jersey and New York, and then expanding into New England and the Middle Atlantic states. In 1997, the company had less than 100 screens, but planned on expanding to 300 by 2000.[112]

Smaller still, but also niche driven by changing demographics, was a chain of complexes owned by former professional basketball star Magic Johnson. Johnson started in 1994 with a 50-50 partnership with Sony to develop Magic Johnson Theaters in predominantly Black middle-class neighborhoods. The first complex was in Los Angeles and the second was built in Atlanta. Then a third opened in Houston, Texas, and a fourth in Carson, California. Getting the films, with Sony's backing, was easy; securing prime space in shopping centers was far more difficult. Targeting an emerging African American middle class is the chain's special niche.[113]

And in rarer cases, the art house strategy was still at play in 1999. Typical in this vein was Laemmle Theatres, a family-owned chain of two dozen or so screens located in Los Angeles, California. Two generations of Laemmles—son of the founder, Robert, and his son Gregory—stick to their niche of foreign films. After 40 years in the business, the low cost family operation successfully counters the Hollywood blockbuster with foreign and independent film screenings. Laemmle also rode the wave of growing interest in films of all sorts, and doubled in size during the 1990s. This is proof that this sector of the film business is not as concentrated as the production and distribution side dominated by the Big Six.[114]

These examples represent the range of companies, but they hardly present a comprehensive analysis of every theater circuit in the United States. See the Web site at www.boxoffice.com for a complete up-to-date listing. The theatrical market reamins far too fluid—with numerous deals, mergers, and takeovers every year—that there will surely continue to be new entrants, both large and small. These independent regional chains that mark ownership of this segment of the film industry mean this sector will remain far more open than the major studios.

PAY TV

Broadcast TV channels have been showing old films since the mid-1950s, but by the early 1980s, it was Time Warner's HBO that revolutionized the film business. People paid about $10 a month to see uncut, full-length, noncensored versions of films that had completed their theatrical runs. Fans finally had an alternative to going to a movie house. Yet the demand for pay TV crested in about 1990, as home video grew steadily more important. In 1999, this window was becoming more compressed. But, with nearly $5 billion flowing into the pay TV giants in the late 1990s, this "after market" was surely no trivial portion of the multiple lives of a feature film.[115]

Two of the Big Six dominated pay TV through vertical integration: Viacom with its Showtime and The Movie Channel, and Time Warner with its HBO and Cinemax. HBO had long been the leader. In retrospect, HBO's success should not have been surprising. In one survey, taken in the mid-1970s, in the days before cable television became widespread, sample respondents were asked what they most disliked about film showings on TV broadcast networks. There were only two significant answers: constant advertisement interruptions and the long wait for blockbusters to appear. HBO solved both these problems, and more.

HBO began as a microwave service in 1972. It was not until 1975 when it went to satellite distribution that HBO sparked interest in cable television. In one of the most productive investments in television history, Time Inc. gambled $7.5 million on a five-year lease to put HBO on RCA's satellite, Satcom I, even before the satellite had been launched. HBO commenced satellite national distribution in September 1975, and moved from a base of 300,000 to 6 million subscribers. By giving its subscribers uncut, uninterrupted movies a few months after they had disappeared from theaters, growth during the late 1970s and into the early 1980s proved nothing less than spectacular. By 1983, the company could claim 12 million subscribers, and as a consequence, for Time, Inc., HBO's revenues soon surpassed more fabled publishing activities in terms of profits generated.[116]

In 1976, Viacom, then a major television program supplier and owner of cable systems, created Showtime, and went on to satellite distribution in 1979. Viacom later created a second service, The Movie Channel, to counter Cinemax, seeking to appeal to younger audiences. By the late 1980s, nearly every cable system offered at least one of these four services, with over 90% carrying two or more. If a system had only one pay channel, then odds were that it was HBO. By the end of the 1980s, Time Warner's duo controlled some 60% of the pay television market and Viacom's Showtime and The Movie Channel had to settle for most of the rest.[117]

In 1987, HBO signed a long-term agreement with Warner Bros. studio, which led in part to the merger of Time and Warner. This vertical deal offered the ultimate in exclusivity. Under this arrangement, HBO and Warner Bros. Pictures, Inc. would be part of the same company. But Time Warner also controlled the nation's second largest MSO (multisystem cable operator). Thus, in reaction, Tele-Communications, Inc. (TCI; then the national's largest holder of cable subscribers) purchased an interest in Showtime and The Movie Channel, and infused them with new capital. TCI controlled about one quarter of all cable subscribers, and so guaranteed the future survival of Showtime and The Movie Channel as alternatives to HBO. TCI executives realized that after the 1989 Time Warner merger, HBO possessed a great advantage with its internal direct link to the second largest MSO in the nation. In the 1990s, TCI went one step further and started its own pay TV services, Encore and Starz! With more choices, pay TV subscribership increased to 41 million in 1990. Then the business cycle and the substitution effect of home video caused cable subscribers to abandon pay TV; the totals actually fell in 1991 and 1992. But total subscribers began to increase again, nearing 50 million in 1999.[118]

By the early 1990s, the pay TV business had settled into a predictable pattern. Local cable systems charged subscribers about $10 per month per pay cable movie channel. That revenue was then split between the local franchise (which kept about two thirds) and the pay cable channel (which kept the other one third). HBO in the 1970s had pioneered the scheduling of movies for pay TV: Create an attractive package each month so that subscribing households will continue to pay. The average pay TV service offered between 20 and 50 movies per month, a handful of first runs, but mostly "encores" from previous months. The idea was to give the viewer several opportunities to watch each film, but not to quickly exhaust the top blockbusters. Thus, the success of a pay cable movie channel has been determined not by ratings for a single program, but by the general appeal and satisfaction level for the month as a whole. The test was not ratings, but whether the customers kept on writing their monthly checks. HBO in particular became Time Warner's "cash cow," generating well over $400 million of profit per annum based on revenues of $2 billion.[119]

By the late 1990s, pay TV had a new outlet in DBS (see Chapter 5). For example, according to research conducted by Paul Kagan Associates, pay TV added some 4.6 million units over the first nine months of 1998, with 952,000 coming from cable and the balance from DBS services. (Some households subscribe to as many as five or more different pay TV channels, all counting as units.) Indeed, Kagan research showed that for the period from December 1996 to June 1998, new pay TV units rose by 15.8 million overall, with some 3.3 million in cable and 12.5 million in DBS. And many were not just HBO, Cinemax, Showtime, and The Movie Channel. One estimate placed growth for Starz! and Encore at a combined 3.5 million units through the first nine months of 1999. Of that total, 2.5 million units came in cable homes, with Starz! ahead 1.3 million and Encore up 1.2 million. In 1999, Encore had 12.2 million subscribers, whereas Starz! totaled 8.4 million (contrasting with the HBO/Cinemax total of some 34 million subscribers and the Showtime plus The Movie Channel total of 19 million subscribers). Digital upgrading of cable will probably see in the future the pay TV multiplex, that is, add HBO2, HBO3, and so on. As MSOs rebuild in preparation for the move to digital, they are expanding analog capacity. So as more systems go from 50 to 75 channels, there are opportunities to add more pay subscribers.[120]

But that does not say the 1990s have produced an easy go for pay TV. As the Big Six concentrated more on home video, pay TV has been viewed as more of a weak player. This is evident in that the average pay rate peaked in 1990, and then sagged in real— and nominal—dollars since that time. The average was $10.30 in 1990; by 1996, it had fallen to less than $8.50 (adjusted for inflation). The response to the industry has been multiplexing, so that whereas in 1990 there were 5 pay cable networks, the number grew past 20 in 1994. Over two decades, the big winners have been the Big Six, which incidentally supply the films for pay TV and own most of these services.[121]

Will the public respond when on digital cable systems, the total number of pay TV channels, including the HBO and Cinemax packages, offered by the two services amounts to a dozen? The HBO "mega-brand," to be known as "HBO The Works," will include HBO, the original HBO service; HBO Plus, a counterprogrammed service to HBO; HBO Signature, for the "discriminating light television viewer" (a showcase for original movies, series, and documentaries, as well as theatrical films); HBO Zone, aimed at a "Gen-X sensibility," with films, boxing and programming aimed at the post-Baby Boomer demo; HBO Family; and HBO Comedy. Cinemax has expanded to four channels, collectively known as MultiMAX: Cinemax, the original Cinemax; MoreMAX, with harder-to-find movies, including premieres of foreign and independent films; ActionMAX; and ThrillerMAX. Yet although all cable industry participants acknowledged the need for multiplexing to help them compete with DBS services—which have been highly successful in offering large numbers of pay-per-view channels, drawing customers away from cable—MSOs also feared that more channels will further drive the discounted promotional packages that have resulted in heavy churn in the category. Not surprisingly, HBO's rivals at Encore/Starz! and Showtime/The Movie Channel noted simply that in this case Time Warner was the laggard because it had multiplexed in the mid-1990s. The optimal number that will constitute the apex will be decided early in the next century.[122]

The leading premium networks will then continue to compete for the best movies. HBO, Showtime, and Starz! will grapple to lock in long-term distribution deals with movie makers other than Warner and Paramount, already spoken for by their corporate affiliations. Starz!, with no studio owner, will have to continue to scramble to sign up independent studios before anyone else. Output deals (contracts giving pay networks access to the pay window for all of a studio's releases about 18 months after they leave theaters) have long been preferable to strict cash-for-titles transactions. But pay TV has long fought the battle of exclusives, and the one solution has been to produce original movies.

For example, Showtime has long relied on original made-for pay TV movies. Theatrical films will always be important, but in the main they will become less valuable as pay per view (analyzed later) becomes more prevalent and people use their VCRs more. By 1999, consumers expected to see exclusive, quality, original made-for-pay TV movies on pay TV. For example, Showtime and parent company Viacom fully financed about 36 original films, including a dozen family films. This translates to about three per month, or about half the number of theatrical run in the average month. Still, with all the talk of original pay TV programming, the core of Showtime in 1999 was its attachment to Viacom, and Paramount's blockbusters. On the other side, HBO executives have long stated the $24 million spent to produce *From Earth to the Moon*, an HBO original, represented the equivalent to what they would have payed for a roster of theatrical movies. With a pay TV original, HBO owned every hour of the series in perpetuity without fear of expiring contracts, or the threat of controversy over troublesome content. In 1997, HBO boasted an annual original production budget of more than $500 million. In 1998, HBO spent a staggering $52 million for a 13-episode series about the Apollo space missions.

In short, the big winners in the pay TV battle were the Big Six studios, and Warner and Paramount in particular. Their movies played over and over again, and Time Warner and Viacom had both studios and pay services (as seen in Table 6.11). With few American homes left unwired that wanted cable TV, and literally no home out of DBS range, the other key area will be how fast the world is upgraded to broadband delivery. With that extra space, why not go directly to all pay per view (PPV)? Literally following the theatrical box office model, PPV charged a separate fee for each movie watched, just as people pay an admission fee before entering a movie theater. PPV was innovated during the 1980s. In 1982 there was one PPV service. This grew to four in 1985 and to eight in 1994. PPV represented one of the faster growing segments of the multichannel TV business as the 1990s ended—albeit from a smaller base of homes with addressable convertors or DBS access. Entrepreneurs sought to tempt customers tired of waiting to find blockbuster films in the video store. Just as pay cable services had come into the marketplace because of the limitations of movies presented on over-the-air television, so PPV sought its niche based on the perceived failure of home video. PPV was sold as a convenience service, rotating

TABLE 6.11
Pay Cable Services

Service	Start Date
Time Warner's Home Box Office	December 1972
Viacom's Showtime	March 1978
Viacom's The Movie Channel	December 1979
Time Warner's Cinemax	August 1980
Disney's The Disney Channel*	April 1983
TCI's Encore	June 1991
TCI's Starz!	July 1994

*Disney in 1997 was in the process of converting the Disney Channel into a basic service.
Source: National Cable Television Association Web site at www.ncta.com.

screenings of the same "new" blockbuster film around the clock, but penetration was limited and so its vast potential had not yet been realized (as seen on Tables 6.12 and 6.13). Still the bulk of the monies flowed to the Big Six studios.[123]

Yet, even if the PPV universe expands, no one is sure about how to fit PPV into the release pattern of feature films. The Big Six will remain in the driver's seat, however, whatever direction is taken; they will be able to dictate terms to nonowned cable systems, and to tinker with maximizing revenues on films long fully amortized. Common good would seem to require cooperation. Viacom proposed in 1998 that, given the recent developments in technology and increases in channel capacity, the pay-per-view industry is at the threshold of a potentially revolutionary chapter in its history. Some even publically proposed that the Big Six cooperate to work together to make PPV grow even faster.[124]

In March 1999, a turning point seemed to have been reached as the Big Six announced a huge pay-per-view marketing initiative, committing millions of dollars to promote the value and advantages of PPV. The national promotion marked the first unified studio attempt to create brand awareness for the struggling industry. The studios created a coalition to provide the industry with a unified PPV movie marketing

TABLE 6.12
Pay-Per-View Households and Spending, Cable TV Only Households, 1990–1996

	Number of PPV Capable Households in Millions	Annual Buys Per PPV Household	Average Price Per PPV Movie	Spending on PPV Movies in Millions
1990	15.2	1.5	4.19	$98
1991	17.3	2.1	4.22	138
1992	16.8	2.5	4.35	184
1993	18.1	2.9	4.45	233
1994	19.6	2.8	4.63	253
1995	21.5	3.1	4.51	304
1996	25.4	3.2	4.39	358

Source: *Veronis, Suhler and Associates Communications Industry Forecast*, 9th ed., July 1995, p. 167; 11th ed., July 1997, pp. 202–203.

TABLE 6.13
Pay-Per-View Households and Spending, 1993–1996 (Through Noncable TV Sources)

	Number of PPV Capable Households in Millions	Annual Buys Per PPV Household	Average Price Per PPV Movie	Spending on PPV Movies in Millions
1993	0.7	3.5	$4.00	$10
1994	2.0	4.0	3.65	30
1995	4.3	10.0	3.50	151
1996	5.6	15.0	3.55	297

Source: *Veronis, Suhler and Associates Communications Industry Forecast,* 9th ed., July 1995, p. 167; 11th ed., July 1997, pp. 202–203.

message. The coalition employed major Hollywood stars to tout the benefits and value of PPV through spot ads and other promotional materials. For example, 30-second spots featured stars promoting PPV, followed by clips from upcoming films. There was debate among studio executives as to whether the campaign should be targeted solely to digital PPV users or to the current analog business, but what both operators and cable executives agreed on is the need for a national PPV image campaign. Although the PPV movie business generated nearly $1 billion in 1998, according to Veronis, Suhler, and Associates, it was equally split between cable and DBS and paled in comparison to home video rentals and sales measuring at about 15 times that amount.[125]

HOME VIDEO

Surely the most important transformation in movie watching during the latter half of the 20th century has been the innovation of the video cassette recorder (VCR). Home video, representing the VCR and its tapes, enabled movie fans to program their own theater. No one has to be dependent on the desires of a theater owner or television network programmer. In the convenience of their home, individuals could choose from thousands of films. This freedom (and falling equipment prices) stimulated movie watching to new heights. By the late 1990s, a VCR was second only to a TV set in household penetration, in about 9 of 10 homes. There were thousands of places that would rent and/or sell home videos. The domestic home video market accounted for about 55% of atypical feature film's total revenues, with estimates from various sources placing the total revenue in the $15 to $18 billion range in 1999.[126]

Although the home video market was technically still labeled an ancillary or secondary market, through the 1990s home video was consistently generating more revenue than theatrical box office. This is especially impressive considering that VCR penetration did not exceed 10% until 1984. It seems odd to define home video as an ancillary market because by 1999 home video revenue ranked as essential (as in Table 6.14).[127]

Again, the consistent winners were the Big Six. This revenue stream ranked as their largest single source of revenue. The key change in the 1990s occurred when the two top chains of video stores, Blockbuster and Hollywood Video, began rev-

TABLE 6.14
The Video Market in the USA

	Total Rentals (in millions)	Total Purchases (in millions)
1998	3,979.5	676.3
1997	4,086.5	657.1
1996	4,226.1	735.1
1995	4,194.8	682.9
1994	4,593.9	580.1
1993	4,473.6	462.5
1992	4,481.2	386.8

Source: From Web site at www.alexassoc.com.

enue sharing arrangements with the Big Six movie studios. For nearly two decades, the Hollywood oligopoly sold tapes and then others bought and rented them out without having to share the rents with them. Hollywood began to take a share of most rentals in the same manner as they had long participated in theatrical revenues. For example, previously Blockbuster purchased videotapes and shared nothing; by 1999, it was sharing about 40% of its rental revenue with all studios, including Paramount Pictures (owned by the same parent corporation—Viacom).[128]

History

The history of home video is short, but it offers a vital example of technological innovation in the film business. In little more than a decade after the 1976 introduction of the Betamax and the VHS alternative, rentals and sales of movies on tape surpassed the theatrical box office take. Home video combined the best of the box office approach of movie economics, and the convenience of television watching at home. Unlike advertising-based broadcast and cable television, in which the presentation of films is geared to the desires of advertisers, home video is geared to the desires of the individual fan. Home video proved superior to pay TV as well, because the customer could choose when to run the tape. With the HBO-innovated system of monthly payment collection, films are shown over again until the new month begins.[129]

It took a decade, but the major Hollywood studios figured out how to dominate home video. Whether rentals or sales, the blockbuster movie drove the business. In the 1980s, people seemed to prefer simply going down to the local video store and renting a copy. As the 1990s progressed, customers faced lower purchase prices, and could simply pick up a copy at a store. For the best and worst of Hollywood's past and present, the VCR enabled a repertory and multiplex experience at home, with all the moneys flowing back to the Big Six. The coming of home video added an additional "window" (in industry terms), and with skillful adjusting of the windows and time between them, the Big Six employed admission price discrimination to extract the optimal amounts of moneys from greater fan interest.[130]

Sony introduced videotape for the home with its Betamax in 1975. Sony's monopoly was short lived. In 1977, Matsushita of Japan introduced a technically incompatible system, the Video Home System (VHS). Matsushita charged less for the machinery, although it admitted its picture quality was as good as a top Beta system. By as early as 1978, VHS outsold Beta by two to one. Although engineers hailed Beta, the public wanted VHS. Still, the VCR was not an instantaneous success. At first, only true buffs bought a VCR because of price. But from the initial cost of $1200 for a Betamax, the average price fell steadily, falling below $1000 in 1981, and to less than $300 five years later. In 1980, only 2 of every 100 homes in the United States had a VCR. But with the prices coming down and movies becoming available, sales of the apparatus picked up considerably. Buyers in out of the way places such as Anchorage and Fairbanks, Alaska, led the way. This was expected, because they had little access to numerous over-the-air television stations. Surprisingly, however, millions in the nation's largest cities (Chicago, New York, Washington, DC) also began to purchase VCRs. This initially baffled observers because these citizens had the greatest over-the-air television choices. But movie fans were voting for choice.[131]

From 1985 to 1990, the rental market saw revenue increases of greater than 10% every year. By the end of the 1980s, "everyone" had a VCR, and its was a VHS machine. In terms of the war between Beta and VHS, VHS price and the possibility of longer tapes won out. Americans adopted the VCR as quickly as they did television itself. At first the VCR was heralded for its ability to "time shift." People could record a show and watch it at another time. Soon movie watching became the VCR's major function. Watching recent and classic feature films—uncut, uncensored, and at any time one chose—proved the driving force in the long run.[132]

At first the Hollywood powers loathed the machine. They instructed Jack Valenti, head of the MPAA, to publicly declare that the VCR was a parasitical instrument pilfering Hollywood's rightful take at the box office. Valenti asserted that the VCR would kill movie going in the United States, as this new evil machine from Japan would cripple the ability of Hollywood to make top flight movies. It was not until November 1979 that a major studio, Paramount, formally released films on tape. One year later, the rest of the Big Six followed. Looking back, 1980 was the key year, because the major studios commenced forming video distribution subsidiaries. The tape, they thought, should be sold like a hardcover book, bought for a relatively high price and then shelved for repeated use over an extended period of time.

Some Hollywood independents tried to use the innovation of home video to join the ranks of the major studios. Vestron directly targeted the video after market, not seeking to use it to milk more revenues from its well-publicized blockbuster hits. The model was book publishing, releasing directly to the customer via a retail situation. But hits proved hard to fashion. In 1985, Vestron was able to (temporarily) lay claim to second place in video sales. But, in the end, the only way to match the Big Six at their own game was to go into production of feature films. This was precisely where the Big Six held their comparative advantage, and in the long run Vestron never had a chance. Video stores favored pre-sold films, that is, those with the Hollywood publicity and distribution machinery behind them. Vestron created a single hit called *Dirty Dancing* in 1987; other efforts (e.g., *Steel Dawn*, *Earth Girls Are Easy*, and *China Girl*) did not make profits. As a result, Vestron was effectively out of business.[133]

Also during the 1980s, at the retail level, dozens of non-Hollywood innovators took to renting tapes. For example, the Erol's video chain in Washington, DC started as a single television repair shop renting a handful of tapes to their customers who purchased a new VCR (or had one repaired). The first rentals were kept on a single shelf in a manager's office in suburban Arlington, Virginia. In 1981, the company recorded 30,000 rentals; four years later, Erol's recorded 18 million. In 1982, there were seven stores; by 1986, there was more than 100. Gross revenues from tape rentals topped $100 million.

Erol's certainly typified the transformation of the video rental business from a mom-and-pop operation into a vast regional powerhouse. But economic logic dictated that a national chain, to take full advantage of the business strategies Erol's and others had developed, ought to be put in place. Enter Blockbuster Entertainment, a Florida-based company that symbolically overtook Erol's as the nation's number one video chain sometime in late 1988. By 1990, it owned Erol's and many other small operations. Three years later, Viacom purchased Blockbuster Video, and vertical integration by a member of the Big Six was set in place.[134]

Blockbuster Video's growth was indeed spectacular. In 1986, it had only 17 stores; in 1988, it counted 300; by 1990, Blockbuster had more than 1,000 stores and more than $400 million in annual revenue. Blockbuster franchised on a national basis, with big, brightly lit stores with 10,000 or more tapes in stock. Cross-promotions with the likes of Domino's Pizza and McDonalds brought in millions more customers. Blockbuster Video began to open stores in Great Britain, Australia, and Western Europe. Blockbuster purchased many chains and also opened new stores by franchising in the manner of McDonald's.[135]

Rentals totaled close to $10 billion per year by the end of the 1980s. The owners and operators of the late 1980s video rental industry loved holidays, weekends, and bad weather. It was easy and convenient to grab a couple of tapes and snuggle up at home. But success led to a vexing problem. "Everybody" wanted to rent the same tape at the same time. Copies needed to be made with hundreds of "slave" VCRs in real time, demanding a large investment in equipment. Moreover, once Hollywood had sold a tape copy to an entrepreneur, then the studio did not share in the rentals paid by the consumers, reducing its incentive to produce many copies quickly. Indeed, the First Sale Doctrine stated, once a videotape had been sold, the second party owned the material and could do with it what he or she wished. That is, once somebody bought a tape from a Hollywood studio, that person could rent the tape until it wore out—about 200 runs on a reasonably well-kept-up machine. This was still the case in the mid-1990s (as seen from Table 6.15).

Market Structure and Operation

Although through the 1990s, video specialty stores rented the largest amount of tapes, the retail end remained a fragmented market with one dominant player, Blockbuster, accounting for about one third of all rentals. However, they are the only fully national chain. There are a few other chains: Hollywood Entertainment, West Coast Entertainment, Movie Gallery, and Video Update. Hollywood Entertainment ranked as the nation's second largest chain in 1999 with about 1,000 locations and about 5% of the market. Hollywood Entertainment looked to the Internet

TABLE 6.15
Pay Now and Pay Later: Theatrical Box Office, Video Rental, and Video Sales

Film	Box Office Receipts (millions)	Number Rental Videos (thousands)	Number Times Rented (millions)	Number Sold (thousands)
The Birdcage	$124.1	456	19.7	667
Eraser	101.3	494	27.6	645
A Time to Kill	107.3	454	27.1	538
Tin Cup	53.0	345	15.3	418
Executive Decision	56.6	390	18.7	373

Source: Joel Brinkley, "It's a Made for Television Controversy," *New York Times*, October 15, 1997, p. D4.

to challenge Blockbuster, when it spent $100 million to acquire Reel.com, which it hoped would help them build on its 25 million "member" customer base.[136]

The market fragments into small parts, with the top 50 chains accounting for only about 49% of all revenues. The market is dominated by small chains of five stores or less that account for the other 51% of video rental revenues. This is because renting movies is very geographically centered. People are willing to travel a few miles to their local video stores, but are not willing to travel to go to "brand name" stores. Thus, mom-and-pop chains continued to do solid business. In 1998, Blockbuster began to open new stores for the first time in several years—based on the new revenue sharing operations with the Big Six—and so no one can be sure what will happen after 2000.[137]

By the end of the 1990s, the rental market consists of from 25,000 to 30,000 video specialty stores dealing almost exclusively in renting and selling movies. There are an additional 10,000 to 12,000 other stores that rent videos. These are mostly supermarkets, but they also include convenience stores, drug stores, and various other businesses. According to various sources (including *Video Business*, and Alexander and Associates, Inc., a firm that tracks the home video market), the estimates on the revenue from the rental market range from $8.7 to $11.0 billion in 1996 and from $8.4 to $11 billion in 1995. However, in 1997, rental revenue actually declined by 3.3%, but it is expected to recover and grow at 2.5% per year until 2002. Video specialty stores account for about 80% of all rentals; supermarkets accounted for the rest.[138]

The average price to rent a movie was $2.66 in 1996 and the average cost to distribute cassettes is $1.02 per unit. The distributor for non-sell-through titles sold wholesale to retail outlets for $60 to $65 per tape. Using these figures, a movie needs to be rented out about 25 times to turn a profit for the rental store. The wholesale price remained high because of the First Sale Doctrine of the Copyright Act, which meant that once a copyrighted item such as a videocassette was sold to a retailer, the distributor could demand no further compensation beyond the wholesale price. As a result, retailers can sell or rent the item at their will and keep all of the profits. So the movie studios had to charge a high enough price per cassette so that they make a sufficient profit. In fact, before revenue sharing, the major studios only received about 40% of consumer spending on videos. Here is the spill over effect from a successful theatrical release. Fans were much more likely to rent a movie that was a hit in theaters. Retailers prominently allocated shelf space to theatrical hits. An extremely successful film will sell from 500,000 to 600,000 copies (the upper threshold of how many units a film can ship to the rental market in 1999). Alexander and Associates, Inc. determined that an "A" rental title should make its money back on the initial wholesale cost of from $65 to $70 in 4 to 6 weeks. If in 4 to 6 weeks a video is rented 25 times, then that translates into 4 to 6 rentals per week per tape.[139]

Sell Through

The Big Six pushed more hard to sell titles directly to the customer in the 1990s because it meant they would take in more moneys. Experiments with this tactic began in the mid-1980s. For example, Paramount's *Top Gun* (1986) brought in $82 million to the parent company in theatrical rentals, but the tape, priced at a nickel less than $27, sold more than two and a half million copies in its initial thrust and pushed Paramount's revenues from that single blockbuster source to some $40 million. But the corner was turned in Fall 1988 as Universal began to sell *E.T.*[140]

Studies indicated that the majority of people who frequently rent and purchase movies are households with children at home. Children drive the video market. Young children are more likely to watch a movie multiple times and their parents are more likely to let them do so. The parents can choose the movies so that the content is appropriate, something not so easily done with television, and an hour-and-a-half to two-hour movie allows parents to perform other activities. This pushed the sell through market. Whereas adults rent films to watch themselves or with their families, they are very unlikely to buy these movies for themselves. Sell through is to watch over and over again. In 1997, for example, seven of the top 10 sell through titles were animated films and the other three were *Men in Black*, *Star Wars*, and *The Lost World: Jurassic Park*. All of these movies aimed at children of some level. The seven animated films are obviously aimed at younger viewers and the other three are clearly aimed at young, adolescent boys. In the rental market, films aimed at adults perform just as well as children's movies, but this is not true at the sell through level.[141]

Sell through means that direct-to-video movies for children are offered to the sell through market instead of the rental market. These are often sequels to movies that are never theatrically released or series created entirely for video. These include the mega-sellers *The Lion King 2*, *Beauty and the Beast 2*, and *Pocahontas 2*. As a result of this kids-dominated market, Disney is the clear forerunner in the sell through market. Of the top 10 sell through titles in 1997, six were distributed by Buena Vista, Disney's video distribution arm. In 1996, they accounted for 35% of the entire sell through market. Warner Home Video ranked a distant second with 17%.

Demographics can help, but they cannot overcome date of release. It appears that a movie not released during the holiday season stands much less of a chance of being released on a sell through basis. Two great examples of this are *Rush Hour* and *The Waterboy*, which were released only to the video market in February and March 1999. Both were rated PG-13, aimed at teenage boys, and both were huge box office blockbusters, earning $142 million and $162 million, respectively. It is especially

TABLE 6.16
All-Time Top 10 Video Rentals and Sales of 1996

Top 10 Video Rentals	Top 10 Video Sales
1. Star Wars (Fox Video)	1. The Lion King (Disney Home Video)
2. On Golden Pond (ITC)	2. Jane Fonda's Workout (Lorimar)
3. 48 Hours (Paramount Home Video)	3. Jane Fonda's New Workout (Lorimar)
4. The Karate Kid (Columbia Home Video)	4. Callanetics (MCA/Universal Home Video)
5. Romancing the Stone (Fox Home Video)	5. Jane Fonda's Low-Impact Aerobics (Lorimar)
6. An Officer and a Gentleman (Paramount Home Video)	6. Pinocchio (Disney Home Video)
7. Flashdance (Paramount Home Video)	7. Lady and the Tramp (Disney Home Video)
8. Back to the Future (MCA Home Video)	8. Raiders of the Lost Ark (Paramount Home Video)
9. Beverly Hills Cop (Paramount Home Video)	9. The Sound of Music (Fox Video)
10. First Blood (Avid Home Entertainment)	10. Beauty and the Beast (Disney Home Video)

Source: Robert Moses et al., The 1997 A&E Entertainment Almanac (Boston: Houghton Mifflin, 1997), p. 592.

surprising because *The Waterboy* was produced by Disney, easily the most successful studio in the sell through market. The reason for these decisions seems to be season. Both *Men in Black* and *Armageddon* were released during the holiday season when parents shop for their teenage sons. This demand is lacking during the other months of the year.[142]

Thus the biggest problem for sell through was how best to tap into the moneys seen in Table 6.17. There was no better way to introduce a new sell through tape than by a first-run theatrical premiere.

Since 1992, selling directly to the customer has driven the increases in home video revenues (not rentals that drove the revenue increases of the 1980s). This started with family titles (e.g., the various Disney offerings such as *The Lion King*), which were aimed at children for repeated viewings. As of the end of 1995, *The Lion King* at $29.95—with a wholesale price estimated at $15.52—had sold 30 million units for revenues of $566.8 million. Whereas success is measured by video sales if they match domestic box office revenues (and rentals would account for the bulk of

TABLE 6.17
Profile of U.S. Home Video Market

	VCR Households	TV Households	Percent Penetration
1998	84,100,000	99,400,000	84.6%
1997	80,400,000	98,000,000	82.0%
1996	78,800,000	95,900,000	82.2%
1995	75,800,000	95,400,000	79.5%
1994	72,800,000	94,200,000	77.3%
1993	71,687,000	93,100,000	77.0%
1992	70,348,370	93,053,400	75.6%
1991	67,465,686	92,040,500	73.3%
1990	65,356,200	93,100,000	70.2%

Source: Motion Picture Association of America Web site at www.mpaa.org.

the market), *The Lion King* generated nearly twice as much through just video sales. All this was pure profit because the film had been fully amortized based on theatrical revenues around the world.[143]

By the mid-1990s, sales equaled rentals. For all of 1996, consumers spent $21.8 billion on video rentals and purchases, up nearly 6% from 1995. Selling through grew by 7% to $10.4 billion and rentals were up 5% to $11.5 billion. The bulk of purchases continued to be made at retail stores (i.e., Wal-Mart and Kmart), who with nearly one of four purchases were by far the biggest players on the retail sell through side. Blockbuster was third, followed by full service retailer Target and Wal-Mart's Sam's Club. These five accounted for more than half the purchases of videos in 1999. Video rental stores accounted for 18%, led by Blockbuster with its 9% of all video sales.[144]

Indeed, although renting movies was limited to video specialty stores and supermarkets, the range of retail operations that sold movies on tape was much broader, peaking at about 100,000 storefronts selling movies during the holiday season. Every department, electronics, and music store offered movies. And some stores specialize in movies, such as Suncoast Movies. Dozens of Internet sites that tendered movies, such as reel.com and amazon.com, were created. These figures are nearly impossible to estimate. Supermarkets also claim around 12% of the sell through market. But the key factor was that—like the video rental market—the sell through market was dominated by major studio releases.[145]

It is easier for a given store to sell movies instead of rent them. One reason is that there are fewer choices that are for sale than for rent, although more movies were being brought into the sell through market. However, a Wal-Mart and the like needed only to carry the latest sell through videos, because buying a movie seemed to be a different type of purchase than renting. A person consciously chose to go to the video store and take the time to pick out a movie to rent. That person needed many choices to keep them satisfied with that store. With purchases, however, a customer often would see a movie while shopping for other things, and make a spontaneous decision to buy a particular title, whether for themselves or as a gift.

Movies that came out in the sell through format as the 1990s ended proved to be generally of two types: children's movies and box office blockbusters. Because a major studio was only getting about $12 to $15 per tape for sell through versus $65 to $70 per tape in the rental market, this proved to be a classic test of demand elasticity. Will the company sell enough copies in the sell through to make up the much lower price per unit that it would receive? By these numbers, a company must sell about five times as many copies in the sell through market as it would in the rental market. This figure may even be a little low because the marketing costs are much higher for a sell through movie. A studio must take out ads in newspapers, magazines, and on television to let potential consumers know the movie is available. These marketing costs have been known to be as high as $50 million for a popular film. For a rental movie, just having in store advertisements is sufficient to promote a movie, because people rarely enter a video store with an exact idea of the movie they wish to rent.

If a sell through movie needed to sell approximately five times as many copies to equal the revenue gained from selling only to video stores at the higher wholesale price and a successful entry in the rental market sells about a half million copies, then it stands to reason that a movie must sell about three million copies for the economic decision to be sound. If a film does not sell at least three million copies in sell through, then the studio could have made more revenue by only offering the movie at the $70 wholesale price and only selling to video stores. The key to the sell through continued to be a quality known as "repeatability," or a title fans were willing to watch over again. If a movie lacked this "repeatability" quality, then no one will buy it for $15 if they can rent it and watch it once for $3 and be satisfied. Again, for a movie to possess "repeatability," it must be aimed at teenage boys or young children, because these are the consumers who re-watch movies.

The sell through market by 1999 proved extremely lucrative for a successful movie. For a movie released to the rental market, the highest revenue it can be expected to generate for the studio was about 600,000 copies at $67.50 per tape or about $34 to $40 million in revenues. This figure was a nice add-on for an ancillary market, but paled when compared to the hundreds of millions of additional dollars from top sellers such as *The Lion King* or *Titanic*—each of which have sold around 30 million copies through 1999. At $13.50 wholesale per movie, these two movies have each grossed over $400 million from video alone. Although these movies set the extreme, even if a movie could sell about 8 million copies in the sell through market at $13.50 per tape, the studio can generate revenue of $110 million. Even if this movie is a huge box office smash, making $150 million, it must still sell to about 20% of its original viewers to make this kind of money.

For the Big Six, the big problem is bootleggers who copy the film as it nears completion and make it available on the street before the actual movie premieres in theaters. So, in June 1997, while Time Warner's *Batman and Robin* opened in New York City theaters for $7 and $8 (depending on time of day and day of week), it was available any time on the street from illegal vendors for $5 or less. It is almost impossible to know how much Hollywood loses each year from video piracy. The guesstimates always number in the hundreds of millions of dollars. Bootlegs are recorded from theater seats in advance screens for the press, and from editing labs and special effects companies. These "work prints" are stolen. New York City has numerous illegal labs, informal distribution networks, and far flung street sales. But bootleggers can be found in any city, even in front of the offices of the media conglomerates in New York City and the Motion Picture Association of America in Washington, DC.[146]

The Hollywood Oligopoly Wins Again

The Big Six produced and sold most of the movies that made up the vast sums flowing into home video. By 1999, box office revenue accounted, on average, for only about one quarter of domestic revenue generated. And they dominated outside the United States as well, with at least three quarters of the entire non-U.S. market for home video. In all, the total "ancillary" home video moneys flowing were staggering. In 1995, sales plus rentals passed $20 billion. Big Six executives spent as much time calculating where to set sales prices and how long to wait for release after the theatrical run as they did on which movies to "green light." They also closely studied the impact of new technologies; whereas they called satellite to home service (DBS) the "death star" for home video, there seemed to be no evidence for this effect. In fact, the impact of DBS was small. The blips were better explained by scheduling. As Hollywood jockeys for best release position, the top titles continue to drive the market. The boom/bust characteristic of the video market will continue until an impact new technology is innovated, and/or a new window schedule of releasing has been fashioned. Until then (as seen in Table 6.18), the health of renting or buying favorite movies will remain the top generator of revenue.[147]

Indeed, video offered a venue where a relative failure in theatrical exhibition can be rediscovered, and thus lead to millions of added dollars in the revenue life of a feature film. So although *The Shawshank Redemption* did little business in movie theaters, by 1999 it had become a hit with video purchasers. But this exception denotes the long-term trend: If fans "vote" a hit in theaters, then this means significant video rentals and sales; if the film does weak theatrical business, then video revenues are relatively weak as well. But, there are always exceptions, which gives hope to makers of "failed" theatricals. This is where the Internet has played a role, spreading the word through Web pages and movie database rankings.[148]

One trend seemed clear, however: Vertical integration had not paid off. In 1993, Viacom paid billions for Blockbuster Entertainment. It seemed as if Blockbuster was a "cash cow," but that was a false assumption; Blockbuster stagnated. For example, in 1995, cash flow was $785 million; a year later, it stood at $773 million; in 1997, it fell below $600 million. Centralizing distribution and its headquarters to Dallas, Texas, did not help. By 1997, the company that had sold for more than $8 billion was estimated by Wall Street experts to be worth $2 billion. In June 1996, Sumner Redstone visited the video sales offices of his rival five studios and pleaded for lower sales prices to Blockbuster. They did not lower prices.[149]

Blockbuster Video was a great experiment of the 1990s. Since taking over in 1994, Viacom struggled to integrate Blockbuster Video into its Hollywood operation. Indeed, Viacom concentrated on the integration when it sold off Madison Square

TABLE 6.18
Home Video Rentals, 1990–1997

	Rental Transactions (millions)	Rentals Per VCR Household	Average Rental Price	Consumer Spending on Rentals (millions)
1990	2,870	46.7	$2.31	$6,629
1991	3,054	45.9	2.30	7,025
1992	3,140	44.7	2.30	7,223
1993	3,107	42.9	2.42	7,520
1994	3,104	41.7	2.50	7,760
1995	2,925	38.3	2.56	7,489
1996	2,987	38.0	2.62	7,826
1997 (est.)	3,046	37.6	2.65	8,071

Source: *Veronis, Suhler and Associates Communications Industry Forecast*, 9th ed., July 1995, pp. 182–183; 11th ed., July 1997, pp. 202–203.

Garden for $1 billion, its cable MSOs for $1.7 billion, its radio stations for $1.1 billion, and most of book publisher Simon & Schuster for $4.6 billion (see Chapter 3). Indeed, in March 1999, Viacom announced plans for an initial public offering to raise moneys to infuse into Blockbuster Video. By early 1999, Blockbuster looked healthier, but primarily because John F. Antico came on board in July 1997 (from Taco Bell) and cut costs, shuttered 6,000 stores, and fundamentally changed the way Blockbuster did business. Traditionally, Blockbuster bought new video releases for $65 each, and hoped it had bet correctly. By 1999, Blockbuster was tendering only $5 per tape on average and then giving 40% from each rental back to one of the Big Six, in the same manner as theatrical participation. This new participation strategy allowed Blockbuster to stock more winning titles, and guaranteed customers would find the titles they wanted on the shelf. Customers rented fewer tapes in 1998, but they rented more expensive ones, and Blockbuster made more profit.[150]

In April 1999, the Video Software Dealers Association released the results of a $270,000 study on the effects of this recent innovation of revenue sharing. According to data compiled by the researchers at Mars & Company, doubling the number of copies of new releases on video store shelves led to an increase in store revenues of 8%. Bigger chains benefitted the most, and some smaller mom-and-pop stores reported no increase in rentals. If this trend proves long term, it will create pressures toward consolidation of video store retailing. But this prediction is contingent on the stability of the rental video market not being replaced by some newer means of distribution, either a new form (e.g., discs) or a swing to PPV (as analyzed earlier).[151]

Blockbuster became very aggressive, and again started opening new stores, something they had not done in several years. The local chains started to complain. As the 1990s ended, although some smaller chains tried revenue sharing, the studios would not give them the same deal that Blockbuster received. If the studios held the line, and did not offer the same terms to smaller chains, then the large stores would have a major competitive advantage over the mom-and-pop chains. Not only will Blockbuster have enough demand to satisfy all customer needs, but they will be able to charge a lower price because of the economies of scale of operation. Many of the local chains got customer spill over when Blockbuster or another big chain store did not have their movie, but this is unlikely to happen in the future; many small operations will be driven out of business. What is now a very fragmented market will become dominated by a few large chains.[152]

In 1999, the Video Software Dealers Association (VSDA) calculated that about one half of U.S. households—or roughly 100 million people—were still renting videos in a typical month. Home video continued to gross more than the theatrical end, pay TV, or PPV. The hopes were that new technologies (e.g., DVD) would lead to greater sales. Time Warner led the way in pushing DVD around the globe. And a steady stream of mega-hits continued. In 1998, *Titanic* sold a record 32 million copies outside the United States, according to Twentieth Century-Fox executives. And, at an average wholesale price of $15, that sum equaled nearly a half billion dollars. This huge figure might be inflated as part of the *Titanic* hype, but the stakes of additional revenues to the Big Six would surely continue to be considerable.[153]

The video market by the 1990s ranked as the most important ancillary sector of the film industry. Surely it swelled the coffers of those with the big hits of that particular season. For movies with more modest box office revenues, especially those with large budgets that did not perform up to par in the theaters, the video market provided a venue to recoup its losses. This is especially true for movies with superstar actors that perform poorly at the box office. For example, *Sleepers*, a move starring Brad Pitt, Robert DeNiro, and Dustin Hoffman, and directed by Barry Levinson (director of such box office hits as *Rain Man* and *Disclosure*), made about $50 million at the box office. This barely covered its budget, and the film was considered a box office disappointment. However, on home video, it generated an extra $41 million and was number 10 on the top rentals of 1997. Although this figure represented the amount of revenue video stores reported off the film as opposed to the studio revenue, it displays the power of the home video market.[154]

Independents, such as Vestron, are distant memories, but niches do remain. In these cases, sales of 5,000 or more are considered success stories, generally to the educational or informational market that Hollywood has long abandoned. So, for example, California Newsreel, a media arts nonprofit center, has aimed to be a niche distributor of films on African American themes. By 1998, California Newsreel had 40 titles in its catalog and sold an average of 400 to 500 of each—slowly—to the educational market of the libraries and media centers of high schools, colleges, and universities. Of the thousands of video stores, but 200 stock these specialized items. Indeed, Afro-American bookstores have provided the lone consistent noneducational sales channel. Women Make Movies has done similar business for independent films made by and for women. Northeast Historic Film has done likewise for films about and for New England and its population. None of these businesses is a threat to the majors. It simply makes no economic sense for Hollywood to go after this niche business.[155]

THE HOLLYWOOD OLIGOPOLY: OWNERSHIP AND THE FUTURE

The motion picture—seen in a theater, on pay TV, or as home video—will continue to be a vibrant part of media economics. Realistically, in 1999, nothing looms on the horizon to threaten the oligopolistic power of the major studios. The Big Six will continue to enjoy their formidable economic power. Their influence will continue to reach throughout the world, more powerfully than any other mass medium. The oligopoly has learned to thrive in the age of advanced technologies, based on skilled use of media economics. It will continue to operate with its safe and predictable formulae. The Big Six will compete over small differences rather than important considerations of expression. Sequels have a built-in recognition factor, a simplicity of appeal that makes the job of profit maximization much easier than trying to continually locate new films. The homogenization of content and style derives from the oligopoly of the Big Six. And the Big Six will continue their power and this style well into the next century.[156]

Indeed, there seem only two possibilities to disrupt and significantly alter the oligopoly. The first, technical change, always gets the greatest press coverage, but because the oligopoly has survived and thrived many changes (e.g., broadcast TV, cable TV, home video) and turned them into additions to Hollywood power, this seems doubtful. The second possibility is also unlikely. There would need to be government antitrust action forcing the oligopoly to spin off a unit, and thus lose some of its considerable power.

New Technologies

By 1999, nearly every facet of the movie industry had encountered transformation possibilities in recent decades—from production (computerized dinosaurs and other special effects) to distribution (the collection and analysis of box office data) and presentation (a host of alternatives to home video). But even with all the possibilities of digital wizardry and computer video replacing chemical celluloid, the motion picture reels were still made through a chemical film process and then projected onto screens using technology that has changed little. Many predict imminent changes in this 100-year-old process, but the transformations thus far have been small.

First, there are direct changes in the production, distribution, and presentation system. As the 1990s ended, this focused on installing digital projectors in place of celluloid projectors. Reels of 35-millimeter film, which are several feet in diameter and heavy, would be replaced with electronic projectors that use magnetic tape or digital disks. In March 1999, at a meeting of the National Association of Theater Owners, two new electronic projectors (one by Texas Instruments that relies on a chip with more than a million tiny mirrors, and a competing technology using what is called a light valve produced by Hughes-JVC) demonstrated what they can do. The same four-minute film clip was shown on each of the new projectors, as well as a traditional 35-millimeter projector. The technology existed, but no one could predict what audiences might think about the changes, and more importantly, if they would pay extra. Executives argued about who should take that first risky step to pay at least $100,000 per screen (and probably more) to install the new projectors for a system that costs about two thirds more.[157]

On one side, the studios would no longer have to create and ship thousands of reels. Under the old system, each print costs about $2,000, and a major blockbuster requires as many as 5,000 prints. With the new digital systems, entire movies could be sent to theaters by satellite. There would be no wear and tear; no more scratches or fading after a couple of weeks running from noon to midnight. Movies could be shot and edited on traditional 35-millimeter film, but then a *telecine* would make the digitized print, with all subsequent digital copies a "perfect" replica. The new, digital projector would be generating the image from data stored as computer code—the way an audio CD player translates into sounds. Exhibitors could benefit as well. Films could be switched and juggled instantly from screen to screen within a multiplex, and even within complexes in a single chain. If a movie was doing well, then a multiplex cinema could add showings to its other screens with the click of a mouse rather than having to wait days for the delivery of new prints. And, whereas the old system included theatrical digital 8-track sound, proponents of the new system argued there would be at least 12 audio channels.

But major questions remained. The MPAA estimated that the Big Six studios lost about $3 billion a year to illegal copying of films. If a "movie" was sent to theaters through a satellite transmission, then pirates would be able to intercept the signal and steal a "perfect" copy. Cinecomm Digital Camera, one of the companies trying to break into the business in 1999, believed it had a solution to this key problem by encrypting the movie transmission. In addition, to smooth over the huge capital costs of removing the old projectors and installing the new ones, Cinecomm intended to charge the theaters a fee based on the number of showings of each movie. But even if Cinecomm delivered all it promised, executives would not sign up because they did not want to be dependent on a single supplier with a single standard. Change looks like it will be slow in coming, just as it took a decade or more for sound and color to become standard movie house fare.[158]

More likely there will be an early 21st century substitution within "home video." A digital player will replace the VCR tape. In 1999, the Digital Video Disc (DVD) system simply did to video cassette technology what CDs were doing with sound recording and reproduction. In fact, the apparatus looked remarkably similar; early DVD players could play audio CDs as well. DVDs are superior to VCRs in that they require no rewinding and people can jump to any scene in a movie. The assumption is that the price of DVD players will drop, more "software" will be sold, and then consumers will substitute DVD for the VCR as their home entertainment source for movies. Encouraging figures indicate that several million DVD players were in homes by the end of the 1990s, yet there was only a fraction of the number of titles available to be purchased. The Big Six moved slowly because they had spent the 1980s gaining control of the home video market and did not want to lose that control. The locus of action was at Best Buy and Wal-Mart, which could and did sell both the players and the discs.[159]

The advantages of DVD seemed considerable. Each disc can hold the information of a typical full-length (translation: not more than two hours) Hollywood feature film. DVD discs provide far superior sound and picture quality over the VHS videotape system. DVD also promises a longer shelf life, and so can become a preservation medium to store family memories. DVD also enables customers to rapidly access any part of the movie, in the same way that compact audio discs enable listeners to move to their favorite tune. There is no need to rewind or fast forward; slowing down the image is simple and distortion free. In addition, a single DVD can carry up to eight audio tracks and 32 subtitle (or karaoke) tracks, along with alternative takes of a shot.[160]

As 1999 ended, so did DVD's most significant problem. Rival Digital Video Express ("Divx") ended its experiment as a rival system. Divx (pronounced DIV-ix) was developed by Circuit City, and was designed to look like a DVD system save its "rental" only design. A Divx player connected to a phone line to forward films for viewing, and then sent back billing information to a central computer. Twice a month the Divx player called a toll free number at Divx headquarters, sending data on what was watched and billed the consumer's credit card. For a single fee, the consumer was able to view the movie an unlimited number of times for 48 hours after the initial screening. After that time, the consumer paid an additional fee for a second 48-hour viewing period. The discs would automatically—by a time code—erase themselves if the customer did not pay. Between September 1998 and June 1999, Divx had captured 20% of the new market, but lost more than $100 million.[161]

After 2000, DVD and other new technologies will try to capture the home "video" market. In the late 1970s, Beta VCRs seemed to set the standard; but by the mid-1990s, few—outside the professional community—owned a Beta player, even though it provided the most information per square inch of the TV screen. VHS was the consumer's choice. Whether DVD will take off or fade away like the Beta format has yet to be determined as the 20th century closed. What is clear is that the home video market quickly came into being and emerged as one of America's most popular leisure time activities and it will continue to serve this purpose in one technological form or another, all supplied by the Big Six studios.[162]

Finally, there is the possibility of technological effect from the outside. Whether the VCR continues, or DVD players replace them, the Big Six are always looking for new means to sell more "units" in the ancillary market. The late 1990s innovation focused on the Internet. Amazon.com and its competitors—led by reel.com—were converting the Internet into the world's largest video sales center. Why buy only at Blockbuster or the local grocery store when all tapes (or discs) could be browsed from, items selected, and then shipped to the home via the World Wide Web? Expansion of "video" sales via the Internet certainly looked to be a safe prediction for the new century. And for the Big Six this was viewed as "new money." Reel.com did not even go online until 1997, and Amazon.com started even later. In 1999, the Big Six, led by Warner and Disney, began to figure ways to control sales through the World Wide Web, figuring controlling their own Web sites (as in Disney's "GO" network) would mean they could sell directly to the public and not have to share with retail stores.[163]

Antitrust Concerns

In the past, the U.S. federal government sued the major studios and their theatrical chains and opened the market to more competition. For example, this enabled General Cinema to enter the theatrical exhibition business. Vertical integration became a concern in the 1990s. The merger of Loews and Cineplex brought the new company into the focus of the U.S. Department of Justice. At issue was whether these theater chains blocked a "fair" opportunity to play films from other members of the Big Six and were able to use their corporate power to raise ticket prices. In the end, the Justice Department did approve of the Loews and Cineplex merger—so long as 85 screens were sold. This signaled that there was some concern, but only on the margin.[164]

Even 1999's *The Phantom Menace* was not shown everywhere because of disputes among the Big Six and their vertical divisions. For example, the distributor, Twentieth Century-Fox, could not come to terms with Loews Cineplex and so the top screens on Manhattan's Upper West Side did not premiere the film. Loews Cineplex decided not to screen the predicted hit at its Lincoln Square complex, reputed to be the nation's top grossing cinema, because Fox simply demanded too much (in this case, a minimum fee whether or not the film was a hit). This and other "anomalies" in the system were what caused the Department of Justice to open a preliminary investigation of anticompetitive practices of the Big Six in 1999.[165]

The Big Six have so much power they will not let internal squabbles lead to any antitrust action. They have developed an enormous amount of economic power; they wish to remain in control of creating vast profits. But direct governmental intervention seems unlikely. The focus of public outrage and public policy seems directed solely toward television and the Internet. The Big Six will continue to define the basic ownership and operation of the film industry well into the next century.[166]

NOTES

1. Joseph Periera, "Star Wars Merchandise Launch Draws Thousands of Shoppers on the First Day," *Wall Street Journal*, May 4, 1999, p. B13; Ron Grover, "The Force Is Back," *Business Week*, April 26, 1999, pp. 74–78; Daniel S. Wood, "The 'Star Wars' Myth—and a One Month Wait," *Christian Science Monitor*, April 13, 1999, pp. 1, 4; Bruce Orwall and John Lippman, "From Creator of 'Star Wars,' a New Legal Force," *Wall Street Journal*, March 10, 1999, pp. B1, B6.
2. " 'Menace' Debut Sets Record," *The Washington Post*, May 21, 1999, p. C6; "As 'Star Wars' Opens, Many Gauge Payoff," *Wall Street Journal*, May 20, 1999, p. B2; Bruce Orwall and John Lippman, "Return of the Franchise," *Wall Street Journal*, May 14, 1999, pp. B1, B6; Thomas E. Weber and Stephanie N. Mehta, "Web, Telephone Prove No Match for 'Star Wars,' " *Wall Street Journal*, May 13, 1999, p. B1.
3. Paul Kagan Associates, *Kagan's Media Trends '96* (Carmel, CA: Paul Kagan Associates, October 1996), p. 145.
4. Lynn Hirschberg, "Michael Ovitz Is on the Line," *New York Times Magazine*, May 9, 1999, p. 49.
5. Compare this to what was the case in the late 1980s as summarized in Jeffrey B. Logsdon, *Perspectives on the Film Entertainment Industry* (Los Angeles: Seidler Amdec Securities, Inc., 1990).
6. John Lippman, "Hollywood Sets Records Again at the Box Office," *Wall Street Journal*, December 31, 1998, p. B2. See, for current data, the Web site of the Motion Picture Association of America at www.mpaa.org.
7. Marc Graser, "F/x Costs, Complications Confounding Pic Budgets," *Variety*, March 29–April 4, 1999, pp. 7, 16.
8. For background on agents, see Frank Rose's *The Agency* (New York: HarperBusiness, 1995).
9. See the latest edition of the *International Motion Picture Almanac* (New York: Quigley Publishing Company) for a concise review of the year in review for the Hollywood major studios.
10. See this theory described in F. M. Scherer and David Ross, *Industrial Market Structure and Economic Performance* (Boston: Houghton Mifflin, 1990), pp. 199–220.
11. This financial portrait is based on various charts of data found at the Web site of the Motion Picture Association of America at www.mpaa.org.
12. See weekly *Variety* issues for June and July 1997.
13. Leonard Klady, "H'wood's B. O. Blast," *Variety*, January 5–11, 1998, pp. 1, 96.
14. For the history of any movie company, see *Hoover's Guide to Media Companies* (Austin, TX: Hoover's Business Press, 1996). For a contemporary capsule of the company see Hoover's Web site at www.hoovers.com. Know that for detail—without charge—one needs to consult the Web site of the U.S. Security and Exchange Commission, known as EDGAR, at www.sec.gov. Seek out the most recent annual report and most recent 10-K report.
15. See Alan B. Albarran and John Dimmick, "Concentration and Economics of Multiformity in the Communication Industries," *Journal of Media Economics* 9.4 (1996), pp. 41–50.

16. Dyan Machan, "Mr. Valenti Goes to Washington," *Forbes*, December 1, 1997, pp. 66, 68, 69–70; Paul Karon, "MPAA's 75th Year Under Fire," *Variety*, September 22–28, 1997, pp. 11, 16; Tom Birchenough, "Valenti Visit Jump Starts Russian Anti-Piracy Fight," *Variety*, July 28–August 3, 1997, pp. 9, 14. The *Fortune* appraisal can be found as Jeffrey Birnbaum, "Washington's Power 25," *Fortune*, December 8, 1997, pp. 144–148, 152. Juliet Eilperin's "Movie Studios Still in the Picture for Rogan," *Washington Post*, March 27, 1999, p. A4, offers a fascinating case study of the power and influence of the MPAA. For the current activities of the MPAA, see its Web site at www.mpaa.org.

17. "Average Pic Costs $59.7 Mil.," *Film Journal International*, April 1997, p. 6; "Star Wars Edges Past E.T.," *Film Journal International*, March 1997, p. 8.

18. Ronald Grover, "This Mickey Mouse Case Should Disappear," *Business Week*, May 17, 1999, p. 48.

19. Graser, "F/x Costs," pp. 7, 16.

20. The quotation and a fine survey of the current state of Hollywood production can be found in John Voland, "L.A. Production Pace Means Battle for Space," *Variety*, November 17–23, 1997, special Los Angeles issue, p. 10.

21. This historical analysis comes from Douglas Gomery, *The Hollywood Studio System* (New York: St. Martin's, 1986).

22. Biographers of Lew Wasserman's clients usually properly credit him. For James Stewart's appreciation, dip into the dozens of citations in Donald Dewey's *James Stewart: A Biography* (Atlanta: Turner Publishing, 1996). Alfred Hitchcock was another longtime Wasserman client, as can be seen in Donald Spoto's *The Dark Side of Genius: The Life of Alfred Hitchcock* (Boston: Little, Brown, 1983), and Stephen Rebello's *Alfred Hitchcock and the Making of Psycho* (New York: Dembner Books, 1990). In both books, we learn Hitchcock vacationed with Wasserman, exchanged advice about finances and in the end became a major stockholder of MCA.

23. Bernard F. Dick, *City of Dreams: The Making and Remaking of Universal Pictures* (Lexington: University Press of Kentucky, 1997), pp. 203–222.

24. The addition of television production significantly transformed Hollywood. But this transformation was no simple, straightforward matter. Consider that two celebrated "firsts," neither of which led to long-run successes for their enterprises. In 1954, Howard Hughes sold RKO's library of movies to TV and broke a cooperative logjam. Yet, this cash infusion only offered only a one-time fix for RKO, and soon thereafter Hughes' company was out of the production business. A year later, Warner Bros. innovated studio production of TV series with *77 Sunset Strip*, *Maverick* and *Cheyenne*. But, this pioneering effort did not revitalize Warners, and within a decade the company was sold to outsiders (Seven Arts from Canada, and then later to Kinney from New York).

25. Lew Wasserman's role in the remaking of Universal Pictures has been examined in Bernard F. Dick, *City of Dreams: The Making and Unmaking of Universal Pictures* (Lexington: University Press of Kentucky, 1997), Chapter 10.

26. This modern history is expanded on in Douglas Gomery, "The Economics of Hollywood: Money and Media," in Alison Alexander, James Owers and Rod Carveth (eds.), *Media Economics: Theory and Practice* (Hillsdale, NJ: Lawrence Erlbaum Associates, 1998), pp. 175–184.

27. For a summary of this during the 1980s, see *The Velvet Light Trap*, Spring 1991 ed. (issue no. 27), "The 1980s: A Reference Guide to Motion Pictures, Television, VCR and Cable," pp. 77–88.

28. The blockbuster and its marketing is the subject of Justin Wyatt, *High Concept: Movies and Marketing in Hollywood* (Austin, TX: University of Texas Press, 1994).

29. John Lippman, "Hollywood Hit by Sharp Boost in Movie Costs," *Wall Street Journal*, March 11, 1998, pp. B1, B6; John Lippman and Eden Shapiro, "Warner Bros. Cancels Films, Cuts Budgets," *Wall Street Journal*, April 23, 1998, pp. B1, B13; Elizabeth MacDonald, "Hollywood's Accounting Ways May Lose Special Effects," *Wall Street Journal*, August 11, 1998, pp. B1, B4.

30. Dan Margolis, "Solons Fight for States' Rights in Battle for Prod'n," *Variety*, June 30–July 13, 1997, pp. 11, 22. And there will never be a shortage of publicly subsidized projects to somehow get a share of the millions spent on film production. See, e.g., Charles V. Bagli, "DeNiro and Miramax Plan a Film Studio at Brooklyn Navy Yard," *New York Times*, April 29, 1999, p. A25.

31. Lisa Gubernick, "Hollywood Prospects for Gold on Broadway," *Wall Street Journal*, April 14, 1998, pp. B1, B4.

32. For a contemporary picture of modern distribution, read Caclie Rohwedder, "Ein Popcorn, Bitte: Hollywood Studios Invade Europe," *Wall Street Journal*, November 5, 1997, pp. B1, B11; and Don Groves, "O'Seas Biz Has H'W'D Hopping," *Variety*, August 4–10, 1997, pp. 9, 14. Douglas Gomery, *Shared Pleasures: A History of Motion Picture Presentation in the U.S.* (Madison: University of Wisconsin Press, 1992), treats the history and development of movie presentation—in theaters and on TV—in some detail.

33. Chris Petriken, "Pix Ad Spend Up," *Variety*, March 31, 1999, on Web site at www.variety.com.

34. See Tino Balio's two versions of this analysis in " 'A Major Presence in All of the World's Markets': The Globalization of Hollywood in the 1990s," in Steve Neale and Murray Smith (eds.), *Contemporary Hollywood Cinema* (London: Routledge, 1998), pp. 58–73; and "Adjusting to the New Global Economy: Hollywood in the 1990s," Albert Morin (ed.), *Film Policy: International, National and Regional Perspectives* (London: Routledge, 1996), pp. 23–38. See, for older research on this global issue, Asu Aksoy and Kevins Robbins, "Hollywood for the 21st Century: Global Competition for Critical Mass in Image Industries," *Cambridge Journal of Economics* 16 (1992), pp. 1–22.

35. Bruce Orwall, "Summer's Reel Story: Revenue From Films Wasn't So Exciting," *Wall Street Journal*, August 29, 1997, p. B2.

36. The changing relationships of theater owners versus the Big Six studios, and their effects of vertical integration are neatly summarized in Standard and Poors Industry Study: "Movies & Home Entertainment," typically done in May of the year under consideration.

37. Reports of Entertainment Data, Inc., although proprietary, can be found in media reports, and are regularly summarized in weekly *Variety* in its "film" section. This brief profile of Entertainment Data, Inc. is based on material found on the company Web site at www.entdata.com.

38. Gomery, "The Economics of Hollywood," pp. 175–183, deals extensively with the theory and practice of this price discrimination.

39. Don Groves, "Boffo Year for O'Seas Markets," *Variety*, April 21–27, 1997, pp. 9, 16; Don Groves, "O'Seas Video Takeout Makes Comeback Bid," *Variety*, March 3–9, 1997, pp. 9, 22. See also Gomery, *The Hollywood Studio System*, for historical background on the ascendency of Hollywood as a global media power.

40. See Gomery, "The Economics of Hollywood," pp. 175–183.

41. See John Lippman, "NBC's Standoff with Hollywood Studios Jeopardizes Next Fall's Program Lineup," *Wall Street Journal*, October 19, 1998, p. B10; and "Producer's Scorecard," *Electronic Media*, September 7, 1998, p. 10. Sora K. Park, in "Trends in the Supply of Television Programs for Network and Syndication Markets," *Feedback* 40.2 (Spring 1999), pp. 14–20, misses this crucial connection, and thus underrepresents the growing concentration in this sector of the television industry.

42. Erwin A. Blackstone and Gary W. Bowman, "Vertical Integration in the Motion Picture Industry," *Journal of Communication* 49.1 (Winter 1999), pp. 123–140, outlines some of these issues in the 1990s, and while making certain untenable assumptions still comes to the conclusion that the benefits are substantial.

43. The legal basis of this and how this leads to greater and greater power for the major studios is a central theme of John W. Cones, *The Feature Film Distribution Deal: A Critical Analysis of the Single Most Important Film Industry Agreement* (Carbondale, IL: Southern Illinois University Press, 1997).

44. Joan Warner, "A New Breed of Blue Chips," *Business Week*, July 7, 1997, pp. 52–92; Gustavo Lombo, "Creating American Jobs," *Forbes*, July 28, 1997, pp. 222–224.

45. Standard & Poor's Industry Surveys, "Movies & Home Entertainment," February 27, 1997, pp. 1–3.

46. The annual edition of *International Motion Picture Almanac* (New York: Quigley Publishing Company) provides a succinct and up-to-date history of the studio. For recent financial information see the company Web site at www.disney.com—part of the "GO" network owned by Disney.

47. Leonard Klady, "Disney Revives Family Feud," *Variety*, October 6–12, 1997, pp. 9, 12, offers a fine summary of Disney as 1997 closed. For the longer picture see three books: *The Disney Touch* by Ron Grover (Homewood, IL: Business One Irwin, 1991), *Prince of the Magic Kingdom* by Joe

Flower (New York: John Wiley & Sons, 1991), and *Storming the Magic Kingdom* by John Taylor (New York: Alfred A. Knopf, 1987).

48. Bruce Orwall, "Pixar and Disney Set Exclusive Deal For Five New Films," *Wall Street Journal*, February 25, 1997, p. B10.

49. Andrew Hindes, "Will Baptists Break Mouse House Walls?," *Variety*, June 23–29, 1997, pp. 5, 10.

50. Daniel Lyons, "The Odd Couple," *Forbes*, March 22, 1999, pp. 52–53; Tim Carvell, "Who Says They're Independent?," *Fortune*, April 14, 1997, pp. 28–30; Peter Bart, "Macho Moves of Miramax," *Variety*, January 22, 1996, p. 8.

51. Monica Roman, "New Chapter Written for Miramax," *Variety*, December 1–7, 1997, pp. 7, 17; Bruce Orwall, "Disney Hopes to Cash In on Miramax Unit's Cachet," *Wall Street Journal*, August 25, 1997, p. B4. See also Justin Wyatt, "The Formation of the 'Major Independent': Miramax, New Line, and the New Hollywood," in Steve Neale and Murray Smith (eds.), *Contemporary Hollywood Cinema* (London: Routledge, 1998), pp. 74–90.

52. See Chris Petriken, "Pix Ad Spend Up," *Variety*, March 31, 1999, at Web site at www.variety.com—and information summarized in the 1998 Disney Annual Report found on the corporate Web site at www.disney.go.com.

53. Much of the internal working of Disney's movie business were exposed during an open trial where former studio chief Jeffrey Katzenberg sued Disney for monies he claimed were owed from past productions. In open testimony Michael Eisner found himself on the witness stand explaining the inner workings of a company he long had managed. See, for examples, Bruce Orwall, "Hostility Between Disney's Eisner and Katzenberg Explodes in Court," *Wall Street Journal*, May 5, 1999, p. B8, and Peter Bart, "Venting Their Rage," *Variety*, May 3–9, 1999, pp. 4, 102.

54. Martin Peers, ". . . as Bashful Mickey Gets Grumpy," *Variety*, May 3–9, 1999, pp. 1, 102; Robert McGough and Bruce Orwall, "Disney: Lion King's Roar Stays Hoarse," *Wall Street Journal*, April 29, 1999, pp. C1, C2; Bruce Orwall, "Disney Names Movie Distribution Head, Looks to Hasten Digital Delivery of Film," *Wall Street Journal*, April 2, 1999, p. B4; Bruce Orwall, "'Armageddon,' Missing Disney Targets, Draws Less Than Astronomical Numbers," *Wall Street Journal*, July 6, 1998, p. A20.

55. The annual edition of *International Motion Picture Almanac* (New York: Quigley Publishing Company) provides a succinct and up-to-date history of the studio.

56. Martin Peers, "Those Sumner Time Blues," *Variety*, April 28–May 4, 1997, pp. 1, 119.

57. Peter Henne, "A Classic Opportunity," *Film Journal International*, February, 1999, pp. 8, 10.

58. Mark Caro, "'Titanic' Broke All the Rules—And Now Records at the Box Office," *The Chicago Tribune*, January 12, 1998, Section 5, pp. 1–2 offers the best capsule summary—as 1998 began—of this unexpected triumph in movie economics.

59. "Viacom's $ Woes," *Film Journal International*, December, 1997, p. 6; John Lippman, "Today, Paramount Means Just Half," *Wall Street Journal*, November 18, 1998, pp. B1, B4. To keep up with future deals see the Viacom Web site at www.viacom.com.

60. The annual edition of *International Motion Picture Almanac* (New York: Quigley Publishing Company) provides a succinct and up-to-date history of the studio.

61. John Lippman, "Ticket Receipts Are Lackluster for 'Godzilla,'" *Wall Street Journal*, May 26, 1998, p. B11; Dan Cox, "Sony Swallows a Bitter Pill," *Variety*, November 21, 1994, p. 7; Nancy Griffin and Kim Masters, *Hit and Run: How Jon Peters and Peter Guber Took Sony for a Ride in Hollywood* (New York: Simon & Schuster, 1996).

62. Peter Bart, "How Sony Got Tony," *Variety*, July 28–August 3, 1997, pp. 4, 72.

63. Bruce Orwall and John Lippman, "Cut! Hollywood, Chastened By High Costs, Finds A New Theme: Cheap," *Wall Street Journal*, April 12, 1999, pp. A1, A15; Dan Cox and John Voland, "Sony's Coming Out Party," *Variety*, November 24–30, 1997, p. 29; "Sony Tops $1 Billion for '97," *Film Journal International*, October, 1997, p. 8; John Lippman, "Sony Pictures, Clarifying Management, Names Wynne as Studio's Co-President," *Wall Street Journal*, November 10, 1997, p. B17; Tsunao Hashimoto, "The Sony Group's New Management Structure," *Japan Update*, November 1997, pp. 12–13.

64. Larry M. Greenberg, "Cineplex Odeon and Sony's Loews Agree to Movie Theater Merger," *Wall Street Journal*, October 1, 1997, p. B6.

65. John Lippman, "New Sony Pictures Head Woos Stars, Rescues Godzilla," *Wall Street Journal*, March 18, 1997, pp. B1, B15.

66. The annual edition of *International Motion Picture Almanac* (New York: Kyogle Publishing Company) provides a succinct and up-to-date history of the studio. See also Martin Peers and Chris Petrikin, "Get Ready for the Rupe Group," *Variety*, July 21–27, 1997, pp. 1, 50.

67. Andrew Hindes and Martin Peters, "H'Wood Rivals Do the Splits," *Variety*, August 3–July 28, 1997, pp. 1, 74; Chris Petrikin, "Fox Taking Titanic Risks," *Variety*, June 1–May 26, 1997, pp. 1, 92; John Lippman, "'Titanic' Nears Port, Piloted by Feuding Studios," *Wall Street Journal*, November 21, 1997, pp. B1, B6; John Lippman, "After 'Titanic,' Fox Sees Smoother Sailing," *Wall Street Journal*, May 5, 1998, pp. B1, B4.

68. Chris Petriken, "Pix Ad Spend Up," *Variety*, March 31, 1999, at Web site at www.variety.com.

69. See, for example, John Lippman, "'Titanic' Expected to Net $200 Million, with High Estimates Near Twice That," *Wall Street Journal*, February 23, 1998, p. B7.

70. Chris Petrikin and Anita M. Busch, "Is New Regency Deal in Murdoch's Game Plan?," *Variety*, July 28–August 3, 1997, p. 4; "New Regency Fox Deal," *Film Journal International*, October, 1997, p. 8.

71. "Independent Returns: How Investors Have Fared," *Wall Street Journal*, May 15, 1998, p. W5; Bruce Orwall, "Hollywood Champs: Cheap Little Flicks," *Wall Street Journal*, November 11, 1998, pp. B1, B4.

72. Alex Ben Block, *Outfoxed* (New York: St. Martin's Press, 1990), and William Shawcross, *Murdoch* (New York: Simon & Schuster, 1992), provide good background on Murdoch and his corporate building as of the early 1990s.

73. Don Groves, "Rupe's Son Doesn't Lach New Challenges," *Variety*, March 22–28, 1999, p. 4; Adam Dawtrey, "Elisabeth Murdoch: Rupert's Sky Pilot," *Variety*, April 14–20, 1997, p. 106; Mark Woods, "Lachlan Murdoch: A News Man Broadens," *Variety*, April 14–20, 1997, p. 106. Don Groves, "Heir Power," *Variety*, September 8–14, 1997, p. 8 examines the much speculated succession to Rupert Murdoch by his children.

74. The annual edition of *International Motion Picture Almanac* (New York: Kyogle Publishing Company) provides a succinct and up-to-date history of the studio.

75. Dan Cox, "U's Slate: Imagine-Ation," *Variety*, November 17–23, 1997, pp. 9, 15.

76. Bruce Orwall, "With the Help of a Mummy, Universal Comes Back to Life," *Wall Street Journal*, June 4, 1999, pp. B1, B3; Martin Peers and Benedict Carver, "Swap Meet Feels the Heat," *Variety*, April 12–18, 1999, pp. 1, 78; Patrick M. Reilly, Seagram's Filmed Entertainment Division To Report Operating Loss of $65 Million," *Wall Street Journal*, December 10, 1998 p. B15; Bruce Orwall, "Universal Chief Quits in Wake of Movie Flops," *Wall Street Journal*, December 1, 1998, pp. B1, B4; Eden Shipiro and Bruce Orwall, "Bronfman Takes Reins at Universal," *Wall Street Journal*, November 17, 1998, pp. B1, B4; Martin Peers and Brendan Kelly, "U Posts Loss World Despite 'Park' Revs," *Variety*, November 10–16, 1997, p. 10; Monica Roman, "October Lifts Its Pic Sights," *Variety*, August 18–24, 1997, pp. 7, 13; Ronald Grover, "Universal's Soon-To-Be-Lost World," *Business Week*, June 23, 1997, p. 66.

77. The annual edition of *International Motion Picture Almanac* (New York: Kyogle Publishing Company) provides a succinct and up-to-date history of the studio.

78. Connie Bruck, *Master of the Game: Steve Ross and the Creation of Time Warner* (New York: Simon & Schuster, 1992) stands as an extensive account of the life and accomplishments of the creator of Time Warner.

79. John Lippman, "Warner's 'Weapon' Gets $34.4 Million in Solid Opening," *Wall Street Journal*, July 13, 1998, p. B8; John Lippman, "Worried Warner Bros. Seeks Aid From Batman," *Wall Street Journal*, June 20, 1997, pp. B1, B7. See also Justin Wyatt, "The Formation of the 'Major Independent': Miramax, New Line, and the New Hollywood," in Steve Neale and Murray Smith (eds.), *Contemporary Hollywood Cinema* (London: Routledge, 1998), pp. 74–90.

80. See, for example, Benedict Carver, "Reversal of Fortunes: Warner Bros. Succeeds at Mating Dance. . . ," *Variety*, May 3–9, 1999, pp. 1, 101.

81. John Lippman and Eben Shapiro, "Warner Bros. Cancels Films, Cuts Budgets," *Wall Street Journal*, April 23, 1998, pp. B1, B8.

82. Thomas Schatz, "The Return of the Hollywood Studio System," in Erik Barnouw, et al., *Conglomerates and the Media* (New York: The New Press, 1997), emphasizes merchandising and on p. 106, note 43 reports the millions of dollars at stake by compiling data reported in *Variety*.

83. John Lippman and Richard Gibson, "Warner Bros. Taps McDonald's Official to Run Studio's Movie Marketing in U.S.," *Wall Street Journal*, April 1, 1998, p. B6.

84. Martin Peters, "TW Stock Singing Despite Off Notes in Music, Pix," *Variety*, December 1–7, 1997, p. 4; Eben Shapiro, and John Lippman, "Film Flops, Dated Tunes Bedevil Warner Co-Chairmen," *Wall Street Journal*, December 4, 1997, pp. B1, B8.

85. Peter Bart, "Levin Gets the Last Laugh," *Variety*, April 19–25, 1999, pp. 1, 61.

86. Andrew Hindes, "Three for the Road," *Variety*, September 1–7, 1997, pp. 1, 86 nicely summarizes the attempts at cracking the "Big Six" during 1997.

87. Dan Cox, "Dream Team in Pricey Scheme," *Variety*, December 15–21, 1997, pp. 1, 92; Bruce Orwall, "DreamWorks Has Modest Victory With Debut Feature," *Wall Street Journal*, September 29, 1997, p. B10; Bernard Weintraub, "Don't Say No to Jeffrey," *The New York Times Sunday Magazine*, June 30, 1996, pp. 20, 22–23; Ronald Grover, "Light! Camera! Anxiety!," *Business Week*, September 15, 1997, p. 44; Ronald Grover, "Plenty of Dreams, Not Enough Works?," *Business Week*, July 22, 1996, pp. 64–66; Ronald Grover, "They're Stuffing Money Through the Studio Gates," *Business Week*, March 6, 1995, p. 38.

88. "MGM Is Revamping United Artists Label for Low-Budget Fare," *Wall Street Journal*, June 8, 1999, p. B11.

89. Martin Peers and Benedict Carver, "Lion Tries to Regain Its Throne," *Variety*, May 3–9, 1999, pp. 6, 100; Bruce Orwall, "With New Cast, MGM Aims for Revival," *Wall Street Journal*, May 3, 1999, p. B2; Bruce Orwall, "MGM, on the Selling Block Once Again, Stops New TV Work, Considers Layoffs," *Wall Street Journal*, August 7, 1998, p. B7; Rex Weiner, "Leo's Born Again—Again," *Variety*, June 30–July 13, 1997, pp. 1, 76; Bruce Orwall, "MGM Directors To Discuss Timing of Public Offering," *Wall Street Journal*, August 1, 1997, p. B2; David McClintick, "Third Try at the Club," *Forbes*, December 15, 1997, pp. 218–221, 226, 228–230, 234, 236–237; Martin Peters, "Lion Roars Down Bumpy Road," *Variety*, November 17–23, 1997, pp. 18, 23; Bruce Orwall, "Kerkorian To Buy 30% of MGM Issue for $75 Million," *Wall Street Journal*, November 11, 1997, p. B6; "MGM Gets Tepid Response To Initial Stock Offering," *Wall Street Journal*, November 14, 1997, p. B6.

90. See Douglas Gomery, *Shared Pleasures: A History of Movie Presentation in the United States* (Madison: University of Wisconsin Press, 1992) for the background on how this vertical integration strategy worked in the past, and how it seemed to be working as the 1990s commenced.

91. "Cineplex Odeon Merges with Loews," *Film Journal International*, November, 1997, p. 8; Larry M. Greenberg, "Cineplex Odeon and Sony's Loews Agree to Movie Theater Merger," *Wall Street Journal*, October 1, 1997, p. B6.

92. Monica Roman, "Shari Redstone: Family Unity," *Variety*, April 14–20, 1997, p. 106; Andrea Fuchs, "Vamos Al Cine!," *Film Journal International*, March 1997, pp. 14, 16, 18, 199; Monica Roman, "Exhibs Adding Fuel to Urban Renewal," *Variety*, April 21–27, 1997, pp. 9, 16.

93. Steven Lipin and Bruce Orwall, "KKR, Hicks Muse To Buy Regal Cinemas," *Wall Street Journal*, January 20, 1998, pp. A3, A6; Bruce Orwall, "Theater Consolidation Jolts Hollywood Power Structure," *Wall Street Journal*, January 21, 1998, pp. B1, B8. See the latest edition of *International Motion Picture Almanac* (New York: Quigley Publishing Company) for a review of the year in exhibition, and the news deals and the latest mergers.

94. For the history and immediate impact of this case see Michael Conant, *Antitrust and the Motion Picture Industry* (Berkeley: University of California Press, 1960).

95. Christopher Grove, "Showbiz Runs in the Family," *Variety*, December 22, 1997–January 4, 1998, pp. 38, 54.

96. Roy Furchgott, "Maybe Nobody Does Read the Reviews," *Business Week*, November 24, 1997, p. 8. For more on the daily changes in the theatrical side of the motion picture business read *Boxoffice* magazine most easily found through its Web site at www.boxoff.com.

97. Margaret Webb Pressler, "The Silver-Screening of Washington," *The Washington Post*, November 1, 1997, pp. A1, A10.

98. Kevin Lally, "Regal's Reign," *Film Journal International*, March 1999, pp. 198, 200; Eric S. Hardy and Steve Kichen, "Lies, Damn Lies, and Corporate Growth Rates," *Forbes*, November 3, 1997, pp. 246, 270, 282, 294.

99. Steven Lipin and Bruce Orwall, "KKR, Hicks Muse To Buy Regal Cinemas," *Wall Street Journal*, January 20, 1998, pp. A3, A6; Martin Peers, "Hicks Picks Pix Tix, Buys UA Chain," *Variety*, November 17–23, 1997, p. 18; Bruce Orwall and Alejandro Bodipo-Memba, "Hicks, Muse Reaches Definitive Pact To Buy United Artists Theatre Group," *Wall Street Journal*, November 13, 1997, p. B10; Bruce Orwall, "UA Theatre Circuit Is Screening Its Options as Consolidation Nears," *Wall Street Journal*, August 19, 1997, p. B6; "Regal Acquires Cobb Circuit," *Film Journal International*, July 1997, p. 8; David Schaum, "Entertainment Digest," *Film Journal International*, November 1997, p. 197; "Regal Opens 38 Screens Plus FunScape," *Film Journal International*, July, 1997, p. 144.

100. "Carmike's Venture," *Film Journal International*, May 1997, p. 6; for current information see the company's web site at www.carmike.com.

101. Anita Sharpe, "Last Picture Show," *Wall Street Journal*, July 12, 1995, p. A1; Jennifer Reingold, "Carmike Cinemas: It Always Plays in Peoria," *Financial World*, March 14, 1995, p. 51; Jennifer Pendelton, "Chain Sees Possibilities in Midst of Recession," *Variety*, March 30, 1992, p. 51.

102. Barry Henderson, "AMC Bets on Theater Allure Over Couch," *Kansas City Business Journal*, March 25, 1994, p. 3.

103. Kevin Helliker, "Monster Movie Theaters Invade Cinema Landscape," *Wall Street Journal*, May 13, 1997, pp. B1, B13.

104. Andreas Fuchs, "Welcome to Planet Movies," *Film Journal International*, September 1997, pp. 12, 14, 102.

105. Andreas Fuchs, " 'Front Row' Mitchells," *Film Journal International*, November 1997, pp. 148, 150, 152, 154.

106. Dennis Blank, "The Movie Theater is a Steakhouse," *Business Week*, May 17, 1999, p. 8; "Redford in General Cinema Pact," *Film Journal International*, October, 1997, p. 8; David Schaum, "Entertainment Digest," *Film Journal International*, November 1997, p. 82; Jeffrey Krasner, "GC Net Drops As Box Office Proves Tepid," *Wall Street Journal*, August 20, 1997, p. B12; "General Cinema at 75," series of articles written by and about the company, *Variety*, December 22, 1997–January 4, 1998, pp. 37–54.

107. Bruce Orwall, "Hicks Muse Terminates Its Agreement To Buy United Artists for $300 Million," *Wall Street Journal*, February 23, 1998, p. B7. See also the United Artists' corporate Web site at www.uatc.com.

108. Sandy George, "Aussie Players: A Comprehensive Look," *Film Journal International*, April, 1999, p. 32. For more on Hoyts see *Boxoffice* magazine Web site at www.boxoff.com.

109. Robert La Franco, "My Multiplex Is Bigger Than Your Multiplex," *Forbes*, February 24, 1997, pp. 50–52.

110. Peter Henne, "Dueling Megaplexes," *Film Journal International*, June 1997, pp. 10, 82; Ronald Grover, "Now Playing on Screen 29. . . ," *Business Week*, July 7, 1997, p. 46.

111. Nancy D. Holt, "Attack of the Giant Theaters," *Wall Street Journal*, March 4, 1998, p. B8; Andrew Fuchs, "First Class Moviegoing," *Film Journal International*, June 1998, pp. 24, 26. See the latest *Film Journal* and *Boxoffice* trade publications for descriptions of the newest megaplexes.

112. Dwight Oestricher, "Clearview Cinema Offers a Mixed Fare of Films for Generally Affluent Groups," *Wall Street Journal*, September 29, 1997, p. B9G.

113. Monica Roman, "Exhibs Adding Fuel to Urban Renewal," *Variety*, April 21–27, 1997, pp. 9, 16; Ann Carrns, "Magic Johnson's Theaters: Slow Motion," *Wall Street Journal*, July 9, 1997, pp. B1, B8; "Magic Johnson Opens in Carson, CA," *Film Journal International*, December 1997, p. 128.

114. Peter Henne, "The Laemmle Difference," *Film Journal International*, August 1997, pp. 22, 153.

115. See "Video Retailers: An Annual Report in the Home Video Market 1997; Industry Overview," *Video Business*, July 14, 1997, p. S8 plus the vast amount of information found on the National Cable Television Association Web site at www.ncta.com.

116. The history of HBO is vividly told in George Mair, *Inside HBO* (New York: Dodd, Mead, 1988), and Curtis Prendergast, *The World of Time Inc: The Intimate History of a Changing Enterprise*,

1960–1980 (New York: Atheneum, 1986). See also the HBO at 25 special section in weekly *Variety*, November 3–9, 1997, pp. 35–80.

117. For more on this history see Douglas Gomery, *Shared Pleasures* (Madison: University of Wisconsin Press, 1992).

118. This survey is based on "Pay Cable: 1978–1995," and "Current Estimates," found as part of the excellent Web site of the NCTA at www.ncta.com.

119. Elizabeth Lesley Stevens, "Call It Home Buzz Office," *Business Week*, December 8, 1997, pp. 77, 80.

120. Mike Reynolds, "Few Cable Gains For Premium TV," *Cable World*, November 30, 1998, Web site at www.cableworld.com.

121. Information from National Cable Television Association Web site at www.ncta.com.

122. Charles Paikert, "HBO Unveils 'The Works' Multiplex," *MultiChannel News*, April 13, 1998, Web site at www.multichannel.com.

123. Kim Mitchell, "The State of Pay TV," *Cable World*, October 13, 1997, pp. 22, 30. Regina Mathews," "Pay Nets Eye Land Grab for Titles," *MultiChannel News*, November 30, 1998, Web site at www.multichannel.com. See also Patricia E. Bauer, "Young and Impulsive: Pay-Per-View Projected Growth," *Channels*, May, 1987, pp. 50–51.

124. Matt Stump, "Kagan: Cable's PPV Revenue Expected To Hit $1.8B By 2001," *Cable World*, April 21, 1997, p. 35. See also the complete special supplement "PPV 2000" as part of *Multichannel News*, April 7, 1997.

125. R. Thomas Umstead, "PPV-Movie Push," *Multichannel News*, March 8, 1999, Web site at www.multichannel.com.

126. See "The Market: An Annual Report on the Home Video Market 1997; Industry Overview," *Video Business*, July 14, 1997, p. S4; Dan Alaimo, "Keeping Pace in the Race: Supermarkets Share of the Video Market," *Supermarket News*, April 13, 1998, p. 53. For current data see the statistical portrait found on the Motion Picture Association of America Web site at www.mpaa.org.

127. "Video Spending Will Grow at 6.3% Rate, Veronis, Shuler Says," *Video Week*, November 9, 1998, p. S4.

128. FCC, In the Matter of Annual Assessment of the Status of Competition in Markets for the Delivery of Video Programming, Fifth Annual Report, Adopted: December 17, 1998; Released: December 23, 1998 on www.fcc.gov, pp. 68–69, which relies on Kagan data, as well as Adams Media Research, Video Software Dealers Association research, and information from the Motion Picture Association of America.

129. This abbreviated history is based on Gomery, *Shared Pleasures* (Madison: University of Wisconsin Press, 1992).

130. See B. C. Klopfenstein, "The Diffusion of the VCR in the United States," in Mark R. Levy (ed.), *The VCR Age: Home Video and Mass Communication* (Newbury Park, CA: Sage, 1989), pp. 21–39; C. A. Lin, "The Function of the VCR in the Home Leisure Environment," *Journal of Broadcasting and Electronic Media*, 36.3, pp. 345–351.

131. For a wonderful journalistic account of the invention and innovation of the VCR and Hollywood's reluctance see James Lardner, *Fast Forward: Hollywood, the Japanese, and the Onslaught of the VCR* (New York: W. W. Norton, 1987).

132. During the innovation and diffusion of home video a body of literature did arise seeking to understand its implications in the Hollywood feature film marketplace. See, for example, Richard Butsch, "Home Video and Corporate Plans: Capital's Limited Power to Manipulate Leisure," in Richard Butsch (ed.), *For Fun and Profit: The Transformation of Leisure into Consumption* (Philadelphia: Temple University Press, 1990), pp. 215–235; Gladys D. Ganley and Oswald H. Ganley, *Global Political Fallout: The First Decade of the VCR, 1976–1985* (Norwood, NJ: Ablex, 1987); Frederick Wasser, "Flexible Home Entertainment: Hollywood's Response to Home Video," unpublished PhD Dissertation, University of Illinois, 1996.

133. "Vestron Claims Major Status," *Variety*, January 4, 1984, p. 57; Megumi Komiya and Barry Litman, "The Economics of the Prerecorded Videocassette Industry," in Julie R. Dobrow (ed.), *Social and Cultural Aspects of VCR Use* (Hillsdale, NJ: Lawrence Erlbaum Associates, 1990), p. 29; Anne Thompson, "Another Indy Bites the Dust," *Los Angeles Weekly*, August 4, 1989, p. 1.

134. James D. Moser (ed.), *International Television & Video Almanac—1997*, 42nd edition (New York: Quigley Publishing Company, 1997), p. 15A.

135. Bruce C. Klopfenstein, "The Diffusion of the VCR in the USA," in Mark R. Levy (ed.), *The VCR Age: Home Video and Mass Communication* (Newbury Park, CA: Sage, 1989), pp. 21–39.

136. See "The Annual Report on the Home Video Market," *PRC News*, August 10, 1998, p. 3; "Hollywood Entertainment: On-Line Video Marketer Bought for $100 Million," *Wall Street Journal*, July 31, 1998, p. B12.

137. David Segal, "Fast Forward Deals: Blockbuster Video Thrives on Arrangements With Studios," *Washington Post*, September 15, 1998, pp. C1, C12.

138. Dan Alaimo, "Keeping Pace in the Race: Supermarkets Share of the Video Market," *Supermarket News*, April 13, 1998, p. 53; Alexander and Associates Web page at www.alexassoc.com.

139. See Web site of Alexander and Associates at www.alexassoc.com.

140. Dan Steinbock, *Triumph and Erosion in the American Media and Entertainment Industries* (London: Quorum Books, 1995), pp. 112–114; "Video Spending Will Grow at 6.3% Rate, Veronis, Shuler Says," *Video Week*, November 9, 1998, p. S4.

141. "Video Spending Will Grow at 6.3% Rate, Veronis, Shuler Says," *Video Week*, November 9, 1998, p. S4.

142. Marcy Magiera and Amy Innerfield, "Buena Vista and Warner Lead in 1996 Video Market Share," *Video Business*, January 13, 1997, p. 6.

143. Paul Kagan Associates, *Kagan's Media Trends '96* (Carmel, CA: Paul Kagan Associates, October, 1996), p. 106.

144. Seth Goldstein, "Home Video Finds a Lower Spot on Media Food Chain," *Billboard*, October 25, 1997, p. 92; Seth Goldstein and Eileen Fitzpatrick," "Sell-Thru Vid Sector Moves Beyond 'G'-Title Stronghold," *Billboard*, July 12, 1997, pp. 1, 99; Don Jeffrey, "Home Video Sell Through Numbers Up At Year's End," *Billboard*, April 5, 1997, pp. 6, 93.

145. Dan Alaimo, "Keeping Pace in the Race: Supermarkets Share of the Video Market," *Supermarket News*, April 13, 1998, p. 53.

146. See Web site at www.mpaa.com.

147. See "Top 10 Video Titles," and "Coming Attractions," both regularly found on the Web site of the Video Software Dealers Association at www.vsda.com. Annual reports of the estimated number of videos rented and sold can be found on the Web site of Alexander & Associates at www.alexassoc.com.

148. Stephen Schurr, "Shawshank's Redemption: How a Movie Found an Afterlife," *Wall Street Journal*, April 30, 1999, pp. B1, B4.

149. "Video Retailers: An Annual Report in the Home Video Market 1997; Industry Overview," *Video Business*, July 14, 1997, p. S8; Stephanie Anderson Forest, Gail Degeorge, and Kathleen Morris, "The Script Doctor Is In at Blockbuster—Again," *Business Week*, July 28, 1997, pp. 101–102.

150. Richard Siklos, "Blockbuster Finally Gets It Right," *Business Week*, March 8, 1999, pp. 64, 66; Leslie Cauley, "Blockbuster Set to Boost Cache of New Movies," *Wall Street Journal*, January 14, 1999, p. B8; Eben Shapiro, "Blockbuster's Return Is on Fast Forward," *Wall Street Journal*, April 7, 1998, p. A3; Eben Shapiro, "Blockbuster Seeks a New Deal with Hollywood," *Wall Street Journal*, March 25, 1998, p. B1, B6; Brett Sporich, "Blockbuster Tries Revenue Sharing," *Multichannel News*, April 20, 1998, p. 62.

151. Paul Sweeting, "Widening the Video Gap," *Variety*, April 5–11, 1999, p. 18. See also Web site at www.vsda.com.

152. David Segal, "Fast Forward Deals: Blockbuster Video Thrives on Arrangements With Studios," *Washington Post*, September 15, 1998, pp. C1, C12.

153. See Don Groves, "Clearer Picture for O'Seas Vid," *Variety*, February 22–28, 1999, pp. 9, 15. DVD was surely a hot new technology during the late 1990s, but no one then was sure of its future impact. See John Voland, "Compu-phile Confab Soars with DVD Demos," *Variety*, November 24–30, 1997, p. 16; Paul Karon, "Helmers Hail Era of Digital Videodisc," *Variety*, November 10–18, 1997, pp. 5–6.

154. "Video Spending Will Grow at 6.3% Rate, Veronis, Shuler Says," *Video Week*, November 9, 1998, p. 4.

155. See *NVR Reports*, issue #21, Winter 1998, the entire issue, for the case studies of five independents.

156. See the work of Jonathan D. Levy and Florence O. Setzer, economists at the FCC, most easily accessed as Jonathan D. Levy, "Evolution and Competition in the American Video Marketplace," in Albert Morin (ed.), *Film Policy: International, National, and Regional Perspectives* (London: Routledge, 1996), pp. 39–61. Earlier reports by both Levy and Setzer include "Broadcast Television in a Multichannel Marketplace," Working Paper 26, FCC's Office of Plans and Policy, 1991 & "Measurement of Concentration in the Home Video Markets," FCC Office of Plans and Policy Staff Report, 1982.

157. Peter Henne, "Introducing the Dream Catcher," *Film Journal International*, March, 1999, pp. 52–53.

158. Nick Wingfield, "Farewell to Film," *Wall Street Journal*, March 22, 1999, p. R13. The same issues surrounded the coming of sound during the late 1920s as Douglas Gomery analyzed in "The Coming of Sound: Technological Change in the American Film Industry," in Elisabeth Weis and John Belton (eds.), *Film Sound: Theory and Practice* (New York: Columbia University Press, 1985), pp. 5–24.

159. James D. Moser (ed.), *International Television & Video Almanac—1997*, 42nd edition (New York: Quigley Publishing Company, 1997), pp. 15A–16A; FCC, In the Matter of Annual Assessment of the Status of Competition in Markets for the Delivery of Video Programming, Fifth Annual Report, Adopted: December 17, 1998; Released: December 23, 1998 on www.fcc.gov, pp. 69–70; Daniel Greenberg, "Video Discontent: DVD Wants to Replace Videotape," *The Washington Post*, September 25, 1998, p. A42.

160. Edward Baig, "Movies: Be Happy, Film Freaks," *Business Week*, May 26, 1997, pp. 172–173.

161. Evan Ramstad, "Circuit City Pulls Plug on Its Divx Videodisc Venture," *Wall Street Journal*, June 17, 1999, p. B10.

162. Evan Ramstad, "In HDTV Age, Successor to VCR Is a Long Way Off," *Wall Street Journal*, April 8, 1999, pp. B1, B10.

163. Eben Shapiro, "Web Retailers Are Racing to Sell Videotapes," *Wall Street Journal*, October 2, 1998, pp. B1, B4.

164. Bruce Orwall and John Lippman, "U.S. Probes the Links of Film Studios, Theaters," *Wall Street Journal*, February 8, 1999, p. B8; Bruce Orwall, "Cineplex Odeon-Loews Merger Is Backed by Regulators, with Sales of Theaters," *Wall Street Journal*, April 17, 1998, p. B6.

165. Bernard Weintraub, "Manhattan's Loews Screens Won't Show 'Star Wars,' " *The New York Times*, May 15, 1999, p. A7; Andrew Hindes, "Exhibs Prep for Digital 'Shootout,' " *Variety*, March 8–14, 1999, pp. 9, 16.

166. Lisa Gubernick, "The VIP Rooms," *Wall Street Journal*, December 11, 1998, pp. W1, W4–W5; John Lippman, "MovieFone Sees Internet Growth Ticket," *Wall Street Journal*, February 3, 1999, p. B14.

7

The Online Information Industry

Benjamin M. Compaine

The previous chapters on the traditional media industries have refrained from projections about growth rates of advertising, circulation, viewership, or whatever. The online industry, particularly as a consumer medium, however, does not have the history and maturity that even the cable industry had in 1999. Although the basic Internet dates to 1968, its use as a popular medium for news, entertainment and information dates to 1994 with the introduction of the graphical browser from Netscape. Thus, at the time of this writing, the Internet and its components were at a very early stage of growth: perhaps comparable to broadcast television in the 1950s. As with TV, there is every reason to expect that online information will become cheap, ubiquitous and popular. But as with the TV industry in the early 1950s—when TV screens were small, black and white and expensive, and when installing one with an antenna outside required some degree of aptitude or hiring a technician—the online industry in 1999 will probably look rather primitive in a few decades.

Thus, departing cautiously but clearly from this volume's practice of staying grounded in today's and yesterday's data, this chapter employs more prediction and speculation. The authors agree with the contemporary critique that online advertising will grow from 1998 level to become a formidable competitor for advertising expenditures sought by older media, and that time spent online will be noticed in the viewership or readership levels of older media. This chapter therefore includes the leap of faith, that although the Internet was not a major player as measured by audience or media revenues in 1998, it will be by the time this is being read and in years thereafter. Consequently, it is worthy of considerable attention.

EARLY INDICATORS OF ONLINE AS A FORCE IN MASS COMMUNICATION

The online information industry dates back to the 1960s. Until the early 1990s, however, electronic information retrieval was almost exclusively used for business applications. The Lexis/Nexis legal and news database started by Mead, a paper company; Dialog, started by defense contractor Lockheed; and various credit-reporting services were among the earliest and priciest players.

In 1979, the British Post Office, which then ran the telephone system, introduced Prestel in the United Kingdom. It was a consumer online service that combined the television set as a dumb terminal, connected via dial-up telephone lines to a central computer database. Data was accessed via a keypad similar to today's television remote controls. The system was menu driven: Users had to "drill down" from screen to screen using numbered menu choices to find ever-more-specific information. What was most innovative was the use of color and graphics, although primitive by today's standards. At its peak in 1986, Prestel had about 74,000 subscribers in the United Kingdom and monthly "frame" accesses of about 11 million.[1]

Prestel spawned a rush to similar, although technologically incompatible, ventures: Telidon in Canada, Viewtron and Viewdata in the United States, and most prominently, Minitel in France. All were closed, proprietary systems. All were based on powerful (for the time) central computers to send data to dumb terminals. Only Minitel survived to maturity, but only because Minitel was a project of the French government, which bought and gave away millions of special terminals to French households.[2]

After these failures, it was not until the spread of personal computers and low cost modems that the online world started to filter to small business and the home. Even then, the major event in the realization of online, real-time information dates back to 1994, the year in which the first commercially available graphical browser created the conditions for the Internet and its World Wide Web to be launched on its way as a mass medium. Since then, the growth of the Internet has been unlike virtually any other communication medium in history.

The Internet emerged in the second half of the 1990s as a phenomenon that can only be described in orders of magnitude of change:

- In 1995, an estimated 18 million Americans were online. In 3 years, that was up 244% to 62 million. In mid-1999 it was 106 million, more or less, or 40% of the adult U.S. population.[3]
- Advertising on the Internet, barely visible in 1996 at $267 million, more than tripled to $907 million in 1997 and had reached almost $3 billion in 1999.[4]
- Data sent over the Internet was doubling every 100 days.[5]
- At the end of 1996, about 627,000 Internet domain names had been registered. A year later, the number of domain names had reached 1.5 million. In 1998 alone Network Solutions registered over 1.9 million domain names.[6]
- In 1996, Amazon.com, as an Internet bookseller, recorded sales of less than $16 million. It sold $608 million worth of books and CDs in the first half of 1999, as much revenue as all of 1998.[7]
- In January 1997, Dell Computer was selling less than $1 million of computers per day on the Internet.[8] The company reported reaching daily sales of $30 million less than 30 months later.[9]
- At the start of 1994 there were 20 newspapers worldwide with online editions. In 1999, there were 4,220. About one-third of these were outside the United States.[10]

With this kind of evolution—if that is even the right word—the Internet (or Internets) may already be very different even in two or three years from the publication of this book. Unlike the mature media industries, the Internet and its components are in such nascent form that most accounts of the players or their position in the industry are likely to be outdated before the ink dries on this page. But the nature of the technologies behind the Internet do suggest several general positions that are likely to remain true:

1) The Internet itself is not and is not likely to be "owned" by anyone or even a small group.
2) The business models for making the Internet a paying proposition were not well formed circa 1999.
3) The Internet is likely to recast as nonissues many of the concerns of pricing or concentrated control of the traditional media segments.
4) In the foreseeable future, nothing on the Internet is likely to kill off any of the other media. It will provide new competition for user time and advertiser expenditures. There will be a further blurring of the boundaries among media (e.g., is video over the Internet "television?"). Older media will have to adapt to the changes in media information landscape to survive. And if history is a guide, they will.

WHO OWNS THE INTERNET?

There was a joke of sorts making the rounds in 1998 that Bill Gates, the co-founder of Microsoft and at the time reportedly the richest man in the world, tried to buy the Internet. The problem was that he could not find out to whom to make out the check.

Indeed, unlike older media models based on proprietary systems and tangible assets, the Internet is a collection of technologies, hardware, software and systems that does not lend itself to concentrated control. There are many places to learn about the history and architecture of the Internet and the development of the World Wide Web.[11] The very short story is that the U.S. Defense Department's Advanced Research Project Agency (ARPA) initiated the ARPANet as a tool for linking academics doing defense and security work with military contractors. Critical was the plan to create a network that had redundant communications paths, so that even a natural disaster or nuclear explosion at one or several links would not bring down the system.

Moreover, the initial Internet was designed to use much of the existing telecommunications infrastructure. And lastly, it adopted the Transmission Control Protocol/Internet Protocol, a standard set of rules that allows computers on different networks to communicate with one another. This was a public domain protocol that worked across various proprietary computer operating systems and "platforms."

There are, to be sure, some major players. To best understand their role, it is first necessary to explain the components of the Internet.

Telecommunications: Backbone and Retail POPs

The bits that compose the text, sound and pictures that traverse the globe are carried over a telecommunications platform that is much like—and in places is congruent with—the traditional telephone network. Users from homes and small offices have used dial-up telephone lines to call into Internet Service Provers (ISPs) who connect to the Internet "backbone" providers. These latter have the high bandwidth facilities that merge the data packets from many users to and from the servers around the world. Larger businesses and institutions may have higher speed connections to ISPs or even into the backbone directly.

POP stands for "point of presence." These are the nodes to which users connect to gain access to the Internet. When consumers have their modems dial a phone number and "log on," they are dialing into a POP. A corporate network may have a high speed line, such as a 1.5 mb T-1, to a POP as well.

The telecommunications side of the Internet is highly competitive at all levels. Although the national backbone business was consolidating in 1999, the retail ISP business was adding players. In 1999, there were 44 national backbone providers, up from 36 in 1998, though a much smaller number was predominant. Figure 7.1 shows that three providers—Cable & Wireless, MCI/Worldcom and Sprint—accounted for 73% of the 6,639 connections from all ISPs. However, this was down from 1997 when the top three—MCI, Sprint and UUNET—accounted for 80% of 4,445 total connections. The number of ISPs, essentially the oft-described on-ramps to the Internet, continued to increase throughout 1998. From 4,354 in Fall 1997 to 4,855 in 1998 and 5,078 in 1999.[12]

As most of what has been offered on the Internet, whether e-mail, chat groups or World Wide Web browsing is essentially "free," the cost of the monthly ISP fee is the major ongoing expense, for both individuals and institutions. Thus, availability and pricing of ISP service is the first point of interest for competition. Most ISPs had some sort of measured usage service until 1996, when AT&T introduced its national WorldNet service at a flat rate of $19.95 for unlimited usage. Most ISPs were forced to follow. Ironically, in 1998 AT&T found itself in the position of being one of the first to retreat from this offering, limiting users to 150 hours a month, with additional hourly charges for extra hours. However, at an average of five hours per day, this quota did not dramatically affect most consumers.

Table 7.1 identifies many of the largest national Internet Service Providers. America Online, which had its start as a proprietary consumer online service and only incidently became an ISP, was by far the largest, with more than 17 million in 1999.

These national ISPs were among 184 in 1999 (up from 109 in 1998) that had a presence in at least 25 area codes.[13] They competed with about 5,000 more local ISPs, offering businesses and consumers in almost any telephone exchange access to anywhere from one to dozens of ISPs with varying packages of price, service and features. In those cases where users were not within a local call of a POP, most of the national services offered access to 800/888 dial-up lines, usually at about $6 per hour. (However, local toll rates and some interexchange call plans in many jurisdictions

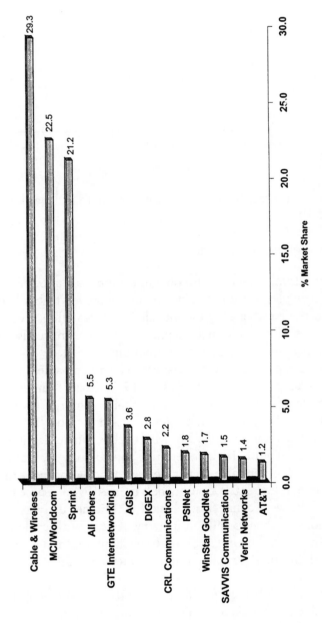

FIG. 7.1.   Market Share of Connections by Internet Backbone Providers, 1998
Source: *Directory of Internet Service Providers*, Winter 1998–Spring 1999, on Web site at
boardwatch.internet.com/isp/spring99/pg5a.jpg, accessed November 18, 1998.

TABLE 7.1
Largest ISPs in the United States, 1998

Internet Service Provider	Subscribers (000)
America Online	15,000
Microsoft Network	2,000
CompuServe Interactive Services (AOL subsidiary)	1,150 (U.S. only)
AT&T WorldNet Service	850
Prodigy	790
Earthlink (includes Sprint)	710
GTE Internetworking	660
Mindspring	393
Cable & Wireless (formerly MCI)	310

Sources: *Boardwatch Magazine*, various issues online; company press releases; Hoover's Online, November 1998. All numbers are estimates.

were less than that, so at times it would be less expensive to make a "long distance" call to a distant POP).

Developments in Telecommunications

The most prominent development in telecommunications as it affected the Internet was the variety of new players using alternative and improved technologies to provide connection to the backbone. These included cable, satellite, electric utilities and terrestrial wireless. The traditional telephone companies have also introduced their own, faster "pipes" such as Digital Subscriber Line (DSL).

The early leader among the new players were cable companies, which started offering access over upgraded cable systems in 1997. Road Runner, an alliance between MediaOne and Time Warner, attracted sizable minority investment from Microsoft and Compaq.[14] It had 125,000 subscribers in October 1998. The other early player was AtHome, started in 1995 by MSO Tele-Communications Inc. (now AT&T) and venture capital firm Kleiner Perkins Caufield & Byers. It attracted additional investors from 15 other cable companies, accounting for more than 50% of homes passed by cable. It had 210,000 subscribers in late 1998.[15] These two and several smaller cable ISPs were connecting about 1,000 homes daily as 1998 ended, leading to projections of about 3 million users by 2002.[16] With cable passing well over 90% of households in the United States (see Chapter 4) and a year head start over high bandwidth alternatives, cable is likely to remain a prominent competitor in Internet access.

Satellite services offer global reach and minimize the expense of upgrading existing telephone or cable plant and equipment. In its first generation implementation, through the DirectPC service of Hughes Electronics, the relatively large down stream potential was tempered by the need for a conventional modem and telephone connection for upstream communications.[17] Pricing was also not very competitive with cable or telephone competitors, suggesting that DirectPC, at least, was targeting its service to rural users who would be least likely to have access to the competition.

Meanwhile, telephone companies were hopeful that the DSL technology that made possible broadband transmission speeds possible over existing copper wiring would become the preferred route for end users. The various former Bell companies, as well as GTE, MCI and AT&T, among others, all had plans to offer some form of DSL to their local customers. The advantage of DSL over high speed alternatives from the cable companies was that it used the existing telephone wiring. Investment needed to be made only at the central office. For the cable companies, all their plant, up to the entrance to the consumer's dwelling, required upgrade. On the other hand, as DSL had advanced at the end of the 1990s, the technology worked only to homes and offices within 10,000 feet (about 4 miles) of a central office. Whereas this was not a problem for most dense urban areas, it could leave many suburban residences and office parks, not to mention rural areas, out of the loop.

The cable and DSL-based transmission technologies both provide two major features that are important to the viability and usability of the Internet as a mainstream medium. First, and most obviously, is *bandwidth*. Whereas engineers may have good technical descriptions of bandwidth, for the end user it comes down to speed: how many bits per second come into the receiving device. If the traditional dial-up lines and modems acted like a garden hose, DSL and cable transmission could be likened to a fire company's hose. Attached to the same water main, a bucket will fill up faster with the latter than the former (other factors, such as the velocity of water in the main, being equal). Whether retrieving a 49 k text and photo of a news headline or downloading a 4 mb update of a computer program, the cable or DSL connection will be much faster than even the 53 kps modems that were the fastest available in 1998.*

A factor affecting effective bandwidth is *compression*. By using both hardware and software techniques, various technologies have made it possible to trasmit more types of content at any given transmission. For example, once DBS services began transmitting digitally, they were able to squeeze five to six video channels in the same space that it had taken to send one analog channel.[18]

High bandwidth (generally meaning at least 500 kps circa 1999, although the bar gets raised as the technologies improve) greatly expands the potential uses of the Internet. Following are some possibilities and implications for players and stakeholders. They are not predictions of what will come.

- It makes real-time audio and even video transmissions feasible. The quality of the sound, the size and quality of the image improve while the problems of latency in the packet network become less visible. Alongside developments in user-writeable optical and digital mass storage devices (such as DVD), this has implications for traditional broadcasters, cable networks, motion picture distributors, book publishers and recording studios.

---

*The difference between a dial-up connection and the wide bandwidth options would generally be far more noticeable in the 4 mb download than in the much smaller text and photo file. In part, that is due to the overhead of getting the attention of the server on which the requested information resides and the set up time for establishing the path from the server to the requester's terminal. This overhead is roughly the same regardless of the type of telecommunications service used. Thus, high bandwidth holds a much greater edge when accessing large files or wide bandwidth streams, such as streaming video.

- It means that software may be sold increasingly by downloads, instead of in physical form. This includes music and videos as well as computer programs. It further makes it technically (although not necessarily market) feasible to eliminate much of the complexity of installing and maintaining software by having only the relevant pieces of a program downloaded on an as-needed basis. This could have implications for software retailers as well as manufacturers of many types of computer components.
- It may result in greater real-time interactivity among Internet users. With high speed connection, video/computer games may be played in real time among participants next door or across the world. Video conferences or just video chats may be as simple as has been placing a phone call. Work at home may become practical for more types of functions and people. This could affect manufacturers and distributors of entertainment software.

Second, and perhaps as important, is *connectivity*. Both DSL and cable connections act like the network connections people are used to in office environments. Whenever the computer (or network device) is turned on it has access to the network. To send or receive e-mail, to access a Web page or to engage in real-time "chat" only requires the appropriate keyboard, mouse or spoken command. This greatly increases the convenience of using online services. If users were truly online all the time, then they are more likely to use the system.

In the dial-up connection world, each time a user wanted to go online, they had to engage in a time-consuming dial-up, handshake and log on process. This was not conducive to frequent checking of e-mail or spontaneously checking on stock prices. Some households, with multiple telephone lines, may have kept their dial-up connection live for extended periods. But telephone companies as well as ISPs regarded this as an expensive type of connection and found ways of discouraging it, either by charging for extended time on the network or by automatically disconnecting users after some period of inactivity.

However, all these and other technologies have been evolving rapidly, so any prediction of winners and losers can change with the next technology breakthrough—or innovative application. More critical in the context of media control and competition is that there are multiple alternatives for high bandwidth connections. Whereas every home may not have access to all the options, there seems to be enough to provide what looked to be a competitive environment for high speed data to reach the home and small businesses.

CONTENT PROVIDERS

Of all the industries covered in this volume, the online business is clearly the fastest growing, albeit from the smallest base. Whereas the business models for older media are well established, the business model for online was still evolving. Early attempts focused on charging consumers: Knight-Ridder and Times Mirror charged cable-like monthly fees for their early videotext services. America Online, CompuServe and Prodigy followed this model with their PC-based services in the early 1990s. Newspapers in Atlanta and Los Angeles opened pre-Web proprietary sites in the mid-1990s with few takers. Similarly, most attempts to charge consumers for content via the Internet fizzled.

The actual revenues attributed to the online industry are imprecise. It was estimated that total expenditures for Web site advertising was about $900 million in 1997 and about $3 billion in 1999. One well-respected source guessed that online advertising expenditures would grow to $6.5 billion by 2002, compared to an estimated $16.4 billion for cable and other subscription video services.[19]

Online revenue directly from consumers is another matter. The trend into the end of the 1990s was away from a paid subscription model and increasingly toward "free" advertiser-supported sites from most content providers. Knight-Ridder's Mercury Center initially charged subscribers to its San Jose newspaper as little as $2.95 per month for the Web-based service. Even with its Silicon Valley base of operations, it attracted fewer than 10,000 people before being shut in 1998. At the time it was receiving about 6 million "page views" per month. Shortly after going to a free service page views jumped 67%, allowing it to raise its advertising rates.[20]

USA Today tried charging $4.95 a month when it was introduced online and reportedly languished with under 2,000 subscribers months later. Most other newspaper and media sites never tried to charge. Instead, the model has been to try to rely on advertising revenues to cover costs and profits. The notable exception circa 1999 was the Wall Street Journal's online edition. From a standing start in 1996 it had more than 330,000 paid subscribers near the end of 1999. Perhaps more telling was that 70% of those subscribers were not subscribers to the print edition. At the time they paid $60 annually, as compared to about $175 for a year's subscription to print the newspaper.[21]

A handful of other consumer-oriented information providers were trying to make the user-paid model work.

ECONOMICS OF ONLINE

Closer to Broadcasting Than to Print

The costs associated with typesetting, printing and distributing a newspaper or magazine represents from 30% to 40% of the cost of doing business for publishers. This includes not only the variable costs of production but the capital cost of printing presses. In the case of online access, much of that cost is passed on to the user: Whereas creation of a printed product requires the provider to assume all capital and distribution costs, to be online requires the user to assume many capital costs in the form of a device, such as a personal computer. Users also pay directly for distribution, in the form of a connection that provides access to the Internet.

Thus, at least in relation to print, the online model looks more like the old broadcasting economic model: the user assumes much of the capita cost (TV set, radio, PC) and distribution cost (cable service/telecommunications costs). The marginal cost of additional viewers online, subject to capacity of servers and access lines, is close to zero. This contrasts with a print product or CD, where there are measurable costs of raw materials, production equipment and distribution. The print information provider therefore needs less revenue in the online world than under the old model to provide equal or even greater service and still maintain a comparable profit.

The online model has opened the door to countless information providers. Granted, many are and will remain small and obscure. But not necessarily without influence on the media in general. In the print world, small, quality journals—such as political magazines in the tradition of *The Nation* or *The Weekly Standard*, or medical journals, such as the *New England Journal of Medicine*—have on occasion set the agenda for the major media far out of proportion to their immediate circulation. Similarly, many small information providers on the Internet settle into similar roles. Perhaps a precursor to this model was the role of "The Drudge Report," a one-man Web service that broke the story about Monica Lewinsky and President Clinton early in 1998. Although *Newsweek* had been working on the story for months, it may or may not have published anything. Or it may have downplayed what it published. Matt Drudge, the site's freelance producer, wrote up what he had heard and published it on his site. It started an avalanche, as the major media ran with the story.[22]

THE ONLINE BUSINESS MODELS

The economic models for Internet media were still evolving in 2000. What seemed to be happening was that the robustness of the Internet as a distribution mechanism would sustain multiple models, including but not limited to:

- *Subscribers pay some, advertisers pay some.* The newspaper model is to derive all or most revenue from advertisers. Magazines tend to derive substantial revenue from advertisers and readers, but the model varies based on type of periodical. Only a few online services had been able to use this model, the *Wall Street Journal Interactive* site being most prominent.
- *Subscriber/users pays all.* The book publishing model is to depend on readers (or intermediaries like libraries or schools) to provide all their revenue. Theatrical film, premium and pay-per-view cable networks follow this as well. Online, this has been the model for the business-oriented research services, such as Lexis-Nexis, Westlaw and Dialog, and the financial data services, such as Bloomberg.
- *Advertiser pays all.* Broadcasting is advertiser supported, as are most cable networks. After some fits and starts, this seemed to become the most prominent model for online sites. Online's slice of the advertising pie was still small in 1998, but it was expanding rapidly. Moreover, advertisers need not be limited to paying simply for exposure.

  The unique qualities of online makes it possible for advertisers to pay based on the number of times a viewer actually "clicks" on their ad and even more if they buy something or otherwise use the information at the site. Indeed, like a shopping mall operator that collects a percentage of stores' rents against a minimum rent, any information provider can strike a deal to get a percentage of the transactions generated by ads at its site.

THE IMPORTANCE OF THE ONLINE MEDIA

Whether online media is a viable long-term option in the media mix is critical in determining the degree of competition or concentration of the mass media. And whether it is today or will be in the near future is in part a function of the economics of online and in part the social-cultural nature of using online media as partial replacement for traditional print, radio and video.

The economics of online involve the consumer's capital cost (i.e., equipment and its upkeep) and the operating costs (i.e., subscription and connection fees). The social-cultural factors address the McLuhanesque nature of screens versus paper, keyboards or dictation versus pens and pencils. The two are related: If wireless connections and paper-like reading devices are economical (we know they are technologically feasible), then the some of the social-cultural nuances could be diminished.

The following pages focus on the economics of online, although the section on electronic ink (p. 475) suggests where the technology could go next. There is a developing literature with discussion and insights on the social and cultural nature of online.[23]

Consumer Costs

There is a cost to consumers even when the content is "free." Users must pay, in some form, for any information they access via the media. For broadcast television and radio, the direct cost is periodic investment in television and radio receivers, antenna and occasional repairs.[24] Readers, listeners and viewers must subscribe to newspapers and magazines, purchase books and records, subscribe to cable, rent videos or a pay-per-view showing. Table 7.2 identifies examples of the monthly costs of some of these media. Consumer spending on media was estimated to be an average of more $48 per month per person in 1999, not including online access.[25]

The monthly total is realistic as an average: $31 for a cable subscription, $15 for the newspaper, $10 for a few magazines for different family members, $25 for a few paperback books for parents and kids (more if a bestseller hardcover is included), $30 for a family night at the movies (popcorn not included), $15 for five or six video rentals for the month plus perhaps a few CDs.

In addition, households need one or more televison sets and radios; the average household had 2.3 television sets and 5.6 radios in 1996.[26] More than 82% of households had video cassette players (VCRs), four times the penetration of 10 years earlier.[27] Indeed, consumers increased the proportion of their personal consumption expenditures on media from 2.5% in 1980 to 2.9% in 1996.[28]

Just as consumers had to buy radios, phonographs, televisions and VCRs to make use of previous waves of new media technologies, to make use of online media they must have access to other devices. Initially these were personal computers but supplemented by less expensive options such as dedicated set-top boxes. One brand was WebTV, a Microsoft subsidiary that used the TV set as the display.[29] And, from home, consumers must have telecommunications access to the Internet, via a telephone line, cable wire or wireless. Does cost create a barrier?

The simple answer is, of course. Any cost is a barrier. The real question involves whether it is a fatal or unfair barrier given the standard of living (referring here to the United States, but applicable to societies of similar wealth). How does access to the Internet compare to the cost and value of other media? Figure 7.2 looks at the costs of television sets from 1950 to 1998. The measurement is in number of weeks of work at the average weekly pay from private sector wage earners. In essence, it shows that the first television sets were expensive: equal to 3.6 weeks of earnings. By

TABLE 7.2
Monthly and Capital Cost of Traditional Media, 1998

Medium	Monthly Cost	Capital Cost
Daily newspaper subscription		
Atlanta Journal & Constitution	$17	$0.00
Pottstown (PA) Mercury	14	
Wall Street Journal	15	
USA Today	10	
Cable Television, standard tier	$31 (1998 national ave.)	$350 (per 27" TV set)
Home Box Office	9.95	
Pay per view movie	3.95	
Pay per view special event	19.95 and up	
Direct Broadcast Satellite	$30 (1999 DirecTV Total Choice)	$150 for dish and one receiver
		$350 (per 27" TV set)
Books		
Bag of Bones, Stephen King	$28 list, $19.60 discount	$0.00
	16.50 (paper)	
Technologies of Freedom, Pool	$25 list, $17.47 discount	
Silver Palate Cookbook	$50 (paper)	
Statistical Abstract of the U.S.	$5 list, $4 discount	
Babe—The Gallant Pig		
Magazine subscription		
PC Magazine	$2.90 (2 issues)	$0.00
Fortune	5.00 (2 issues)	
Atlantic Monthly	1.25 (1 issues)	
Time	4.30 (4.3 issues)	
Consumer Reports	2.00 (1 issue)	
Total consumer spending on all media	$49.33	

Sources: Newspapers: From each newspaper's Web site, February 10, 1999. Cable: Seth Schiesel, "FCC Notes Lack of Cable TV Competition," *New York Times Interactive*, January 14, 1998, plus estimate update. Magazines: From Web sites, February 11, 1999. Book: From Amazon.com, February 10, 1999. DBS: From DirecTV price list at Web site, February 10, 1999. Hardware cost from Circuit City advertisement, February 7, 1999.

the late 1990s, the cost had declined to under four days of work. Meanwhile, the quality improved as well. From 9-inch black-and-white screens with high maintenance tubes to 27" solid state color and remote control, the cost by any measure fell continuously and substantially throughout the decades.

The cost of the hardware associated with online information has followed even a steeper declining curve. Table 7.3 shows examples of the costs associated with access to the Internet in 1999. Based on historical trends, the capital cost of hardware is likely to decrease in both current and real dollar terms, the cost of access fees is likely to decline more slowly, and the cost of information is likely to stay constant or decrease as the audience online expands.

Figure 7.3 charts one of the measures of computer costs over the decade of the 1990s, the decline in computer processing costs. It is consistent with Moore's Law. As the story goes, in 1965, Gordon Moore, a founder of Intel, which has developed most of the central processing units (CPUs) used in personal computers, was preparing a speech. When he started to graph data about the growth in memory chip performance, he realized there was a striking trend: Each new chip contained roughly

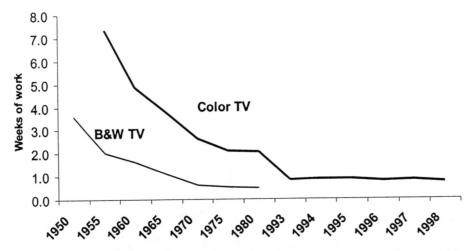

FIG. 7.2.   Cost of Television Sets, Selected Years, 1950–1998
Sources: Television set prices, 1950–1976: Christopher Sterling and Timothy Haight, *The Mass Media: Aspen Institute Guide to Communications Industry Trends* (New York: Praeger Publishers, 1978), pp. 360–362. 1979–1983: *U.S. Statistical Abstract*, 1985, p. 777, from *Merchandising, 62nd Annual Statistical and Marketing Report*. 1993–1996: U.S. Bureau of the Census, Current Industrial Reports, Manufacturing Profiles, annual. Wages: U.S. Bureau of Labor Statistics, *Employment and Earnings*.

TABLE 7.3
Capital and Operational Costs for Consumer Internet Access, 1999

Access device:	Street price (Feb., 1999):
Personal computer*	$878
Dedicated Web-TV device**	$160 with keyboard
Internet service providers:	**Monthly cost:**
American Online	$21.95 unlimited use
	19.95 with annual contract
	4.95 for 3 hours + 2.50/hour
Erols.com (regional)	$19.95 month unlimited use
	13.95 month on 2 year contract
MediaOne.Net—cable	$29.95 unlimited for cable subscribers
	39.95 for non cable subscribers
Bell Atlantic 640kps DSL	$39.95, plus $275 for modem
Internet-accessed content providers:	**Monthly cost:**
The Atlanta Journal-Constitution online	$0.00
The Mercury (Pottstown, PA)	0.00
The Wall Street Journal Interactive	5.00
USA Today online	0.00
ZDNet (includes *PC Magazine* & others)	0.00
U.S. Statistical Abstract	0.00
Consumers Report	2.00
Time, Fortune, Newsweek	0.00

*Compaq Presario 2286, 32 mb w/ CD-ROM, 56K modem, 15″ monitor. PC Connection catalog, v. 207, February 1999.
**At Proactive Web Marketing at www.pactive.com/, February 5, 1999.
ISP charges: from company Web sites, February 5, 1999.

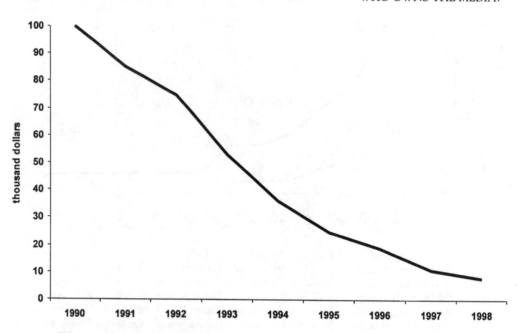

FIG. 7.3.   Cost of MIPS, 1990–1998
MIPS = million instructions per second.
Source: Eva Freeman, "No More Gold-Plated MIPS: Mainframes and Distributed Systems
Converge," *Datamation*, March 1998. Data from Hitachi Data Systems.

twice as much capacity as its predecessor, and each chip was released within 18 to
24 months of the previous chip. If this trend continued, he reasoned, computing
power would rise exponentially over relatively brief periods of time.

Moore's observation described a trend that was maintained for at least 35 years. It
was the basis for many planners' performance forecasts. In 26 years, the number of
transistors on a chip had increased more than 3,200 times, from 2,300 on the 4004
in 1971 to 7.5 million on the Intel Pentium II processor that was the standard in
1999.[30] Meanwhile, other components also decreased in cost while increasing in
capacity: mass storage, modems, CD-ROM drives, even monitors. Between 1996 and
1998 alone, the retail cost of the personal computer fell nearly 23% annually.[31]

This brought the retail price of Web-ready full-featured (for the time) personal
computers to about $600 or about 1.4 weeks of average weekly earnings. This level
was not reached for color television sets until the mid-1980s. By 1999, Web-enabled
PCs were offered for free. They might be provided in return for recipients supplying
personal demographic information and willingness to be exposed to added advertising as they use the Web.[32] Or they are provided to consumers willing to sign a long-
term contract with an Internet Service Provider.[33]

CONSUMERS WILL PAY, BUT FOR WHAT?

The early consumer online services (e.g., CompuServe, Prodigy and America
Online) were subscriber-fee supported. Many newspapers attempted subscription
services, several through an association with Prodigy. The *Los Angeles Times*, *Atlanta*

Journal and Constitution, Tampa Tribune, New York Newsday and the *Washington Post* were among those who tried subscription-only services. The *L.A. Times'* TimesLink and the *Journal and Constitution's* Access Atlanta reportedly had as many as 20,000 subscribers, but the others never reached 9,000.[34] Many information providers who set up on the World Wide Web thought they could sustain a subscriber model for access to all or most of their site: *USA Today*, the *San Jose Mercury*, the Microsoft-funded online magazine, *Slate* among them. One by one they reverted to advertiser only support. In 1999, abandoning its 10-month attempt to attract subscribers at $19.95 annually, *Slate's* publisher wrote "that by making *Slate* free our audience will grow substantially and this will make us more attractive to advertisers." On the Web, "paid subscriptions for content (other than smut and investments) simply have not grown as expected."[35]

Among the major media, only two types of information providers had early success in finding substantial revenues from subscribers—that is, where the revenue from subscribers would more than compensate for any additional advertising revenue that could be gained by having a free site with greater traffic and therefore higher advertising rates. One was those sites with sexually explicit materials. The other area was money and financial information.

Sex

The sex content sites have been reportedly been profitable. Some charge flat monthly fees, upward of $20 per month. Some sites have pay per view, charging by the minute for real-time "performances." The sex content sites promoted themselves with millions of "spam" e-mail messages. With e-mail list brokers offering files with one million e-mail addresses for as low as $700, these high margin promoters inundated the Internet with teasers for their sites.

More mainstream sites included Playboy Online, the Web division of *Playboy* magazine. In addition to typical advertising-supported Web access to some of the print magazine's content, Playboy Online started offering subscriptions to its Cyber Club in 1997 at rates ranging from $6.95 per month to $60 for one year. In late 1998, it reported 29,000 subscribers and revenue at the rate of $7.2 million annually. Still, Playboy reported it was losing money on Cyber Club.

Business and Finance

Financial and business information is the other area that has been viable in the user-pays model. This model was firmly established in the business sector, where timely access to financial data has measurable value and returns. Reuters, Telerate, Quotron and Bloomberg are among past or present players who placed terminals on hundreds of thousands of desks and sold access to data on stock, bond, futures and options markets. Subscription rates were often hundreds of dollars per month per terminal.

Online access to textual information goes back to the 1970s. Mead Data Central (then a subsidiary of Mead Corp., a paper manufacturer) started Lexis in 1973 as a searchable database of virtually all federal and state legal opinions. It was joined in 1979 by Nexis, a service that could search the full text of newspapers, in particular the *New York Times*. Lexis-Nexis was bought by Reed-Elsevier in 1994 for $1.5 billion and in 1998 had revenue of well over $1 billion.

Dialog claims it became the world's first commercial online database service in 1972. It grew out of the need of Lockheed, the aircraft manufacturer and defense contractor, to use computer technology to keep track of its vast instruction manuals. In 1981, it became a separate subsidiary of Lockheed. Knight-Ridder acquired it in 1988 for $353 million. In 1997, Knight-Ridder sold Dialog for $420 million to a small online database provider in the United Kingdom, M.A.I.D., which renamed the combined company Dialog Corporation. Like Lexis-Nexis, Dialog is marketed to the corporate and library markets, rather than to individual consumers. Dialog, for example, charges per access fees, with a $75 per month minimum, plus a $12 per month membership. Most databases cost from $60 to $90 per hour to access.

At the consumer level, TheStreet.com was an investor-oriented Web site whose co-founder and investor was Martin Peretz, owner of *The New Republic*. At $9.95 per month or $99.95 annually, TheStreet.com had 37,000 subscribers in early 1999, or indicated annual revenue of $3.7 million, exclusive of advertising revenues. The site included some free areas, but only subscribers had access to columnists and analysis of investment activity. In 1999, the New York Times Co. purchased an 8% stake in The Street.com. Softbank was another minority investor.

The *Wall Street Journal Interactive* (WSJI) was probably the most successful subscriber site in 1999. And it most closely followed the traditional newspaper model, with substantial revenue from both subscribers and advertisers. In 1996, when the site first opened with several months of free access, WSJI registered 650,000 users. Fewer than 5% initially converted to paid later in the year. But by 1999 the WSJI had more than 330,000 subscribers, by far the largest paid subscriber base on the Internet.[36] Based on some assumptions about advertising revenue from the site, revenue for the Interactive edition was likely at the rate of $20 million annually and growing.

Consumer Reports Online, the Web complement to Consumers Union's *Consumer Reports*, reported it had about 200,000 paying subscribers to its site at the end of 1998.[37] Consistent with the magazine's policy of not accepting advertising, the site is totally user supported. With subscriptions ranging from $2.95 per month to $19.95 annually for magazine subscribers, Consumers Union had revenue of an estimated $3 to $4 million in 1998 from its online operation.

ADVERTISERS ONLINE

In 1997, when total advertising expenditures in all media was $187 billion, online advertising was $900 million, or about 0.5% of the total.[38] This rose to 0.9% in 1998 and was projected to be about 1.4% in 1999. According to the projection used in Figure 7.4, by 2002 online's share of advertising was anticipated to reach about 3.2% of advertising expenditures in the United States. This growth rate, if realized, was far greater than that for cable television through the 1980s and 1990s. In 1997, for example, cable still accounted for only 2.8% advertising, as compared to 19.9% for broadcast television.

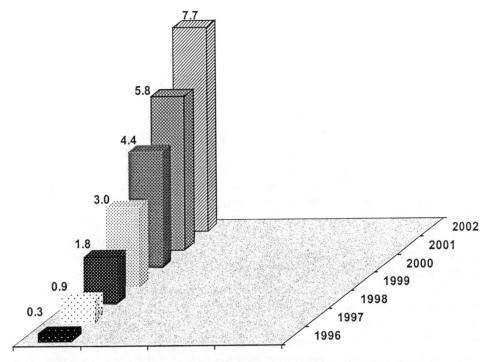

FIG. 7.4.   Online Advertising Expenditures, Projected to 2002 (in billions)
Source: Advertising revenue, 1996–1998: Internet Advertising Bureau; Projected revenue,
1999–2002, Jupiter Communications, Inc., New York.

Both the amount and rate of increase is important to the online business. If, indeed, many of the information providers on the Internet depend on advertising revenue, then the slice of the pie they get will help determine the attraction of being online to old and new players alike. For the older players in particular, their ability to segue from their existing businesses to online revenue streams may make the difference between thriving, surviving or having to sell out.

Historically, advertising has varied within a range slightly above 2% of gross domestic product in the United States (somewhat less in the rest of the industrialized world). Analysts were projecting, however, that a variety of factors were pushing this percentage to the high end of its historic range.[39] If the advertising pie grows faster than the economy in general, then older media could remain healthy in absolute revenues even as their share gets nibbled at by the faster growing online industry.

It is not clear which segments of the traditional media are more at risk in losing share. Newspapers may be one, which would help explain why the publishers have been in the forefront of establishing Web sites with the publications' logo. Some radio and television outlets, including cable networks, could be at risk as more consumers have access to enough bandwidth to make Web video and audio sites viable competitors for narrowcast programming. Thus, the Fox News Network, which lagged behind Cable News Network in access to cable homes, was more aggressive in establishing real-time feeds via the Internet than was its more established cable competitor, which seemed to be content with a text-based site.

MEASURMENT OF CONCENTRATION

Notions of concentration of ownership and control over the Internet are dogged by the different rules and measures that must be applied to Internet-related media and older, more established media. Competition in the print segment has been measured using metrics such as the percentage of total circulation accounted for by a publisher, or the proportion of industry revenue or advertising expenditures. And consumer video and audio has used audience share as well.

These measures might be acceptable surrogates for concentration, but they break down when applied to the Internet. With daily newspapers, most consumers have very limited choices. In Des Moines, Iowa, one can buy the *Register* or be without a local newspaper. A household could subscribe to the only cable provider or one of two satellite television providers or be limited to a handful of over the air stations. A prospective author of a book on the history of the West Indian banana trade may find a willing publisher in, at best, a dozen university presses.

But the Web vastly expands options for both the information consumer and the provider. For consumers who previously may have needed the daily newspaper as a source for learning about real estate for sale or local hockey scores or movie times, the WWW opens the door to dozens or even hundreds of options. Table 7.4 is part of a search in the Yahoo! index simply for the term "Des Moines." Among other links is one to other daily online newspapers in Iowa.

For the prospective author, the options include evolving forums for online publishing. This takes several forms. One is the development of online journals. Like print journals, they have an editorial process. But, unlike print journals, they are not constrained by the economics of page limits as a determinant of what is worthy of "publication." Another option is third-party publication. Various think tanks, university programs and private organizations have traditionally provided access to their publications but in limited quantity, with minimal publicity and most availability to the wider public. With online sites, organizations with limited budgets can make their publications available to all who seek them. Another option is self-publication. In 1999, the Internet was already filled with personal Web sites that encompassed the frivolous, the learned and serious, even defamatory writings. They were from published authors and those who had never before ventured beyond their own thoughts.[40] Audio and video as well as text and graphics were available.[41] For the first time, anyone could publish or "broadcast" without a license, without a large bankroll, and with potential access to the entire Internet audience.

Given the openness and accessability of the Internet, what would indicate concentration? Would it be the percentage of total accesses accounted for by the owners of 10 or 20 largest sites, if that could even be measured (virtually every URL requested by anyone anywhere would have to be captured)? And the methodology to create a valid sample of users is still evolving. The following tables are based on usage for a sample of more than 10,000 computers. But even the companies doing

TABLE 7.4
Search for "Des Moines" in Yahoo!, February 4, 1999

Search Result Found **9** categories and **151** sites for **Des Moines**

Inside Yahoo! Matches

Financial Info: (Symbol:PDM) last 23 3/8 change +1/4**News:** PDM Forms Alliance with
Larsen and Toubro To Pursue Engineering and Construction Projects in India -
more . . . **Community:** PITT-DES MOINES Message Board

Yahoo! Category Matches (1 - 9 of 9)

Regional: U.S. States: Iowa: Cities: **Des Moines**
Regional: U.S. States: Iowa: Metropolitan Areas: **Des Moines** Metro
Regional: U.S. States: Iowa: Cities: West **Des Moines**
Regional: U.S. States: Washington: Cities: **Des Moines**
Regional: U.S. States: Iowa: Counties and Regions: **Des Moines** County
Regional: U.S. States: Texas: Cities: The Woodlands: Business and Shopping: Companies:
Construction: General Contractors: Commercial: PDM - Pitt-**Des Moines, Inc.**
Recreation: Sports: Hockey: Ice Hockey: Leagues: Junior Leagues: United States Hockey
League (USHL): Teams: **Des Moines** Buccaneers
Regional: U.S. Cities: Iowa: Cities: **Des Moines**: Business and Shopping: Companies: Internet
Services: Access Providers: DSMnet - **Des Moines** Internet
Regional: U.S. States: Iowa: Cities: **Des Moines**: Real Estate: Iowa Realty - **Des Moines**

Yahoo! Site Matches (1 - 11 of 151)

Science: Biology: Zoology: Zoos
• Blank Park Zoo - **Des Moines, IA**
News and Media: Newspapers: Browse By Region: U.S. States: Iowa: Complete Listing
• DesMoines Register.com - subscribe to the paper, write a letter to the editor, contribute to the news.
Regional: U.S. States: Iowa: Cities: **Des Moines**: Education: K-12
• **Des Moines** Public Schools
Regional: U.S. States: Washington: Cities: **Des Moines**: Community
• City of **Des Moines** - photographs of the city and information about services and government.
Regional: U.S. States: Iowa: Cities: **Des Moines**: Community: Government
• City of **Des Moines** - government information and services.
Society and Culture: Crime: Law Enforcement: Police Departments: Local Departments
• **Des Moines, IA** - Police Department - includes information on vice/narcotics,
• criminal investigation, patrol, administrative services, legal advisor, research & development, profession-
al standards, and more.
Regional: U.S. States: Iowa: Cities: **Des Moines**: News and Media: Newspapers
• DesMoinesRegister.com - subscribe to the paper, write a letter to the editor, contribute to the news.
Arts: Organizations
• Metro Arts Alliance of Greater **Des Moines** - working to increase awareness and participation in cultur-
al events throughout greater **Des Moines**, Iowa. Calendar, artist and agency listings.
Business and Economy: Labor: Unions: Countries and Regions: North America: International Union of
Operating Engineers
• Local 234 - **Des Moines, IO**
Society and Culture: Religion and Spirituality: Faiths and Practices: Christianity: Churches: Nondenomi-
national
• First Church - **Des Moines, IA** - an Open Bible Standard church.
Recreation: Sports: Hockey: Ice Hockey: Leagues: Youth Leagues
• Greater **Des Moines** Youth Hockey Association

Click here NOW for iMALL

advanced search - help **Other Search Engines** Alta Vista - HotBot - Infoseek - Deja News - Lycos - More . . .
Yellow Pages - People Search - City Maps - Get Local - Today's Web Events & Chats - Image Surfer -
More Yahoos Copyright © 1994-99 Yahoo! Inc. - Company Information - Help

the measuring admit that this sample is too small to accurately measure sites that may have many accesses but only from limited geographic areas or outside the United States. Users from business sites and behind "firewalls" cannot be monitored. Popular sites that are locally cached are undercounted.[42]

The Top Web Sites, 1999

In the young and dynamic Internet world, the top companies and the most popular sites can change in a month, yet alone a year or two. The following picture is thus a snapshot, circa late 1999. What it says is at that instant, the well-known, established media companies were just a small part of the vast content available via the Internet.

Table 7.5 identifies the most popular Web sites and their owners. The measurement is one of several that might be used to judge the significance of a site. In this

TABLE 7.5
Most Visited Web Sites, September 1999

Rank	Web Site	% Reach	Owner
1	Yahoo.com	50.7%	Yahoo!: public
2	AOL.com	44.9	AOL: public
3	MSN.com	44.5	Microsoft: public
4	Netscape.com	31.0	AOL: public
5	Microsoft.com	30.9	Microsoft: public
6	Geocities.com	30.5	Yahoo!: public
7	Go.com	29.8	Disney: public
8	Excite.com	22.2	Excite@Home: public
9	Hotmail.com	21.5	Microsoft: public
10	Lycos.com	21.2	Lycos: public
11	Passport.com	20.5	Microsoft: public
12	Amazon.com	17.8	Amazon.com: public
13	Anglefire.com	17.5	Lycos: public
14	Tripod.com	16.3	Lycos: public
15	Real.com	16.0	RealNetworks: public
16	ebay.com	15.8	eBay: public
17	Altavista.com	14.9	Altavista: CMGI
18	Bluemountainarts.com	14.4	Excite@Home: public
19	About.com	12.8	About.com: public
20	Looksmart.com	12.7	Looksmart: public
21	Hotbot.com	12.5	Lycos: public
22	Snap.com	12.1	NBCi: public
23	Goto.com	11.5	Goto: public
24	ZDNet	11.3	Ziff-Davis: public
25	Xoom.com	11.2	NBCi: public

Sources: Cols 1–3: Mediametrix; Col 4: multiple news and financial sources
Top 25 Web Sites http://www.mediametrix.com/PressRoom/Pres_releases/10_20_99.html
Data were based upon a sample of 11,000 people who used the web during the month of September, 1999. The statistical margin of error is +/− one percentage point. "Reach" is a measure of unduplicated audience, expressed as a percentage of all web users, and is often interpreted in the following manner: "In the month of September, 1999, approximately 50.7% of all people who used the web (from home or office) went to Yahoo!.com at least once during the month." The universe of users in September 1999 was 63.4 million.

case, the ranking is based on the proportion of the universe of Web users who visited the site in September, 1999. Measuring Web usage in 1999 was relatively primitive, despite the potential of accurate measurement made possible by computer technologies. The capability for extremely accurate knowledge of who is visiting each Web site has been diluted by substantial concerns over privacy. Thus, Web sites have generally been limited in the amount of personal information they are willing to request from site visitors.

In 1999, the most popular Web sites were America Online (AOL, the most successful of the early proprietary consumer online services) and the sites that started as search engines but had transformed themselves into "portals." These were locations that users often set as their initial screens when they started their Web browsers. Although they differ slightly, they tended to be user-customized to some extent and tended to promote quick access to breaking news, sports, stock and financial information, weather, technology and entertainment information, as well as e-mail and "yellow pages."

Up to 1999, traditional media companies were not well represented among the most used Web sites. Only General Electric's NBC (through investments in NBC Internet and a half interest in MSNBC), Disney and Ziff-Davis (ZDNet) were major players. Nontraditional players included AOL, and a clutch of start-ups that rode the breathtaking expansion of the Internet in the 1990s: Yahoo, Excite, Lycos, etc. The only other established player in the top 25 was Microsoft, which started its own service called MSN, was co-founder of MSNBC and acquired Hotmail. Two of the most visited sites were essentially store fronts: Amazon.com and auction facilitator eBay.

By other measures of rank, traditional media players showed up with greater frequency, but still did not dominate any list. Table 7.6 is a ranking that aggregates all sites owned by any given entity. This list adds Time Warner and Viacom, both with substantial entertainment promotion sites for their Warner and Paramount studio sites, respectively. The Weather Channel, from the cable network, is number 22. It is the only one of the predominately news and information sites or companies that cracked the top tier by itself.

News Sites

Just as television news shows get smaller audiences than most entertainment programming, so news-oriented Web sites in 1999 were not among the most visited of Web sites. Moreover, on the Web, all news sites compete on an even field with each other: Those that are run by newspaper companies, broadcast news operations, cable news networks, magazine publishers and by nontraditional players all compete with one another for audiences with no natural geographic boundaries. A Philadelphia native living in Boston can reach the *Inquirer*'s Web site as readily as the *Boston Globe*'s. A noncable subscriber can use CNN's Web site. And a Penn State alumnus can follow the details of that university's football team in the student *Collegian*.

By the same token, advertisers are able to reach audiences in new ways: a vendor of Penn State insignia goods can advertise with the *Collegian*'s online site. Real estate agents may find it worthwhile to include banners tailored to users based on

TABLE 7.6
Most Visited Properties and Owners, September 1999

Rank	Web Site	% Reach	Owner
1	AOL sites	78.1%	AOL: public
2	Yahoo! sites	57.2	Yahoo!: public
3	Microsoft sites	52.7	Microsoft: public
4	Lycos sites	41.1	Networks/Lycos: public
5	Go Network	31.4	Disney: public
6	Excite@Home	22.8	Excite@Home: public
7	Amazon	17.9	Amazon.com: public
8	Time Warner	17.3	Time Warner: public
9	RealNetwork sites	15.8	RealNetworks: public
10	Altavista.com	15.4	CMGI: public
11	eBay	14.9	Xoom: public
12	Go2Net Network	14.6	Go2Net: public
13	LookSmart	13.8	LookSmart Ltd.: private
14	Bluemountain.com	13.6	Excite@Home: public*
15	ZDNet sites	12.9	Ziff-Davis: public
16	About.com sites	12.6	About.com: public
17	CNET	12.4	CNET: public
18	Snap Sites	11.6	NBCi: public
19	Xoom.com sites	11.1	NBCi: public
20	Goto.com	10.9	Goto: public
21	Juno.com	10.8	Juno Online Services: public
22	Weather Channel	10.0	Landmark Communications: private
23	AT&T sites	9.3	AT&T: public
24	Viacom sites	8.3	Viacom: public
25	InfoSpace	7.9	InfoSpace.com: public

*Bluemountain.com was subsequently purchased from Blue Mountains Arts Publishing Co. by Excite@Home.

Sources: Cols 1–3: Mediametrix; Col 4: Hoovers.Com; multiple online news and financial sources.

Top 25 Web Properties accessed November 19, 1999 at site www.mediametrix.com/PressRoom/Press_Releases/10.20.99.html. Data were based upon a sample of about 11,000 people who used the web during the month of September. Universe of online users was 67.1 million. "Reach" is a measure of unduplicated audience, expressed as a percentage of all web users, and is often interpreted in the following manner: "In the month of September 1999, approximately 78.1% of all people who used online services (From home or office) went to sites or pages owned by America Online at least once during the month."

the basic data in the "cookies" and registration information that users may be willing to provide in exchange for free access to a site. News from around the world is now available on the Internet, usually free of charge. By one tabulation, there were 4,220 newspapers of all varieties available online as of November 5, 1999.[43] This number includes dailies, weekly, speciality, campus, alternative newspapers, in any language, throughout the world. Some were very elaborate sites, others just repackaged some or all of the print newspaper.

All but three of the top 50 magazines in the country (as defined by paid circulation) had a Web presence as of January 1998.[44] Nearly 900 TV stations across the United States had Web sites, although many were purely promotional.[45] About 145 U.S. cable channels (including CNN, HBO, MTV and Singlevision) had Web sites of varying depth.[46]

Table 7.7 identifies the most frequented news sites in 1998 and 1999. The measurement method used, however, would likely underrepresent the audience for sites with geographically sizable but national small audiences.[47] Still, the reach of the Internet changes many of the rules about competition: The traditional regulatory, distribution and capital barriers to entry are largely eliminated on the Internet, circa 1999. Of the 25, 4 are sites that have no old media roots (Go Network, NewsWorks, Yahoo!, Headbone.com). Five others are related to essentially television programs (MSNBC, CNET, The Weather Channel, Fox News, BBC Online).

Table 7.7 also helps bring substance to the notion of the World Wide Web. Six of the top 25 news sites were based outside North America. As the United States and Canada had a disproportionately large number of those accessing the Internet in 1998, it will be useful to track the usage trends as the rest of the world reaches parity.

A compilation such as that in Table 7.7 differs from similar lists in the other segments of the media industry in that it is far more cross-cutting. Identifying the

TABLE 7.7
Most Visited News Sites 1999 and 1998

11/99	7/99	11/98	Web Site	Owner (Public Co. in italics)
1	2	12	MSNBC	*General Electric and Microsoft*
2	7	2	USA Today	*Gannett*
3	6	6	CNET*	CNET
4	1	1	Time Warner**	*Time Warner*
5	3	19	The Weather Channel	Landmark Communications
6	18	NA	FOX News	*News Corp.*
7	4	8	BBC Online	British Broadcasting Co. (UK)
8	8	8	Go Network	*Disney*
9	20	15	The Wall Street Journal	*Dow Jones*
10	10	16	NewsWorks***	NA
11	NA	NA	Los Angeles Times	*Times Mirror*
12	11	21	The New York Times	*The New York Times Co.*
13	25	NA	The Sydney Morning	*Fairfax Holdings* (Australia)
14	12	NA	The Detroit Free Press	*Knight Ridder*
15	NA	NA	United Media	*E.W. Scripps*
16	13	18	Financial Times	*Pearson plc* (UK)
17	NA	NA	India Express.Com	Indian Express Group (India)
18	16	NA	The Philippine Star	Philstar Daily, Inc. (Philippines)
19	19	9	Washington Post	*Washington Post Co.*
20	18	NA	Yahoo sites	*Yahoo!*
21	17	NA	The Times of India	Bennett, Coleman & Co. Ltd. (India)
22	NA	NA	Mercury Center	*Knight Ridder*
23	NA	NA	Dallas Morning News	A. H. Belo
24	NA	NA	Dawn	Dawn Group (Pakistan)
25	16	NA	Headbone.com	Headbone Interactive, Inc.

*Includes CNET, Search.Com, News.Com and Download.com
**Includes Pathfinder, CNN, Warner Bros. sites
***Site unavailable November 19, 1999
NA: not applicable, usually because not rated in top 25 in that listing.
Source: Web21, http://www.web21.com/newspaper, accessed, November 19, 1999, July 27, 1999 and December 12, 1998.

largest newspapers does not compare the relative circulation of newspapers to, say, the viewership of the largest television networks. For example, ratings for CNN on a weekday averages about 370,000 households.[48] This is minuscule by national TV audience size, where audiences are often 15 million households for a broadcast network TV show. But 370,000 would put CNN into the top ranks of daily newspaper circulation.

Over the Internet, sites initiated by broadcasters, newspaper publishers, cable networks and everyone else compete with one another. Old measures of dominance and concentration were, at least in 1999, meaningless in the Internet age. Morever, the nature of the top news sites shifted in the nine months covered in Table 7.7. Gone from the top 25 were Philadelphia Online, ABC News and the ONION, among others. Far more prominent were international news sites, usually in English. This change may be an indicator of better measurement, of greater penetration of the Internet outside North America, of increased access by U.S. residents and visitors to news sources in their native country, of more organizations developing and promoting Web sites, as well as improved measuring techniques.

NEW PLAYERS AND COMPETITORS

Many of the Web sites with the largest audience in the late 1990s were dubbed "portals" by the trade press. These grew out of the early indexing and search engine sites that became popular as the "home page" for many users. Given the vastness of resources available online, the search engines were popular to help many users find their way around the online world. These large volumes of users helped the search engines become the locus of much of the advertising revenue in the early days of the Web. Quickly, the search engine entrepreneurs devised strategies to attract more users and keep them at the site longer. They started providing links to news headlines, sports scores, weather, entertainment news and the like. They took advantage of the power of computers to allow users to somewhat customize their own homepage. In exchange for some information about themselves, users were provided targeted information, such as the weather based on the user's zip code. The same information could help advertisers target their messages as well: ads directed at skiers in the Northeast or Rockies, ads for golf or lawn services in warmer climates.

The critical role of the portal sites for the attention of users was bolstered by survey research that found "almost half of online users . . . access news via search engines or directory Web sites."[49] The same research also suggested that consumers' preference for collecting news on these entry sites has also lead to another trend: As "search engines pull stories straight from the 'wires,' news services such as Associated Press, Bloomberg, and Reuters are becoming more familiar to consumers."[50]

The following is the barest sampling of the thousands of new players—or rejuvenated players—in the media landscape as the result of the Internet. Reuters is included because it is an example of an old-time player that found a new "retail" business via the online world and was a leader in seizing the opportunity. America Online, which is an old timer in the online world, was able to make the transition from a pay-as-you-go proprietary online service to a flat rate, Internet-based provider of services and information. Yahoo!, Excite@Home, Lycos, InfoSeek and LookSmart were quintessential start-ups, with revenue in 1998, shown in Table 7.8, just edging into a range where they can be taken seriously—and ripe for acquiring or being acquired. Bloomberg, CNET and Hoover's are examples of new information companies that started their lives with one expectation, but quickly grasped the Web and shifted all or some of their efforts to this newer medium.

Omitted are far more: Microsoft, whose Microsoft Network in 1995 had been feared by some prognosticators as the death knell for America Online, was still struggling to play a role in the media business with its MSN.com portal; Netscape, the 1994 start-up that commercialized the Web browser but found it could not sustain a business plan of selling it against Microsoft's free Internet Explorer; Dun & Bradstreet, a $2 billion company that makes many of its databases available to clients online.

America Online

Is America Online a portal, an Internet service provider, a publisher, or an online shopping mall? It is or has been some of each, and more or less. A direct descendant of an early 1980s pioneer consumer online service called The Source, AOL outlasted a host of better financed competitors (e.g., CompuServe, for many years owned by H&R Block and Prodigy, started by Sears, CBS and IBM), newer and well-financed competitors (e.g., Microsoft Network) and the challenge of the open Inter-

TABLE 7.8
Revenue of Selected Online Players, 1996–1998

	1998 Revenue (est. in millions)	1997 Revenue (in millions)	1996 Revenue (in millions)
Traditional Companies Online			
Reuters Group plc	$5,032	$4,762	$4,990
America Online[1]	2,600.0	1,685.2	1,093.9
Thomson Corporation*	2,382	2,097	
Bloomberg L.P.	1,500.0	NA	NA
Bridge Information Systems	1,330.0	572.0	NA
Reed-Elsevier*	1,059	979.8	NA
Associated Press	465.0	441.4	417.9
Primark	435.0	397.9	277.1
New Internet Companies Online			
Yahoo!	190.0	67.4	19.1
Excite@Home	160.0	50.2	14.8
InfoSeek	75.0	34.6	15.1
Lycos[2]	56.1	22.3	5.3
CNET	54.0	33.6	14.8
SportsLine USA	29.0	10.3	2.4
Hoover's	5.5	NA	NA

[1]Fiscal year ending June 30.
[2]Fiscal years ending Jul 31.
NA = not available
*Electronic publishing portion of total revenue.
Sources: Annual Reports and Hoover's Online profiles. Industry estimates for Bloomberg and Hoover's.

net to its own proprietary network model. Its longtime economic mode had been a fixed $9.95 per month for five hours of use, plus $2.95 for each additional hour. When AT&T was the first major ISP to offer unlimited Internet access for $19.95 per month in 1996, AOL's model was undercut. With some glitches, AOL managed to adapt to the open-ended usage paradigm. By 1999, AOL was by far the largest entity on the Internet, with 17 million subscribers accessing its own proprietary content, seamlessly mixed in with material from the World Wide Web. It also acquired CompuServe in 1998 along with its 2 million users. In all, it accounted for Internet access for 60% of those online in the United States in 1999.

Also in 1999, it completed its acquisition of Netscape. Although Netscape was primarily associated with commercializing the Mosaic graphical Web browser developed in 1994 at the University of Illinois, it was gradually transforming itself into a publisher of a portal site. Whereas in 1995 only 2% of Netscape revenue came from Web site revenue, that increased to 7% in 1996, 18% in 1997 and 27% in the third quarter of 1998.[51] Thus, AOL and Netscape were both compliments and competitors.

Reed-Elsevier

With ownership equally split between Britain's Reed International and the Dutch Elsevier NV, Reed-Elsevier derives half its revenue from North American operations.[52] The largest segment of Reed-Elsevier's online business is the Lexis-Nexis service it acquired from Mead Corp., the paper manufacturer, in 1997. Its science journals and selected trade magazines have introduced new online services, such as *Chemical News & Information* and *Air Transport Intelligence*. Reed-Elsevier estimated that 20% of its total revenue was derived from electronic publishing (the basis for the figures in Table 7.8) and expected that proportion to increase to 30% in the medium term.[53]

Thomson Corporation

Thomson has been divesting itself of newspapers while bolstering its businesses that utilize online information services. In the 1990s, it acquired the Institute for Scientific Information, the largest commercial scientific research database. In 1994 it added Information Access Company (a reference database service), which Ziff Communications sold. In 1995 and 1996 it sold 74 newspapers in the United States and Canada. In 1996 it acquired legal publisher West Publishing Co. whose WESTLAW database was a direct competitor to Reed-Elsevier's LEXIS.[54] By 1998 Thomson derived 38% of its $6.3 billion in information and publishing business revenue from electronic products.[55]

Associated Press

The Associated Press (AP) is operated as a cooperative, owned by 1,550 member newspapers. It is the world's oldest (founded 1843) and largest news organization, with 237 bureaus worldwide.[56] For most of its history, the AP was a wholesaler of news: Its clients were newspapers and later radio and television news organizations. Each client made its own decisions on what materials to use and how to edit it. When Reuters and others made their feeds available to consumers on the Web, the AP had a dilemma. If it provided direct access to consumers, it undercut its value to its client/owners. If it did not, then it could lose revenue opportunities as well as prestige. In 1996 it introduced "The WIRE," which essentially gave individual Web users access to AP stories through its own site. AP continued to utilize the Internet for its paying clients as well. In 1995 it began offering online access to its photo archive, with more than 400,000 photos. Public access to the AP wires is just one example of how the Internet may be able to remove layers of gatekeepers to news and information.

Bridge Information Systems

Bridge is not widely known outside the financial community. Founded in 1974, it became second only to Reuters (and ahead of Bloomberg) in 1999 as a worldwide provider of financial information.[57] Bridge's customers are institutional investors, brokers and stock exchanges. Besides basic financial data, it provides news feeds and transaction services. Bridge tripled its size in 1998 when its acquired Dow Jones Markets, divested by Dow Jones. Bridge gathers information from more than 200 exchanges for its clients in more than 100 countries.

Softbank

A major and low profile player in the content portion of the Internet is Softbank, based in Japan. Softbank made its presence known in the United States with the purchase of magazine publisher Ziff-Davis, then purchased massive Comdex, the mega trade show for the computer industry. But through a series of strategic and high risk investments, shown in Table 7.9, Softbank became a substantial minority investor in many of the nascent Internet firms that sprouted with venture capital after 1996.

Yahoo! started life as a search site and transformed itself to a portal. E*Trade is an online brokerage. Geocities, subsequently acquired by Yahoo!, was the leading provider of free Web home pages to users. USWeb Corp., worked with Fortune 500 companies to develop Web sites. And CyberCash was in the business of providing secure transactions for financial transactions on the Web. What all these investments had in common, with the exception of Ziff-Davis, was that they were not basically content companies. Softbank withdrew from investing in companies that wanted to sell content over the Internet when several did not work out. "Every time we'd do a content deal, I'd feel great about it," explained the head of Softbank's investment company. "Then nine months later we'd be trying to figure out who could buy the company and take it off our hands."[58]

Bloomberg

Michael Bloomberg started his company in 1982, marketing a financial terminal that was designed to manipulate bond data. It was not until 1990 that Bloomberg began its owns news gathering operation. In 1992, it bought a New York radio station and converted it to an all news format. In 1994, it started a cable TV network as well as a financial magazine. By 1998, it had its consumer offerings through agreements with companies such as America Online and CNET. Bloomberg was 80%

TABLE 7.9
Softbank Holdings Internet Investments, 1999

Investment	% Ownership
Yahoo!	30%
E*Trade	28
Geocities	22
Yahoo! Japan	60
Ziff-Davis	72
US Web	8
CyberCash	6

Source: "Softbank Hits $12 Billion Jackpot on Its Various Internet Stakes," *Wall Street Journal*, February 3, 1999.

owned by its founder (initial investor, financial services provider Merrill Lynch, owned the rest). It had an estimated $1.5 billion revenue in 1998.

CNET

CNET was started in 1992 to provide cable TV programming on technology and computers. USA Network, which took a 5% stake in the company, was its first client. Shortly after CNET Central began its USA Network run in 1995, CNET started an Internet version. Subsequently it expanded to six television programs and multiple Web sites. CNET uses a combination of its own reporters plus outside services, such as Bloomberg, for content for its Web sites.

Although CNET, Inc. is a publicly owned company, about 60% is owned by its three founders, which includes its two top executives plus Paul Allen, a founder of Microsoft. NBC bought a 5% take in CNET in 1998 as part of its investment in CNET's SNAP portal service.

Primark

Primark was a holding company for a natural gas utility. Starting in 1988, it sold off its utility holding and became a collection of information companies for finance and business. Among its subsidiaries is Disclosure (through which much of the stock ownership data in Chapter 8 was accessed); EDGAR Direct, acquired from Dow Jones in 1999, which provides online access to filings with the Securities and Exchange Commission (also used extensively for this research); and Baseline Financial Services, which provides financial information for money managers. Much of the information that had originally been published in hard copy, on CD-ROM or via proprietary online networks has been migrated to Internet access, by subscription.

Yahoo!

Yahoo! is the prototypical Internet story: In 1994, two graduate students tinkered around for their own amusement and developed a method for indexing and searching Web sites. Their friends and their friends' friends started to use it. In 1995, it went commercial and became so synonymous with Web searching that Ziff-Davis arranged to use its name for a magazine about the Internet.

Yahoo! differed from the start from the search engines that followed it. Yahoo! is actually an indexing service, relying on an editorial staff to assign sites to one of its many subcategories.

Yahoo! had more traffic than any site on the Internet in 1999 (and in 1998 second in advertising revenue only to Netscape, which had a built in advantage because its own site was the default home page on every copy of its browser). It was also the first to start to add news, sports and other "substance" to keep the interest of those who used it only for searching. In 1999, it purchased GeoCities for $5 billion in stock. GeoCities was a site at which computer users could create and store their own Web pages. It claimed a population of 3.5 million individual sites in 1999.

In 1996, Yahoo! was one of the first of the Internet companies to issue its stock publicly. In a year in which its total revenue was $19 million, its value based on its initial public stock offering $300 million—and it more than tripled by the end of the day. Revenue for 1998 was $190 million.[59] About 30% of Yahoo!'s stock was owned by Softbank, the Japanese company that is the principal owner of Ziff-Davis, the magazine publisher. The two student founders owned more than one quarter of the company.

Excite

Excite, Inc. was another of the search engines turned portal. The original plan, initiated in 1994, was to develop a software tool to help users manage the vast amount of information on the Internet. In 1995, Excite was turned on to the public and became the second most trafficked search engine next to Yahoo! America Online had a 12% ownership stake, a legacy of its sale of its own Webcrawler search engine to Excite. Financial software manufacturer Intuit owned about 13% in 1998. In 1999, however, AtHome, a service that provided cable modem service, purchased Excite in a transaction valued at $7.5 billion. AtHome, in turn, was financed by a coalition of cable companies, including TCI. In 1999, AT&T acquired TCI and its 40% stake in AtHome, making AT&T a substantial minority owner of the combined Excite@Home. Excite gets most of its current news and sports news form Reuters, some from UPI and its technology news provider is Ziff-Davis' ZDNet.

Lycos

Lycos started its young life as a Web search engine developed by a researcher at Carnegie Mellon University. The company was formed in 1995, about the same time that Microsoft became one of the first to license its search engine technology. Subsequently, Lycos raised venture capital, then went public. With its financing, it was able to purchase the components of a comprehensive portal site: Tripod and Angelfire were sites that allowed users to create and share their personal home pages. WhoWhere? started life as the online equivalent of the white pages phone book. In purchasing Digital Wired in 1998, Lycos bought the online segment of *Wired*, the pioneering print magazine about the wired culture itself sold to the Newhouse magazine interests. Digital Wired put Lycos into the information-gathering business, as it employed a staff of reporters and editors. It includes Hotwired.com, a daily chronicle of the intersection of Web technology and Wired.com, a source for daily news and analysis of the technologies, companies and people driving the information age. In 1999, USA Networks failed in a bid to merge a major portion of its holdings with Lycos.

InfoSeek

InfoSeek was started in 1994 and went online in 1995 as a search engine. In 1998, Walt Disney Co. bought a 43% interest in InfoSeek (for $70 million, an amount roughly equal to InfoSeek's total revenue for the year). Armed with fresh capital, in 1999 InfoSeek launched a new portal, Go.com. Go has many of the same features as other portals: somewhat user definable sections for current news, sports, weather and entertainment. Other than reusing material from ABCNews.com, it created no original news or information. Disney subsequently bought the rest of InfoSeek and changed its name to GO Network.

LookSmart

LookSmart had its roots in Australia, but received its start-up funding from Reader's Digest in 1996. The founders subsequently bought back their interest. LookSmart has tried to differentiate itself with information value added: It claimed to have an editorial staff and a proprietary database, which was updated daily with links to top quality Web sites, selected and reviewed by their editors and organized intuitively into 12,500 categories.

Hoover's

Hoover's is not a portal, but it is an example of a start-up publisher that took advantage of the explosion of the consumer online industry in the late 1990s. It started as The Reference Press in 1991 with one book, "Hoover's Handbook 1991: Profiles of Over 500 Major Corporations." However, its founders quickly saw the coming of electronic distribution and early on struck deals with American Online, CompuServe and LEXIS-NEXIS. Although continuing with some print products, it concentrated its efforts in electronic information. By 1998, this privately held company (Time Warner, Media General and Infoseek are among minority owners) had 20,000 individual subscribers (at $14.95 per month or $110 per year) and a database of more than 13,500 company profiles from around the world. Its profiles are written by its own editorial staff.

SportsLine USA

SportsLine is a good example of the type of content-rich sites that were spawned by the opportunities of the Internet. It was started by entrepreneur Michael Levy in 1994 and launched in mid-1995. SportsLine provided sports programming on the

Internet, including live coverage of events; sports news and analysis; up-to-the-minute scores, stats, and odds; real-time celebrity interaction; and sales of sports merchandise. Among its funders was venture capital investor Kleiner Perkins, 10%; cable operator MediaOne Group, 10%; and broadcaster CBS, 22%. CBS's investment was part of an alliance with SportsLine that included renaming the site CBS SportsLine. For its stake, CBS was to spend $57 million in advertising on the site and promote it on its own sports programs. It had the option to increase its ownership to 33% of the company. One feature of the site is 24-hour daily talk "radio" shows, including call-in segments.

Reuters

The portal sites had many similarities. One (and again this is likely to evolve over time) was their common initial alliance with the same service to provide most of their news: Reuters. This is the British news and financial information company that traces its beginnings to telegraphing stock prices between Paris and London in 1851. But as a news service, its presence in the United States was minimal after the Associated Press and even the weakened United Press International (UPI). Perhaps because it had less to lose, it made a strategic decision in the Web's earliest days to provide its news wire to online publishers. The AP, on the other hand, owned collectively by its newspaper publisher subscribers, was concerned about providing "retail" online distribution. Newspaper publishers were concerned that the AP would, in effect, be competing against the newspapers.

Because of it's "first in" presence in the online world, Reuters became the only or primary source for the news articles that were available on the home pages of the millions of users of Lycos, Excite, Netscape, Yahoo and InfoSeek.

TRADITIONAL MEDIA INVESTMENTS IN ONLINE MEDIA

As should be obvious, established media players, although rarely in the forefront of the online world, were not ignoring it. Whether seen as a grand opportunity or as a response to a threat (or some of each), media companies have been and are continuing to try to find ways to be involved.

The most obvious is in creating their own sites. Virtually every major newspaper and hundreds of smaller ones had a Web presence. Most consumer and many trade magazines had sites, ranging from those with complete contents (e.g., Newhouse's *Wired*) to sites with a small selection of online content (e.g., Pearson's *Economist*).

Table 7.10 includes a sampling of the outside investments and acquisitions of some media companies. A comprehensive list was neither feasible nor fruitful: Even for public-owned companies, small investments or investment through separate investment funds are difficult to track. Moreover, given the rapid developments with online media, this listing would be hopelessly outdated by the time the first copies of this book came off the press. The value of Table 7.10 is to indicate that older media were, on a selective basis, investing in the new start-ups. And assuming further growth, they would increase their investments over time.

TABLE 7.10
Examples of Media Company Investments in Online Sites, 1999

Media Company	Site and Investment*
CBS, Inc.	MarketWatch.com (financial news)—38%
	Sportsline.com (sports news)—18%
New York Times Co.	TheStreet.com (financial news)—8%
Tribune Co.	America Online (electronic publishing)—2%
	CareerPath (recruiting service)—16%
	Classified Ventures (classified ad)—33%
	Digital City, Inc. (network of American Online and Internet local interactive services)—20%
	Excite, Inc. (Internet search engine)—4%
	InfoBeat, Inc. (e-mail service provider)—13%
	Open Market, Inc. (Internet commerce software and products)—3%
	Peapod (online grocery shopping and delivery)—11%
	Tribune Interactive Network Services (Internet Web site content)
	iVillage, Inc. (online network targeting women)—8%
Hearst	CareerPath.com (recruiting service)
	Women.com (Internet site geared towards women)—50%
General Electric (NBC)	MSNBC (Internet and cable news site)—50%
	Snap.com (portal)—60%
	CNET (news and information)—5%
	CareerPath (recruiting service)
Walt Disney Co.	InfoSeek (portal and search)—43%
Time Warner	Hoover's (business information)—minority stake
Times Mirror	Auctionuniverse (online auctions)
	CareerPath.com (recruitment service)
	CitySearch (local information)
	Hollywood Online (entertainment news)—100%
	ListingLink (real estate classified)
	Pointcast (personal news service)
Newhouse (Advance Publications)	RainorShine.com (weather)
	Yucky.com (kids)
Cox Enterprises	CareerPath.com
Knight-Ridder	Under 20% interest in:
	CareerPath.com (recruiting service)
	SaveSmart (online promotions)
	PointCast (personal news service)
	SportslineUSA (online sports)
	ZIP2 (directories)

*Excludes wholly owned and integrated sites initiated by the media company. Equity stake indicated when known, as of February 1999.

Sources: Hoover's Online, individual company press releases and reports, *Business Week*, *The New York Times on the Web* and *The Wall Street Journal Interactive*.

Many of the early deals are relatively small. A typical example was the minority investment of CBS, Inc. in MarketWatch.com and Sportsline.com. Knight-Ridder planned to invest up to $25 million annually, in most cases acquiring no more than 20% of any such venture. "The dumbest thing we could do," said Knight Ridder's chairman, Anthony Ridder, "is sit back and wait for competitors to figure out the revenue streams online."[60]

Partnerships (as opposed to outright acquisitions) of media companies with Web-based information providers were mutually beneficial: the links helped the media companies dabble in content and formats their main publications may not have been able to duplicate. And the Web sites gain the advertising power and established credibility of the established media. An analyst for a media-investment firm suggested that "all of these Internet companies are realizing that the traditional media companies can give them the distribution that they need . . . and can help them to build their brand name faster than they can do strictly through the Internet."[61]

Just a Snapshot

Some of these or thousands of other players may already be gone or will not be around in five years: There will be combinations, consolidation and failures. The established media players knew they had to have a Web-based presence or risk leaving opportunity on the table for their competition.

THE INTERNET AND COMPETITION

Although the business models and uses for the Internet will evolve and change over the years, several elements differentiate the Internet from all media that have come before it.

- By its nature it is global. There is no other medium, other than perhaps short wave radio, that has the global reach of a Web site accessed via the Internet. Print material can be mailed, but the time lag and the cost make this unavailable as a regular and mass form of distribution. Television and radio are local or at most national in reach. Direct broadcast satellite could be global, but would require cooperation of multiple satellite operators to make it happen.
- It is universally accessible. This was not quite accurate, but almost. In theory, and usually in practice, any user with a terminal (PC or other device with basic tehnologies) and a phone line (wired or wireless) or cable connection can access an Internet service provider and then have access to any URL in the world. A few governments have tried to filter out certain domains for political or cultural reasons. In the United States, where the First Amendment applies to the Internet, the few attempts to limit even indecent sites has met with legal objections. Universal access does not automatically mean universally affordable. However, the cost of dissemination of information available electronically via the Internet is substantially less than distribution by physical and mechanical means. This should lower the economic barriers to access.
- It is relatively oligopoly-proof. Conspiracy theorists could likely construct a scenario where a small worldwide cabal could eventually control all content available online. But the distributed nature of the Internet makes this far less likely than even unfulfilled scenarios of an oligopoly of more traditional media, where such events would be more feasible. This is not to say that there will not be large dominant players. There will be. Yet the ease of entry (i.e., no licencing requirements or high initial capital requirements, ease of access to distribution channels) would seem to ensure that there will always be a surfeit of voices providing audio, video and text news, entertainment and information for those users who want it.

- It opens up new opportunities for new players, while challenging the business models of established players. Music that can be downloaded and stored permanently on digital media (CD, DVD, etc.) is of concern to the five major record companies as well as retail music stores. Video that may be accessed at any time can upset the provider control of video (as when tens of millions must tune it at the same time to watch the evening news. What if the video stream could be started 4 minutes or 29.5 minutes later?)

The nature of the impending competition no doubt has many traditional media players scrambling for ways not to be left behind. This explains such alliances (as already noted in this chapter) and the many that will be evident in succeeding years. The forthcoming developments in communications and computer technologies—those already known in 1999 though not yet widespread—can only further the threats and opportunities presented to both old and new players.

The Economics of Mergers and Acquisitions

The world of mergers and acquisitions is not always as straightforward as it seems from afar. Although the acquisition of one newspaper by another or a chain of radio stations by a television broadcaster may be relatively simple, combinations involving different industries is far more complex, both financially and in corporate culture. In 1993, a tentative mega-merger between Bell Atlantic and TCI fell apart over two issues: the gap in corporate culture between a regulated common carrier phone company and a free-wheeling cable operator, and the effect of the merger on the stock value of Bell Atlantic.[62] In 1999, however, AT&T, having been gradually freed from telephony regulation since its 1984 divestiture, did undergo a complex merger with TCI (although the long-term impact remained to be evaluated).

Nor is it a given that the large, established media companies have the resources to buy up the fledgling Internet companies. There were issues of valuations of Internet companies that made them very expensive for older media companies to acquire, whereas there are some disincentives for Internet companies in merging with traditional media companies.

On the one hand, there is a natural attraction of many of the young Internet companies to align with media firms. To get consumers to their Web sites, they need content. And it is the traditional media companies, that is, publishers and broadcasters, who have content.

On the other hand, Internet companies have been valued by investors much higher than they do traditional media companies.[63] Table 7.11 provides some examples in 1999. What this shows is that at that date, based on the closing price of the stock of each of these corporations, multiplied by the number of common shares outstanding, the market value of Yahoo! was roughly the same as CBS. Yahoo!, however, had only 3% of the revenue of CBS. Yahoo! had a value the same as Viacom and 40% greater than News Corporation. Similarly, it shows that America Online, with just over 10% of the revenue of Walt Disney Co., was, according to the marketplace, worth the same value (about $71 billion).

The value of these and other Internet-based companies had been highly valued in 1998 and 1999 because of their rapid growth and their potential. This gave them the

TABLE 7.11
Comparison of Financial Indicators of Selected Media and Internet Companies, 1999

	1998 Revenue	Market Value February 17, 1999
CBS	$ 6.8	$26.1
Walt Disney	23.0	71.5
Viacom	14.4	23.1
News Corp.	12.8	15.0
Yahoo!	0.2	25.6
America Online	2.6	71.4
Amazon.com	0.6	14.8
AtHome	0.05	10.2

Source: Hoover's Online at www.hoover.com, accessed February 18, 1999.

resources to acquire or merge with other companies on very favorable terms, despite their small absolute size. When USA Network agreed to merge some of its operations with Lycos in 1999, it was a $2.6 billion revenue company with about $77 million in net income in 1998. Its properties included the USA and Sci-Fi Networks, the Home Shopping Network, 18 major market television stations and Ticketmaster. Lycos ran a group of Web sites, including the Lycos portal, Anglefire.com. Hotwired and WhoWhere?, with total 1998 revenue of $56 million and a net loss of $97 million. Yet, according to the terms of the deal, Lycos would have ended up owning 30% of the combined company. That is, instead of owning 100% of a $56 million company, they owned 30% of a $2.6 billion company. That was the leverage of high valuation. Even so, Lycos stockholders felt they still were not getting sufficient value and the deal fell apart.

And shortly thereafter, as the USA Network/Lycos merger agreement came undone, NBC, owned by General Electric, merged some of its fledgling online investments with Internet start-up Xoom.com. The new company, called NBCi, initially operated its service as Snap.com (one of NBC's earlier online investments). NBC's finanacial strategy was to create NBCi independent of the General Electric Company. In doing so, it hoped the shares of NBCi could acheive the lofty levels of Yahoo! and the other major high fliers of that time. If successful, it will be able to use those shares to acquire other Internet companies at prices that would be unthinkable if General Electric actually had to pay cash. Or, as one contemporary analyst put it, "How do you buy an overvalued Internet company? With overvalued Internet assets, of course."[64]

Old media companies without some Internet invesments to spin off into separate public companies, intrigued as they may be in the Internet, may be hesitant to trade their own shares for a flyer into the little tested world of Internet valuations, at least until they feel confident in the long-term viability of their possible partners.

There is every reason to predict that there will be a continuation of mergers and alliances of the older and the newer media companies. Noted one analyst, "As the Internet companies continue to mature, and as they continually seek content, they will ultimately butt heads with some of the traditional media companies. In the end, all of these guys need something to get you to sign on to their Web site."[65]

CONTINUED TECHNOLOGICAL INNOVATIONS

At a seminar sponsored by the American Academy of Arts and Sciences in 1982, a trade book editor rejected the notion of electronic media replacing "The Book." She said, "Who would want to curl up in front of the fireplace to read *War and Peace* on a CRT?"[66] Who indeed? But this editor could not think beyond the then-current technology. The video displays circa 1982 where mostly monochrome, with resolution so crude that one could see the dots that formed the letters. Although *War and Peace* and novels may be among the last types of substance to find their ways into an electronic format, the larger point is that communication and computer technology has made and will continue to undergo rapid change, which includes devices and transmission becoming smaller, faster, cheaper and better. For the Internet to give traditional media true competition will take further but predictable developments: higher resolution displays, greater portability, increased bandwidth and improved ease of use.

Displays

Reading from a video screen may not be a comfortable as print, but displays have progressed far from the green screen cathode ray tubes (CRTs) of the 1980s. The resolution on today's CRTs are approaching that of print, with millions of gradations of colors possible. In addition, flat, high resolution, thin screens of various technologies (gas plasma, liquid crystals) have become commonplace on laptop computers and, increasingly, have become economical alternatives for the desktop.

Portability

Portability depends on both the size and weight of the device and the capability to get online information to users wherever they are.

One of the drawbacks of online information was that it tied the user to a fixed location. The typical online terminal required both an electric power cord and a wire tied to a communications port. Thus users did not have the portability of a newspaper, magazine, books or even a radio. But here too technology makes a difference. Full featured computers weigh under three pounds, and screens larger than a sheet of letter paper are commonly available. At the same time that the devices get lighter and better, their prices keep decreasing.

The other piece of portability requires cutting the power and communications cords. Batteries give laptops two to five hours of use, but newer and smaller devices—sometimes called "palmtops" with smaller screens—offer battery life of six to eight weeks under moderate use. The other part of the equation for portability is wireless communications. Although nationwide paging and other low bandwidth services were commonplace, the capability to receive and send e-mail and get more bit-intensive downloads has been slower in arriving. In 1999, consumer devices weighing less than one pound were being marketed in combination with wireless connectivity at a transmission rate that made online information retrieval possible and affordable to many. These early devices started selling at $500, with wireless service at $10 per month.[67]

Voice Recognition

The keyboard has been the primary device for input to a computer to the online world. A mouse, trackball or glide pad have improved the keyboard by providing some short cuts. But after decades of promises and the tantalizing images of science fiction, smart devices that can reliably understand conversational speech have emerged. Microprocessors have become fast enough and memory cheap enough that consumers will increasing find that their dictation, spoken questions and commands can replace the cumbersome keyboard for input. Products that were available in 1999 included software sold by IBM as "ViaVoice" and by Dragon Systems as "Naturally Speaking." These and other products may come and go. With reliable voice recognition (and the technically less challenging voice synthesis), the degree of skill needed to be "computer literate" will start to sound as silly as terms that could have been used in the past, like "telephone literate" or "television literate."

Search Engines

Perhaps the greatest asset of the Internet was also its biggest headache: its vastness. Anyone can publish, but how does one find the content? One response in 1997 was the introduction of "push" software. The idea was that rather than users having to actively seek out information online, users could determine what types of information they want and it would be sent to them automatically. Advertisers were attracted to this model because they would know who was receiving their ads as well as what the "circulation" was.

Another approach was the development of "search engines." Yahoo! created the field and its was swiftly followed by Webcrawler, Excite, Lycos, HotBot, among others. The need for these services was affirmed by the high volume of traffic these sites attracted (as seen in Table 7.3). Search engines worked in two ways:

- Purposive indexing. This is done by Yahoo!, which has teams of indexers that evaluate tens of thousands of sites and assigned them categories, such as those seen in Table 7.2.
- Automated indexing. Most search engines, such as Alta Vista and HotBot, work by locating URLs (usually from URLs submitted to them or by following links from URLs they contact) and, using their proprietary algorithms, indexing each site without human intervention.

Many professional Web site developers add their own "metatags" that some search engines look for as the basis of their indexing decisions.[68] This could help users by assuring that the Web pages were indexed according to terms the creators felt appropriate. This technique was also misused by some site developers (especially sex sites) that would embed dozens or even hundreds of popular search words into the tags to increase the chance of the site being listed in a search even if unrelated to searcher's objective. Search engines are getting better at weeding out extraneous material.

And therein is another development in the evolution of technologies for the Internet. Search engines are constantly getting better. They are, to use an overworked term, getting more intelligent. The skill of understanding search "strategies" that librarians learn, the skill of mastering Boolean search protocols are and will increasingly give way to systems that can parse natural language queries. A prototype of this approach was The Electric Library (www.elibrary.com), a site from Infonautics Corporation. Aimed at home and school research, it searched hundreds of newspapers, magazines, broadcast transcripts, books, even maps and pictures, based on natural language questions.

Compression

As introduced earlier in the chapter, techniques keep evolving for cramming more useful data in less space or over any given bandwidth. The first hard disk drives for PCs in the early 1980s were an astounding—for the time—5 mb. Over the years, the hard disk drives themselves actually got smaller, whereas the data storage capability increased by orders of magnitude (while cost per mb declined). Converting to digital transmission from analog had opened up the floodgates to compression, to the point where crude but recognizable video was able to be sent over normal telephone lines, received by modems that cost under $75.

In music, providing music in high quality via the Internet would allow a growing inventory of pirated music to be digitized, copied, passed along on the Web and played on computers with compact disc quality sound. But, it also allowed new musicians to find their own audiences rather than depend on getting the ear of a traditional record label.

Implications of Technological Convergence

Just as the arrival of the Internet required the convergence of numerous telecommunications, computer and software technologies in both cost and capabilities, so will the future value of the online world depend on continued convergence. Technologies are creating more viewable, lighter and more energy efficient devices. Voice recognition and more intelligent search procedures are reducing the specialized skills needed to use the devices. And the costs for both the devices and access have been declining. All trends suggest that online information sending and receiving will indeed become a substantial avenue for both old and new players to engage in the media business.

A criticical factor to remember in a discussion of the technolgoy underlying this component of the media is that it is available to anyone. Lightweight, inexpensive video cameras that consumers were able to buy in the 1990s took video out of the exclusive hands of broadcast stations. They made it possible, for example, for countless "civilians" to capture video from air disasters to police beatings to home movies. Some of this found its way onto community cable stations and now onto the Internet.

These infrastructure technologies keep emerging, often with significant potential. For example, software was introduced in 1999 that made it possible to make textual searches of video. So, a Web site catering to the public (as well as professional news organizations) could enter questions or words, and search against all the video speeches made by specific candidates for office. Public affairs cable network C-

SPAN planned to do just that: It announced a program to "digitize the major speeches of the candidates, and then sic Virage's [the developer] software on the files. Visitors to the C-SPAN Web site (www.c-span.org) will be able to type in, say, 'Social Security reform,' and see video clips of each of the candidate's pronouncements about the issue."[69] Technologies such as this greatly undermine the power of traditional media sources, allowing consumers to search across many sources to find what they want, what they did not know they wanted, what they should know, and even trip over material they should not know about.

Unk-Unks and E-Ink

And then there are the *unk-unks*, that is, the unknown unknowns. These are the developments that trade book editors in 1982 nor most anyone else even anticipates. The World Wide Web is an example. The Internet was known in 1980. But it was not on the radar screen of media strategists, regulators, or most anyone outside of a relatively small circle of academics and defense contractors. Thus, anyone looking to provide a model for online information services looked at closed proprietary systems as the expectation. The development of the World Wide Web by Tim Berners-Lee and his colleague at CERN in Switzerland was an unk-unk. The development of the Mosaic graphical browser was an unk-unk. Even in 1994, AT&T was building a proprietary consumer information service, Exchange, and Microsoft was creating the proprietary Microsoft Network (MSN). Exchange was closed down in 1995 and MSN was quickly morphed to an open Web model.

E-Ink stands for electronic ink. It is an example of what may be an unexpected development that changes the expectations for forecasters. Electronic ink is a "smart" material that changes its image when exposed to an electric field. Thus, surfaces coated with electronic ink can be updated continually with new information. But unlike existing electronic displays, electronic ink maintains the cultural "look and feel" that people associate with paper. Images using electronic ink have the sharpness and brightness of ink on paper. Yet it requires only a minute amount of energy to update the display, and once applied, the image can be retained for weeks without additional power. Although there are many potential uses for such a coating, the expectation is that this process may be used to create electronic paper with real pages that can be leafed through and read on the beach or on the bus. They could typeset themselves with the daily headlines and classified ads or with the text of *War and Peace*.

Combining electronic paper (an oxymoron?) with wireless connectivity to the Internet would create new opportunities for print, while retaining the cost advantages of electronic distribution. The bottlenecks of capital and physical distribution are eliminated, the cost of a sophisticated terminal is reduced and the cultural familiarity of print would be retained.

This is not a prediction that electronic ink will in fact lead to all this. The value of this scenario is as a reminder that the economic and technological models of today may not be those of tomorrow or the day after. If not electronic ink, then it will be something else that nobody knew about and had not even thought about as this book was put together.

SUMMARY AND DISCUSSION

As has been reiterated throughout this chapter, the Internet was changing so rapidly at the time this was being written that definitive statements about its role, about the players and about its future were highly speculative. Its widespread use has raised many issues for policymakers and scholars, among them privacy of individual information, security of transactions, impact on politics and political forms, application of intellectual property rights, implications for First Amendment rights in the United States and freedom of speech issues globally. Still being worked out are who will be the winners and losers—among the older media players, infrastructure providers and equipment manufacturers.

Yet a vague shape of the Internet (or Internets) was coming into focus by 2000. First, by its nature, it is global and universally accessible. It will be difficult, if not impossible, for any nation to stop the communications provided by the Internet at its borders short of denying access altogether. Despots may try to limit the number of nodes and who has access to the connections, but satellite and other wireless connections will undercut such efforts. Moreover, as the former Soviet Union learned, it is impossible to create a prosperous economy in the Information Age without reasonable access to the flow of information. It would be analogous to running an industrial economy without ready access to coal and oil.

Second, the Internet is oligopoly proof, at least at the content end. That is, no matter how popular or dominant any dozen or 100 major information providers may become, it is hard to create a scenario that would preclude equal access to virtually unlimited information sites and forums at very nominal cost.

Third, the telecommunications and computer technologies that have converged to make online information and entertainment viable are not fixed. They are evolving much faster than anything seen in the technologies associated with print and even broadcasting. And by their nature, the technologies are creating goods and services that are continually becoming smaller, faster, cheaper and better. Whether it is voice recognition that can complement keyboards or electronic paper that may be an alternative to flat screen displays or broadband data communication channels that may merge with traditional broadcasting and cable, the trends point to a greater opportunity for online services for consumers and businesses.

The single bottleneck that could hamper the potential of online is in the control of the access points and the telecommunications backbone. Given that multiple cable, telephone and wireless providers are competing to serve as the access point for users, the short-term scenario suggests sufficient options for users. In the longer run, it will likely be necessary to keep this piece of the structure open through structural and/or behavior regulation. Control of the Internet backbone is the most likely to work toward limited competition, as it is the most capital intensive piece of the infrastructure. Common carrier regulation can keep access available and the vast capacity of the infrastructure should help ensure that high utilization at low cost will be the pricing model employed.

The online world is one in which established players with substantial financial resources have little advantage over small and nimble start-ups. There is no set business model. Everyone is feeling their way. There seems to be a surfeit of entrepreneurs willing to try something new, whether it is streaming video, electronic ink or a virtual bookstore. It was an entrepreneur starting Amazon.Com that established the leading electronic commerce site. Barnes & Noble, although a leading player in the traditional book-selling world, had to play catch up, with no indication that it would overtake Amazon. It was Hoovers and not Dun & Bradstreet that became the premier provider of company information to consumers online and TheStreet.com, not McGraw-Hill, that created a popular, subscriber-based investor information site.

The inescapable consolidation between and among the older and newer media players will almost inevitably result in a net gain in the number of players than in the era prior to the Internet. It would take a dark and sinister scenario to conclude otherwise. The very structure of the Internet bypasses the choke-points of highly restricted spectrum that created initial scarcity in broadcasting or the substantial capital costs and regulatory barriers for competition in cable distribution and the capital and distribution bottlenecks that limited start-ups in many segments of print. In the past, the underfunded had access to an audience only within the sound of their voice. With the Internet, that audience can be global, limited only by their willingness to find their audience.

NOTES

1. See, for example, Richard Hooper, "Prestel, Escher, Bach: Changes Within Changes—Lessons of a Videotex Pioneer," in Benjamin M. Compaine, *Issues in New Information Technology* (Norwood, NJ: Ablex Publishing Co., 1988); and Efrem Sigel, ed., *Videotext: The Coming Revolution in Home/Office Information Retrieval* (White Plains, NY: Knowledge Industry Publications, 1980).
2. Benjamin M. Compaine, "Is Minitel a Good Model for the North American Market?" *Network World*, September 11, 1989.
3. All data from CommerceNet/Nielsen surveys. Accessed via NUA Internet Surveys at www.nua.ie/surveys/how_many_online/index.html, November 17, 1999. One could quibble over the accuracy of the user numbers, as different surveys have found different numbers of involvement. For example, definitions of "people connected" is slippery. Does it include people who have access through connections at businesses? How are multiple family members counted? Some samples include children age 12 or older, others 16 or older and so on. But there must be something significant going on out there when we look at the number of bits transmitted (relatively easy to measure), amount of commerce—someone is buying this stuff—and the volume of "hits" that media sites and others are reporting. And everyone's measure was rapidly growing from period to period.
4. 1996 and 1997: Internet Advertising Bureau, on Web site at www.iab.net. 1998: Estimate from Jupiter Communications at NUA Internet Surveys Web site, "Estimate for Web Advertising by Research Houses, 1996–2002," on Web site at www.nua.ie/surveys/analysis/graphs_charts/comparisons. Other estimates for 1999 ranged from $1.6 billion to $4.7 billion.
5. "Large Scale Network Caches Provide More Bandwidth for Your Money," on Web site at www.inktomi.com/products/traffic/tech/economics.html, November 17, 1998.
6. 1996–1997: "The Emerging Digital Economy," U.S. Department of Commerce, April 1998, p. 2. 1998: "Network Solutions Registers Record Number of Web Addresses in 1998" on Network Solutions' Web site at netsol.com/news/1999/pr_199901/2b.html.
7. Company financial statements for second quarter, 1999 (SEC Form 8-K, July 21, 1999); Doreen Carvajal, "Amazon Surge May Reflect the New Math of the Internet," *New York Times*, January 11, 1999, pp. C1, C13.

8. Amazon.com, Inc. financial statements.

9. "Michael Dell Says Online Sales Represent a Fraction of Internet's Massive Business Potential," Dell Press Release, Aug. 25, 1999 accessed Nov. 18, 1999 at Web site www.dell.com/us/en/gen/corporate/press/pressoffice_us_1999.html.

10. "Current Database Statistics," *Editor & Publisher* Web site at emedial.mediainfo.com/emedia/statistics.htm. Current to Nov. 5, 1999.

11. If the link is still good, a good and brief description of the Internet is at Jack Rickard, "The Internet—What Is It?" *Boardwatch Magazine's ISP Directory*, Winter 98/Spring 99. You can try the online link at boardwatch.internet.com/isp/spring99/internetarch.html. Hal Varian, the Dean of the School of Information Management and Systems at the University of California at Berkeley kept a site with many useful links to relevant articles and other sites at www.sims.berkeley.edu/resources/infoecon/.

12. Bill McCarthy, "Introduction to the Directory of Internet Service Providers," *Boardwatch Magazine's Directory of Internet Service Providers*, Winter '98/Spring '99, on Web site at boardwatch.internet.com/isp/spring99/introduction.html, November 20, 1998 and 11th ed. on Web site boardwatch.internet.com/isp/index.html. The number of connections to backbone provers exceeds the number of ISPs because many ISPs are served by multiple backbone providers.

13. "National Dial-up Access Provider," *Boardwatch Magazine Directory of Internet Service Providers*, on Web site at boardwatch.internet.com/isp/nsp/index.html, November 20, 1998.

14. "Cable Internet Service Providers," *Cable Datacom News*, on Web site at CableDatacomNews.com/cmic5.htm, November 2, 1998.

15. Ibid.

16. "Cable Modem Market Stats and Projections," *Cable Datacom News*, at Web site at CableDatacomNews.com/cmic16.htm, November 20, 1998.

17. Downstream refers to data being sent from servers to the users. Upstream is from the user to a server or another user.

18. Joel Brinkley, "Some Broadcasters Back Away From HDTV Programming Pledge," *New York Times Online*, August 18, 1997, on Web site at www.nytimes.com/library/cyber/week/081897hdtv.html, accessed August 18, 1997.

19. *Communications Industry Forecast*, 12th ed. (New York: Veronis, Suhler & Associates, 1998).

20. Steve Outing, "Mercury Center Revisited: Portal Vision," *E&P Interactive*, July 22, 1998.

21. "Dow Jones & Company Announces Strong Gains in Third Quarter Earnings," *Business Wire* release of Dow Jones press release.

22. Jonathan Alter, "The Endgame," *Newsweek*, February 8, 1999. Accessed February 5, 1999, on Web site at www.newsweek.com/nw-srv/printed/us/na/na0306_5.htm.

23. Benjamin M. Compaine, "The New Literacy: Or How I Stopped Worrying and Learned to Love Pac-Man," in Benjamin M. Compaine, ed., *Understanding New Media* (Cambridge, MA: Ballinger Publishing Co., 1984); Benjamin M. Compaine, "Information Technology and Cultural Change," in Compaine, ed., *Issues in New Information Technology*. Sherry Turkle, *Life on the Screen: Identity in the Age of the Internet* (New York: Touchstone Books, 1997).

24. Even the programming that is apparently "free" has some cost in the form of marketing costs that are part of the prices we pay for goods and services that advertise. How much that cost really is and how much different prices would be if there were no advertising (and hence less competition and thus hypothetically perhaps higher prices for many goods and services) is left to another venue.

25. *Statistical Abstract of the United States, 1998*, p. 572, Table 914. Source of data is *The Veronis, Suhler & Associates Communications Industry Report*, annual.

26. Ibid., p. 573, Table 915.

27. Ibid.

28. Calculated by adding books, newspapers and magazines, video, audio and computer products, radio and TV repair and motion picture theater admission by personal consumption expenditures. From U.S. Bureau of Economic Analysis data in *The U.S. Statistical Abstract*, 1985 and 1998.

29. John Markoff, "Microsoft Deal to Aid Blending of PCs and TVS," *The New York Times Interactive*, April 7, 1997, on Web site at www.nytimes.com/library/cyber/week/040797webtv.html.

30. "What is Moore's Law?" Intel Corporation Web site at www.intel.com/intel/museum/25anniv/hof/ moore.htm, accessed February 12, 1999.

31. James Padinha, "Taking PC Prices Out of the Equation," TheStreet.com, February 3, 1999, on Web site at www.thestreet.com/comment/economics/713190.html.

32. Don Clark, "Free-PC to Offer Free Computers in Exchange for Exposure to Ads," *Wall Street Journal Interactive*, February 8, 1999, on Web site at interactive.wsj.com/articles/SB918431496866451000. htm.

33. Margaret Kane, "ISP Offers Free PCs to Subscribers," *ZDNet*, February 17, 1999, accessed February 19, 1999, on Web site at www.zdnet.com/zdnn/stories/news/0,4586,2210090,00.html.

34. Steve Outing, "TimesLink's Strategic Move to the Web Was Inevitable," *E&P Interactive*, October 5, 1995. Accessed January 11, 1999, on Web site at www.mediainfo.com/ephome/news/newshtm/ stop/stop106.htm.

35. Alex Kuczynski, "Slate Ends Its 10-Month Experiment with Subscriptions," *The New York Times on the Web*, February 15, 1999, on Web site at www.nytimes.com/library/tech/99/02/biztech/articles/ 15slat.html.

36. See note 31.

37. "Consumer Reports Online Gives a Behind-the-Scenes Cybertour of Its Testing Labs," *Business Wire*, November 11, 1998, on Web site at www.businesswire.com/webbox/bw.111198/873325.htm.

38. Total advertising: "Facts About Newspapers, 1998," Newspaper Association of America. Internet advertising: Internet Advertising Bureau.

39. "PW Media Conference: Bullish Ad Outlook Sets Stage" (New York: PaineWebber Research Note), December 8, 1998. This reported on the presentation of Robert Coen, a longtime advertising industry analyst for the McCann-Erickson agency. This document and others from the 1998 PaineWebber Media Conference was available as a .pdf document on Web site at www.painewebber. com/media/whatsnew/index.html.

40. As one example of a self-published site with a variety of content, if it's still available, see Web site at www.rjgeib.com.

41. A phenomenon of xcam sites was perhaps a precursor. For example, Jennicam started simply as a site where a video camera sent a new picture every 30 seconds of whatever was in front of it. It was situated in a young women named Jenni's apartment. Over time, this site grew more elaborate and added short video clips and a link to a personal real-time "show." Production values were minimal—but it was spontaneous and unfiltered. Jennicam was at www.jennicam.org.

42. About caches: American Online and other large ISPs store many of the most requested sites on their own servers. When a user of that service requests one of these URLs, instead of traveling via the Internet to the host server, it is "short stopped" at the ISPs server and sent back to the requester. This increases access speed for users and reduces traffic on the Internet backbone. But the original information provider therefore may not know the full extent of the popularity of their material. The notion of intellectual property issues involved in caching is another issue.

43. See note 10.

44. *The Emerging Digital Economy*, Secretariat on Electronic Commerce, U.S. Department of Commerce, Washington, DC, A4-4.

45. "Current Database Statistics as of December 3, 1998," *Editor & Publisher* Media Info Link, on Web site at www.mediainfo.com/ephome/npaper/nphtm/statistics.htm, January 4, 1999.

46. Compiled at UtimateTV.Com, www.ultimatetv.com/tv/us/, January 4, 1999.

47. In 1999, Web21 collected data from many different sources. They primarily used the logs from proxy servers. These logs were FTP'd to Web21 on a daily basis and represented the surfing patterns of over 100,000 users worldwide. Approximately 60% of the sample was from North America and 40% was from international countries. Universities, businesses and home users were all represented, but AOL, Prodigy and CompuServe users were not represented. Web21 tracked single-page views only, not images or frames. Web21 is part of GO2NET. It excludes its own sites from the rankings.

48. Timothy Noah, "Beating Swords into TV Shares," *U.S. News & World Report*, December 1, 1997, on Web site at www.usnews.com/usnews/issue/971201/1cnn.htm.

49. "Portals Emerge as Dominant Source for Online News," New York, Jupiter Communications, December 8, 1998, on Web site at www.jup.com/jupiter/press/releases/1998/1208a.html.
50. Ibid.
51. Netscape financial reports, accessed from Web site at www.netscape.com/comprod/investor, January 11, 1999.
52. Company Profile from Disclosure's Global Access, on Web site at www.disclosure.com/dga/search.cgi, March 9, 1999.
53. Reed-Elsevier Annual Reports, 1999 and 1997 accessed at www.reed-elsevier.com.
54. Company profile from Hoover's Online, on Web site at www.hoovers.com/premium/profiles/41609.html, accessed March 9, 1999.
55. Thomson Corporation Annual Reports, 1998 and 1997 accessed on Web site at www.thomcorp.com.
56. "AP Today: Facts and Figures," accessed March 9, 1999, on Web site at www.ap.org/pages/aptoday/index.html.
57. Bridge Information Systems, company profile from Hoover's Online, accessed on Web site at www.hoovers.com/premium/profiles/42781.html, March 9, 1999.
58. George Anders, "Softbank Hits $12 Billion Jackpot on Its Various Internet Stakes," *Wall Street Journal*, February 3, 1999, p. B-1, on Web site at interactive.wsj.com/articles/SB917994007337296500.htm.
59. With revenue in 1999 of about $550 million Yahoo's capitalized value on November 19, 1999, was an incredible (except in Internet dollars) $44.7 billion. This was roughly the same as aircraft manufacturer Boeing, with $56 *billion* in sales.
60. Richard Siklos, "Knight Ridder and New Media: If You Can't Beat 'Em . . . ," *Business Week*, January 18, 1999, on Web site at www.businessweek.com/1999/03/b3612082.htm.
61. Brian Steinberg, "New York Times to Buy Stake in Web Publisher TheStreet.com," *Wall Street Journal Interactive Edition*, February 22, 1999, at interactive.wsj.com/articles/SB919728196550652500.htm.
62. David Kline, "Infobahn Warrior," *Wired 2.07*, July 1994, on Web site at www.wired.com/wired/archive/2.07/malone.html; and David Kline, "Align and Conquer," *Wired 3.02*, February 1995, on Web site at www.wired.com/wired/archive/3.02/smith.html, both accessed February 12, 1999.
63. Covering this subject is tricky. This is a case where the fast pace in the evolution of the Internet business makes any statement about what is happening *now* (1999) conceivably very outdated by 2003—or earlier. But the basic principle here—that businesses in the different sectors of the general "media" industry are often valued quite differently, making glib pronouncements on who is likely to acquire whom unpredictable for the casual observer.
64. Alex Berenson, "Who's Xoomin' Who?" May 10, 1999, *The Street.Com* accessed May 11, 1999, on Web site at www.thestreet.com/tech/internet/745312.html.
65. Paul M. Sherer and Kara Swisher, "Wall Street Ponders Mergers Of Web and Traditional Firms," *Wall Street Journal*, February 5, 1999, p. C-1. Quote of Louis G. Zachary Jr., a managing director at Credit Suisse First Boston.
66. Personal recollection of B. Compaine who participated in the seminar. CRT is a cathode ray tube—essentially the typical video display of the time.
67. Kristen Kennedy, "3Com's Palm VII Will Offer Functions Once Relegated to Larger, Pricier Units—Wireless Features Key to Next-Gen Palmtop," *Computer Retail Week*, December 7, 1998, accessed February 2, 1999, on Web site at www.techweb.com/se/directlink.cgi?CRW19981207S0007. This article reported an initial price of $800. By November 1999 the list price was down to $499.
68. Amy Cowen, " Spotlight Your Site: Tapping the Traffic Stream," Web Marketing Information Center, accessed February 4, 1999, on Web site at www.hp.com/Ebusiness/index_spotlight.html.
69. Lee Gomes, "Start-Up Virage Takes Lead in Making Video Searchable," *Wall Street Journal*, July 22, 1999, p. B4. Also accessed on July 22, 1999, on Web site at interactive.wsj.com/articles/SB932597839476672451.htm.

8

Who Owns the Media Companies?

Benjamin M. Compaine

The preceding seven chapters identified the major players in each of the traditional and evolving media segments: broadcasting, cable and digital broadcast satellite (DBS) television, radio and music, theatrical film, newspapers, magazines, book publishing and online. Each chapter described the degree of competition within each segment and identified the companies that owned or controlled the brand names.

This chapter has two objectives. First, it pulls together into a comprehensive table the leading media companies across the industry boundaries, cross-tabulated to show what segments in which each company plays a major role. Second, this chapter identifies who actually owns these companies. With few exceptions, most of these organizations are publicly owned. That is, their stock is owned by individuals and investment institutions. Organizations are run by managers, but managers are rarely the owners. Although senior management generally has considerable latitude in day-to-day operations, they are often more constrained in strategic direction by the interests of their major stockholders.

MEDIA HOLDINGS OF THE LEADING MASS MEDIA ENTERPRISES

In the 1982 edition of *Who Owns the Media?*, 62 companies were recognized as being a leading firm in one or more media industries. Table 8.1 lists 90 companies, including 5 record companies, 2 DBS providers and a list of online services, most operated by companies that did not exist in 1995 (yet alone in 1982).

The basis for determining which are the dominant firms differs from segment to segment and is subject to varying interpretation. For newspapers, it is those companies that account for the largest proportion of aggregate circulation. For magazines, it is the largest groups by circulation or revenue. Broadcast television and radio are measured by the groups with the largest audiences. For cable MSOs and networks, it is subscribing households. For book publishers, booksellers and motion picture and recorded music distributors, it is proportion of industry revenues. For the electronic publishing segment, it is those firms whose Web site or sites, in aggregate, account

TABLE 8.1

Leading Firms in One or More Media Segments, 1998

	Newspapers	Magazines	Broadcast TV	Cable MSO	Cable Nets	DBS	Radio	Film Production & Distribution	Film Exhibition	Recorded Music	Electronic Info Services	Book Publishing	Book Selling
Leader in Seven Segments													
Time Warner		*		*	*			*		*	*	*	
Leader in Five Segments													
News Corp.	*	*	*					*				*	
Viacom			*		*			*	*			*	
Walt Disney Co.		*	*		*		*	*					
Leader in Three Segments													
CBS			*		*		*						
Cox Enterprises	*			*			*						
Sony								*	*	*			
Thomson Corporation	*										*	*	
USA Network			*		*						*		
Leader in Two Segments													
A. H. Belo	*		*										
Amazon.com											*		*
Bertelsmann										*		*	
Comcast				*	*								
Gannett	*		*										
General Electric (NBC)			*		*								
Hearst	*	*											
Newhouse	*	*											
Reader's Digest		*										*	
Reed-Elsevier		*									*		
Seagram								*		*			
Softbank (Ziff-Davis)		*									*		
Tele-Communications, Inc.				*	*								
Tribune Co.	*		*										
Leader in One Segment													
Adelphia Cable				*									
AMC Theatres									*				
American Association of Retired Persons		*											
AOL											*		
Associated Press											*		

482

Table 8.1 (Continued)

	Newspapers	Magazines	Broadcast TV	Cable MSO	Cable Nets	DBS	Radio	Film Production & Distribution	Film Exhibition	Recorded Music	Electronic Info Services	Book Publishing	Book Selling
AtHome											*		
Barnes & Noble													*
Blue Mountain Arts											*		
Bonneville International							*						
Books-A-Million													*
Borders Group													*
Bridge Information Systems											*		
Broadcast.com											*		
Cablevision Systems				*									
Carmike Theatres									*				
Century Communications				*									
Charter Communications				*									
Chris-Craft Industries, Inc.				*									
Cinemark USA									*				
Clear Channel Communications							*						
CNET											*		
Compaq											*		
Crown Books													*
C-SPAN					*								
Dow Jones & Co.	*												
E. W. Scripps	*												
EchoStar Communications						*							
EMI Group										*			
Emmis Broadcasting							*						
Falcon Cable Television				*									
Freedom Communications	*												
General Cinemas									*				
Hachette-Filipacci		*											
Hicks Muse, Tate & Furst							*						
Harcourt General												*	
Houghton Mifflin												*	
Hollinger, Inc.	*												
Hughes Electronics						*							

(Continued)

Table 8.1 (Continued)

	Newspapers	Magazines	Broadcast TV	Cable MSO	Cable Nets	DBS	Radio	Film Production & Distribution	Film Exhibition	Recorded Music	Electronic Info Services	Book Publishing	Book Selling
International Data Group		*											
Jacor Communications							*						
Jones Intercable				*									
Knight-Ridder	*												
Lenfest Communications				*									
Lifetime Television					*								
LookSmart Ltd.											*		
Marcus Cable				*									
McClatchy Newspapers	*												
McGraw-Hill	*											*	
MediaNews Group	*												
MediaOne				*									
Meredith		*											
National Geographic Society		*											
Microsoft											*		
New York Times Co.	*												
Paxson Communications			*										
Pearson PLC												*	
Petersen Publishing		*											
Primark											*		
Primedia		*											
RealNetworks, Inc											*		
Regal Theatres									*				
Reuters Group											*		
Spanish Broadcasting System							*						
Telemundo Group			*										
Times Mirror Co.	*												
Xoom.com, Inc.											*		
Yahoo!											*		

Note: Inclusion as a major player in this table is based on the identification of the companies according to the criteria described in the text. In most cases they are drawn from each company's standing as of 1998. Because it is about a rapidly changing industry, chap. 7, Online Information Industry, was updated in many cases to reflect company standing in late 1999. However, for consistency, Table 8.1 remains a snapshot as of late 1998. Given the divestitures, acquisitions and start-ups this book has discussed, it will always be outdated.

for the largest percentage of all Internet users accessing within a month and those players with the greatest electronic publishing revenue.

Other measures could have been used, such as percentage of advertising revenues or number of stations or publications. However, the measures used here were selected as representing the most valid proxy for the most frequently cited concern over media competition: the degree of diverse sources of news, culture and information available to consumers. The selected metrics are most appropriate for approximating dominance—or lack of dominance—of some number of media players across the different segments.

The number of dominant players also varies from segment to segment. In recorded music there are the top five, with about 80% of the market and everyone else. In theatrical film, there are six studios that account for the 90% of the box office. On the other hand, including the 15 largest newspaper publishers still only accounts for 44% of daily circulation and the 10 largest cable system operators reach under 50% of TV households. Thus, the number of players in Table 8.1 is somewhat arbitrary, but is meant to substantially represent the largest companies in each segment. It provides a useful snapshot into the degree of competition within and across media segments.

Table 8.1 provides several insights.

- Only one company, Time Warner, spans half the segments. Time Warner, known for its magazines, books, film and music businesses, is nonetheless a no-show in the major segments of newspapers and broadcasting.
- Three firms—News Corp., Disney and Viacom—span five or four segments. News Corp., which at one time owned a substantial group of U.S. newspapers, sold off most, including the *Boston Herald*, to concentrate on building a television station group that they needed as the base for the Fox Network. Disney divested itself of the newspapers and trade magazines (Fairchild and Chilton) that came along in the Capital Cities/ABC acquisition and has no cable system operation to backstop its cable networks. To reduce debt from its acquisitions, Viacom sold off its cable franchises, its radio station group and parts of its book publishing to concentrate on its 50% owned TV network, the United Paramount Network (UPN).
- Five companies are major players in as many as three segments: Bertelsmann, Cox, Sony, Newhouse and USA Network. Bertelsmann replaced Newhouse in the book publishing arena by purchasing Random House from Newhouse. USA Network has been cobbled together with some old media (televison stations), some newer media (the Home Shopping Network), and the newest, online through its association with Ticketmaster Online-Citysearch. CBS (broadcast and cable networks, radio) squeaks in to this group by virtue of its aquisition of The Nashville Network, the eighth largest cable network measured by households with access to it.
- Fourteen firms show up in two segments, including such well-known and visible names as Newhouse (newspapers and magazines), Hearst (magazines and books), Gannett (newspapers and broadcasting) and newcomer Amazon.com. The latter is both a popular Web site in itself, as well as a new major force in bookselling.
- The remaining 67 names in Table 8.1 are major stakeholders in only one of the old or new media segments. Despite often being substantial players in their segments, their presence is minor or nonexistent across the media spectrum. This includes many news-

paper publishers, including the New York Times Co. E. W. Scripps, Knight-Ridder and Dow Jones.

One of the changes in the media industry since 1980 is that it has become more "pure." That is, in 1980, a small but significant proportion of the largest media companies were small parts of larger industrial companies or conglomerates: Westinghouse Broadcasting was a small part of Westinghouse, which made nuclear powerplants and electrical equipment; Scott & Fetzer sold vacuum cleaners door to door and owned World Book. Gulf + Western (conglomerate), Plough (pharmaceuticals), General Tire and General Electric were among others. By 1999, less than a handful of nonmedia companies had major media properties: General Electric still owned NBC. Microsoft had cable and online interests. Seagrams, a beverage company (liquor and Tropicana), was divesting itself of its nonmedia businesses. Westinghouse acquired CBS, then shed its industrial companies and renamed the remaining company CBS. Gulf + Western turned itself into Paramount Pictures and became part of Viacom.

Despite the seeming constant stream of mergers and acquisitions that attract headlines, there have been only modest shifts in the role of major players in the media industry between 1980 and 1998. They are contrasted in Table 8.2. Time merged with Warner and the combination appears across the chart. But News Corporation did not even show up as a player in 1980. By 1986, it had created what had been a longtime goal of policymakers—a viable fourth broadcast network with a different slant than the older three. In 1980, CBS was one of only three commercial networks and on any given night had 30% of the television audience. It had a stable of consumer magazines and book imprints. In 1998, it was one of six broadcast networks, and was happy with 15% of the audience. It is the major owner of radio stations and is feeling its way in the online world.

TABLE 8.2
Comparison of Holdings of Selected Media Companies, 1980 and 1998

Company	Segments with Leading Status, 1980	Segments with Leading Status, 1998
Time Warner	Magazines, book publishing, cable MSO, cable network	Magazines, book publishing, cable MSO, cable network, film, music, online
Newhouse	Newspapers, magazines, cable MSO, book publishing	Newspapers, magazines
CBS, Inc.	TV broadcasting, radio, magazines, book publishing	TV broadcasting, radio, cable network
News Corp.	(Not a significant presence in U.S.)	Magazines, TV broadcasting, cable network, book publishing, film
Times Mirror Co.	Newspapers, book publishing, cable MSO	Newspapers
Cox Enterprises	Newspapers, TV broadcasting, cable MSO	Newspapers, TV broadcasting, radio
Hearst	Newspapers, magazines	Newspapers, magazines
Tribune Co.	Newspapers, TV broadcasting	Newspaper, TV broadcasting, online
Viacom	Cable MSO	TV broadcasting, film, book publishing, online
Walt Disney Co.	Film	Magazines, TV broadcasting, cable network, radio, film, online

In 1980, Disney was the weak eighth-place Hollywood studio. It was better known for its theme parks than as a film maker. In 1998, it was a major player as a cable network, in film, broadcasting and magazines, as well as online. On the other hand, the various interests of the Newhouse family were consolidated primarily into newspapers and magazines. It sold off its book publishing operation, Random House, as well as its broadcasting stations. It has minor investments in cable systems and programming. Cox Enterprises is in fewer traditional media segments, as is Times Mirror. Viacom has expanded beyond its original television and cable roots.

The number of media companies that were considered among their top firms in their segments in 1980 and were still around in 1998 was relatively small. Table 8.3 identifies the leading firms in both years. Only 22 out of the 65 firms from 1980 were still in business and among the leaders in one or more segments in 1998. A few from 1980, like Playboy Enterprises and Scholastic, were still independent firms in 1998 but were not in the top tier of firms in their business segments. In most cases, however, the 1980 companies chose to sell themselves to others. Of these, many exist as subsidiaries or brands: Columbia Pictures is now Sony Pictures; Twentieth Century-Fox is owned by News Corp; Warner Communications is now part of Time Warner; Prentice-Hall is within Simon & Schuster, which is part of Viacom. In other cases, the old firm was merged into a new entity and disappeared: Continental Cablevision was merged with the cable acquisitions of the former Bell company, US West, and was then spun off as an independent publicly owned company, MediaOne; it and Tele-Communications were acquired by AT&T. Field Enterprises was absorbed by Hollinger.

The list of 1998 firms that were not present in 1980 also includes different stories. A. H. Belo was around with newspapers and broadcasting, but was not a major player in either. Comcast and Adelphia were small cable systems and Barnes & Noble was a small bookseller. News Corp. owned a few newspapers and Bertelsmann was a major presence only in Europe. Many other companies did not exist. Obviously, the Internet companies were not born. Amazon and Yahoo! did not exist. High power earth satellites were not available, thus there were no DBS firms. But even in the more established areas, new players have replaced older ones. Primedia and Hachette-Filippachi replaced CBS, Ziff-Davis and Macmillan at the top of the magazine publishing segment. MediaNews and Hollinger came in to pick up some newspapers that others did not want.

There are several, perhaps seeming contradictory, conclusions that may be drawn from examining this ebb and flow (see Tables 8.2 and 8.3).

- In some cases, the big got bigger. ABC merged with Capital Cities, then into Disney. Time and Warner merged, then took in Turner Broadcasting, with Cable News Network. Viacom acquired Paramount, Simon & Schuster and Prentice-Hall.
- In other cases, the big got smaller or disappeared. CBS divested its magazines and books; Macmillan sold off its books and magazines; Newhouse retreated from cable operations, Times Mirror got out of the book publishing business and Knight-Ridder divested itself of specialized information services as well as minor broadcasting, cable and book publishing operations.

TABLE 8.3
Additions and Subtractions From Largest Media Company Lists, 1980 and 1998

On 1980 List Only	On 1998 List Only	1980 and 1998
Twentieth Century-Fox	A. H. Belo	Bonneville International
ABC Cos.	Adelphia Cable	CBS
Allied Artists	AMC Entertainment	Compaq
American Multi-Cinemas	Amazon.com	Cox Enterprises
Avco-Embassy	American Association of	Dow Jones & Co.
Capital Cities	Retired Persons	E. W. Scripps
Communications	AOL	Gannett
Charter Co.	AtHome	General Cinemas
Columbia Pictures	AT&T	General Electric
Continental Cablevision	Barnes & Noble	Hearst
Doubleday	Bertelsmann	Knight-Ridder
Encyclopaedia Britannica	Blue Mountain Arts	McGraw-Hill
Field Enterprises	Books-A-Million	Meredith
Gaylord Communications	Borders Group	New York Times Co.
Grolier	Broadcast.com, Inc.	Newhouse
Gulf + Western	Cablevision Systems	Reader's Digest
Harcourt Brace Jovanovich	Carmike Theatres	Thomson
Inner City	Century Communications	Time Warner
Macmillan	Charter Communications	Times Mirror Co.
MCA	Chris-Craft Industries, Inc.	Tribune Co.
Metromedia	Cinemark USA	Viacom
Playboy Enterprises	Clear Channel	Walt Disney Co.
Plitt Theatres	Communications	
Plough Broadcasting	CNET	
Prentice-Hall	Comcast	
RCA	Compaq	
RKO General	Crown Books	
Rogers UA	C-SPAN	
Cablesystems	EchoStar Communications	
Sammons Communications	EMAP Petersen Publishing	
San Juan Racing	EMI Group	
Scholastic	Emmis Communications	
Scott & Fetzer	Falcon Cable Television	
SFN Cos.	Freedom Communications	
Storer Broadcasting	Hachette-Filipacci	
Taft Broadcasting	Hicks Muse, Tate & Furst	
Tele-Communications	Hollinger, Inc.	
Trinagle Publications	Hughes Electronics	
UA Theatre Circuit	Jacor Communications	
United Cable	Jones Intercable	
Warner Communications	Lenfest Communications	
Westinghouse	Lifetime Television	
	LookSmart Ltd.	
	Marcus Cable	
	MediaNews Group	
	MediaOne	
	McClatchy Communications	
	Microsoft	
	News Corp.	
	Paxson Communications	
	Pearson PLC	
	Primedia	

(Continued)

TABLE 8.3 *(Continued)*

On 1980 List Only	On 1998 List Only	1980 and 1998
	RealNetworks, Inc.	
	Regal Cinemas	
	Reiman Publications	
	Rodale Press	
	Seagram	
	Softbank	
	Sony	
	Spanish Broadcasting System	
	Telemundo Group	
	USA Networks	

Sources: 1998: Table 8.1; 1980: *Who Owns the Media?*, rev. ed., 1982, Table 8.1.

- Large mergers get the headlines, but there is a steady profusion of newer players that come along to take advantage of opportunities created by the mergers. When Disney acquired Capital Cities/ABC, it became owner of some daily newspapers that did not fit its long-term plan. It sold some of these to Knight-Ridder. Knight-Ridder, needing to raise money to pay Disney, turned around and sold off some of its newspapers that it was not willing to support. MediaNews Group, formed in 1983, has picked up papers sold off by Knight-Ridder, Gannett and small chains.

- The list has become more international. Although few U.S.-based firms are major players globally, the United States is attracting interest from abroad. News Corp. is based in Australia and has substantial interests in Europe and Asia as well as North America. Bertelsmann is headquartered in Germany. Reed-Elsevier is a Dutch–English joint venture. Pearson PLC and EMI Group are based in London. Softbank has its base of operations in Japan. In 1980, on the other hand, no major media player was based outside North America.

WHO OWNS THE MEDIA COMPANIES

One task is to identify the corporate entities that are the media industry. That was the subject for the previous seven chapters, summarized in Table 8.1. But companies are composed of people and every organization has owners. It might be a government, a union, employees, a family or a larger group of stockholders. In the United States, media companies fall almost exclusively into the last two categories.

Private and Publicly Owned Firms

Most of the largest companies are publicly held, meaning that anyone can buy stock and have a vote, however large or small, on major corporate decisions. Publicly owned firms have a fiduciary duty to their stockholders, meaning they must protect the value of their investment. Several of the largest companies, however, are privately held, closely controlled by families, who are usually founders or their decedents. Their responsibility is to private interests, rather than to public ones.

who want to keep dominant ideology

The boundary between public and private ownership is not as sharp as might first appear. Many firms that are nominally publicly owned are still controlled by families or a small group of investors. Sometimes it is through family trusts. In many cases, there are multiple classes of stock, with greater voting power vested in the stock accessible only to the trust or founders, although all classes may share in the growth and profits of the company. In other cases, the original investors simply own substantial (although not necessarily a majority) amounts of the common stock. Among the prominent public firms where control is closely held are Times Mirror Co. (Chandler family), the New York Times Co. (Sulzberger family), Knight-Ridder (Knight and Ridder families), as well as Dow Jones (Bancroft decedents), News Corp. (Murdoch family) and the Reader's Digest Association (DeWitt trusts). Using various classes of stock and trusts, the owners have been able to at least partially gain the advantages of public ownership, while maintaining nominal voting control over their company.

Chapter 1 discusses the public versus private corporate structure, specifically regarding newspapers. However, the same analysis pertains to all media segments (and industry in general). There is nothing inherently better or worse about being publicly or privately owned. Public companies generally have access to greater financial resources and can therefore, should they choose, expand faster, invest in new equipment and services, weather downturns, invest in research and development and offer employees from key managers to entry-level newcomers a piece of ownership and with it incentives to make the company profitable. Profits come from a variety of strategies. They may come from cost-cutting. But, among the most successful companies over time, they come from products and services that are better than, cheaper than and/or more innovative than those of the competition. On the other hand, public companies have to report on their performance every three months. To attract investment, they may also need to show that they generate a better return than alternative uses of investors' money. For some companies, at some times, this pressure may encourage emphasis on short-term objectives that may not be consistent with long-term goals.

Private companies have a different set of strengths and weaknesses. On the plus side, managers typically do not have to keep one eye on outsiders. They may be able to make decisions faster, invest for the long term, ignoring such concerns as earnings per share and return on investment. Managers at private companies, especially media companies, may be able to pursue editorial objectives without having to answer to an outside Board of Directors. On the other hand, privately owned companies, without access to the equity markets, may find it difficult, even if they are profitable, to invest in new products or technologies. They are often unable to attract the top executives because they cannot offer the same incentives to share in the success of their company without a stock option plan. And, the flip side of not having to answer to outside stockholders for editorial policy is that the owners may pursue their personal social or political agendas with little restraint (a plus or a minus depending on how any observer feels about that agenda).

Access to investment capital is a particular advantage for public companies, especially when technologies are rapidly changing in an industry. In the 1970s and early

1980s, there was a wave of privately held newspaper firms selling to publicly owned companies, in part due to the investments they needed for advanced computer systems in the newsroom, for updated production equipment and presses. In the 1990s, all cable companies needed to upgrade their plan to offer digital services. Faced with the high capacity digital DBS services and telephone companies implementing high speed broadband transmission, the cable industry was facing substantial investment needs. Publicly owned companies were better equipped to accept investments than those in which the few controlling shareholders wanted to maintain control. In 1997, Microsoft invested $1 billion for a minority stake in Comcast. In 1998, Microsoft and computer maker Compaq each invested $212 million in Roadrunner, a start-up bankrolled by Time Warner and MediaOne to provide high speed Internet access to consumers. With these investments they were "hoping their cash injections and attention will help spur cable companies to make good on their oft-repeated promises to turn their cable-TV lines into seamless communications highways capable of handling all manner of digital traffic and interactive fare."[1] The handful of privately held companies, such as Falcon Cable and Lenfest, were not in a financial structure to participate.

Even the largest publicly owned players in the telecommunications sector were being stretched by the financial needs, leading to more than one merger. In supporting the reasoning for its planned merger with AT&T in 1999, TCI gave as its top reason:

> Delivery of new services through the cable infrastructure, such as local telephony, interactive television through the advanced set top devices or boxes and high-speed Internet access, will require the expenditure of significant capital investments in order to upgrade the cable plant and equipment of TCI's cable systems and also will require technology skills that TCI possesses only in limited amounts.[2]

Table 8.4 identifies the ownership structure of the organizations in Table 8.1 Overall, about two thirds (i.e., 64) were nominally publicly owned. Nominally, that is, because many of these, as indicted previously, were substantially controlled by a small class of stock. Table 8.5 further identifies the individuals and institutions that are the major stockholders of a selection of the largest media companies. Two indicators of how dispersed or closely held the stocks are is seen both in the proportion of ownership by insiders—officers and directors of the company—and in the total number of shareholders. For example, Adelphia Cable, the fifth largest cable system operator in 1999, was very much controlled by the foundling and managing Rigas family. At the other extreme, AT&T and General Electric, of which NBC is a very small part, had more than 3.5 million and half a million stockholders, respectively, with insiders accounting for less than 0.1% of the total. Walt Disney Co. is also among the most widely held in the world, with 658,000 stockholders (including many children who were given a few share as presents). Despite various stock options, insiders own only 1.5% of the company's common stock.

Insider stock ownership does not necessarily tell the entire story. Because of the various classes of stock and the conditions attached to them, insiders may have

TABLE 8.4
Corporate Structure and Control of Major Media Organizations, 1998

Public or Privately Held (Private in italic)	Number Shareholders	% Controlled by Officers and Directors
Adelphia Cable	164	73.4%
A. H. Belo	20,084	16.3
Amazon.com	2.304	46.7
AMC Entertainment	n.a.	6.5
American Association of Retired Persons	—	—
America Online	4,408	2.7
Associated Press	—	—
AT&T	3,500,000	under 0.1%
Barnes & Noble	2,018	30.7
Bertelsmann (Germany)	—	—
Blue Mountain Arts	—	—
Bonneville International	—	—
Books-A-Million	25,300	26.7
Borders Group	4,506	6.5
Bridge Information Systems		
Broadcast.com, Inc.[1]	36,782	n.a.
Cablevision Systems	927	59.6[2]
Carmike Cinemas	744	6.9
CBS	113,024	1.9
Century Communications	919	3.8
Charter Communications	—	—
Chris-Craft Industries, Inc.	4,089	38.1
Cinemark USA	—	—
Clear Channel Communications	622	15.3
CNET	226[3]	40.8
Comcast	4,144	2.0
Compaq (Alta Vista)	89,000	1.6
Cox Enterprises	—	—
Crown Books	230	n.a.
C-SPAN	—	—
Dow Jones & Co.	16,130	27.5
E. W. Scripps	5,018	61.8
EchoStar Communications	2,280	3.7
EMAP Petersen Publishing (UK)	n.a.	n.a.
EMI Group (UK)	n.a.	n.a.
Exite@Home	911	66.0[4]
Emmis Communications	n.a.	4.9 (A) 70.1 (B)
Falcon Cable Television	—	—
Freedom Communications	—	—
Gannett	14,000	1.7
General Cinema	2,845	n.a.
General Electric (NBC)	543,000	0.2
Hachette-Filipacci Medias (France)	n.a.	n.a.
Harcourt General	1,645	21.8
Hearst	—	—
Hicks Muse, Tate & Furst	—	—
Hollinger International (Canada)	239	48.2
Houghton Mifflin	5,500	3.8
Hughes Electronics[5]	n.a.	n.a.
International Data Group	n.a.	n.a.
Jacor Communications	1,600	n.a.
Jones Intercable	1,841	13.5
Knight-Ridder	11,373	3.6
Lenfest Communications	—	—
Lifetime Television	—	—

(Continued)

TABLE 8.4 (Continued)

Public or Privately Held (Private in italic)	Number Shareholders	% Controlled by Officers and Directors
LookSmart Ltd.	—	—
Marcus Cable	—	—
McClatchy Co.	2.307	59.1 (A) 78.8 (B)
McGraw-Hill	n.a.	1.4
MediaNews Group	—	—
MediaOne	543,084	0.6
Meredith	1,900	26.5
Microsoft	70,491	32.0
National Geographic Society	—	—
New York Times Co.	11,635	21.6
Newhouse (Advance Publications)	—	—
News Corp. (Australia)	25,832	0.1[7]
Paxson Communications	502	43.0
Pearson PLC (UK)	n.a.	n.a.
Primark	7,302	18.4
Primedia	268	6.7
Reed-Elsevier	38,000+	n.a.
Reader's Digest	2,501	n.a.
RealNetworks, Inc.	404[3]	57.6
Regal Cinemas	—	—
Reuters Group (UK)	25,769	n.a.
Seagram (Canada)	7,167	30.6
Softbank (Japan)	54,690	n.a.
Sony	183,720	n.a.
Spanish Broadcasting System	—	—
Tele-Communications	n.a.	n.a.
Telemundo Group	—	—
Thomson (Canada)	n.a.	n.a.
Time Warner	25,000	1.0
Times Mirror Co.	4.236	9.5
Tribune Co.	5,855	1.9
USA Network	30,000	23.1
Viacom	28,532	18.8
Walt Disney Co.	658,000	1.5
Yahoo!	2,350	27.6

[1]Acquired by Yahoo!, April 1999.
[2]Effective voting power of Class A and Class B combined.
[3]Does not reflect effect of subsequent public offering.
[4]Total for all "insiders."
[5]Controlled by General Motors.
Sources: Numer of shareholders from 10K reports, generally 12/31/98 Insider ownership from Proxy reports, generally March 1998. Accessed via Disclosure Global Access at www.disclosure.com and Edgar Online at www.edgar-online.com.

greater influence than the percentages indicate. At the McClatchy Co., for example, the closely held Class B shares elect 75% of the Board of Directors and have one vote per share on other matters. The more widely available Class A shares elect the rest of the Board and have one tenth of a vote per share on other matters. All stockholders share equally in dividends, if any.[3]

In addition, it is not necessary to own or control even a majority of the stock in large companies to exert substantial control. With most of the stock widely held, a substantial minority block closely held can usually have deciding influence in company policy. One notable example is Australia-based News Corporation. The Murdoch family, through an investment company, owned about 31% of this publicly traded company in 1998. But with the remainder of ownership scattered among 123 institutions and hundreds or thousands of individuals, the Murdoch family is generally in control.[4]

Although multiple classes or large closely held blocks of stock have been used to help the founding families to maintain control over their company while still being able to tap the broader financial markets, they must give up most of the privacy that comes with running a private company. All public companies must follow very specific disclosure requirements of the Securities and Exchange Commission. Their books must be essentially open to pubic scrutiny; the details of their acquisitions and investments must be openly vetted, and their fiduciary responsibility to all outside stockholders must be respected. In short, even when a publicly traded company is closely controlled, it must be responsible to broader interests than if it were a private company.

The Role of Financial Institutions

Table 8.6 is the reverse of Table 8.5. It identifies the institutions that have invested most consistently in media companies. It shows some of their largest holdings, but far from all. Much of the savings of Americans is not in savings banks but in various investments. Many Americans have invested in stocks and bonds, in effect buying pieces of corporations. But by far the largest portion of savings in the United States is in the form of pension and retirement plans, IRAs, and private investments in mutual funds. This money is in turn invested in the equity and debt of global business. This is relevant in the understanding of who owns the media because so much of the media is owned, indirectly perhaps, but in the interest of tens of millions of working people.

The largest mutual fund manager in 1999, Fidelity Investments, had under its numerous funds and plans $600 billion in assets in 1999. The second largest, Vanguard Funds, had $420 billion. The College Retirement Equity Fund, the manager of the savings plan for most university faculty and staff, managed about $240 billion.[5] The California Public Employees Retirement System (CalPERS), the largest public institutional investor in the United States with assets in 1999 in excess of $151 billion, provides for more than 1 million current and retired public employees in California.[6]

Financial institutions include bank trust departments, insurance companies, pension funds and mutual stock funds. In the case of bank trust departments, securities are bought and held for customers who have trust funds or similar accounts, for which the bank has a fiduciary responsibility. They are held for many individuals, some of whom chose to vote their stock themselves, others of whom allow the bank to vote their shares. Mellon, Barclays, State Street and Bankers Trust are among the bank holding companies with a high level of media company investment.

Although the records may show that a particular institution is the holder of record, generally banks do not own the stock themselves. Similarly, other institu-

TABLE 8.5
Largest Stockholders of Selected Media Companies, 1998

Adelphia Cable	Rigas Family	64.30%[1]
	Capital Research	4.90
	Janus Capital	3.68
	Denver Investment Advisors	2.20
	Northwestern Mutual Life	1.47
	62 Institutions	34.76
Amazon.com	Jeffrey Bezos & family	41.00
	John Doerr	12.00
	Deutch Bank Securities	14.39
	Kleiner, Perkins, Caufield & Byers	11.40
	Bowman Capital	3.04
	Essex Investment Management	2.57
	104 Institutions	39.80
AOL	Fidelity Management & Research	8.72
	Putnam Investment Management	5.24
	Janus Capital	4.96
	American Century Investment	3.07
	J. P. Morgan	2.96
	Stephen M. Case	1.30
	369 Institutions	72.60
AT&T	Fidelity Management & Research	0.05
	Barclays Bank	0.03
	Capital Research & Management	0.03
	College Retirement Equities	0.02
	Merrill Lynch & Co.	0.02
	834 Institutions	45.80
Bertelsmann	J. Mohn GmbH	46.61
	R. Mohn Verwaltungs	42.65
	Zeit-Stiftung Eblin & Bucerius	10.74
CBS	Fidelity Management & Research	9.06
	Putnam Investment	4.88
	Janus Capital	3.19
	Barclays Bank	2.77
	College Retirement Equity Fund	2.63
	354 Institutions	56.80
Chris-Craft Industries, Inc.	Sigel family	>50.00[2]
	Gamco Investors	7.46
	Capital Research	4.82
	Boston Partners Asset Management	4.42
	Gabelli Funds	4.14
	Private Capital Management	3.40
	111 Institutions	65.48
Clear Channel Communications	L. Lowry Mays	15.00
	B. J. McCombs	11.00
	Putnam Investments	8.90
	Fidelity Management & Research	5.05
	Morgan Stanley Dean Witter	4.57
	Jennison Associates Capital	3.05
	American Express Financial	3.01
	265 Institutions	64.37
Comcast	Brian and Ralph Roberts	15.80
	Fidelity Management & Research	9.88
	Wellington Management	8.77
	Capital Research	6.11

(Continued)

TABLE 8.5 *(Continued)*

	Vanguard Group	3.29
	Loomis Sayles & Co.	2.79
	113 Institutions	63.59
Dow Jones & Co.	Jane C. Macelree	8.60
	James H. Ottaway, Jr.	7.80
	Capital Research	7.68
	Roy Hammer Esq.	7.55
	Chrisopher Bancroft	6.40
	State Street Corp.	6.27
	Franklin Resources	4.08
	200 Institutions	79.77
Gannett	University of California	3.59
	Equitable Companies	3.30
	Barclays Bank	3.26
	Wellington Management	3.14
	Tukman Capital Management	3.14
	507 Institutions	72.60
General Electric	Fidelity Management & Research	3.67
	Barclays Bank	2.92
	Banks Trust	1.75
	State Street Corp.	1.54
	Mellon Bank Corp.	1.26
	110 Institutions	18.80
Hollinger International	Conrad Black & Family	>50.00[2]
	Bankers Trust	3.98
	State Street Research & Management	3.19
	Moody Aldrich & Sullivan	2.68
	Barclays Bank	2.08
	Mellon Bank	1.94
	106 Institutions	52.57
Knight-Ridder	Southeastern Asset Management	13.06
	Harris Associates	12.10
	T. Rowe Price	3.5
	Barclays Bank	2.82
	Mellon Bank	2.22
	213 Institutions	76.51
McClatchy Newspapers	McClatchy Family	>50.00[2]
	Private Capital Management	2.94
	Wellington Management	2.79
	Primecap Management	2.12
	Gamco Investors	1.67
	Pitcairn Group	1.00
	72 Institutions	65.45
New York Times Co.	Sulzberger family	16.00
	Barclays Bank	1.18
	Mellon Bank	1.15
	Lazard Freres	1.02
	275 Institutions	52.84
News Corp.	Murdoch Family	30.86
	Capital Research & Management	1.06
	Southeastern Asset Management	0.91
	123 Institutions	5.36
Primedia	Kohlberg Kravitz & Roberts	84.60
	Shapiro Capital Management	2.43
	Cimco Inc.	0.94

(Continued)

TABLE 8.5 *(Continued)*

	51 Institutions	1]
Reader's Digest	Wallace-Reader's Digest Funds	7[
	Employee Stock ownership plans	7.90[3]
	Brandes Investment Partners	4.20
	T. Rowe Price	4.04
	Fidelity Management & Research	2.30
	Franklin Resources	2.10
	Federated Investors	1.84
	113 Institutions	43.23
Seagram	Bronfman Family	34.52
	Southeastern Asset Management	4.19
	J. P. Morgan & Co.	4.11
	Barclays Bank	2.56
	Institutional Capital	2.49
	Primecap Management	1.55
	216 Institutions	26.22
Sony	Dodge & Cox	1.00
	Primecap Management	0.62
	114 Institutions	3.51
Time Warner	R. E. Turner	11.70
	Capital Research	10.6
	Fidelty Research & Management	6.90
Times Mirror Co.	Chandler Family	>50.00[3]
	Fidelity Research & Management	15.60
	Soros Management	9.93
	Putnam Investments	6.62
	Times Mirror Employees Stock Ownership	5.09
Tribune Co.	McCormick Trust-Cantigny Foundation	18.37
	Northern Trust[4]	11.04
	John A. Levin & Co.	3.70
	Fidelity Management & Research	2.92
	Barclays Bank	2.80
	Bankers Trust	2.08
	Putnam Management	1.92
	292 Institutions	52.84
USA Network	Capital Research	5.02
	Denver Investment Advisors	2.96
	Montgomery Asset Management	2.22
	Putnam Investment	2.17
	Fidelity Management & Research	2.08
	123 Institutions	58.37
Viacom	Gamco Investors	6.20
	Capital Research	5.27
	Gabelli Funds	3.24
	Fidelity Management & Research	3.19
	Federated Investors	1.33
	91 Institutions	24.61
Walt Disney Co.	Barclays Bank	2.92
	Bankers Trust	1.88
	State Farm Mutual	1.81
	Capital Research	1.65
	State Street Corp.	1.42
	799 Institutions	42.30
Yahoo!	Fidelity Management & Research	4.37

(Continued)

TABLE 8.5 *(Continued)*

Amerindo Investment Advisors	3.07
Morgan Stanley Dean Witter	2.20
Bowman Capital	1.10
Dawsam-Samberg Capital Management	1.06
154 Institutions	25.08

NOTE: Many media companies have two or more classes of stock. Typically, one class is restricted to company founders and/or their families. Another category is more widely held and traded. The former often has "super" voting rights, giving its holders the ability to elect the majority of the Board of Directors. Both classes share in the profits and dividends, if any. All data in this table are for the publicly traded common stock of each firm.

[1]Equivalent voting power taking into account conversion of Class B shares to Class A.

[2]Complex corporate strcuture. Indicates individual and/or family does control more than 50% of the equivalent voting power. Total of all institutionally held stock plus family stock may exceed 100% because former refers to the percent of traded stock, usually Class A.

[3]Represents Class B stock, which holds all voting power. In response to tax laws, the two funds reduced their aggregate holdings of Class B stock to 50% in 2000.

[4]Trustee for Employee Stock Onwership Plan.

Sources: SEC 13F filings, accessed via Disclosure Global Access at www.disclosure.com; SEC forms 10K and 14DEF Proxy reports. Most data is from September 30, 1998.

tional holders of record do not necessarily vote their stock in a block. For example, the Capital Group shows up in Table 8.5 as a major holder of media companies. It manages more than 10 million customer accounts and provides investment services for thousands of banks, trust companies, corporations and retirement plans. It oversaw $275 billion in assets, virtually all of it owned by its clients.[7]

Life insurance companies invest some of their assets in common stocks. These investments not only contribute to the returns that get paid out in death benefits to policyholders, they are also used to support the annuities the companies sell. The returns on these investments generally lower the premiums that policyholders would have to pay if company investments were restricted to lower yielding fixed income investments. Travelers, Equitable Companies, Northwestern Mutual and State Farm are among the insurance companies with major media company portfolios.

Mutual funds invest in a portfolio of stocks and bonds. They do vote their shares in accordance with the best interests of the many stockholders in the mutual fund. Besides Fidelity and Vanguard, Putnam, Janus and American Century are mutual fund groups that have historically seen the media sector as a favorable one for investment.

Pension funds, both public and private, invest in stocks and bonds to optimize their assets, the better to fund higher payouts to their retirees. Besides CREF and CalPERS, other pension funds with sizable media holdings are the Texas Teacher Retirement System, the California State Teachers Retirement System and the New York State Teachers Retirement Plan, as well as smaller funds from cities and states.

Other types of institutions are stockholders of the media companies. University endowments, employee stock ownership plans and charitable foundations may all have sizable stakes. In 1998, the University of California owned 0.4% of General Electric and 0.9% of Walt Disney Co., the IBM Retirement Plan held 0.1% of Adel-

TABLE 8.6
Major Institutional Holders of Media Companies, 1998

American Century Companies	Adelphia Cable	0.51%
	AOL	6.22
	CBS	1.07
	General Electric	0.59
	The New York Times Co.	0.37
	News Corp.	0.21
	Viacom	0.15
American Express Financial	AOL	1.62%
	CBS	2.22
	Clear Channel Communications	3.01
	Gannett	1.53
	General Electric	0.55
	The New York Times Co.	0.67
Bankers Trust	Amazon.com	0.36%
	AOL	1.85
	CBS	1.81
	Chris-Craft	0.86
	Clear Channel Communications	1.32
	Dow Jones	1.17
	Gannett	1.69
	General Electric	1.75
	Hollinger	3.98
	Knight-Ridder	1.80
	McClatchy	0.39
	The New York Times Co.	0.69
	Primedia	0.51
	Reader's Digest Association	0.62
	Tribune Co.	2.08
	Walt Disney Co.	1.88
	Yahoo!	0.40
Barclays Bank PLC	Amazon.com	0.35%
	AOL	3.37
	AT&T	0.03
	CBS	2.77
	Chris-Craft	1.27
	Clear Channel Communications	2.58
	Dow Jones	3.67
	Gannett	3.36
	General Electric	2.92
	Hollinger	2.08
	Knight-Ridder	2.82
	McClatchy	0.74
	The New York Times Co.	1.18
	Primedia	0.52
	Reader's Digest Association	1.20
	Seagram	2.56
	Tribune Co.	2.80
	USA Network	1.02
	Viacom	0.13
	Walt Disney Co.	2.92
	Yahoo!	0.38

(Continued)

499

TABLE 8.6 *(Continued)*

California Public Employees Retirement System (CalPERS)	Chris-Craft	0.97%
	Comcast	2.23
	Dow Jones	0.54
	McClatchy	0.41
	Viacom	0.25
The Capital Group (includes Capital Research & Management and Capital Guardian	Adelphia Cable	5.95%
	AOL	2.06
	AT&T	0.03
	Chris-Craft	4.82
	Comcast	7.31
	Dow Jones	7.68
	Gannett	1.04
	News Corp.	1.27
	Time Warner	10.60
	USA Network	5.02
	Viacom	5.27
	Walt Disney Co.	1.65
College Retirement Equity Fund (CREF)	CBS	2.63%
	Clear Channel Communications	2.52
	Comcast	2.31
	Gannett	0.98
	General Electric	1.03
	Primedia	0.76
	Tribune Co.	1.24
	Viacom	0.68
	Walt Disney Co.	0.87
	Yahoo!	0.75
Equitable Companies	AOL	3.70%
	CBS	2.15
	Gannett	3.30
	General Electric	0.82
	News Corp.	0.23
	Tele-Communications	2.50
	USA Network	1.15
	Walt Disney Co.	1.32
Fidelity Management & Research	Adelphia Cable	0.32%
	Amazon.com	1.52
	AOL	8.72
	AT&T	0.05
	CBS	9.06
	Chris-Craft	1.26
	Clear Channel Communications	5.05
	Comcast	9.88
	Gannett	1.64
	General Electric	3.67
	Knight-Ridder	1.37
	The New York Times Co.	0.34
	News Corp.	0.35
	Reader's Digest Association	2.30
	Time Warner	6.90
	Times Mirror	12.70
	Tribune Co.	2.92

(Continued)

TABLE 8.6 (*Continued*)

	USA Network	2.08
	Viacom	3.19
	Walt Disney Co.	0.97
	Yahoo!	4.37
Gamco Investors	Chris-Craft	7.46%
	McClatchy Co.	1.67
	Reader's Digest	0.99
	Seagram	0.49
	USA Networks	1.78
	Viacom	6.20
Janus Capital	Adelphia Cable	3.68%
	Amazon.com	0.47
	AOL	4.96
	CBS	3.19
	Clear Channel Communications	2.54
	Tele-Communications	1.18
Mellon Bank	AOL	0.98%
	CBS	0.68
	Clear Channel Communications	0.96
	Dow Jones	0.74
	Gannett	1.89
	General Electric	1.26
	Hollinger International	1.94
	Knight-Ridder	2.22
	McClatchy Co.	0.51
	The New York Times Co.	1.15
	Primedia	0.25
	Seagram	0.75
	Times Mirror	1.63
	Viacom	0.19
	Walt Disney Co.	0.90
Putnam Investments	AOL	5.24%
	CBS	4.88
	Clear Channel Communications	8.90
	McClatchy Co.	0.54
	Tele-Communications	1.64
	Times Mirror	5.39
	Tribune Co.	1.92
	USA Network	2.17
State Street Corp.	CBS	1.33%
(not affiliated with State	Clear Channel Communications	1.231
Street Research & Management	Dow Jones	6.27
	Gannett	1.75
	General Electric	1.54
	Knight-Ridder	1.49
	The New York Times Co.	0.72
	Primedia	0.43
	Reader's Digest Association	0.44
	Seagram	1.07
	Tribune Co.	1.53
	Walt Disney Co.	1.42

(Continued)

TABLE 8.6 (Continued)

T. Rowe Price	Chris-Craft	2.73%
	Dow Jones	1.85
	Knight-Ridder	3.50
	Reader's Digest	4.04
	Tribune Co.	1.91
Travelers	AOL	0.87%
	CBS	0.86
	Dow Jones	2.96
	Gannett	1.28
	General Electric	0.73
	Seagram	0.45
	Sony	0.26
	USA Network	1.19
	Walt Disney Co.	0.76
	Yahoo!	0.60
Vanguard Group	CBS	1.22%
	Clear Channel Communications	1.19
	Comcast	3.29
	Dow Jones	1.16
	Gannett	1.29
	General Electric	1.23
	Knight-Ridder	1.20
	The New York Times Co.	0.53
	Primedia	0.30
	Seagram	1.07
	Tribune Co.	1.27
	Viacom	0.16
	Walt Disney Co.	1.17
Wellington Management	AOL	0.87%
	CBS	0.42
	Comcast	8.77
	Gannett	3.14
	McClatchy Co.	2.79
	Walt Disney Co.	0.52

Source: See note Table 8.5.

phia Communications, Harvard University owned 1.7% of the Reader's Digest Association and Times Mirror employees owned more than 5% of the company.

In some cases, individual investors and pensions funds, both large and small, contract with outside management firms to advise them on investments and handle the buying and selling of securities. The Capital Group, for example, is a holding company that includes Capital Guardian Trust Co., which is a trustee and investment manager for large institutional accounts. It also includes Capital Group International and is adviser to the American Funds Group.

What are the implications for the media companies stemming from the sizable investment of financial institutions? Traditionally, there has been little effect in the direct control by way of the voting of the stock of the institutional holders. That changed modestly in the 1990s, however.

Historically, investment managers choose to buy stock or debt in a company after carefully evaluating the current management, the company's past performance and its potential for future growth. They looked at its line of business and strategic vision. Rarely does this type of investment target the short term. Investments are made for years, even decades, often with small additions or subtractions to individual holdings based on current value of the security and cash needs (e.g., pension payouts) of the institution. Institutional investors are not operating managers; they do not have the knowledge or inclination to dictate policy, editorial or otherwise, to the firms in which they have an interest. They make an investment based on what the company is doing, not what they want it to do.

Nonetheless, there has been a small but growing movement among some institutional investors to become more active in shaping corporate policies. The most influential was CalPERS, the largest public retirement system in the United States, which has concluded that " 'good' corporate governance leads to improved long-term performance. CalPERS' also strongly believes that 'good' governance requires the attention and dedication not only of a company's officers and directors, but also its owners. CalPERS is not simply a passive holder of stock. We are a 'shareowner,' and take seriously the responsibility that comes with company ownership."[8]

Such activism tends to focus on general corporate governance, openness and accountability, not the editorial or operating policies of their companies. For example, in 1999 CalPERS voted against one of the nominees as an outside (nonmanagement) director for Walt Disney's corporate board. As he was the architect for much of Disney's building, they thought there might be a conflict of interest. It also voted in favor of three proposals put forward by other shareholders and opposed by the Disney Board, including one that would have required Disney to issue a report on how well its international suppliers adhered to the company's own code of conduct policies.[9] Although rarely would even an institutional investor have enough control to determine votes, the position of larger players such as CalPERS may influence other stockholders.

Some decision-makers of publicly owned companies would attest to an indirect role that institutional investors have in shaping their policies. Executives, who often own stock themselves, as well as holding stock options, are generally rewarded based on the long-term price of their company's stock. This factor may be considered in deliberations on a wide variety of decisions, from how much money to allocate to editorial coverage, to investments in expansion, equipment and the level of dividends. This interest creates needs to fulfill short-term expectations for earnings and long-term requirements for viability and growth. Institutional investors look to long-term growth. They are not concerned with the controversial—or lack of controversial—content of movies or books or television shows. To the extent that an institution does have a propensity for or aversion to the type of content that is consistent with a public company, they would tend not to invest or to sell off their holding rather than try to influence the direction of management.

This decision-making process is at the heart of the private enterprise system in general and, just like any other economic system, it has its benefits and drawbacks. Those who believe that investing institutions should use their clout as media owners to encourage better or more cultural programming may also have to accept an outcome in which some institutions use their activism to promote a version of "better" or "cultural" that is different from what they had in mind. Whether it is a government, employee or some other group, the controlling forces will expect the media to reflect their values, which may or may not be the "right" ones. The best innoculation to these pressures seems to be the overwhelming pluralism of the public ownership of the media companies.

WHO THEN OWNS THE MEDIA?

The media industry is not an abstract concept. It is composed of thousands of larger and smaller companies. In back of each one are owners. It might be an individual, several partners, a family or thousands of investors.

There is an ebb and flow in the identity of the largest media companies: Smaller companies merge to become larger ones. Large companies acquire or merge with others to become larger. New companies emerge in new media segments or to challenge the existing regime. A list in 1920 similar to that of Table 8.1 would have been much shorter; there were, after all, only newspaper, magazine and book publishers then. It would have included names that were well known and considered "dominant" at the time: Munsey, Curtis, Pulitzer. A list in 1960 would not have included names such as MediaOne, Viacom or Tele-Communications. In 1980, as illustrated in Table 8.3, News Corporation, Broadcast.com, Bloomberg Financial and Amazon.com, among others, either did not exist or were too insignificant to be noted. In many ways, information technology has helped to create its own democratic process in the world of media gateways.

And, of course, Table 8.1 does not come close to exhausting the universe of firms with significant or influential media holdings. The *New England Journal of Medicine*, owned by the Massachusetts Medical Society, is one of many publications that help set the agenda, in this case on health care, far out of proportion to any measure of circulation or wealth.[10] Some Web sites similarly have an influence on the more popular media, although they may not be among the most popular sites as measured by users. For example, there is this reference to such politically oriented sites as "Capitol Hill Blue" and "American Politics":

> A year after the gossipy Web site run by Matt Drudge became a bookmark in Washington computers [for breaking a sorry about the relationship between Monica Lewinsky and President Bill Clinton that *Newsweek* knew about but was not prepared to release yet], other, more partisan Web sites are becoming early warning systems for the mainstream press. Like talk radio, they are filled with free-form invective. . . . They offer previews of coming attractions from places where conspiracy is king.[11]

Tables 8.4 and 8.5 in this analysis provide data that points to a structure that shows, far from an oligarchy of a tight group of owners, that media companies are largely controlled either by their founders and their descendants or, in more cases, by a substantial number of institutional investors. These investors are interested not in control but in long-term growth and increased value to fulfill their responsibilities to their millions of beneficiaries. There is breadth in the holdings of these institutional investors in that most institutions prefer to diversify by taking a portfolio approach: relatively small investments in a wide range of industries and companies within those sectors.[12] The portion not held by institutions, family and employees is held by individuals for their own accounts, including IRAs and other tax-favored retirement accounts. In the case of companies like General Electric, Time Warner and Walt Disney, there may be tens of thousands of such stockholders.

Whether or not this diversity of ownership is sufficient to maintain both the appearance and actuality of pluralism in content and pricing of the media is ultimately up to every individual to decide. From their own perspectives, Chapters 9 and 10 address the question, "How few is too few?" or its corollary, "How many are too many?" For in the world of unlimited virtual bandwidth, the curse of who owns the media may be in its unwieldy anarchy rather than in the feared controlled oligopoly.

NOTES

1. "Microsoft and Compaq Buy Matching RoadRunner Stakes," June 15, 1998, *The Wall Street Journal Interactive*, on Web site at interactive.wsj.com/edition/current/articles/SB897933322173988500.htm, accessed June 30, 1998.
2. "The Merger of AT&T and TCI," AT&T Proxy Statement/Prospectus, January 8, 1999, pp. 34–35.
3. U.S. Securities and Exchange Commission Form DEF 14A for McClatchy Newspapers Inc. filed on March 28 1997, accessed at www.edgar-online.com/bin/getsec/index.pl?doc=A-822043-0000950008-97-000093, March 5, 1999.
4. Cruden Investments held 30.86% of News Corporation shares, according to Disclosure's "Ownership and Subsidiaries" report, on Web site at www.disclosure.com/dga/search.cgi, accessed March 1, 1999.
5. Sandra Ward, "Playing with Fire," *Barron's Online*, January 11, 1999, accessed March 5, 1999, on Web site at www.tiaa-cref.org/siteline/Playing.htm.
6. CalPERS Web site, "Facts at a Glance," at www.calpers.ca.gov/about/factglan/factglan.htm, investment as of February 10, 1999. Accessed March 6, 1999.
7. The Capital Group Companies, on Web site at www.capgroup.com/gig/crmc.html, accessed March 7, 1999. Assets as of December 31, 1999.
8. CalPERS Shareholder Forum, on Web site at www.calpers-governance.org/forumhome.asp, accessed March 8, 1999.
9. "Proxy Voting Decisions," on Web site at www.calpers-governance.org/alert/proxy/disney.asp, accessed March 8, 1999. Voted at Walt Disney Co. annual meeting held February 23, 1999.
10. As just one example or many, in 1997 the *Journal* published studies as well as an editorial critical of "Phen-Fen," a potent drug combination that turned out to have serious side effects. Gregory D. Curfman, "Diet Pills Redux," *New England Journal of Medicine* 337.9 (August 28, 1997). Following that issue, hundreds of articles in the popular press, from local newspapers, to the newsweeklies and major TV news shows, followed with extensive coverage and the FDA withdrew approval of the drugs for weight loss. A search of *The Wall Street Journal Interactive Publications Library* yielded the

maximum 200 articles it retrieves for any search. Searched terms ("Phen," "Fen" or "Redux," and "New England Journal") on March 8, 1999.

11. Felicity Barringer, "Partisan Web Sites Gain Some Media Credibility," *The New York Times On the Web*, March 8, 1999, at www.nytimes.com/library/tech/99/03/biztech/articles/08web.html.

12. A mutual fund (technically a Regulated Investment Company) cannot have more than 25% of its total assets accounted for by one company (with some technical exceptions). If it violated this rule (Title 26, Subtitle A, Chapter 1, Subchapter M, Part I, Sec. 851 of the Internal Revenue Code), then it will lose its favorable tax status as an investment company. See Web site at www.fourmilab. ch/ustax/www/t26-A-1-M-I-851.html.

9

Interpreting Media Ownership

Douglas Gomery

The ownership of the mass media in the United States is of vital interest. These vast institutions influence what we know, the images of ourselves and the bulk of the way we amuse and entertain. The production and distribution of newspapers, books, magazines, television, radio, music, movies, and increasingly the Internet (i.e., the mass media) require great expense and frequently generate enormous profits. No research in mass communication can ignore questions of mass media ownership and the economic implications of that control. Mass media businesses routinely take in and spend vast sums of money. The mass media in the United States, and elsewhere in the world, seek to maximize profits, and thus can safely be studied as economic institutions. Whereas owners and managers go about maximizing profits, this key assumption still functions best as a starting point. Then the question becomes: What is the best way to go about trying to make sense of the ownership and operation of mass media industries?

Media economics should move into the center of communications study by offering powerful and flexible methods by which to analyze mass media industries in the context of core concerns of the communication process. Marxist "critical studies" and free market empiricism lack appeal because they ask people to analyze a subject when they already "know" a predetermined answer. From critics from the left, the mass media assume an all-encompassing conspiracy by monopolists. A cursory examination of the contemporary magazine and Internet industries undercuts any such monolithic image. Such a "critical analysis" is a simplistic, incomplete and narrow discussion, the product of fitting examples to predetermined conclusions based on a single set of values.

By contrast, conservative free market advocates assume that efficient operation represents the paramount, and often sole, goal for any enterprise, even those so vital to democracy and quality of life as mass communication and mass entertainment. Studying the economics of mass communication as though simply contemplating the toaster or pencil industries offers a far too narrow perspective. They see no reason for any government intervention. But the mass media at least create negative externalities. Critics from all sides have long found problems with the media and asserted a plethora of corrective regulations by which to improve industry operation and content production. Analysis of media economics ought not to be restricted to only today's problem industries; the complete range of media industries and institutions, including the Internet when that achieves mass status, needs to be regularly analyzed to establish a base from which to understand and evaluate the workings of the mass media.[1]

This new emphasis on media economics needs to have at its core the study of changing conditions of quality, hereafter referred to as the study of performance. This perspective favors a model for media economic analysis that not only examines questions of "who owns the media" (economic structure) and "how the corporations operate in the real world" (media conduct), but also a methodology that looks directly in the end at how well the mass media perform in modern society. Based on the pioneering work found in industrial organization economics, the basic conditions of an industry should be established and defined, its major players (structure) should be established, the behavior dictated by this structure (conduct) should be defined, and finally the core questions of industry performance should be evaluated, and when necessary, a set of alternative possible public policies should be proposed.[2]

In the end, I posit an institutional economic model. If we are to move past mere efficiency as the sole criterion of proper policy and thus the use of pure microeconomics as the lone tool for analysis of media companies, we must begin with the problem, in particular, recognizing that the broadcasters, for example, are not simple firms reducible to equations but large complex social, cultural and political institutions, with vast growing multinational power. Communication corporations are most complex because they do not "simply" make automobiles, they make and distribute the communications of culture and politics. When Congress grants them an exclusive monopoly as a broadcaster, it is necessary to be aware of all the ramifications of that, both as an economic phenomenon and as a social, cultural and political manifestation.[3]

Economists need to deal with the real world, not some idealized model—even if we are frustrated by all the complexities involved. We need empirical studies, but we also need studies of trade-offs that are value laden as well. We need to analyze the interconnectedness of society and the economy, and not reduce the criterion of what is valued as simply what is most efficient. We need to accept that economic behavior and cultural action are intertwined, and that people are conditioned by culture, and then change and respond. This feeds into the economics, particularly when that economic system is the production and distribution of that very culture.

That is, in the beginning—at the end—we need to acknowledge that the history of the institutions plays a vital role, and that institutions vary by ownership, market conditions and technological change. Thus value is determined by a social context, as well as an economic context of media corporate ownership. Here is where we can see that some markets—especially those media markets that are so vital to culture and democracy—sometimes fail. New technology does not always appear so as to offer alternatives when monopoly conditions exist. Information is not always perfect; uncertainty sometimes is the case rather than the assumed perfect flow on information so the consumer can make rational choices. Sometimes barriers to entry prevent competitors from offering superior products or services. The value cannot always be accurately reflected in its price. Customers have a hard time factoring in advertising costs into product or services advertised on the mass media.

Central to institutionalists lies the consideration of where the social and economic and political factors intertwine. Tastes are not given, but learned from all three of these institutions as well as other situations. In addition, institutionalists look to history and see trends. Value in culture and society is not always simply reflected by price. The problem is that institutional economics offers less than simple solutions, such as that offered by market clearing neoclassical economics, or the rulings of monopoly capitalists. One must accept that capitalism will in its history offer problems that then need to be understood in their full context, with economics as a necessary component of the analysis, but not sufficient to a complete understanding. Qualitative and quantitative data ought to be applied.[4]

Simply listing who owns the media institutions is not enough. Here we connect with the vital problem of industry boundaries, which arises from buyers shifting from one group of sellers to another, as well as sellers shifting their activities from one product or service to another. Any attempt to classify mass media firms in the U.S. economy—let alone those in the world—runs into boundary definitional difficulties, but in the end one makes a decision. Drawing boundaries too widely lumps together producers who are insensitive to other's actions. Drawing them too tightly leads to the opposite problem. There is also the problem of geographical boundaries. Although tackling global mass media would seem to be most advisable in this modern age, its study would simply become never-ending.[5]

Even listing the top firms is hard because we need to somehow accurately count and figure the share of each seller. It is easier to talk about more or less concentrated ownership than to try to quantify the precise share, or control, of each player—or indeed the distribution of the sellers in the industry as a whole. A monopoly of one dominant company, or an oligopoly of a handful of dominant sellers, can be more easily studied than an industry like book publishing where there are clearly 10 or so top players, but 50,000 total book publishers. However, I assume trying to get a sense of the ownership is needed and necessary—as hard as that may be.

One needs to hypothesize and understand how a particular form of industrial structure leads to certain corporate conduct. We need a system for media economics analysis of the linkage among structure, conduct and performance that leads to discussions of the need for public policy reformulations. Examining performance of media industries ought to be the ultimate step in media economics analysis. It is at the level of performance analysis that communication scholars and citizens should and can take interest in media economics. We need to foster a connection between media economics and the longtime concerns of our field, whether this deals with questions of how to best promote diversity or how best to foster freedom of speech and discussion. If we can link the study of the economics of ownership and corporate behavior to the communication qualities we desire, communication scholars can begin to make recommendations for policy change that the players in real-world public policy discussion will take seriously.[6]

The study of economics is supposed to be objective and positive, not something dealing with normative issues. However, as issues of media freedom and audience choice, of proper news objectivity and depth, continue to swirl, we should stop being afraid to combine empirical research and normative concerns. What defines good media performance has long assumed an outcome of competitive pressures and a plethora of voices, a flourishing marketplace of ideas. But this purely competitive (to use the economics term) ideal is rarely met in the modern world. We need to combine media economic analysis and normative analysis to see how we might deal with public policy concerns about the mass media. Economic analysis can best help us make more informed choices of appropriate government action and assess the range of policy influences and effects.[7]

Before we grapple with the difficult questions of performance, however, we need to closely examine the economics of market structure and conduct. First, the analysis of economic structure seeks to establish the number of buyers and sellers in a market, to identify barriers to entry to potential new competitors, to isolate the effects of horizontal and vertical ownership patterns and to study the consequences of conglomerate control.[8]

One of the key needs for determining competition is first determining the relevant market. This can be applied to the product market and the geographic market. The distinctions are particularly critical for many media, which are geographically local, while being part of a broader product market. The more that products are reasonably interchangeable, the more likely it is that they should be considered as the same product market. This applies both from the perspective of consumers (demand) and potential market entrants (supply). So after the product market is determined, the geographic market is addressed. Traditionally, the geographic market may be a city, a region or the entire country. Increasingly, there may be a global component as well.[9]

Most daily newspapers, cable systems and television and radio stations are distinctly local, whereas the remainder of the mass media is national and international in scope. Here are goods and service that can be substituted for, depending on the nature of what they offer. So, for example, at the turn of the 20th century, the customer who wanted "news" needed to purchase a newspaper. But as the century passed, first came radio, television, cable TV and then the Internet. Relative to the population, once substitutes came online, newspaper readers declined, and although the state of the newspaper industry at the end of the 20th century remained profitable, circulation per household has been falling since the advent of television. Even for buyers of newspapers, the amount of time spent with them is down. There are fewer cities than ever with fully competing newspapers each day.

Thus, in analyzing competition for narrow media industry segments, it is critical to distinguish what the standard for the relevant market might be. There remain dozens of cable operators, but the household in any given locality has from the start generally had only one choice (enforced legally by the monopoly franchising power of local governments). Whereas media compete for advertisers and buyers, I think that breaking them down by traditional industry remains the most useful segmentation. Each retains certain characteristics. Classified advertising does not work well on television; films cannot be viewed in a magazine. Some are related, such as where and when one can view a film—a theater, pay TV and home video. Consumers and advertisers collect possible options for them, constrained by the medium's characteristics and their funds. It may seem like we are approaching a world of "one media," yet in economic reality there exists a defined collection of media businesses competing for customers—mass media industries.[10]

Taking up market structure requires the key variables that wind themselves through the analysis, even as one considers seller concentration at the top of the list. How does a firm become dominant? It can offer different products and services that are seen as superior to buyers. In the 1990s this became "branding," but whether called product differentiation or branding, this is key to the success of any commercial enterprise. The corporation can fashion barriers to entry to keep out rivals. Here, for the mass media as they have operated for more than a century, the scale economies (leading to low relatively costs) have long ranked as top barriers that new, smaller competitors cannot match. Thus, corporations try to become the first in the market, and set up a vast network to reap economies of scale, and make it harder for the second or later movers to compete. The corporation can recognize historical change and technical inventions and respond to the market demand they can create, by diversifying or vertically integrating or trying a combination of business strategies to continue industry domination and maximize profits in the long run. It is not easy to rank these elements in importance, but product differentiation and barriers to entry would seem to rank at the top of most economist's lists.[11]

Market structure and conduct in the media world fall into four categories: monopoly, oligopoly, monopolistic competition and those in some transition phase. Before I analyze these four, note that they are paid for in two distinct ways. On the one hand, there is direct payment. Books, popular music, movies and pay TV sell their wares directly to the public. On the other hand, there is the world of indirect payment characterized by advertisers "buying" audiences. Television, radio, magazines and newspapers rely on advertising dollars to create the bulk of their revenues. These media may have a small initial charge (e.g., the subscription price of a newspaper), but advertising fees generate the bulk of the revenues.[12]

The important difference here for the study of industrial conduct is that with direct payment customers are able to telegraph directly their preferences. For advertising-supported media, the client is the advertiser, not the viewer or listener or reader. Advertisers seek out media that can best help sell products or services; advertisers desire placement in media that can persuade customers who can be convinced to change their buying behavior and have the means to execute new purchases.

Given this duality of revenue generation, the industrial organization economic model postulates that the structure of a media industry determines the particular characteristics of its economic behavior—monopoly, oligopoly, monopolistic competition and pure competition. Lacking any examples of the latter, I turn to the former, recognizing some are in a transitional phase in 1999.

MONOPOLY

In a media industrial monopoly, a single firm dominates. The basic cable television franchise and the single community daily newspaper provide two examples of media monopoly. To take advantage of this power and exploit economies of larger scale operation, cable television and newspaper corporations collect their monopolies under one institutional umbrella. A monopoly fosters economic behavior familiar to any subscriber to cable television, or wishes there was some other local newspaper. In any local jurisdiction, there is typically but one cable television choice and one local newspaper. If one does not like the lone cable TV operator or newspaper owner's offerings and prices, then the choices are not to subscribe or to move. The monopoly cable company has little incentive to keep prices down, to add channels or to offer high quality service. The newspaper cannot cover all subjects, and thus makes choices some (or a lot) of the population in its local area will not like. This is a product of being a monopolist and seeking to maximize profits with no effective competition.[13]

U.S. newspapers in the 1990s were by-and-large monopolies. Although there are fewer advertising dollars for newspapers, they are split among fewer establishments. Circulation is lower, but declines are not uniform. In cities where a single publisher remains, circulation is higher, although at less than the combined circulation of the two papers that used to be there. For the most part, the newspaper groups of 1998 were the same as in 1980: Gannett, Knight-Ridder, Lee Enterprises and McClatchy among them. Indeed, some seem to be getting out of the business. For example, Thomson, which had owned more newspapers than any other group, has sold off many of its papers to concentrate in financial information. Harte-Hanks has divested all its papers to focus on direct marketing.[14]

The problem is that for most communities there is but a single dominant newspaper. Here is a local product, that over the past decades, has seen one newspaper takeover cities from Washington, DC and Philadelphia to small towns and communities. The market for a national audience and national advertising is confined to a handful of newspapers best exemplified by USA Today. From the perspective of a local retailer or real estate broker, whether the local paper is one of dozens owned by a group or the only daily newspaper property of a local family, the issue is almost universally the same: If the local daily newspaper is the most efficient medium for them to reach their market, they have but one choice. Similarly, for the local resident, who feels it useful to read about the local sports teams, the issues in town government, the developments on the school board or the sale items at the supermarket that week, there have been few alternatives to buying the daily newspaper, regardless of the ownership. And with advertising concentrated in one newspaper, it is expensive and highly unprofitable in the short run to start a second, competitive newspaper.[15]

Surely, large monopoly newspapers can hire the top talent and report stories with more resources than small independent newspapers facing competition. But the ability or opportunity to do this does not guarantee that they do. Newspaper owners profit maximize as do other corporations, and thus it is up to the owners and managers to determine how much to invest in longer stories, which are costly to produce. This is a difficult balancing act, and with no competition from other local news organizations for longer stories—as TV has never done this—the performance of newspapers is best seen as preservation of its monopoly through some prestige in prizes but not so much as to draw away from maximizing profits. Whereas more than

500 cities and towns had two or more competing newspapers in the 1920s, including 100 cities with three or more papers, by 1998 that figure had decreased to 34 cities, including those with federally mandated (permitting lower costs through economies of scale of operation) joint operating agreements. Only New York, the nation's largest city, could maintain more than two.[16]

Cable television operates from a monopoly basis as well. In the 1990s, there were a limited number of additional cable "overbuilds" where the incumbent cable operators faced such a competitor. TV used to be "free;" now cable operators openly talk of separating out popular networks (e.g., ESPN) and changing $1 to $4 a la carte per month for that set of channels alone. Add in all those pay channels and pay-per-view events and bills for all the choices cable TV offers can frequently mean a three-figure monthly bill. The average cable customer was paying more. At the end of 1998, the Federal Communications Commission (FCC) reported that cable rates rose more than four times the rate of inflation. According to the Labor Department's Bureau of Labor Statistics, between June 1997 and June 1998, cable prices rose 7.3% as compared to a 1.7% increase in the Consumer Price Index used to measure general price changes. A portion of these rate increases is attributable to capital expenditures for the upgrading of cable facilities (up 21% over 1996), an increased number of channels and nonvideo services offered and increased programming costs (license fees increased by 18.4% and programming expenses increased by 20.9%, reported the FCC).[17]

The cable television franchise provides a classic example of a media monopoly. The core of the cable television operation—where the programming meets its customers—is the basic local franchise. And cable television franchises are monopolies (except in rare cases of so-called overbuilding, where two cable systems are built covering the same area) for their legally defined area. That monopoly forms the economic power of the cable television business through government protection. Once one owner has obtained a legal franchise, for a defined period of time no competitor can arise to challenge the franchise holder. To take advantage of significant economies of operation, corporations collect franchises under one corporate umbrella, creating a multiple system operator (MSO), where a number of cable franchises are collected together under a common owner and reap significant economies of scale. An MSO can have a single accounting department, a single sales force, a single repair division, for example, and spread these and other fundamental costs across the various franchises, and thus have lower per franchise costs with constant revenues and hence higher profits. In the 1990s, a handful of cable television's multiple system operators controlled the vast amount of cable systems and monopolized the cable television business.[18]

After a look at the top multiple system operators—AT&T, Time Warner and Comcast—the key point is that the monopoly-based MSOs dominated by a wide margin. Indeed, in 1999, AT&T, Time Warner and Comcast ranked as the "Big Three" in the cable MSO business. Together they controlled more than half of all the customers subscribing to cable TV. The remainder of the top 10 controlled about one third as many. The Big Three also owned shares in nearly all the important cable TV networks. They exemplified vertical integration. But two pretenders existed, who copied the AT&T,

Time Warner and Comcast model, and sought to challenge them. Neither were as big or as vertically integrated, but these two companies did have programming interests and MSO size advantages that made them closer to the Big Three than the long list of small mom-and-pop MSOs. Cox and Cablevision Systems are about equal in size, and with a major merger or two, they could move up to challenge the Big Three.[19]

The 1990s innovation of direct broadcast satellite service commenced on in July 1994 when DirecTV, backed by the deep pockets of owner Hughes (owned by automobile giant General Motors), began selling dozens of channels that could be captured through an easy-to-install pizza-sized dish. Within a couple of years, four million mostly rural Americans had signed up; one study found that early adopters cut their video cassette renting by 70%, and instead watched movies on direct broadcast satellite (DBS)—a classic case of the substitution effect. Because this analysis showed that about 34% of video cassette recorder (VCR) households account for about 75% of total tapes rented, the introduction of DBS was successfully off and running. The 1990s class of DBS services permitted households to receive digitally compressed signals, up to 200 per customer. Without digital compression, only 32 channels would come through and DBS—as it was during the failed innovative attempts in the 1980s—would not be perceived as a product equal to cable, but more like a multichannel multipoint distribution system (MMDS) and its limited number of channels. DBS expanded choice with not only the full complement of the various cable services, but also additional sports feeds and pay-per-view movies.[20]

But with DirecTV's acquisition of first USSB, and then PrimeStar, the DBS industry in 1999 stood at two firms—DirecTV and Echostar. It would seem a safe bet that DirecTV would emerge after 2000 as the lone DBS alternative to cable. From a beginning in 1994, Hughes built on its experience as a manufacturer of communications satellites. DirecTV served as a natural extension of Hughes' existing business. DirecTV enlisted manufacturer Thomson of France to develop the 18-inch dishes and receivers in return for an exclusive contract to manufacture and sell the first million. Congress then helped. In the 1992 cable act it required cable programmers to charge equitable rates to DBS, as a way to boost an alternative to cable. DirecTV did so well that Hughes began selling off its military contractor and its electronics supplier divisions to focus exclusively on commercial satellite operations. Still, by the close of 1997, DirecTV had posted more than $300 million in losses, and it did not begin to show profits until 1999.[21]

OLIGOPOLY

A handful of firms dominate in an oligopoly, the most heralded example being the longtime 3 (now more) television networks. But there are other oligopolies, including the 5 major music record labels, the 6 commanding major Hollywood studios and the 10 major book publishers. If there is a ownership pattern that best categorizes the mass media industries, it is one where sellers are few in number.[22]

Oligopolists are mutually interdependent. When they cooperate they can act like a monopolist; yet cooperation comes only with a handful of issues such as expanding the marketplace possibilities for all or keeping out new and powerful competitors. Oligopolists work together to fashion positive governmental policies toward their industry, and thus to keep out potential competitors. Nothing unites a media oligopoly more than a threat from the outside. Simply put, oligopolists tend to seek and agree on an informal set a rules for competition, restricting the game of profit maximizing to themselves.[23]

Here is where we confront the media conglomerate. To maintain their positions of power in recent decades, media oligopolies have diversified, both vertically and horizontally. Disney, for example, owns and operates a famous movie studio and a set of theme parks, as well as a television network (ABC), a score of successful television and radio stations, two sports cable TV networks (ESPN and ESPN2) and more. Because of this diversification, Disney is not dependent on the business cycle of a single operation. Unprofitable subsidiaries can be reconstructed and repositioned with funds generated from other profitable ongoing businesses. This enables an oligopoly to offer a high barrier to entry. Disney's potential rivals lack this conglomerate protection.[24]

An oligopoly sees its small number of firms operate in reaction to each other. The metaphor is a poker game with five or six players. Each player knows a great deal about what the other is up to, but does not possess perfect knowledge. Take the case of the four dominant over-the-air television networks. When NBC offers a new comedy at a particular time on a particular day, its rivals counterprogram. This leads to some experimentation, but all too often this only means a numbing generic sameness where like programs (e.g., comedies, dramas or soap operas) face off against each other. Because there is no calculable, predictable mathematical solution (as in the case of monopoly or pure competition), economic theorists have a great deal of trouble modeling oligopolistic behavior. The outcomes of oligopolistic corporate interplay depend on how many firms there are, how big they are in relation to each other, past corporate histories and sometimes the whims of individual owners. Here is where institutions and their specific types of ownership come into play.[25]

The *Wall Street Journal* recognized the power of the oligopoly in 1999 with "Lets Play Oligopoly! Why Giants Like Having Other Giants Around." Along with the Big Three of beverages, tobacco and automobiles, music's Big Five highlighted the story. The *Journal* led: "If you want to understand the big force underlying the past decade [1990s] of mega-mergers, here's one word: oligopoly. Everywhere you look, industries are sorting themselves out into their own version of the Big Three auto makers." And this, experts told the *Journal*, would soon happen globally as well. And giant corporations seem to prefer this because an oligopoly allows them to retain a degree of competition without ceding too much control through regulation invariably aimed at pure monopolists. That is, they like controlled competition with a few players. Oligopolies more easily come to common standards, seem competitive on the surface and permit some entry on the margins. Surely oligopoly was the most common market structure for mass media ownership in the 1990s.[26]

The Hollywood film industry long has stood as an oligopoly. In 1999 there were six members (in alphabetical order): Disney (owned by the Walt Disney Corporation), Paramount Pictures (owned by Viacom), Sony Pictures (owned by Sony),

Twentieth Century-Fox (owned by News Corporation), Universal Pictures (owned by Seagram) and Warner Bros. (owned by Time Warner). All competed to produce and release the top hits, but all cooperated to make sure the game remained only amongst themselves. Who was on top which year varied, but only these majors premiered possible blockbuster hits in multiplex theaters during the 1990s, and they surely will well into the future. In 1998, two of the Big Six, Viacom's Paramount Pictures and the Disney studio, exceeded $1 billion in world box office revenues. Twentieth Century-Fox, Sony and Warner Bros. all gathered in about three quarters of a billion dollars each. Whereas in the 1990s mergers defined new owners, the structure of the institution of Hollywood's Big Six did not change. They were the dominant motion picture makers and distributors, and maintained barriers to entry to protect their oligopoly.[27]

In the late 1990s, each of the Big Six studios effected a different business strategy, reflecting the personality of the studio chief as well as the financial condition and strategic objectives of the parent company. For example, Disney represented the well-oiled machine, fashioning almost paramilitary operations, but succeeding less as the 1990s ended. Michael Eisner tried to continue his amazing streak of making Disney's profits grow quarterly. Sony was still seeking to make its grand experiment of marrying a movie studio and an electronics maker consistently profitable, but it was still not working; as a result, its Japanese owners looked for and tested new business strategies.[28]

The oligopoly power is most obvious in the activities of the Big Six's trade association, the Motion Picture Association of America (MPAA), where the six deal with common concerns—from rating films to smoothing the way for international distribution to protecting their valuable copyrights around the world. Although critics of the film industry usually focus only on the MPAA's ratings system, its longtime head, Jack Valenti, earns his $1 million a year salary by helping the Big Six expand revenues from around the world. Valenti can more often be found abroad, far from his home office at 16th and "I" Street in Washington, DC. One poll ranked the MPAA as the 18th most powerful lobby in Washington, DC in 1997. Valenti's total association budget would make and market but a single modest blockbuster, but the Big Six know it is money well spent to protect their turf and expand their markets.[29]

Likewise, the music industry was dominated by a handful of dominant firms. Whatever the sales venue, most of the music vendors sold came from the Big Five. Through volatility of styles and genres, the production and distribution oligopoly of the Big Five held. The innovation of the compact disc (CD) and the Internet did not lessen its collective power. Indeed, as the 20th century ended it seemed to actually increase it. The only real question each year was: Who ranked where in terms of sales?[30]

Seagram's Universal Music Group stood atop the music business in 1999 because of its purchase of Polygram, a former member of the oligopoly. Overnight, for $10 billion, the Big Six shrunk to the "Big Five." Here was a liquor company, based in Montreal, Canada, re-inventing itself into a music (and movie) company. Seagram included many labels and stars (i.e., Counting Crows, Nirvana, Bobby Brown, Vince Gill, Reba McIntyre, George Strait, Mary J. Blige and the Wallflowers).

The Warner Music Group did well with its music division in the mid-1990s, and followed Seagram on the Big Five list in 1999. The Warner Music Group functioned as a division of the vast, multinational media conglomerate, Time Warner, the sole member headquartered in the United States. Warner labels included Warner Brothers, Reprise, Giant, Sire, Elektra, Atlantic, Atco, Curb, Rhino, and so on. Its stars of the late 1990s included Metalica, R.E.M., Eric Clapton, Green Day and Madonna.

The Sony Music Group had been established when longtime oligopoly member CBS sold out in 1988. This electronics giant could sell music with its audio equipment. As the 1990s ended, its labels were doing very well—with Columbia (Bob Dylan, Mariah Carey, Will Smith, Barbra Streisand), Epic (Michael Jackson, Pearl Jam, Billy Joel), 550 Music (Celine Dion, Ben Folds Five) and Work Group (Fiona Apple, Jamiroquai) leading the way.

The Bertelsmann Music Group is a division of a privately held German company with well-known labels (i.e., RCA, Arista, Zoo and Windam Hill) and stars (i.e., Whitney Houston, ZZ Top, TLC, Kenny G., Crash Test Dummies, Ace of Base and Toni Braxton). The Bertelsmann Music Group entered the music business in 1986 by purchasing the former RCA Victor Company, and BMG surely played a key role for parent company, Bertelsmann AG, in generating billions of dollars of sales worldwide. With headquarters in Germany, but with the music group headquartered in New York City, media operations include businesses in music, television, film, video, interactive entertainment and direct marketing, as well as compact disc and cassette manufacturing.

The EMI Group PLC had been, until 1996, a division of Thorn EMI PLC (formally Electrical and Music Instruments), a vast British media and manufacturing conglomerate. EMI centered around Capitol Records, and made millions of dollars in profits from sales of records by the Beatles and Pink Floyd.

Like their counterparts in the motion picture industry, the Big Five regularly took in $7 of every $8 spent. On the other side of the equation was Edgar Bronfman Junior, who in 1998 paid more than $10 billion for one of the oligopolists just to have greater access to the world market (estimated at $30 billion per year).[31]

The Big Five worked together through the Recording Association of America (RIAA), founded in 1952 to protect the property interests of its member clients. Collectively the Big Five resist proposed government restrictions, fight piracy and struggle against tariffs and trade restrictions abroad. The RIAA's awards—gold, platinum and multiplatinum records—gain the vast proportion of publicity, but economic issues are paramount. Consider that, for example, half the association's employees work in the antipiracy division. In 1997, for example, its lawyers filed suits against music archive sites on the World Wide Web that offer full-length copyrighted recordings. The RIAA stressed that sound recordings represent a powerful contribution to the U. S. balance of trade. The RIAA helped the Big Five move into China, the most populous nation on the planet. The RIAA also battled cheap copies that flooded the world from the Netherlands, Germany and Sweden, summing to more than 100 million illegal CDs per annum.[32]

For the book industry, 10 firms dominated, but many firms participated. In the 1990s, book publishing, in the end, must be judged as a loose and open oligopoly, with the tightest control in trade and educational publishing. But, entry possibilities existed for all categories of books in niches from religious to children's publishing. With 10 dominant firms, but thousands of other publishers, one can properly lament some concentration in trade and educational publishing, but this market structure was nowhere as tightly controlled as movies and music (analyzed earlier). In particular, the one exception is educational publishing, which is concentrated in the hands of six or so companies. Brining a textbook requires lots of up-front capital and so there are real barriers to entry. These three- to five-year up-front costs are substantial, and thus there are really no mom and pop textbook companies. This highly profitable segment is dominated by McGraw-Hill, Viacom, Inc., Harcourt General, News Corporation and Pearson PLC.[33]

Domination can most easily be appreciated by glancing at the *New York Times* bestseller list, and seeing the same publishers year after year. In 1996, for example, the leader in bestsellers (as complied by *Publishers Weekly*) was Advance's Random House (by 1998 owned by Bertelsmann AG), followed by Bertelsmann's various imprints, Viacom's Simon & Schuster, News Corporation's HarperCollins and Time Warner's various imprints. These five had most of the books, most of the weeks on the hardcover lists and market shares from 20% to 13%. The same five dominated mass paperback bestseller lists. *Publishers Weekly* found that approximately 90% of the top fiction titles were by writers who had previously enjoyed bestseller status. For nonfiction, the top sellers included titles by and about famous people in the news, followed by how-to-do titles.[34]

Change was the order of the day in the late 1990s, but it did not mean the move toward an industry characterized as competitive—filled with small firms, free entry and exit. In March 1998, for example, Bertelsmann AG became the largest publisher in the world when it acquired Advance Publication's (also private) Random House—then the largest trade publisher in the United States—and moved to the point of selling an estimated 40% of all the trade books sold in the world under its Dell Doubleday and other labels. The Bertelsmann AG deal, worth an estimated $1.5 billion, rocketed Bertelsmann AG into first place in sales of trade books in the United States. This was one of many deals, but its costs meant that no small publisher could gain this share of the market. The $1.5 billion paid attested to the cost of entry.

But this is not to say that there were thousands trying to play in publishing. "Desk top publishing" sought to break the trade book Boston to New York to Washington, DC editorial axis. By 1997, there were presses located in every state in the union, with sizable distribution arms working to get their products in the hands of desiring customers. Thus, more books have been published as the 20th century ended; fully half of the titles ever published in the United States issued since 1970. In the 1990s, it has settled in at about 100 new titles issued per day, with a set of major publishers managing to capture the bulk of this market. An oligopoly topped the book industry, but more than 50,000 small presses came afterward, all offering books aimed at a certain niche of readers.[35]

Finally, broadcast television has long operated as an oligopoly, which is best symbolized by the three, then four, and in the 1990s, six television networks. But with the innovation of cable TV and DBS, discussed earlier, these networks captured a smaller share of viewers. Nonetheless, their economies of scale enabled them alone to offer the most expensive first-run prime time programming, and to dominate sports coverage as well. Even with all the change, the average audience rating of one of the network's nightly evening news broadcasts is five times what CNN draws. Do not forget that the major broadcast networks regularly deliver the top-rated programs. And this ought to continue as four of the six were owned and operated by Hollywood studio production factories, all part of vast media conglomerates: Disney owning ABC, Twentieth Century-Fox owning the Fox television network, Warner Bros. (owned by Time Warner) owning the WB television network and Paramount Pictures (owned by Viacom) owning UPN.[36]

That broadcast television is still a vital oligopoly can best be seen as outsiders willing to pay millions of dollars to get in the game. Although there are no absolute formulas for valuing broadcast properties, stations change hands often enough so that at any given time, the going rate in the market can be fairly easily determined— measured in millions of dollars. For a top 10 market, this meant more than a half billion dollars. In small markets, for example, the Meredith Corporation agreed to pay $435 million for stations in Orlando, Florida; Greenville, South Carolina; and Portland, Oregon. The value of the expected profits from a license was going up, not down. We can get some sense of what this high profit rate might be by examining the selling process of top 50 market television stations far over what the replacement value of their nonlicense inputs. This extra payment reflects the discounted value of the expected excess profits and is thus a sort of bid (as at an auction).[37]

MONOPOLISTIC COMPETITION

Monopolistic competition denotes a marketplace where there are many sellers, but for any specific product (or service) there are but a few competing products. Today's magazine industry is monopolistically competitive; the radio industry was until the mid-1990s. For example, although there are thousands of magazines, they can be grouped by identifiable genres, from hobbyist quarterlies to scandal sheets to seriously monthlies. Within a single genre, only a small number of publications compete for a reader's purchase and attention. The same "competition" can be said to have been at work—in large media markets prior to the consolidation caused by the Communications Act of 1996—for radio broadcasting, with their range of familiar formats (from "Album-Oriented Rock" to "Country" to "All-News").[38]

The magazine industry serves as a model of a robust, but constantly re-invented, business. Whereas television eroded the market for mass consumption advertising, it provided the direct impetus for two of the most successful magazines of all times: first *TV Guide* and later *People*. Personal computers and professional wrestling, for example, have generated dozens of highly popular and profitable periodicals. This industry is simply far easier to enter than newspapers, television, music or movies. That is not to say that there are not media conglomerates owning scores of popular magazines, but as special interests change, new niche magazines emerge. This occurs because there are no economies of scale of distribution to operate as a barrier to entry; the U. S. Postal Service handles delivery.

Both consumer magazines and professional and business magazines serve the need of advertisers who wish to reach a defined audience interested in defined products and services. The best indication of this specialization is that the number of magazines has been growing. In 1950, there were almost 6,600 periodicals of quarterly or greater frequency. In 1998, the number was over 11,800, although with deaths and births of many publications, the actual number of different titles is no doubt much greater. Whole categories spring up to meet new interests, with automobile enthusiasts, fix-it-uppers, private pilots, grooms and brides-to-be, horse breeders, antique collectors, political junkies, sports enthusiasts, computer programmers and media economists. This industry is highly fragmented, so much so that no one company or group of companies dominates it. The largest general circulation magazine in 1997, *Readers Digest*, accounted for 4.1% of per issue consumer magazines sales; *TV Guide* accounted for virtually the same figure in 1980 at 4.2%, at which time it was the largest magazine (excluding association periodicals). Yet, by definition, each magazine does not compete with all other magazines. Each competes within its niche arena by catering to a distinct audience segment. *Country Weekly* does not compete with the *New Republic*; the *American Journalism Review* does not compete with *PC Week*. Magazines offer the purest remaining example of monopolistic competition: many similar products, but each one perceived as being different enough from the others to create its own unique market. The distinction may be by geography (Washingtonian or New York) demographics (*Jet* or *Seventeen*), or a multitude of ways to divide up the people and their interests and concerns.[39]

TRANSITIONING INDUSTRIES

Some industries, like radio and the Internet, are in the midst of transition. Radio had long been categorized as an example of monopolistic competition, but after the 1996 Telecommunications Act, the radio market was moving toward an oligopoly. On the other hand, the Internet surely was as open an industry as the media offered as late as the mid-1990s, but with developing categories of e-commerce and portals for information seeking, the Internet seems headed toward monopolistic competition sometime after 2000.

Through the mid-1990s, radio broadcasting had been more decentralized and thus considered a monopolistically competitive industry. That is, there were many stations offering closely competitive "products," or formats, particularly in major markets. These were substitutes for each other. So there might be a couple of Country stations, and although not perfect substitutes, research showed that the average person tuned into a score of stations—through button selections on the automobile radio—and selected among those substitutes. Further, each substitutable station in the market sought to differentiate their on-air product in the mind of the listener by way of different combinations of music, different disc jockeys and personalities, and by different marketing tactics. And FCC rule demanded decentralized ownership.

But, in 1996, ownership rules were relaxed and chains developed collections of stations numbering in the hundreds. With this concentration of ownership, decisions of formats were made within the same group, and so the economics of monopolistic competition disappeared, and radio broadcasting began verging toward a classic oligopoly—particularly within bigger markets.[40]

Radio broadcasting used to be TV's down home cousin, a collection of stations with many owners, and a plethora of formats from which to choose. The Telecommunications Act of 1996 set off the greatest merger wave in history. CBS took over Infinity Broadcasting; Hicks Muse, a Dallas investment firm, acquired more than 400 stations. In a telling metaphor, Infinity's founder, Mel Karmazin, noted: "It's like combining two ocean front properties." He meant that the new empire would not be some mom-and-pop collection of rural stations in small towns, but would own 7 outlets in New York City, 6 in Los Angeles, 10 in Chicago, 8 in San Francisco and 4 in Washington, DC.[41]

Radio proved important because of its local domination. A collection of popular stations in a city could mean millions of dollars in advertising. In 1997, for example, CBS controlled more than one third of all advertising dollars poured into radio in Boston, half in Philadelphia, one fifth in Washington/Baltimore, one quarter in St. Louis and Los Angeles and one third in Dallas/Ft. Worth and Detroit. Wall Street analysts recognized this, and solidly supported the mergers that led to Hicks Muse, CBS and Clear Channel, the largest collections of radio stations in history, and a redefinition of the radio industry in the United States during the 1990s. By 1999, radio was dominated by this "Big Three." Disney's ABC and Cox followed as part of major media conglomerates. Because radio operates locally, the Washington, DC market provides an example of the new ownership in a top 10 market. Through the mid-1990s, change in ownership was the order of the day. Hicks Muse's Evergreen and CBS moved into the nation's capital to acquire stations in a populous and well-off market. Thanks to strong Washington demographics, although the market was eighth in population reached, it was sixth in advertising dollars spent. The Washington radio community had not seen such an "invasion" since the early days of radio when NBC and CBS established major outlets in the nation's capital. After the dust cleared in 1999, eight stations controlled by Hicks Muse and Westinghouse/CBS accounted for more than one third of all advertising dollars (and nearly that in listener share). Eight companies controlled about 90% of the total ratings and revenues.[42]

The Internet and its components were at a very early stage of growth in the 1990s, starting from free entry and exit. But as the industry matures, it seems headed toward certain sites dominating with certain categories (e.g., the magazine industry). Some celebrate the openness of the Internet, but all entrants seek to become a monopoly. In 1999, portal sites, more and more taken over by major media companies as InfoSeek by Disney, see this as the key strategy. Will the Internet become a monopoly? Most would argue no, but that does not ensure that it will emerge as a purely competitive industry.[43]

In 1999, the most popular Web sites were those of America Online (AOL), the most successful of the early proprietary consumer online services, and the sites that started as search engines but had transformed themselves into "portals." These were locations that users often set as their initial screens when they started their Web browsers. Major media giants were seeking to dominate this entry and thus dominate the Internet. Disney, through Infoseek and its "Go" network, and General Electric's NBC, through investments in the SNAP portal and a half interest in MSNBC, sought to add the Internet to their already sizable media divisions and operations. Microsoft, Yahoo! and other smaller operations sought to make the Internet not simply an extension of already existing media corporations. With more than 4,000 companies providing access to the Internet as 1999 ended, even Microsoft's network had but one eighth of AOL's customers. Only AT&T WorldNet, MindSpring and Earth-Link were one sixteenth the size of AOL.[44]

But early in industry history, success stories rang in everyone's ears. For example, Yahoo! offers the prototypical ease of entry and early success story. Founded by two graduate students who developed a method for searching Web sites for their friends, they incorporated in 1995. In 1996 Yahoo! went public, and within a year its total revenue per annum fell far below the value of its stock. Yahoo! differed from the start because it offered an indexing service, relying on an editorial staff to assign categories and subcategories. By 1998, Yahoo! was generating more hits than rival portals as users valued its indexing service, news summaries, sports scores and other content. In 1999, Yahoo! purchased GeoCities for $5 billion in stock, and thus added the ability for users to create and store their own Web pages. Investors were betting on the future as the stock price soared, but this was an uncertain wager.[45]

Major media companies did not sit by long, and by 1999 began to work to make the Internet—particularly through portal sites—an oligopoly. Sellers online started with books, but by 1999 all media products, from home videos to CDs, were sold directly to the customers. Given that multiple cable and telephone companies were competing to serve as the access point for users, this industry was still evolving. Whereas control of the Internet backbone seemed to be the likely constraint toward limiting competition, the use of the Internet and its status as a mass medium remained in doubt. With only one third of households online, the early years of the 21st century will offer the Golden Age for grabbing market share, and establishing oligopolistic power—if possible. Media economists will surely write more about this industry as the 21st century progresses.[46]

PERFORMANCE

Analysis of economic structure (and conduct) initiates and logically leads to analysis of performance. Indeed, what media scholars and critics care most about are the economic linkages to media performance. Remedies are proposed when proper performance of the industry is judged not to be up to standard. We need to select performance criteria that are as precise as possible: How well has a media industry functioned when compared to some ideal standard? If there is market operational failure, then is there a regulatory remedy to correct that failure? The former question is treated under performance later, saving the development of public policy options for the following unit.

Six media performance norms encompass most judgments. They are discussed in order of ease of use. That is, the first criteria considered are easier to deal with than those further down on the list. These are all value judgments and the order does not reflect my priorities. But the discussion has to begin somewhere, so as to make this analysis explicit and not tied to my own or someone elses per se:[47]

1) Media industries ought not to waste resources; that is, they should be as efficient as possible. Monopolists waste resources in order to maintain their position of power. However, what about control by a few firms? Many argue that this is just as bad, acknowledging that these industries regularly cooperate through powerful trade associations and thus hardly represent "lean and mean" business operations. However, whereas free market economists focus on only this performance criterion, media economics ought to weigh others.[48]

2) Media industries ought to facilitate free speech and political discussion. A democracy needs freedom of expression to make it work and the mass media ought to be open enough to promote debate of all points of view. The marketplace of ideas calls for criteria of factualness, accuracy and completeness.[49]

3) Media industries ought to facilitate public order. In times of war, violence and crime, how should the media be regulated (if at all) to ensure differences? This is a growing area of concern as the media easily jump across national (and local) boundaries.[50]

4) Media industries ought to protect and maintain cultural quality, offering some role of the media diversity. Can advertising-generated revenue companies develop quality programming, and not simply dish up more sensationalism? Here the issue of use of television in elections becomes paramount.[51]

5) Media industries ought to bring to the marketplace new technologies as quickly as possible. It has long been known that monopolies and collusive oligopolies resist the innovation of new technologies in order to protect their highly profitable status quo positions.[52]

6) Media industries ought to be equitable. Should members of groups in society be shut out of the mass media industries either as employees and managers, or as consumers? Executives and managers are uniformly White males. For consumers, access is becoming more restrictive as a larger share of the mass media go to direct payment. If television is an important link in democracy, how will our process of government change when one third do not have access to cable or DBS television?[53]

But, applying these six criteria consistently and fairly and equitably across all the mass media is difficult. Critics often select potions to use for their judgments. So, for example, in a simple, but narrow analysis, according to Ben H. Bagdikian, we ought to confront the potential harm in concentrated ownership as most persons are shut out of the creative process.[54] Bagdikian expresses fears that the media in general, and newspapers and television in particular, are increasingly controlled by a new kind of central authority over information—a monopoly pure and simple. Yet a closer look—industry by industry—hardly reveals that a handful of men and women control what the rest of us read, see and hear. Central to Bagdikian's overarching media monopoly is the newspaper business; in that industry (and cable TV) Bagdikian is right. But to argue the other media industries are monopoly is patently absurd, as the bulk of this book demonstrates. For Bagdikian and others, analyzing oligopolies is simply too hard; mischaracterizing them as monopolies is easier.

Profit maximizers are more explicit. *Business Week*, in its annual March report of publicly traded companies (which are part of the Standard & Poor's 500), uses eight criteria: total return for the year, total return for past three years, sales growth of the year, sales growth for three years, profit growth for the year, profit growth for past three years, net margin and return on equity. For the *Business Week* report published on March 29, 1999, for the 1998 year and prior, the leading U.S.-based companies are covered in our book in the following order: 7 AOL, 20 Ameritech, 35 Wal-Mart, 44 General Electric, 49 Bell Atlantic, 63 Gannett, 73 Comcast, 96 AT&T, 120 McGraw-Hill, 131 Tribune, 151 Clear Channel Communication, 171 New York Times, 214 Meredith, 216 Walt Disney, 231 Time Warner, 232 Knight-Ridder, 240 MediaOne Group (in 1999 taken over by AT&T), 289 King World (in 1999 taken over by CBS), 316 CBS, 323 Harcourt General, 328 Viacom, 423 Times Mirror and 455 Dow Jones. This list does not include foreign-based companies and private companies, but it does measure success for corporations.

But for communications scholars, I assert the mass media should not be mislabeled as monopolies, not judged as "just another business" to be measured by the *Business Week* criteria, but because they supply the vast majority of common information and common entertainment, they ought to be judged by all six criteria—and more, if applicable. We ought to worry about maintaining universal service, the creation of propaganda and about the maintenance of a single mass taste culture. We will have in the future to worry more about bridging information and media gaps, about securing political involvement, about maintaining creativity, independence, and diversity, and about minority rights and cultural identity.

For me diversity is a key, particularly for what is known as the political economy approach. We ought to applaud the innovation of new cable networks, from Black Entertainment Television (BET) for African Americans to Lifetime for females, from Univision for Hispanics to Discovery for documentary fans. Yet recognize that this plethora of choices does have a downside. In 1998, Fox's Family Channel unit announced two new cable networks, the Boyz Channel and the Gilrz Channel. The Boyz Channel would feature karate and lasers, whereas the Girlz Channel would feature baby sitting tips and relationship building. It was a simple step to advertising segmentation and possible polarization, rather than interaction between females and males.

History points to some government rule-making. For example, affirmative action rules set up in 1969, which measured a company's balance of minority employees against the percentage of minorities living in the broadcast TV market, led to more female, African American and Hispanic faces and voices on television. In 1998, the Commission, under pressure from a Republican-led Congress, softened these rules to look favorably on more females and minorities. The previous rules had led to some success in that in 1998 minorities made up one fifth of broadcast industry employees, and more than one quarter of those in the cable business, about the level in the U.S. population. By this same FCC survey, women in 1998 made up two fifths of broadcast TV workers, and about the same percentage in the cable TV business, while women made up just over half the population of the United States.[55]

The evidence demonstrating more diversity is harder to come by for top executive positions, but surely the percentages have been lower than examining all employees. Yet progress has been made on at least one front—female executive promotions. There is evidence of a new generation of executives, who earned MBAs and established themselves while working up the chain of command. They may have lower profiles than their pioneer predecessors, but in 1998 Nancy Tellen was president of CBS's entertainment division, Patricia Fili-Krusel was president of ABC Daytime, Laurie Younger was chief financial officer of ABC, Anne Sweeney was the head of the Disney Channel, Susanne Daniels was executive vice president for entertainment at the WB television network, Judith McGarth was the head of MTV and Cyma Zhargami was the head of Nickelodeon. The new world of cable TV offered many opportunities to gain experience and move up the ladder. We hope such progress toward equal representation is manifest for African Americans and Hispanics in television as well.[56]

We all ought to consider our criteria for proper performance, and then if ownership and conduct are judged acceptable or better, we ought to argue to leave things alone and let profit maximization work. But if we judge failures exist in market ownership and/or operation, we ought to advocate public policy (discussed in the following section). But before ending the analysis of performance, note that sometimes the failures are not internal to the industry, but external. Part of the consideration of the public interest is to recognize that there are negative externalities. That is, the traditional microeconomic model assumes that a decision by a firm has no external effects on another firm, but communications is a system where there are many situations where external or third-party effects are important—positively and negatively. Communications systems break down space and positively tie us together; but they also cause disconnections, paranoia and social volatility. For instance, Robert Kuttner persuasively links the erosion of civic life through the 20th century with the agenda setting power of the mass media in general, broadcast television in particular. The broadcasters have argued for the positive externalities—assuming that they alone by continuing free, advertising-based system television link a nation in vital ways. But with the list of concerns and special cases in the 1996 Act—particularly worries about obscenity and violence in Title V—a policy must be shaped that takes into account not only concerns of broadcasters, but the whole plethora of concerns in society, and this is particularly the case with the possible externalities for children's TV viewing.[57]

The importance of externalities is carefully laid out by James Hamilton. Looking at the market for television violence, he judges this an example of market failure whereby television violence generates negative externalities. Which costs spill over to members of society and are not born by the industry. He compares this with environmental pollution, because a firm that generates the hazardous waste may not incorporate the full costs to society of its corporate decisions when its spillover effects are not calculated as part of what it needs to produce, distribute and present the product to the public. Here negative TV externalities work both in the manner as well as possible solutions. A means needs to be created, so the polluting corporation internalizes all the costs (corporate and societal). If broadcasters, cable casters and DBS deliverers do not fully incorporate all the costs to society (such as increased levels of aggression and crime), then Hamilton argues that a means ought to be constructed to make them do so by restricting such programming to certain parts of the day, or label the programming or even pay a tax to put it out. The theory of externalities underscores how the damage to society as a whole that arises from television violence remains outside the calculations of most programmers, producers and viewers calculated in the typical microeconomic analysis of television.

The recognition that television violence, as but one example of a negative externality, suggests that the optimal amount of violence is not zero, reinforces that the externalities need be considered in any policy analysis. Hamilton notes that one way to reduce damages from violence on television would be to use the license system because programmers use violence as part of their quest to maximize profits. Hamilton assumes there is monopoly profit in the system and so the broadcaster obtaining a free license would not be made worse off. Cable MSOs at least must pay a "franchise fee" that is often used by communities for public projects, including offering alternative programming. This assumes that the optimal amount of violence is not zero, but that costs and benefits need to be weighed and policy options considered.[58]

PUBLIC POLICY

The history of the mass media in the United States suggests that it is necessary to choose among media industry monopolies, oligopolies or situations of monopolistic competition. That is, it will be necessary to choose among less than perfectly desirable market structures and conducts. Idealists speculate on a world of one media industry; realists know that in modern capitalism corporations will operate differently within industry market structures that are not purely competitive. Once we understand media industry structure and conduct, we will need to be clear what performance criteria we wish to prioritize and work from there. The media economist can play a central role by evaluating proposals for regulation and analyze their effects on structure, conduct and performance. However, the media economist should not seek to impose performance criteria. Media scholars can help specify what appropriate criteria might be.[59]

Negative externalities do offer the lone examples of market failures. Market failures are endemic in the structure and conduct of monopolies and oligopolies, and in the form of restricted output, can encourage poor management, can lead to lower spending on research and development and can lead to negative externalities. There are three principle ways to deal with this failure—to nationalize, to regulate and to use taxes and/or government spending and rule making to encourage more competitive-like operations. Nationalization is rare, but it did give us Public Broadcasting System (PBS) and National Public Radio. The FCC has regulated broadcast radio and television since 1934. Congress has passed tax breaks to encourage minority ownership of television and radio stations. But the deregulatory movement of the 1980s and 1990s has discouraged use of all three of these methods in all but a few cases, and instead looked to the Department of Justice and the Federal Trade Commission to enforce existing antitrust laws.[60]

We should take this task of media economics, broadly defined, very seriously. Societies of the future will be dependent on complex electronic information networks offering information and communication. There will be globalization of distribution. We need to help judge proper performance and tender (if necessary) corrective public policy actions.

Should we offer strong countervailing governmental power? Should we let the free market tap the energies (and rewards) of technical innovation? Or should we, as we do at present, seek to optimize the mixture of a regulated and unregulated media world?

We will have to, in the future, worry about many channels, with greater ease of access and growing expense of use. For the media of the future, it will be important to bridge information and media gaps, secure political involvement and maintain creativity, independence and diversity about social solidarity and minority rights, about cultural autonomy and identity. Media economics is useful when sorting through these thorny public policy questions.[61]

We need to rationally adopt public policies to facilitate all citizens having access to many channels and sources, offering different content, alternative voices. We will need know how the common structures of message production and distribution and presentation effect audiences. Thus, in the future we need, on an industry-by-industry basis, to examine the structure, conduct and performance of changing media economics.

Before jumping into policy recommendations, consider the data necessary to make these decisions. The media, however, present problems in gathering such data. In the 1990s, government statistics were harder to come by. And industry-generated numbers were limited. So, for a telling example, no one really knows how many books are published each year. It is estimated that more than 50,000 titles are published annually, but some analysts go as high as 70,000 titles. With many small publishers starting and ceasing operations each year, there is no central authority that can establish the figure precisely. Magazine publishing is the same way. The great diversity of publishers and publications has its counterpart in a paucity of detailed information about the industry. Publishers are extremely close-mouthed about the economics of their operations; only a small minority report to the Publishers Information Bureau, an industry clearinghouse for advertising and circulation data.

Also recognize that private and public corporations may operate differently. Public companies generally have access to greater financial resources, and can therefore be more flexible choosing to expand, contract or stay pat. On the other hand, public companies have to report on their performance every three months, to prove to the Wall Street analytical community they may generate a better return than an alternative use of an investor's savings. This encourages a greater emphasis on short-term profit maximization. Private companies, particularly family or individual owned, can ignore outsider advise and look to the long run. Owners can make decisions faster, and ignore quarterly pressures to raise earnings per share. Managers at private companies, especially media companies, may be able to pursue editorial objectives without having to answer to a stockholder-voted board.

Although it is possible to identify who actually owns these media companies. With few exceptions, most of these organizations are publicly owned and thus the ownership is widely diffused. There are exceptions, such as Rupert Murdoch and Sumner Redstone. This is where the debate of managerial control comes in (e.g., the work of Adolph Berle and Gardiner Means). Organizations are run by managers, but managers are rarely the owners. Whereas senior management generally has considerable latitude in day-to-day operations, they are often more constrained in strategic direction by the interests of their stockholders' expectations. Yet the stockholders rarely do more than vote out management, or pay them considerably for their fine efforts.[62]

Even in public companies there can be private-like control. There may be a single dominant owner (e.g., Murdoch with News Corporation, the Graham family with The Washington Post, and Sumner Redstone and Viacom). The Securities and Exchange Commission (SEC) takes 5% stock share as some control; the FCC cuts it off at 25% to determine control. These owner-dominated public companies offer the exception. More typically is an AT&T and General Electric, of which NBC is a very small part, which had more than 3.5 million and one half million stockholders, respectively, with insiders accounting for less than 0.1% of the total. Disney is also among the most widely held in the world, with 658,000 stockholders (including many children who were given a few share as presents). Certainly Disney offers classic management control, with Michael Eisner having a powerful role, even if he and other insiders own less than 2% of the company's common stock.

In addition, it is not necessary to own or control even a majority of the stock in large companies to exert substantial control. With most of the stock widely held, a substantial minority block closely held can usually have deciding influence in company policy. One notable example is Australia-based News Corporation. The Murdoch family, through an investment company, owned about 31% of this publicly traded company in 1998. But with the remainder of ownership scattered among 123 institutions and countless individuals, the Murdoch family is generally in control.

This leads to the issue of managerial compensation. In companies controlled by a small set of stockholders or those dominated by management, sometimes the remuneration of this can seem excessive. Great management offers a very valuable skill, but should that be rewarded with hundreds of millions of dollars per annum? Is Michael Eisner worth more than $100 million in salary and stock options per year? Corporations operated well in the 1960s, paying top executives 35 times what the average worker made, and in the 1990s that figure jumped to more than 100 times. Foreign corporations pay nowhere close to that latter amount. But this surely represents management control of a corporation, as managers pick board members who consider some remuneration that is not out of line.[63]

Surely media managers were among the best paid of all corporate executives, far greater than the size of their enterprises might predict. In Business Week's annual poll released in April 1999, Michael Eisner of Disney led with total pay for 1998 of $575,592,000, followed in second place by CBS's Mel Karmazin at $201,934,000 and GE's Jack Welch in sixth place at $83,664,000. Even Business Week had to ask if Eisner was worth it? Forbes, in its May 1999 issue, asked the same thing? Defenders properly pointed out that most of this "pay" was in stock options and thus the stock price had to be kept up to cash in such staggering amounts. Critics asked: Why wouldn't more pay for average workers and something less for the CEOs making the company more profitable?

But analysts must work with the statistics at hand, must differentiate private versus public companies as best as they can and must factor in ownership control versus management control. Most rabid neoclassical economists would argue that monopolists sustaining barriers to entry and thus no effective competition is in the long run in the best interest of U.S. citizens. The Sherman and Clayton antitrust acts and the Federal Trade Commission Act exist as part of the U.S. laws. Thus when a monopoly problem is identified, then alternative solutions ought to be considered and tested. But as politics changes, interpretations do as well, and the policies to deal with mergers and their effects on competition, and the policies to deal with restraints of trade come through case law precedents, or exceptions made to these basic laws.[64]

But making good public policy is difficult. Consider the case of trying to prop up a second newspaper in monopoly communities. The Newspaper Preservation Act was passed in 1970, in effect providing an exemption to the antitrust laws for 44 newspapers to effect 22 joint agreements to share costs of all inputs save editorial staff. Since then, agreements must be approved by the Justice Department on a case-by-case basis. This has kept a second newspaper in business for a decade or so.

The proponents of the legislation argued that two separate editorial voices were a better alternative than the single voice that would exist if an otherwise marginal paper were forced out of business or taken over entirely by the stronger paper. The opposing view has been voiced not only by many small, independent dailies, but by the *New York Times* and the Newspaper Guild as well, contending that daily and weekly papers in suburbs offered effect substitutes for failing city newspapers, and thus government assistance was not needed. Critics of the Newspaper Preservation Act have cited in particular the changing interpretations of the Act by the Justice Departments of succeeding administrations. Some papers have done "creative accounting" to help make the newspaper look less profitable.

The fine line that the Justice Department must walk in determining the applicability of the Newspaper Preservation Act for new applicants has made interpretation of the Act a variable in the political arena, as in the case of one of the most contentious of all petitions for a joint agreement between the Detroit papers in 1986. This followed years of spirited competition between Knight-Ridder's *Free Press* and the *Evening News*, purchased by Gannett in 1985. The *Free Press*, was the second place paper for years, accounting for about 35% of the advertising linage of the two papers in 1986. In 1979, Knight-Ridder executives determined to spend whatever it took to overtake the *News*. The paper slashed advertising rates and held down subscription prices. The *News* matched the *Free Press* and both papers lost money in the battle. To hold on to circulation, the *News* continued selling for $0.15 weekdays, less than any other Gannett paper and lower than the more prevalent $0.25. The *Free Press* reported annual losses of between $11 million and $14 million between 1981 and 1986. An alternative solution would seem to be called for, or a recognition that news can be acquired from a variety of means. Thus, the

Newspaper Preservation Act has outgrown its usefulness as public policy, and is indeed anticompetitive.[65]

Enforcing the antitrust laws sometimes makes no difference in the long run. In 1938, for example, the Justice Department sued the then "Big Eight" major studios, and in 1948 the U.S. Supreme Court forced the movie majors to sell their theatrical chains in order to open the market to more competition. This decree remained in existence until the Justice Department of the administration of President Ronald Reagan—in its deregulatory zeal—declared the new competition from pay TV and home video effective competition and vacated the decree. In the long run, however, the Big Six of Hollywood simply took over these pay TV and home video "rival" venues, and instead of offering competition, they took back the movie business, and gained more power than they ever had in 1938. The oligopoly was never broken.

In a few cases, there has long been direct government regulation. For radio and television broadcasting, based on the 1934 Communications Act, the FCC has allocated licenses and enforced a plethora of rules and regulations set in place by Congress and the president. We are still living with the FCC; indeed, in 1996, the most sweeping of the revisions of that Act was signed into law. The law had many consequences, some of which are only beginning to be appreciated today. But surely the 21st century will experience further, not yet anticipated, consequences (and amendments).[66]

But for radio broadcasting, it lifted the ownership limits so that single companies would be taking in more than half of all revenues going into radio advertising. The U.S. Department of Justice under president William J. Clinton objected under antitrust statutes, and pressed several cases objecting to such mergers. But economies of scale will continue to push these radio consolidations, and so the Justice Department will remain an important player. As of the late 1990s, the Department of Justice had negotiated a number of consent decrees. For example, in Cincinnati, Jacor agreed to sell and thus at the time saw its share of the advertising dollars fall from 53% to 46%; and CBS, as a result of its Infinity takeover in nine separate markets, agreed to divest stations to push down its dominant share of the radio advertising revenues.[67]

The 1996 Telecommunications Act anticipated that for the most pervasive of the mass media, television, new technological delivery systems would challenge the oligopoly power of the broadcast networks and monopoly power of the cable TV industry. But as of 1999, DBS provided a single option, and although customers had a choice, it was hardly very competitive. Indeed, the conundrum in the 1990s no longer rested with the expanding universe of broadcast television, because most people watched the broadcast networks not through broadcasting but from cable delivery: Were cable operators acting alone or acting together to exercise market power in the purchase of video programming? Observation over the 1990s indicated that MSOs had an incentive to coordinate their decisions in the upstream market for the purchase of programming on a national or regional level, and they were very successful at this. There seems no reason to expect MSOs not to continue to seek to control the flow and price of valued inputs through exclusive distribution contracts or monopsonistic pressure, and in turn to deter entry and competition in the marketplace, and limit the diversity of cable programming, reducing the number of voices available to the public.[68]

As of mid-1998, the FCC also noted the following horizontal relations. AT&T's TCI had a 10% ownership interest in Time Warner, Inc. and all of its subsidiaries, including a 10% ownership interest in Time Warner Cable—the nation's second largest MSO—and a 10% ownership interest in Time Warner/Turner programming services. MediaOne, later acquired by AT&T, had a 25% ownership interest in Time Warner Entertainment, L.P., which included a 25% ownership interest in Time Warner Cable. Furthermore, Comcast Corporation had acquired Jones Intercable, then the nation's eighth largest MSO with 1.5 million subscribers. The major cable companies work together in joint deals, thus expanding their collective power and raising barriers to entry.[69]

In the end, three years after the passage of the 1996 Telecommunications Act for multichannel video, cable had seven eighths of the market, and DBS the rest. Indeed, whereas DBS continued its expansionary trend during the 1990s, the market share of cable decreased from 87% in June 1997 to 85% in June 1998. Using the market shares for each technology, the estimate of the HHI is 7,015, a decrease from the HHI of 7,567 for 1997. Nevertheless, an HHI of 7,015 remained several times greater than the 1,800 threshold at which a market may be considered "highly concentrated," even by the conservative standards set during the height of the 1980s deregulatory era.[70]

Indeed, as the 1990s ended, cable was working on new methods to capture more power, led by clustering, a process by which MSOs consolidated system ownership within separate geographical regions. Clustering provided a means of reducing costs and attracting more advertising, but it also significantly raised barriers to entry to potential overbuilders. During 1997, there were more than 100 such cable transactions, with a total market value of approximately $22.2 billion involving approximately 11 million subscribers. A similar pattern continued in 1998 and 1999, reflecting even greater power through economies of scale. AT&T's TCI, for example, aggressively pursued clustering, and so in the Chicago metropolitan area, at the end of 1999, through swaps and acquisitions had gained control of 9 of 10 cable subscribers.[71]

DBS never provided the array of alternatives that might benefit the customer. It should not be expected that DBS prices will continue to rise as has been the case with cable prices. The power of the entrenched industry can be seen in its continual ability to raise prices to customers. In one 1996 survey for systems in and around Washington, DC, it was found that rates were going up from 7% to 15% per annum, well beyond the inflation rate of 3%. Spiraling price increases began in the late 1980s. Responding in October 1992, Congress, over President George Bush's veto, passed a law designed to restrain rate increases. The FCC issued regulations and hired 160 new employees in an effort to cut customer's prices by an average of 17%. Prices fell for a time, but when the industry realized there was no real competition coming from the Baby Bells, it began to exercise its monopoly power again by pushing up prices. Double-digit price increases became the norm, signaling the truest measure of the little impact of the promised competition.[72]

At the heart of all radio and TV legislation has been a "public interest" obligation. Such an obligation could be extended to cable companies and the DBS operator. Then this obligation would have to be enforced. What defines this "public interest" has always been controversial, with at least three considerations at work: ownership restrictions, content restrictions and protections of certain spaces for political debate. The 1996 Telecommunications Act did not revoke broadcaster's public trusteeship, continuing a trend that began with the 1992 Cable Television Consumer Protection Act, which contained a clause (47 U.S.C. 335) intended to impose traditional public interest obligations in the new world of DBS. This debate over obligations of "public interest" ought to define the debate for proper radio and TV policy after 2000.[73]

Critics will continue to find the media wanting, and so proposals will be made to improve performance of the media industries. I hope we have helped with such debates by establishing the ownership and conduct of important media industries, which is the first step in making public policy that will help, not hurt, their performance.

NOTES

1. Douglas Gomery, "The Centrality of Media Economics," *Journal of Communication* 43.3, pp. 190–198.
2. See F. M. Scherer and David Ross, *Industrial Market Structure and Economic Performance* 3rd ed. (Boston: Houghton Mifflin, 1990), for the best synthesis of this approach.
3. See Paul Auerbach, *Competition: The Economics of Industrial Change* (London: Basil Blackwell, 1988), pp. 9–11.
4. See Randy Alberda, Christopher Gunn and William Waller, *Alternatives to Economic Orthodoxy* (London: M. E. Sharpe, 1987), pp. 263–265; Andrew R. Schotter, *Microeconomics* (New York: HarperCollins, 1994), pp. 1–12.
5. For a listing of global media of the late 1990s and their possible negative effects, see Edward S. Herman and Robert W. McChesney, *The Global Media: The New Missionaries of Corporate Capitalism* (London: Cassell, 1997), particularly pp. 70–105.
6. My guide to issues and concerns of media performance is Dennis McQuail, *Media Performance* (Newbury Park, CA: Sage, 1992).
7. Robert M. Entman, "Newspaper Competition and First Amendment Ideals: Does Monopoly Matter?" *Journal of Communication* 35.3 (1985), pp. 147–165.
8. For analysis of the role of the media conglomerate, see Douglas Gomery, "Media Economics: Terms of Analysis," *Critical Studies in Mass Communication* 6.1 (1989), pp. 43–45. See also Erik Barnouw et al., *Conglomerates and the Media* (New York: The New Press, 1997), which analyzes the effects of media conglomerates and finds the organizational system generally wanting.
9. Application of the antitrust laws in the 1980s and 1990s is the subject of John E. Kwoka, Jr., and Lawrence J. White (eds.), *The Antitrust Revolution: Economics, Competition, and Policy*, 3rd ed. (New York: Oxford University Press, 1999).
10. Scherer and Ross, pp. 74–76, 581–586.
11. Ibid., pp. 278–285, 395–407.
12. See Robert G. Picard, *Media Economics: Concepts and Issues* (Newbury Park, CA: Sage, 1989).
13. Gomery, "The Centrality of Media Economics," pp. 190–198; Joseph E. Stiglitz, *Principles of Micro Economics* (New York: W. W. Norton, 1993), pp. 395–422.
14. See Jack Bass, "Newspaper Monopoly," *American Journalism Review*, July/August 1999, pp. 64–86.
15. John Morton, "Small Dailies Are Dying in California," *American Journalism Review*, May 1998, p. 76.

16. See Robert G. Picard and Jeffrey H. Brody, *The Newspaper Publishing Industry* (New York: Allyn & Bacon, 1997).

17. Douglas Gomery, "Cable TV Rates: Not a Pretty Picture," *American Journalism Review*, July/August 1998, p. 66.

18. Patrick R. Parsons and Robert M. Frieden, *The Cable and Satellite Television Industries* (New York: Allyn & Bacon, 1998), pp. 195–237; David Waterman and Andrew A. Weiss, *Vertical Integration in Cable Television* (Cambridge: MIT Press, 1997), pp. 152–157.

19. Douglas Gomery, "Phone Giant Elbowing into Cable," *American Journalism Review*, July/August 1999, p. 90.

20. Parsons and Frieden, pp. 147–151; Robert N. Wold, "United States DBS History: A Long Road to Success," *Via Satellite*, September 1996, pp. 32–34, 36, 38, 40, 42, 44.

21. Douglas Gomery, "The Making of a Satellite Behemoth," *American Journalism Review*, May 1999, p. 82.

22. See Picard, *Media Economics*.

23. Stiglitz, pp. 423–445.

24. The theory of oligopoly is very complex and oftentimes seemingly unsettled. To begin to read about this important type of market structure and conduct, start with James Friedman, *Oligopoly Theory* (Cambridge: Cambridge University Press, 1983); and Scherer and Ross, pp. 199–316.

25. Gomery, "The Centrality of Media Economics," pp. 190–198.

26. G. Pascal Zachary, "Lets Play Oligopoly! Why Giants Like Having Other Giants Around." *Wall Street Journal*, March 8, 1999, pp. B1, B10.

27. John Lippman, "Hollywood Sets Records Year Again at the Box Office," *Wall Street Journal*, December 31, 1998, p. B2; the Web site of the Motion Picture Association of America at www.mpaa.org.

28. For more on this, see Douglas Gomery, "The Economics of Hollywood: Money and Media," in Alison Alexander, James Owers and Rod Carveth (eds.), *Media Economics: Theory and Practice* (Hillsdale, NJ: Lawrence Erlbaum Associates, 1998), pp. 175–184.

29. Dyan Machan, "Mr. Valenti Goes to Washington," *Forbes*, December 1, 1997, pp. 66, 68, 69–70; Jeffrey Birnbaum, "Washington's Power 25," *Fortune*, December 8, 1997, pp. 144–148, 152.

30. Ed Christian, "WEA Regains No. 1 in Album Market Share for '97," *Billboard*, October 18, 1997, pp. 55–56, 62, offers a comprehensive report as 1997 ended. Regular reports can be found in the middle of the month (about the 18th or 19th) of January, April, July and October in *Billboard*—online at Web site www.billboard.com—from SoundScan compiled information.

31. Richard Siklos, "Can Record Labels Get Back Their Rhythm?," *Business Week*, July 27, 1998, pp. 52–53.

32. Robert S. Greenberger and Craig S. Smith, "CD Piracy Flourishes in China, and West Supplies the Equipment," *Wall Street Journal*, April 24, 1997, pp. A1, A13; Linton Weeks, "Turning Up the Power," *Washington Post*, July 30, 1997, pp. C1, C2. See RIAA Web site at www.riaa.com.

33. Patrick M. Reilly, "Luring Today's Teen Back to Books," *Wall Street Journal*, March 24, 1999, pp. B1, B4; Doreen Carajal, "As Booksellers Shuffle, Readers Depart," *New York Times*, May 3, 1999, p. C13; Standard & Poor's Industry Surveys, "Publishing," February 6, 1997, pp. 8–9.

34. Jim Milliot, "Book Sales Topped $20 Billion in 1996 but Growth Rate Slows," *Publishers Weekly*, March 3, 1997, p. 11; Daisy Maryles, "How the Winners Made It to the Top," *Publishers Weekly*, January 6, 1997, pp. 46–49.

35. Standard & Poor's Industry Surveys, "Publishing," April 23, 1998, p. 1; "How We Got to Here, 1973–1997," *Publishers Weekly*, July 1997, special issue, pp. 14–16.

36. This was not so much different from the listing *Broadcasting & Cable* magazine published in 1993 when Capital Cities/ABC was first, CBS second, NBC third, Tribune fourth, Fox fifth, Home Shopping Network sixth and Chris-Craft seventh. See "Top Television Groups," *Broadcasting & Cable*, March 22, 1993, pp. 29–30.

37. Harold L. Vogel, *Entertainment Economics: A Guide for Financial Analysis* (Cambridge: Cambridge University Press, 1994), p. 171; "Meredith Buys First Media TVS," *Broadcasting & Cable*, January 27, 1997, p. 8 summarizing FCC data.

38. Douglas Gomery, "Tune In: Radio's Still a Big Player," *American Journalism Review*, December 1996, p. 44.

39. See Samir A. Husni, "Influences on the Survival of New Consumer Magazines," *Journal of Media Economics* 1.1 (Spring 1988), pp. 39–50; and Charles P. Daly, Patrick Henry and Ellen Ryder, *The Magazine Industry* (New York: Allyn & Bacon, 1997).

40. For the case of radio as a monopolistically competitive industry, see Gomery, "The Centrality of Media Economics," pp. 190–198.

41. Douglas Gomery, "Radio's Hot, and So Is Thomas Hicks," *American Journalism Review*, March 1998, p. 50.

42. Marc Fisher, "Colors of the Radio Spectrum," *Washington Post*, December 3, 1996, pp. E1, E7; Paul Fahri, "For Radio Stations, Does Big Mean Bland?," *Washington Post*, "Washington Business," July 1, 1996, p. 5.

43. Taking a snapshot of the Internet at any point in the late 20th century is a risky proposition, but John V. Pavlik's *New Media Technology: Cultural and Commercial Perspectives*, 2nd ed. (New York: Allyn & Bacon, 1999) tries, but only sees it in transition.

44. Leslie Walker, "Rivals Cede Throne to AOL," *Washington Post*, April 8, 1999, pp. E1, E6.

45. Kara Swisher and Evan Ramstad, "Yahoo! Plans to Buy Internet Broadcaster," *Wall Street Journal*, April 1, 1999, pp. A3, A8; John V. Pavlik's *New Media Technology: Cultural and Commercial Perspectives*, 2nd ed. (New York: Allyn & Bacon, 1999), pp. 41–42.

46. For a fine survey as of the mid-1990s, see "The Info Tech 100," *Business Week*, June 21, 1999.

47. These criteria I developed from Dennis McQuail's *Media Performance* (Newbury Park, CA: Sage, 1992).

48. Scherer and Ross, pp. 19–29, 661–667.

49. See Richard A. Schwartzlose, "The Marketplace of Ideas: A Measure of Free Expression," *Journalism Monographs*, No. 110, December 1989.

50. See Robert W. McChesney, *Corporate Media and the Threat of Democracy* (New York: Seven Stories Press, 1997).

51. See Robert W. McChesney, *Rich Media, Poor Democracy* (Urbana: University of Illinois Press, 1999).

52. See Scherer and Ross, pp. 614–621, 630–637, 652–654.

53. Gomery, "The Centrality of Media Economics," pp. 190–198.

54. See Bagdikian's *The Media Monopoly*, 5th ed. (Boston: Beacon Press, 1997).

55. "FCC Eases Affirmative Action Rules After Court Struck Down Old Guides," *Wall Street Journal*, November 20, 1998, p. B6

56. For a fine survey of this approach in 1999, see Gerald Sussman, "Special Issue on the Political Economy of Communication," *Journal of Media Economics* 12.2 (1999), pp. 85–89.

57. Kuttner discusses the effects of mass media in *Everything for Sale* (New York: Knopf, 1996). That children are a special focus of advertising is best described in James U. McNeil, *Kids as Customers: A Handbook of Marketing to Children* (New York: Lexington Books, 1992). The many publications of the Center for Media Education identify the effects on mass media on children and is most easily accessed through the non-profit Web site at www.cme.org.

58. James Hamilton, *Channeling Violence: The Economic Market for Violent Television Programming* (Princeton: Princeton University Press, 1998), pp. 3–7, 30–39, 293–321.

59. Gomery, "The Centrality of Media Economics," pp. 190–198.

60. Stiglitz, pp. 177–178, 446–468, offers a clear guide to the theory of market failure. PBS was created to address the market failures perceived in broadcast television in the late 1960s. For an evaluation of its success, see a 1993 report from the Twentieth Century Fund entitled *Quality Time?*

61. Scherer and Ross, pp. 411–448, 661–685.

62. For summaries of the pioneering work of Berle and Means, see Auerbach, pp. 91–94; and Scherer and Ross, pp. 42–43.

63. Stiglitz, p. 570.

64. Scherer and Ross, pp. 448–488.

65. See Kenneth C. Baseman, "Partial Consolidation: The Detroit Newspaper Joint Operating Agreement," in Kwoka and White, pp. 25–44.

66. Patricia Aufderheide's *Communications Policy and the Public Interest: The Telecommunications Act of 1996* (New York: Guilford Press, 1999) offers a fine survey of the effects of the 1996 Act. For the FCC's position on the 1996 Telecommunications Act, as the 20th century ended, see an evaluation by its chair William E. Kennard, "The Telecom Act at Three," *Media Law & Policy* 7.2 (Spring 1999), pp. 1–6.

67. Joel I. Klein, "DOJ Analysis of Radio Mergers," presented at ANA Hotel in Washington, DC, February 19, 1997, a statement from the Acting Assistant Attorney General of the United States in charge of the Antitrust Division, 18 pages mimeo. See also Donna Petrozzello, "Justice Looks at Rochester Radio," *Broadcasting & Cable*, September 9, 1996, p. 10; Elizabeth A. Rathbun, "Justice Caps Radio Ownership," *Broadcasting & Cable*, August 12, 1996, p. 9.

68. FCC, *In the Matter of Annual Assessment of the Status of Competition in Markets for the Delivery of Video Programming*, Fifth Annual Report. Adopted: December 17, 1998. Released: December 23, 1998, on www.fcc.gov, pp. 94–96.

69. Ibid., p. 96. See also Martin Peers, "Giants Chow Down Indies," *Variety*, September 15–21, 1997, pp. 31, 33.

70. FCC, pp. 80-8, C-1–C-3.

71. Ibid., pp. 89–90.

72. Cable World Staff, "MSOs Map 1998 Rate Hikes," *Cable World*, December 8, 1997, pp. 1, 150; Paul Fahri, "Cable TV Rates Going Up Sharply," *Washington Post*, May 18, 1996, pp. A1, A9; Chris McConnell, "FCC Zeros in on Cable Competition," *Broadcasting & Cable*, December 15, 1997, p. 16; John M. Higgins, "Cable Ramps Up Rates," *Broadcasting & Cable*, December 8, 1997, pp. 6–7.

73. Willard D. Rowland, "The Meaning of 'the Public Interest' in Communication Policy," *Communication Law and Policy* 2.4 (Fall 1997), pp. 363–396.

10

Distinguishing Between Concentration and Competition

Benjamin M. Compaine

OWNERSHIP AND THE NEW MEDIA LANDSCAPE

In January 1998, a reporter for *Newsweek* magazine was sitting on a big story. It certainly was racy, and it would likely help sell magazines. It involved politics and sex. According to the journalist's sources, the president of the United States, Bill Clinton, had a sexual relationship with a young White House employee in the Oval office itself.

But he and his editors were not ready to release the story in print just yet. It was probably for good journalistic and ethical reasons: It involved the President, so they wanted to be sure of their sources and of the accuracy of the account. A conspiracy theorist, however, might suggest darker motives. *Newsweek* is owned by the same company that owns the *Washington Post*. Were the owners concerned that in publishing this story they could anger the President and his staff, drying up much needed sources for that newspaper?

Other mainstream media outlets had whiffs of what the *Newsweek* reporter knew, but they held back from publishing or broadcasting because of concern about ethics or reputation.

Matt Drudge heard the rumors as well. He heard that Michael Isikoff, the *Newsweek* reporter, was working on this story. Drudge was a freelance writer with no formal journalism training—not even a college degree. The closest he was to the mainstream media was as a clerk at the CBS gift shop in Hollywood. Drudge's father bought Matt a computer during a visit with his son in the mid-1990s. Drudge was soon exchanging gossip on Internet news groups. He started collecting e-mail addresses from these exchanges and began an e-mail list with what he dubbed "The Drudge Report." First he had 100 names, soon it was 5,000 and then 100,000 names. His Web site by the same name was born. It specialized in political gossip, not reporting.

In 1998, Drudge was running his Web site from his $600 a month apartment, using a modest computer based on an outdated Intel 486 microprocessor.[1] That January he did not have the corporate or ethical burdens carried by Michael Isikoff and his colleagues. "The Drudge Report," on the Web, published a story about what

Newsweek was holding back: the story of Bill Clinton and Monica Lewinsky. Now in the public domain, the mainstream media picked up the story. Two pieces of history were made that day. The most obvious are the forces it unleashed that lead to the impeachment of a President of the United States for only the second time. But it also made media history. Although not the first time that the mass media were goaded into running a story after its break in the small media or even the Internet, it was by far the biggest and most consequential.

This chapter starts with this story because the ultimate theme of this book is that the old rules, the classic *verities* about the media and its control, have changed. The outlines were already there when the last edition of this book was published in 1982. It pointed to the blurring of the boundaries among the traditional media:

> The information dissemination process is rapidly changing. Computers and connected terminals in homes and offices increasingly allow users to *select* the information they wish to receive, at precisely the time they wish to use it. Computers have made it economically feasible to mail identical, "personalized" messages to millions of recipients using the postal system that at one time was reserved for point-to-point communication. The telephone can give countless users almost simultaneous access to the same computer data base. The telephone and computer are also being combined to provide "electronic mail," perhaps doing for mail what the Xerox machine did for memos. Video and audio cassette recording devices allow individuals to record broadcast programs for replay at a time of their own choosing.[2]

By the end of the ensuing decade, "The Drudge Report" received more visitors each day than the weekly circulation of *Time* magazine.[3] Matt Drudge had some insight on the connection between these two: the relation between the big established media companies and the very small:

> What's going on here? Well, clearly there is a hunger for unedited information, absent corporate considerations. As the first guy who has made a name for himself on the Internet, I've been invited to more and more high-toned gatherings such as this . . .
>
> Exalted minds—the panelists' and the audience's average IQ exceeds the Dow Jones—didn't appear to have a clue what this Internet's going to do; what we're going to make of it, what we're going to—what this is all going to turn into. But I have glimpses . . .
>
> We have entered an era vibrating with the din of small voices. Every citizen can be a reporter, can take on the powers that be. The difference between the Internet, television and radio, magazines, newspapers is the two-way communication. The Net gives as much voice to a 13-year-old computer geek like me as to a CEO or Speaker of the House. We all become equal.[4]

WHAT *IS* GOING ON HERE?

When U.S. media pundit A. J. Liebling wrote that freedom of the press belongs to those who own one, he summed up the emotion that separates the media business from virtually any other enterprise. The press—or today more generically the mass media—stands not simply for the power to convey information, but more crucially for the assumed ability to shape attitudes, opinions and beliefs. The media are the vehicles for education and propaganda. Who controls these outlets and what the players' intentions are for their use has been a contentious issue at least since the 15th century, when both Church and State recognized the potential of the printing press and immediately sought to control it.

From time to time in recent history, public policy has become concerned with apparent trends toward concentration in one branch or another of the media industry. Since the 1930s, various federal bodies have legislated, adjudicated or regulated such areas as ending newspaper–television cross-ownership, breaking up theatrical film distribution–exhibition combinations, limiting broadcast station ownership, prohibiting most television network program ownership and preventing telephone ownership of cable.[5]

In the opening years of the 21st century, the issue remains salient. The stakes have risen higher than ever, as ownership has broken out of national boundaries. The United States has long had a major media presence in much of the world through the preeminence of Hollywood in film and television production. British, German, Dutch, French, Japanese and Australian players have become prominent in the United States, initially in publishing, then in all aspects of media.

The substance conveyed by the media can no longer be stopped at national boundaries by customs services. A dial-up telephone connection between computers can transfer information in seconds. A videocassette or disc can be easily smuggled and inexpensively duplicated, and a television program can be transmitted by satellite across thousands of miles for reception by an antenna that can be purchased by anyone at a local electronics store. In 1999, $600 worth of computing equipment and $20 monthly access to an Internet Service Provider could produce a Web site with a global access that only a decade before required hundreds of thousands of dollars for equipment and distribution.

There appear to be two trends pulling in opposite directions. One trend, suggested by a reading of the headlines, is that there is a new round of consolidation within the media industry. This would imply a lessening of separately owned outlets for information. At the same time, the trend of smaller, faster, better and cheaper information-related technologies appears to be generating the ability to create, store and transmit many types of information faster and less expensively, with greater "production values" than ever before. This trend would appear to imply that there is opportunity for a greater number of information outlets.

MEDIA FREEDOM

The mass communications industry is unique in the American private enterprise system because it deals in the particularly sensitive commodities of ideas, information, thought and opinion. Especially since the development of the broadcast media, we have become aware of the power of being able to simultaneously reach millions of individuals in the United States as well as throughout the world with a message or an image. The mass media are perceived as opinion makers, image formers and culture disseminators.

At the same time, the media in the United States have a degree of autonomy that exists nowhere else in the world. Although there are other nations that have a relatively free press, the United States was unique through the 20th century in allowing all forms of transmission of information to be privately owned. There is no government ownership of any significant newspaper, magazine or book publisher, television or radio station or network, other than some specialized publications issued by the Government Printing Office. The telephone lines and satellites may be subject to some government regulation, but they are all privately owned.

Above all, the very foundation of the governmental system, the Constitution, singled out the press for special treatment: "Congress shall make no law . . . abridging the freedom of speech, or of the press. . . ." It may be argued that this absolute prohibition was written in an era of a handful of weekly colonial papers, a few books and magazines, laboriously turned off hand presses at the rate of 200 sheets per hour. At the start of the Revolutionary War there were only 35 weekly newspapers in the Colonies, going into a total of about 40,000 homes.[6] The *Connecticut Courant* had what was described as the "amazing circulation of 8000 . . ."[7]

Yet, the politicians of that era were not ignorant of the power of the press. Thomas Paine's *Common Sense* pamphlet sold 120,000 copies in its first three months, and his views spread to virtually every literate American.[8] This one publication is given much of the credit for helping to bring patriots watching from the sidelines into the revolutionary movement. The authors of the Bill of Rights were probably well aware of the power of the press when they wrote that document.

The notion of diversity of political opinion lay behind the press freedom clause of the First Amendment. The fear at the time was that only government might have the power to limit that diversity. But today, there is concern in some quarters that the range of opinions to which the public has access is being limited by large media conglomerates.

The media have evolved into big businesses, just as other small businesses have changed and expanded with the technology of the Industrial Revolution, the enormous population growth of the nation and the complexity of dealing in a massive economy. Some commentators continue to be concerned that the modern media are becoming increasingly concentrated in the hands of a small group of corporate executives who may try to control what and how information is gathered and distributed to the populace.[9] *See note!*

BLURRING BOUNDARIES OF MEDIA INDUSTRIES

The media are the structures through which much communication takes place. Starting with the printing press—and at an increased pace in the past 150 years— more of our communication has become *mass* as technology has created the machinery to promote the mass media industries. These include the older, print-based media—books, newspapers and magazines—as well as the electronic mass media— film and radio and television broadcasting. Historically, mass communication industries have been characterized by a *one to many* model. The primary communication flow was one way. Print and broadcasting were mass communication. Telegraph and telephone, although used by a mass of people, were largely *one to one* or point to point, thus not mass communication. Whether the Internet is an instrument of mass communication is yet to be resolved, having characteristics of both one to many and point to point. It is the perfect case study of blurring boundaries, as established media players, traditional telephony stakeholders and old line regulators try to sort out the implications.

Mass communication historically has had certain characteristics that differentiate it from other forms of communication. First, it was directed to relatively large, heterogeneous and mostly anonymous audiences. Second, the messages were transmitted publicly, usually intended to reach most members of the audience at about the same time. Finally, the content providers operated within or through a complex, often capital-intensive industry structure.[10] Point-to-point forms of communication, such as telephone or letter mail, traditionally have had only the third of these characteristics.

Digital technologies and the Internet infrastructure undermines those long-held characteristics. Digital means that text, audio and visual information are in the identical and interchangeable format of bits. The Internet, while relying on a complex and overall expensive structure, is more like the highway system to which it is often compared than to a printing press or broadcast network. It is owned by hundreds of thousands of entities, but it works like the switched telephone network as a whole to connect hundreds of millions of users. Thus, the media arena, which in an earlier era could be described as encompassing industries known as newspaper, film, books, television, etc., today must recognize less precise boundaries for the term *mass*.

More crucially, the traditional media industries are finding a blurring of the boundaries among themselves. For example, a television set may get its picture and audio at any given moment from a broadcast signal, a coaxial cable signal, a video cassette, an optical disc or a telephone line. What then is the relevant medium? A person viewing the screen may not even know what the conduit is at any moment.

The changing media environment that makes a precise definition of the media arena difficult also means that competition may be coming from new, less traditional players, such as telephone companies, computer firms, financial institutions and others involved in the information business. This suggests not only a broadened arena for conflict in the marketplace, but in the regulatory environment as government agencies seek to identify their territory.

AN ALTERNATIVE MEDIA FRAMEWORK

Blurring media boundaries have made the conventional industry classifications decreasingly relevant for public and private policymakers. Both corporate strategists and federal regulators are finding that rather than concern themselves, for example, with ownership patterns in the cable industry, the real issue may lie in the pathways of disseminating a *package of content* that serves the functional needs of the traditional video audience. This may or may not be a cable industry service.

This was highlighted with AT&T's acquisition of cable operators TCI in 1998 and then MediaOne in 1999. "Regulators also think that these deals, despite their size, make for tough challenges under federal antitrust laws, partly because the lines between these businesses have blurred with the rise of superfast computers, digital pipelines and the Internet."[11]

Thus, it is appropriate to revisit the media using an alternative classification scheme. Policy decisions are increasingly based on a framework other than the traditional descriptions.

Substance, Process and Format

The "media" actually covers several discrete types of activities. First there is the *content*, or *substance*, itself and then the *process* by which it is gathered, stored and transmitted. Finally, there is the *format* in which the substance is displayed for the user. For example, the substance of an economic report from the Federal Reserve Board may be gathered and stored as digital data, as analog renderings on a magnetic audio cassette or as images on celluloid. It may be sent via paper on trucks to door steps or over the air as radio waves or a bits over a wire. Ultimately, it may be read as text, heard as audio and watched as video. Players in the media industry may be involved in any or all of these activities.

Understanding the media as a bundle of *substance, process* and *format* may help in loosening the traditional boundaries that have been in place, such as "the newspaper industry" or "the radio industry." There was a time not long ago when the Rolling Stones and other "classic hits" could be heard only two ways: by obtaining a record/CD (tangible commodity) or listening to the song from a radio fed by an FCC licensed broadcaster. In the first case, the media company that recorded the Rolling Stones, for example, may also have produced and distributed the album. In the second case, a different media company, which had no hand in the creation of the substance, may have chosen to play the recording created by the recording company. In both cases, the substance was essentially the same, the process differed and the format was the same.

In this example, today the substance and format remain similar but there are even more processes—and thus more media companies who can provide the process (read "transmission") piece. The music may be distributed by a provider using the TCP/IP Internet protocol to microprocessor-controlled devices that may or may not look like conventional computers. It may be by wired or wireless, but not broadcasting as defined in the past. Similarly applicable are descriptions of newspaper-like text or television-like video substance.

The media, in their various formats, provide *substance* that has been categorized as news, entertainment and all types of information, including advice, instruction, advertisements, statistical data, etc. Substance, then, is the information that is provided by the supplier and received by the user. Certain media formats tend to specialize in offering specific types of substance, but most media supply some of each. Newspapers, for example, along with their hard news, provide personality profiles as features, crossword puzzles for entertainment, a list of polling places as notices. Whereas most televised programming is largely entertainment, important news and information content are prominent as well.

Process encompasses both the handling and transmitting of information; processing functions include gathering, creating and storing information. A newspaper reporter, for example, researches and writes an article, probably using a keyboard or voice recognition, then stores it in computer memory for editing, hyphenation and justification by a computer geared to typesetting and layout. Process further encompasses the transmission conduits for information, such as broadcasting, coaxial cable, mail and private parcel delivery, microwave, circuit switched and packet switched telephony and so on.

Format, as used in this context, refers to the form in which the substance is made available to the user. This may be as hard copy, such as words or pictures on paper. It may be electronic/visual (e.g., that created on a video display), and may consist of text as well as pictures. It may be a mechanical/visual representation, such as that resulting from motion picture projection or microforms. It may be aural, such as sounds created by a vibrating speaker cone. In many cases, several formats are combined.

Traditionally, the "media" have been defined primarily by their formats. That is, a newspaper is a manufactured product consisting of ink on newsprint; a book is ink on better quality paper and bound between discernable covers. But more recently, we have been accepting process labels to denote the medium (e.g., cable and video-cassette). Here, then, are apples and oranges. Neither videocassettes nor cable are media in the same sense as newspapers, magazines or books: Videocassette is to substance as paper is to book. The former are alternative means of delivering substance. They are still "television," although they are not broadcasting, which itself is a transmitting option. The process, therefore, should not be muddled with a format in defining a medium.

The substance, process, format distinction most obviously applies in evaluating vertical combinations. But as consumers as well as regulators become more conversant with the changes being wrought by the digital world, the basis for defining the boundaries of heretofore distinct industry boundaries is also likely to require substantial re-evaluation.

SIZE AND SCOPE OF THE MEDIA BUSINESS

Figure 10.1 is a map of the information business. On it are placed some of the products and services that are part of that industry. The axes of the map are Services and Products (north–south) and Form and Substance (east–west). The products–services axis was chosen largely because companies and economists traditionally have viewed industrial activity in this manner. Displaying corporate activities along this axis helps highlight some facets of vertical integration. It also facilitates display of the fact that traditional notions of "product" and "service" may be blurring into a middle ground of "systems," whereby customers mix and match products and services in order to achieve a desired end. Progression along this axis from the product extreme to the service extreme also may be viewed as increasing customer dependence on supplying institutions. The Form–Substance axis was chosen because it helps distinguish those companies that traditionally have viewed themselves as pro-

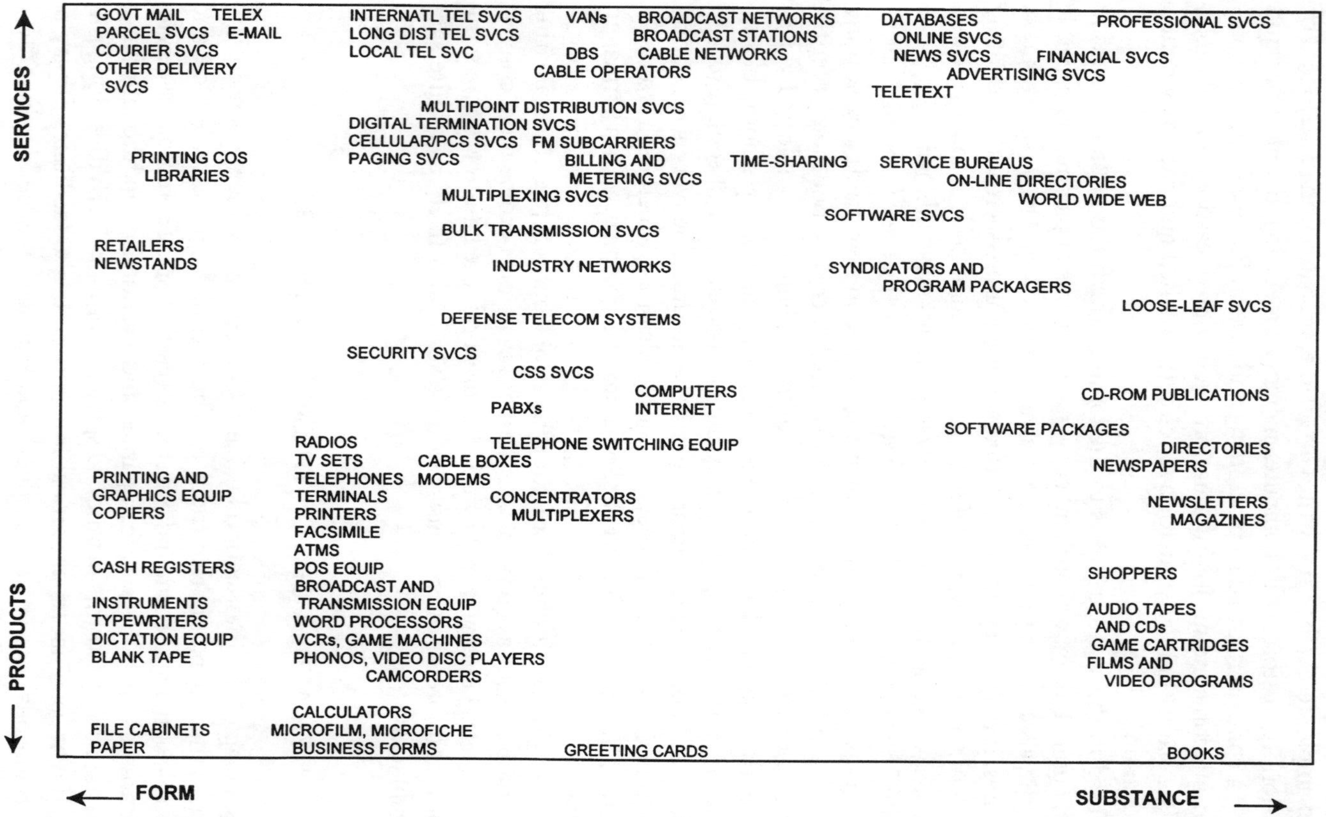

FIG. 10.1. The Information Business MAP, 1999.
Sources: Program on Information Resources Policy, Harvard University, 1986. Updated by author 1999.

SERVICES

PRODUCTS

FORM →

SUBSTANCE →

GOVT MAIL TELEX E-MAIL
PARCEL SVCS
COURIER SVCS
OTHER DELIVERY
SVCS

INTERNATL TEL SVCS VANs BROADCAST NETWORKS
LONG DIST TEL SVCS DBS BROADCAST STATIONS
LOCAL TEL SVC CABLE OPERATORS CABLE NETWORKS

DATABASES PROFESSIONAL SVCS
ONLINE SVCS
NEWS SVCS FINANCIAL SVCS
ADVERTISING SVCS
TELETEXT

MULTIPOINT DISTRIBUTION SVCS
DIGITAL TERMINATION SVCS
CELLULAR/PCS SVCS FM SUBCARRIERS TIME-SHARING SERVICE BUREAUS
PAGING SVCS BILLING AND ON-LINE DIRECTORIES
METERING SVCS WORLD WIDE WEB

PRINTING COS
LIBRARIES

MULTIPLEXING SVCS

SOFTWARE SVCS

DIRECTORIES
NEWSPAPERS

CD-ROM PUBLICATIONS

RETAILERS
NEWSTANDS

BULK TRANSMISSION SVCS

INDUSTRY NETWORKS

SYNDICATORS AND
PROGRAM PACKAGERS

LOOSE-LEAF SVCS

NEWSLETTERS
MAGAZINES

SOFTWARE PACKAGES

DEFENSE TELECOM SYSTEMS

SHOPPERS

SECURITY SVCS

CSS SVCS

COMPUTERS
INTERNET

PABXs TELEPHONE SWITCHING EQUIP

AUDIO TAPES
AND CDs
GAME CARTRIDGES
FILMS AND
VIDEO PROGRAMS

RADIOS CABLE BOXES CONCENTRATORS
TV SETS MODEMS MULTIPLEXERS
TELEPHONES
TERMINALS
PRINTERS
FACSIMILE
ATMS

PRINTING AND
GRAPHICS EQUIP
COPIERS

POS EQUIP
BROADCAST AND
TRANSMISSION EQUIP

CASH REGISTERS

INSTRUMENTS WORD PROCESSORS
TYPEWRITERS VCRs, GAME MACHINES
DICTATION EQUIP PHONOS, VIDEO DISC PLAYERS
BLANK TAPE CAMCORDERS

GREETING CARDS

CALCULATORS
MICROFILM, MICROFICHE
BUSINESS FORMS

FILE CABINETS
PAPER

BOOKS

ATM - Automatic Teller Machine
COS - Companies
CSS - Carrier "Smart Switch Services"

DBS - Direct Broadcast Satellite
SVCS - Services
PABX -Private Automated Branch Exchange

POS - Point of Sale
VAN - Value Added Network

544

ducers of information (such as publishers), and those companies that provide means for recording information and transmitting it. Progression along this axis from the Form extreme might best be visualized in terms of increasing "information value-added" or in McLuhanesque terms, from medium to message.

The businesses that make up the media industry occupy roughly the extreme right quadrant along the Process–Substance axis and vertically span the range of both products and services. The media include the virtually pure service function of the news wire services used by publishers, as well as the pure products called books or magazines. But they also stretch two thirds of the way toward the process limit in the services, reflecting the broad range of transmission vehicles that are available as distribution conduits. To the extent that information services increasingly use the telecommunications networks to transmit computer-based content, the line could be extended even further to the left. Indeed, given the substantial reliance of magazine and book publishers on the Postal Service and private delivery services, it could be argued that the media extend completely along the horizontal axis as well. The demarcation criteria in 1999, however, may be based on the extent to which the conduit operator has responsibility for content. Cable and broadcast operators do make content decisions, whereas in 1999 the telephone companies and the Postal Service remained common carriers and thus exercised no substantial content decisions.

The entire media and entertainment business accounted for about one third of the total information industries revenue of an estimated $947 billion in 1996. Table 10.1 is useful for providing some context to the information industries, summarizing the major components and their relative sizes to each other and to the U.S. economy in general.[12] In this interpretation, the information industry covers communications services, including Internet access and satellite, in addition to the sectors listed in the table; professional information services, which covers computer systems integration, information retrieval and credit report services; hardware and software manufacturing, covering telephony customer premises equipment, television studio equipment, computers and peripherals, prepackaged software as well as household audio and video equipment; and the media, as identified in the table. Among the observations derived from this data:

- Between 1987 and 1996, the information industry grew at nearly twice the rate of the overall economy as measured by Gross Domestic Product (GDP).
- The Media and Entertainment sector grew nearly 50% faster than the economy as a whole, but not as much as the information industry as a whole.
- Rates of growth varied dramatically within the Media and Entertainment sector. The mature print business underperformed the economy, with growth rates ranging from 2.6% (newspapers) to 4.9% (periodicals).
- The motion picture sector, which included increasing revenue from video cassettes and cable networks, was the fastest growing media segment.
- Overall, Media and Entertainment were a smaller portion of the information industry in 1996 (30.4%) than in 1987 (34.3%).

The growth rate of the economy and the media industries are crucial data points for understanding some of the effects of industry mergers. It is critical to recognize

TABLE 10.1
Revenues of the Media and Information Industry, Selected Years 1987–1996

	1987	1995	1996	Ave. Ann. Growth Rate
Total Comm Svcs	130.9		225.8	8.1
Local telephone	84.9		108.3	3.1
Long dist telephone	44.8		82.0	9.2
Cellular telephony	1.2		26.4	233.3
Media and Entertainment	155.0		287.5	9.5
Movie	7.2		22.4	23.5
Broadcast TV	22.9		36.0	6.4
Cable TV	13.6 (a)		37.6	22.1
DBS	N.A.		2.8	N.A.
Broadcast radio	7.2		12.1	7.5
Music	6.3 (b)		12.3	10.6
Newspapers	31.9		39.5	2.6
Periodicals	17.3		25.0	4.9
Book pub & print	19.9		27.5	4.2
Professional Info Svcs	128.4 (c)	193.4	212.9 (d)	10.1
Advertising Services[a]	18.3	28.6		7.0
Direct Mail Services	4.7	8.5		10.1
Postal Service[a]	35.9	54.5		6.5
Computer prog svcs	N.A.	37.5		N.A.
Data processing	N.A.	31.1		N.A.
Hardware and Software	97.7	196.1	220.8 (d)	12.6
Total Information Industries[d]	452.0	869.4	947.0 (d)	12.2
GDP	4692.3	7253.8	7636.0	6.8
Info Indus as % GDP	9.6	12.0	12.4 (d)	

Note.   a = 1988; b = 1989; c = 1990; d = 1987 and 1996 total estimated and may not total from segment subtotals. N.A. = not available or not applicable.

Source: Derrick C. Huang, "Size, Growth and Trends of the Information Industries, 1987–1996," Chapter 11 in B. Compaine and W. Read, eds. *The Information Resources Policy Handbook*, (Cambridge, Mass: The M.I.T. Press, 1999), pp. 347—361.

that consolidation of players in an otherwise expanding industry may have a different outcome on pricing and market control than consolidation in a stagnant or declining industry sector.

DETERMINING MEDIA CONCENTRATION

Chapter 8 described who, literally, owned the media companies. But that is only part of the larger picture of whether the mass media industries or any segment has a degree of concentration that would be in some way detrimental to some vaguely defined political, social, economic and cultural interests of society. This is by far a more difficult question to answer definitively than the relatively specific tabulation of who owns what entity. Moreover, in the interest of good journalistic balance and fairness, it should be equally valid to ask whether the media were in 1999 or were likely in the foreseeable future to be too diffuse, decentralized and competitive.

The implications of concentration are the more typically voiced. Ben Bagdikian seems to have best articulated this concern in writing that "our view of the social-political world is deficient" if there is a regular omission or insufficient inclusion or certain elements of reality. And that is happening, he believes when "the most important institutions in the production of our view of the real social world," the mass media, are becoming "the property of the most persistent beneficiaries" of the mass media's biases.[13] Although corporations "claim to permit great freedom" for their editors and producers, he asserts that these businesses "seldom refrain from using their power over public information."[14] Moreover, as Bagdikian accurately concludes, it is not the total number of outlets that matters, but the number of owners.

Thus, it would seem that when it comes to the media industry, there are at least two thresholds in the continuum from monopoly to unfettered competition. First, there is the conventional antitrust standard. This is primarily the realm of lawyers and economists, of concentration ratios, Lerner and of Herfindahl–Hirschmann indexes. Second, there is the sociopolitical standard, the one that says we need to ensure diversity of sources, accessability by consumers and uncontrolled distribution. There are no known indexes, curves or standards for this measurement of competition. It tends to be on an "I'll know it when I see it" basis. Presumably, however, it is the sociopolitical standard that the antitrust standard is intended to promote: As the media approaches concentration that gets closer to the antitrust trip-wire, it is more likely that there will be the threat of narrowness and omissions that Bagdikian and others worry about.

To that end, this chapter first examines the economic and antitrust version of the media world. Then it returns to address some of the sociopolitical concerns. Ultimately, it is left to each reader to determine how few is too few in the measurement of media owners.

TYPES OF OWNERSHIP PATTERNS

It is beyond the scope of this book to provide a primer on the microeconomic elements of monopoly and competition. For such a basic overview for noneconomists there are several excellent sources.[15] Two concepts are immediately helpful to understanding past and future alliances in the media industry.

Ownership concentration and industry competition can be split along two dimensions, each with different implications. One is horizontal integration, the other is vertical integration. Introduced here, they are taken up later in this chapter.

Horizontal Integration

The most typical form of media horizontal integration is that of a single firm owning more than one entity in a single medium. The firm then becomes a chain owner of newspapers or magazines or of cable systems, etc. This was traditionally the most frequently occurring form of media combination and has been the subject of the greatest share of scrutiny by regulators and economists. For the most part, horizontally integrated firms own properties either in geographically discrete areas or that are directed to different audiences. An example of the former would be a firm that owned television stations in Boston, Philadelphia and Detroit. The second case would be a firm that publishes magazines for skiers, for photographers and for gourmet cooks. There are also media conglomerates, or firms that are horizontally integrated in more than one medium (e.g., Time Warner, News Corporation or Viacom).

Another form of horizontal integration involves what is called *cross-ownership*, where a firm controls more than one medium in the same market. Such would be the case of a newspaper and a television station owned by the same firm in the same city.

Vertical Integration

Firms that are completely vertically integrated control the product or service from raw material to final distribution. They bring together raw materials (or ideas), combine them into a product and service and market them. Full vertical integration occurs when businesses representing several sequential stages of production that could be separately owned are instead directed by a single firm. An example is a publisher that owns a paper mill, has its own staff of writers and editors, performs its own typesetting, runs its own presses and even handles its own delivery to the customer.

Both the economic and social impact of vertical combinations are much more difficult to measure than horizontal combinations. Many of the largest mergers in the media industry in the 1990s were primarily vertical combinations, including Disney with Capital Cities/ABC.

Using the content/process/format framework, a vertically integrated media firm would likely be both the content creator and the content processor. This would encompass most daily newspapers, but fewer weekly newspapers, not many magazine publishers and almost no book publishers. Unlike daily newspapers, these others tend to contract out typesetting (although the decreasing cost of electronic typesetting equipment has caused many companies to make this an in-house function) and with very few exceptions, contract for printing. Physical delivery to newsstands, retailers or to the subscriber is often by third-party distributors. For many years, television networks had been forced to separate programming (except news) from transmission. Those restrictions were removed in the mid-1990s as competition with the increasingly vertically integrated cable industry eroded the rationale for these controls.

The Internet has largely undermined the integration of content and delivery in the online sphere. Although early online providers may have used proprietary telecommunications for connecting with customers, the Internet emerged in the second half of the 1990s as an open delivery system, much like the postal system is for all print players.

Most attention in the media ownership area has focused on horizontal integration: large newspaper chains, limits on the number of broadcasting stations under a single owner, questions of whether the size of multiple system cable operators should be limited. The issue of the permissible degree of cross-ownership in a geographical area has been a longtime concern in the public policy arena. Vertical integration has become a central issue for debate, such as in the cable system/programming area.

THE ECONOMIC NATURE OF INFORMATION

Although this book incorporates the work of many economists, it is not an economist's approach to understanding the structure of the media industry. The study of the media is actually an attempt at understanding the status of the flow of content—of information. It is the communication process itself that ultimately has meaning for society. It has been challenging for economists to get a handle on the nature of information: What is it, how is it used, what is its value and how can—or should—it be allocated?

In the traditional manufacturing environment, economists have pointed to the "law of diminishing returns" or organizational barriers to suppport practical limits on enterprise size. In the new digital world of information, there is growing recognition for a "law of increasing returns." If accurate, this is an inflection point in the understanding of bigness and its economic consequences.

The term *marketplace*, as in "marketplace of ideas," is frequently applied to describe the ideal environment for information. But describing the information marketplace is a different order of problem than characterizing the marketplace for toothpaste, or even for newspapers. Conventional measurements do not suffice when dealing with the amorphous and inexact concept of information. For example, how can a monetary value be placed on the information an airline pilot uses to guide a jet that is not in sight of land to a precise destination (i.e., the weather reports, the navigational aids, the on-board computer read-outs, etc.), not to mention the knowledge and intuition gained by years of accumulated experience?

"Marketplace" seems to presuppose information is indeed a commodity, like cotton, paper or hamburger. This may be a reasonable assumption, but it must be tested in light of other economic approaches to its nature. For example, at the other extreme, information may be viewed as a theoretical construct, having features unlike other commodities and therefore requiring unique treatment. In between, there is an alternative that grants some commodity-like characteristics to information, but recognizes other distinctive features as well. For example, typical commodities are tangible, but information may not be. Most commodities lend themselves to exclusivity of possession, but information can be possessed by many individuals at the same time without any other being deprived of it. In addition, there is frequently little or no marginal cost to the provider of information in reaching a wider audience.[16]

This last viewpoint is the one that is accepted for the purpose of this book. It considers information a "public good." One key characteristic of public goods is that of essentially no marginal cost associated with adding distribution. An example is a television broadcast. Once the fixed costs of production have been incurred and the show is sent out over the air, there is no difference in expense to the broadcaster whether 1 household or 21 million households tune in to the show. Thus, broadcast television (and radio) can be given away. However, advertising is not sold at its marginal cost, because that would be zero.

The "product" of the media differs from most commodities, which are private goods. Every orange, for instance, has a cost, and each one adds weight in shipment.

Selling more oranges means adding more orange trees, etc. There can be a real marginal cost—the expense of growing and shipping one more orange.

In print media, the informational content is really the public good, and the physical product (i.e., paper and ink) is a private good. In many cases, the cost of producing the first copy constitutes the bulk of total cost, just as in broadcasting the production is virtually the total cost. Costs of editorial staff, typesetting and plate making are all necessary whether the print run will be 100 or 100,000. The incentive, therefore, for broadcasters and publishers is to increase circulation or audience for a product, because that adds little or nothing to marginal costs while justifying higher marginal revenue from advertisers in the form of higher advertising rates. The public good aspect of information is what encourages television networks and syndicated shows, as well as the desire for a firm to trade up from stations in smaller markets to larger ones. News services and print syndicates are encouraged by the same economic facts. Information provided over the Internet is a public good. The critical characteristic here is that many users can have the same data or information without depriving another from having it. The same cannot be said for a newspaper. If I have the physical paper, you cannot have it. But I can read an online newspaper at the same time as thousands of others.

COMPETITION IN THE MEDIA ARENA

One of the key needs for determining competition is first determining the relevant market. This can be applied to the product market and the geographic market. The distinctions are particulary critical for many media, which are geographically very local, while being part of a broader product market.

Section 7 of the Clayton Antitrust Act, along with years of court interpretations, makes determination of "line of commerce" (or product market) and "section of the country" or (geographic market), the first step in any determination of concentration.[17] The more that products are reasonably interchangeable, the more likely it is that they should be considered as the same product market. This applies both from the perspective of consumers (demand) and potential market entrants (supply). After the product market is determined, the geographic market is addressed. Traditionally, the geographic market may be a city, a region or the entire country. Increasingly, there may be a global component as well.[18]

Most daily newspapers, cable systems and television and radio stations are distinctly local for the geographic markets. Periodicals are for the most part geographically national or regional. Film, recordings, books and television programming are, for the most part, national in their geographic market.

Thus, in analyzing competition for narrow media industry segments, it is critical to distinguish what the standard for the relevant market might be. There remain dozens of cable operators, but the household in any given locality has from the start generally had only one choice (enforced in part by the economics of building a cable system, but as well by the monopoly franchising power of local governments). Similarly, the residents and merchants of most cities and towns have only a single daily local newspaper to buy or advertise in. Although there are 9,000 radio stations, a given locality may reliably have access to 10 or 40 that have transmitters in the area. Thus, whereas it may be useful to aggregate the overall market "power" of a newspaper or cable chain, the degree of competition at the local level needs to be considered separately from the less geographically based media. One reason why the Internet is such a break with old media is that it has virtually no geographical market limitations.

Quite relevant to the issue of local competition for specific media, however, is the degree of *substitutability* among media. If an advertiser is not satisfied with the pricing or service of the local newspaper, what options does it have? If a household is displeased with the local cable operator, then what reasonable alternatives, if any, exist?

This was the central point of Theodore Levitt's enduring concept of "marketing myopia." To prevent marketing myopia demands that a firm carefully determine its field of operations. For example, decades ago the railroads conceived themselves (as did the regulators) as being in the railroad business. The relevant antitrust question was the market share of competing railroads. But with the expansion of the Interstate Highway System in the 1950s and 1960s, all railroads started losing tons of freight to trucks, as well as passengers to cars and airlines. The relevant market turned out to be "transportation." So it is with beverage containers: steel, aluminum, glass, plastic, cardboard. Could a single manufacturer in the aluminum can and the glass and plastic businesses be considered monopolists? Would a buyer (e.g., say Coke or Pepsi) in fact have a choice and be able to bid one against the other?

And so it might be with the media. Granted, each medium is not perfectly interchangeable with another. Classified advertising does not work well on television; music cannot be played in a magazine. However, there is probably more fungibility than not. Daily newspaper circulation has declined steadily (as measured by household penetration), and the percentage of adults who claim to get most of their news from television has increased. Are those trends related? DBS service is a close alternative to cable. Video cassette and disc sales and rentals compete with movie theaters as well as premium and pay-per-view service. Direct mail competes with newspapers.

Again, these do not need to be perfect substitutes, at all times, for all types of content. Cardboard containers compete with glass or plastic containers for juice, but not for carbonated beverages. The overlap is substantial, not perfect. Similarly, consumers and advertisers may find some bundle of options that erodes the notion of a local cable, newspaper or broadcaster bottleneck. And, here again, the Internet is changing everything. Bits (i.e., video, text, audio and graphics) have become increasingly fungible, so that audio and video can be part of the Web site of a newspaper, whereas text is now part of the Web site of a television station's site.[19]

Criteria for Ascertaining Antitrust

Starting with the Sherman Antitrust Act in 1890, Congress has taken legislative steps targeted at the breakup and prevention of industry concentration. Authority for implementing antitrust policy is shared by the Justice Department and, since the Clayton Act in 1914, the Federal Trade Commission.

There is a rich history of antitrust activity. For the most part, antitrust cases are seldomly clear cut and frequently involve years, if not decades, of fact finding, negotiation, trial and appeals. In the media industry, one of the first antitrust cases was

Associated Press v. United States. In this case, the U.S. government sued the newspaper cooperative on antitrust grounds for its restrictive policies for membership. The Associated Press argued that it was both protected by the First Amendment and immune from the Sherman Act, because newspapers were not engaged in interstate commerce. The Supreme Court clearly placed newspapers within the jurisdiction of antitrust legislation, holding that "freedom to publish is guaranteed by the Constitution, but freedom to combine to keep others from publishing is not."[20]

In a 1948 ruling, the Court ruled against the vertical integration of Paramount Pictures as a motion picture distributor and theater chain. In a consent degree, Paramount had to divest its theater chain.[21] For decades, the Paramount decision was the basis for restricting vertical integration between producer/distributors of motion pictures and exhibition.

Chapter 1 discussed two types of newspaper antitrust cases. In the case of the joint operating agreement between the two daily newspapers in Tucson, Arizona, the Supreme Court upheld a judgment that charged the two papers with price fixing, profit pooling and market allocation.[22] This was the catalyst for the Newspaper Preservation Act that Congress passed, essentially giving newspapers a dispensation from this form of otherwise anticompetitive behavior, in the interest of the greater benefit of preserving limited competition. The other case involved the Times Mirror Co., owner of the *Los Angeles Times*, which was ordered to divest the neighboring newspaper in San Bernardino, although another larger chain, Gannett, faced no obstacle in being the new purchaser.

New Technologies and Consumer Behavior and Media Markets

The courts and ultimately the antitrust litigators in government have recognized changing technologies and consumer media user patterns. As far back as 1975, the Justice Department argued that, in certain circumstances, newspapers, television stations and radio stations compete and, therefore, should be included in the same product market.[23] In *Satellite Television v. Continental Cablevision*, the Court of Appeals held that "cinema, broadcast television, video disks and cassettes, and other types of leisure and entertainment-related businesses for customers who live in single-family dwellings and apartment houses" were reasonably interchangeable and constituted a single product market.[24] Another Appeals Court decision, in *Cable Holdings of Georgia v. Home Video, Inc.*, found that consumers perceive cable television, satellite television, video cassette recordings and free broadcast television to be reasonable substitutes.[25] Thus, the relevant market definition was that all "passive visual entertainment" was reasonably interchangeable by consumers and constituted a single product market.[26] As a result, the Court upheld a merger between two cable companies.

Similar reasoning by the courts ultimately eroded and broadened the definition of the product market for first-run films in the *Syufy* case in 1989.[27] At issue was the alleged concentration of ownership of motion picture theaters in Las Vegas. The defendant, Syufy Enterprises, argued that its competition was not just movie theaters but video cassette rentals, cable and pay TV. With evidence that owners of video cassette recorders (VCRs) and subscribers to cable did attend first-run theaters less often than non-VCR and cable consumers, the Court agreed that the relevant competitive market was greater than just the market share of movie house attendance. This determination has lead to a lessening of federal oversight of vertical integration in the motion picture industry.[28]

The reality of the new mix of the media is suggested in a case study of a film, *The Shawshank Redemption*. It was produced and released in 1994 by Castle Rock Entertainment, a small studio that subsequently became part of Time Warner. Despite some excellent reviews, its initial theatrical release produced a rather poor $18 million in box office receipts. Here's how other media affected *Shawshank*:

> Broadcast TV: The attention from several Academy Award nominations (the ceremony viewed by millions on television) enabled it to bring in another $10 million in 1995.
>
> Cable TV: Cable network TNT heavily promoted the movie as part of its "New Classics" campaign.[29]
>
> Internet: About a dozen Web sites devoted to "Shawshankmania" were created by individuals. In the evaluation of film critic Roger Ebert, "The Web has become an 'important element in any film reaching cult status, because people who like it can find a lot of others who agree with them. Movie lovers with specialized tastes no longer feel isolated.' "[30]

With these other media in play, *The Shawshank Redemption* became the top video rental in 1995.[31] It was the top movie on the Internet Movie Database list, ahead of *Godfather*, *Star Wars* and *Schindler's List* in 1999.[32]

Cable television, videos and the Internet have all given movies more avenues to reach viewers by—and, in turn, they have given audiences more say in a movie's long-term appeal. "There are just so many more ways to discover a movie than there used to be," says Martin Shafer, a principal at Castle Rock Entertainment.[33]

Flowing from such examples, there is growing recognition by the courts that in determining economic concentration there is the need for broadened product market definitions for the media industry, transcending the traditional boundaries of standard industry codes.

Beyond Economics: Social and Political Criteria

The crux of much of the debate over whether the media are becoming less competitive mirrors a basic controversy in antitrust law in general. That is, whether a measure of concentration should be solely along economic grounds (entry and efficiency analysis) or should include an evaluation of social and political implications as well. This argument was central to the Celler–Kefauver Amendment to Section 7 of the Clayton Act, passed by Congress in 1950.[34] In the ensuing decades, these concerns have waxed and waned in the salience of the executive agencies as well as the Court.

The Chicago School

The approach that advocates a largely economic approach has been identified as the Chicago School. It holds that the economic criteria for antitrust are paramount: to promote economic efficiency, to keep prices close to cost, to minimize undesirable accumulation of private wealth, to use resources most effectively. Proponents of the Chicago School emphasize the potential benefits that may come from mergers, rather than dwelling on the possible noneconomic consequence of these activities. Benefits may include economies of scale, technological and product-related synergy, superior management, coordinated research and development, lower transportation and transaction costs and the reduction of excess capacity.[35]

In the media arena, the Chicago School would support the advantage of mergers in the cable industry, where many small, inefficient cable systems are being gathered into large, often geographically contiguous ventures. These larger entities may gain greater bargaining leverage with the movie studios and programming providers, lowering the per household cost of acquiring programming. The merged companies may have the capital resources and geographic base to create integrated video, voice and data telecommunications systems that can compete with the incumbent and heretofore monopoly regional telephone companies.

The Multivalued Approach

The view that political and social values need to be more implicitly accommodated in measuring antitrust has been labeled the Multivalued Approach. In his article examining antitrust as applied to media mergers, Peter Nesvold explained:

> Many proponents of the Multivalued Approach justify this broadened definition by arguing that Congress [in the Celler–Kefauver Amendment] wished to avoid not only economic, but also social losses from mergers. These proponents maintain, for example, that Congress sought to protect small businesses, prevent the loss of communities' local economic independence to large, absentee corporations, and preserve the social and civic ties that bind communities together.[36]

This would clearly be the model advocated by Bagdikian and others for the media. The Multivalued Approach would hold that ideals such as localism, multiple voices and access are at least as important as the economic efficiency of cable systems or newspaper production.

The criteria for determining the sufficiency of competition, or its converse, the degree of concentration in the media, may thus be summarized in a simple matrix, as in Table 10.2. It combines the narrow or broadened approach to market definitions required by Section 7 of the Clayton Act with the Chicago School vs. the Multivalued Approach suggested by the Celler–Kefauver Amendment. Using this model, media ownership may be analyzed across product lines using economic criteria alone or factoring in social and political criteria, or vertically along economic or sociopolitical lines, factoring in product boundaries.

With this increasing pattern of multiple media as the model, the old notion of judging concentration based on individual media segments is probably moot. Court rulings starting with *Syufy* substantially undermine arguments for employing either block one or two in Table 10.2. The proliferation of news, sports, entertainment, database, music and video accessible via the Internet should further end narrow product market or even geographic market determinations in most cases.

TABLE 10.2

Matrix for Criteria for Determining Media Competition or Concentration

	Economic (Chicago School)	Socio/Political (Multivalued)
Narrow product market	1. Degree of concentration determined by economic criteria within a traditional media industry segment.	2. Degree of concentration determined as well by noneconomic considerations, such as effects on labor, preservation of small businesses, number and diversity of political decision-makers
Broadened product market	3. Degree of concentration determined by economic criteria, but relevant boundaries expanded to include reasonably substitutable media, such as cable for broadcast, online for newspaper.	4. Degree of concentration determined as well by noneconomic considerations, but against boundaries expanded to include reasonably substitutable media.

The impact of trends in media ownership must therefore incorporate the broadened market definitions. This leaves essentially at issue the criteria for measuring and judging if the media are becoming unduly concentrated, which is largely a question of whether the relevant criteria are mostly economic (the effect on prices and efficiency) or social and political.

Evaluating the Chicago School Approach

Although "multivalued" might seem to be a concept that should always be favored over a narrower, unidimensional approach, there are several good reasons to be suspicious of the term in the media industry context. The largely economic criteria for judging media competition holds several advantages:

- Economic criteria tend to be relatively identifiable, quantified and validated.
- They are less likely to run into First Amendment barriers.
- In many ways, they are reasonable surrogates for socio-political criteria.
- They may be less susceptible to "the law of unintended consequences."

Quantified and Valid

Economic criteria have long been the only or primary criteria for determining concentration in all industries. Although the congressional debate over the Celler–Kefauver Amendment to Section 7 of the Clayton Act suggested that social and political criteria should be considered in antitrust proceedings, the amendment itself did not include such language. Measures of efficiency and entry to an industry are measured by such criteria as the percentage of industry revenue accounted for by the largest players, as well as by the more complex Herfindahl–Hirschmann Index.

In the most conservative determination of oligopoly, proposed by Carl Kaysen and Donald Turner, the eight largest firms would have at least $33^1/3\%$ of sales and the 20 largest at least 75%.[37] This is called a type II oligopoly. From an antitrust viewpoint, an industry must reach a type I oligopoly, at which time the eight largest firms have 50% of receipts and the 20 largest at least 75%, before the concentration allows firms to charge prices and make profits above competitive levels and to misallocate resources.

Economists have been able to determine at what point there are few enough firms in a market (product or geographic) to allow them to charge noncompetitive price and to use resources in ways that are unproductive and inconsistent with the allocation of resources of firms in a competitive situation. This "misaollocation" is from an economist's viewpoint. In fact, monopolists have also been known to funnel resources into socially beneficial projects. For example, Bell Laboratories under the old monopoly AT&T was known for work in pure science. Many of its researchers were given free reign to study areas that had no reasonable relation to telecommunications. The elaborate system of cross-subsidies that allowed local and rural residential phone service to be priced well below cost was created under the monopoly. After AT&T was thrown into a competitive marketplace as an outcome of the antitrust suit it settled in 1982, it eliminated most of its basic research at Bell Laboratories. The cross-subsidies have had to be replaced largely by regulatory requirements for items called access line charges, access fees and universal service fund charges. In short, monopolists and oligopolists may use some of the expanded profitability for social benefit, regardless of their motivation.

First Amendment "Immunity"

Whenever there is talk of regulating the media, the discussion invariably turns to the First Amendment protections afforded the media. Despite occasional attempts by media companies to use this as a shield against regulation, such as being required to pay minimum wage to newspaper deliverers or opening Associated Press membership to competing newspapers in a city, the courts have been clear that media companies are businesses and are subject to general rules that apply to all commerce. Thus, the media are subject to the same rules of combinations and concentration as oil refiners or pencil manufacturers. Should a special set of tests be applied to media companies that try to measure effects of mergers on "diversity" of content providers or the impact on political discourse, then First Amendment concerns become far more salient.

Ithiel de Sola Pool, in his classic book *Technologies of Freedom*, expressed concern that the propensity of government, with good intentions, to regulate communications media, was actually cause to worry. Although addressing regulation of electronic media in particular, his warning and optimism are more general:

> Lack of technical grasp by policy makers and their propensity to solve problems of conflict, privacy, intellectual property, and monopoly by accustomed bureaucratic routines are the main reasons for concern. But as long as the First Amendment stands, backed by courts which take it seriously, the loss of liberty is not foreordained.[38]

Pool was essentially concerned that trying to find a way to achieve social and political objectives through special regulation of the media, beyond the economic standards applied to business, could be of greater harm than any possible benefit that might be derived—unintended consequences.

Unintended Consequences

The media industry is not the only arena with unintended consequences of regulation. But it has had its share. Broadcasting has from its start been regulated by the federal government with a much heavier hand than the print media. Much of the basic underpinning for this has been what every communication student learns in Broadcasting 101: The spectrum is a limited resource. It essentially belongs to society but is given to broadcasters to use for free, in return for which there is a "public trustee" responsibility in its use. However, it can be argued that the spectrum was scarce because demand exceeded supply. This is almost invariably the case when a good with value is given away for free. If a market price had been assigned to spectrum from the start (which in effect is done when licenses are bought and sold later on), then it would be no more or less scarce than are pencils, VCRs or Lexus automobiles. Moreover, it may have been put to different uses initially if those who obtained it had to pay for it.[39] The up-front cost may have resulted in some users sharing its use. For example, one firm may have purchased the weekday daytime rights to a specific frequency, another firm for evening use and yet a third for weekend use.

In another case, the FCC's policy of promoting localism in broadcasting lead to a system of assigning the rather limited section of VHF spectrum that was initially designated for television in such a way as to make it reusable within a geographic region. In trying to ascertain that every small city had at least one local channel, and faced with interference from assigned adjacent channels in the same area, the United States ended up with only three or at most four VHF channels available in any community. This assured that there was room for only three national networks. If frequencies had been assigned on a regional or national basis, then there likely would have been six or more channels available to every household from the start of television broadcasting.

As Pool noted, "While the intent of regulation is often to provide some modest protection for the weak, the ultimate outcome is often more protection of the strong." The policy of localism "protects an oligopoly of broadcasters in every city."[40] Or at least it did until competition came along by allowing some big players, initiated by News Corporation, to acquire more local stations and get a waiver from other regulations.[41] In effect, the consequence of encouraging new big players in the market was to provide greater competition than when they were kept out by the consequences of regulatory policies.

Pool, as well as Krattenmaker and Powe, cited repeated cases where regulation of the media had consequences different than, and in some cases counter to, their intended ends. This is not an argument to avoid all regulation. It suggests that where there are other options that may be employed, they should be seriously considered. These other methods (in the case at hand, economic-based criteria) need not be perfect, only less cumbersome and perhaps more predictable in their outcome.

Economic Criteria as Reasonable Surrogate

If one accepts the points that social and political measures are likely to introduce highly subjective (e.g., what's the "public interest"?) criteria that may, at any rate, collide with First Amendment protections, then what standard remains? The traditional economic criteria for concentration may, in fact, be a reasonable surrogate measure. The relevant question may not be "Is the media industry becoming *more* concentrated?" Rather, it may be "What is a sufficient number of competing players such that we may feel reasonably comfortable that a wide range of political, cultural and political interests can find accessible outlets?" A further corollary but critical question is, "Regardless of the number of players, is there sufficient opportunity and wherewithal for new players to enter the media industry?" That is, are there unreasonable financial or regulatory barriers to entry?

The HHI Index

Among the various economic measures of concentration, the Herfindahl–Hirschmann Index (HHI) is one of the more robust because "it reflects . . . the number and size distribution of firms in a market, as well as concentration of output."[42] It is calculated by squaring the market share of each player in the industry. Generally, an HHI score of greater than 1,800 indicates a highly concentrated industry. Under 1,000 is considered unconcentrated, with scores in between degrees of moderate concentration.

In an example of an industry with 10 providers, it can differentiate between a playing field where the market is relatively equally divided and one where a few players hold most of the revenue. In example A, the three largest players account for 30%, 25% and 20%, respectively, of industry sales. The remaining seven divided up 25% about equally. It has an HHI of 2,014, which is highly concentrated. In example B, the largest firm has a 15% market share, the second firm 12%, the third 10% and the seven remaining firms roughly divide the rest. The HHI in this industry is 1,036, which is a low concentration.

One study applied the HHI to the book publishing industry from 1989 to 1994.[43] These years followed several decades of apparent consolidation from mergers, including the 1970s period that helped inspire the Federal Trade Commission to investigate media concentration in 1978. Seen in Table 10.3, during the period studied, the 14 largest book publishers accounted for 75% to 80% of total book industry revenue, but with downs and ups over the years. The fragmented nature of the industry is seen in the HHI. Even at the its highest, in 1994, the HHI indicated a very competitive industry, well below even the low boundary of oligopoly. The study went on to calculate the effect of a single company controlling the 25% to 20% of the industry revenues not accounted for by the 14 in the study. This would have resulted in an HHI of 931 in 1994—a drop from 1,101 in 1989, below the minimum for low concentration. This research further documented that over the decades of mergers the volume of new titles published grew dramatically, a sign of great competition, adding credibility to the HHI data of a highly competitive market.

A similar type of analysis may be applied to the television broadcasting segment. Table 4.2 identified the 20 largest media companies by broadcast revenue in 1997. In that year, those companies had an aggregate of $23.9 billion in broadcast revenue. CBS and NBC each accounted for about 20% of the total, ABC 19% and Fox 11%. From Table 4.4, these four accounted for 60% of the revenue of the top 20 broadcasters, which in turn had the dominant share of the total broadcast market. But,

TABLE 10.3
HHI for Book Publishing, 1989–1994

	% of Industry Revenue by 14 Largest Publishers	HHI Index
1989	74.6	454
1990	78.6	488
1991	73.7	443
1992	74.6	450
1993	76.0	464
1994	80.0	511

Source: Albert N. Greco, "The Impact of Horizontal Mergers and Acquisitions on Corporate Concentration in the U.S. Book Publishing Industry, 1989–1994," *Journal of Media Economics*, 12.3, pp. 172–173.

contrary to what might have been assumed, this share, and the HHI, was actually lower in 1997 than in 1994, before the wave of mergers in response to the liberalized ownerships standards of the 1996 Telecommunications Act.

Table 10.4 suggests that television broadcasting is a moderately concentrated industry—no surprise. But it further shows that over this period the concentration, as measured by HHI, also decreased by nearly 12% among the 20 largest companies. The revenue share of the top four and top 10 players was lower. This is largely due to the mergers at the bottom of the industry, creating stiffer competition for an industry that, until 1986, was dominated by only three networks and limited to many small groups that could have no more than seven stations each. A rough estimate is that, in 1980, the three largest players (the networks) held an industry share similar to that of the four major networks in 1997.[44] These are small changes, but at the very least they suggest a different outlook than the intuitive one created by merger announcements.

Trends in Media Concentration, 1986–1997

Nonetheless, focusing on trends in a specific market segment is a distraction from the prevailing trends. With the continued blurring of the boundaries of the old media as all become essentially digital in nature, the product market distinctions have become essentially meaningless. Broadcasters compete with programming that is available

TABLE 10.4
Revenue Share and HHI of Largest Broadcasters, 1994–1997

	Total Revenue Top 20 (billion)	Share Top 4	Share Top 10	HHI
1994	$18.9	72.6	87.8	1553
1995	18.0	71.5	86.3	1455
1996	20.6	72.2	86.4	1432
1997	23.9	70.9	86.7	1372

Sources: *Advertising Age*, August 17, 1998, August 18, 1997, August 19, 1996, accessed July 12, 1999, on Web site at adage.com/dataplace/100_LEADING_MEDIA_COMPANIES.html.

only over cable: Few viewers with cable (the majority) care or even know the difference. Cable operators that provide Internet access and switched telephone service blend with telephone companies offering their own high speed data services and video. Thousands of newspapers have World Wide Web sites that are accessible not only by the hometown residents but by anyone, anywhere. Radio broadcasters are also available via Internet, and other programmers, without any government license, are available via the Internet, including those with portable wireless connection. Record manufacturers are facing Internet delivered music. It is quite difficult to sustain a fiction of old boundaries: that is, that newspapers compete only with newspapers and the local TV stations only compete with the few others in the market. It is through the merger of digital technologies, more than mergers of companies, that has brought "all modes of communications into one grand system."[45]

How does the overall media industry look based on concentration percentages as well as the HHI? Table 10.5 identifies the 50 largest media companies in 1986 and

TABLE 10.5
Media Revenue of the Largest Media Companies, 1986 and 1997

Parent Company	1997 Media Revenue (mil)	% Total	Parent Company	1986 Media Revenue (mil)	% Total	HHI 1997	HHI 1986
1 Time Warner	22,283	9.22	CBS	4,714	5.61	85.03	31.52
2 Disney	17,459	7.22	Capital Cities/ABC	4,124	4.91	52.20	24.13
3 Bertelsmann	9,525	3.94	Time	3,828	4.56	15.54	20.79
4 Viacom	9,051	3.75	Dun & Bradstreet	3,114	3.71	14.03	13.76
5 Sony	8,253	3.42	GE (NBC)	3,049	3.63	11.66	13.19
6 News Corp	7,695	3.18	Warner Comm	2,849	3.39	10.14	11.51
7 TCI	6,803	2.82	Gannett	2,802	3.34	7.93	11.14
8 Thomson	5,849	2.42	Times Mirror	2,684	3.20	5.86	10.22
9 Seagram	5,593	2.31	Newhouse	2,371	2.82	5.36	7.97
10 Polygram N.V.	5,535	2.29	Gulf + Western	2,094	2.49	5.25	6.22
11 CBS	5,363	2.22	Knight Ridder	1,880	2.24	4.93	5.01
12 GE (NBC)	5,153	2.13	Tribune	1,830	2.18	4.55	4.75
13 Reed Elsevier	4,902	2.03	MCA	1,829	2.18	4.12	4.75
14 Gannett	4,730	1.96	Hearst	1,688	2.01	3.83	4.04
15 Reuters	4,729	1.96	McGraw Hill	1,577	1.88	3.83	3.53
16 Cox	4,591	1.90	New York Times	1,565	1.86	3.61	3.47
17 Newhouse	4,250	1.76	Cox	1,544	1.84	3.09	3.38
18 EMI Group	4,088	1.69	News Corp	1,510	1.80	2.86	3.23
19 MediaOne	3,586	1.48	Coca Cola (Columbia)	1,374	1.64	2.20	2.68
20 McGraw Hill	3,534	1.46	Readers Digest Assoc	1,255	1.49	2.14	2.23
21 Times Mirror	3,298	1.36	Washington Post Co	1,162	1.38	1.86	1.92
22 Pearson	3,066	1.27	Dow Jones	1,135	1.35	1.61	1.83
23 Knight Ridder	2,879	1.19	Thomson	1,000	1.19	1.42	1.42
24 New York Times	2,866	1.19	Thorn EMI	959	1.14	1.41	1.30
25 Hearst	2,800	1.16	Viacom	932	1.11	1.34	1.23
26 Tribune	2,720	1.13	Westinghouse	839	1.00	1.27	1.00
27 Readers Digest	2,662	1.10	Harcourt Brace Jovanovich	800	0.95	1.21	0.91
28 Dow Jones	2,573	1.06	Thomson	756	0.90	1.13	0.81

(Continued)

TABLE 10.5 *(Continued)*

Parent Company	1997 Media Revenue (mil)	% Total	Parent Company	1986 Media Revenue (mil)	% Total	HHI 1997	HHI 1986
29 Hollinger	2,538	1.05	Storer Communications	649	0.77	1.10	0.60
30 Dun & Bradstreet	2,154	0.89	Tele Communications	646	0.77	0.79	0.59
31 SBC Comm	2,110	0.87	Maclean Hunter	638	0.76	0.76	0.58
32 Cablevision Sys	1,949	0.81	Macmillan	611	0.73	0.65	0.53
33 BellSouth	1,934	0.80	Harte Hanks Comm	576	0.69	0.64	0.47
34 Washington Post	1,799	0.74	Disney	512	0.61	0.55	0.37
35 AOL	1,685	0.70	Affiliated Publications	401	0.48	0.49	0.23
36 Primedia	1,488	0.62	Amer Television & Comm	569	0.68	0.38	0.46
37 Sprint	1,454	0.62	A.H. Belo	399	0.48	0.38	0.23
38 Grupo Televisa	1,446	0.60	Houghton Mifflin	321	0.38	0.36	0.15
39 Harcourt General	1,376	0.60	Lorimar-Telepictures	757	0.90	0.36	0.81
40 A.H. Belo	1,284	0.57	Media General	431	0.51	0.32	0.26
41 Hughes Electronics	1,277	0.53	Meredith Corporation	507	0.60	0.28	0.36
42 E.W. Scripps	1,246	0.53	MGM/UA	355	0.42	0.28	0.18
43 Ziff Davis	1,154	0.52	Multimedia	372	0.44	0.27	0.20
44 PrimeStar	1,097	0.48	Orion Pictures	328	0.39	0.23	0.15
45 Rogers Comm	958	0.45	Pulitzer Publishing	329	0.39	0.21	0.15
46 Media General	910	0.40	Southam	530	0.63	0.16	0.40
47 Torstar	894	0.38	Taft Broadcasting Co.	490	0.58	0.14	0.34
48 Meredith	830	0.37	Turner Broadcasting	507	0.60	0.14	0.36
49 Houghton Mifflin	797	0.34	Advo-Systems	460	0.55	0.12	0.30
50 USA Networks	796	0.33	Berkshire Hathaway	400	0.48	0.11	0.23
Total Industry (mil)	241,650			83,961		268.11	205.89

Sources: 10-K Reports, Hoovers Online, private company estimates from *Forbes Private 500; Veronis Suhler & Associates, Communications Industry Report*, 5th (1986 data) and 16th editions (1997 data).

1997 by the revenue from their media activities. In most cases, this is 100% of their revenue. For a few companies, the parent company has much greater revenue. For example, NBC's revenue in Table 10.6 was about 6% of parent General Electric's revenue.

Using 1986 as the base year for comparison is appropriate as it was the first year after the Federal Communications Commission eased the number of television stations under the ownership of a single firm from 7 to 12. It was in that year that News Corp. launched the first successful challenge to the long dominance of the older three commercial networks, opening the gates to new competition in broadcasting. The timing of the Fox network a year later was not coincidental. The ability of News Corp. to gain ownership of local stations in 12 major markets gave it the core of network affiliates. In the early 1990s, the FCC's restrictions on broadcast networks owning a financial interest in prime time programming were phased out. In early 1996, the Telecommunications Act substantially eliminated the size of broadcast radio groups and further loosened restriction on television station group ownership.

Tables 10.5 and 10.6 evaluate media ownership as a single industry. Unlike Table 8.1, which evaluated the dominant companies based on their standing in each media

TABLE 10.6

Concentration of Media Industry Revenue by Number of Companies, 1986 and 1997

	% of Industry Revenue 1997	% of Industry Revenue 1986
Top 50	81.81	78.67
Top 20	59.16	56.79
Top 8	35.97	32.35
Top 4	24.13	18.79

Source: Derived Table 10.5. If mergers that were pending in 1999 between Viacom and CBS and between Seagram and Polygram had been in effect in 1997 (assuming no divestitures of any lines of business of the participants), the top 50 would have been 82.13%, top 20, 61.80%, top 8, 40.37% and top 4, 27.02%. The HHI would be 295 instead of 268.

segment, Table 10.6 aggregates all media companies based on media industry revenues. The highlights are:

- As measured by revenue, there was very little change in media concentration between 1986 and 1997. In the former period, the top 50 accounted for about 79% of revenue. By the end of the period, it edged up to under 82%. The change in concentration among the top 20 and top 8 was similarly small. Only at the top four level has there been a sign of greater concentration (see next item).

- At the very top, the two largest companies (CBS and Capital Cities/ABC) accounted for 10.5% of industry revenue in 1986. The top duo in 1997 (Time Warner and Disney, with most of Capital Cities/ABC) had 16.4% of industry revenue. This is the only economic measure by which the notion of increased concentration of ownership of the media had substantive backing. But it was prior to Disney selling off substantial parts of the newspaper and magazine properties that were part of the acquisition.

- The HHI increased from an extremely low 206 in 1986 to a still very low 268 in 1997. Thus, whereas this measure did show some increased concentration, with HHI levels of under 1,000 indicating low concentration, the media industry remains one of the most competitive major industries in U.S. commerce.

- There has been a substantial turnover in the companies in the top 50 and even the top 12. CBS, the largest in 1986, was 11th in 1997. Dun & Bradstreet, Gannett, Times Mirror, Newhouse, Knight-Ridder and Tribune Co. are firms that were still around but had dropped from the top tier. Gulf + Western become Paramount and was acquired by Viacom. New to the top tier in 1997 were Bertelsmann, Viacom (with Paramount), Sony, News Corp., TCI, Thomson, Seagram (with MCA) and Polygram.

- Indeed, fully half the names in the 1997 list were not in the top 50 in 1986. In some cases, they were too small in 1986 but grew rapidly (e.g., Cox Enterprises, Cablevision). In other cases, they were new to the U.S. market (e.g., Bertelsmann, News Corp.). Others reflect new owners and new names for old players (e.g., Sony, which renamed Columbia Pictures; Seagram, which renamed MCA). Yet others were companies that are totally new to the media industry or did not exist (e.g., AOL, SBC Communications, Hughes Electronics/DirecTV).

- Of the 25 names from 1986 that were no longer in the top 50 in 1997, 15 disappeared as the result of mergers and acquisitions. The other 10 simply did not grow fast enough to stay at the top. They are identified in Table 10.7.

TABLE 10.7
Change in Firms on Largest 50 List, 1986 and 1997

Top 50 Companies 1986 Merged/Acquired by 1997	Top 50 Companies 1997 Not in 1986 List
Capital Cities/ABC with Walt Disney Co.	Bertelsmann
Warner Communications with Time Inc.	Sony Pictures (formerly Columbia)
Gulf + Western with Viacom	News Corporation
MCA with Seagrams	Seagram
Westinghouse Broadcasting with CBS	Reed-Elsevier
Storer Broadcasting	Reuters
MacLean Hunter	Cox Enterprises
Macmillan, pieces sold to various	EMI
Affiliated Publications with New York Times Co.	MediaOne
American Television & Comm	Pearson
Lorimar Telepictures with Time Inc.	Hollinger
Multimedia	SBC Communications
Orion Pictures	Cablevision Systems
Taft Broadcasting	Bell South
Turner Broadcasting with Time Warner	America Online
	Primedia
	Sprint
	Grupo Televisa
	E.W. Scripps
	Hughes Electronics (DirecTV)
	Rogers Communications
	USANetworks
	Ziff-Davis
	Torstar

- The total media industry's revenue nearly tripled in the 1986–1997 period, while the economy as a whole did not quite double.[46] Thus, bigger media companies did not necessarily grow in relative size. See the percentage of media revenue in Table 10.2.

- The role of synergy in mergers may play themselves out differently depending on management as well as product factors. For example, in 1986, Capital Cities/ABC and Disney added together accounted for 5.5% of media revenue. Time plus Warner plus Lorimar Telepictures plus Turner Broadcasting were 9.0%. After its merger with Capital Cities/ABC, in 1997 Disney was at 7.2% of revenue, and the combined Time/Warner/Turner was 9.2%. In relative terms, therefore, Disney showed much greater true growth, perhaps due to synergy among the pieces. That is, above and beyond its growth from mergers, it generated growth greater than the overall media industry. Time Warner increased its relative size only marginally beyond what the combined companies would have been.

- There has been a pronounced shift in the nature of the players in Table 10.5. In 1986, 5 of the top 12 companies (Gannett, Times Mirror, Newhouse, Knight-Ridder, Tribune) were best known as newspaper publishers, although with substantial other print and electronic media interests. A sixth (Capital Cities/ABC) also had a group of large city newspapers. By 1997, there were no newspaper publishers in the top tier. Thomson, which still had a large division composed of very small dailies, received most of its revenue from electronic information services, magazines and books. It was in the process of divesting itself of its newspapers. News Corp., which owned the *New York Post* and

Boston Herald, among others in its early years in the United States, was largely out of that business in the U.S. as well. Thus, electronic media owners were displacing the old guard print media at the top of the media industry.

The Complexities of Media Combinations: It's Not Always Obvious What Is Good or Bad

"News Corp. buys Twentieth Century-Fox."

"News Corp. buys Metromedia's broadcast stations."

"News Corp. acquires a 20% interest in New World Communications."

"AT&T buys TCI and MediaOne."

Sounds ominous to anyone concerned with media concentration. The knee jerk reaction when there is a large merger is often that it is bad. At least this is frequently the implication of headlines, of the critics who are interviewed and maybe the general public. On the other hand, financial analysts may support mergers on the grounds of promoting greater efficiencies, expanding geographic or product markets or bringing in superior management. (Financial analysts may also be skeptics, wary of unproven synergies or overpayment by the acquiring firm).

As in much of life, reality is more complex than the either/or modes that often seem to be the only choices. The acquisitions of News Corporation contributed to its ability to launch the first successful national television network in 40 years, a goal of television's harshest critics for most of that period.

The consolidation in the cable industry was actually less about cable television than about telecommunications. AT&T bought TCI not because it wished to be in the television business, but to be in the local telephone exchange business (again). And the cable industry already had wires running past 95% of U.S. households. Thus, the goal of creating true local exchange competition for the monopoly local telephone companies was being served by consolidation of relatively small and scattered cable systems into larger, more contiguous and financially capable entities to compete with the entrenched Bell companies. And along the way, if the Bells saw that their exchange telephone revenue was being attacked by the cable companies, then perhaps that would give them more incentive to offer video services themselves.

The Paradox of Vertical Integration

One of the most misunderstood aspects of media combinations is vertical integration. Simply stated, this is where a single entity owns multiple elements in the production and/or distribution channel. One example is a cable system operator that has an interest in one or more programming services. Vertical integration is supposed to bring synergy and with that greater profit than if the entities operated separately. Sometimes this may be the case. But media companies have learned that this is not always true.

For example, in the 1970s and 1980s, many book industry combinations involved trade hardcover publishers with mass market paperback publishers, such as Doubleday (hardcover trade) and Bantam (paperbacks). These combinations were thought to be desirable because paperback publishers often bid hundreds of thousands or even millions of dollars to get the rights to bestsellers. Why not keep the money all in house? Yet, in many cases, hardcover publishers found they could do better by continuing to have open auctions for paperback rights to its bestsellers. If their own "captive" paperback imprint only thought a book was worth $300,000, but an unaffiliated publisher was "fool" enough to bid $500,000, then they were better off selling outside. Doubleday, which published mystery author Stephen King's bestsellers *The Shining* and *Pet Cemetery*, sold the paperback rights of each to New American Library, rather than to one of its own paperback imprints.

Vertical integration in television would include a broadcast network and a program production studio under the same corporate roof. In 1998, Warner Bros.' TV unit produced the top-rated drama, *ER*. At that time, Time Warner, which was struggling to get its fledgling WB television network noticed and profitable, might well have decided to schedule *ER* on the WB network to that end. Instead, it renewed the rights to rival NBC. It realized that the $13 million per episode it was worth to that General Electric unit was far greater than it could get by showing the program on its own affiliates.

The tug between staying in house or selling on the outside is generally resolved pragmatically: which has the greatest profit potential. In 1997, Twentieth Century-Fox television developed a show, *Two Guys, a Girl and a Pizza Place*. When it could not find a good slot in their own network's schedule, they sold it to rival ABC, where it became a modest success. It outperformed the Fox show in the same time slot. Although selling its own show to another network may have undercut Fox, the network, it was a winner for Fox, the studio. Fox's Entertainment group president said at the time, "Instead of allowing it to flounder, we allowed it to flourish elsewhere, and if it does turn out to be a long term success, it will be an asset for the corporation."[47]

Indeed, the entire notion of mergers motivated by visions of vertical integration have been questioned by some economists. Drawing on the substance, process, format model described earlier, what we call "the media" actually consists of two types of companies. One is involved in the creation and production of substance. The second is involved in its distribution and packaging process. Most daily newspapers combine both functions. But most magazine and book publishers are in the content business. They leave the distribution channel operation to others (distributors such as Ingram and bookstores or online resellers for books, national distributors and wholesalers, newsstands and the U.S. Postal Service for magazines). Cable operators, for the most part, have been in the distribution business, but some have participated in the content business, although usually by minority investment in various cable networks.

"Content is most valuable when it seeks and receives the widest possible distribution. . . . [A]n information distribution/packaging company . . . functions best when it has unfettered access to all possible content sources at competitive prices and can assemble the best mix for its chosen market."[48] Good content has little trouble finding distribution. Low and mediocre quality faces greater hurdles. Indeed, John Malone, who was head of the TCI cable operation before it was sold to AT&T

(as well as chief executive of Liberty Media Group, an investor in programming), characterized vertical mergers in the media as "like saying you need to own a share of stock in a diary to get milk. Money buys programming."[49]

The usual rationale for vertical mergers, such as Disney (content) with Capital Cities/ABC (distribution) is that the former can readily feed into the latter. But as Doubleday (with Stephen King books) and Warner Bros. television (with *ER*) and Fox (with *Two Guys* . . .) learned, good material can readily find a home and bring in significant revenue. The converse would suggest that the in-house distribution arm will get struck with content for which the outside will not pay. Whereas it might get distributed by the captive distribution company, such as the ABC network for a Disney show, it might not be the programming that a truly independant programming director would have chosen. That would not be good business decision making. And, in fact, most of these vertically integrated content and distribution entities do work at arms length. Then why bother with vertical integration?

It is this business rationale that is likely to limit many of these types of mergers—or undo them years later when they do occur. It was this form of decision making that lead AT&T to divest itself of its longtime manufacturing subsidiary, Western Electric (renamed Lucent Technologies) in 1997. The separation of Western Electric from AT&T had been a longtime goal of antitrust forces. It lead to the Consent Decree with the Justice Department in 1956. But, in the end, it was a totally voluntary, pragmatic decision by AT&T's Board of Directors. They reasoned that Western Electric could sell more to AT&T's competitors as an independent company, while at the same time AT&T was freer to pick and choose its equipment from the global vendors who might offer products or services better or cheaper than what its in-house manufacturer could offer.

In the real world of business, sometimes what looks like monopoly power from the outside can drag down profits, development and growth when looked at from the inside. Eventually, savy managers divest as well as acquire.

POLICY IMPLICATIONS OF THE TRENDS IN MEDIA OWNERSHIP

Policy, of course, is determined by more than lofty ideals of what is right or wrong, what is best for society or what is technologically feasible. In the case of media concentration and ownership issues, policy combines at least four separate factors: the legal, economic, socio-political and technological.

Legal Factors

Those who have followed the attempts of successive Congresses in trying to rewrite the Communications Act of 1934 are well aware of the political booby traps in policymaking. Any time a part of a bill deregulated one piece of the pie, some new player appeared to either claim injury or a piece of the pie itself. The broadcasters hoped to hinder the cable business, the cable operators wanted to cripple the direct broadcast satellite (DBS) industry and the long distance telephone companies had their goals in restraining entry of the regional Bell local exchange carriers onto their turf. The outcome, the Telecommunications Act of 1996, was therefore written in general terms, leaving much of the decision making to the Federal Communications Commission (FCC).

The process of changing FCC policy can be torturously slow, especially when the guiding document is as vague as the 1996 Telecommunications Act. A simple content analysis of the wording of the Telecommunications Act tells a tale: Deregulation was mentioned twice; regulation (and its derivatives), 202 times; fair or unfair, 35 times; reasonable or unreasonable, 37 times; the "FCC shall," 94 times; and the "FCC may," 30 times. The Act called for 80 proceedings to be initiated by the FCC.[50] This wording lead to continued reliance on the courts, administrative proceedings and appeals by the losing parties.

Developments such as the ownership and use of digital spectrum for introduction of digital television has been hampered by lack of legislative and regulatory resolve. In the case of digital TV, local station license holders were required to implement digital broadcasting in exchange for being given free digital spectrum. Alternatively, the new spectrum could have been split among new and additional owners, vastly dispersing control over broadcasting. Questions of who should have access to cable and telephone company systems for offering high speed Internet connections was another legal process with implications for control over access to new media outlets.

Economic Factors

Although it may be a pleasant fantasy (except to the incumbents) to wish there could be 2 or 3 independent newspapers in every city or 15 radio stations in every town and village, the reality is that the economic infrastructure does not support such dreams. Indeed, the limitation on the number of radio stations in most parts of the country is not due to spectrum scarcity any more than the number of newspapers in a town is related to lack of printing presses. There is just not a large enough economic base to support more broadcasters or newspapers. The implications of this reality for public policymakers was recognized in a congressional staff report in 1981. It noted that "Since scarcity due to economic limitations does not provide a rationale for regulating other media, a strong argument can be maintained that such a rationale should not be a basis for broadcast regulation either."[51]

Similarly, it may be argued that the tendency toward mergers and acquisitions in cable is in large measure the result of the economic demands being made of cable systems. Initially, there were the costs of wiring entire towns and cities, the poorer areas along with the middle-class neighborhoods. Local franchise authorities often required the cable operator to provide neighborhood studios and programming funds for public access channels, link the city's educational facilities as well as the government offices together and remit a franchise fee to the city in addition. In the late 1990s, there were massive new investments to provide expanded channel capacity for all the new program services, for digital services and most recently for switched telephony. Small firms could not handle these demands. So the older cable systems combined with larger, better financed systems.

The role of increased competition is an economic force as well. Among the competitive factors that have been identified in this book that are changing the economic models of the media are the doubling in the number of broadcast television networks since 1985, the availability of cable to over 90% of households, the vast number of channels available to the 75% of households that have cable or satellite services and the news, entertainment and information available on the Internet. Meanwhile, none of the old industries have faded away. But new industries and players have been added: the online aggregators lead by America Online but including Yahoo!, Excite and Lycos; the financial services players, such as Bloomberg and Intuit; the Internet Service Providers, including the regional Bell telephone companies; and others, such as Microsoft with both content (financing the *Slate* online magazine) and aggregation, with the Microsoft Network. E-commerce has a profound economic impact on many of the older media: Books or toys sold by online merchants erode the sales of retailers who might have to cut down their newspaper or magazine advertising schedule. On the other hand, the online merchants have been paying some of those same publishers for banners and similar links from their Web sites.

Socio-Political Factors

Social factors are related to political factors. In this case, the real question is, "How much diversity is enough?" And a corollary question is, "How is that determined?"

If it is generally agreed that the antitrust standard for concentration as applied to the media would be insufficient to fulfill the objective of having many unaffiliated "voices," there is no acceptable guideline for what constitutes too few voices. It cannot be seriously proposed that the mass communications business must be so structured that any person or group can have unlimited access to whatever medium for whatever purpose for whatever period of time they so desire. Short of that impractical standard, what is acceptable and how can that be determined?

The issue of media control is particularly important to many critics and analysts because of the presumption of the media content's great influence on mass society. Those who control the media, goes the argument, establish the political agenda, dictate tastes and culture, sell the material goods and in general manipulate the masses. Whereas there is certainly great power in the media, for two related reasons its strength may also be overemphasized.

First, so long as there are reasonably competing media sources as there are today, these can cancel each other out. Why is it that everyone does not eat Wheaties or use Exxon gasoline? Second, there are media other than the "big" media that can be very effective, especially for reaching easily identified groups. Indeed, replacing the fear that society is the victim of a few mass media moguls is a new specter of such a fragmented media landscape that society becomes captive to narrows interests, following the news groups on the Internet and the myriad of Web sites from which individuals assemble their own, almost unique stew of content.

The use of media in the 1978 Iranian revolution was an early prototype case study.[52] In the typical *coup d'etat*, the rebel forces are supposed to takeover the television and radio stations. The government meanwhile imposes censorship in the press. The Iranian revolution succeeded without the Ayatollah Khomeini overrunning a single broadcast facility. The Shah had control of all the media to the day he left. The revolutionary forces relied quite effectively on the "small" media. Khomeini used audio tapes to get his message to the mullahs, who in turn spread the word in the mosques. The Xerox machine, Everyman's printing press, was used to distribute his instructions. And the telephone was used to coordinate efforts between Teheran and exile headquarters in Paris.

During the uprising in Tiananmen Square in China in 1989, it was widely reported that the students used faxes to distribute their positions and events to the news media and to communicate with the expatriate Chinese community abroad. The latter were able to monitor the live accounts from CNN that were not available locally in China and thus fax back news available in San Francisco, but not blocks away from where the demonstrators were located.

Now, the Internet has taken its place among the applications of information technologies in a political setting. Here is how one report started:

> As rebellions broke out across Indonesia . . . protesters did not have tanks or guns. But they had a powerful tool that wasn't available during the country's previous uprisings: the Internet.
>
> Bypassing the government-controlled television and radio stations, dissidents shared information about protests by e-mail, inundated news groups with stories of President Suharto's corruption, and used chat groups to exchange tips about resisting troops. In a country made up of thousands of islands, where phone calls are expensive, the electronic messages reached key organizers.
>
> "This was the first revolution using the Internet," said W. Scott Thompson, an associate professor of international politics at the Fletcher School of Law and Diplomacy at Tufts University.[53]

Still, the perception no doubt persists that the mass media are all powerful in the industrialized world, so this factor will be a dominant force in determining policy.

Technological Factors

Technological factors are addressed last to emphasize that they are only one of many interacting factors. With the rapid advancement in developments of microprocessors, telecommunications processes and software, it sometimes seems that the communications world is technology driven. The preceding sections indicate that technology interacts with other forces. History seems to provide several lessons about the role of technology in change.

First, technology is rarely adopted for its own sake. It must fulfill some need. Off and on from the 1960s, the Bell System and its successor tried to introduce Picture-Phone' service. It did not catch on. Also, during the 1960s and 1970s, the educational establishment tried to implement computer-aided instruction. It too failed miserably. In 1978, the government-owned telephone system in Great Britain, looking at its underutilized network, initiated an electronic data base service for the home market, dubbed Prestel. They expected it to have 100,000 households sub-scribing by the end of 1980. It had fewer than 10,000.

Second, whereas is was not unusual for some technology to take five or more years to get from discovery to commercial availability, the rate of time to the marketplace seems to have contracted. That gives existing industry participants less time to adjust. The ubiquitous telephone was not in place in 50% of U.S. households until 1946, 70 years after its invention. But the graphical browser for hypertext was invented in late 1990 and introduced in 1991. The working version of Mosaic, the first browser for PCs and Macintosh computers, was made available mid-1990s and its commercial version, Netscape, was available in 1994. By 1998, 83 million U.S. adults—40% of the over 16-year-old population—had access to the Internet.[54]

Finally, there is an important difference between that which is technologically feasible and what is economically viable. Indeed, the technological graveyard is lit-tered with better mousetraps that failed because they cost too much. What the tech-nology will do, at what price and what it will replace are questions that must be resolved as part of the policy-making process. One example was the uncertainty about digital television and high definition television in 1999. The original motiva-tion of moving to digital TV was to make it feasible to provide a wide, high defini-tion picture while using the same bandwidth (6 MHZ) as older analog transmission. However, using bandwidth compression, it was also feasible to use the 6 MHZ of dig-ital space to offer four or five digital channels at a similar resolution and size as the NTSC standard. Should high resolution be employed to show the "talking heads" of a newscast just because it is available? Or should it be used at the discretion of video distributors, based on audience considerations, for events such as action movies or sporting events? The answer may well help determine how many channels of video are available to consumers and who may have the ownership of them.

GOVERNMENT INVOLVEMENT

Over the decades, the three agencies of the U.S. government most regularly involved in monitoring the status of competition in the media industries have been the U.S. Department of Justice (DOJ), the Federal Trade Commission (FTC) and the Federal Communications Commission (FCC). The former have statutory author-ity over antitrust, whereas the FCC has specific authority for broadcasting and cable through its mandate to safeguard "the public interest."

One critical question that has faced these agencies over the years was to what degree they could and should be more concerned about concentration in the media than other industries due to the First Amendment implications that complement the usual economic concerns of antitrust. Should a stricter standard apply to the media than to other industries because of the media's position in U.S. society and the importance of having many channels available for speech? Can free speech be separated from the economic structure that controls the media? Should the govern-ment promote diversity and independence to avoid having to regulate?

In the media merger waves of the 1970s, 1980s and 1990s, federal antitrust enforcers have shown themselves willing to approve more and larger deals than ever. But they have exacted a price: The FTC and the Justice Department, reluctant to incur the expense of taking big cases to court with unpredictable outcomes, have instead fashioned intrusive settlements that let big deals go ahead only after agreeing to meet certain conditions that will enhance long-term competition or avoid future antitrust litigation. Merging companies eager to get their deals approved have agreed.

Many experts trace the evolution of settlements rather than litigation to congressional passage of the Hart–Scott–Rodino Act in 1976. It required companies planning mergers of a certain size to notify the Justice Department and FTC and give them any information they request. These inquiries can be enormous and stretch out over many months. For example, when Time Warner concluded a deal to buy Turner Broadcasting, the companies spent six months gathering documents and answering FTC questions. The law gives enforcers great leverage. But it also forces them to make their concerns clear before filing lawsuits to block deals. The law essentially sets the ground rules for the government and companies to sit down and talk, instead of rushing into court.[55]

The negotiations prior to merger approval have changed the way mergers get approved, and have sometimes given competitors leverage to get something themselves. The 1996 Time Warner-Turner deal, for instance, was announced at the same time that NBC was shopping for channel space for MSNBC, its cable news channel joint venture with Microsoft. At the request of NBC, the FTC required that Time Warner cable systems carry another major news channel to compete with Turner's CNN. Not surprisingly, this turned out to be MSNBC. In addition, the FTC's final order approving the merger had a provision requiring Time Warner to report deliberations on some of its most strategic decisions in programming. It also contained a provision requiring Time Warner to sell programming at a price pegged to a benchmark set by the FTC.[56] Thus, rather than simply approve or disapprove mergers on an all-or-nothing basis, the FTC and DOJ have taken a more regulatory course that tries to accommodate combinations and help competition at the same time. With the exception of the motion picture industry in the late 1940s, the Justice Department has seen little cause to bring broad antitrust actions against the mass media industries comparable to the suit that broke up AT&T in 1982 or the major action initiated against computer software giant Microsoft in 1998. Individual firms have been affected, as in the case where Times Mirror Co. had to divest itself of the *San Bernardino (CA) Telegram* on the grounds that it would lessen competition. Perhaps the most important Justice Department industrywide action outside of film was the 1945 Associated Press case, which clearly placed newspapers and other media within the jurisdiction of antitrust legislation (see Chapter 1).

In 1979, the antitrust division of the Justice Department investigated the merger between newspaper giant Gannett and Combined Communications, with its extensive broadcast holdings. However, a top Justice Department official admitted:

> The antitrust laws do not flatly prohibit media conglomerates any more than they prohibit other kinds of conglomerates. Under present law, some measurable impact on

competition in some market must be proven before a merger or acquisition will be held to violate the antitrust laws. Indeed, the courts have been generally reluctant to condemn conglomerate mergers where such an impact has not been shown, regardless of the social or other objections that have been asserted.[57]

IMPLICATIONS FOR STRATEGY

Business Strategies

Technologies are changing the basis on which current media enterprises have been built. Consumers now have a far greater set of options for their personal media mix than at any time in history. There are not just three television networks, but dozens, via cable and DBS services. There is not just one newspaper but many, via national newspapers and the entire World Wide Web. There are not just a handful of movie theater screens but thousands, via the video store.

So, for example, a newspaper publishing company that persists in restricting itself to printing its product in the conventional method and distributing it over traditional conduits may find both advertising and readership being eroded by competition from other firms providing similar services but utilizing a more efficient or consumer-acceptable technology, such as an Internet-based service.

Consider the 1998 and 1999 acquisitions by AT&T of TCI and MediaOne. It made AT&T the country's largest cable operator while furthering consolidation in the top tier of multiple system operators. But AT&T did not make these acquisitions so it could become a cable operator. Rather, it was a strategy to speed "a huge roll-out of AT&T-branded local phone service that will offer consumers their first true alternative to the Baby Bells."[58] That is, there would be greater *concentration* in cable as a consequence of providing greater *competition* in the heretofore monopoly local telephone business.

In essence, what is happening in the media and related arenas is that the previously discrete and readily identifiable segments are coming closer together into a more fluid industry, leading to dissolution of old groupings and crystallizing of new. Media participants are increasingly using the computer for information storage and retrieval. They are using telephone lines, cable and satellites for transmitting information. In 1982, *Who Owns the Media?* anticipated what has come to pass: The old common carriers, such as American Telephone and Telegraph (AT&T) "are looking increasingly like information providers, either in the form of viewdata services or by providing information directly (such as the weather, stock market information, or sports calls over a special telephone number). As all manner of information-providing firms are increasingly using the same technologies, information consumers will gradually shed their traditional perceptions of the media forms as distinct and discrete entities."[59]

Through their understanding and exploitation of the fluid nature of the substance process/format mix, businesses and entrepreneurs of all sizes have increasingly through the 1990s availed themselves of the opportunity to break out of their traditional molds. The more savy information providers have reevaluated their customers not as newspaper readers or magazine subscribers, etc., but as *information consumers*

whose interest is in the unique usefulness of the substance paired with the convenience and economics of a mix-and-match variety of processes and formats. At home
at breakfast: pick up the newspaper. At the office: log onto the Internet site. In the
car: tune in the radio. On a plane flight: tune on the digital playback device or
video equipment laptop computer.

Information providers may discover that many customers will not stick with a particular format given their greater options and the strengths of different formats and
processes to optimize the utility of a specific type of information. And those incumbents who have refused or been slow to foresee the change have been candidates for
merging or being acquired by those who better see the opportunities. In other cases,
entrepreneurs, such as the founder of Bloomberg Financial or those who started the
Internet-based VerticalNet.com, have shown the established players where the opportunities lay.

Implications for Public Policy

Government policymakers are faced with similar challenges to long-standing practices. At the top of the list are decisions on defining the product and geographical
boundaries for the old and new media industries. It is perhaps nonproductive in the
longer run to focus on the concentration of media ownership using conventional
concepts of newspapers, television, magazines, etc. Rather, the criteria that government policymakers must be concerned with instead may be a more generalized goal:
encouraging diversity of conduits for information and knowledge. Do the major
news weekly magazines have direct competition from all newspapers, local and
national televised news programs and all news cable and radio programmers? Do
motion picture distributors compete with book publishers and certain periodicals?
Do special interest magazines, already knocking heads in price with mass market
paperback books, compete for advertiser dollars, consumer dollars and time with
video programming?

Questions and More Questions

There remain further questions that need to be considered in the discussion of policy formation. A selection of such questions includes:

- Does increased diversity and access imply greater quality? What happened when the
  FCC took 30 minutes of prime time programming from the three networks (via the
  Prime Time Access Rule) and forced this time on the individual stations? The costs of
  single market productions resulted in few quality shows and opened up the market to
  syndicators of low cost game shows of little substance and great popularity. On the other
  hand, cable television has spawned the Discovery and History Channels, among other
  quality and small audience niches. The plethora of film releases and multiscreen cinema seems to have created room for both higher culture from the likes of Miramax and
  Sony Classic Pictures as well as more fluff movies aimed at teenagers.
- Who should be the arbiter of what type of programming or content is most desirable for
  society? Much of the criticism of the old broadcast networks centered on the supposedly
  mindless grade of the programming. However, when given a choice, the viewing public

has "voted" by the way it clicks the remote. Many of the top-rated shows have outper-formed presentations of supposedly higher intellectual content. But the sheer volume and variety of books, magazines and video seems to be pushing publishers and programmers in directions that seem to fill increasingly smaller niches of all variety and quality.

- How much control by any firm or group of firms must be manifest before we are threat-ened with perceivable restraints on true access to a broad spectrum of opinion and information? Most crucially, how can this be measured? On the one hand, there is a point at which some combinations may have to be limited. On the other hand, there can be no credence given to the argument advanced by some that every opinion or cre-ative idea has a right to be heard through the mass media. However, anyone with a few dollars can make up a picket sign or hand out leaflets at City Hall or create a Web page or post a message to dozens or even hundreds of Internet News Groups. Often, such viewpoints get aired by becoming news. Even not-for-profit university or other subsi-dized presses must employ some criteria of value to a specific market in determining which offerings to publish. Can concentration of ownership be measured by the total number of media properties? By the number of households reached by the media owned by a given firm? By the geographical concentration of the firm's properties?

More Concentration or Greater Competition?

Perhaps the safest and least contentious conclusion is that nothing in this book will settle any debates on whether the mass media are unduly concentrated, heading toward dangerous concentration or are and will likely remain sufficiently competi-tive. The answers depend on what is to be measured, whether it can be measured and what judgment policymakers want to apply to the findings. Indeed, the debate rages between the two authors of this work.

The Argument of Greater Concentration

Looked at in small, industry-specific pieces, there is indisputably consolidation in some media segments and status quo in others. Cable operators have combined, as the industry matured from its early mom-and-pop operations to a big business with high capital costs. Radio broadcasters went on an acquisition binge after most restrictions on ownership were lifted in 1996. As the limits on broadcast license ownership were gradually lifted, there were mergers permitted under the new thresh-olds. Daily newspaper chains have become marginally more concentrated. The film distribution and recorded music industry have long been relatively concentrated and have not become less so in recent years. Motion picture theater circuits have con-solidated (as have retail booksellers).

Thus, the argument that there is more concentration in these industries in 1999 than in the past can be substantiated.

The Argument of Greater Competition

Looked at as a single industry, there can be little disagreement that there is more competition than ever among media players. The issue could be stopped with a sin-gle word, *Internet*. But it goes beyond this development.

The combination of Twentieth Century-Fox with News Corporation's television stations helped create a fourth television network. The wiring of the cities with coaxial cable has created an infrastructure for scores of programers and hundreds of channels. The introduction of satellite receivers for the price of what a terrestrial home TV antenna used to cost has provided a measure of competition for cable operators. Computerized data-based management has provided direct mail with even greater accuracy as an option for advertising in newspapers and magazines. As seen in Table 10.5, the owners of these outlets remain many, diversified and in constant flux.

But it is and will be the Internet that ultimately appears to erode many of the old notions of bottlenecks. Users can easily and cheaply access essentially any newspaper from almost anywhere. Musicians that are not offered any or decent recording contracts can distribute via the Internet. (And listeners who cannot find the type of music they like can probably find it on the Internet.) Publishers who may not have titles that fit into the bookstore chain's inventory can get ready distribution via online booksellers or sell economically direct to customers. Home sellers and car dealers and anyone else dependent on local newspaper classified ad rates can use online options instead. Government agencies, public service organizations—indeed, any organization or individual with a message that it cannot get covered in the traditional media—can get it out, often with startling speed and coverage, using the Internet. Conversely, consumers of all stripes who want some type of information can—sometimes with little effort, sometimes with the need for search skills—find most of what they may want. This includes specific needs (e.g., how to find out more about Lyme disease) to pure browsing. And there is every indication that the capability to disseminate as well as the ability to aggregate will get more accurate and require lower skill levels.

The difference between the Internet and newspapers, books, records or television is that it can be all those things. There may be large players who continue to provide content, packaging and promotion that make them popular providers via the Internet. Unlike the older media, there are not the high regulatory and/or capital barriers to entry using the Internet. If it is diversity, accessability and affordability that are society's goal for the media, then the Internet appears to have laid the foundation for its success—for better or worse.

A Self-Administered Test on Competition
Versus Concentration

T. S. Eliot wrote that the world will end "Not with a bang but a whimper." It is similar with the media industry. We will not wake up one morning to find all newspaper publishers gone or 18 new networks broadcasting. Even the World Wide Web, while developing at breathtaking speed compared to the centuries of evolution of print, can be seen in a context of years, rather than weeks or months.

Nonetheless, the media environment and therefore the industry is changing. Even the familiar print products of newspapers and magazines and books, whereas they look generally the same as ever, are produced with technologies that were not available a half a century or even two decades ago. Anyone reading this book already knows that the options for distributing substance have multiplied substantially: from centuries of print only to all forms of electronic outlets. From limited channels of broadcast to a surfeit of broadcast frequencies (multichannel microwave, high frequency satellite, side bands and subcarriers) to a proliferation of coaxial and fiber optic cable. The common and ordinary phone line carries enough data to enable sound and video with hardware priced at mass audience-affordable prices.

With these changes come an inevitable—that is not a loosely selected term—flux in the media industry, among the media players. Successful proprietors are encouraged by family, stockholders or managers to apply their formulas with less successful companies. Owners that get tired of being in business or who cannot keep up with the competition may sell their businesses, totally or piecemeal. And, as in any endeavor that involves frail humans, there are those owners, managers and employees who will be more competent, more professional, more ethical, than others. Indeed, some may be hungry for power, influence, self-promotion—whatever motivations can be found in people anywhere.

It is for this reason that there is concern whenever the number of so-called voices seems to shrink due to a merger. Ultimately the questions to ask yourself are: Are there more or fewer voices available to me today than 15, 25 or more years ago? And, is it easier or harder, are the regulatory barriers higher or lower, is it more expensive or less expensive, to gain access, in whatever format, to any audience of one or one million than in 1900? in 1950? in 1990?

There are numerous ways to fashion an answer. Chapters 8 and 9 also suggest several. However, beyond the percentages and ratios, there is a much simpler test that any reader can try. It is likely that those readers who remember television before the early 1980s will respond somewhat differently than younger readers. The test is this: Do you have more choices in what you watch, read and hear today than 10 or 15 or 20 years ago? Then, by using the data provided in this and the previous nine chapters, judge whether these choices were controlled by fewer, more or about the same number of owning entities as in the past? This is the essence of *Who Owns the Media?*

CONCLUSIONS

In the 18th-century, the populace of major U.S. cities had access to a few skimpy weekly newspapers. They were priced at levels placing them out of the reach of the ordinary citizen. A circulation of 3,000 was impressive. The papers may each have been individually owned, but people still had access at best to just one or two local papers. In some cities, there began to appear public libraries with a few books. By 1900, the newspaper was flourishing, as were a few national magazines. Already there were chains and conglomerates, owned by Hearst, Munsey, Scripps and Pulitzer. Nonetheless, people had to get their information from a few daily newspapers (of questionable objectivity), a few magazines and books. Even with a wide range of ownership, it is not likely that individuals had the diversity of sources, from as great a variety of producers, as Americans have today.

The value for democracies, for marketplace economies, for establishing communities beyond geographic boundaries all require a vigorous flow of varied ideas and information. The conditions that promote this also give reign to unpopular, unsavory and even potentially dangerous information flows—from legally permissible but distasteful art to indecent and hate speech, to instructions on building bombs. Free flow of information means just that: the high brow, the important, the inane and the hurtful.

The intent of this study has not been to propose a course of action that should be taken. The authors themselves differ on what, if anything, would be appropriate political, social or cultural responses to the changes in the structure of the media industry.

This final chapter, however, has attempted to indicate the complexity of the issue of concentration as well as the many variables that must enter into any policy-making decisions. Foremost, there is the critical definition of concentration. This involves not only the differentiation between the traditional antitrust standard and a broader social-economic-political concept, but an agreement on what the relevant market should be: each media segment or the mass communications industry. If, in fact, the concern is with diversity of media voices (i.e., the social-economic-political concept for defining concentration), then by the same reasoning it is consistent to support the broader mass communications industry, reinforced by the blurring of the boundaries among its traditional segments, as the proper designation of the market.

In deciding to accept or modify the rules under which the information business continues to develop, there are several trends that need be kept in mind. These were first identified in the 1982 edition of *Who Owns the Media?*[60]

First, the economy of the United States is mammoth and keeps growing. Gross Domestic Product, at \$2.5 trillion in 1982, was \$8.5 trillion in 1998. It can only be idealistic or nostalgic as to believe that the small business entities of previous eras are as appropriate today. For any institution to provide competent and efficient service to a nation of more than 220 million people and to portions of the globe requires considerable resources. In this context, the largest of the media companies are mere pixels in the economic tapestry.

Second, the United States, more than ever, is part of a world that is growing more economically competitive. The economic wherewithal of the increasingly integrated European Community, Japan and the Pacific Rim and South America are certainly at or striving for parity with the United States. Many developing nations, such as Singapore and South Korea, are anxious to exploit their labor strengths and our technology. In the future, Africa may become a more viable economic engine. U.S. information providers are facing stiff competition in world markets as a result. Artificially scaled-down institutions will not be able to win their share of the world market.

Finally, the accomplishments and the promise of the Internet structure, as well as other information technologies, may be providing some of the crucial pieces that will put the media business in the position to foster political and social change worldwide. Seers have been notoriously unable to successfully predict the eventual social outcomes of new technology. Neither film nor the record player revolutionized the education process as Edison had so explicitly predicted. The telephone and telegraph did not spell the end of written communication, as the Postmaster General of the United States expected it would in 1873. But after decades of development, the ubiquity and instantaneousness of television and radio have had profound if not always quantifiable impacts on the political process, social *mores* and cultural values. There is every reason to expect the evolution of the Internet to have further profound (if not specifically predictable) consequences for these factors as well as the economic structure of the media industry itself.

Given the vast array of separate entities with holdings in the mass communications industry, society may be in for some unmasking of long-held myths surrounding the media. One, for example, seems to have equated greater diversity of ownership and content with presumed higher quality of content. If the proliferation of television, books and Web sites reveals anything, it is that greater diversity means just that: more low brow shows, trash journalism, pandering politics to go along with opportunities for finding more thoughtful and quality outlets for analysis, entertainment and information. Diversity cuts all ways.

In the tension that tends to exist between government and the press, Thomas Jefferson is often cited: "Were it left to me to decide whether we should have a government without newspapers or newspapers without government, I should not hesitate to prefer the latter." Jefferson continued to subscribe to this priority despite being viciously attacked by the press during his presidency. This may be a critical lesson to keep in mind as society wrestles with the new unabridged media environment that has emerged. Initial attempts to control the new diversity, such as the Communications Decency Act in 1996, were turned back by the courts.[61]

Who owned the media in 1978 or 1982 or 1998? The answer is the same: thousands of large and small firms and organizations. These are not necessarily the same firms: some old, some new, some combined. They acquire, merge, divest, start up. They are controlled, directly and indirectly, by hundreds of thousands of stockholders, as well as by public opinion. The mass communications business is profitable, as it must be to survive. It is an industry changing its boundaries from one defined by format (i.e., books, television, newspapers, etc.) to one defined by function (i.e., collecting and disseminating information).

The media industry in the 21st century will be transformed by the array of systems that came together in the last decades of the 20th century. The need to fill increasingly limitless outlets, the ability of any user to have access to any computer database, the possibility of aiming an antenna into the heavens and thereby having access to the programming of dozens of firms in this country and perhaps worldwide, may make today's concerns over concentration of media ownership different than concerns of an earlier era where media resources were more finite. The old media firms have been and will continue to be joined by new firms and other industries to create a media marketplace that may be noted more for information overload and fragmentation than for concentration and scarcity.

Epilogue

The chapter began with a story about Matt Drudge taken from the newest media conduit, the Internet. All roads seem to lead back there. This one was offered by Philip Meyer, a longtime newspaper reporter, academic and author of the classic book, *Precision Journalism*. In a 1998 column he wrote:

There was a time in the USA when a few prestigious media could control the agenda for almost everyone else. Editors looked to *The New York Times* for clues to their daily definition of news. . . .

But media power is no longer so concentrated. The Internet has fixed that. Freedom of the press used to belong to those who could afford to own one.

Now everyone with a computer has a shot at being an agenda-setter—Matt Drudge, Salon magazine, Rudy Brueggemann.

Rudy who? Five years ago, Brueggemann did an investigative project on environmental racism in the area of Holly Springs, N.C., near Raleigh. The town got picked for more than its fair share of landfills, he argued, because its residents were disproportionately poor, black and powerless.

He wrote this in 1993 as one of the requirements for his master's degree in journalism at the University of North Carolina at Chapel Hill and tried to get it published in a local medium. No luck there. So he put it aside and went out to Seattle to work as a writer, photographer and on-line editor. Last spring, he decided to publish his five-year-old thesis himself on the Internet. (You can read it at http://www.oz.net/~rudybrue/wagthedog.html). Holly Springs residents found it, mobilized, finally got the attention of local media and are now in the process of making a more effective fight against the latest plan for landfill expansion.

Concentrated media power is breaking up. . . .[62]

NOTES

1. Matt Drudge, "Anyone with a Modem Can Report to the World," transcript of speech to the National Press Club, Washington, DC, June 2, 1998. Accessed May 5, 1999, on Web site at www.frontpagemag.com/archives/drudge/drudge.htm.
2. Benjamin M. Compaine, et al., *Who Owns the Media? Concentration of Ownership in the Mass Communications Industry*, 2nd ed. (White Plains, NY: Knowledge Industry Publications, Inc., 1982), p. 3.
3. Drudge transcript.
4. Ibid.
5. For a historical review of such concerns and efforts, see Compaine, et al., *Who Owns the Media?*
6. Edwin Emery and Michael Emery, *The Press in America*, 4th ed. (Englewood Cliffs, NJ: Prentice-Hall, 1978), p. 69.
7. Ibid., p. 70.
8. Ibid., p. 68.
9. This is an old concern. In 1946, Morris Ernst, in *First Freedom* (New York: Macmillan), expressed the fear of increasing concentration of news outlets. He pointed out that there were fewer newspapers then than in 1909 (1,750 vs. 2,600) and fewer owners in relation to total number of papers. He did not address the rise of radio or the beginnings of television.
10. Reed H. Blake and Edwin D. Haroldson, *A Taxonomy of Concepts in Communication* (New York: Hastings House, 1975), p. 34.
11. Brian Gruley, "Why Trustbusters Often Allow Telecom Mergers to Go Through," *Wall Street Journal*, May 10, 1999, p. 1.
12. The table itself has some important gaps and must be used with care. In the original table from which this is drawn (see Source note for table), some industry segments did not have data for some years. Given the large size of the information industry, we filled in these missing data points with interpolated estimates and assumptions to provide some reasonable conclusions about trends and relative growth in this following description.
13. Ben H. Bagdikian, *The Media Monopoly*, 4th ed. (Boston: Beacon Press, 1992), p. xxiv.
14. Ibid., p. xxxi.

15. In particular, see Alan B. Albarran, *Media Economics: Understanding, Markets, Industries and Concepts* (Ames, IA: Iowa State University Press, 1996). See specifically Chapter 1.

16. Benjamin M. Compaine, "Shifting Boundaries in the Information Marketplace," *Journal of Communication* 31.1 (Winter 1981), pp. 132–133.

17. Clayton Act of 1914, ch. 323, § 7, 38 Stat. 730, 731–32 (1914). There are two other statutes that comprise the core of federal antitrust law: The Sherman Anti-Trust Act of 1890. Section 1 of the Sherman Act forbids contracts, combinations and conspiracies that are in restraint of trade. Section 2 of the Sherman Act prohibits monopolization, attempts to monopolize and conspiracies to monopolize. The other principal antitrust statute is the Federal Trade Commission Act of 1914, which, as amended, prohibits "unfair methods of competition" and "unfair or deceptive acts or practices."

18. The detailed legal and economic analysis of antitrust are beyond the scope of this section. For the basic economic concepts such as cross-elasticities, especially as applied to the media, see Albarran, *Media Economics*. The legal analysis drawn on here is from H. Peter Nesvold, "Communication Breakdown: Developing an Antitrust Model for Multimedia Mergers and Acquisitions," on Web site at www.vii.org/papers/peter.htm.

19. See, for example, the text that is part of ABC or CNN's sites (but not part of their traditional television broadcasts) or the audio and video at "newspaper": sites such as the *New York Times* or *Philadelphia Inquirer*. This convergence completely blurs the distinctions of the traditional media.

20. *Associated Press v. United States* 326 U.S. 1 (1945) at 20.

21. *United States v. Paramount Pictures*, 334 U.S. 131.

22. *Citizen Publishing Co. v. United States*, 394 U.S. 131 (1969).

23. According to Nesvold, note 365 (citation omitted): "See *In re Multiple Ownership*, 50 F.C.C.2d at 1056 n.11. According to the DOJ, newspapers, television stations and radio stations are all engaged in the same business of attracting audiences and selling them to advertisers. Whereas the DOJ does acknowledge that the three are not interchangeable for all advertisers, it asserts that the three are far more alike than they are different. Also, at least one commentator has suggested that there is some substitutability between news on the radio and on other media. In New York City, for example, consumers may obtain local news, social calendars and sports information from: local newspapers, including the *New York Post* and *New York Newsday*; news radio stations, including WINS Radio, 1010 AM; and New York 1, a 24-hour all-news cable channel that focuses on events within and concerning New York City."

24. 714 F.2d 351 (4th Cir. 1983), *cert. denied*, 465 U.S. 1027 (1984).

25. 825 F.2d 1559 (11th Cir. 1987).

26. Ibid., at 1563.

27. 712 F. Supp. 1386 (N.D. Cal. 1989), *aff'd*, 903 F.2d 659 (9th Cir. 1990).

28. Nesvold, at note 353.

29. TNT, part of Turner Broadcasting, became part of Time Warner in late 1996, well after the decision to promote the movie.

30. Stephen Schurr, "Shawshank's Redemption," *Wall Street Journal*, April 30, 1999, p. B4.

31. Ibid.

32. Accessed May 3, 1999, on Web site at www.imdb.com.

33. Shurr, "Shawshank's Redemption," p. B1.

34. In its opinion in a landmark antitrust case unrelated to the media, The Supreme Court wrote:

> The dominant theme pervading congressional consideration of the 1950 amendments was a fear of what was considered to be a rising tide of economic concentration in the American economy. . . . Throughout the recorded discussion may be found examples of Congress' fear not only of accelerated concentration of economic power on economic grounds, but also of the threat to other values a trend toward concentration was thought to pose. *Brown Shoe Co. v. United States*, 370 U.S. at 351-16.

35. See Nesvold, at note 244.

36. Nesvold, following note 251.

37. Carl Kaysen and Donald F. Turner, *Antitrust Policy: An Economic and Legal Analysis* (Cambridge, MA: Harvard University Press, 1959), p. 27.

38. Ithiel de Sola Pool, *Technologies of Freedom* (Cambridge, MA: Harvard University Press, 1983), p. 251.

39. Ibid., pp. 113–116, as well as Thomas G. Krattenmaker and Lucas A. Powe, Jr., *Regulating Broadcast Programming* (Cambridge, MA: MIT Press, and Washington, DC: AEI Press, 1994), pp. 52–55.

40. Pool, p. 242.

41. News Corporation benefitted by being exempt from the financial interest and syndication rules until the FCC finally abandoned them altogether starting in 1993. See Krattenmaker and Powe, p. 98.

42. S. A. Rhodes, "Market Share Inequality, the HHI and Other Measures of the Firm Competition of a Market," *Review of Industrial Organization*, 10, pp. 657–674. See also A. Golan, G. Judge and J. Perloff, "Estimating the Size Distribution of Firms Using Government Summary Statistics," *Journal of Industrial Economics*, 44, pp. 69–80. This study demonstrated the efficacy of the HHI in a study of 20 industries.

43. Albert N. Greco, "The Impact of Horizontal Mergers and Acquisitions on Corporate Concentration in the U.S. Book Publishing Industry, 1989–1994," *Journal of Media Economics*, 12.3 (1999), pp. 165–180.

44. This is drawn from *Who Owns the Media?*, 2nd ed., Table 6.6, subtracting estimated nontelevision revenue and adjusting for inclusion of only 16 rather than 20 firms in the 1980 data.

45. Pool, p. 28.

46. Media industry revenue was up 188% in current dollars (from Table 10.2), and GDP was up 83% in current dollars (from Table 715, *1998 Statistical Abstract*).

47. Jefferson Graham, "If 'Party' Doesn't Eat it Up, 'Pizza' Likely to get Reorder," *USA Today*, April 22, 1998, p. 3D.

48. Rajendra S. Sisodia, "A Goofy Deal," *Wall Street Journal*, August 4, 1995, p. A-9. Sisodia was writing in response to the recently announced combination of Disney and Capital Cities/ABC.

49. Ibid.

50. Benjamin M. Compaine, "Regulatory Gridlock and the Telecommunications Act of 1996," National Cable Television Association Academic Seminar Keynote Address, Atlanta, GA, May 2, 1998. Accessed April 28, 1999, on Web site at www.cablecenter.org/Main/INSTITUTE/speech.cfm?SelectedSpeech=8.

51. U.S. Congress, "Telecommunications in Transition: The Status of Telecommunications in the Telecommunications Industry," report by the Majority Staff of the Subcommittee on Telecommunications, Consumer Protection and Finance, U.S. House of Representatives, November 3, 1981, pp. 310–325.

52. Majid Tehranian, "Iran: Communication, Alienation, Evolution," *Intermedia*, March 1979, p. xiii.

53. David L. Marcus, "Indonesia Revolt Was Net Driven," *Boston Globe*, May 23, 1998, p. A1.

54. Estimates of Internet use (which may include e-mail but not necessarily World Wide Web) vary, depending on definitions of "use" and what age groups are included. This survey was done by Intelliquest and was accessed April 29, 1999, on Web site at www.nua.ie/surveys/?f=VS&art_id=905354866&rel=true.

55. John R. Wilke and Bryan Gruley, "Feds Approve More Big Deals, But Companies Pay a Price," *The Wall Street Journal Interactive*, March 4, 1997, accessed Match 4, 1997, on Web site at interactive5.wsj.com/edition/current/articles/SB857432325842726500.htm.

56. Ibid.

57. I. William Hill, "Justice Department Probes Gannett-Combined Merger," *Editor & Publisher*, March 24, 1979, p. 11. Quotes John H. Shenefield, then Assistant Attorney General for antitrust.

58. Leslie Cauley, "AT&T Is Testing its Mettle as a Local Service Provider," *Wall Street Journal*, July 16, 1999, p. 1.

59. Compaine, et al., *Who Owns the Media?*, p. 7.

60. Ibid., pp. 493–494.

61. *Reno v. American Civil Liberties Union*, 117 S.Ct. 2329, 138 L.Ed.2d 874 (1997).

62. Philip Meyer, "Clinton-Crazy? No, Net Floods Us with News," *USA Today*, October 4, 1998, Opinion column, News section.

Afterword

February 2000

The phone rang at Ben Compaine's office one Arctic-cold day in early January 2000. It was Linda Bathgate, our editor at Lawrence Erlbaum Associates, Publishers. "What are you going to do about the AOL-Time Warner merger," she wanted to know. "Nothing," he replied. There was a long silence at the other end. He explained further.

They discussed the fact that, because this was going to be a printed a book, it couldn't have the latest data in a continually changing landscape. Latching on to the landscape theme he went on. "In a way it's like a photograph. It captures what the camera saw at one instant: the ocean crashing on the rocks, or my daughter blowing out the candles on the cake for her ninth birthday. But a photograph doesn't capture a reality beyond the instant of snapping the shudder."

We did agree that we could add an Afterword: a few pages at the very last minute before the book has to be fixed for final page proofs. Still, it doesn't buy us much. The main part of the manuscript was finished in the summer of 1999, Most of the data was available through the end of 1998. But the very first readers would not see this book until mid 2000 and most readers will be seeing this months or years later. The outcome of the AOL-Time Warner deal, or the CBS-Viacom merger or Softbank divestiture of Ziff Davis will be history, superseded by emergence of new players, combinations and spin offs.

THE DEALS KEEP FLYING

That said, following is sampler of the major activities just since we "completed" the book.

Ziff-Davis Divestiture and Transformation

Ziff-Davis had been owned by the Japanese technology venture company Softbank. Its stable of computer and Internet related magazines made it the sixth largest periodical publisher in the United States.[1] It also was one of the major Interest players with its ZDNet sites. In 1998 Softbank sold off Ziff-Davis as a publicly-owned company in which it still had a substantial interest. Since then Ziff-Davis began a transformation from a publishing company to an Internet technology media source. In 1999 it announced the sale of its publishing unit to Will Stein & Partners, a private investment firm. It also sold its ZDTV cable television channel to Vulcan Ventures. In 2000 the remaining company became ZDNet, Inc., a publicly owned company. Softbank initially had a 45% stake in the new company.

CBS-Viacom Merger

Although not a done deal—the companies were still awaiting approvals from the FCC and Justice Department—the merger of the two companies was the largest media deal ever when announced in 1999 ($37 billion in stock at the time). CBS, which had only recently been divested by Westinghouse, was technically being acquired by Viacom. In many ways it followed a pattern set by the Disney/ABC merger. CBS has essentially stripped itself down to a television network and a group of radio and television stations. Viacom had a major film studio—Paramount—as well as its extensive cable holdings, its own television stations, and a 50% share in the UPN network. The combined entity was being analyzed as a more vertically integrated entity, better able to compete with Time Warner, Disney, and News Corp. It was expected that regulatory approval would require, at a minimum, selling off about 16 broadcast stations among them as well as Viacom's share in UPN.

Time Warner-EMI Joint Venture

Time Warner and Britain's EMI Group announced in 2000 that they intended to form a joint venture to which they would each contribute their record and music publishing businesses. Based on global revenues, EMI was the third largest and Warner Music the fourth largest music company. The planned venture, Warner EMI Music, would be very close in size—and perhaps a bit larger—than the largest in the industry, Seagram's Universal. However, the deal needed approval of regulators in both the European Union as well as the United States Initial analysis of its approval prospects were mixed. For example, one antitrust attorney was quoted as saying that he expected the merger to face few regulatory hurdles, largely because the combined company would still face stiff competition from Universal, as well as Sony Corp.'s Sony Music Entertainment and Bertelsmann's BMG Entertainment. "A merger that just reduces the number of music recording companies from five to four without giving Time Warner a monopoly ... this one may raise a few questions but it will go through... ."[2] But another legal expert came out differently. Because it's unclear how potential antitrust concerns could be settled, he said, "If I had to handicap it, I'd probably say that it is more likely than not that the government is going to try to block (the merger)."[3] The key difference in the analysis was the role of the Internet. The lawyer who was skeptical about approval added "If they can persuade the government that these (current) market shares are really irrelevant, because the market is going to change so much with the Internet, then maybe the government would look at it differently."

AOL-Time Warner Merger

The Godzilla of media mergers up to this writing was the planned combination of Time Warner with America Online. Besides it being the largest merger of all time—based on the value of the stock of the two companies—it had the added significance of essentially being the acquisition of the largest traditional media company by a much smaller new media company. In 1998, Time Warner's media revenue of $26.8 billion was five times AOL's $5.6 billion. But as the deal was structured, AOL stockholders would end up with 55% of the shares. The merger was proclaimed by many analysts as a harbinger of the 21st century: new players making their mark at the highest levels of the media pyramid.

The merger of these two companies was not a done deal. It faced not only the usual FTC and Justice Department antitrust scrutiny but shareholder scrutiny as well. Time Warner shareholders would be contributing 80% of the assets of the new company. In 1999 a proposed merger between Internet company Lycos and traditional media company USANetworks fell apart when Lycos shareholders rebelled against the dilution of their stock's value. Still, just the attempt of the management of the venerable Time Warner to agree to be the junior partner with AOL, barely 15 years old at the time, signaled an inflection point in the landscape of the media industry.

Thomson Corporation Divests Newspapers

As reported initially in Chapter 1, Thomson continued its divestiture out of the newspaper business. At one time it owned more dailies in the United States and Canada than any other publisher. In 2000 it planned to sell the rest of its dailies except the *Toronto Globe & Mail*. Some of its larger papers with more than 50,000 circulation included *The Tribune* in Mesa, Ariz.; *Connecticut Post*, in Fairfield County; and the *Canton* (Ohio) *Repository*. It planned to invest the proceeds in the electronic and Internet-information operations that had become its focus in the last decade.[4]

UPDATE ON TRENDS AND MARKET FORCES

The rapid evolution of the Internet has continued to upset many of the former verities of the competition in the media world. Just the proposal for a combination of Time Warner and AOL confirmed expectations that the traditional and newer formats were blurring. There are others:

- The estimated number of Internet users continued to vary widely based on definitions and methodology. Still, a good estimate was that at the end of 1999 there were well over 100 million users in the United States (actual users, including access through work or school). AOL, the largest internet service provider, passed 21 million subscribers in early 2000. It reported that its subscribers were spending more than 1 hour daily online. Although the final numbers were not available, all indications were that online shopping in 1999 well exceeded the $3 billion that some analysts had projected, and may have been twice that.
- "Vanity" publishing—paying a publisher to publish one's book instead of being paid—is not new. But married with the reach of the Internet, advances in short run printing and online booksellers, it has taken on increased potential for expanding its viability for authors as well as publishers. Iuniverse.com was one service offering authors the opportunity to publish—in bound hard cover—their books for as little as $99.[5] Books could be ordered online and printed on demand, as ordered. They were also available at bricks and mortar Barnes & Noble Superstores. Iuniverse.com also had a program to republish out of print works that authors had rights to. They also had agreements with Harvard and Columbia presses to offer books those publishers felt merited their imprimatur but they could not economically justify to print in the usual speculative process.
  Thus, access of both authors and consumers for books—hard copies—has gone beyond the traditional publisher gatekeepers.
- Internet radio continued to find an audience. According to one study, close to 12% of the population has sampled Internet radio by late 1999, and Microsoft's entry into the arena through its promotion of the service may give further credibility to the trend.[6]
- Even the mergers in the already consolidated music industry have their upside, according to several executives at Internet music. They see the latest mergers as the first major step toward a new music distribution system. They expected the likely mergers and the ensuing artist cuts to make

many acts more wary of major labels and more willing to sign with independent companies and Internet start-ups.[7]

- "Personal" music. Numerous sites let Internet users access music that was not on major labels—or may be from performers without a label at all. For example, LAUNCH.com was a venture-capital funded start-up that provided users personalization capabilities to create comprehensive and interactive online music communities. In early 2000 it offered a roster of over 1000 music videos that were available on request, or by user-created custom playlists of selected videos that ran back-to-back.[8]

- Many of the established media companies were "spinning off" their Internet ventures in separate, publicly-owned companies. NBCi was created through the combination of Snap, XOOM.com, NBC.com, NBC Interactive Neighborhood, AccessHollywood.com, VideoSeeker, and a 10% equity stake in CNBC.com. GE, through NBC, held a large but less than majority interest in the entity. The New York Times Co. was creating a "tracking stock" of its Internet interests, which included The New York Times on the Web as well as boston.com, NYToday.com, WineToday.com, GolfDigest.com and Abuzz. Disney combined its digital operations, including Infoseek and Disney.com, into the Go Network, in which it held a 72% interest.[9]

The list of the major media companies will continue to change. Our listing in the 1982 volume, for example, did not include either America Online, which did not exist, or News Corp., which was barely a player in the United States. Although mergers will continue, there is every indication that so will the influx of new players. We ended the Preface with a summary of the strategic value of this book: to help readers understand *why* these things happen as well as what *contexts* may be appropriate for analyzing their import." The day-to-day ebb and flow is a natural part of the evolution of the media industry.

NOTES

1. Kevin Max, "Ziff-Davis Agrees to Sell Publishing Unit for $780 Million," NYTimes.com/TheStreet.com, December 6, 1999, accessed February 2, 2000 at http://www.nytimes.com/library/tech/99/12/biztech/articles/07ziff-sale.html.
2. Colleen Debaise, "Antitrust Scrutiny Seen for Time Warner, EMI Music Deal," *Dow Jones Newswires*, January 24, 2000, Accessed February 2, 2000 at http://interactive.wsj.com/edition/past/summaries/menu/html.
3. Ibid.
4. Mark Heinz, "Canadian Publisher Thomson Puts Up Newspapers for Sale," *The Wall Street Journal*, February 16, 2000. Accessed Feb 16, 2000 at http://www.interactive.wsj.com.
5. http://www.iuniverse.com accessed February 3, 2000
6. Aaron J. Moore, "An Internet Radio Breakthrough," Office.com, January 28, 2000, accessed January 28, 2000.
7. Neil Strauss, "Music Mergers Herald a Shift to the Internet," *The New York Times*, January 26, 2000. Accessed January 26, 2000 at http://www.nytimes.com/library/tech/00/01/biztech/articles/26time-emi.html.
8. http://www.launch.com, accessed February 17, 2000.
9. http://www.nbci.com and Hoover's Online, http://www.hoovers.com

Author Index

A

Adelson, Andrea, 130, *144*, 310, 317, *353, 354*
Aeppel, Timothy, 235, *278*
Aksoy, Asu, 377, *428*
Alaimo, Dan, 411, 415, 418, *433, 434*
Albarran, Alan B., 6, 55, 62, *137*, 195, 275, 298, 352, 366, 426, 547, 550, *580*
Alberda, Randy, 509, *532*
Alexander, Alison, xxi, *xxii*
Alexander, P.J., 319, *354*
Alter, Jonathan, 446, *478*
Alvarado, Manual, 214, *276*
Anders, George, 133, *145*, 463, *480*
Anderson, J. A., 47, *59*
Archer, C., 292, *351*
Arvidson, Cheryl, 174, *191*
Ashley, Godfrey, 294, *351*
Atwood, Brett, 337, 346, 347, 349, 356, *358*
Auerbach, Paul, 508, 528, *532, 534*
Aufderheide, Patricia, 205, *276*, 530, *534*

B

Baer, W., 201, *275*
Bagdikian, Ben H., 17, *56*, 523, *534*, 547, *579, 580*
Baig, Edward, 424, *435*
Baker, John F., 108, 122, *142, 143*
Baker, Stephen, 236, *278*, 308, *352*
Balio, Tino, 377, *428*
Ballantine, Betty, 66, *137*
Bannon, Lisa, 109, *142*
Barbato, Joseph, 118, *143*
Barnouw, Erik, 510, *532*
Barrett, Amy, 255, *280*
Barringer, Felicity, 43, *58*, 109, 134, *142, 145*, 176, *191*
Bart, Peter, 387, 388, 397, *429, 431*
Barthold, Jim, 267, 272, 282, *283*
Baseman, Kenneth C., 529, *534*
Bass, Jack, 512, *532*
Bauer, Patricia E., 410, *433*
Beam, Randy, 45, *58*
Bear, John, 66, *137*
Beatty, Sally, 236, *278*
Becker, Lee, 45, *58*
Berenson, Alex, 471, *480*
Bernstein, Elizabeth, 130, 131, *144*

Besen, S. M., 203, 207, *276*
Bhargave, Sunita Wadekar, 124, *143*
Bianco, Anthony, 69, 132, *138, 145*
Bibb, Porter, 62–63, *137*
Biddle, Frederic M., 134, *145*, 269, *282*
Birchenough, Tom, 366, *427*
Birnbaum, Jeffrey, 366, *427*, 516, *533*
Bishop, Robert L., 20, *56*
Blackstone, Erwin A., 379, *428*
Blake, Reed H., 541, *579, 580*
Blank, Dennis, 404, *432*
Bleyer, Willard G., 12, *56*
Block, Alex Ben, 392, *430*
Blumenstein, Rebecca, 255, 256, *280*
Blumenthal, Karen, 312, *353*
Bodipo-Memba, Alejandro, 310, *353*, 402, *432*
Boehm, Enrich, 338, *357*
Boehm, Eric, 288, *350*
Bogart, Dave, 80, 131, *139, 145*
Borstell, Gerald, 44, *58*
Bounds, Wendy, 101, *141*
Bowman, Gary W., 379, *428*
Breznick, Alan, 269, 270, *282*
Brinkley, Joel, 443, *478*
Brody, Jeffrey H., 39, *57*, 513, *532*
Brotman, S. N., 203, *276*
Brown, Sara, 222, *278*
Bruck, Connie, 94, *140*, 395, *430*
Bryant, Adam, 246, *279–280*
Burnett, 349, *358*
Burnett, Robert, 320, *354*
Busch, Anita M., 392, *430*
Busterna, J., 200, *275*
Busterna, John C., 39, *58*
Butsch, Richard, 413, *433*

C

Cadet, Ron, 346, *358*
Caro, Mark, 388, *429*
Carrns, Ann, 406, *432*
Carton, Barbara, 106, 129, *141, 144*
Carvajal, Doreen, 64, 74, 80, 85, 86, 87, 88, 89, 98, 99, 104, 108, 109, 122, 125, 128, 135, *137, 138, 139, 140, 141, 142, 143, 144, 145*, 438, 477, 518, *533*
Carvell, Tim, 385, *429*

587

Subject Index

S

San Bernardino Sun, 52
San Bernardino Telegram, 52, 571
Satellite
    Internet, 442
    radio broadcasting, 318
    television. *See* Direct broadcast satellite (DBS)
Satellite Television V. Continental Cablevision, 552
Saturday Evening Post, 152
Scholastic Corporation, 74, 114–115, 487
Scott & Fetzer, 486
Scripps, E.W., 11
Scripps League newspapers, 23
Scripps-McCrae, 11
Seagram Company Ltd., 486
    profile, 393
    Universal Pictures. *See* Universal Pictures
Seagram's Universal Music Group, 330–332, 516
    profile, 331
Search engines, 460, 473–474
Seattle Times, 33
Securities and Exchange Commission, 494, 528
SFX Broadcasting, 304–305
Shawshank Redemption, 553
Sherman Anti-Trust Act, 200, 529, 551
Shop at Home Inc., 227
Showtime, 407, 409
Simon & Schuster, 62, 79, 91
    electronic publishing, 96
    mergers & acquisitions, 66–67, 74, 83
Simon & Schuster Consumer Book Group, 94–95
Sinclair Broadcasting Group Inc., 225, 244
Slate, 451
Social values, in determining competition, 554–555
Sociopolitical factors, policymaking and, 568–569
Softbank, 184, 463, 583
    TheStreet.com, 452
Sony Corporation
    film industry, 365, 366, 371, 398
    Magic Johnson Theaters, 406
    media holdings, 485
    profile, 336, 389
Sony Music Group, 334–337, 346, 348–349, 517
Sony Pictures, 388–390
    oligopoly, 515–516
    Telemundo Group Inc., 226
SoundScan, 347–348
Southam, Inc., 11, 14
Spanish Broadcasting System, 316
Sports programming, 214, 264–265
SportsLine USA, 467–468
Springer GmbH, 88
St. Martin's Press, 108
Star Wars: Episode I — The Phantom Menace, 359, 425–426
Start-ups, magazine, 174–175
Starz!, 407, 408
State Farm, 498
State Street, 494
Steck Vaughn Publishing Corporation, 103
Stock swaps, 34
Stockholders
    media company, 489–494, 495t–498t
    newspaper industry, 32
Stowe, Harriet Beecher, 65–66

Substance. *See* Content
Suffolk Sun, 23
Sundance Cinemas, 404
Sunset Books, 92, 93
Superstores, 67
Syndication, 217–218
Syndication rules, 203, 204–205
Syufy case, 552–553

T

Tacoma City Light, 267
Tampa Tribune, 451
Target stores, book sales, 130–131
Tax Reform Act, 34
Taxes, 33–34
TCA Cable TV, 263
Technology. *See also* Digital technologies
    educational, 106–107
    as factors in policymaking, 568–569
    implications of, 474–476
    innovations, 472–474
Telecommunications, Inc. (TCI), 208, 273–274, 407
    AT&T's acquisition of, 256–257, 470, 491
Telecommunications Act of 1996, 205, 209, 222, 228, 521, 532
    affect on radio, 287, 297–300
    policy development & wording, 567
Teleconnect, 179
Telemundo Group Inc., 217, 226
TeleNoticias, 235
Telephone companies. *See also* Baby Bells
    cable service, 209
    and DSL, 443
Telephony, 256
Television industry. *See also* Specific network
    advertising, 2, 194–196, 206, 214–217
        movie, 372–373, 375
        targeted, 220
        top, 219
        types of, 218
    affect of cable on, 209–210
    concentration, 195, 222, 228–230
    cost of TV sets, 447, 449f
    future of, 270–272
    HHI for, 558–559
    history of, 197–202
    mergers & acquisitions, 195, 208, 228, 229
    minor companies, 245–247
    network affiliation, 204, 218
    networks & distribution, 216–217
    oligopoly, 518–519
    parent companies, 229t
    pay TV. *See* Pay TV
    presentation to the public, 218–220
    prime time, 194, 203, 204, 213, 215–216
    production, 213–214
    radio advertisements for, 292
    ratings & revenue, 214–216
    regulations, 198–205
    relations with film industry, 370, 371, 372–373
    spectrum space, 198–199
    station web sites, 458
    syndication, 217–218